DICTABLANDA

AMERICAN ENCOUNTERS/GLOBAL INTERACTIONS
A series edited by Gilbert M. Joseph and Emily S. Rosenberg

This series aims to stimulate critical perspectives and fresh interpretive frameworks for scholarship on the history of the imposing global presence of the United States. Its primary concerns include the deployment and contestation of power, the construction and deconstruction of cultural and political borders, the fluid meanings of intercultural encounters, and the complex interplay between the global and the local. *American Encounters* seeks to strengthen dialogue and collaboration between historians of U.S. international relations and area studies specialists.

The series encourages scholarship based on multiarchival historical research. At the same time, it supports a recognition of the representational character of all stories about the past and promotes critical inquiry into issues of subjectivity and narrative. In the process, *American Encounters* strives to understand the context in which meanings related to nations, cultures, and political economy are continually produced, challenged, and reshaped.

DICTABLANDA

POLITICS, WORK, AND CULTURE IN MEXICO, 1938–1968

PAUL GILLINGHAM and BENJAMIN T. SMITH, editors

Duke University Press   Durham and London   2014

© 2014 Duke University Press
All rights reserved
Printed in the United States of America on acid-free paper ∞
Designed by Heather Hensley
Typeset in Quadraat by Westchester Publishing Services

Library of Congress Cataloging-in-Publication Data
Dictablanda : politics, work, and culture in Mexico, 1938–1968 /
Paul Gillingham and Benjamin T. Smith, editors.
pages   cm—(American encounters/global interactions)
Includes bibliographical references and index.
ISBN 978-0-8223-5631-8 (cloth : alk. paper)
ISBN 978-0-8223-5637-0 (pbk. : alk. paper)
1. Mexico—Politics and government—1946–1970. 2. Mexico—History—
1910–1946. 3. Mexico—History—1946–1970. I. Gillingham, Paul, 1973–
II. Smith, Benjamin T. III. Series: American encounters/global interactions.
F1235.D53 2014
972.08'2—dc23

Duke University Press gratefully acknowledges the support of the University of Pennsylvania,
Department of History, which provided funds toward the publication of this book.

CONTENTS

vii PREFACE | *Paul Gillingham*

xv ACKNOWLEDGMENTS

xvii GLOSSARY OF INSTITUTIONS AND ACRONYMS

1 INTRODUCTION | *Paul Gillingham and Benjamin T. Smith*
The Paradoxes of Revolution

45 **HIGH AND LOW POLITICS**

47 CHAPTER 1 | *Alan Knight*
The End of the Mexican Revolution? From Cárdenas to Avila Camacho, 1937–1941

70 CHAPTER 2 | *Roberto Blancarte*
Intransigence, Anticommunism, and Reconciliation: Church/State Relations in Transition

89 CHAPTER 3 | *Thomas Rath*
Camouflaging the State: The Army and the Limits of Hegemony in PRIísta Mexico, 1940–1960

108 CHAPTER 4 | *Rogelio Hernández Rodríguez*
Strongmen and State Weakness

126 CHAPTER 5 | *Wil G. Pansters*
Tropical Passion in the Desert: Gonzalo N. Santos and Local Elections in Northern San Luis Potosí, 1943–1958

149 CHAPTER 6 | *Paul Gillingham*
"We Don't Have Arms, but We Do Have Balls": Fraud, Violence, and Popular Agency in Elections

173 **WORK AND RESOURCE REGULATION**

175 CHAPTER 7 | *Michael Snodgrass*
The Golden Age of Charrismo: Workers, Braceros, and the Political Machinery of Postrevolutionary Mexico

196 CHAPTER 8 | *Gladys McCormick*
The Forgotten Jaramillo: Building a Social Base of Support for Authoritarianism in Rural Mexico

217 CHAPTER 9 | *Christopher R. Boyer*
Community, Crony Capitalism, and Fortress Conservation in Mexican Forests

236 CHAPTER 10 | *María Teresa Fernández Aceves*
Advocate or *Cacica*? Guadalupe Urzúa Flores: Modernizer and Peasant Political Leader in Jalisco

255 CHAPTER 11 | *Benjamin T. Smith*
Building a State on the Cheap: Taxation, Social Movements, and Politics

277 **CULTURE AND IDEOLOGY**

279 CHAPTER 12 | *Guillermo de la Peña*
The End of Revolutionary Anthropology? Notes on *Indigenismo*

299 CHAPTER 13 | *Andrew Paxman*
Cooling to Cinema and Warming to Television: State Mass Media Policy, 1940–1964

321 CHAPTER 14 | *Pablo Piccato*
Pistoleros, *Ley Fuga*, and Uncertainty in Public Debates about Murder in Twentieth-Century Mexico

341 CHAPTER 15 | *Tanalís Padilla*
Rural Education, Political Radicalism, and *Normalista* Identity in Mexico after 1940

360 CHAPTER 16 | *Jaime M. Pensado*
The Rise of a "National Student Problem" in 1956

379 FINAL COMMENTS | *Jeffrey W. Rubin*
Contextualizing the Regime: What 1938–1968 Tells Us about Mexico, Power, and Latin America's Twentieth Century

397 Select Bibliography

427 Contributors

429 Index

PREFACE | *Paul Gillingham*

This book is about power in a place beyond dichotomies of democracy or dictatorship, namely modern Mexico. The authors come from distinct disciplines and different historiographical traditions, have diverse research interests, and were brought together without any single theoretical *diktat*. It was in part the very breadth of interests and approaches that suggested their incorporation, in a deliberate search for academic biodiversity. We encouraged disagreement. This approach to collaborative work has been dubbed a dog's breakfast.[1] We hoped instead for a cat's cradle: a skein of threads that, when drawn tight, might reveal a pattern.

Initially the only evident common factor was a shared curiosity in the no man's land of historicizing power in the mid-century, those three decades between 1938 and 1968 when dominant party rule coalesced and peaked. A preference for controlled eclecticism over theoretical monoculture did not, however, mean the absence of a framework.[2] We sought contributors whose work fell into one of three broad categories: high and low politics; work and resource regulation; and culture and ideology. These thematic choices presupposed an organizing concept: that the relations between rulers and ruled were characterized by authoritarianism, competitive politics, and resistance, making Mexico an early variant of a *dictablanda*, a hybrid regime that combines democratic and authoritarian elements; and that such hybrid regimes are profoundly complex, dynamic, and ambiguous, demanding heterodox approaches.[3] They reflected a debt to those scholars who have made empirical cases for the ability of everyday subjects to resist the projects of the powerful, shaping their lives in constant haggling with authority; for the state as a masque; and for the causal significance of popular culture in determining dynamic political outcomes.[4] They also reflected the proposition that this was not the whole story.[5]

We posited that cultural and materialist explanations were not so much dichotomous as complementary[6] and that struggles for power encompassed additional phenomena. Some were previously hidden. Cumulative case studies and once-unobtainable sources, notably declassified intelligence, revealed the underestimated violence deployed by both rulers and ruled; the related salience of popular *political* inputs; the enduringly central role of petty authoritarianism, also known as *caciquismo*; and the way that local autonomies and a fragmented public sphere—"many Mexicos"—might strengthen rather than weaken central power. Other phenomena were more obvious and as such might be undervalued by the seductive episteme of the hidden. They should not be: laws, institutions, and budgets were more than façades under which deeper causal mechanisms lurked. Moreover, the importance of an economic model that overtly privileged towns at the expense of countryside was unmistakable. Finally—and critically—we were struck by the ubiquitous phenomenon of actors who shifted fluently along a spectrum of resistance to, tolerance of, and alliance with the state.

The resulting framework identifies three arenas of power: the political, the material, and the cultural.[7] It conceptualizes power as the ability to do things, to get other people to do things, and/or to stop other people from doing things. This draws on two resistance-centric definitions: that of Max Weber, who deemed power an actor's capacity "to carry out his will despite resistance," and George Tsebelis's idea of veto players, those "individual or collective actors whose agreement (by majority rule for collective actors) is required for a change of the status quo."[8] In between the extreme outcomes of imposition or veto lies negotiation, in itself both a process and an outcome: a statement of a balance, albeit skewed, of power.

Negotiation was central to rule in Mexico, but that does not imply the preeminence of a consent-based cultural hegemony because negotiation in hybrid regimes involves violence past, violence present, and the fear of violence in the future. This is incompatible with one type of Gramscian hegemony, which opposes hegemony to "authority" and "dictatorship," quarantines it from violence, and stresses instead its consensual core.[9] It is compatible with Gramsci's alternative idea of hegemony as the balance (or "dual perspective" or "dialectical unity") of "force and consent," which, when effective, establishes a "compromise equilibrium" between rulers and ruled.[10] Yet advancing this is (as Michael Taussig observed regarding social construction) "nothing more than an invitation, a preamble to investigation," rather than a conclusion.[11] As Kate Crehan suggests, "rather than being a precisely bounded theoretical concept, hegemony for Gramsci simply names the problem—that of how the power relations underpinning various forms of inequality are produced and reproduced—that he is interested in exploring. What in any given context constitutes hegemony can only be discovered through careful empirical analysis."[12] The question is not whether Mexican elites achieved stability, however rudimentary, on a national level through a balance of force and consent; they did. The questions, rather, are where that balance fell, how it was struck, and how it swayed from time to time and from place to place.

We discuss these questions in specific terms in the introduction. In general terms, gauging answers to those questions involves all three arenas of power: the political, the material, and the cultural. There is no single independent variable that provides a comprehensive explanation for the processes of state formation and its outcome. The three are, rather, tightly interwoven. For example, the political function of any state's management of economic resources is coalition-building, but in Mexico, at all levels, those resources were leveraged by a cultural phenomenon: the pervasive revolutionary rhetoric that gave the excluded some hope of joining such coalitions in the future. Revolutionary nationalism did provide something of a common language for both hegemonies and counter-hegemonies, but that language was underpinned by violence. Everyday people were coerced into nationalist ceremonies by the threats of fines or jailing; archaeological artifacts were appropriated by platoons of soldiers despite village protests; journalists and Catholic militants, or *agraristas* and teachers, could face beatings or assassination.[13] Bribery—lunches for marches—was also salient. Moreover, rulers and ruled were polyglot, and in addition to the common language of revolutionary nationalism (which some refused to speak) there were other common languages that were tactically adopted as political mores shifted, such as the rhetorics of democracy and development. To see economic processes at work shaping culture, cultural forces shaping economies, and politics—both formal and informal—at the intersection of the two; to posit that causal primacy varies from case to case, when it can be pinned down at all; and to note a high prevalence of equifinality—different processes leading to similar outcomes—is not a "live-and-let-live" conceptual mush. It is a reasonable reflection of the case studies we have.

Mexican historiography is highly dependent on case studies for the obvious epistemological reasons of a large and diverse territory and population. This should not shut the door on systematic comparison both across and beyond Latin America.[14] Deviant case studies, exploring the exceptions that test the rule, can revise broad generalizations, as regional histories of revolution demonstrated.[15] Most likely (those where a theory should if anywhere work), least likely (those that should lie beyond the limits of a theory), and crucial case studies can test, extend, and even suggest theories. These may be less grand and more middle-range: universal but comparatively narrow proposals of social processes founded on the concrete, the specific, and the time-sensitive.[16] Yet such generalizations are particularly apt for Mexico in the mid-century, with its neither-fish-nor-fowl relationships of power. As Fernando Coronil observed, "fragmentation, ambiguity, and disjunctions are features of complex systems"[17]; in Mexico and other hybrid regimes the fragmentation and the ambiguity are not just down to complexity but also form part of the ruling class's strategies of domination: divide, confuse, and rule. The limitations of methodology are, in other words, perhaps less limiting in Mexico than elsewhere. At the same time history's strengths—broad and deep empiricism, the explanatory richness that creates, and a sophisticated appreciation of the diverse rhythms and causal effects of time—might allow historians of Mexico to advance more universal discussions.[18]

It is difficult (but not impossible) to generalize about the frequency of the processes of domination and resistance that studies in this field are starting to trace. But in identifying and tracing the multiplicity of those processes, combining case studies, qualitative overviews, and basic cliometrics, we might come up with a coherent model of mid-century Mexico. That model is neither of a system based on consensual cultural hegemony nor one of Althusser's Repressive State Apparatuses, such as bureaucratic authoritarianism.[19] The essays in this book argue that force was real, strategically applied, and successfully masked. It also was exercised by both rulers and ruled. It went hand in hand with a certain degree of consent: one produced by economic growth and a coalition-building distribution of resources, by political accommodation, and by culture. The outcome was not stasis but rather something like a chemist's dynamic equilibrium, in which reactions move in opposite directions at broadly similar speeds.

This can be described by the term *dictablanda*: the combination of *dictadura* (dictatorship) with the switch of *dura* (hard) for *blanda* (soft). This has, as Jeffrey Rubin argues, a powerful, untranslatable resonance. It also enjoys a record of some usage inside Mexico, bypassing the more misleading labels of the democracy with adjectives, the perfect dictatorship, or even the PRIísta state. Dictablanda, in both popular and general terms, is good to think for mid-century Mexico.[20] In comparative terms, however, Guillermo O'Donnell and Philip Schmitter's definition, which denotes liberalizing authoritarian regimes, without elections, in transition,[21] suggests the need for translation, for a parallel, more precise, and broadly understood category. Translating the dictablanda seems particularly relevant given that Mexico shared some aspects of old Latin American authoritarian states while foreshadowing the post–Cold War genus of hybrid regimes, species of which encompass between a quarter and a third of all contemporary states.[22] In our period Mexico was in many ways a competitive authoritarian regime, a type of civilian regime "in which formal democratic institutions exist and are widely viewed as the primary means of gaining power, but in which incumbents' abuse of the state places them at a significant advantage vis-à-vis their opponents. Such regimes are competitive in that opposition parties use democratic institutions to contest seriously for power, but they are not democratic because the playing field is heavily skewed in favour of incumbents. Competition is thus real but unfair."[23] Some of the characteristics behind the Mexican regime's resilience—the institutionalized circulation of national elites within a single party, a powerful national story, and a deliberately fragmented public sphere, the negotiated nature of rule, the hidden violence, the local electoral contests—might interest political scientists who apply this historically contingent theory to places like contemporary Malaysia, Russia, or Tanzania, extending its ambit beyond the electoral and the elite toward a model of power that is simultaneously comprehensive and disaggregated, one that gives full play to the local and the informal and the cultural: soft authoritarianism.[24]

Notes

1. Barrington Moore, cited in James Scott, Foreword, in *Everyday Forms of State Formation: Revolution and the Negotiation of Rule in Modern Mexico*, ed. Gilbert M. Joseph and Daniel Nugent (Durham, NC: Duke University Press, 1994), vii.

2. For controlled eclecticism, see Alan Knight, *The Mexican Revolution* (2 vols.) (Cambridge: Cambridge University Press, 1986), vol. I, 84. See also Alexander L. George and Andrew Bennett, *Case Studies and Theory Development in the Social Sciences* (Cambridge, MA: MIT Press, 2004), 3–10; Terence J. McDonald, "Introduction," in *The Historic Turn in the Human Sciences*, ed. Terence J. McDonald, 1–17 (Ann Arbor: University of Michigan Press, 1996).

3. Guillermo O'Donnell and Philippe C. Schmitter, *Transitions from Authoritarian Rule: Tentative Conclusions about Uncertain Democracies* (Baltimore: Johns Hopkins University Press, 2013); Larry Diamond, "Elections without Democracy: Thinking about Hybrid Regimes," *Journal of Democracy* 13, no. 2 (April 2002): 21–35.

4. The classics are Mary Kay Vaughan, *Cultural Politics in Revolution: Teachers, Peasants, and Schools in Mexico, 1930–1940* (Tucson: University of Arizona Press, 1997); Jeffrey W. Rubin, *Decentering the Regime: Ethnicity, Radicalism, and Democracy in Juchitán, Mexico* (Durham, NC: Duke University Press, 1997); and Joseph and Nugent, *Everyday Forms of State Formation*.

5. Emilia Viotti da Costa, "New Publics, New Politics, New Histories: From Economic Reductionism to Cultural Reductionism—in Search of Dialectics," in *Reclaiming the Political in Latin American History: Essays from the North*, ed. Gilbert M. Joseph, 17–31 (Durham, NC: Duke University Press, 2001).

6. While, as David Nugent points out, "It is a curious fact that neither of the two approaches to the state that currently inform academic debate—the organizational nor the representational—has had much to say to each other," scholars have long indicated the potential of such dialogues. David Nugent, "Conclusion: Reflections on State Theory Through the Lens of the Mexican Military," in *Forced Marches: Soldiers and*

Military Caciques in Modern Mexico, ed. Ben Fallaw and Terry Rugeley (Tucson: University of Arizona Press, 2012), 240; William Roseberry, "Marxism and Culture," in *Anthropologies and Histories: Essays in Culture, History, and Political Economy*, 30–54 (New Brunswick, NJ: Rutgers University Press, 1991); William B. Sewell, *Logics of History: Social Theory and Social Transformation* (Chicago: University of Chicago Press, 2005); Richard Biernacki, "Method and Metaphor after the New Cultural History," in *Beyond the Cultural Turn: New Directions in the Study of Society and Culture*, ed. Victoria E. Bonnell and Lynn Hunt, 62–94 (Berkeley: University of California Press, 1999); John Tutino, *Making a New World: Founding Capitalism in the Bajío and Spanish North America* (Durham, NC: Duke University Press, 2011), 47–48.

7. This identification of loci of power complements Wil Panster's more process-based model of state formation, which identifies zones of hegemony, zones of coercion, and gray zones in between. Wil G. Pansters, "Introduction," in *Violence, Coercion and State-Making in Twentieth-Century Mexico: The Other Half of the Centaur*, ed. Wil G. Pansters, 3–39 (Palo Alto, CA: Stanford University Press, 2012).

8. Weber as cited in Alan Knight, "The Weight of the State in Modern Mexico," in *Studies in the Formation of the Nation-State in Latin America*, ed. James Dunkerley, 212–53, 215 (London: ILAS, 2002); George Tsebelis, "Decision Making in Political Systems: Veto Players in Presidentialism, Parliamentarism, Multicameralism and Mutipartyism," *British Journal of Political Science* 25 (July 1995): 289–325, 289.

9. Antonio Gramsci, *Selections from the Prison Notebooks* (London: Lawrence and Wishart, 1996), 124, 170, 239. See, for example, Claudio Lomnitz's definition of hegemony as "an institutionalized structure of interactional frames, localist ideologies, and intimate cultures which allow for consensus around a particular regime." Claudio Lomnitz, *Exits from the Labyrinth: Culture and Ideology in the Mexican National Space* (Berkeley: University of California Press, 1992), 40.

10. Gramsci, *Selections from the Prison Notebooks*, 124, 161.

11. Michael Taussig, *Mimesis and Alterity: A Particular History of the Senses* (London: Routledge, 1993), xvi.

12. An analysis that fully recognizes Gramsci's "intense concern with the materiality of power"; a concern that, Crehan argues, has been largely lost in anthropologists' usage. Kate Crehan, *Gramsci, Culture and Anthropology* (Berkeley: University of California Press, 2002), 104, 172–76.

13. Sandra Rozental, "Mobilizing the Monolith: Patrimonio and the Production of Mexico through Its Fragments" (PhD dissertation, New York University, New York, 2012); Carlos Moncada, *Del México violento: periodistas asesinados* (Mexico City: Edomex, 1991); Pablo Serrano Alvarez, *La batalla del espíritu: el movimiento sinarquista en El Bajío, 1932–1951* (2 vols.) (Mexico City: Consejo Nacional para la Cultura y las Artes, 1992), vol. II, 80; Tanalís Padilla, *Rural Resistance in the Land of Zapata: The Jaramillista Movement and the Myth of the Pax Priísta, 1940–1962* (Durham, NC: Duke University Press, 2009).

14. For Latin Americanists' (largely missed) potential to shape theory in the social sciences, see the introduction to Miguel Angel Centeno and Fernando López-Alves, eds., *The Other Mirror: Grand Theory through the Lens of Latin America*, 3–23, 14 (Princeton, NJ: Princeton University Press, 2001).

15. Important works include Luis González y González, *Pueblo en vilo* (Mexico City: SEP, 1984); Heather Fowler-Salamini, *Agrarian radicalism in Veracruz, 1920–38* (Lincoln:

University of Nebraska Press, 1978); Romana Falcón, *Revolución y caciquismo: San Luis Potosí, 1910–1938* (Mexico City: Colegio de México, 1984); Thomas Benjamin and Mark Wasserman, eds., *Provinces of the Revolution: Essays on Regional Mexican History, 1910–1929* (Albuquerque: University of New Mexico Press, 1990); Barry Carr, "Recent Regional Studies of the Mexican Revolution," *Latin American Research Review* 15, no. 1 (1980): 3–14, 7.

16. Harry Eckstein, "Case Studies and Theory in Political Science," in *Handbook of Political Science. Political Science: Scope and Theory*, ed. Fred I. Greenstein and Nelson W. Polsby, vol. 01.7, 94, 137 (Reading, MA: Addison-Wesley, 1975). For a skeptical consideration of Mexico and grand theory, see Alan Knight, "The Modern Mexican State: Theory and Practice," in Centeno and López-Alves, *The Other Mirror*, 177–218.

17. Fernando Coronil, "Foreword," in *Close Encounters of Empire: Writing the Cultural History of U.S.-Latin American Relations*, ed. Gilbert M. Joseph, Catherine C. LeGrand, Ricardo D. Salvatore, vii–xi (Durham, NC: Duke University Press, 1998).

18. Patrick Joyce, "What Is the Social in Social History?" *Past and Present* 206, no. 1 (2010): 213–48, 216.

19. Louis Althusser, "Ideology and Ideological State Apparatuses (Notes towards an investigation)," in *Lenin and Philosophy and Other Essays*, ed. Louis Althusser, 145 (New York: Monthly Review Press, 1972).

20. The term was coined to describe Spanish politics under General Berenguer during the 1930s and subsequently applied to the last years of the Franco regime. By the 1950s it had been adopted by Mexican intellectuals to describe first the Porfirian and later the PRIísta state. It lay at the heart of the stormy exchange between Octavio Paz, Mario Vargas Llosa, and Enrique Krauze of 1990s televised "Encuentro Vuelta," in which Vargas Llosa dubbed modern Mexico the "perfect dictatorship," Paz reacted furiously, and Krauze suggested the compromise of *dictablanda*. (Paz abruptly cancelled the ensuing round table; Vargas Llosa left the country adducing "family reasons.") William D. Phillips, Carla Rahn Phillips, *A Concise History of Spain* (Cambridge: Cambridge University Press, 2010), 246; Daniel Cosío Villegas quoted in Enrique Krauze, *Místico de la autoridad: Porfirio Díaz* (Mexico City: Fondo de Cultura Económica, 1987), 34; Xavier Rodríguez Ledesma, *El pensamiento político de Octavio Paz: Las trampas de la ideología* (Mexico City: Plaza y Valdés, 1996), 414–18.

21. Guillermo O'Donnell and Philippe C. Schmitter, *Transitions from Authoritarian Rule: Tentative Conclusions about Uncertain Democracies* (Baltimore: Johns Hopkins University Press, 2013), 8–14.

22. Andreas Schedler, "The Logic of Electoral Authoritarianism," in *Electoral Authoritarianism: The Dynamics of Unfree Competition*, ed. Andreas Schedler, 1–14, 3 (Boulder, CO: Lynne Rienner, 2006), 3; Diamond, "Elections Without Democracy," 27.

23. Steven Levitsky and Lucan A. Way, *Competitive Authoritarianism: Hybrid Regimes After the Cold War* (Cambridge: Cambridge University Press, 2010), 5.

24. There are several extant types of what might be called authoritarianism with adjectives. While cautious to introduce one more, we think it is useful in this instance to think as splitters rather than lumpers: hegemonic party autocracies, for example, are generally thought of as noncompetitive, whereas competitive authoritarianism does not capture the distinct origins and multiple strategies of domination that characterize mid-century Mexico. Neither does Tocqueville's concept of "soft despotism,"

with its subtle capture of "free agency" in the bureaucratic "networks of small, complicated rules" elaborated by an "immense and tutelary power," which ends up securing "servitude of the regular, quiet, and gentle kind"; and neither does Joseph Nye's formulation of "soft power" as "getting others to want the outcomes that you want." Alexis de Tocqueville, *Democracy in America*, trans. Henry Reeves, vol. II, 392–93 (Cambridge: Sever and Francis, 1863); Joseph S. Nye Jr., *Soft Power: The Means to Success in World Politics* (New York: Public Affairs, 2004), 5–6.

ACKNOWLEDGMENTS

This book grew out of a series of panels that led in turn to a two-day international conference at Michigan State University in 2009. We would like to thank all the departments and individuals who generously supported that conference, in particular Mark Kornbluh, Dylan Miner, Elizabeth O'Brien, Antonio Turok, Lapiztola, Zzierra Krezzia, and Edith Morales Sánchez, together with the Department of History, the Residential College in the Arts and Humanities, the Center for Latin American and Caribbean Studies, the Department of Political Science, the School of Journalism, and the School of Criminal Justice. For the next step of turning the resulting papers into a book we owe warm thanks to Gil Joseph and to Valerie Milholland and Gisela Fosado at Duke University Press, whose backing for this project has been patient and considerable.

We have incurred substantial professional and personal debts along the way—substantial enough, when combined with those of our contributors, to defy detailed listing. The archivists, librarians, interviewees, students, colleagues, and friends who helped us along the way have been fundamental to our work; they know who they are, and how grateful we are to them. Our authors have been much put upon and have responded with tolerance and multiple drafts. Other colleagues have contributed as commentators and critical readers. Heather Fowler-Salamini, Alan Knight, Pablo Piccato, and John Womack Jr. were the original discussants at Michigan State University; they went on to read drafts of the manuscript and make valuable observations and suggestions a second time around, to which Oscar Altamirano, Chris Boyer, Barry Carr, Ben Fallaw, María Teresa Fernández Aceves, Gladys McCormick, Tanalís Padilla, Wil Pansters, Andrew Paxman, Eric Van Young, and Duke's anonymous readers subsequently added. John Womack Jr. asked some difficult—and consequently useful—questions, which we greatly appreciated.

Above all we would like to thank Jolie Olcott and Jeffrey Rubin for their incisive readings of this book, which have significantly shaped its final form.

Finally we would like to thank our families, in particular our wives, who contributed in ways ranging from interviews and translations to technology and contracts.

GLOSSARY OF INSTITUTIONS AND ACRONYMS

Institutions

Agrarian Department	Departamento Agraria (1934–1960); Departamento de Asuntos Agrarios y Colonización (1960–1974)
Attorney General	Procurador General
Department of Agriculture	Secretaría de Agricultura y Fomento (1917–1946); Secretaría de Agricultura y Ganadería (1946–1976)
Department of Defense	Secretaría de la Defensa Nacional (SEDENA)
Department of Education	Secretaría de Educación Pública (SEP)
Department of Foreign of Affairs	Secretaría de Relaciones Exteriores
Department of Health and Social Security	Secretaría de Salubridad y Asistencia
Department of the Interior	Secretaría de Gobernación
Department of Public Works	Secretaría de Comunicaciones y Obras Públicas (1920–1959); Secretaría de Comunicaciones y Transportes (1959–)
Federal Security Directorate	*Dirección Federal de Seguridad,* (DFS)
General Directorate of Political and Social Investigations	Dirección General de Investigaciones Políticas y Sociales (IPS)
Office of the State Prosecutor	Ministerio Público
Treasury	Secretaría de Hacienda

Acronyms

AGN	Archivo General de la Nación
ACPEO	Archivo General del Poder Ejecutivo del Estado de Oaxaca
AHEV	Archivo Histórico del Estado de Veracruz
AHSDN	Archivo Histórico de la Secretaría de Defensa National
ALM	Adolfo López Mateos
AMI	Archivo Municipal de Ixcateopan
BCCG	Biblioteca Carmen Castañeda García
CMGUF	Colección María Guadalupe Urzúa Flores
CNCA	Consejo Nacional para la Cultura y las Artes
CNTE	Coordinadora Nacional de Trabajadores de la Educación
CTM	Confederación de Trabajadores de México
DFS	Dirección Federal de Seguridad
DGG	Dirección General de Gobierno
DGIPS	Dirección General de Investigaciones Políticas y Sociales
FCE	Fondo Cultura Económica
FLACSO	Facultad Latinoamericana de Ciencias Sociales
FO	National Archives, Foreign Office
ILAS	Institute of Latin American Studies
INAH	Instituto Nacional de Antropología e Historia
IPN	Instituto Politécnico Nacional
LC	Presidentes, Lázaro Cardenas
LCA	Liga de Comunidades Agrarias
MAC	Manuel Avila Camacho
MAV	Miguel Alemán Valdés
MIDRF	Military Intelligence Division Regional Files
MRM	Movimiento Revolucionario del Magisterio
NARA	National Archives and Records Administration
NARG	National Archives Record Group
ONIR	Obra Nacional de Instrucción Religiosa
PAN	Partido Acción Nacional
PCM	Partido Comunista Mexicana
PRI	Institutional Revolutionary Party
PRM	Partido de la Revolución Mexicana
PRO	Public Records Office
SCM	Secretaría de Defensa Nacional
SEP	Department of Education

INTRODUCTION | *Paul Gillingham and Benjamin T. Smith*

THE PARADOXES OF REVOLUTION

Revolutions have unintended consequences. In 1910 Mexicans rebelled against an imperfect dictatorship; after 1940 they ended up with what some called the perfect dictatorship.[1] Mexico was ruled by a single—admittedly mutation-prone—party from 1929 to 2000, a record of longevity surpassed only by Liberia's True Whig Party (1878–1980), the Mongolian People's Revolutionary Party (1921–1996), and the Communist Party of the Soviet Union (1917–1989).[2] While everyday people and scholars debated the details of this long-running regime, a compelling story survived the passing of time, governments, and scholarly fashions. This metanarrative held that the revolution had evolved from violent popular upheaval to sweeping social reform in the 1930s. Mexico's new rulers of the Partido Revolucionario Institucional—the PRI—had with that reform signed a revolutionary social contract to reestablish central control.[3] Peasants traded in their radicalism for land grants; a diverse labor movement mutated into a monolithic servant of government. The new state delivered economic growth, political stability, and a discourse—partially fulfilled—of social justice. The years between 1940 and 1968 were consequently a golden age.[4] History, in the pejorative sense of one damn thing after another, ended in 1940.

Yet this vision of a thirty-year *pax priísta* doesn't add up: it "drops history out at every turn."[5] Numerous studies of the revolutionary period have demonstrated that Mexico was nowhere near this sort of synchronic stability in 1940. The state that emerged from Cárdenas's agrarian, labor, and educational reforms was inchoate and often ineffective. The political class remained fragmented, a "loose, heterogeneous, and shifting coalition" of radicals, reformers, moderates, opportunists, and veiled reactionaries. The party's peasant corporatist bloc—still supposed to represent (and control) a majority of the population—was an umbrella organization of little practical import. Vigorous electoral competition endured, particularly in the provinces; managing the 1940 presidential election required a massacre in the capital.[6] Mexico's state apparatus remained underfunded, understaffed, and ill-informed.[7] Although social spending increased, bureaucrats complained that they lacked the competent agronomists, teachers, and indigenous advocates to implement central policies.[8] Socialist education failed, Cárdenas concluded, not just through conservative opposition but also because "the Secretaría de Educación Pública didn't have enough socialist teachers."[9] Furthermore, political factions cannibalized critical government agencies, reorienting them to service local and rent-seeking goals.[10] Popular groups, from the Mayo and Tarahumara in the north, to the Sinarquistas of the Bajío, to the Zapotecs and Triquis of Oaxaca, resisted state integration.[11] And economic elites—ranging from rural ruffians like Manuel Parra to industrial heavyweights like the Monterrey group—used "the weapons of the strong" to press for the reversal of state reforms.[12]

Cárdenas's failure to construct a corporatist *Rechtsstaat* casts doubt on prevailing interpretations of the succeeding decades and leaves the historian with two paradoxes. There is the paradox of revolution: how did millions of Mexicans who made anarchic popular revolution end up as apparently peaceable subjects in the world's most successful authoritarian state?[13] And there is the further paradox of state capitalism. Transitions from revolution to authoritarianism are relatively commonplace; France, Russia, China, and England all underwent similar shifts.[14] Simultaneous, drastic shifts toward highly inequitable economic models are less common. Mexico is extraordinary in that a revolutionary movement, which experimented with collectivist and even socialist modes of production, led to such a deeply inequitable capitalist regime. Mexico experienced strong economic growth across the period: gross domestic product rose at an average rate of 6.4 percent and manufacturing output 8.2 percent per annum. Agricultural production more than trebled. Yet urban real wages declined, only regaining 1940 levels in 1967, and rural wages fell 40 percent.[15] Wage earners, moreover, were not the hardest hit: peasant household income was statistically "not just insufficient but ridiculous."[16] Government policies of retrenched per capita social spending and effectively regressive taxation further increased inequality.[17] In comparative terms, Mexico's Gini coefficient, a compound measure of national inequality in the distribution of wealth, averaged 0.55 between 1950 and 1968. By the end of the 1960s it had risen to 0.58. This outstripped every other Latin American country bar Honduras and Brazil,[18] and was only comparable, outside the region, with the economies of sub-Saharan Africa; the countries of

TABLE I.1. Income Inequality in Mexico and Nine Comparatives, 1968–1970

Country	Mean Gini Coefficient	Year
Mexico	0.58	1968
Brazil	0.58	1970
Colombia	0.52	1970
Chile	0.46	1968
Turkey	0.56	1968
India	0.32	1968
Taiwan	0.29	1968
Japan	0.35	1968
Tanzania	0.39	1969
Sierra Leone	0.61	1968

Source: Klaus Deininger and Lyn Squire, "A New Data Set Measuring Income Inequality," World Bank Economic Review 10 (1996): 565–91, restricted to "high quality" data points.

postcolonial Asia and North Africa all developed significantly more equitable economies in this period (see table I.1).[19] Even after the populist reforms of the 1970s a marked inequality endured, and nutritionists estimated that nearly a third of the population suffered severe malnutrition.[20] Behind upbeat stories of Mexico's extraordinary political and economic models lay a more complicated reality—one masked, relatively successfully, by the cultural managers of the state.

Mechanical Metaphors, Messy Realities

The success story of the "revolution made government" was written by Mexican politicians, "official" historians, and social scientists such as Frank Brandenburg, whose influential work was dedicated to "the visionaries of the Revolutionary Family."[21] It was not unanimously accepted in Mexico, where people across classes, regions, and ideologies bitterly criticized the postrevolutionary state. Politicians struggled under the fire of what James Scott called "the weapons of the weak": gossip, slurs, satirical songs, black jokes, and other means of character assassination.[22] Discourse deemed them "vampires"; when President Adolfo Ruiz Cortines flickered across a cinema screen his gigantic image met with cries of "Dracula!"[23] From joke to threat was no big step. A peasant told his village treasurer that he "was a whoreson just like the other municipal authorities and very soon they'd get fucked up."[24] Even the president was not immune to the subversive violence of gossip. In 1948 a spy inside the miners' union reported one worker saying "that the President of the Republic and the bunch of bandits who surround him were to blame [for the economic crisis], that they were sick of it and should exercise direct action against the Government, and that Chapultepec woods had lots of fine trees to go and hang every last one of them."[25] The listeners laughed, perhaps a bit nervously. They might also have laughed at Abel Quezada's cartoons, in which bandolier-festooned revolutionaries sliced golf shots, or new elites wore diamonds on their noses and sported names like *Gastón Billetes*.[26] In the theaters and cinemas they could see comedians like Cantinflas or Palillo flirting with similar dissidence or hear Rodolfo Usigli's bitter denunciations of revolutionary cant.[27] If they read Carlos Fuentes or Mariano Azuela they could be shocked by the cynical intermarriages of pre- and postrevolutionary elites, knowing exchanges skewered as "give me class and I'll give you cash."[28] The government could restrain popular revisionism, but it could not end it.

Across the mid-century, historians including Daniel Cosío Villegas, Jesús Silva Herzog, Jorge Vera Estañol, and Moisés González Navarro all imported some of that popular revisionism into the early historiography of the revolution.[29] Others subsequently reconstructed some of the tricky juggling acts underlying elite endurance in power.[30] Yet these were exceptions, and until recently most historians ignored the period after 1940, leaving interpretation to anthropologists, sociologists, and, above all, political scientists. The latter's models of state/society relations were ambiguous from the start: was Mexico a democracy or a dictatorship? Such incertitude was exemplified in Brandenburg's work, which evolved in the late 1950s from considering Mexico a "one-party democracy" to concluding that it was a "liberal authoritarian" system.[31] As the 1960s ended—with the landmark student massacre at Tlatelolco and without alternation in power—uncertainties dwindled. By the 1970s broad consensus held that Mexico was an authoritarian state, where a powerful corporatist party exercised tight social control through its three class-defined subentities, which marshaled peasants, workers, and the middle classes in massive support, part coerced and part founded on the social compact of revolutionary reform.[32] And Mexico was a hyper-presidentialist state in which a single man and his coterie monopolized national power.

These interpretations and their everyday counterparts drew heavily on mechanical metaphors: the country was run by *el sistema, la maquinaria oficial,* the party machine, "a political solar system," in which Mexicans "rotated around the presidential sun and his electoral machinery."[33] Less mechanical metaphors were similarly sweeping: Mexico was, commonplace held, a Leviathan state.[34] Its immediate past, particularly in the *época de oro* before 1968, was one of static and uncontested domination over an apathetic people.[35] Such ideas were not wholly to the distaste of Mexican elites: the PRI elite's "image of invincibility" was a key tool for survival.[36] Across the period both sympathetic and skeptical analyses centered on these two assumptions: that the postrevolutionary state was powerful, dominating a largely unresisting population, and as a consequence was—by the standards of both the Mexican past and the Latin American present—exceptionally stable.

Such assumptions begged clear questions of class conflict and resistance: how had the state either hidden or bypassed them? These interpretive problems led historians to reconsider state formation from a cultural perspective, embracing the poststructuralist textual analyses and anthropology-inflected works of European cultural historians. In doing so, they challenged "reified" Marxist or Weberian examinations of the state "as a material object of study," preferring Philip Abrams's interpretation of the state as an "a-historical mask of legitimating illusion."[37] In the most influential formulation of this shift, Gilbert Joseph and Daniel Nugent leaned selectively on the work of Derek Sayer and Philip Corrigan to argue that the state's power derived not from its laws, its institutions, its armed forces, or even its broad capitalist underpinnings, but rather from "the centuries-long cultural process which was embodied in the forms, routines, rituals, and discourses of rule."[38] As state formation was "nothing less than a cultural 'revolution,'" it was festivals, comic books, education programs, and murals—rather than parties, bureaucracies, or systems of land tenure—that created the modern Mexican state.[39]

At the same time, historians drew on the insights of subaltern studies theorists to investigate the relationship between these state-building efforts and popular culture, arguing that peasants neither blithely accepted nor bitterly rejected revolutionary cultural shifts.[40] Instead, they argued that country people tactically negotiated, appropriated, and reformulated state discourses and rituals. Eliding cultural interpretations of the state and a sophisticated conception of popular responses, scholars concluded that this hegemonic process of appropriation and negotiation produced "a common material and meaningful framework for living through, talking about, and acting upon social orders characterized by domination" and that this framework underpinned the postrevolutionary state's endurance.[41] It was neither "a shared ideology" nor a low-rent "false consciousness" but rather a shared language that led to a consensus on the cultural bases for (and scope of) political action.[42]

This approach had several advantages. In analytical terms it reestablished the sheer messiness of reality, meshing neatly with studies of *caciquismo*.[43] It stressed that resistance existed in everyday forms, outside of set-piece battles, and argued cogently for its impact. In so doing it unearthed multiple examples of popular inputs to state formation, corrected earlier concepts of popular passivity, and continued social historians' traditional appreciation of the difficulty and complexity of achieving order. It furthered Nora Hamilton's pathfinding analysis, lowering estimates of elite autonomy and stressing the flimsiness of central power.[44] Finally, it argued that hegemonic discourses over revolution, nation, and gender both subsumed and were shaped by counter-hegemonic voices, a process that channeled resistance and hence, ironically enough, helped to explain the state's apparent stability.[45]

Yet employing cultural hegemony as an exclusive framework for understanding PRIísta dominance also has constraints because reality is complicated in conceptual terms as well. Reducing the state to a "mask" and the process of state formation to a cultural revolution or a series of discursive acts can promulgate a model of the state as one-dimensional as earlier reifications. As Mary Kay Vaughan observed, the new cultural history requires "those practicing it [to] combine culturalist approaches with continued attention to economic processes and to layers of political power."[46] Festivals, rituals, state narratives, and discourses did all play fundamental roles in distorting visions of the state, shaping popular opinion and elite policy, and generating some consensus. But contrary to Abram's original formulation, which works best as constructive challenge rather than stand-alone theory, the state—for all its flaws—did exist as a "social fact"; the state, to paraphrase Alan Knight, had weight.[47] It was a series of political-bureaucratic institutions with dedicated personnel who developed an array of distinct interests, preferences, and capacities.[48] Some of those bureaucratic institutions—the Banco de México, the Secretaría de Hacienda, the Departamento Agrario— were considerably more Weberian than others, such as the Secretaría de Communicaciones e Obras Públicas or the Departamento General de Investigaciones Políticas y Sociales. The state both reflected and regulated economic relations. While it was never a simple instrument of bourgeois rule, as tax collector, investor, and policy-maker it formed what Bob Jessop terms a "social relation": not just a product, but also a generator of various class strategies.[49] Revolutionary nationalism may have mitigated the political impact of growing inequality, but state fiscal and economic policy bankrupted peasants, impoverished the urban poor, and benefited the rich. Circuses were important; so too was bread; and so too were guns.

The rapidly expanding historiography of the last decade or so tacitly reflects this realization. There are four principal themes that have drawn historically minded Mexicanists to this period, namely national and elite politics, popular politics and violence, religion and the right, and culture. The study of elites spans individuals; *camarillas*, such as the Grupo Atlacomulco; critical analyses of (long-overlooked) institutions such as the Supreme Court and the Secretaria de Hacienda; and critical conjunctures, such as the Henriquista campaign of the early 1950s and the textbook conflict of the 1960s.[50] Building on the regional studies of Cardenismo, works on popular politics and violence comprise analyses of social movements, caciquismo, governorships, and increasingly guerrilla campaigns and state repression.[51] Scholarship on religion and the right, which cover Sinarquismo, the PAN (Partido Acción Nacional), and Protestant sects, amply demonstrates how enduring divisions over state land reform and anticlericalism shaped the succeeding decades.[52] Finally, works on culture, from comics to Cantinflas to rock 'n' roll, pick apart the intimate ties between the state and the media industry and suggest the multiplicity of responses of Mexico's new generation of cinema-going, radio-owning, record-collecting mass media consumers.[53] Much remains to be done, and smart, hybrid works, mixing high and low politics, labor and identity, such as those of Steven Bachelor, Gabriela Soto Laveaga and Ariel Rodríguez Kuri, may show the way forward.[54] For the moment, though, despite the recent flurry of publications, fundamental questions over sources, approaches, chronologies, and overarching frameworks remain.

Historicizing Authoritarianism: Problems and Possibilities

In looking for answers there is no shortage of data. Historians of the mid-century face a data flood: one driven by archival liberalization (and the new technology to deal with it), the possibilities of oral histories, the post-war surge of print production, and a new level of government and international agency technocratic output. Moreover, these years saw a dramatic expansion of the social sciences, and Mexico proved an area of positive fascination for both foreign and domestic scholars. Their work needs to be engaged with: it provides both irreplaceable data and analyses that fell from favor yet anticipate, in cases, our own. Merely reviewing such a body of sources is one challenge. Sorting the reliable from the unreliable is another. This is particularly the case with the two most positivist groups of sources, namely statistics and intelligence.

PRIístas relied heavily on the positivist magic of numbers. Governors claimed to have implemented imaginary land grants and built hypothetical roads; the statistical blizzards of presidential reports systematically and dramatically inflated agricultural production figures.[55] Some sneered: the Agriculture Secretary, one journalist wrote, "knew how to make such marvellous, eloquent statistics that the hungriest, after reading them, would be full up and burping chicken."[56] (Forty years later the bitter jokes continued: cartoonists invented a statistics ministry called the Secretaría de Verificación Nacional del Discurso Estatal, SEVENDE for short.)[57] But politicians were right to bet on a residual popular faith in statistics, and spies eavesdropping in cafés found that statistics claiming increased production "caused the best impression."[58] Historians need to beware the same trap. Quite often the state had no way of counting accurately, or it counted with a pronounced optimism.[59] Yet a rough-and-ready cliometrics remains valuable. Even unbelievable statistics reveal what rulers wanted the ruled to believe; they are as useful as cultural artifacts as they are useless for straightforward representation. Furthermore, grassroots or backdoor statistics—those assembled by local bean-counting or induction—can tell us what the state either didn't want known or couldn't itself know. Chris Boyer's chapter, for example, estimates deforestation through the backdoor of the volume of timber transported by rail. Finally, some statistics of questionable absolute worth are of great relative worth. Pablo Piccato's official homicide statistics do not believably reflect real murder rates (although they may well reflect the state's systematic massaging of those rates), but they do believably indicate their long-term decline.

Mexico's intelligence archives pose a similar mixture of problems and possibilities. They have multiple uses: spies wrestled with the same problems of the unknown provinces as historians do now, and they enjoyed the advantage of actually being there in trying to resolve them. They were given unambiguous—unfortunately, usually verbal—briefs: one inspector in San Luis Potosí was asked, "Why are there unopposed candidates? Why do they have overwhelming political power? Through the townsmen's fear of the authorities? Through the indifference of the voting masses? For other reasons?"[60] Questions like these—and some of their answers—offer insights not just into politics, but also into the federal government's priorities and *mentalité*. Some of the raw data collected by agents also are useful for social, cultural, and economic history. Yet the darker corners of the PRIísta state are now in some ways too accessible, the intelligence archives one-stop shops on an archival motorway. This poses three problems. One is what psychologists call the availability heuristic: "the tendency to judge the frequency or likelihood of an event by the ease with which relevant instances come to mind."[61] Another follows Hibbert's stricture that people who "rely excessively on information from secret sources . . . are bound to receive a distorted view of the world."[62] Finally, these agencies were marked by amateurism, clientelism, and political bias. For much of the 1940s and 1950s they remained small, ad hoc, and amateurish agencies. In 1952 the state could only spare fifteen Gobernación agents to oversee the contested federal elections throughout the country; in 1957 the staff of one service seems to have totaled all of twenty-eight agents.[63] Even in police states, intelligence material demands careful contextualization, and with a handful of agents, many of whom were incompetent, Mexico was no police state.[64]

The host of competing voices in these and other sources demand (and enable) creative triangulation and elegant research design. Michael Snodgrass, for example, analyzes the growing subordination of miners and metalworkers in the North before shifting to rural Jalisco, where he explores one of the rewards of union acquiescence: privileged entry to the limited good of the Bracero Program. Piccato uses an unholy mix of tabloid crime reporting and intelligence to examine murder as an optic onto—and a critical exchange with—the state. Wil Pansters's least-likely case study selects the most notoriously *cacical* region of the period, San Luis Potosí, to investigate the balance of power between local actors and state representatives, reasoning that conclusions regarding popular inputs in such unpromising circumstances are generalizable across the country. Gladys McCormick's most-likely case study of Zacatepec, one of Mexico's largest peasant cooperatives, reasons that the processes of domination are most likely to be revealed among those who cooperated in a zone of endemic rebellion. These and other contributors move fluently from the micro to the macro and from detailed case studies to the broadest sustainable conclusions; their work shares Eric Wolf's idea that society is "a totality of interconnected processes, and [that] inquiries that disassemble this totality into bits and then fail to reassemble it falsify reality."[65]

The combination of local and national, popular and elite realities is complemented by a heterodox approach that strives to avoid cultural or economic reductionism. Some essays center on culture: Andrew Paxman's analysis of mass media, Jaime Pensado's tracing of student protest, and Guillermo de la Peña's examination of *indigenismo*. Others seem more political or materialist: Thom Rath's work on the military, Benjamin Smith's analysis of the state's fiscal impotence, or Roberto Blancarte's overview of church/state relations. In reality these and the other authors were characterized by their explorations of the interstices of culture, economics, and politics. While Rath's chapter demonstrates civilian governments' continuing dependence on the military, it is equally concerned with the causal impact of a linguistic phenomenon: the mystifying discourse of demilitarization. Paxman's enthusiasm for media production and consumption is intertwined with the institutional and business histories of culture. Snodgrass's work on the political economy of unionized and transnational labor ends up outlining a "culture of migration"; Pansters's history of Gonzalo N. Santos's political reach begins by considering that literary gunman's textual strategies. Such an integrated scholarship—studying local and national actors in tandem, blending grassroots and elite sources, considering among others linguistic, institutional, electoral, infrapolitical, and economic variables—is particularly indicated for hybrid regimes like Mexico, where neither Namierite nor subaltern approaches capture the complexities and subtle dialectics of history.[66]

Toward a Model

Moving from different starting points, these essays add up to a working model of PRIísta Mexico. Future debates are foreshadowed in the following chapters. Certain basic agreements also are evident. Some are not startling: restatements, rediscoveries, or refinements of earlier scholars' work. Others are less anticipated. Taken together, they suggest that the diversity, dynamism, and contradictions of mid-century Mexico are best captured in a series of mid-range theories and an emic label: *dictablanda*.

Perhaps the most basic agreement (unsurprising given the predominance of historians) was that time mattered. While prior studies were dominated by more synchronic disciplines, our contributors emphasize what William Sewell Jr. calls "the temporalities of social life," the understanding that outcomes are contingent "not only upon a wide range of other actions, trends, or events, but also upon the precise temporal sequence in which these occur."[67] This reveals how different social processes with diverse temporalities—from long-running trends to sudden individual decisions—affected the entire period, for the decades between 1938 and 1968 were extremely dynamic. Mexicans experienced shifts at all three levels of the *annaliste* concept of time, imagined as an ocean marked by the rapid movements of surface flotsam, by the tides of mid-level change, and by the deep, slow-moving currents of the *longue durée*.[68] At the surface *sexenios* moved from left to right and, to a lesser extent, back again. The tides of growing industrialization and fluctuating control in the provinces ran fast. Finally, the period witnessed two bursts of that rarest brand of change, marked shifts in longue durée patterns. After three centuries of stability the population trebled in three decades. People flocked to the growing cities: by 1960 more Mexicans lived in cities than in the countryside.[69] Simultaneously, in part consequently, people fundamentally reshaped their environments: whether through deforestation, irrigation canals, land grabs by squatters, or developmentalist macroprojects. Such objective shifts were complemented by shifts in subjective experiences of time. These ranged from the adoption of mechanical time—by the 1950s a majority of tenement dwellers in downtown Mexico City owned watches—to the pacifying acceleration of time that Paxman tentatively links to high consumption of mass media.[70] They included the PRIístas' adept management of boom and bust cycles of hope, drip-feeding Mexicans with politicians who proclaimed renewed political and social reform. This may well have delayed popular classification of the state as authoritarian, its economy inequitable, its revolution past.

Reintroducing time begs the questions of periodization, continuity, and change. Current schemes end the revolution in 1940 and the "golden age" in 1968. These traditional watersheds are here to stay, in part because they also are embedded in popular memory, products of a nostalgia that invoked (and invokes) Cardenismo as a critique of PRIísmo, and the early PRI as a critique of the later PRI. In analytical terms they need to be qualified. Across the mid-century there was no steady progression into authoritarianism but rather a series of lurches in the dynamic balance of power between rulers and ruled and a series of turning points. The "beginning of the end" of the revolution came in 1938, Knight argues; from a Church perspective, Blancarte demonstrates that it occurred even earlier. The government of the early 1940s was more tight-fisted, repressive, and conservative than its predecessor, a shift that stretched beyond peasant and labor politics to encompass phenomena as diverse as teacher training and conservation strategy.[71] Pent-up political demand after the war, however, shaped the early PRI and lent electoral substance to its modish rhetoric of democracy. Both mode and substance largely died across Latin America in the late 1940s, and Mexico was no exception. The 1950 end to party primaries restricted competitive politics; 1952 proved the last threatening presidential election for thirty years[72] yet also marked the end of the army's overt meddling in presidential politics. The year 1959 saw not just the repression of the railroad workers' strike but also a mass extinction of the biggest regional caciques,[73] a purge of the army's top regional commanders and—a year later—the nationalization of the Jenkins film monopoly.[74] The early 1960s combined increasing antisystemic revolt and increasing authoritarianism with increased land grants and increased avenues for limited electoral pluralism; a modicum of proportional representation in 1963, a brief fling with primaries in 1965. Such ambiguities—a defining characteristic of a dictablanda—leave room for debate over the significance of each shift. One argument is clear and runs across several chapters: 1968 was a turning point more in perception than in reality.[75] Military repression had never left the countryside and urban protests had never ended. As Pensado demonstrates, multiple pro-democracy student movements—countered with soldiers—stretched back over a decade. Imagining the golden age as a clearly bounded period is as much a function of the ideological remembering of time as of dramatic historical rupture.

The most revision-proof aspect of the golden age is macroeconomic. Between 1940 and 1970 the state implemented protectionist and investment policies designed to develop key industries and stimulate the economy. This project—Import Substitution Industrialization (ISI)—generated impressive growth and one of the lowest import coefficients in Latin America. Quality of life indicators such as literacy and longevity rose alongside the economy.[76] Yet the former originated in the 1930s and the latter was in part a product of global medical advances. Mid-century economic growth was quantitatively strong but qualitatively weak. Government investment channeled growth toward two sectors: manufacturing and export agriculture.[77] Development also was geographically concentrated: between 1940 and 1955 more than three quarters of industrial value added occurred in the north or Mexico City.[78] In northern cities wages were more than double the national average.[79] Yet huge swathes of the urban population remained outside the country's explosive economic growth, forced to earn low wages in a (largely unmeasured) informal economy; urban women remained particularly marginalized.[80] Rural workers, above all, paid the bills for ISI. Population growth was not matched with land or credit; the agrarian reform was curtailed amid accusations of congenital low productivity. The role of agriculture was to supply export crops to the north and cheap food to the cities, permitting the low urban wages that enabled industrialization. The state supported agribusiness through massive irrigation projects and tax breaks and credits, policies that—combined with price controls—undermined *ejidatarios* and smallholders.[81] Between 1939 and 1947 the purchasing power of agricultural workers declined 47 percent; corn prices, adjusted for inflation, fell 33 percent between 1957 and 1973.[82] Meanwhile fiscal policy failed to redistribute wealth from richer urban to poorer rural zones. The "Mexican miracle" presupposed, in short, a systematic transfer of resources from countryside to city and from south and center to north.

Why did peasants accept this? The second clear consensus of this volume is that many did not. Rural communities across Mexico protested vigorously and at times violently against stolen elections; against crooked politicians, tax collectors, alcohol inspectors, or forestry wardens; and against enduring poverty. Insurgencies did not begin in the 1960s: they were a constant during the earlier period.[83] The state consequently relied on violence, exercised by *pistoleros*, policemen, and soldiers, far more than is traditionally appreciated. The petty undeclared counterinsurgencies of the 1940s gave way in the 1950s to repression of peasant movements linked to *Henriquismo* or the Unión General de Obreros y Campesinos de México (UGOCM), peaking with the crushing of the 1961 Gasca rebellion.[84] Even—perhaps especially—petty local rebellions or jacqueries could be met with extreme, performative violence. In 1955 villagers from La Trinitaria, Chiapas, rebelled, citing high corn prices and local corruption; an army captain beheaded five of them in the main square.[85] In 1956 Triquis from northwest Oaxaca murdered a lieutenant and two soldiers who had raped a local woman; the army called in planes to bomb the village.[86] In 1957 soldiers in Cuaxocota, Puebla, countered plans for an *ejido* with beatings, mass arrests, and the threat to burn the village.[87] This was all in the mid-1950s, generally considered to be the most peaceful stretch of the mid-century. Such unequivocal object lessons in state terror were, as one soldier told a spy, "standard (if secretive) practice." The army was critical to rural order: in the early 1950s, Rath finds, some 20 percent of *municipios* held small garrisons, and conflict zones often were ruled by unelected councils headed by an officer.[88] State violence was carefully masked—deployments often began by night, soldiers killed while dressed as peasants—and carefully targeted. It continued the tradition of decapitating social movements by selectively killing their cadres.[89]

Yet there was more to violence than draconian repression, and popular violence sometimes secured popular demands. A Mexican variant of what Eric Hobsbawm dubbed collective bargaining by riot obtained, as rulers and ruled haggled through choreographed low-intensity violence, which ranged from street fights to riots to simulacra of rebellion.[90] Collective bargaining by riot characterized both electoral and economic protests, and even the most radical, antisystemic mobilizations often led to concessions once they had been repressed. The 1965 guerrilla attack on an army base in Ciudad Madera, Chihuahua, led to the army hunting down and killing the attackers, but it also led to a tour of inspection by ex-president Cárdenas, which in turn generated a major redistribution of land.[91] When local agrarian protests threatened to spread across regions of high-yield agricultural production the government would sometimes revive the agrarista largesse of the 1930s. In 1957 Jacinto López and the UGOCM invaded the sugar latifundias of Los Mochis, Sinaloa, and the lands of the U.S.-owned Cananea Cattle Company in Sonora, invasions that spread to the Yaqui and Mayo valleys, the Laguna, Colima, and Nayarit.[92] Although soldiers arrested López, President López Mateos responded by expropriating the Cananea lands and creating seven ejidos covering a quarter of a million hectares.[93] Collective bargaining by riot was time-honored practice: it was obtained in resource regulation and in the local elections, and it was salient in the PRI's retreat from power in the 1990s.[94] It applied to both policy and personnel choices, was partially protected by revolutionary rhetoric, and underlay much co-option by the state.

The main mass beneficiaries of state co-option were workers. As Kevin Middlebrook details, the state largely subordinated labor by engineering union cacicazgos between 1949 and 1951. Yet although that subordination held down real wages, it was offset by new social benefits: subsidized food staples, housing, health care, and eventually worker profit-sharing.[95] As Snodgrass demonstrates, the sheer range of those benefits outweighed, in popular memory, the high costs of repression; it was—again paradoxically—a "golden age of charrismo."[96] Moreover, economic co-option stretched far beyond ownership of the means of production or benefit packages. One of the hallmarks of the period was the "dramatic expansion" of state control over the access points to a mixed economy, epitomized in legislation such as the 1950 Law on Federal Executive Powers in Economic Matters.[97] Governments could buy consent by direct and indirect means; both involved rigging the competition for limited resources, broadly defined as any generator, whether tangible or intangible, of wealth. Intensive direct incentives to cooperation—state benefits, development funding—rewarded relatively narrow sectors, above all unionized labor, bureaucrats, and soldiers. Yet government revenues were exiguous, and such benefits were perforce limited: the state had to pay market price (in cash) for the Cananea expropriation.[98] As Boyer, Snodgrass, Paxman, and McCormick all show, less tangible resources were many and ranged from the natural—water, forestry, grazing—to the institutional, such as licenses for transport businesses, cantinas, television and radio stations, factories, imports and exports, street vendors, bureaucratic sinecures, or *bracero* permits. Government permits were ubiquitous: one cartoonist drew a policeman demanding that the three kings produce their permit to distribute Christmas presents.[99] Regulating such a wide range of resources cost the state relatively little, while tactically ceding access to local, national, and export markets purchased support across classes, spanning the unemployed who got street vendors' permits, the workers and peasants who were granted bracero permits, the middle classes who received transport concessions for taxis, buses, trucks, and drugs plazas,[100] and the major industrialists who won favorable shares of national import and export quotas.[101] (Permit-givers at all levels— from crony capitalist presidents like Rodríguez or Alemán down to the lowest bureaucrat—also personally profited from controlling entry to the broadest range of economic activity.) Failure to support the government could be punished by blocking that entry: Azcárraga waited a decade for his TV concession after backing Almazán.[102] This regulation of resources was critical in building coalitions of consenters on the cheap because it lent Mexico one of the main advantages of a gatekeeper state: the counteracting of state weakness by the stabilizing, coalition-building tool of controlling access to capitalist markets.[103]

The third consensus of this book's case studies is that rowdy mass politics never ended in the cities, where in between large-scale, set-piece confrontations and everyday forms of resistance a mid-range rumbling of dissent and mobilization persisted. During the early 1940s protests focused on the combination of spiraling food costs and ostentatious corruption.[104] The harvest crisis of 1943 precipitated bread riots in Mexico City and Monterrey; two years later, dissidents blockaded downtown Xalapa to protest the price of bread.[105] In the later 1940s urban grievances turned toward taxes, and social movements—some nominally attached to fly-by-night parties or unions—emerged to veto fiscal increases.[106] During the 1950s and 1960s the focus of urban discontent shifted to student organizations from Puebla, Michoacán, Sonora, and San Luis Potosí.[107] Throughout the period, squatter (*paracaidista*) organizations invaded private lands, demanded services and ejidos, and rejected state regulation. Governments were forced to respond, importing grain, desperately attempting to control food prices, punishing high-taxing state officials, titling lands, and dishing out water and electricity. These measures were costly and often ineffective. Lasting alliances between the state and single-issue movements were slow to build and unreliable. It took twenty years of repeated ad hoc concessions to co-opt the market women of Oaxaca City into the official apparatus of the Confederación Nacional de Organizaciones Populares (CNOP), and even then they occasionally held the government to ransom.[108] Although Ernesto Uruchurtu built thousands of market stalls for traders, in 1966 they turned on the mayor and helped topple him when he tried to dislodge paracaidísta groups.[109] Some researchers conducting fieldwork in the 1970s observed a well-regimented party, lording it over a populace committed to "conformity to the rules rather than manipulation of them" and avoiding "violent or clearly illegal forms of political action."[110] Others, slightly earlier, did not: in the late 1960s, for example, Carlos Vélez-Ibañez witnessed groups of "*viejas chingonas*" burning down mortgage offices and throwing managers into sewage ditches in Ciudad Nezahualcóyotl.[111] Collective bargaining by riot was not confined to the countryside.

As the last example suggests, and several of our contributors demonstrate, these movements also saw women enter the political sphere with increased force. The revolution ushered in a new wave of feminists, who linked demands for voting rights with broader social claims. Some sought to work within the system, exchanging conditional loyalty for economic benefits, forming their own unions, and supporting state-linked cacicazgos.[112] Others joined the Partido Comunista Mexicano (PCM) and harassed the government for female suffrage from the outside.[113] At the other end of the ideological spectrum, Catholic women's groups mobilized against government anticlericalism, especially socialist schools.[114] Improving church-state relations, the co-option of leaders, and the political demobilization of World War II probably combined to suffocate more radical demands.[115] But, during the succeeding decades, these left- and right-wing discourses and organizational structures percolated down to the urban and rural poor. In the process, peasants, workers, street vendors, and paracaidísta housewives blended and reconfigured previously polarized ideals and redirected them toward immediate goals. In Morelos, women provided foot soldiers for Rubén Jaramillo's radical agrarismo.[116] In the 1940s in Oaxaca City women harnessed the organizational power of the Acción Católica Mexicana (ACM) to press the government to cut taxes and fulfill its promise of greater democracy, which they defined as having their newly granted vote actually count.[117] By the 1960s, women also embraced the new biopolitics of fertility. Despite Catholic opprobrium,

Mexican women overwhelmingly accepted the use of contraception, which they adopted in soaring numbers across the 1970s, in some cases whether their husbands liked it or not.[118]

Elites were forced to react to this new level of power and treated women as a distinct political category. They established female branches of the PRI, publicly endorsing a handful of female deputies and *cacicas*, and channeled social spending toward women's organizations.[119] Mexican women developed longer school careers than women in countries of comparable wealth, which translated into significantly lower infant mortality.[120] The Secretaría de Salubridad y Asistencia concentrated its paltry funds on constructing hospitals, kindergartens, and education centers for poor working mothers.[121] Throughout the country community organizers, such as Celia Ramírez, head of the Unión de Mujeres de las Colonias 20 in the Federal District, and Guadalupe Urzúa Flores, the "advocate of the outcasts" of Jalisco, gained government support.[122] Offers of state largesse and political leadership brought results. As María Teresa Fernández Aceves argues, second-generation female leaders, by securing unevenly distributed social services, assured widespread female backing for the PRI after full suffrage was granted in 1952. Women could also be, as Heather Fowler-Salamini points out, caciques of much the same stripe as their male counterparts: the leaders of the Veracruz coffee sorters negotiated notable benefits for their constituents while simultaneously grafting and getting seats on the Córdoba town council.[123] Some PANistas brokered similar deals. Genoveva Medina, cacica of the Oaxaca City stallholders association, drafted her union into the PRI after accepting a seat in congress.[124] By the mid-1950s, the growing numbers of working women, suffragettes, aspirant caciques, and militant Catholics all offered conditional support to the PRI. As a result, women voters in general, Blancarte reminds us, left PRIísta fears of their generic opposition unfulfilled.

PRIísta hopes for cultural engineering through education, on the other hand, generated ambiguous results. Rafael Segovia found the schoolhouse to be the main space for political discussion.[125] However, the contents of many such discussions were often critical of the state. As Tanalís Padilla notes, by the 1960s "the very schools the revolutionary government had once designed to create a loyal citizenry were now producing its most militant foes." Guerrilla leaders from Chihuahua and Guerrero were teachers; Subcomandante Marcos's parents were *maestros rurales*.[126] The cities were the most educated zones, where the state lavished its greatest efforts in controlling the public sphere. Yet city-dwellers seemed skeptical from the start. Café gossip was virulent and all-encompassing: presidential untouchability did not obtain over a coffee or a beer.[127] That gossip translated into political opposition is clear not just in informal politics but also in election results. Unmanipulated figures show Alemán winning a mere 59 percent in Mexico City in 1946; more manicured numbers still showed the PRI facing consistent and substantial opposition in both the center-west and north.[128] Cultural production and reception reflected, in short, the double-edged legacy of revolutionary discourse, an instrument of both control and contestation.

Various authors question the state's control of the public sphere and of mass media in particular. Some were overtly controlled by the government: *El Nacional* billed itself as "the official organ of the government" (in sales pitches pressuring town councils to subscribe).[129] The government credit agency Nacional Financiera (NAFINSA) owned 51 percent of the shares in Clasa Films Mundiales SA, which made many of the newsreels.[130] From 1955 on there was only one television provider, TSM (later Televisa), whose owner declared the network "part of the governmental system" and the President "his boss."[131] Wartime censorship agencies endured, supposedly controlling everything from newsreels to comics. The censors' work was supplemented by an array of covert control strategies that targeted the mainstream, officially pluralist press. The government used advertising contracts, soft loans, and its control of newsprint through a state monopoly supplier, PIPSA, to induce compliance. Most of the time this worked.[132] Survey data from the 1940s to the 1970s suggest a certain core belief in the national state—in abstract—that may be causally linked to this virtual world of state-approved mass media.[133] As Paxman argues, however, that world was not just a product of dominant party social engineering but also straightforward profit-maximizing; in ceding much control to the private sector the state also bet on the controlling effect of sheer quantity rather than on hegemonic quality alone.

Media control was also a lot more partial than generally thought. Censorship agencies enjoyed mixed results: newsreel and film censorship was dynamic and effective, while comics flourished despite the best efforts of the cultural bureaucrats.[134] There were backdoors to effective social commentary, as Piccato's analysis of the national crime pages demonstrates. There was a muckraking oppositional press *en provincia*. Newspapers such as *La Verdad de Acapulco*, *El Diario de Xalapa*, *El Chapulín* in Oaxaca, *El Informador* in Guadalajara, *El Sol del Centro* in Aguascalientes, and Tampico's *El Mundo* and Apizaco's *Don Paco* all managed, at times at least, to follow profoundly critical editorial lines. They constituted a fourth estate. They were joined by traveling corrido sellers, modern-day troubadours equipped with thin sheets of popular songs, which were read out and sung in markets, cantinas, and town squares. Many such Mexican *samizdat* explicitly criticized the state, from the *Corrido del bracero*, which decried the "brutal taxes/the fines and donations/the vile monopolies/of repulsive individuals," to the *Corrido de Jaramillo*, which warned prospective peasant leaders that presidential hugs might be followed by a "jaramillazo": a bullet and a coffin.[135] They were, the U.S. embassy concluded, "truly a mass medium."[136] Furthermore, even when bureaucrats could control the medium, they were unable to regiment reception. Vélez-Ibañez described the atmosphere at a cinema in Ciudad Nezahualcóyotl as a cacophony of "boos, jokes, plays on words, whistling, commentaries, flatus, shuffling of feet . . . munching, belching, name calling, and cursing at friends, all combined with the sound track of the movie." There was also "laughter (usually at the most inappropriate times)."[137]

Such humor is interesting both as a constituent of and an optic onto state-society relations. Earthy ranchero jokes were a key recruiting tool for politicians from Alvaro Obregón through Ezequiel "Scarface" Cruz to Vicente Fox.[138] Gonzalo N. Santos claimed to be a lifelong Obregonista because of a joke: when a general commiserated with Obregón on the loss of his arm, Obregón replied, "Thanks a lot, brother, but it would've been worse if they'd cut my cock off." "This man," enthused Santos, "really was one of us, because he really spoke like us! This one had to be our *jefe.*"[139] At the same time, equally earthy jokes were a medium of subversion. They were not hard to find: on one bathroom wall rhyming couplets described the PRI as "a total son of a bitch . . . like this cubicle, smelling of shit."[140] Not all attacks were abstract: corridos nicknamed Alemán ("the biggest thief of all") Ali Baba, while jokers mocked President Díaz Ordaz's ugliness and the elderly Ruiz Cortines's sexual weediness.[141] During the successful 1952 movement to rid Oaxaca of an unpopular governor, guitar-wielding comics urged on female protestors, deriding rural heavies as impotent bumpkins.[142] Even *relajo*—relatively mild and nonsensical communal wordplay and mockery designed to deflate serious situations—could focus discontent.[143] When cultural missionaries arrived in the small town of Tezoatlán, Oaxaca, they publically catalogued the "many advantages" of their outfit, listing the "many ploughs," "many crops," and "many educated citizens" they had bestowed on other fortunate villages. In the midst of the speech, the local priest interjected "*muchos maestros, mucha mierda,*" deflating the missionaries' serious tone and causing the meeting to disintegrate into "obscene jokes and name-calling."[144]

If humor occupied the intersection of politics and culture, what were its functions? The stock answer is resistance; jokes are widely accepted as one of the key weapons of the weak. Contemporary elites sometimes agreed. During the late 1940s a blend of devaluation, inflation, and baroque corruption proved a boon for aspirant satirists, who took street humor to the boards of Mexico City's cabaret bars, mobile playhouses, and official theaters.[145] Most performances passed without interference. But if the authorities suspected that critiques were sweepingly systemic or that dramatists had directly insulted the president, then repression was swift: performances were closed, actors were jailed. Alemán ordered Usigli's acid denunciation of contemporary politics, El gesticulador, to shorten its run.[146] Government thugs shut down Roberto Blanco Moheno's attack on state corruption, El cuarto poder, after only a few shows.[147] Other heavies smashed the printing presses of Presente, the most critical magazine of the time.[148] The somewhat simian Gustavo Díaz Ordaz gave the most celebrated demonstration of state humorlessness, closing down El Diario de México for switching captions beneath his portrait and that of the monkeys at the local zoo.[149]

Other PRIístas, though, tolerated and even participated in the cynical, oft-obscene, and profoundly black humor of the age. Many seemed to bet that by embracing that subversive humor they might draw its satiric sting and even establish new if *inconfesable* solidarities with their constituents. Santos's claim that his methods of *"encierro, destierro y entierro"* meant he needed gravediggers not bureaucrats, or that "in this state, the only politician who is allowed to steal is me," may have played well with his ranchero supporters while demonstrating more widely that he was "more bastard than dickhead."[150] Other in-jokes had their roots in the interiors of government offices rather than the fireside banter of the revolution, but they were no less rhetorically effective. Tuxpan politician César Garizurieta's gag that *"vivir fuera del presupuesto es vivir en error"* or Mexico City mayor Carlos Hank González's observation that "a poor politician is a poor politician" undoubtedly enraged some of the ruled; they may well have persuaded others that the politicians were "*muy gente*" or "one of us."[151] The reception of jokes like these (and their political impact) is self-evidently speculative. Yet their prevalence strongly suggests that they were not just matters of taste but also deliberate instruments to foster what Michael Herzfeld has called cultural intimacy, "the recognition of those aspects of a cultural identity that are considered a source of external embarrassment but that nevertheless provide insiders with their assurance of common sociality, the familiarity with the bases of power that may at one moment assure the disenfranchised a degree of creative irreverence and at the next moment reinforce the effectiveness of intimidation."[152]

FINALLY, IT IS demonstrable that PRIístas, even when not cracking jokes themselves, appreciated the benefits of letting others do the same. Satire can vaccinate against more serious disorder; hence medieval elites' tolerance of carnival excess, which actually "maintain[ed] local society in working order."[153] Censorship in Mexico alternated with periods of comic laissez-faire, when authorities allowed satirical newspapers like Presente, cabaret acts like Jesús Martínez "Palillo," columnists like Carlos Monsiváis and Renato Leduc, cartoonists like Abel Quezada or Rius, and writers like Jorge Ibarguengoitía to ridicule with only limited interference. At the same time, government agents only rarely persecuted popular satire on the street. PRI leaders understood that much of the humor directed at the government served to express frustration in a nonthreatening manner: that the ability to pay a handful of centavos, sit before Ahí está el detalle, and watch Cantinflas mock the *apretado* elites could lend them legitimacy, while tolerating outbreaks of popular *relajo* merely acknowledged the lack of real revolutionary purpose behind the disorder.[154] According to Palillo, President Alemán believed that "it was good that criticisms of a government occurred in a play and were designed to make people laugh, instead of building up hatred and provoking strikes, marches, and coups d'état as in South America."[155]

The deployment and management of humor is, in short, a microcosm of the blend of force and consent inside mid-century Mexico. Mexico was not Romania, where a famous joke went, "What did they give the winner of the national comedy awards? Fifteen years."[156] As Roland Barthes argued, though, "a little confessed evil saves one from acknowledging a lot of hidden evil."[157] Elites tolerated cutting café jokes at the same time as they killed peasant leaders, toppled local governments, winked at suspicious suicides, banned left-wing parties, and cut many Mexicans out of their economic model. That ambiguity, that interspersion of hard and soft power, of coercion and co-option and the shifting coalitions they built, are captured in a final joke of sorts: the dark, paradoxical pun of the dictablanda.[158]

Authoritarianism with Adjectives

In Juan Linz's classic definition, an authoritarian system is one "with limited, not responsible, political pluralism, without elaborate and guiding ideology, but with distinctive mentalities, without extensive or intensive political mobilization, except at some points in their development, and in which a leader or occasionally a small group exercises powers, within formally ill-defined limits but quite predictable ones."[159] Mexico breaks these criteria in several key areas. It did lack elaborate ideology, being characterized above all by hard-nosed pragmatism, and it did have a distinctive mentality in the culture of revolutionary nationalism. In part because of that culture, however, its "limited pluralism" was often quite responsible, as elites juggled the competing interests of a broad range of social sectors. Party membership was impressive—by the early 1960s nearly 25 percent of the population belonged to the PRI[160]—but it reflected neither extensive nor intensive political mobilization; as Carlos Madrazo pointed out, the crowds at mass rallies were "herds," affiliated with the PRI without choice or conviction and "forced" to attend.[161] There was some intensive mobilization in the frequent elections—across the twentieth century Mexico held well over eighty thousand elections[162]—but it was generally that of dissident factions or opposition parties in those local societies where representative politics persisted; power was distributed across society, well beyond the narrow bounds of a national leadership.

Neither did Mexico reproduce the mechanisms of power that characterize other nondemocratic states. As Knight observes, totalitarian states—the USSR, Nazi Germany, or Spain in the first decade of Franco's power—are characterized by overt, systematic, and massive violence against the ruled; Mexico was not. Other authoritarian states relied heavily on extensive secret police forces, such as the estimated fifty thousand employees of Brazil's Serviço Nacional de Informações; Mexico did not.[163] The James Bond fallacy—that a spy agency might rely on a single agent to do everything—was actually realized in 1940s Mexico: at one point one man, Colonel Manuel Rios Thivol, ended up dealing with a large proportion of the government's crises.[164] Most authoritarian states retain large armies: Pinochet's Chile, for example, contained eleven soldiers for every thousand citizens.[165] Mexico in the early 1950s had all of two soldiers per thousand.[166] Finally, the unwritten rules meant that elite powers were indeed "formally ill-defined . . . but quite predictable." Yet most authoritarian regimes are characterized by the stagnation of their elites, as strongmen and their coteries cling to power across decades. Mexico, in contrast, held to a constitutional mandate prohibiting re-election and smoothly circulated political elites every six years. Applying authoritarianism to mid-century Mexico clearly demands adjectives. Looking for them is not scholastic hair-splitting but rather a logical imperative: how can we discuss the *sui generis* nature of Mexican history without positing a genus in the first place?

Bureaucratic is not one of these adjectives. Like Argentina and Brazil, Mexico combined "high modernization" with decreasing real wages and attempts to control society through corporatist organizations. Unlike these countries, Mexico was not run by a narrow coalition of bureaucrats, large landowners, industrial bourgeoisie, and military. Landowners and soldiers were comparatively less significant in formal politics; the industrial proletariat was at least partially included, with a broad range of perks offsetting lower wages[167]; and peasants, for all their declining wealth, had greater bargaining possibilities for coveted roads, schools, and rural health clinics. Furthermore, the "black fiscal economy" of tacitly sanctioned tax evasion and loan default allowed governments to extend this broad (if conditional) coalition on the cheap.[168] As a result, even after historians unearthed significant levels of violence in Mexico, extreme coercion did not have the same "crucial importance" as in bureaucratic authoritarian regimes.[169] While the Argentine *junta* killed an estimated thirty-two per one hundred thousand, Mexico's official homicide rate at the same time was thirteen per one hundred thousand.[170] Authoritarianism is a well-populated genus, though, and two species do describe much of mid-century Mexico's political reality: electoral authoritarianism and competitive authoritarianism.

Electoral authoritarian regimes are those that "play the game of multiparty elections by holding regular elections for the chief executive and a national legislative assembly. Yet they violate the liberal-democratic principles of freedom and fairness so profoundly and systematically as to render elections instruments of authoritarian rule rather than instruments of democracy.[171] Competitive authoritarian regimes are a subset in which there is "real but unfair" competition in elections. Neither is a perfect fit. Elections were more than "instruments of authoritarian rule"; at the same time, there was no real competition for executive power in Mexico after 1952, as one mass party was banned and the other's candidates failed to win more than 15 percent of the vote.[172] Yet the other central aspects of the competitive authoritarianism model were all present. Elections were "arenas of contestation through which oppositions [could] legally—and legitimately—challenge incumbents," who "[were] forced to sweat." The opposition did participate with "both votes and thugs"; the cost of toleration was comparatively low, the cost of suppression quite high; the circulation of elites provided the means for recovery after losing. Civil liberties were "nominally guaranteed and at least partially respected." While informal institutions—smoke-filled rooms—were often the main sites of decision-making, the PRI also "[packed] judiciaries, electoral commissions, and other nominally independent arbiters and [manipulated] them via blackmail, bribery, and/or intimidation." Finally, informal means of coercion were extremely important and ranged from the discretionary application of the law to the part-privatized, deniable violence that was salient but, like its critical military twin, subject to a "certain invisibility."[173]

Yet the PRI arrived at this outcome through wholly different processes than those driving contemporary competitive authoritarianism. This is usually the product of a balance of exogenous pressures toward democratization and endogenous abilities to resist both foreign and domestic opposition through "incumbent organizational power."[174] Neither applies to Mexico.

The United States fundamentally shaped Mexico's economy—through export markets, direct foreign investment, and consumer culture—albeit to an extent that remains open to debate.[175] In political terms, however, there was at best brief exogenous pressure on Mexico to democratize; for most of the period U.S. pressure on Latin American states was exerted in the opposite direction. In more general terms, a debate is implicit in the growing research on Mexico's international conjuncture: did the Cold War change all that much?[176] While several authors incorporate exogenous factors in their analyses, this book does not dedicate a specific chapter to international relations; as such our argument is preliminary. We would, however, identify four main questions. Did the Cold War change the language of politics? Did it increase the degree of external—and particularly U.S.—influence? Did it radicalize Mexican society? Did it substantially redirect Mexican political development?

Following these lines, we posit that external linkages were not critical. It is obvious that contemporary actors adopted the dramatic language of the times. Alemán should have his term extended to ten years, opined one editorialist, as "the Cold War has to become a hot war."[177] "Germany and Japan," a Henriquista general told his followers, "had wanted to go through Mexico to attack the United States, and Russia would surely try the same thing."[178] Normalistas listened to Radio Havana and held vigils for Che; even normalista socialites "were filled with socialist ideas."[179] Yet it is not at all obvious that exogenous discursive influence translated into strategic or political influence. In terms of security, Mexico received exceptionally low amounts of aid, arms, and training from the United States: out of the sixty-one thousand troops the United States trained in Latin America in the 1950s and 1960s, only 659 came from Mexico, despite U.S. aspirations to greater influence.[180] (This is unsurprising, perhaps, given that Mexico's war planners identified the United States as their main external threat.[181]) In terms of policy, Mexico frequently demonstrated its autonomy, whether refusing to join the General Agreement on Trade and Tariffs, renegotiating the terms of the foot-and-mouth campaign, winking at Castro's training in Mexico, condemning the Bay of Pigs, or recognizing Castro's government.[182] Such foreign policy decisions were made for domestic rather than foreign purposes and consumption.[183] As for communist influence, the PCM was, as Barry Carr points out, strikingly weak, numbering—by U.S. sources, which are unlikely to undercount—all of sixteen hundred members in 1950 (and that before a 1953 schism created the dissident Partido Obrero-Campesino Mexicano). The party's Thirteenth Congress in 1960 brought together all of seventy-six delegates in a disused brothel.[184] The Confederación de Trabajadores de América Latina (CTAL), Mexico's would-be continental labor anti-imperialists, received a grand total of thirty thousand dollars a year in Soviet subsidies.[185] The Cold War did become more significant in the later 1960s, and the success of the Cuban Revolution did inspire guerrilla warfare on the left and mass demonstrations, tragicomic attempted coups, and low-level terrorism on the right. Yet guerrilla movements remained small: at their 1970s peak, intelligence counted 1,860 fighters scattered between 29 different groups.[186] There were, moreover, no direct links between Cuba and Mexican guerrillas. By the standards of the 1910s or 1920s, mid-century governments were markedly more autonomous than their predecessors.

As for the radicalization of society, in Mexico the Cold War largely failed to inspire what Greg Grandin has termed the "politicization and internationalization" of everyday life.[187] For the majority of Mexicans the Cold War may instead have depoliticized everyday life. At the political extremes left- and right-wing groups remained wedded to pre-existing rhetoric, alliances, and organizational structures. Rubén Jaramillo's peasants were disenfranchised Cardenistas, the occasional burst of Marxist rhetoric as much a product of the CNC of the late 1930s as of international communism.[188] Genaro Vázquez and Lucio Cabañas were revolutionary nationalists first, Cuban-style socialists very much second.[189] Although the U.S. embassy and the Mexican government dressed up Celestino Gasca's 1961 rebels as Che-reading revolutionaries, the blend of military officers, middle-class democrats, and angry peasants better resembled the 1940 Almazanista electoral alliance.[190] The Movimiento de Liberación Nacional (MLN) was a classic Cardenista organization, well-meaning, inclusive, and ramshackle, its rhetoric "written within the vocabulary of reformist movements."[191] Even anticommunist rebels, like the "últimos cristeros" who attacked Huajuapan's garrison and Ciudad Hidalgo's town hall in 1962, harked back to an earlier era and comprised radicalized members of the ACM.[192] What polarization did exist proved if anything a political windfall for the PRI. By exaggerating the threat of armed revolt and repressing both left and right, the government pushed Mexicans toward the political center. Cárdenas withdrew his support from the MLN and took state employment as the head of the Río Balsas irrigation project.[193] The new leader of the PAN, Adolfo Christlieb Ibarrola, pulled back from the party's policy of paranoid McCarthyism, ordered activists to withdraw from conflictive local elections, and accepted the PRI's offer of watered-down electoral reforms.[194] Foreign policy, which balanced broad support for U.S. hemispheric defense with the right of Latin American countries to self-determination, exacerbated this shift, not only appeasing internal pressure groups but also solidifying the PRI's reputation for maintaining the peace.[195] Gazing north to a United States embroiled in Korea and then Vietnam or south to a war-torn Guatemala, many Mexicans lauded their government's pacific if inconsistent policies, feeling, perhaps, that Mexico remained "the best place to watch history from the ringside seats."[196]

The other major factor in stabilizing competitive authoritarianism is a reasonably powerful state. Assessed through Joel Migdal's schema of state characteristics—the power to penetrate society, extract resources, regulate social relationships, and appropriate resources—PRIísta Mexico was little stronger than its Cardenista predecessor.[197] The state had the technology and organization to extract resources and enjoyed some successes in penetrating society in material terms, including an expanding bureaucracy, social services, rising school enrollment; in the cultural terms of disseminating revolutionary nationalism, crafting an image of inevitability for the party, and providing a common language for political debate; and in the political terms of recruiting a mass party membership. Yet the quality of that penetration was equivocal. Bureaucrats' cognitive capacity remained low, to the extent that basic geography sometimes escaped them; thus, in a fit of absentmindedness, Ometepec, Guerrero, was once relocated to Oaxaca, while Zirándaro was moved to Michoacán.[198] Basic data collection remained woeful, particularly in the south: one economist complained that data collection in Oaxaca rarely covered more than 40 percent of the territory, in Guerrero perhaps 70 percent.[199] Bureaucracies were bigger, but they often were cannibalized by caciques or local interest groups and redirected away from state projects toward regional or rent-seeking goals. At the serrano extremes, entire regions used *indigenismo* to carve out parallel, contradictory autonomous powers such as the Consejo Supremo Tarahumara.[200] Mexico continued to fail in the most basic regulation of social relationships, namely Weber's "monopoly of the legitimate use of violence"[201]: everyday Mexicans protested against extrajudicial and/or privatized violence that encompassed preelectoral beatings, assassination, and petty massacre. As Piccato points out, "impunity . . . was more tangible in everyday life than presidential power."[202] Finally, critically, Mexico lacked the fundamental capability to appropriate resources. Traditional resistance to taxation combined with easy evasion to generate "incredibly low" revenues. In 1950 Mexicans paid the lowest taxes in Latin America—a region, as Miguel Angel Centeno pointed out, where the state was a "fiscal dwarf"—and little changed during the next fifty years.[203] Measured against the benchmarks of earlier scholarship, self-presentation, or extraregional comparative cases, the Mexican state was rather weak.

Yet while the long-term fate of contemporary competitive authoritarianism is murky, that of Mexico's historical parallel was exceptional longevity. Some of the answers to the paradoxes of authoritarianism and enduring inequality are to be found in force: both physical violence and the resulting violent imaginaries that multiplied its impact. Half-hidden force inhabited all three arenas of power, from straightforward political repression to cultural control to the key transfer of resources from countryside to city, which helped buy off an urban population that could not be controlled militarily and that never completely bought the state's legitimacy. In the provinces caciques, gunmen, and soldiers were central to the exercise of power and the maintenance of authoritarian capitalism. Troops were sent to occupy ejidos, chase local dissidents or insurgents, and break strikes, from the oilfields of Poza Rica to the sugar mill at Zacatepec to the mines of Nueva Rosita to the hospital corridors of Mexico City.[204] They did more than just monitor elections:

they arrested leaders, beat protesters, toppled opposition ayuntamientos, and *in extremis* waded into marches and street fights to lethal effect. At key junctures the army was used in capital cities: troops were deployed against students in Oaxaca in 1952, Mexico City in 1956, Chilpancingo in 1960.[205] Even high-ranking politicians could suffer overt military pressure. One officer made the attorney general publicly retract insinuations of extrajudicial executions; army patrols surrounded Henríquez Guzmán's house before the 1952 transfer of powers.[206] Well before Tlatelolco, state domination relied on violence significantly more than traditionally realized; brute force that was managed through careful targeting, concealment, and deniability. At critical junctures and in critical places—Mexico City in 1940, Baja California in 1962, municipios across the country when popular mobilization took hold—violence had causal primacy in sustaining PRIísta rule.[207]

Yet while force was a sine qua non of PRIísta survival, consent weighed heavier in the balance as economic, cultural, and political accommodation attenuated the paradoxes of authoritarianism and inequality. In the economic arena, elites channeled the rewards of growth to key sectors, directly in the form of jobs in industry, salaries, and services and indirectly through regulating access to resources and, in particular, fast-growing national and international markets. Against a background of global postwar boom, demographic growth, infrastructural development, and the spread of consumer culture, acting as a gatekeeper to those markets helped build large coalitions on the cheap. Urban populations certainly did not buy state discourse wholesale, but faced with a series of economic dilemmas they did opt in large numbers for a grudging, conditional consent. Consent also was favored by the cultural legacy of revolution: a common language of power, a certain residual faith in a revolutionary state, and, on both sides of power, the memory of revolutionary apocalypse.[208] Mexico is the only country in Latin America that might fit the European bellicist model of state formation, whereby "states make wars and wars make states"[209]; but Mexico's own Great War, the revolution, seems to have promoted a more pragmatic and resigned approach to the countercurrents of regional autonomy.[210] At the intersection of culture and economics lay the practice of politics, in which institutional design and the high cost of repression favored co-option and the second chances that prevented elite exits. These rights were not granted free, although some PRIístas clearly were shrewd institutional designers; they also were gained by popular mobilization and by the veto power to which politicians and policies at all levels were subject. Consent was in part a product of the involuntary laissez-faire of a weak state, whose elites often were incapable of imposing their will; of the considerable cultural, local, and ethnic autonomies that weakness permitted; and of the dialectic of state formation that weakness imposed. And that weakness, enforced flexibility, and inability to control local societies helped lend the state, for all the inequality of its economy, greater long-term stability than Latin America's harder and heavier authoritarian monoliths.

"One of the easiest ways to define a concept," Linz concluded, "is to say what it is not."[211] Mexico was not a perfect dictatorship: governments were too flexible yet institutional, popular inputs too great, and consent too negotiated to qualify as dictatorial, while politicians' frantic juggling and frequent recourse to violence made Mexico nothing like Orwell or Huxley's smooth-running dystopias. Neither was Mexico a classic, bureaucratic, or electoral authoritarian state. Among extant concepts, mid-century Mexico lay closest to competitive authoritarianism. Yet the processes underlying that outcome were utterly different. Mexican stability was not the product of a heavily political equation of external pressure versus sheer state power. External pressure for democratization was—with the brief exception of the mid-1940s—entirely absent. The aims, mechanisms, and results of Mexican state power were subject to multiple vetoes, which meant that quite often elites could not impose their will in the teeth of resistance and that the adroit exercise of soft power was critical. Single-factor theories—whether structural Marxism, cultural hegemony, or straightforward authoritarian repression—do not explain the ensuing balance of power as well as a historically contingent application of several middle-range theories. These span the circulation of elites, caciquismo, weapons of the weak, collective bargaining by riot, and local polyarchies; the interplay of hegemony, counter-hegemony, and cultural autonomy; and the cheap coalition-building characteristic of a gatekeeper state. This messy reality, with its contradictions, ambiguities, and considerable diversity, is captured when cultural, economic, and political analyses meet in a suitably contradictory term, *dictablanda*. Or, in comparative terms, soft authoritarianism: the combination of, on the one hand, a monopoly of national political office, carefully cultivated but thin cultural hegemony, lop-sided economic pay-offs, and resource regulation; and, on the other, hidden repressive violence with local autonomies, competitive if unequal elections, and salient popular bargaining and veto power. This produces unusually broad coalitions of political actors who shift fluently between opposition to, tolerance of, and support for a nondemocratic state. That shifting is central to the inherently ambiguous realities and legacies of a dictablanda, profoundly political ambiguities that in 2012 allowed the PRI out of the wilderness and back into Mexico's corridors of power.

Notes

1. Mario Vargas Llosa, "La dictadura perfecta" in *Desafíos a la libertad*, 171–76 (Madrid: El Pais, 1994).

2. Beatriz Magaloni, *Voting for Autocracy: Hegemonic Party Survival and Its Demise in Mexico* (Cambridge: Cambridge University Press, 2006), 1.

3. Thomas Benjamin, *La Revolución: Mexico's Great Revolution as Memory, Myth and History* (Austin: University of Texas Press, 2000), 137–49.

4. Arthur Schmidt, "Making it Real Compared to What? Reconceptualizing Mexican History since 1940," in *Fragments of a Golden Age: The Politics of Culture in Mexico Since 1940*, ed. Gilbert M. Joseph, Anne Rubinstein, and Eric Zolov, 23–66, 23–33 (Durham, NC: Duke University Press, 2001).

5. Jeffrey Rubin, "Popular Mobilization and the Myth of State Corporatism," in *Popular Movements and Political Change in Mexico*, ed. Joe Foweraker and Ann L. Craig, 247–67 (Boulder, CO: Lynne Rienner, 1990), 266.

6. Alan Knight, "Cardenismo: Juggernaut or Jalopy?" *Journal of Latin American Studies* 26, no. 1 (February 1994): 73–107, 79; Jeffrey Rubin, *Decentering the Regime: Ethnicity, Radicalism, and Democracy in Juchitán, Mexico* (Durham, NC: Duke University Press, 1997), 52–54; Ben Fallaw, *Cárdenas Compromised: The Failure of Reform in Postrevolutionary Yucatán* (Durham, NC: Duke University Press, 2001), 97–108; Adrian Bantjes, *As if Jesus Walked the Earth: Cardenismo, Sonora, and the Mexican Revolution* (Wilmington, DE: Scholarly Resources, 1998), 62–67, 192–203; Ben Fallaw, *Religion and State Formation in Postrevolutionary Mexico* (Durham, NC: Duke University Press, 2013); Emilio Portes Gil, *Autobiografía de la Revolución Mexicana* (Mexico City: Instituto Mexicano de Cultura, 1964), 633–34; Ariel José Contreras, *México 1940: Industrialización y crisis política: Estado y sociedad civil en las elecciones presidenciales* (Mexico City: Siglo XXI, 1977); Albert L. Michaels, "The Crisis of Cardenismo," *Journal of Latin American Studies* 2, no. 1 (1970): 51–79.

7. Alan Knight, "The Weight of the State in Modern Mexico," in *Studies in the Formation of the Nation-State in Latin American*, ed. James Dunkerley (London: ILAS, 2002), 212–53.

8. James W. Wilkie, *The Mexican Revolution: Federal Expenditure and Social Change Since 1910* (Berkeley: University of California Press, 1967), 158–59.

9. Cited in Rogelio Hernández Rodríguez, *La formación del político mexicano: el caso de Carlos A. Madrazo* (Mexico City: Colegio de México, 1991), 38.

10. Fallaw, *Cárdenas Compromised*, 125–57; Fallaw, *Religion and State Formation*; Stephen Lewis, *The Ambivalent Revolution: Forging State and Nation in Chiapas, 1910–1945* (Albuquerque: University of New Mexico Press, 2005), 119–36; Alexander Scott Dawson, *Indian and Nation in Revolutionary Mexico* (Tucson: University of Arizona Press, 2004), 163–64; Bantjes, *As if Jesus Walked the Earth*, 109–22; Paul Gillingham, "Ambiguous Missionaries: Rural Teachers and State Facades in Guerrero, 1930–1950," *Mexican Studies/Estudios Mexicanos* 22, no. 2 (summer 2006), 331–60; Benjamin T. Smith, "Inventing Tradition at Gunpoint: Culture, Caciquismo and State Formation in the Región Mixe, Oaxaca (1930–1959)," *Bulletin of Latin American Research* 27, no. 2 (April 2008): 215–34.

11. N. Ross Crumrine, *The Mayo Indians of Sonora* (Tucson: University of Arizona Press, 1977), 151–56; Julia Cummings O'Hara, "Transforming the Sierra Tarahumara: Indians, Missionaries and the State in Chihuahua, Mexico, 1890–1960" (PhD dissertation, University of Indiana, 2004); Agustín García Alcaraz, *Tinujei: Los Triquis de Copala* (Mexico City: Centro de Investigaciones y Estudios Superiores en Antropología Social, 1997), 171–89; Rubin, *Decentering the Regime*, 45–63; N. L. Whetton, *Rural Mexico*

(Chicago: University of Chicago Press, 1948), 482–522; Jean Meyer, *El sinarquismo: un fascismo mexicano?* 1937–1947 (Mexico City: Editorial J. M. Ortiz, 1979); Pablo Serrano Alvarez, *La batalla del espíritu, el sinarquismo en el Bajío Mexicano (1934–1951)* (2 vols.) (Mexico City: Consejo Nacional para la Cultura y las Artes, 1992), vol. I.

12. Antonio Santoyo, *La mano negra: Poder regional y estado en México (Veracruz, 1928–1943)* (Mexico City: Conaculta, 1995), 136–42; Thomas Benjamin, *A Rich Land, a Poor People: Politics and Society in Modern Chiapas* (Albuquerque: University of New Mexico Press, 1989), 201–4; Alex M. Saragoza, *The Monterrey Elite and the Mexican State* (Austin: University of Texas Press, 1988), 192–209.

13. Kevin Middlebrook, *The Paradox of Revolution: Labor, the State, and Authoritarianism in Mexico* (Baltimore: Johns Hopkins Press, 1995), 290; Magaloni, *Voting for Autocracy*, 14, 19, 81.

14. Middlebrook, *The Paradox of Revolution*, 5.

15. Clark Reynolds, *The Mexican Economy: Twentieth-Century Structure and Growth* (New Haven, CT: Yale University Press, 1970), 84; Roger Hansen, *The Politics of Mexican Development* (Baltimore: Johns Hopkins Press, 1971), 8, 72, 74; Mike Everett, "The Role of the Mexican Trade Unions, 1950–1963" (PhD dissertation, University of Washington, 1997), 196; Jeffrey L. Bortz, *Industrial Wages in Mexico City, 1939–1975* (New York: Garland Publishers, 1987); Jeffrey L. Bortz and Marcos Aguila, "Earning a Living: A History of Real Wage Studies in Twentieth-Century Mexico," *Latin American Research Review* 41, no. 2 (2006): 112–38; Roger Bartra, *Caciquismo y poder político en el México rural* (Mexico City: Siglo XXI, 1975), 6.

16. Arturo Warman, cited in Tanalís Padilla, *Rural Resistance in the Land of Zapata: The Jaramillista Movement and the Myth of the Pax Priísta, 1940–1962* (Durham, NC: Duke University Press, 2008), 166.

17. In 1963, the poorest 70 percent of Mexicans earned just 27.5 percent of national wealth, a drop of more than 4 percent since 1950. Hansen, *The Politics of Mexican Development*, 83, 87; Ifigenia Navarrete, "La distribución del ingreso en México, tendencias y perspectivas," in *El perfil de México en 1980, La economía y la población*, ed. Jorge Martinez Ríos (Mexico City: Siglo XXI, 1971), 37.

18. Klaus Deininger and Lyn Squire, "A New Data Set Measuring Income Inequality," *World Bank Economic Review* 10 (1996), 565–91. This is among the countries for which Deininger and Squire possess "high quality" data for the period.

19. Deininger and Squire, "A New Data Set Measuring Income Inequality," 565–91. Incorporating the estimates and incomplete survey data (the only available for much of the world in this period), outside the Americas, only Rhodesia, Gabon, Kenya, Zambia, Sierra Leone and Nigeria had higher Gini coefficients.

20. M. Szekely, "Pobreza y desigualdad en Mexico entre 1950 y 2004," *El Trimestre Económico* 72, no. 4 (October–December 2005): 913–31, 916.

21. Frank Brandenburg, *The Making of Modern Mexico* (Saddle River, NJ: Prentice Hall, 1964), vi; Schmidt, "Making It Real Compared to What?," 23–68.

22. James C. Scott, *Weapons of the Weak: Everyday Forms of Peasant Resistance* (New Haven, CT: Yale University Press, 1985).

23. It was noted that he actually resembled Boris Karloff rather than Bela Lugosi. Peñalosa Varo to Alemán, May 18, 1944, AGN/DGG-2/311 G(9)2 exp. "elecciones para gobernador" vol. IV; Calvario to Catalán Calvo, January 2, 1945, AGN/DGG-2/311 M(9)

caja 4B; Taylor to Foreign Office, October 25, 1951, FO371–90820/AM1015/8; *The San Diego Union*, July 2, 1952.

24. Acta, October 14, 1948, Archivo Municipal de Ixcateopan (AMI), 1948.

25. Inspector no. 37 to Ortega Peregrino, August 5, 1948, AGN/DGIPS-111/2–1/260/82.

26. A loose translation might be "Chuck Cash." Abel Quezada, *El mejor de los mundos imposibles* (Mexico City: CNCA, 1999), 80–81.

27. Jeffrey M. Pilcher, *Cantinflas and the Chaos of Mexican Modernity* (Wilmington, DE: Scholarly Resources, 2001), 154; PS-16 to Gobernación, August 3, 1948, AGN/DGIPS-111/2–1/260/82; Rodolfo Usigli, *El gesticulador (pieza para demágogos en tres actos)* (Mexico City: Editores Mexicanos Unidos, 1985), 53, 65, 107; Enrique Krauze, *La Presidencia Imperial: ascenso y caída del sistema político mexicano (1940–1996)* (Mexico City: Fabula, 1997), 159.

28. Carlos Fuentes, *La región más transparente del aire* (Mexico City: Fondo de Cultura Económica, 1996 [1958]), 50, 281; Mariano Azuela, *Nueva burguesía* (Mexico City: Fondo de Cultura Económica, 1985).

29. Daniel Cosío Villegas, *La Crisis de México* (Mexico City: Clio, 1997 [1947]); Jorge Vera Estañol, *La revolución Mexicana: orígenes y resultados* (Mexico City: Porrúa, 1957); Jesús Silva Herzog, *Un ensayo sobre la revolución Mexicana* (Mexico City: Cuadernos Americanos, 1946); Stanley Ross, ed., *Is the Mexican Revolution Dead?* (New York: Knopf, 1966); David C. Bailey, "Revisionism and the Recent Historiography of the Mexican Revolution," *Hispanic American Historical Review* 58, no. 1 (February 1978): 68, 70–71.

30. Notably Olga Pellicer de Brody and José Luis Reyna, *Historia de la Revolución Mexicana, 1952–1960: El afianzamiento de la estabilidad política* (Mexico City: Colegio de México, 1978) (see also vols. 17–22 in the same series); Carlos R. Martínez Assad, *El henriquismo, una piedra en el camino* (Mexico City: Martin Casillas, 1982); Soledad Loaeza, *Clases medias y política en México: la querella escolar, 1959–1963* (Mexico City: Colegio de México, 1998); Wil Pansters, *Politics and Power in Puebla: the Political History of a Mexican State, 1937–1987* (Amsterdam: CEDLA, 1990); Rafael Loyola Díaz, ed., *Entre la guerra y la estabilidad política: El México de los 40* (Mexico City: Consejo Nacional para la Cultura y las Artes, 1990); Hernández Rodríguez, *La formación del político Mexicano*; Armando Bartra, *Los herederos de Zapata: Movimientos campesinos posrevolucionarios en México, 1920–1980* (Mexico City: Ediciones Era, 1985); Barry Carr, *Marxism and Communism in Twentieth-Century Mexico* (Lincoln: University of Nebraska Press, 1992); Serrano Alvarez, *La batalla del espíritu*; Ricardo Pozas Horcasitas, *La democracia en blanco: el movimiento médico en México, 1964–1965* (Mexico City: Siglo XIX, 1993); Hector Aguilar Camín and Lorenzo Meyer, *In the Shadow of the Mexican Revolution: Contemporary Mexican History, 1910–1989*, trans. Luis Fierro (Austin: University of Texas Press, 1993)

31. Brandenburg, *The Making of Modern Mexico*, 164.

32. Luis Reyna and Richard S. Weinert, eds., *Authoritarianism in Mexico* (Philadelphia: Institute for the Study of Human Issues, 1977); Evelyn P. Stevens, "Mexico's PRI: The Institutionalization of Corporatism?," in *Authoritarianism and Corporatism in Latin America*, ed. James M. Malloy (Pittsburgh: University of Pittsburgh Press, 1977), 227–58; Judith Alder Hellman, *Mexico in Crisis* (New York: Holmes and Meier, 1983).

33. Krauze, *La Presidencia Imperial*, 136.

34. Donald J. Mabry, "Changing Models of Mexican Politics: A Review Essay," *The New Scholar* 5, no. 1 (1976): 31–37.

35. Pablo González Casanova, *Democracy in Mexico*, trans. Danielle Salti (London: Oxford University Press, 1970), 24–30, 103, 119–20, 127; Evelyn Stevens, "Protest Movement in an Authoritarian Regime: The Mexican Case," *Comparative Politics* 7, no. 3 (1975): 376; Richard S. Weinert, "Introduction," in Reyna and Weinert, *Authoritarianism in Mexico*, xiii; Roderic Ai Camp, *Politics in Mexico* (Oxford: Oxford University Press, 1993), 12.

36. Magaloni, *Voting for Autocracy*, 9, 26, 52.

37. Philip Abrams, "Notes on the Difficulty of Studying the State," *Journal of Historical Sociology* 1, no. 1 (1977), 58–89, 77; Gilbert M. Joseph and Daniel Nugent, "Popular Culture and State Formation in Revolutionary Mexico," in *Everyday Forms of State Formation: Revolution and the Negotiation of Rule in Modern Mexico*, ed. Gilbert M. Joseph and Daniel Nugent, 3–23 (Durham, NC: Duke University Press, 1994), 19. See also Ana Alonso, "The Politics of Space, Time and Substance: State Formation, Nationalism, and Ethnicity," *Annual Review of Anthropology* 23 (1994): 379–405.

38. While Corrigan and Sayer stressed the importance of laws as moral regulators in Great Britain, this was seemingly lost in translation into a Mexican setting (Joseph and Nugent, "Popular Culture," 20).

39. Joseph and Nugent, "Popular Culture," 19. Key works include Anne Rubenstein, *Bad Language, Naked Ladies, and Other Threats to the Nation: A Political History of Comic Books in Mexico* (Durham, NC: Duke University Press, 1998); William H. Beezley, Cheryl English Martin, William E. French, eds., *Rituals of Rule, Rituals of Resistance: Public Celebrations and Popular Culture in Mexico* (Wilmington, DE: Scholarly Resources, 1994); Mary Kay Vaughan and Stephen E. Lewis, eds., *The Eagle and the Virgin: Nation and Cultural Revolution in Mexico, 1920–1940* (Durham, NC: Duke University Press, 2006); Mary Kay Vaughan, *Cultural Politics in Revolution: Teachers, Peasants, and Schools in Mexico, 1930–1940* (Tucson: University of Arizona Press, 1997).

40. Florencia Mallon, "The Promise and Dilemma of Subaltern Studies: Perspectives from Latin American History," *The American Historical Review* 99, no. 5 (December 1994): 1491–515; Joseph and Nugent, "Popular Culture," 21; Daniel Nugent and Ana María Alonso, "Multiple Selective Traditions in Agrarian Reform and Agrarian Struggle: Popular Culture and State Formation in the Ejido of Namiquipa, Chihuahua," in Joseph and Nugent, *Everyday Forms of State Formation*, 209–46; William Roseberry, "Hegemony and the Language of Contention," in Joseph and Nugent, *Everyday Forms of State Formation*, 355–66; Ranajit Guha, "On Some Aspects of the Historiography of Colonial India," in *Mapping Subaltern Studies and the Postcolonial*, ed. Vinayak Chaturvedi, 1–7 (London: Verso, 2000); David Arnold, "Gramsci and Peasant Subalternity in India," in Chaturvedi, *Mapping Subaltern Studies*, 24–49; Rosalind O'Hanlon, "Recovering the Subject: Subaltern Studies and Histories of Resistance in Colonial South Asia," in Chaturvedi, *Mapping Subaltern Studies*, 72–115.

41. Roseberry, "Hegemony and the Language of Contention," 365.

42. Vaughan, *Cultural Politics in Revolution*, 7, 22, 42.

43. Alan Knight, "Caciquismo in Mexico," in *Caciquismo in Twentieth-Century Mexico*, ed. Alan Knight and Wil Pansters, 1–51 (London: ILAS, 2005).

44. Nora Hamilton, *The Limits of State Autonomy: Post-revolutionary Mexico* (Princeton, NJ: Princeton University Press, 1982).

45. Jocelyn Olcott, *Revolutionary Women in Postrevolutionary Mexico* (Durham, NC:

Duke University Press, 2005); Florencia Mallon, "Reflections on the Ruins: Everyday Forms of State Formation in Nineteenth-Century Mexico," in Joseph and Nugent, *Everyday Forms of State Formation*, 69–106, 81–89.

46. Mary Kay Vaughan, "Cultural Approaches to Peasant Politics in the Mexican Revolution," *Hispanic American Historical Review* 79, no. 2 (May 1999): 274.

47. Peter Bratsis, "Unthinking the State: Reification, Ideology, and the State as a Social Fact," in *Paradigm Lost: State Theory Reconsidered*, ed. Stanley Aronowitz and Peter Bratsis, 247–67 (Minneapolis: University of Minnesota Press, 2002).

48. For a more subtle appreciation of the role of state institutions, see Vivien Schmidt, "Institutionalism," in *The State: Theories and Issues*, ed. Colin Hay, Michael Lister, and David Marsh, 98–117 (London: Palgrave, 2006).

49. Bob Jessop, *State Theory: Putting the Capitalist State in Its Place* (Cambridge: Polity, 1990).

50. Loaeza, *Clases medias y política en México*; Rogelio Hernández Rodríguez, *Amistades, compromisos y lealtades: líderes y grupos políticos en el Estado de México, 1942–1993* (Mexico City: Colegio de México, 1998); Stephen R. Niblo, *Mexico in the 1940s: Modernity, Politics, and Corruption* (Wilmington, DE: Scholarly Resources, 1999); Miguel González Campían and Leonardo Lomelí, *El Partido de la Revolución: Institución y conflicto (1928–1999)* (Mexico City: FCE, 2000); Elisa Servín, *Ruptura y oposición: El Henriquismo, 1945–1954* (México: Cal y Arena, 2001); Luis Aboites Aguilar, *Excepciones y privilegios: Modernización tributaria y centralización en México, 1922–1972* (Mexico City: Colegio de México, 2003); María Antonia Martínez, *El despegue constructivo de la Revolución: Sociedad y política en el alemanismo* (Mexico City: Editorial Miguel Angel Porrúa, 2004); Ricardo Pozas Horcasitas, "La democracia fallida: La batalla de Carlos A. Madrazo por cambiar el PRI," *Revista Mexicana de Sociología* 70, no. 1 (2008): 47–85; Ariel Rodríguez Kuri, "Los años maravillosos. Adolfo Ruiz Cortines," in *Gobernantes mexicanos*, ed. Will Fowler (Mexico City: Fondo de Cultura Económica, 2008); Jonathan Schlefer, *Palace Politics: How the Ruling Party Brought Crisis to Mexico* (Austin: University of Texas Press, 2008); Rogelio Hernández Rodríguez, *El centro dividido: La nueva autonomía de los gobernadores* (Mexico City: Colegio de México, 2009); Ariel Rodríguez Kuri, "Adolfo López Mateos y la gran política nacional," in *Adolfo López Mateos: La vida dedicada a la política* (Mexico City: Gobierno del Estado de México, 2010); Alejandro Quintana, *Maximino Ávila Camacho and the One-Party State: The Taming of Caudillismo and Caciquismo in Post-Revolutionary Mexico* (Lanham, MD: Lexington Books, 2010); José Antonio Caballero, "Amparos y Abogángsters: La justicia en México entre 1940 y 1968," in *Del nacionalismo al neoliberalismo, 1940–1994*, ed. Elisa Servín (Mexico City: Fondo de Cultura Económica, 2010); Nichole Sanders, *Gender and Welfare in Mexico: The Consolidation of a Postrevolutionary State (1937–1958)* (University Park: Pennsylvania State University Press, 2011).

51. Armando Bartra, *Guerrero bronco: Campesinos, ciudadanos y guerrilleros en la Costa Grande* (Mexico City: Ediciones Era, 2000); Alicia Olivera Sedano, Rina Ortiz Peralta, Elisa Servín, and Tania Hernández Vicencio, eds., *Los matices de la rebeldía. Las oposiciones políticas y sociales* (Mexico City: INAH, 2010); Rubin, *Decentering the Regime*; Sergio Aguayo Quezada, *La Charola: Una historia de los servicios de inteligencia en México* (Mexico City: Grijalbo, 2001); Donald C. Hodges and Ross Gandy, *Mexico under Siege: Popular Resistance to Presidential Despotism* (London: Zed Books, 2002); María del Carmen Ventura Patiño, *Disputas por el gobierno local en Tarecuato, Michoacán, 1942–1999* (Zamora: Co-

legio de Michoacán, 2003); Verónica Oikión Solano and Marta Eugenia García Ugarte, *Movimientos armados en México, siglo XX* (Morelia: Colegio de Michoacán, CIESAS, 2003); Alan Knight and Wil Pansters, eds., *Caciquismo in Twentieth-Century Mexico* (London: Institute for the Study of the Americas, 2006); Salvador Román Román, *Revuelta Cívica en Guerrero 1957–1960* (Mexico City: INERHM, 2003); Laura Castellano, *México Armado, 1943–1981* (Mexico City: Ediciones Era, 2007); Eric Zolov, "¡Cuba sí, Yanquis no! The Sacking of the Instituto Cultural Mexico-Norteamericano in Morelia, Michoacán, 1961," in *In from the Cold: Latin America's New Encounter with the Cold War*, ed. Gilbert M. Joseph and Daniela Spenser, 181–210 (Durham, NC: Duke University Press, 2007); Padilla, *Rural Resistance*; O'Neill Blacker, "Cold War in the Countryside: Conflict in Guerrero, Mexico," *The Americas* 66, no. 2 (2009): 214–52; José Carmen Soto Correa, *El rifle sanitario, la fiebre aftosa y la rebelión campesina* (Mexico City: Instituto Politécnico Nacional, 2009); Benjamin T. Smith, *Pistoleros and Popular Movements: The Politics of State Formation in Postrevolutionary Oaxaca* (Lincoln: University of Nebraska Press, 2009); Aaron W. Navarro, *Political Intelligence and the Creation of Modern Mexico, 1938–1954* (University Park: Pennsylvania State University Press, 2010); Robert Alegre, "Las Rieleras: Gender, Politics, and Power in the Mexican Railway Movement, 1958–1959," *Journal of Women's History* 23, no. 2 (2011): 162–86; Wil G. Pansters, "Zones of State-Making: Violence, Coercion, and Hegemony in Twentieth-Century Mexico" in *Violence, Coercion, and State-Making in Twentieth-Century Mexico: The Other Half of the Centaur*, ed. Wil G. Pansters, 3–41 (Palo Alto, CA: Stanford University Press, 2012); Paul Gillingham, "Who Killed Crispín Aguilar? Violence and Order in the Postrevolutionary Countryside," in *Violence, Coercion, and State-Making*, ed. Wil Pansters, 91–111; Fernando Herrera Calderón and Adela Cedillo, eds., *Challenging Authoritarianism in Mexico: Revolutionary Struggles and the Dirty War, 1964–1982* (New York: Routledge, 2012).

52. Soledad Loaeza, *El Partido Acción Nacional: La larga marcha, 1939–1994: Oposición leal y partido de protesta* (Mexico City: Fondo de Cultura Económica, 1999); Yolanda Padilla Rangel, *Después de la tempestad: La reorganización católica en Aguascalientes, 1929–1950* (Zamora: Colegio de Michoacán, 2001); Daniel Newcomer, *Reconciling Modernity: Urban State Formation in 1940s León, Mexico* (Lincoln: University of Nebraska Press, 2004); María Luisa Aspe Armella, *La formación social y política de los católicos mexicanos: La Acción Católica y la Unión Nacional de Estudiantes Católicos, 1929–1958* (Mexico City: La Universidad Iberoamericana, 2008); Jason Dormady, *Primitive Revolution: Restorationist Religion and the Idea of the Mexican Revolution, 1940–1968* (Albuquerque: University of New Mexico Press, 2011); Benjamin T. Smith, *The Roots of Conservatism in Mexico: Catholicism, Society, and Politics in the Mixteca Baja, 1750–1962* (Albuquerque: University of New Mexico Press, 2012).

53. Jacinto Rodríguez Munguía, *La Otra Guerra Secreta: Los Archivos Prohibidos de la Prensa y el Poder* (Mexico City: Random House Mondadori, 2007); Fernando Mejía Barquera, *La industria de la radio y la televisión y la política del estado mexicano (1920–1960)* (Mexico City: Fundación Manuel Buendía, 1989); Alex Saragoza, "Behind the Scenes: Media Ownership, Politics, and Popular Culture in Mexico (1930–1958)," in *Los intelectuales y el poder en México*, ed. Roderic Ai Camp (Mexico City: Colegio de México, 1991); Eric Zolov, *Refried Elvis: The Rise of the Mexican Counterculture* (Berkeley: University of California Press, 1998); Michael Nelson Miller, *Red, White, and Green: The Maturing of Mexicanidad, 1940–1946* (El Paso: Texas Western Press, 1998); Rubenstein, *Bad Language, Naked Ladies, and Other Threats to the Nation*; Joy Hayes, *Radio Nation: Communication,*

Popular Culture, and Nationalism in Mexico, 1920–1950 (Tucson: University of Arizona Press, 2000); Gilbert M. Joseph, Anne Rubinstein, and Eric Zolov, eds., *Fragments of a Golden Age: The Politics of Culture in Mexico Since 1940* (Durham, NC: Duke University Press, 2001); Pilcher, *Cantinflas and the Chaos of Mexican Modernity*; Claudia Fernández and Andrew Paxman, *El Tigre: Emilio Azcárraga y su imperio Televisa* (Mexico City: Grijalbo-Mondadori, 2001 [rev. ed.]); John Mraz, *Looking for Mexico: Modern Visual Culture and National Identity* (Durham, NC: Duke University Press, 2010); Anne Rubenstein, "Mass Media and Popular Culture in the Postrevolutionary Era," in *The Oxford History of Mexico*, ed. Michael Meyer and William H. Beezley (New York: Oxford University Press, 2010); Paul Gillingham, *Cuauhtémoc's Bones: Forging National Identity in Modern Mexico* (Albuquerque: University of New Mexico Press, 2011).

54. Steven J. Bachelor, "Toiling for the 'New Invaders': Autoworkers, Transnational Corporations, and Working-Class Culture in Mexico City, 1955–1968," in Joseph, Rubenstein and Zolov, *Fragments of a Golden Age*, 273–326; Ariel Rodríguez Kuri, "Secretos de la idiosincracia: Urbanización y cambio cultural en México, 1950–1970," in *Ciudades mexicana del siglo XX: Siete estudios históricos*, ed. Carlos Lira Vasquez and Ariel Rodríguez Kuri, 19–56 (Mexico City: Colegio de México, 2009); Gabriela Soto Laveaga, *Jungle Laboratories: Mexican Peasants, National Projects, and the Making of the Pill* (Durham, NC: Duke University Press, 2010).

55. Moisés T. de la Peña, *Guerrero Económico* (2 vols.) (Mexico City: n.p., 1949), vol. 2, 611; *El Popular*, October 8, 1952; "President Alemán's Message on the State of the Nation, Economic Aspects," September 12, 1951, NARG-712.21/9–1251.

56. Clipping from *El Mundo*, in I-184 to Gobernación, May 11, 1944, AGN/DGIPS-100.

57. That is, for sale. El Fisgón y Helguera, *El sexenio me da risa: la historieta no oficial* (Mexico City: Grijalbo, 1994), 22.

58. Gobernación report, September 2, 1948, AGN/DGIPS-132/2–1/303"1948."

59. Knight, "The Weight of the State," 216–17.

60. Instructions to S. Pavón Silva, April 1948, AGN/DGIPS-797/2–1/48/392.

61. Roy F. Baumeister and Brad J. Busman, *Social Psychology and Human Nature* (Belmont, CA: Thomson Higher Education, 2008), 144.

62. Reginald Hibbert, "Intelligence and Policy," *Intelligence and National Security* 5, no. 1 (January 1990), 118.

63. "Relación de los inspectores de la DGIPS comisionados en diversos estados de la República para observar el desarrollo de las elecciones de poderes federales," June 1952, AGN/DGIPS-814/2–1/52/70; request for identity cards, Lince Medellín to Dir. Gen. Administración, January 11, 1957, AGN/DGIPS-1993B-2–1/"57"/86.

64. For a sample of usefully contextualized reports, see "Spy Reports: Content, Methodology, and Historiography in Mexico's Secret Police Archive" special issue of the *Journal of Iberian and Latin American Research* 19, no. 1 (July 2013), ed. Tanalís Padilla and Louise E. Walker.

65. Eric Wolf, *Europe and the People Without History* (Berkeley: University of California Press, 1982), 3.

66. Middlebrook, *The Paradox of Revolution*, 29; Magaloni, *Voting for Autocracy*, 24.

67. William B. Sewell, *Logics of History: Social Theory and Social Transformation* (Chicago: University of Chicago Press, 2005), 1–12.

68. Fernand Braudel, *The Mediterranean and the Mediterranean World in the Age of Philip II* (Berkeley: University of California Press, 1996), vol. I, 19–21.

69. INEGI, *Estadísticas Históricas de México* CD-ROM.

70. Oscar Lewis, *The Children of Sánchez: Autobiography of a Mexican Family* (New York: Basic Books, 1963), xvi–xvii.

71. Padilla, chapter 15, and Boyer, chapter 9, this volume.

72. Gillingham, chapter 16, this volume.

73. Hernández Rodríguez, chapter 14, this volume.

74. Paxman, chapter 13, this volume.

75. A conclusion not far removed from that of Carlos Monsiváis, who concurred with Paz in seeing 1968 as "un año axial" while recognizing its primary significance as perceptual: ". . . *a la luz del 2 de octubre la historia de los años recientes cobra otra significación. Un acto represivo ilumina un panorama* . . ." [the history of recent years takes on another meaning in the light of October 2. A repressive act reveals a landscape . . ."]. Carlos Monsiváis, *Días de Guardar* (Mexico City: Ediciones Era, 1970), 16–17.

76. Enrique Cárdenas and Rosemary Thorpe, "Introducción," in *Industrialización y Estado en el America Latina, La Leyenda Negra de la Posguerra*, ed. Enrique Cárdenas, José Antonio Ocampo, and Rosemary Thorpe, 9–57 (Mexico City: El Trimestre Económico, 2003), 40; Guillermo A. O'Donnell, *Modernization and Bureaucratic-Authoritarianism: Studies in South American Politics* (Berkeley: University of California Press, 1979), 38–40.

77. Calvin P. Blair, "Nacional Financiera, Entrepreneurship in a Mixed Economy," in *Public Policy and Private Enterprise in Mexico*, ed. Raymond Vernon, 192–240 (Cambridge, MA: Harvard University Press, 1964); Cynthia Hewitt de Alcántara, *La modernización de la agricultura Mexicana* (Mexico City: Siglo XIX, 1978).

78. Paul Yates, *El desarrollo regional de México* (Mexico City: Banco de México, 1962), 49.

79. National Border Program, *Programa Nacional Fronterizo* 1 (1961): 6.

80. Reynolds, *The Mexican Economy*, 18; Larissa Adler de Lomnitz, *Networks of Marginality: Life in a Mexican Shanty Town* (New York: Academic Press, 1977), 12–13.

81. Blanca Torres, *Hacia la utopía industrial* (Mexico City: Colegio de México, 1984), 28, 41; Rodolfo Stavenhagen, *Neolatifundismo y Explotación,: de Emiliano Zapata a Anderson Clayton & Co.* (Mexico City: Editorial Nuestro Tiempo, 1975); Hewitt de Alcántara, *La modernización de la agricultura*.

82. Salomón Eckstein Raber, *El ejido colectivo en México* (Mexico City: Fondo de Cultura Económica, 1966), 70; INEGI, *Estadísticas Históricas de México* CD-ROM; Jeffrey H. Cohen, "Transnational Migration in Rural Oaxaca, Mexico: Dependency, Development, and the Household," *American Anthropologist* 103, no. 4 (December 2001): 954–67, 957.

83. Padilla, *Rural Resistance*, 7–8, 139–60; Elisa Servín, "Hacía el levantamiento armado: Del henriquismo a los federacionistas leales en los años cincuenta," in *Movimientos armados en México*, ed. Oikión Solano and García Ugarte, vol. I, 307–32.

84. Which, although short-lived, spread across seven states: Puebla, Veracruz, Oaxaca, Chiapas, Guerrero, Estado de México, and Coahuila. Servín, "Hacía el levantamiento armado," vol. I, 310.

85. Rath, chapter 3, this volume.

86. Gutierrez Tibón, *Pinotepa Nacional, mixtecos, negros y triquis* (Mexico City: Universidad Autónoma de México, 1961), 138–40.

87. Thomas Rath, "Introduction," *Myths of Demilitarization in Postrevolutionary Mexico, 1920–1960* (Chapel Hill: University of North Carolina Press, 2013).

88. Rath, chapter 3, this volume.

89. Heather Fowler-Salamini, *Agrarian Radicalism in Veracruz, 1920–1938* (Lincoln: University of Nebraska Press, 1978), 144–45.

90. Eric J. Hobsbawm, "The Machine Breakers," *Past and Present* 1, no. 1 (1952): 57–70, 58–59; Padilla, *Rural Resistance*, 141.

91. Victor Orozco Orozco, "La guerrilla chihuahuense de los sesenta," in Oikión Solano and García Ugarte, *Movimientos armados en México*, vol. 2, 337–60, 353.

92. Pellicer de Brody and Reyna, *Historia de la Revolución Mexicana*, 123–40.

93. Angel Bassols Batalla, *El noreste de Mexico: Un estudio geográfico-económico* (Mexico City: UNAM, 1972), 548–51; Eckstein Raber, *El ejido colectivo en México*, 165–68; Steven E. Sanderson, *Agrarian Populism and the Mexican State: The Struggle for Land in Sonora*, (Berkeley: University of California Press, 1981), 157.

94. Magaloni, *Voting for Autocracy*, 269.

95. Middlebrook, *The Paradox of Revolution*, 107–55.

96. Snodgrass, chapter 7, this volume.

97. Susan M. Gauss, *Made in Mexico: Regions, Nation, and the State in the Rise of Mexican Industrialization, 1920s–1940s* (University Park: Pennsylvania State University Press, 2010), 5, 185–86.

98. Pellicer de Brody and Reyna, *Historia de la Revolución Mexicana*, 9.

99. Mraz, *Looking for Mexico*, 165.

100. Michael Lettieri, "Wheels of Government: The Alianza de Camioneros and the Political Culture of PRI Rule, 1929–1981" (PhD dissertation, UCSD, 2014); Terrence E. Poppa and Charles Bowden, *Drug Lord: A True Story. The Life and Death of a Mexican Kingpin* (El Paso, TX: Cinco Puntos Press, 2010), 42–43.

101. Gauss, *Made in Mexico*, 166, 185–90.

102. Paxman, chapter 13, this volume.

103. Mexico was not a gatekeeper state, however. It was not recently a colony, and it enjoyed more national autonomy, a more diversified economy, a larger institutional apparatus, and a more effectively powerful national identity than do such states. For the concept, see Frederick Cooper, *Africa since 1940: The Past of the Present* (Cambridge: Cambridge University Press, 2002), 5, 156–90; Javier Corrales, "The Gatekeeper State: Limited Economic Reforms and Regime Survival in Cuba, 1989–2002," *Latin American Research Review* 39, no. 2 (2004): 35–65.

104. Paul Gillingham, "Maximino's Bulls: Popular Protest after the Mexican Revolution," *Past and Present* 206 (February 2010): 145–81.

105. Enrique Ochoa, *Feeding Mexico: The Political Uses of Food Since 1910* (Wilmington, DE: Scholarly Resources, 2000), 86, 82.

106. Manuel Perló Cohen, "Politica y vivienda en México 1910–1952," *Revista Mexicana de Sociología* 41, no. 3: 769–835, 816–20.

107. Pensado, chapter 16, this volume; Eric Zolov, "¡Cuba sí, Yanquis no!," 214–52; Nicolás Dávila Peralta, *Las Santas Batallas: El Anticomunismo en Puebla* (Puebla: Gobierno del estado de Puebla, 1978); Rafael Santos Cenobio, *El movimiento estudiantil en la UAS (1966–1972)* (Culiacán: UAS, 2005).

108. Smith, *Pistoleros and Popular Movements*, 397.

109. Diane Davis, *Urban Leviathan: Mexico City in the Twentieth Century* (Philadelphia: Temple University Press, 1994), 167–73; John C. Cross, *Informal Politics, Street Vendors and the State in Mexico City* (Palo Alto, CA: Stanford University Press, 1988), 160–87.

110. Wayne Cornelius, *Politics and the Migrant Poor in Mexico City* (Palo Alto, CA: Stanford University Press, 1975), 205; Douglas Butterworth, "Two Small Groups: A Comparison of Migrants and Non-Migrants in Mexico City," *Urban Anthropology* 1 (spring 1972): 41.

111. Carlos Vélez-Ibañez, *Rituals of Marginality: Politics, Process, and Culture Change in Urban Central Mexico, 1969–1974* (Berkeley: University of California Press, 1983), 121.

112. Heather Fowler-Salamini, *Working Women, Entrepreneurs and the Mexican Revolution* (Lincoln: University of Nebraska Press, forthcoming); Enriqueta Tuñón Pablos, *¡Por fin . . . ya podemos elegir y ser electas!* (Mexico City: CONACULTA, 2002); María Teresa Fernández Aceves, "En-gendering Caciquismo: Guadalupe Martínez, Heliodoro Hernández Loza and the Politics of Organized Labor in Jalisco," in Knight and Pansters, *Caciquismo in Twentieth-Century Mexico*, 201–27; Victoria E. Rodríguez, *Women's Participation in Mexican Political Life* (Boulder, CO: Westview Press, 1998); Sara Buck, "The Meaning of the Women's Vote in Mexico, 1917–1953," in *The Women's Revolution in Mexico, 1910–1953*, ed. Stephanie Mitchell and Patience A. Schell, 73–98 (Lanham, MD: Rowman and Littlefield, 2007).

113. Olcott, *Revolutionary Women in Postrevolutionary Mexico*; Jocelyn Olcott, Mary Kay Vaughan, and Gabriela Cano, eds., *Sex in Revolution: Gender, Politics, and Power in Modern Mexico* (Durham, NC: Duke University Press, 2006); Andrew Grant Wood, *Revolution in the Street: Women, Workers, and Urban Protest in Veracruz, 1870–1927* (Wilmington, DE: Scholarly Resources, 2001); Piedad Peniche Rivero, "El movimiento feminista de Elvia Carrillo Puerto y las igualadas: Un liderazgo cultural en Yucatán," in *Dos mujeres fuera de serie: Elvia Carillo Puerto y Felipa Poot*, ed. Piedad Peniche Rivero and Kathleen R. Martín (Mérida: Instituto de la Cultura de Yucatán, 2007); Gabriela Cano, "Debates en torno al sufragio y la ciudadanía de las mujeres en México," in *Historia de las Mujeres en España y América Latina del siglo XX a los umbrales del Siglo XXI*, ed. Isabel Monrat, 535–51 (Madrid: Editorial Cátedra, 2006).

114. Patience Schell, *Church and State Education in Revolutionary Mexico City* (Tucson: University of Arizona Press, 2003); Kristina A. Boylan, "Gendering the Faith and Altering the Nation: Mexican Catholic Women's Activism, 1917–1940," in *Sex in Revolution*, ed. Olcott, Vaughan, and Cano, 199–224; María Teresa Fernández Aceves, "Guadalajaran Women and the Construction of National Identity," in *The Eagle and the Virgin*, ed. Lewis and Vaughan, 297–313; Valentina Septién Torres, "Guanajuato y la resistencia católica en el siglo XX," in *Integrados y marginados en el México posrevoluciónario: Los juegos de poder local y sus nexus con la política nacional*, ed. Nicolás Cárdenas García and Enrique Guerra Manzo, 83–119 (Mexico City: Universidad Autónoma Metropolitana, 2009).

115. Blancarte, chapter 2, this volume; Fowler-Salamini, *Working Women*, chapter 6; Armella, *La formación social y política de los católicos mexicanos*.

116. Padilla, *Rural Resistance*, 161–83.

117. Smith, *Pistoleros and Popular Movements*, 275–77.

118. Carlos Brambila, "Mexico's Population Policy and Demographic Dynamics: The Record of Three Decades," in *Do Population Policies Matter? Fertility and Politics in*

Egypt, India, Kenya, and Mexico, ed. Anrudh K. Jain (New York: Population Council, 1998), 157; Luis González y González, *Pueblo en vilo* (Mexico City: SEP, 1984), 311–12.

119. Roderic Ai Camp, "Women and Political Leadership in Mexico: A Study of Female and Male Political Elites," *The Journal of Politics* 41, no. 2 (1979): 417–41.

120. Arundh Jain, "Population Policies That Matter," in Jain, *Do Population Policies Matter?*, 6.

121. Buck, "The Meaning," 88–89; Sanders, *Gender and Welfare in Mexico*, 73–89.

122. Armando S. Cisneros, *La ciudad que construimos: Registro de la expansión de la ciudad de México, 1920–1976* (Mexico City: UAM, 1992), 140.

123. Fowler-Salamini, *Working Women*, chapter 6.

124. Although she ended up a *suplente*. National Anthropological Archive, Ralph L. Beals Collection, Box 60, interview with Juan Medina, June 13, 1966.

125. Rafael Segovia, *La politización del niño mexicano* (Mexico City: Colegio de México, 1975), 15–16.

126. Gabriel García Márquez and Roberto Pombo, "The Punchcard and the Hourglass: An Interview with Subcomandante Marcos," *The New Left Review* 9 (May/June 2001): 69–79, 77.

127. Assorted reports, July–August 1948, AGN DGIPS-94/2–1/131/802, AGN DGIPS-101/2–1/131/1012; Mraz, *Looking for Mexico*, 165–66.

128. Navarro, *Political Intelligence*, 144; Rogelio Ramos Oranday, "Oposición y abstencionismo en las elecciones presidenciales, 1964–1982," in *Las elecciones en México: evolución y perspectiva*, ed. Pablo González Casanova, 166–86 (Mexico City: Siglo XXI, 1985).

129. El Nacional to presidente municipal Ixcateopan, February 20, 1948, AMI-1945.

130. Martínez, *El despegue constructivo*, 59.

131. Fernández and Paxman, *El Tigre*, 277, 323, 412, 418, 508–9.

132. An exception was El Día, founded in 1962.

133. Tiempo poll, May 1942, reproduced in Joe Belden, "Mexico's Public Opinion Poll," *The Public Opinion Quarterly* 8, no. 1 (spring 1944); Gabriel A. Almond and Sidney Verba, *The Civic Culture: Political Attitudes and Democracy in Five Nations* (Newbury Park, CA: Sage Publications, 1989), 310–11, 363; Segovia, *La politización del niño mexicano*, 55–59; Magaloni, *Voting for Autocracy*, 73.

134. Rubenstein, *Bad Language, Naked Ladies, and Other Threats to the Nation*, 95–97, 110–28.

135. "El Corrido de los braceros," June 4, 1944, Archivo General del Poder Ejecutivo de Oaxaca (AGPEO), Gobernacion; Miguel Angel Gallo, *La Satira Política Mexicana* (Mexico City: Ediciones Quinto Sol, 1987), 259.

136. Raine to State, February 24, 1950, NARG-712.00/2–2450.

137. Vélez-Ibañez, *Rituals of Marginality*, 76.

138. Ernest Gruening, quoted in Jürgen Buchenau, *The Last Caudillo: Alvaro Obregón and the Mexican Revolution* (Chichester, UK: John Wiley and Sons, 2012), 124; Paul Friedrich, *The Princes of Naranja: An Essay on Anthropological Method* (Austin: University of Texas Press, 1986), 45, 50, 185; Julia Preston and Samuel Dillon, *Opening Mexico: The Making of a Democracy* (New York: Farrar, Straus and Giroux, 2004), 178.

139. Gonzalo N. Santos, *Memorias* (Mexico City: Grijalbo, 1986), 167.

140. Armando Jiménez, *Picardía Mexicana* (Mexico City: Libro Mex, 1960), 119.

141. "Los Participaciones," 1948, AGN/DGIPS-III/1/1948; Samuel Schmidt, *Antología del Chiste Político* (Mexico City: Aguilar, 1996), 22.

142. "Corrido de los Cuerudos," 1952, Hemeroteca de Oaxaca, Colección Manuel Mayoral Heredia.

143. Jorge Portilla, *Fenomología del relajo y otros ensayos* (Mexico City: Fondo de Cultura Ecónomica, 1984). See also Roger Bartra, *The Cage of Melancholy: Identity and Metamorphosis in the Mexican Character* (New Brunswick, NJ: Rutgers University Press, 1992), 140–42.

144. Tomás Salazar Paz, "Problemas sociales y jurídicas de las poblaciones indígenas de la Mixteca" (BA thesis, UNAM, 1963), 71.

145. Armando de María y Campos, *El Teatro de Género Chico en la Revolución Mexicana* (Mexico City: Biblioteca del Instituto Nacional de Estudios Históricos de la Revolución Mexicana, 1956), vol. I, 423–24.

146. Peter Beardsell, *A Theatre for Cannibals: Rodolfo Usigli and the Mexican Stage* (Rutherford, NJ: Associated University Presses, 1992), 61.

147. Robert Blanco Moheno, *Memorias de un Reportero* (Mexico City: Costa Amic, 1965), 294–95.

148. Mraz, *Looking for Mexico*, 161–65.

149. Enrique Krauze, *Mexico: Biography of Power* (New York: Harper Perennial, 1998), 686–87.

150. Claudio Lomnitz-Adler, *Exits from the Labyrinth: Culture and Ideology in the Mexican National Space* (Berkeley: University of California Press, 1992), 196; Krauze, *La presidencia imperial*, 243.

151. Roger Bartra, *Anatomía del mexicano* (Mexico City: Random House Mondadori, 2005), 121; Guillermo de la Peña, "Corrupción e Informalidad," in *Vicios públicos, virtudes privadas: La corrupción en México*, ed. Claudio Lomnitz-Adler, 113–27, 120 (Mexico City: CIESAS, 2000).

152. Michael Herzfeld, *Cultural Intimacy: Social Poetics in the Nation-State* (London: Routledge, 2005), 3.

153. Baroja, cited in Emmanuel Le Roy Ladurie, *Carnival: A People's Uprising at Romans* (New York: George Braziller, 1979), 311–16.

154. Portilla, *Fenomología*.

155. Gilberto Ramos Camacho, "Este era Palillo," in *Leyendas, tradiciones y personajes de Guadalajara*, ed. Helia García Pérez, 150–61 (Guadalajara: H. Ayuntamiento Constitucional de Guadalajara, 1996), 157.

156. C. Banc and A. Dundes, *First Prize: Fifteen Years! An Annotated Collection of Romanian Political Jokes* (Teaneck, NJ: Fairleigh Dickinson University Press, 1986).

157. Roland Barthes, *Mythologies* (Paris: Seuil, 1957), 41–43.

158. Paradox is revealingly ubiquitous in this volume, variously deployed to describe taxation, indigenismo, elections, media policy, and regional strongmen.

159. Juan J. Linz, *Totalitarian and Authoritarian Regimes* (Boulder, CO: Lynne Rienner, 2000), 159.

160. Joy Langston, "Why Rules Matter: Changes in Candidate Selection in Mexico's PRI, 1988–2000," *Journal of Latin American Studies* 33, no. 3 (August 2001): 497.

161. Inaugural speech, quoted in Hernández Rodríguez, *La formación del político mexicano*, 126–27.

162. Paul Gillingham, "Mexican Elections, 1910–1994: Voters, Violence, and Veto Power," in *The Oxford Handbook of Mexican Politics*, ed. Roderic Ai Camp, 53–76 (New York: Oxford University Press, 2011).

163. David Mares, "The National Security State," in *A Companion to Latin American History*, ed. Thomas Holloway, 386–405 (Oxford: Blackwell, 2011); David Fleischer and Robert Wesson, *Brazil in Transition* (London: Praeger, 1983), 127.

164. For Rios Thivol's packed 1947 schedule, see AGN/DGIPS-84/Manuel Rios Thivol/111.

165. Alfred Stepan, *Rethinking Military Politics* (Princeton, NJ: Princeton University Press, 1988), 74.

166. Dirección General de Estadística, *Séptimo censo general de población 6 de junio de 1950 résumen general* (Mexico City, 1953); reports on the Mexican Army, 1951, 1953, FO-371/97547 and FO-371/109037.

167. Snodgrass, chapter 7, this volume.

168. Smith, chapter 11, and Paxman, chapter 13, this volume.

169. O'Donnell, *Modernization and Bureaucratic-Authoritarianism*, 90–99.

170. Mares, "The National Security State," 399; Piccato, "Estadísticas del crimen en México: Series históricas, 1901–2001," http://www.columbia.edu/estadisticascrimen/EstadisticasSigloXX.htm; INEGI, *Estadísticas históricas* CD-ROM.

171. Schedler, "The Logic of Electoral Authoritarianism" in *Electoral Authoritarianism*, ed. Andreas Schedler, 3 (Boulder, CO: Lynne Rienner, 2006).

172. Until 1982. Gillingham, "Mexican Elections, 1910–1994," 53–58.

173. Steven Levitsky and Lucan A. Way, *Competitive Authoritarianism: Hybrid Regimes After the Cold War* (Cambridge: Cambridge University Press, 2010), 3–32.

174. Levitsky and Way, *Competitive Authoritarianism*, 20–26.

175. While economic historians have revised the conclusions of the *dependentistas* in theoretical, quantitative, and qualitative terms, there remain important hidden inputs including the use of *prestanombres* to disguise U.S. firms, the government's masking of U.S. private credit to fund the Banco Ejidal, and the (deeply) discretionary application of the law on domestic ownership. For classic statements of the dependista argument, see José Luis Ceceña, *México en la órbita imperial* (Mexico City: Ediciones El Caballito, 1970); Enrique Semo (coordinator), *México, un pueblo en la historia, vol. 5, Nueva Burguesía, 1938–1957* (Mexico City: Editorial La Patria, 1989); James D. Cockcroft, "Mexico," in *Latin America: The Struggle with Dependency and Beyond*, ed. Ronald H. Chilcote and Joel C. Edelstein, 222–304 (New York: John Wiley and Sons, 1974). Most revisions of dependentista theory have focused on the late nineteenth and early twentieth centuries. Stephen Haber, Armando Razo, and Noel Maurer, eds., *The Politics of Property Rights: Political Instability, Credible Commitments and Economic Growth in Mexico, 1876–1929* (Cambridge: Cambridge University Press, 2003); Stephen Haber, ed., *How Latin America Fell Behind: Essays on the Economic Histories of Brazil and Mexico, 1800–1914* (Palo Alto, CA: Stanford University Press, 1997). For hidden inputs and the problems of highly quantitative approaches to economic history, see Pablo González Casanova, *Internal Colonialism and National Development* (St. Louis: Social Science Institute, 1965), 207–8; Ceceña, *México en la órbita imperial*, 245–70; Judith Adler Hellman, *Mexico in Crisis* (New York: Holmes and Meier, 1971), 65–66; Ramón Eduardo Ruiz, *Mexico: Why a Few Are Rich and the People Poor* (Berkeley: University of California, 2010), 160–64; Nicole

Mottier, "What Agricultural Credit and Debt Can Tell Us About the State in Mid-Century Mexico," paper presented at the 126th American Historical Association Annual Meeting, Chicago, January 5–8, 2012.

176. In their case studies of armed resistance and state repression, Tanalís Padilla, Alejandro Aviña, and Aaron Navarro posit that the Cold War was deeply influential; O'Neill Blacker, Renata Keller, and José Luis Piñeyro are more skeptical, whereas Roberto Blancarte stresses the *sui generis* manifestation of anticommunism in Mexico. See Padilla, chapter 15, this volume; Navarro, *Political Intelligence*; O'Neill Blacker, "Cold War in the Countryside," 181–210; Renata Keller, "A Foreign Policy for Domestic Consumption: Mexico's Lukewarm Defense of Castro, 1959–1969," *Latin American Research Review* 47, no. 2 (2012): 100–119; José Luis Piñeyro, "Las fuerzas armadas y la guerrilla rural en México: pasado y presente," in *Movimientos armados en México*, ed. Oikión Solano and García Ugarte, vol. 1, 69–90, 71–74; Blancarte, chapter 2, this volume. In synthetic terms, Gil Joseph concludes that the United States' Cold War aims and capacities were "mediated through, and substantially muted" by the PRI; Friedrich Katz likewise argues for Mexican exceptionalism; and Pablo Piccato warns against the risk of totalizing explanations that risk subordinating "local and national processes to the polarity of global powers." Gilbert M. Joseph, "What We Now Know and Should Know: Bringing Latin America More Meaningfully into Cold War Studies," in *In from the Cold: Latin America's New Encounter with the Cold War*, ed. Gilbert M. Joseph and Daniela Spenser, 3–46, 26 (Durham, NC: Duke University Press, 2008); Friedrich Katz, "La guerra fría en América Latina," in *Espejos de la guerra fría: México, América Central y el Caribe*, ed. Daniela Spenser, 11–31 (Mexico City: CIESAS, 2004); Pablo Piccato, "Comments: How to Build a Perspective on the Recent Past," *Journal of Iberian and Latin American Research* 19, no. 1 (July 2013): 92.

177. *El Universal*, June 2, 1950.

178. Inspectors RMA and VRA to Gobernación, October 13, 1952, AGN/DGIPS-104/2–1/131/1071.

179. Padilla, chapter 15, this volume.

180. The United States was admittedly significant in the formation of the Dirección Federal de Seguridad. Piñeyro, "Las fuerzas armadas y la guerrilla rural"; Navarro, *Political Intelligence*, 179–86.

181. Mónica Serrano, "The Armed Branch of the State: Civil-Military Relations in Mexico," *Journal of Latin American Studies* 27, no. 2 (May 1995): 425.

182. Lorenzo Meyer, "La Guerra fría en el mundo periférico: el caso del régimen autoritario mexicano. La utilidad del anticomunismo discreto," in Spenser, *Espejos de la Guerra fría*, 95–117.

183. Keller, "A Foreign Policy for Domestic Consumption," 100–119.

184. NARG-812.00B/439, "Political Conditions in Mexico from March 16, 1950, through April 15, 1950," NARG-712.00/4–2150; Carr, *Marxism and Communism*, 176–95, 220.

185. Compare this to the "nearly four million dollars" that the U.S. spent on covert action in Chile to prevent the victory of a Socialist or Communist in the 1964 presidential election. Patrick Iber, "Managing Mexico's Cold War: Vicente Lombardo Toledano and the Uses of Political Intelligence," in *Journal of Iberian and Latin American Research* 19, no. 1 (July 2013), 15; *Hearings Before the Select Committee to Study Governmental*

Operations with Respect to Intelligence Activities (Washington D.C: U.S. Government Printing Office, 1976), 161.

186. Sergio Aguayo Quezada, "El impacto de la guerrilla en la vida Mexicana: algunas hipótesis," in *Movimientos armados en México*, ed. Oikión Solano and García Ugarte, vol. I, 91–98, 91–92.

187. Greg Grandin, *The Last Colonial Massacre: Latin America in the Cold War* (Chicago: University of Chicago Press, 2004), 17.

188. Padilla, *Rural Resistance*, 91–98.

189. Blacker, "Cold War in the Countryside," 191–96, 207.

190. Servín, "Hacia el levantamiento armado," 314–15.

191. Olga Pellicer de Brody, *México y la revolución cubana* (Mexico City: Colegio de México, 1972), 107.

192. *El Imparcial*, November 30, 1962; *La Prensa*, November 21, 1962.

193. Kate Doyle, "After the Revolution: Lázaro Cárdenas and the Movimiento de Liberación Nacional," National Security Archive Electronic Briefing Book no. 124, accessed September 1, 2012, http://www2.gwu.edu/~nsarchiv/NSAEBB/NSAEBB124/.

194. Loaeza, *Clases Medias*, 392–94; Jean Meyer, "La Iglesia Católica En México," in *Conservadurismo y Derechas en la Historia de México*, Erika Pani (coord.), vol. 2, 599–647, 637 (Mexico City: Fondo de Cultura Económica, 2009); AGN, DFS, 100–1–18 H26 MRE, Informe of Manuel Rangel Escamilla, November 30, 1962.

195. Lorenzo Meyer, "La Guerra fria en el mundo periferico: El caso del regimen autoritario mexicano: La utilidad del anticomunismo discreto," in Spenser, *Espejos de la Guerra fría*, 95–117.

196. As Abel Quezada had observed thirty years earlier. Quezada, *El mejor de los mundos imposibles*, 321.

197. Joel S. Migdal, *Strong Societies and Weak States: State-society Relations and State Capabilities in the Third World* (Princeton, NJ: Princeton University Press, 1988), 4–9.

198. Follow up to Regino to Alemán, August 10, 1949, AGN/MAV-542.1/975; Liga to Alemán, November 17, 1947, AGN/MAV-551.2/7.

199. Smith, *Pistoleros*, 2; Moisés T. de la Peña, *Guerrero Económico*, vol. 2, 425.

200. De la Peña, chapter 12, this volume.

201. Hans Heinrich Gerth and Charles Wright Mills, *From Max Weber: Essays in Sociology* (New York: Oxford University Press, 1958), 78, 334.

202. Piccato, chapter 14, this volume.

203. INEGI, *Estadísticas históricas* CD-ROM; O'Donnell, *Modernization and Bureaucratic-Authoritarianism*, 140; Miguel Angel Centeno, *Blood and Debt: War and the Nation-State in Latin America* (University Park: Pennsylvania State University Press, 2002), 6; Smith, chapter 11, this volume.

204. Betancourt to Alemán, December 30, 1946, AGN/MAV-609/4; McCormick, chapter 8, and Snodgrass, chapter 7, this volume; Gabriela Soto Laveaga, "Shadowing the Professional Class: Reporting Fictions in Doctors' Strikes," *Journal of Iberian and Latin American Research* 19, no. 1 (July 2013): 31.

205. *Buro de Investigaciones Políticas*, March 31, 1952; Pensado, chapter 16, this volume; Castellanos, *México Armado*, 108–11.

206. Piccato, chapter 14, this volume; Inspectors VRA, RGM, and RMA to Gobernación, November 30, 1952, AGN/DGIPS-104/2–1/131/1071.

207. U.S. Consul Tijuana to state, September 24, 1962, NARG-712.00/9–2462.

208. As many as one in ten Mexicans may have died from violence, famine, or disease between 1910 and 1920. Robert McCaa, "Missing Millions: The Demographic Costs of the Mexican Revolution," *Mexican Studies/Estudios Mexicanos* 19, no. 2 (summer 2003): 367–400, 396–97.

209. Centeno, *Blood and Debt*, 2–17.

210. Mexico stands out in Latin America for experiencing two major international wars since Independence (three if we accept Aguilar Camín's description of the revolution as a war "between two distinct nations with parallel resources," i.e., Sonora and the center). Hector Aguilar Camín, *La Frontera Nomada: Sonora y la Revolución Mexicana* (Mexico City: Siglo XXI, 1977).

211. Linz, *Totalitarian and Authoritarian Regimes*, 50.

HIGH AND LOW POLITICS

CHAPTER 1 | *Alan Knight*

THE END OF THE MEXICAN REVOLUTION?

From Cárdenas to Avila Camacho, 1937–1941

"How [revolutions] end," Hobsbawm once wrote, "seems to have interested recent students much less than how they begin."[1] This may be because histories of revolutions are often written by scholars sympathetic to revolution, who are therefore more interested in finding out how revolutions start than how they stop or can be stopped. Or it may simply be that beginnings are easier to identify and thus to scrutinize. In the case of Mexico, we can date the start of the revolution with some precision: November 18, 1910 (note that the Mexicans began their revolution two days early, the scheduled date being November 20); although, of course, the causes and, if we wish to use the concept, the "precursor movement" take us back into the Porfiriato. But when did the revolution end? It could be argued that, if the outbreak of serious revolutionary violence marks the beginning, then the end should be signaled by the last successful armed rebellion, that of 1920. Indeed, Hobsbawm, following Atkin (hardly an expert guide), suggests that the triumph of Obregón marked "the 'end' of the . . . Mexican revolution" in the "minimal" sense that 1920 saw "the end of effective threats to the new regime."[2] However, if we conventionally define revolutions as processes of relatively rapid and radical sociopolitical change, then we would have to take a broader and more inclusive view—after all, the fall of Carranza did not end the process (in fact, it accelerated it), and a definition of "the Revolution" that excluded Cardenismo would, as Hobsbawm notes, seem strangely distorted.[3] He proposes, therefore, a sensible "maximum criterion": "the establishment of the 'new framework' within which the country's historical evolution henceforth takes place."[4]

But when we take a broader view, the problem of closure becomes more acute; while some revolutions end with a bang (i.e., a dramatic counterrevolution of the kind that Stolypin engineered in Tsarist Russia in 1905 and Huerta attempted in Mexico in 1913), many others end with a whimper—a prolonged, wheezing exhalation of revolutionary breath. In that case, "closure" cannot be precisely dated and—as I shall argue—any analysis of "closure" requires us to disentangle a skein of different themes. Regarding Mexico, debates about the "death" of the revolution are nothing new.[5] They have even entered public debate and discourse: José López Portillo famously proclaimed himself "the last president of the Revolution" (conclusion: the revolution ended in or around 1982). Rather more consensus attaches to the view that the revolution ended about forty years earlier. It was then—in or around 1940—that "revolution" gave way to "evolution."[6] By the later 1940s, Daniel Cosío Villegas declared, the revolution was spent; its last breath had been wheezily exhaled: "the goals of the Revolution have been exhausted to such a degree that the term revolution itself has lost its meaning."[7] This is the chronology I will adopt (whatever its intrinsic merits, it conveniently slots this chapter into the volume). I will therefore address the period straddling the Cárdenas/Avila Camacho succession, the period that, arguably, saw the revolution come to an end. First I will try to justify the chronology, identifying the changes that took place in respect of policies, perceptions, and personnel; I then will attempt a causal explanation of these changes.

The Revolution was multifaceted and, chronology aside, there may be further disagreement as to which policies were diagnostic of "the Revolution." And, if we can't in some sense define "the Revolution," we can hardly decide when it died—an inquest needs a body. Some scholars take the 1917 Constitution as definitive; however, as we all know, the Constitution was often honored in the breach; the basic political armature that was carried over from the 1857 Constitution (division of powers, free elections, civil rights) remained more myth or aspiration than guide to practical Mexican politics. Democracy—conventional, representative, "Dahlian" democracy (what Krauze would later call "democracy without adjectives")[8]—thus remained elusive, more a rallying cry of the opposition (notably the Vasconcelista opposition of 1929) than a defining feature of "the Revolution." Furthermore, democracy of this kind does not help us demarcate "the Revolution" from what came after, since, despite a good deal of rhetoric to this effect, there is scant evidence that the transition of the 1940s brought significant "democratization." Indeed, *democracy* came to be used by both Avilacamachistas and Alemanistas as a code word for conservatism, civilian government, or support for the Allied cause in World War II, in which respect they followed a broader Latin American trend (note the opposition to Bolivia's Movimiento Nacional Revolucionario [MNR], which culminated in Gualberto Villaroel swinging from a lamppost in the Plaza Murillo in La Paz in July 1946).

As against the liberal-democratic provisions of the constitution, the "social" clauses, exemplified by articles 27 and 123, were both more distinctive (they were absent in 1857 and were genuinely radical and innovative) and more consequential (they had practical results). While we might agree with Marte R. Gómez that land reform was not just a question of hectares redistributed, we can still take the scale and speed of the *reparto* as roughly indicative of agrarian radicalism: 1m hectares under Obregón, 3m under Calles, 18m under Cárdenas, 6m under Avila Camacho.[9] Furthermore, if we factor in considerations of land quality, irrigation, credit, protection of private property (often rather euphemistically termed *pequeña propiedad*), and peasant "empowerment"—the most elusive but not the least important—we can see a notable loss of momentum after 1940. So, too, with labor reform and working class mobilization. The 1930s saw the Federal Labor Code; a rising tide of strikes, some of national significance; the creation of the Confederación de Trabajadores de México (CTM); an improvement in real wages, at least between 1932 and 1937; and radical experiments in workers' control. In contrast, the 1940s witnessed greater control from the top (culminating in the *charrazos* of the late 1940s), falling real wages, fewer strikes, a weakening of the CTM, and the abolition of workers' control.

An additional key strand of the revolution—neither conventionally liberal-democratic nor socioeconomic—was cultural Jacobinism, evident in articles 3 and 130, and the prolonged battle between church and state, which, in turn, fueled the Cristiada of the 1920s and the socialist education program of the 1930s. Some revolutionaries, like Francisco Múgica, combined social reform and Jacobinism; some, like Cárdenas, favored the first, whereas others, like Calles and Garrido Canabal, favored the second; and quite a few, over time, distanced themselves from both (e.g., Cedillo, Amaro, Almazán; I discuss this "revolutionary apostasy" in conclusion). Either way, Jacobinism played an important part in revolutionary politics through the 1920s and 1930s, but by the 1940s it had radically declined. Avila Camacho made his peace with the church (a process of détente that Alemán was keen to continue after 1946); socialist education was soon wound up; and, in the key education ministry, old-style anticlericalism gave way to a mushy consensual conservatism. The global conjuncture helped: having displayed its patriotic credentials at the time of the (1938) oil nationalization, the church was "definitely included in the unification of the war effort" after 1942.[10]

If agrarianism, labor reform, and anticlericalism were broadly diagnostic of the revolution—that is, the *revolución hecha gobierno* of the period after 1915—the same cannot be said, with similar confidence, of nationalism, as some might suppose. First, nationalism was much older than the revolution; it had inspired—among others—the generation of patriotic liberals who restored the republic in the 1860s. Furthermore, many of the revolution's enemies—including Federal Army officers and Catholic activists—were, in their own way, just as nationalistic as the revolutionaries they opposed. Even economic nationalism—which could be seen as a hallmark of the revolution, evident in article 27, and the ensuing conflict with the oil companies—is a debatable marker: first, because there were clear stirrings of Porfirian economic nationalism before 1910; second, because revolutionary economic nationalism often was halting and ambivalent; third, because other Latin American governments—who had no time for land reform and little time for labor reform—were not averse to economic nationalist measures; and fourth, because the retreat from revolution that—as I shall conventionally argue—took place after 1940 did not signal an abandonment of economic nationalism. The regime of the PRI, which took a different tack with respect to land, labor, and the church, nevertheless maintained high tariffs, regulated foreign investment, and promoted the "Mexicanization" of the economy.[11]

The shift in policy—perhaps, even, of "national project"—which occurred after 1940 was a cumulative, piecemeal process, whose full significance only became clear over time, with the benefit of hindsight. But it was apparent from early on. A closer focus on the end of the Cárdenas presidency suggests that the turning point came not in 1940, but in 1937–38 (again, this is no revelation; I am echoing a kind of scholarly consensus, albeit a fairly recent one). The 1937–38 turning point has been stressed by students of both national political economy and regional history.[12] At that point, Cardenismo lost momentum, the loose Cardenista coalition began to fragment, reform stalled, and the Right made a comeback.

Contemporary observers soon saw the straws in the wind. President Cárdenas was seen to be tracking to the center, being "prepared to take a stand against the more outrageous demands of labor," as a result of which labor disputes declined.[13] He continued to row back on official anticlericalism, declaring in March 1940 that he had "no intention . . . of attacking religious sentiment and of weakening the affections and respect of children towards their parents."[14] His speeches assumed a more defensive character, taking their cue from conservative scaremongering: "*no hay pues un gobierno comunista en México*," he reassured listeners.[15] (We may compare this with the bold tones of his famous "fourteen points" speech of February 1936, when he outspokenly challenged the industrial bourgeoisie in Monterrey on its own turf.)[16] By early 1940, Cárdenas was something of a lame duck, and criticism of his administration became more overt and belligerent.[17] Once Avila Camacho assumed the presidency, Cárdenas adopted a low profile: although he continued to exercise influence behind the scenes (and would do so for decades), he did not, like Calles, publicly query the policies or challenge the power of his chosen successor(s).[18] Avila Camacho, of course, accelerated this shift to the Right. As a candidate, he famously declared his Catholicism to be "very moderate" in his public speeches, he seemed to promise "all things to all men"; so conservative and conciliatory was his campaign rhetoric that it became difficult to distinguish the candidate of the official Partido de la Revolución Mexicana (PRM) from the candidate of the opposition Partido Revolucionario de Unificación Nacional (PRUN), Almazán.[19] Once elected, Avila Camacho soon spoke out in favor of ejidal privatization, family values ("filial devotion and brotherly love"), and class harmony (a throwback to the old nostrums of 1920s Callismo).[20] Symbolic change also came quickly. By 1942, it was noted, "the red and black flag seldom flies and salutes are no longer given with the clenched fist."[21]

Of course, checklists of formal policies are far from the whole story. As the example of nationalism suggests, policies—or "policy positions"—do not necessarily come with bold labels proclaiming their location on a left/right, progressive/conservative, revolutionary/non revolutionary (or antirevolutionary) continuum. Nationalism can be left or right, progressive or conservative, depending on historical circumstances; the same is true of plenty of other "isms" (liberalism, corporatism, even Catholicism). Land and labor reforms are less ambiguous because they carry class connotations, hence—assuming that they are authentic—they also carry progressive, redistributionist connotations (in terms of both property and power). The question to ask is: *cui bono*? Who (objectively) benefits from a given policy? And—a related but not identical question—how are policies (subjectively) perceived? Here, there is good evidence that contemporary observers saw the 1930s as a period of radical change; that toward the end of the decade they detected—for better or worse—a swing to the Right, that is, to policies that curtailed redistribution and popular empowerment, and that this perceived shift proved to be real (as I have already suggested) and enduring. By 1940, business opinion was quietly rejoicing that the "ultra-radical regime" of Cárdenas was coming to an end and, since "the great majority of thinking people are now sick of socialism and of the resultant ruin it has brought to the country," it was confidently expected that "the trend over the next few years will be to the right."[22] "Communism"—which some critics dated back to the 1917 Constitution—was now said to be "dying" in Mexico, and, it was thought, "whoever becomes the next president of Mexico, the administration will turn to the Right."[23]

The contemporary observers got it roughly right; at least, my impression is that observers who favored the shift got it right (perhaps because the wish was father to the thought), while those who did not favor it were less percipient, thinking it to be, perhaps, a temporary aberration. Some of those, like Lombardo Toledano, seem to have remained willfully blind to the sea of change taking place around them. Thus, just as the Left had swum with the tide a decade before—at a time when the depression had struck and, soon, Cárdenas would wrest power from Calles—so, in the early 1940s, did the Right find the tide of history flowing in their favor.

A third calculus of change involves people, or personnel. Shifts in ruling elites indicate change and are a means whereby change is brought about. The most obvious concerns the presidency: the transition from Cárdenas to Avila Camacho (and the rapid collapse of Francico Múgica's presidential candidacy) clearly signaled both a shift to the center-right and ensured that the shift would likely continue through the following *sexenio*. Avila Camacho—said to be "about as colourful as a slab of halibut"—was a known centrist, a revolutionary insider who had patiently worked his way up through the ranks of the military, relatively untouched by conspicuous success or scandal.[24] He came from a respectable poblano family; like many revolutionary leaders he had a devout mother and a devout wife and, of course, he had a flamboyant older brother, Maximino, known for his outspoken right-wing views, lavish lifestyle, and visceral hostility to the revolutionary Left, notably Lombardo. As state caciques, the Avila Camachos had successfully combated the CTM while promoting their own brand of patriotic poblano machine politics.[25]

The first Avila Camacho cabinet displayed a clear shift to the right. Maximino was not (yet) included, but the new president took steps to balance left and right, Cardenista loyalists (like García Téllez) and allies of right-wing bosses like Portes Gil and Abelardo Rodríguez (such as Rodríguez's erstwhile secretary and biographer, Francisco Gaxiola, who became Secretary of the Economy).[26] There was talk of Rodríguez himself—the preeminent "revolutionary" impresario—also becoming a minister, but he was too busy making money and preferred to pull strings behind the scenes. Another rumored cabinet appointment was that of Luis Cabrera, the old organic intellectual of Carrancismo, by now an acerbic critic of Cardenismo and Communism and, as it happened, a fellow poblano who had tutored the Avila Camacho kids. Not coincidentally, the old *jefe máximo* himself, Plutarco Elías Calles, soon returned from his four-year exile in the United States to effect a grudging reconciliation with Cárdenas.[27]

As usual, the new president had long coattails and the sexennial cycle brought changes of personnel throughout the political system. Twenty-one new supreme court justices were named; only two were reckoned to be Cardenistas and some were said to have been supporters of Almazán.[28] Lombardo Toledano quit the leadership of the CTM to pursue his grand Latin

American labor project, the Confederación de Trabajadores de América Latina (CTAL). While he continued to pronounce on Mexican politics—even sending the new president what was seen as a presumptuous questionnaire designed to elicit Avila Camacho's views on key issues—his influence soon waned; his critics, like Maximino and Portes Gil, became more outspoken; and even his old enemy Luis Morones, boss of the Confederación Regional Obrera Mexicana (CROM), ventured to "emerge from obscurity."[29] Lombardo was, of course, succeeded by Fidel Velázquez, and we know how the story went. At the time, Don Fidel seemed a colorless figure, even a puppet of Lombardo (contemporary observers were keen on detecting political puppetry).[30] But this interpretation was soon questioned and it became clear that Fidel Velázquez and his allies would lead the CTM in a different direction. Meanwhile, beneath this surface froth, a more substantial change of the tide was taking place. On the basis of careful prosopographical calibration, Rod Camp sees 1940 as a turning point, a "natural demarcation" between a previous political generation in which working class offspring comprised a significant (25–30 percent) of office-holders and a new one in which they were few (4 percent).[31]

At the state and local levels, too, the period saw significant shifts. These were not necessarily simultaneous. For all its burgeoning power, which had been confirmed by Cárdenas's triumph over Calles, the presidency was far from all-powerful and the national presidential cycle was not faithfully and immediately reflected in the provinces. Cárdenas, as we know, was stymied in Yucatán, contributed to the rightward drift of politics in Sonora under Yocupicio and Guanajuato under the "green" faction, and had to coexist not only with Governor Alemán in Veracruz but also with unsavory Alemanista allies like Manuel Parra and his *mano negra* mafia.[32] As Cárdenas's term neared its end, the resurgence of the Right and fragmentation of the Cardenista coalition became more widespread. In Chiapas, as already mentioned, Cárdenas imposed his political will in 1936, but within two years the revival of Pinedismo closed the "Cardenista window of opportunity" and the local Cardenistas, obliged to moderate and prevaricate, became increasingly "demoralized and disaffected."[33]

Elsewhere, the circa 1940 watershed saw the removal of the old revolutionary generation and the installation of new elites, allied to the Avilacamachista "center": in Querétaro, where 1940 saw the collapse of both "the agrarista forces of the sierra and the osornistas of the lowlands"; in Durango, where, in the same year, the fall of Governor Calderón signaled the new "*rectificación avilacamachista*" (thus, an end to land reform, guarantees for the private sector, and the renaming of schools "to eliminate any red or alien flavour"); in Guerrero, where Governor Berber fell early in 1941; and in the Estado de

México, where in 1942 the assumption of the governorship by Isidro Fabela marked the beginning of the long hegemony of the Grupo Atlacomulco.[34] At the local level, too, a politico-generational shift was evident as the generation of the revolution—San José de Gracia's "generation of the volcano"[35]—gave way to a new generation, generally more civilian, middle-class, and deferential toward the "center." Local feuds remained endemic to local politics,[36] but in many places old rancors subsided, politics became less polarized, and central control was augmented.

If we accept that a sociopolitical change took place, perceived by contemporaries and confirmed by later historians, how do we explain it? First, generational change was inevitable. The major leaders of the revolution were born in the 1880s; those who—unlike Madero, Zapata, and Villa—survived the original hecatomb were, by the 1930s, well into their fifties, and, not least because of the hard living of the armed revolution and the good living of the post-revolution, they did not age well: Almazán (b. 1891) was reckoned to be too "fat, sick and rich" to chance an armed uprising when he was—arguably—defrauded of the presidency in 1940.[37] Cedillo, who did attempt a quixotic rebellion in 1939, was also in poor shape, which is why he felt obliged to demonstrate his physical vigor by pirouetting in the presence of the U.S. military attaché.[38] Cárdenas (b. 1895), who had joined the revolution as a teenager, was that bit younger and, of course, sober and clean-living; hence he could survive another thirty years, serving as Secretary of Defense in the 1940s and thereafter as the leftist conscience of the PRI. But by the 1940s most of the revolutionary leadership was getting old and weary; like Almazán, they preferred to enjoy their final years in prosperous peace and comfort.[39]

Generational change also was evident in the regime's concern for youth: back in 1934, Calles had famously proclaimed the need to inculcate revolutionary values and loyalties in young Mexicans who had never fought in the revolution. The revamping of the official party in 1938 also responded to the perceived need to incorporate a new generation—a generation that was not only young but also largely civilian. Even the unpopular obligatory military service was seen, rather optimistically, as a means to instill discipline and patriotism in the younger generation. But perhaps what worked in France would not necessarily work in Mexico, and the school, rather than the barracks, remained the chief crucible of nationalism.[40] Female suffrage—promised in the 1930s but postponed to the 1950s—promised the mass inclusion of women into official politics (women had, of course, played a major role in opposition, especially Catholic opposition, movements).[41] Within the PRM, the new "popular" sector soon waxed, while the military sector waned. Taken together, these trends represented a largely top-down policy of political assimilation, recruitment, and control. The revolution got off its horse and sat itself down behind a paper-strewn desk. Gobernación supplanted Defensa Nacional as the anteroom of the presidency. The party increasingly became a vehicle for control rather than mobilization; its components, which in the 1930s had retained ample local and regional autonomy, lost power to the center (which is not to say, of course, that the PRM/PRI became an omnipotent Leviathan: we are all believers in Swiss cheese these days).[42]

Generational change is inevitable, but it is not inevitable that successive political generations should move in a discernible direction—in this case, to the center and Right. They may move Left; they may also scatter in different directions. Mexico's rightward drift depended on particular factors, which, by way of conclusion, I will sum up under four headings: the routinization of the revolution; domestic economic factors; domestic political factors; and the international context. The first is, perhaps, a "structural" explanation, the rest are more conjunctural (I would say "contingent," but that has possibly misleading connotations of chance and randomness).

If revolutions are major sociopolitical upheavals associated with (but not reducible to) violence, they necessarily have a limited shelf-life. Of course, the violent upheaval must be accompanied—or swiftly followed—by substantial socioeconomic change (without which there is no "revolution"). But both the violence and the change are bound to peter out—unless, that is, the country descends into the kind of enduring confrontational violence that Colombia suffered after 1948. Trotsky's notion of "permanent revolution," therefore, is historically questionable. It is true that Mao and the Chinese Communist Party, fearful of falling prey to bureaucratic inertia, attempted recurrent revivalist campaigns, such as the Cultural Revolution. However, not only were those campaigns costly failures, they also gave way, eventually, to a relatively stable one-party capitalist authoritarianism—a system that bears comparison with that of the old PRI. Quite different revolutions—the French, the Bolivian—also renounced their origins, following the Tocquevillean path to enhanced authoritarianism or collapsing amid their own internal contradictions.

Unlike the Bolivian MNR, the regime of the PRM/PRI did not collapse,[43] but—with the possible exception of Echeverría's burst of "late populism"[44]—it did not make strenuous efforts to recover its early radicalism, at least not at the national level. Clearly, there were plenty of local and sectoral protests that appealed to the original spirit and goals of the Mexican Revolution: for example, the insurgencies of Rubén Jaramillo and Lucio Cabañas, syndical protests by the railwaymen in the 1950s and the electricians in the 1970s, and, most recently, the neo-Zapatista rebellion in Chiapas. But they all turned the discourse—the "public transcript"[45]—of the revolution against the "revolutionary" regime that, they convincingly alleged, had long ago abandoned it.

By the 1950s, therefore, the PRI looked a lot more institutional than it did revolutionary. That evolution was, as I have suggested, quite common for postrevolutionary regimes. In the particular case of Mexico, we can see several pressures determining that evolution. If we consider the political elite, their motives have already been touched upon. The older generation of veterans were aging and intended to enjoy the fruits of their revolutionary labors. However, added to this rationally self-interested attitude was a notable disenchantment with the revolution as it had developed under Cárdenas—a trend palpably evident in the role of revolutionary bigwigs in the radical Right opposition (which I discuss below). Almazán, Amaro, and Cedillo—the three divisional generals who, in alliance with Cárdenas had defeated Calles in 1935–36—all went over to the opposition: Almazán put up a bold show in the 1940 election, Amaro veered into extreme anti-Left activism, and Cedillo famously led the last major military revolt against the government. Their common complaint was that Cárdenas had led the revolution down the road of Bolshevism, that he was, in Cedillo's words, "the Dictator modelled on Stalin."[46] All three were virulently hostile to Lombardo and the CTM, whom they criticized for being corrupt, Communist, and power-hungry; meanwhile Lombardo and the CTM led the charge against Cedillo in San Luis Potosí and against Almazán in the dirty election of July 1940. (The first offensive proved a good deal more successful than the second.) This phenomenon of revolutionary veterans turning against the regime and alleging the "betrayal" of the revolution was quite widespread and would continue for years, culminating in the abortive presidential campaign of Henríquez Guzmán in 1952.[47] Thus, by 1939–40, we find Gildardo Magaña and Antonio Díaz Soto y Gama, both of proven Zapatista lineage, adopting a similarly critical, conservative line, whereas old Carrancistas and Callistas like Dr. Atl, Francisco Coss, and Manuel Pérez Treviño veered so far to the Right that they approached the politically fashionable territory of fascism.[48]

This phenomenon—what I have perhaps glibly termed *revolutionary apostasy*—derived not just from the de-radicalizing effects of age or wealth; it also reflected a perception, and perhaps an understandable perception, that the revolution for which these veterans had originally fought and sacrificed had veered in a new, leftist, alien, and unwelcome direction. Consider agrarian reform. Whatever might have been the opinions of Amaro or Almazán (the latter, even in his brief Zapatista days, had a reputation for opportunism),[49] the agrarian credentials of Cedillo, Magaña, and Soto y Gama were solid. By the 1930s, however, they had concluded that the revolutionary land reform—premised on the *ejido*, now also the collective ejido—was basically wrong and did not meet the demands and aspirations of the peasantry. Organized labor, too, now seemed strident, socialistic, and excessively internationalist. Matters were made worse by the fact that agrarian leaders, "socialist" teachers, and, above all, labor leaders (like Lombardo) were usually not revolutionary veterans with the scars to prove it but younger men (and even women) who had come up through the mass civilian organizations of the revolution and who spouted a new class-conscious and anticlerical discourse, larded with references to the proletariat and international Communism. The veterans no doubt exaggerated, but they felt a genuine generational and cultural grievance against these sloganeering civilian upstarts. In agrarian matters, this subjective sentiment derived from an objective reality: the veterans had fought for specific agrarian causes (in Morelos or San Luis) and they had a decided preference for freehold land ownership; the Cardenista agrarian reform, in contrast, was sweeping, radical, and, in some cases, collectivist.

The veterans' reaction would have mattered less had they not enjoyed a measure of popular support. It is clear that by the late 1930s the Cardenista coalition, hastily assembled during the battle with Calles in 1935–36, was tending to fragment. Both agraristas and workers became more critical of the administration and more disposed to listen to its opponents. We may posit both structural and contingent reasons for this popular disenchantment. It was a feature of the Mexican agrarian reform—as of others—that once peasants had successfully mobilized and acquired land, their radical commitment tended to fade.[50] After all, they had got what they wanted; they now concentrated on cultivating their own gardens. Hence the bucolic picture that Redfield (and others) painted of Morelos in the 1920s.[51] This outcome was more likely in situations where agrarian veterans had secured a "primary" reform— that is, a reform won by hard, bottom-up struggle. In contrast, the more sweeping "secondary" reforms of the 1930s had a more top-down and official quality. Some, it is true, were the fruits of long hard struggle: in the Laguna or at Lagos de Moreno in Jalisco.[52] But many were pushed through, hastily and even provocatively, by the Cardenista state. Some peasants—tenants, sharecroppers, and resident peons—were victims; some ejidos fell prey to internal disputes and factionalism,[53] and in a good many cases ejidal grants led to conflicts between communities, which fell to feuding over disputed land. Thus, when Erasto Urbina and his cohorts brought land reform to the Chiapas highlands, they "hurriedly and often violently created dozens of ejidos . . . [and] conflicts typically ensued within and between communities over competing claims."[54] The sweeping and hasty Yucatán reparto displayed similar defects.[55] In addition, the ejido, being a conditional land grant, proved an adept instrument of political clientelism.[56] We should not necessarily assume that every busload of *ejidatarios* brought in to sway an election or flag-wave for the revolutionary cause was a reluctant rent-a-crowd; but some certainly were, and resentment against such political manipulation was exacerbated when the Bank of Ejidal Credit seemed to assume the role of master and exploiter in place of the expropriated *hacendado*.[57]

In those (few but important) cases where trade unions also became owners or co-owners of the mean of production, a somewhat similar structural tension arose. Railway workers, briefly charged with running the industry, were required to tighten their belts and make job cuts.[58] And Petróleos Mexicanos (PEMEX)—a nationalized, although not a worker-controlled, company—also had to conform to market conditions in difficult times.[59] In both cases, sectors of organized labor that had broadly supported Cárdenas were alienated and, like many trade unionists (the sugar workers of Los Mochis or those of Guadalajara, "a great part [of whom] are against Avila Camacho"),[60] supported Almazán in the contentious 1940 election.

Conjunctural factors also contributed to the splintering of the Cardenista coalition. On coming to power, Cárdenas inherited a resurgent economy and rising government income. In 1937, however, the economy stalled (in part, Mexico fell victim to the "Roosevelt recession" of that year). At the same time, Cárdenas's social programs—agrarian reform and socialist education—began to strain government finances. Thus, a deficit of 21 million pesos (5.5 percent of government income) in 1936 rose to 66 million (15.1 percent) in 1938, after which it fell modestly in response to budget cuts.[61] Land reform also slowed.[62] This clearly was not a story of runaway inflation or irresponsible "economic populism,"[63] but it meant that spending had to be cut (hence in part the disillusionment of both ejidatarios and workers in state industries), and the government was accused of contributing to rising inflation. Certainly, prices were now rising, especially the prices of staple foodstuffs (for which lazy and inefficient ejidatarios were blamed, probably unfairly).[64] Trade union leaders, including Lombardo, denounced price inflation and called, largely in vain, for government measures to counter it.[65] At the same time, the petroleum expropriation, for all its patriotic fanfare, carried an economic price; as the oil companies boycotted PEMEX, the peso sank and business confidence wavered. Cardenista reform, which had ridden on the back of the (relatively) fat years of 1934–36, now had to cope with lean times, which speeded the "demobilization of the progressive coalition" and stoked the fires of opposition, to which I now turn.[66]

Hugh Campbell usefully distinguished between the "secular" and "clerical" radical Right, which enjoyed a marked resurgence in the later 1930s.[67] The secular Right has been touched on: it was led largely by aging caudillos, disaffected with the course of the revolution under Cárdenas. It was anti-Left, anti-trade union, anti-ejido, anti-Cárdenas, and anti-Lombardo. In some cases, it was also anti-Semitic.[68] Its positive claims were scant; it suffered from the chronic fragmentation of caudillo politics—too many would-be leaders, mutually antagonistic, chasing too few followers. As breakaways from the Partido Nacional Revolucionario (PNR), fire-breathing leaders of the radical Right, like Amaro, were bereft of patronage and failed to mobilize extensively.[69] Even more clearly, armed rebels like Cedillo stood little chance of repeating their exploits of 25 years earlier, still less of emulating Francisco Franco (as some hoped that Cedillo would).

The sole exception was Almazán, a more moderate exponent of the Right, who capitalized on general discontent and, arguably, was the more popular candidate in 1940. (Proof, yet again, that elections are usually lost by unpopular administrations rather than won by popular oppositionists). But Almazán was not allowed to win and, if the electoral machine of the PRM and CTM proved inept and clunking in July 1940, it was at least a machine, which Almazán did not have. As later schisms were to show (1952 being a classic example; perhaps 1987–88, too), breakaways from the official party were risky and provoked tough responses. But the rise of the secular Right was a further symptom of the malaise within the "revolutionary family," and it contributed to both the tense rumor-filled atmosphere of Mexican politics in 1938–40[70] and the government's decision to track to the center to assuage discontent.

The clerical Right was much more numerous and noisy. Following the (partial) defeat of the Cristeros, the Catholic Church had experimented with a range of organizational strategies. Indeed, its roster of successive, overlapping, and competing associations at times resembles the state's own acronym soup—evidence, it seems, of the rival "massification" taking place and of the lack of tight central coordination on both sides, notwithstanding the authoritarian tendencies of the two rivals. Rome and the hierarchy sought to convert Acción Católica into an effective vehicle of top-down control, which would resist official anticlericalism without provoking a violent reaction from the state.[71] But, at the same time, in response to the renewed anticlericalism of the early 1930s, the hierarchy sponsored the formation of the more militant and clandestine Legions who, in somewhat mysterious fashion, mutated into the Base, which in turn became the "trampoline" for the Unión Nacional Sinarquista (UNS), founded in 1937.[72] The UNS soon became a genuine mass organization, a movement (it could not function as a party) that challenged the Cardenista state; proposed a radical, theocratic alternative to the corrupt liberalism, freemasonry, and Marxism of the day; and drew massive support, especially in the traditionally Catholic center-west of the country.[73] It dwarfed the secular radical Right and, despite a good deal of internal division, maintained a measure of organizational cohesion in common opposition to the state. Since it could not contest elections, however, it could not challenge for political power, and, as the "second" Cristiada showed, an armed confrontation with the state was bound to fail. Violence devolved to the local level and took the form of attacks on federal schools and "socialist" teachers, which elicited violent reprisals in return. Rome, ever apprehensive about autonomous lay militancy, sought to control and curtail the Sinarquistas. The bishops and some well-to-do Catholics also were leery of what they saw as a provocative and even utopian Catholic populism; hence they engineered the ouster of Salvador Abascal, the charismatic Sinarquista leader (the Sinarquistas were great believers in the "leadership principle"). Sinarquismo thus generated a good deal of sound and fury, raising hopes and fears of a Catholic integralist uprising roughly analogous to Spain's nationalist revolt. But the circumstances were very different: the Mexican army, born of the revolution, might not care for Cardenista radicalism, but Cárdenas was one of their own (and made sure the army was looked after); hence there was no likelihood that Cedillo—or Almazán—could play Franco to the Sinarquistas' Carlists. The UNS flourished well into the war, when Avila Camacho—whose Catholicism was on public record—banned the organization in the name of national security.

But not all the Right was "radical." Probably the most successful Right was the business Right, a more discreet, urban, and urbane force for conservatism. They were at odds with the PRM and had not yet found themselves a formal niche within the party's new corporate structure. Beyond the Bajío, business disliked the demotic demagogy of the Sinarquistas, but they had three remaining avenues of protest. First, they could use their economic leverage: the threat of capital flight or investment strikes that, in the straitened circumstances after 1937, the government could not ignore. Hence Cárdenas's efforts to placate business (for example, by assuring them that the oil expropriation was a one-off), efforts that Avila Camacho redoubled, offering guarantees to industry and landowners alike.[74] Since the Cardenista reforms had never propelled Mexico out of its capitalist orbit, the "structural dependency" of the Mexican state on the private sector remained. Second, if the state had grown stronger, so too had business, thanks to vigorous economic growth coupled with enhanced corporate power and organization. The workers might be newly "massified" in the CTM, but the bosses, too, had their burgeoning business associations—notably the Confederación Patronal de la República Mexicana (COPARMEX), in which the Monterrey group was predominant.[75] The Monterrey group alone possessed formidable regional resources, as they had shown in their battle with Cárdenas in the mid-1930s. They successfully resisted the inroads of the CTM, sustained their own labor unions, and made strategic alliances with neoleonés politicians.[76] Monterrey was far from typical, but, third, such defensive politicking was evident throughout Mexico, as businessmen chose not to confront the Cardenista state head-on (as the Cristeros or Sinarquistas attempted), but rather to colonize the PRM, either by running for office themselves or, more usually, by backing preferred, pro-business políticos. A good (early) example was the Vallina family of Chihuahua.[77] Significantly, the Avilacamachista *cacicazgo* in Puebla also resisted the CTM while sponsoring client unions and establishing close relations with local businessmen like William Jenkins.[78] It may not be an exaggeration to suggest that, if Tabasco was, in Cárdenas's phrase, the "laboratory of the Revolution" in the 1930s, Puebla proved to be the laboratory of the post-1940 revolution: conservative, patriotic, tolerant of the church, and friendly toward business.

Of course, business (especially northeastern and Bajío business) also supported the infant Partido Acción Nacional (PAN), born in 1939 and destined to mount a more decorous, elitist, and technocratic opposition to the revolutionary state than the UNS.[79] If the Sinarquistas had numbers, the PAN had contacts in high places. Before the 1980s, however, it could not seriously challenge the state; it was "no more than a nuisance."[80] Hence it served to complement—not to substitute for—the primary political weapon of business, big and small: the discreet colonization of the PRM/PRI and the use of the so-called weapons of the strong, which got business a sympathetic hearing without requiring overt or independent political mobilization. This happy *modus vivendi* worked to mutual advantage for the best part of fifty years, before the economic crisis of the 1980s and López Portillo's disastrous nationalization of the banks broke the relationship and impelled business into a closer and more combative alliance with the PAN.

It is finally worth noting that these domestic dynamics were overlaid by international considerations. While the Mexican economy became more introverted—according to the logic of *desarrollo hacia adentro*—its politics displayed a notable extroversion, with foreign models, ideologies, and conflicts acquiring an unusual salience. Mexico's leaders claimed that their revolution was peculiar (and that claim would form the basis for frequent denunciations of "exotic doctrines"), but they were keen to pick up on foreign examples. Even Cedillo—not the most cosmopolitan of caudillos—is said to have returned from a trip to Europe an ardent admirer of both Mussolini and Kemal Ataturk.[81] Cárdenas, who lacked a university education and had scarcely set foot outside Mexico, was, with respect to models and inspiration, dourly Mexican. But he had a lively and committed interest in foreign affairs, and hence his famous support for the Spanish Republic, his offer of asylum for Republican refugees (as well as Trotsky), his support for the League of Nations, and his condemnation of both imperialist aggression in Ethiopia and

Manchuria and Soviet aggression against Finland (a conflict that, like the Spanish Civil War, had particular resonance in Mexico).[82] Since Cárdenas and his government favored democracy and popular frontism against fascism (and Lombardo and the PCM looked fondly on the USSR), their conservative critics—now including Vasconcelos—sympathized with the fascist cause. The secular radical Right, as we have seen, adopted fascistoid forms and even indulged in a measure of anti-Semitism, whereas the clerical—or, better, the Catholic—Right was predictably strong for Franco, even, in some cases, for the Vichy of Marshal Pétain.[83] This "extroversion" gave an additional twist to Mexican politics, linking local and national issues to the grand global struggles being played out in Europe and Asia. It also made the government, again, cautious: Cárdenas did not want to risk a Franquista-style insurrection; he had to keep the army sweet (which, as the Cedillo revolt showed, he managed to do),[84] and he was leery of Lombardo's flirtations with Moscow. A final crucial consequence was improved relations with the old enemy to the north, the United States. Cárdenas and Franklin D. Roosevelt agreed on the need to combat fascist aggression, especially where it seemed to threaten the Americas. Hence the United States' docile reaction to oil expropriation—which, had it happened ten or fifteen years earlier, would no doubt have produced more strident saber-rattling. Indeed, in 1940, the United States was seen as a guarantor of the Cárdenas government against potential rebels.[85] For his part, Cárdenas was keen to placate the United States and was ready to enter into mutual defense negotiations. Again, Avila Camacho accelerated a policy of détente which had been begun by his predecessor, and World War II, which Mexico entered in 1942, generated an unprecedented degree of economic integration between the two neighbors.

To conclude: According to the old formula, the revolution—the phase of social reform and state-building undertaken by the winners of 1910–20—came to an end around 1940. That remains true, but we can perhaps be a little more precise and date the end—or, at least, the beginning of the end—to 1937–38. The high point of social reform coincides roughly with the Cárdenas sexenio, but not exactly; again, strictly sexennial history should be avoided, for not only did the end come earlier, the radical phase also began before Cárdenas took office. This is obviously true of the cultural radicalism—the anticlerical Jacobinism—of the early 1930s, which Cárdenas took steps to restrain (thus, Graham Greene's diatribe was out of date even when he penned it).[86] But it is also true of socioeconomic reform, which can be seen emerging from the crisis of the depression: the Federal Labor Law of 1931, the new Agrarian Code of 1934, Pani's deficit-financing and, most important, the renewed militancy of both unions and agrarian activists, which preceded 1934, but which was further encouraged by Cárdenas's presidential campaign and subsequent conflict with Calles.

Timing apart, the causes of de-radicalization were both structural and contingent. A loss of revolutionary momentum—the routinization of revolution, if you like—was probably inevitable, as was the sheer physical decline of the revolutionary generation. But many members of that generation now adopted more conservative postures: the elites got rich while lamenting the Communistic deviations of Cardenismo and Lombardismo and the betrayal of the revolution that they brought. Popular groups, too, veered to the Right (if that conventional terminology can be used): the post-reform peasantry, possessed of its ejidos, now had to confront not the landlord and latifundista, but the bureaucrats of the Ejidal Bank and PRM/PRI políticos who wanted their votes. To a lesser degree, workers in the new state sector (oil and railways) found that the state was no longer a useful ally but a demanding taskmaster. The economic downturn of 1937, swiftly followed by the petroleum nationalization, provided additional contingent factors that obliged the government—never a profligate practitioner of "economic populism"—to cut spending and restrain reform.

If we sum up the story, we might invert the usual question and ask not why the Mexican Revolution achieved so little, or why it ran out of steam so soon, but why it managed, not least in its Cardenistic incarnation (a weaker incarnation than many used to imagine), to achieve what it did: significant social reform, successful institution-building, and the maintenance of a measure of social peace and order during a period of world crisis without—if we pluck contemporary examples from the Soviet Union, Nazi Germany, Spain, and Brazil—recourse to Gulags, concentration camps, massacres of priests, or harsh repression of labor.

Notes

1. E. J. Hobsbawm, "Revolution," in *Revolution in History*, ed. Roy Porter and Mikulás Teich (Cambridge: Cambridge University Press, 1986), 21.

2. Hobsbawm, "Revolution," 25. Note that many experts on Mexico also tacitly subscribe to this view by labeling the period after 1920 "postrevolutionary."

3. Hobsbawm, "Revolution," 30.

4. Hobsbawm, "Revolution," 24.

5. Stanley Ross, ed., *Ha muerto la Revolución Mexicana?* (2 vols.) (México City: Sep/Setentas, 1972).

6. Howard F. Cline, *Mexico. Revolution to Evolution, 1940–1960* (New York: Oxford University Press, 1962). Compare Luis González y González, *Pueblo en vilo: Microhistoria de San José de Gracia* (México City. Colegio de México, 1972), 196, which, perhaps sensibly, dates a shift from the "destructive" to "the constructive phase of the Revolution" ca. 1941.

7. Daniel Cosio Villegas, *Ensayos y notas* (2 vols.) (Mexico City: Editorial Hermes, 1966), vol. I, 113.

8. Enrique Krauze, *Por una democracia sin adjetivos* (Mexico City: Joaquín Mortiz, 1986).

9. James W. Wilkie, *The Mexican Revolution: Federal Expenditure and Social Change Since 1910* (Berkeley: University of California Press, 1973), 188. Gómez's comment—that land reform was "not a simple question of theodolites, tapes and measurements" but also involved, we might paraphrase, political dialogue and mobilization—appears in a letter to Cárdenas, November 18, 1939, Archivo General de la Nación, Mexico, Presidentes/LC, 562.11/222.

10. Bateman to Foreign Office (FO), October 12, 1942, FCO Records, National Archives, Kew Gardens, London, FO 371/30571, A9964.

11. Foreign direct investment as a percentage of gross domestic product stood at 117 percent in 1910; by 1940 it had fallen to 30 percent; and by 1946 it had slumped to 10 percent, at which (approximate) level it remained throughout the years of PRI hegemony (1946–70) (Van Whiting, *The Political Economy of Foreign Investment in Mexico* [Baltimore: Johns Hopkins University Press, 1992], 31–32).

12. Friedrich E. Schuler, *Mexico Between Hitler and Roosevelt: Mexican Foreign Relations in the Age of Lázaro Cárdenas, 1934–1940* (Albuquerque: University of New Mexico Press, 1998), chapter 4; Stephen E. Lewis, *The Ambivalent Revolution: Forging State and Nation in Chiapas, 1910–1955* (Albuquerque: University of New Mexico Press, 2005), 154–55.

13. Davidson to FO, March 5, 1940, FO 371/24217, A2619.

14. Rees to FO, March 9, 1940, FO 371/24217, A2348.

15. *Excélsior*, February 21, 1940, cited in Daniels to State Department, February 21, 1940, State Department Records, Internal Affairs of Mexico, 1940–44, 812.00/30936. Manuel Gómez Morín, a severe but cerebral critic of Cárdenas, qualified the nature of the charge: the Cárdenas government could not be said to be "Communist"; but it was *comunizante* (or, we might say, "fellow-traveling") (*Excélsior*, February 29, 1940, cited in Daniels to State Department, 2/29/1940, SD 812.00/30950).

16. Michael Snodgrass, *Deference and Defiance in Monterrey: Workers, Paternalism and Revolution in Mexico, 1890–1950* (Cambridge: Cambridge University Press, 2003), 202–19.

17. Davidson (admittedly, no friend of Cárdenas) to FO, January 9, 1940, FO 371/24217 A1301, reports criticism of the president being "more openly and generally expressed than any other criticism of the government during the last five years." The rising cost of living and the alleged imposition of Avila Camacho figured in particular (Stewart to State Department, February 9, 1940, SD 812.00/35929).

18. Bateman to FO, November 10, 1942, FO 371/30571, A11019.

19. Davidson to FO, January 9, 1940, FO 371/24217, A1301; Rees to FO, July 8, 1940, FO 371/24217, A2619.

20. Rees to FO, December 13, 1940, FO 371/26067, A281; see also *El Nacional*, December 2, 1940.

21. Bateman to FO, September 28, 1942, FO 371/30571, A9380, citing the conservative magazine *Hoy*.

22. Davidson to FO, January 4, 1940, FO 371/24217, A813.

23. The first observation is that of E. D. Ruiz (ex-Mexican consul-general, New York), cited in Bramwell to FO, August 17, 1940, FO 371/24217, A3818; the second prediction appears in a memo from Duggan to Welles, February 9, 1940, SD 812.00/30927.

24. The halibut simile crops up in different Anglophone sources; Bateman to FO, June 2, 1942, FO 371/30593, A5710, attributes it to the American journalist John Gunther. For a useful resumé of Avila Camacho's career, see Rafael Loyola Díaz, "Manuel Ávila Camacho: El preámbulo del constructivismo revolucionario," in *Presidentes mexicanos (1911–2000)*, ed. Will Fowler (2 vols.) (México City: INEHRM, 2004), vol. 2, 217–38.

25. Wil G. Pansters, *Politics and Power in Puebla. The Political History of a Mexican State, 1932–87* (Amsterdam: CEDLA, 1990).

26. On the new cabinet: Rees to FO, January 16, 1941, FO 371/26067, A281.

27. Bateman to FO, September 28, 1942, FO 371/30571, A9380.

28. Rees to FO, December 31, 1940, FO 371/26067, A611.

29. *El Nacional*, May 31, 1941, cited in Rees to FO, May 31, 1941, FO 371/26067, A611; Davidson to FO, March 5, 1940, FO 371/24217, A2619.

30. Rees to FO, March 4, 1941, FO 371/26067, A2315.

31. Roderic Ai Camp, *Mexico's Mandarins: Crafting a Power Elite for the Twentieth Century* (Berkeley: University of California Press, 2002), 236.

32. Ben Fallaw, *Cárdenas Compromised: The Failure of Reform in Postrevolutionary Yucatán* (Durham, NC: Duke University Press, 2001); Adrian Bantjes, *As If Jesus Walked the Earth: Cardenismo, Sonora and the Mexican Revolution* (Wilmington, DE: Scholarly Resources, 1998); Ben Fallaw, *Religion and State Formation in Postrevolutionary Mexico* (Durham, NC: Duke University Press, 2013); Antonio Santoyo, *La Mano Negra: poder regional y estado en México (Veracruz, 1928–1943)* (Mexico City: Consejo Nacional para la Cultura y las Artes, 1995).

33. Lewis, *The Ambivalent Revolution*, 154–55.

34. María Eugenia García Ugarte, *Génesis del porvenir: Sociedad y política en Querétaro* (Mexico City: FCE, 1997), 438; Pavel Leonardo Navarro Valdez, *El cardenismo en Durango: Historia y política regional 1934–1940* (Durango: Instituto de Cultura del Estado de Durango, 2005), 264–65; Ian Jacobs, *Ranchero Revolt: The Mexican Revolution in Guerrero* (Austin: University of Texas Press, 1982), 134–35; Rogelio Hernández Rodríguez, *Amistades, compromisos y lealtades: Líderes y grupos en el Estado de México* (Mexico City: El Colegio de México, 1998).

35. González y González, *Pueblo en vilo*, 133.

36. For example, Frans J. Schryer, *The Rancheros of Pisaflores: The History of a Peasant Bourgeoisie in Twentieth-Century Mexico* (Toronto: University of Toronto Press, 1980); Paul Friedrich, *The Princes of Naranja: An Essay in Anthrohistorical Method* (Austin: University of Texas Press, 1986).

37. The alleged words of Ramón Beteta, in interview with Betty Kirk, cited by Rees to FO, February 9, 1940, FO 371/24217, A1654. Beteta predicted that Almazán, having declined to fight, will cut a deal with incoming President Avila Camacho, "then he will get some more fat contracts to make him richer still." Sure enough, after noisily protesting his defeat and threatening revolt (from abroad), Almazán returned to Mexico, "looking as if he had aged ten years, tired, slightly hoarse, his face set"; but his ample fortune still was intact. Lombardo, for once, hit the nail on the head: "*es un comerciante*" ("he's a businessman") (Virginia Prewett, *Reportage on Mexico* [New York: E. P. Dutton, 1941], 246).

38. Dudley Ankerson, *Agrarian Warlord: Saturnino Cedillo and the Mexican Revolution in San Luis Potosí* (DeKalb: Northern Illinois University Press, 1984), chapter 8.

39. Luis Javier Garrido, *El partido de la revolución institucionalizada: La formación del nuevo Estado en México (1928–1945)* (Mexico City: Siglo XXI, 1991), 173, 175.

40. Thomas Rath, "'Que el cielo un soldado en cada hijo te dio': Conscription, Recalcitrance and Resistance in Mexico in the 1940s," *Journal of Latin American Studies* 37, no. 3 (August 2005): 507–31.

41. Jocelyn Olcott, *Revolutionary Women in Postrevolutionary Mexico* (Durham, NC: Duke University Press, 2006), 64–65.

42. That is to say, the PRI, or the PRI-state dyarchy, was never as powerful, coherent, and extensive as many students of modern Mexico have supposed; even in its heyday, it was, like Emmental, full of holes.

43. Alan Knight ("The Domestic Dynamics of the Mexican and Bolivian Revolutions," in *Proclaiming Revolution: Bolivia in Comparative Perspective*, ed. Merilee S. Grindle and Pilar Domingo, 54–90 [Cambridge, MA: Harvard University Press, 2003]) develops this comparison.

44. Jorge Basurto, "The Late Populism of Luis Echeverría," in *Latin American Populism in Comparative Perspective*, ed. Michael L. Conniff, 93–111 (Albuquerque: University of New Mexico Press, 1982).

45. James C. Scott, *Domination and the Arts of Resistance: Hidden Transcripts* (New Haven, CT: Yale University Press, 1990), 2, 13.

46. Ankerson, *Agrarian Warlord*, 215.

47. See Elisa Servín, *Ruptura y oposición: El movimiento henriquista, 1945–1954* (Mexico City: Cal y Arena, 2001).

48. Magaña died in 1939, but not before he had, as governor, contributed to a rightward shift in Michoacán state politics, a shift that his brother and successor, Conrado, continued (Verónica Oikión, *Michoacán en la vía de la unidad nacional, 1940–1944* [Mexico City: INEHRM, 1995]). On the views of Coss, Pérez Treviño, and the "violently pro-Axis" Dr. Atl, see Bateman to FO (June 2, 1942, FO 371/30593, A5719) and Daniels to State Department (March 9, 1940, SD 812.00/30961).

49. John Womack Jr., *Zapata and the Mexican Revolution* (New York: Knopf, 1968), 80, 212.

50. Bateman to FO (July 10, 1942, FO 371/30571, A7035) offers a simplistic summation: "the Mexican peasant has gained all he wanted with the break-up of the great estates and so long as his present ownership of the land remains unchallenged, he sees no object in further radical policies." Following the French Revolution, George Rudé suggests, "the peasants . . . gained a new status and a measure of economic security that may possibly account for the persistent conservatism of much of rural France during the early decades of the nineteenth century" (*The French Revolution* [London: Phoenix, 1996], 167).

51. Womack, *Zapata*, 373–74.

52. Ann L. Craig, *The First Agraristas* (Berkeley: University of California Press, 1983).

53. Friedrich, *The Princes of Naranja*, is a classic study.

54. Lewis, *The Ambivalent Revolution*, 155.

55. Fallaw, *Cárdenas Compromised*, chapter 6.

56. Again, it is not difficult to find contemporary—if sometimes unsubtle—reports of agrarian clientelism long before the latter became a staple of revisionist historiography; thus, at the time of the contentious presidential election of 1940, a British con-

sular report from Tapachula, Chiapas, noted that "the only [Avila] Camachistas in the district are those who have received land," the remaining majority (allegedly 80 percent) being for Almazán (report of July 14, 1940, in Rees to FO, July 22, 1940, FO 371/24217, A3817).

57. For example, the allegations of corruption, clientelism, and incompetence made by five ejidos in the Río Mayo Valley of Sonora against BNCE officials on October 20, 1938, in Concha de Villareal (*México busca un hombre* [Mexico City: "Libros y Revistas," 1940], 56–59).

58. Joe C. Ashby, *Organized Labor and the Mexican Revolution Under Lázaro Cárdenas* (Chapel Hill: University of North Carolina Press, 1963), 130–41; Rafael Loyola Díaz, *El ocaso del radicalismo revolucionario* (Mexico City: UNAM, 1991), chapter 2.

59. Ashby, *Organized Labor*, 250–71; Loyola Díaz, *El ocaso del radicalismo revolucionario*, chapter 3.

60. Rees to FO July 8, August 2, 1940, FO 371/24217, A2619, 3818.

61. Wilkie, *The Mexican Revolution*, 28.

62. Nora Hamilton, *The Limits of State Autonomy: Post-Revolutionary Mexico* (Princeton, NJ: Princeton University Press, 1982), 237.

63. As Enrique Cárdenas makes clear in *La hacienda pública y la política económica, 1929–1958* (Mexico City: El Colegio de México, 1994), chapter 3.

64. Since rising food prices were driven by broader inflationary pressures as well as poor harvests in 1939 (Daniels to State Department, January 16, 1940, SD 812.00/30906).

65. Indeed, inflation—coinciding with the run-up to the 1940 election—made overt criticism of the administration more severe and extensive (Daniels to State Department, March 11, 1940, SD 812.00/30962).

66. Hamilton, *The Limits of State Autonomy*, 234.

67. Hugh C. Campbell, *La derecha radical en México, 1929–1949* (Mexico City: Sep/Setentas, 1976). Note also John W. Sherman, *The Mexican Right: The End of Revolutionary Reform, 1929–1940* (Westport, CT: Praeger, 1997).

68. And, like anti-Semitism elsewhere, it projected a world of weird conspiratorial cohabitations: flyers distributed in Mexico City by León Ossorio's Partido Nacional de Salvación Pública alleged that Almazán "is betraying the country, allying himself with (Trotskyist) Diego Rivera and the Jewry which protects him with its wealth," concluding, "Almazánismo and Jewry (judaismo) are one and the same thing" (Daniels to State Department, January 18, 1940, SD 81200/30913). Historiographically neglected, and therefore underestimated, modern—including "revolutionary"—Mexican anti-Semitism is usefully addressed in two monographs: Daniela Gleizer Salzman, *México frente a la inmigración de refugiados judíos, 1934–1940* (Mexico City: CONACULTA-INAH, 2000), and Alicia Gojman de Backal, *Camisas, escudos y desfiles militares: Los dorados y el antisemitismo en México (1934–1940)* (Mexico City: FCE, 2000).

69. According to "first-hand information," Amaro resolved early in 1941 to wait and see how President Avila Camacho tackled the "evils" afflicting Mexico before deciding on his stance; if, after six months, "the Cardenista rabble still held the reins he announced that he would be prepared to 'go to the woods' and fight for the elimination of Communism" (Davidson to FO, March 3, 1941, FO 371/26067, A3886). Needless to say, Amaro never "went to the woods."

70. Alan Knight, "México y Estados Unidos, 1938–40: Rumor y realidad," *Secuencia* 34 (January–April 1996), 129–54; Raquel Sosa Elízaga, *Los códigos ocultos del Cardenismo* (Mexico City: UNAM, 1996), part 3.

71. María Luisa Aspe Armella, *La formación social y política de los católicos mexicanos: la Acción Católica y la Unión Nacional de Estudiantes Católicos, 1929–1958* (Mexico City: La Universidad Iberoamericana, 2008).

72. Pablo Serrano Alvarez, *La batalla del espíritu: El movimiento sinarquista en el Bajío (1932–1951)* (2 vols.) (Mexico City: Consejo Nacional para la Cultura y las Artes, 1992), vol. 1, 131, 152.

73. Jean Meyer, *El Sinarquismo: Un fascismo mexicano? 1937–1947* (Mexico City: Joaquín Mortiz, 1979).

74. On the basis of which guarantees business "confidence is strong that . . . 'happy days' are about to be 'here again' and that prosperity is round a very nearby corner" (Rees to FO, March 10, 1941, FO 371/26067, A2543).

75. Hamilton, *Limits of State Autonomy*, 209, 311. See also Ricardo Tirado, "La alianza con los empresarios," in *Entre la guerra y la estabilidad política: El México de los 40*, ed. Rafael Loyola Díaz, 195–222 (Mexico City: Consejo Nacional para la Cultura y las Artes, 1990).

76. Snodgrass, *Deference and Defiance in Monterrey*.

77. Mark Wasserman, *Persistent Oligarchs: Elites and Politics in Chihuahua, Mexico 1910–1940* (Durham, NC: Duke University Press, 1993), 111–12.

78. Pansters, *Politics and Power in Puebla*; Paxman, chapter 13, this volume.

79. On the origins of the PAN, see Soledad Loaeza, *El Partido de Acción Nacional: la larga marcha, 1939–1994* (Mexico City: FCE, 2000) and Michael J. Ard, *An Eternal Struggle: How the National Action Party Transformed Mexican Politics* (Westport, CT: Praeger, 2003), chapter 3.

80. Duggan to Welles, enclosing report on Mexican politics, February 9, 1940, SD 812.00/30927.

81. Ankerson, *Agrarian Warlord*, 141.

82. While, as several histories demonstrate, the Spanish Civil War elicited great concern and partisanship in Mexico, the Russo-Finnish conflict also aroused interest, as well as more consensual sentiments, since most Mexicans—orthodox Stalinist Communists excepted—sympathized with Finland's plucky struggle against an overbearing (and Communist) neighbor. At a bullfight in Mexico City (where "the crowd . . . on a Sunday is very representative of all classes"), the public gave "a remarkable reception to the ladies who were allowed to . . . make an appeal on behalf of the Finnish Red Cross"; the ladies being "cheered to the echo" as "silver and other coins rained down into the arena from all quarters." Newsreel audiences also were reported to be cheering for Finland; see Rees to FO, January 19, 1940, FO 371/24217, A813.

83. "It is among the people of the Mexican 'old regime,' previously highly privileged and claiming to be hurt by the social advances of recent years, that are now to be found the partisans of the Vichy regime" (Maurice Garreau Donbasle to Comité National Français, London, August 17, 1942, FO 371/30571, A8983). Regarding this relationship, see Denis Rolland, *Vichy et la France libre aux Méxique* (Paris: L'Harmattan, 1990).

84. Senior officers, in particular, were loyal to the regime (and, in many cases, personally hostile to Almazán); among junior officers, however, sympathy for Almazán ran high (Duggan to Welles, enclosing report on Mexican politics, February 9, 1940, SD 812.00/30927).

85. "All (Mexicans) believe the US will aid the Cárdenas administration," for example, in the event of an Almazanista revolt (Duggan to Welles, enclosing report on Mexican politics, February 9, 1940, SD 812.00/30927). The attendance of vice president Wallace at Avila Camacho's inauguration clearly signaled U.S. support for the new administration (Rees to FO, November 15, 1940, FO 371/24217, A4825).

86. Graham Greene, *The Lawless Roads* (London: Heinemann, 1939).

CHAPTER 2 | Roberto Blancarte

INTRANSIGENCE, ANTICOMMUNISM, AND RECONCILIATION

Church/State Relations in Transition

The history of church/state relations after the Mexican Revolution passed through three distinct stages. The first was a time of open confrontation between the triumphant revolutionaries and the church hierarchy, which led to the abolition of the church's corporate status, the elimination of priests' political rights, anticlerical persecution, and the so-called Cristero war. This gave way in the late 1930s to a stage of pacification, and then to a relative reconciliation, which permitted a minimum of peaceful coexistence. This modus vivendi endured across the next three decades, until change within and outside the church, combined with democratizing sociopolitical movements to give rise to a new relationship between church and (what remained of) the revolutionary state.

The constitutionalists were the winners of the Mexican Revolution. They believed, with a certain justification, that the Catholic episcopate had allied itself with the oligarchy and that the Partido Católico Nacional (PCN) had lent de facto support to Victoriano Huerta's coup d'état. Once in power they banned confessional political parties from participating in the Constituent Congress of 1916–17. As a result, the measures imposed by the 1917 Constitution sought the disappearance of religious power in the new society. The denial of legal status to churches, the ban on their possession of properties, the constraints on worship outside of church buildings, the impossibility of constituting political parties with religious overtones, and the prohibitions on priests participating in political activities were all anticlerical (if not necessarily antireligious) measures that were designed to eliminate the Catholic church from the sociopolitical sphere. Such measures and the ensuing strong Catholic opposition eventually gave rise to the Cristero war (1926–29). Although formal conflicts ceased, the introduction of socialist education in 1934 shifted the battlefield to the village school, where rural teachers struggled against priests and pious parishioners for much of the 1930s.[1]

The Birth of the Modus Vivendi

To comprehend the so-called modus vivendi, it is important to appreciate the ideological content and scope of the earlier church-state conflict. The two themes that proved highly divisive during this period were education and social policy. These two issues constitute a thread that can guide us through the labyrinth of détente and dispute between the revolutionary state and the Catholic church.

During the Maximato (1929–34), the Mexican state attempted to impose article 30 of the Constitution, which called for the establishment of lay education and the elimination of religious teaching. Things came to a head in 1934, when the government also changed article 3, which now read that education should be "socialist," "exclude all religious doctrine," and "combat fanaticism and prejudices." The Catholic hierarchy saw the adoption of socialist education as an attempt to sovietize the country and to do away with the church's influence in Mexico. From March 1934 onward the Archbishop of Mexico Pascual Díaz urged Catholics to struggle against the establishment of that education by legal means such as school absenteeism.[2] In November 1935 Mexico's bishops published a pastoral letter following the line laid down in Pius XI's encyclical *Divini illius magistri*. From this document the bishops drew four basic principles of Catholic action in the face of socialist education. No Catholic might be a socialist; nor learn or teach socialism; nor sign up to declarations or formulas that might accept, even tacitly, socialist education; nor accept pedagogical naturalism and sex education.[3]

Yet the ideological battle between church and state was not confined to education. President Cárdenas and his supporters accorded greater importance to the transformation of material conditions than to a revolution in beliefs. They held, like their successors, that economic modernization, industrialization, and urbanization would automatically do away with religious thinking. In contrast, for the church the so-called social question was a moral and religious affair. The church intervened because its leaders believed that "where morality [was] concerned, in social as much as in economic matters, [they were] bound by the higher law of the church."[4] Catholic social doctrine, like its revolutionary counterpart, tried to offer an answer to the social problems caused by the modern relations of production, but one based on Christian morality.

Backed by papal statements, Mexico's Catholic hierarchy tried to disrupt the two basic forces of the Cárdenas government: the worker and peasant movements. To do so, they attempted to influence three areas: the role of the state, property rights, and wages. The theme of property posed the thorniest problem because it was linked to agrarian reform, one of the central pillars of the revolutionary government's political legitimization. Although individual priests might consider some peasant demands just, most stuck to the official line—that the revolutionary government, by replacing large landholdings with *ejidos*, was expressing "the denial of the right to private property, class struggle and the tendency to cultivate a state socialism in Mexico, that might serve as a highway to the dictatorship of the proletariat."[5]

In June 1936 the Mexican episcopate published its first pastoral teaching aimed at the country's workers and peasants. It was a brief exposition of Catholic social doctrine and an utter condemnation of liberalism and, above all, Marxism, which they equated to the state's land reform program. Unionism was not condemned, but warnings were issued against false liberators of the people. It was, in short, a pastoral aimed at warning workers of "the errors that Karl Marx preached" and an effort to announce the church's social doctrine to the masses.[6] In all other respects the pastoral faithfully followed the Vatican line that would be reflected less than a year later in Pius XI's encyclical *Divini redemptoris*, which in Mexico was subtitled "On atheistic communism."[7]

During the 1930s, there was a clear and conflictive division between the revolutionary state and the Catholic church. The conditions for a pact based on ideological affinities or common grounds seemed nonexistent. Yet, political conditions combined with ideological agreements and a relative pragmatism made such an understanding possible. In that respect, paradoxically enough, the Holy See's stance on Mexico was late and untimely: by March 1937, the encyclical's date of publication, circumstances had changed in Mexico and a pragmatic understanding between church and state was already being drafted.

Since early 1936 President Cárdenas's speeches had begun to reflect a significant tailing off in governmental anticlericalism. Between 1936 and 1937, Cárdenas decided to end the antireligious campaign, surmising that it had generated more costs than benefits. The church had become a focus for disagreements between the diverse revolutionary factions, and in some cases anticlerical persecution had been twisted into a means of destabilizing the federal government.

In February 1936, Cárdenas declared in Tamaulipas that fighting the beliefs or creed of any religion was not his government's goal. Shortly afterward he added that the government would not fall into the error committed by previous administrations in considering the religious question a preeminent problem and that it was not the government's job to promote antireligious campaigns.[8] Perhaps more pertinently, he followed up these remarks by declaring to a group of schoolteachers that "henceforth there should be no antireligious propaganda in schools. Our complete attention must be concentrated on solely helping social reform."[9]

In March 1936, the exiled apostolic delegate gave an indirect reply to this first approach. The declaration toned down previous demands and condemned any attempt at armed resistance, stating that the desire of the prelates, priests, and Catholics in Mexico was to "reach by legal means the freedom of a legally sanctioned religion." While awaiting that moment—the apostolic delegate went on—the fact that those in charge of applying the law were not exceeding their mandate and were "interpret[ing] those laws in a friendly and not a sectarian spirit" had generated a positive impression.[10] At the end of the same month, he issued another statement, which heralded the opening of churches in twelve states: "If the opening of churches signifies the first step toward a true liberty based on the law, it should be received with approval; in any case it will be impossible to avoid the opposition of Catholics and the people in general to socialist education, which in the revolutionary mind means atheism and materialism."[11]

The prevailing climate of tolerance allowed the episcopate to weigh the advantages of an agreement, explicit or otherwise, with the state. The chance finally came with the expropriation of the oil companies on March 18, 1938. Facing a series of external and internal pressures, the Cárdenas government needed all the support it could get, and the church obliged. Shortly after the expropriation, José Garibi Rivera, the newly appointed Archbishop of Guadalajara and future Mexican cardinal, exhorted the faithful to contribute what they could to paying off the debt to the foreign oil corporations. The official newspaper El Nacional made it front page news. In its wake, the new Archbishop of Mexico, Luis María Martínez, explicitly backed Garibi Rivera's stance.[12] Finally, on May 1, the other bishops of Mexico confirmed the church's position, declaring that "Catholics are not only allowed to contribute to this end in the way they see most fit, but also such a contribution will be eloquent proof that Catholic doctrine encourages the fulfilling of citizens' rights, and lends a solid spiritual base to true patriotism."[13]

This statement, which buttressed Mexican nationalism with ecclesiastical support, launched the implicit church/state accord and pointed to the rationale beneath the modus vivendi of successive decades. The state would not go back on any articles of the constitution (barring the modification of article 3, which was more an internal matter for the Avila Camacho government), but it would tolerate Catholic education in private schools as well as public manifestations of religion. The church, for its part, would maintain its doctrinal differences with the state, but it would support it in its struggle to improve the social and educational conditions of the pueblo. Furthermore, it would not resist efforts to transform the country's society and economy. The report of the Secretariado Social Mexicano (SSM), published in 1937, summed up this new attitude—declaring that the organization's "main field of work was educational" and admitting that when it came to "socio-economic issues," they could "only intervene indirectly." At the same time, the organization laid out the hope that through "the religious, moral and social education of the workers inside Acción Católica Mexicana . . . a solid and transcendental step [would] be taken in favour of the working class as well as towards the solution of the existing problems of capital and labor in Mexico."[14]

Diverse causes lay behind this accord. Cárdenas himself had been, both as governor of Michoacán and Minister of the Interior, a deeply anticlerical revolutionary. Yet the intensification of the conflict under Plutarco Elías Calles, which ended in the former president's exile, probably hastened Cárdenas's conclusion that hard-line anticlericalism was neither necessary nor terribly popular. At the same time, the death or resignation of Mexico's most intransigent episcopal leaders also helped. Whatever the case, it is clear the "intransigentismo" of the bishops certainly declined and the new hierarchy was disposed to establish a more comfortable relationship with those in power.

Education and the Gestation of Anticommunist Nationalism

Cárdenas's last two years were marked by a retreat from the radicalism of his early presidency. Inflation and the scarcity of state resources, the pressure exerted by American and English companies due to the oil expropriation, and the growth of a powerful opposition all obliged Cárdenas to dilute his program for economic and social change. Despite this, Cárdenas wanted to make the policies adopted by his government permanent. In contrast, Manuel Avila Camacho, the presidential candidate of the PRM, promised during his electoral campaign that he would respect freedom of religion.[15] In the end, an agreement was reached. The government upheld the socialist principles of article 3, although certain aspects of the regulation were watered down.

The Catholic hierarchy, facing a fait accompli, made a direct public statement, which they claimed was driven by pastoral duty and "not in the spirit of creating difficulties or provoking unrest." Here, they raised a protest against the law and once again notified the faithful "concerning their duties in this transcendental matter." In January 1940 they republished the instructions proffered in 1936 by the Vatican secretary of state (and future pope) Cardinal Eugenio Pacelli. In the text, the Vatican representative had confirmed that "the fears that the Mexican Episcopate [had] harboured from the outset [about socialist education were] wholly justified." As a result, he ordered bishops to employ certain measures to combat this threat, such as informing the faithful of the church's teaching regarding social and economic doctrines, forcing private schools to refuse government offers of official recognition, and forbidding parishioners from attending "atheist and socialist schools." He concluded by warning that to do so was not only an "extremely serious threat to the faith and good manners of the youths" but also "a sin."[16]

Yet, by this point the new rules of the game were firmly established. To that end both Cardinal Pacelli and the Mexican bishops warned their flocks off violence, which was "contrary to the Christian spirit," and requested that the faithful only employ "legal means" to combat state impiety. They reminded parishioners that "respect for civil authority in the terms laid down by the church" was "incumbent upon every Christian."[17] The ambiguity of previous years regarding the right to rebellion was fading; even if the fear of a possible reemergence of persecution persisted. The growing conciliatory statements of the official candidate to the presidency, in which he promised absolute "freedom of thought and conscience," opened other possibilities.[18]

Although the first outlines of the modus vivendi were traced out under Cárdenas, it was during the Avila Camacho *sexenio* that this informal accord was clearly defined. The personality and the tone of the new president's statements certainly contributed to this. But external and internal social dynamics solidified this new spirit of conciliation based on national unity as opposed to class conflict. From his first speech as a candidate, Avila Camacho tried to calm the fears of business and church leaders by offering them the vision of a country where "all Mexicans [could] unite, forming a single front, consolidating our material and spiritual wealth."[19]

As he closed his campaign in his home state of Puebla, the PRM candidate made reference to the deepening geopolitical crisis. Here, he pressed for American continental unity and proposed the erection of a "nobler and more just Christian international order." He then repeated his conviction that freedom of conscience should be guaranteed and respected, "definitively leaving behind all religious persecution and [ensuring] that national politics would honour and bolster the high moral values of the Mexican family."[20] Avila Camacho made his most important statement, however, once he was president-elect, two months before taking power: he announced his religious belief, repeated that he was a democrat and not a socialist, and affirmed that the communists would not be part of his government. To a journalist who asked if he was Catholic Avila Camacho answered, "I am a believer." The general then added: "Catholic by origin, [and] by moral sentiment."[21] The journalist also asked: "General, if you are a Catholic, doesn't your Catholicism clash with article 3 of the Constitution?" Avila Camacho answered with a simple no, arguing that the article might clash with fanaticism, but not with Catholicism.

These statements deeply influenced Catholic public opinion. It was the first time that a revolutionary leader had declared himself "a believer."

Between 1939 and 1941 Avila Camacho's own position was bolstered by growing public anticommunism, which had emerged in the wake of the Nazi-Soviet pact. Although anticommunism was set to play an important role in the erection of the church-state modus vivendi, when Germany invaded the USSR his government was forced to tone down its aggressive rhetoric. Church authorities instead turned their attention to the U.S. threat and its religious corollary, Protestantism. Borrowing from the Catholic nationalism of the nineteenth century, ecclesiastic leaders argued for the close relationship of religion and nation, asserting that if Catholicism disappeared, "Mexico [would] have lost its last bulwark against the threat of invasion . . . which comes from the north."[22]

In December 1941, with Avila Camacho already president, Congress approved a new regulation of article 3, practically eliminating its former "socialist" character. The new framework, which licensed greater private participation in education and did not directly attack freedom of belief, allowed the Archbishop of Mexico to issue a statement in which he declared that the "firm and genuine" stance of the Catholic church in Mexico was to abstain from politics and dedicate itself to fulfilling its spiritual mission, "which is above any party, and which extends to all Catholics irrespective of political belief."[23] At the same time, church leaders also backed the government's foreign policy and affirmed that, "in case of doubt one should be with the government." Patriotism, support for the state, and Catholicism had aligned.

While the Catholic hierarchy in Mexico was disposed to support attempts at national unity, it never intended to abandon its stance on the question of education. Consequently, after a new education law was passed in January 1942, Acción Católica, which had greater freedom of action than the episcopate, reiterated its opposition to the lay education system: "The threat is serious, as it is abundantly clear that the new regulations in Article 3 might lead many to think that there are no problems any more. And there are . . . it seems to return to the idea of laicism as a principle, and that will always be the most disastrous shift of all . . . because the naive belief that the matter of schools is already settled is a practical joke that places children in extremely serious danger. . . ."[24]

This would continue to be the church's position in Mexico even after the December 1945 reform of article 3. Although the government eliminated the term *socialist* in favor of a more harmonious and unifying concept of education, the article effectively maintained its lay character, stating that education would keep its distance from any religious doctrine and blocking religious bodies and priests from intervening in primary, secondary, and teacher training schools "and those destined for workers or peasants."[25] Despite this, the Archbishop of Mexico declared that the reform, while preserving the anticlerical tone of the 1917 Constitution, constituted an important step toward freedom "because it clarified concepts and removed the obstacles that through the 1934 reform of the . . . article had unsettled spiritual tranquillity."[26]

In 1941 the Mexican episcopate published a collective pastoral letter to mark the fiftieth anniversary of the encyclical *Rerum novarum*. In the letter the episcopate reviewed and restated the church's social doctrine; it largely avoided analyzing the situation in contemporary Mexico, limiting itself to recounting the history of ecclesiastical participation in advancing workers' rights. The bishops went as far as to claim that, "union organization in Mexico from 1913 to 1924 was almost wholly the work of the church."[27] One of the consequences of this pastoral letter was to revive attempts to form a Catholic union capable of opposing the CTM. In 1946, for example, the Asociación Nacional Guadalupana de Trabajadores was founded.[28] Yet despite this and similar earlier attempts, such as the Confederatión Nacional Católica del Trabajo, the church never managed to establish a rival to the state organizations.

Patriotism, Anticommunism, and the Modernizing Project

As the end of World War II approached, the church took advantage of the official party's rightward shift to redouble its attacks on the PCM and those suspected of sympathizing with the USSR. The anticommunist campaign highlighted the links between church-backed Catholic nationalism and the new Alemán government's project of *mexicanidad*. Both shared a rejection of social models deemed "foreign to national reality." For its part, the church considered itself the founder of Mexican national identity.[29] For the ecclesiastical hierarchy a strong Mexico had to be a Catholic Mexico, as citizenship and Catholicism went hand in hand.[30] Communism by contrast implied treason. At the same time, such an approach also contained considerable wariness of the Protestant threat to the north. As well as attacking communist infiltrators, church leaders also warned politicians and parishioners of the dangers of Protestantism, which they linked to the potential for U.S. social, economic, and political dominance.

Miguel Alemán's political agenda was in many ways closer to that of the church than his predecessor's. Many Alemanista proposals coincided—at least on social questions—with those of the episcopate. In his inaugural speech, Alemán emphasized his respect for freedom "both political and intellectual, of both faith and the press."[31] Furthermore, Alemán shared with the church a desire for the elimination of left-wing unions and the redirection of the party toward anticommunist nationalism.[32] With the weakening of Mexico's Marxist groups, the church and the Alemán government eliminated a common enemy, leaving themselves the sole contenders in the battle to control the masses.

The Alemanista government replaced the wartime doctrine of "national unity" with the idea of *mexicanidad*. From late 1947 onward the PRI party line shifted and politicians proposed a struggle against those who "tend to impose ideas that are out of step with Mexican reality."[33] This ideology of *mexicanidad*, like most Alemanista ideas, coincided with the nationalist position and social doctrine of the Mexican episcopate. The church sought to temper workers' demands and to obtain a fair wage from businessmen, denying class struggle and proposing instead moderation and harmony between the classes. At the same time, the bishops simultaneously called for a politics better suited to "national reality" and a rejection of any meddling by the United States or USSR in the country's internal affairs.

Apogee and Decline of the Modus Vivendi

The absence of open conflict made many conclude that the church had become an accomplice of the government's social project. This was in some ways the case between 1938 and 1950. However, the episcopate quickly identified the disadvantages of such links and began formulating a critique of the state's project that, by the middle of the 1950s, would be open and argumentative. Two central factors influenced this ecclesiastical change of heart: a growing realization of the injustices of the Mexican model of development and an analysis of the pros and cons of the church's cooperation with the state.

By 1950 Mexican society, including the ecclesiastical hierarchy, was beginning to doubt the socioeconomic project of the revolutionary state. As it became increasingly apparent that the Mexican model of development would not solve the problems of economic inequality, the Mexican Church began to deploy a critical discourse that would slowly lead it toward a rupture with the new PRIísta elites. The state had benefited from more than a decade of accord, consolidating its internal organization and forging a firmer position in Mexican society. On the other hand, by 1950 the decline of the Left (both official and unofficial) was an established fact. With its elimination as a contender in the struggle for the ideological control of the masses, the alliance between church and state ceased to make as much sense. The scene was set for a process of mutual distancing.

The fourth year of the Alemán government, 1950, could be considered the peak of the modus vivendi. Yet it also marks a renewed outbreak of hostilities between the priesthood and the state's developmentalist politicians. The episcopate took advantage of the sixtieth anniversary of *Rerum novarum* to produce a collective pastoral letter in May 1951. In the epistle, the ecclesiastical hierarchy resolved to direct its criticism toward "the ruling classes," which in itself marked a change from earlier collective letters that had focused on fighting communism. The episcopate openly attacked any attempt to practice a liberal brand of Catholicism and instead called on the faithful "to live Christianity completely." This was not the first time that the Mexican Church had referred to the problem of the poor, but conceptualizing the problem of poverty as an obstacle to genuine national unity constituted a considerable rupture with the past.

The flourishing of clerical organizations devoted to social questions was a further consequence of this ecclesiastical change of tack. The main tool of this change was the SSM, run from 1952 onward by Father Pedro Velázquez. The SSM had been founded in 1920 on the orders of the Mexican prelates and had, for a time, threatened revolutionary unions. After the Cristero war, state pressure and a lack of ecclesiastical support forced the institution into decline. But, during the 1950s, the SSM returned to the front line of Catholic labor organizing and Velázquez became an important spokesman for the church on social and political issues.

At the same time, probably for personal ideological reasons, the new president Adolfo Ruiz Cortines failed to embrace the informal rapprochement established by his predecessor. Instead, Ruiz Cortines renewed the liberal practice of Mexican presidents in declaring himself in favor of "freedoms of expression, thought, press, belief and criticism"[34] and at the same time establishing a strict separation between the affairs of government and clergy, including in his private life, which had not been established in earlier *sexenios*.[35]

Doctrinal Intransigence and Political Participation

The church in Mexico always protested against the anticlerical provisions of the reform laws and the 1917 Constitution, but never as insistently and systematically as it did from the second half of the 1950s onward. Starting in late 1954, Catholic priests and militants struggled for the abrogation of the anticlerical laws. Furthermore, in addition to attempting to abolish articles 3, 5, 24, 27, and 130 of the constitution, they also pushed for the right to vote and the right to free association, in particular in Catholic labor organizations.[36] The bishops' principal argument held that in Mexico anticlerical laws were "against popular sentiment"[37] and that all Catholics rejected them.

The most evident demonstration of the church's shift during the 1950s was its new attitude toward politics. Since the *arreglos* of 1929 the ecclesiastic hierarchy had remained relatively apolitical. This tendency had been reinforced with the establishment of the modus vivendi and the downplaying of the church's social mission. Yet the new crisis in church-state relations led to the reemergence of a politicized discourse, reflecting a project, perhaps ill-defined, of open support for movements and parties that would defend ecclesiastical beliefs better than the revolutionary government.

In this context, and with an eye to the 1955 elections for federal deputies, Acción Católica began to develop an intensive campaign to politicize the faithful. Much hope was placed on the involvement of women, who were enjoying their first opportunity to vote in federal elections. Given such expectations, the elections provided ambiguous results. The PAN won 6 of the 162 seats on offer in the Chamber of Deputies[38] and in some states, such as the Distrito Federal, significantly expanded its share of the vote. Yet the votes of women, who had doubled the size of the electoral roll, had not unduly favored the opposition—as PANistas expected—but rather had been distributed along much the same lines as those of the men. Nevertheless, ecclesiastical intervention in the 1955 elections was not an abject failure. The results revealed certain gains for the PAN in specific regions. And, perhaps more importantly, renewed church involvement in the political sphere set an important precedent for the future. In this light it is unsurprising that the campaign to legitimate Acción Católica's political participation should be followed by another, after the elections, which centered on the church's right to intervene in all social issues.

The elections were followed by one of the starkest clashes between Catholic hierarchy and liberal groups within the state. The conflict was sparked on October 16, 1956, when the Senate approved a decree declaring the 1957 centenary "Year of the Constitution of 1857 and of Mexican Liberal Thought."[39] Barely twenty-four hours after the publication of this decree, the entire episcopate published declarations defending the civic rights of Catholics. Mexico's bishops used the documents to affirm the following principles: Catholics were duty-bound always to love and obey the church and at the same time to love and serve the *patria*; Catholics were strictly obliged to respect, obey, and cooperate with the civil authorities in all measures laid down for the common good, as long as those authorities did not overstep the mark by demanding obedience to measures contrary to faith and conscience; Catholics should take an interest in public affairs and consequently could belong to political parties, as long as those parties in no way infringed the rights of God and church; and Catholics were obliged to vote for the candidates who best assured the commonwealth and the rights of God and church.

The social and political foundations of the church/state relationship were clearly shifting. Controversy broke out again in March 1957 because of the publication of Father Pedro Velázquez's *Iniciación a la vida política*. The work gained substantial press coverage because of Velázquez's position. The book, which took the form of a manual for political action, aimed to defend the church's right to speak "not only of politics, but also of the morality of politics." The central idea was to persuade Catholics of the need to value politics as an important daily activity. It was, in other words, an attempt to reconstruct the meaning of Mexican Catholicism. The reaction of the state was heavy-handed. In March 1957 Velázquez had to clarify publically the aims of the work. At the same time the ecclesiastical hierarchy managed—at least temporarily—to silence the cleric. According to Jesús García the publication placed in crisis "the modus vivendi and the Nicodemian procedures of communication between the church and the state." The hierarchy, in a desperate bid to maintain the pact, was forced to shut Velázquez up.[40]

Perhaps the hierarchy had not planned a return to such high-profile participation in social and political affairs. However, diverse groups within the institution had gradually and inexorably started to get involved in these areas, albeit without risking a complete break with the state. In spite of broad improvements in economic performance, growing discontent, expressed in a heightened rhythm of economic and political protest movements, marked the final years of Ruiz Cortines's presidency.[41] By 1958 there was little surprise when priests spoke out on social or political matters, something unthinkable a decade earlier. The modus vivendi established in 1938 had become something very different.

The period 1959 to 1968 also was characterized by a growing climate of anticommunism. Both church and state helped to construct this political environment. Anticommunism had never been central to the ideology of the Mexican Revolution, but the state now used it to bring wayward worker and peasant groups into line. The church often took the lead, keeping the politicians in line by vocally accusing state representatives of communist affiliation. Fidel Castro's victory and his hostility to the Cuban church had confirmed the growing fears of ecclesiastical hierarchies across Latin America, bringing back the self-defense mechanisms that alarmist papal denunciations had failed to trigger. Among the most important sources of Mexican ecclesiastical anticommunism was the contact with other Latin American prelates through CELAM, the Consejo Episcopal Latinoamericano, created in 1955. At this point, the general opinion of the church in Latin America was that "Catholicism and communism were incompatible"—a judgment that the church in Mexico was all-important in disseminating.[42]

However, in Mexico this struggle against communism developed under special circumstances. Although López Mateos had quickly repressed the railway strike, he showed little hostility to Castro's government, particularly when that government announced to the international press that it was not communist.[43] Yet the nationalist rhetoric of the Mexican Revolution allowed little space for foreign influence or interference. This played into the hands of the church authorities, who during the 1960s directed their anticommunist barbs not at the state—even if it displayed a certain sympathy for the Cuban Revolution—but rather toward an external enemy, personified by Cuba's communist regime, that supposedly was trying to spread disorder, confusion, and eventual revolution in Mexico.

In Mexico the spark that reignited the struggle between the church and communist sympathizers was the U.S.-backed Bay of Pigs. After a series of student protests in support of the Cuban communists at the University of Puebla, the ecclesiastical hierarchy launched a furious public campaign against the communist threat, culminating in mass demonstrations, which the hierarchy rather disingenuously maintained were "of a religious type."[44] These demonstrations were not accidental, but rather geared toward changing state policy. A few months earlier López Mateos had ordered government employees to tone down anticommunist rhetoric and in July 1960 declared that his administration represented the "extreme left" within the constitution.[45]

Evidently the church wished to influence more than Mexico's small bands of communists, which were often little more than phantoms. In reality, the church had as much if not more interest in weakening liberal groups who clung onto the secularist policies embedded in the constitution. Although collective psychosis perhaps persuaded some of the imminence of the communist threat, the Mexican state was little influenced by Russian, Chinese, Cuban, or even Marxist doctrine. The new education plan and the provision of free textbooks, which triggered an enormous anticommunist campaign in 1962, did little more than continue the laicizing tradition of the liberal regimes and the Mexican Revolution.

The Mexican Church, Vatican II, and Church-State Developmentalism

Despite its anticommunism, an inheritance from an antimodernist and antiliberal past, the church could not remain completely above the changing political and social landscape of the 1960s. Within the church itself there were battles to define an ideological orientation. The 1958 election of a new, more liberal pope, John XXIII, shifted the balance (at least temporarily) from intransigence toward reformism. The celebration of the Second Vatican Council (1962–65) had a major impact, introducing theologies of development and liberation and fresh pastoral perspectives that made concessions to secular ideas of social justice. The participation of Mexican bishops, priests, and pious laymen in the discussions of the council allowed the country's church to "open itself to the world" and incorporate new pastoral attitudes from other regions. The publication in April 1963 of *Pacem in terris*—an encyclical announcing greater tolerance toward those who did not share church doctrine—also influenced the position of many Mexican bishops. These doctrinal shifts in Rome modified the Mexican church's stance on the "social question" and moderated the ongoing conflict with the state.[46]

The Mexican church that arose from these changes was neither ultraconservative and traditionalist nor radical and reformist. By the end of 1965, most of the Mexican church was more open to the secular world, and the ecclesiastical establishment, much of it still imprisoned in dreams of religious utopia, was gradually giving way to a new generation of church leaders for whom temporal matters attained new significance. At the same time lay organizations, growing steadily in size and prestige, began a series of profound changes that would further modify church positions. When this process began, at the end of the 1950s, few questioned the absolute control of priests and prelates over the lay organizations. But within a decade it became clear that many of the lay people involved "had something to say" concerning the direction of the church, and by the 1970s many groups were only nominally controlled by the ecclesiastical authorities.

In this context some Catholics proposed cooperating openly with the revolutionary regime to attain greater economic development. Whereas for many Catholics the term *integrated development* had a spiritual and ethical dimension, for President Gustavo Díaz Ordaz the notion was strictly secular and included only a vague acknowledgment of the need for "cultural" development. In any case, the abandonment of anticommunist rhetoric and a growing concern with the problems of underdevelopment brought church objectives into line with those of the state and marginalized their doctrinal differences. The Catholic church sidelined its historical claims and embraced open cooperation with the state and other social actors, with the idea that—in social terms at least—the government project differed little from the ecclesiastical.

Although the Mexican Revolution remained undergirded by a liberal ideology, bishops, priests, and parishioners sought to replace that with a Catholic worldview, in which political duties overlapped with religious ones. One of the main characteristics of the church in the time of Vatican II was the entry of Catholics into national politics. This was most evident in the secular organizations, which enjoyed greater room to maneuver and greater freedom of expression than prelates. Yet this shift was also important for priests and bishops. In these years the Catholic hierarchy, priests, and laymen together entered en masse into public affairs, discussing and acting on a range of social and political problems. Significantly enough, these years also witnessed political turbulence and the attempts of certain social sectors to bring greater democratic participation to the country.

Social and Ecclesiastical Crisis

The year 1966 marked not only the high point of state development but also the beginning of a new era, not only in economic but also in political and social terms. Growing mobilization in universities, schools, and certain social organizations anticipated increasing demands for involvement in the state's decision-making processes. This created an atmosphere of insecurity and mobilization and fed into a press-fuelled return of the collective psychosis of the early 1960s, which saw a communist agitator behind each minor disturbance. Yet the origins of this anticommunist campaign differed from those of 1959–62: government elites, not church prelates, led the campaign. In contrast, the church, influenced by liberation theology, actually grew more critical, moving from a position of unconditional support to a position of "critical support." Although the church never went as far as to question actual cooperation, priests and parishioners did try to *matizar* some of the regime's thinking on social issues.

The change, often barely perceptible, was nevertheless important. The hierarchy now made it clear that the accord with the state had a specific end: the more equitable development of the country. In other words, the church's commitment was not to the state but to Mexico's Catholic people. The reasons for this slight but important change can be found in the transformation that the church had been experiencing during the period after Vatican II. Beyond assimilating some of the council's conclusions, some groups were developing a radical critique of ecclesiastical structures. As a result, while some Mexican prelates were attempting to maintain good relations with the state, they also were being forced to question this strategy by other prelates and groups more in line with the spirit of the council's recommendations.

The situation of the church between 1967 and 1968 can be clearly seen in the episcopate's pastoral letter concerning the development and integration of the country. Although the letter included repeated calls for cooperation with the Mexican state, it also comprised a severe critique of the social, economic, and political situation of the country. The hierarchy reviewed the multiple obstacles to development in Mexico and focused on "a new form of culture and civilization" unresponsive to "the traditional forms of the presence of the church." The hierarchy sustained that the popular sectors were either not organized or seemed "passive and collectively involved in organizations . . . directed towards ends and interests unrelated to the advance and ennoblement of society."

The Mexican episcopate followed this broadside with its first collective criticism of the political system and a coded call for democratization:

In civic and political matters, we should recognize certain advances. But there are obstacles, which get in the way of the development of civic life. On the one hand, there is the lack of community spirit among many citizens, who simply try to find ways to elude unjust laws. On the other hand, the persistence of certain practices of immoral administration also decreases the civic development of the people.

The lack of civic maturity can be seen in the scarce interest of many citizens [in the political process] and the incompetence with which the problems of the political life of the nation are often aired. Many still remain to be convinced of the necessity of placing the common national good over individual interests or those of the group, and systems which discourage the free exercise of citizens' rights abound.[47]

Toward a Conclusion

Church-state relations between 1938 and 1968 rested upon an implicit pact, a modus vivendi built on a common cause between the two institutions. The church, buoyed by an increasingly anticommunist nationalism, supported this pact, as long as the state tolerated the church's own involvement in confessional education. Furthermore, the church agreed to abandon any attempt to influence mass movements, which would now remain in the hands of the corporatist, postrevolutionary state. Beyond their common interests, the modus vivendi also was born of earlier political phenomena: the exhaustion produced by more than twenty years of conflict, persecution, and war and the clash between Calles and Cárdenas. Although this shift did not end the ideological differences between church and state, it did contribute to bringing to Mexico a degree of social peace under the umbrella of an authoritarian state. The elimination of the more radical revolutionary factions and the alliance between these two institutions played an important role in the long-running stability of the Mexican political system.

The church gradually accepted the ideas about social justice advanced by the revolution. At the same time, it made the most of what freedom of action the modus vivendi allowed. Concurrently, the state also benefited from ecclesiastical support in its efforts to attain greater social stability. However, by 1950 the Catholic church had begun to question the regime's political and socioeconomic aims. When it became evident that the model of economic development would not resolve the problems of economic inequality, the church started to criticize the state once again, eventually breaking its accord with the postrevolutionary government.

Between 1958 and 1968 the church undoubtedly experienced a profound internal transformation. There was an abyss between the church before the council, immersed in its dreams of a Christian utopia, and the church after the council, with its vision firmly set on the problems of this world. The church passed little by little from wholesale intransigence to a growing acceptance of the tangible benefits that some secular institutions and individuals could bring to the country's poor and destitute. Shifts in Mexico reflected changes in the rest of the Catholic world. The policy of *aggiornamento* proposed by the Holy See favored greater rapprochement with the Mexican state, one already under way in part because of the perceived communist threat posed by the Cuban Revolution. However, while the Mexican episcopate started to make conciliatory moves, some lay leaders lagged behind and others attempted to act upon the more radical suggestions of Vatican II. These new Catholics stimulated a powerful reformist movement that began to question ecclesiastical institutions and the role of the church in society. Thus, before the student movement began, the church had already completed significant internal change. By 1968 most religious organizations had profoundly modified their attitude toward the modern world and, consequently, toward Mexican society and the state.

As a result, despite professing complete support for the regime—at least between 1963 and 1968—the church assumed an increasingly independent and often critical stance toward the state's model of economic development. As the revolutionary state began to lose legitimacy, this enabled the church to strengthen its social base, particularly among the middle classes. The church for the first time adopted a more radical stance than the government in social policy, as demands for social justice and democratization bled into church pastorals and bishops' epistles. In taking this critical position, old ecclesiastical demands for religious liberty blended with new more "politicized" claims, in which religious liberty was only one of many freedoms necessary for the full development of Mexican society. Thus the ecclesiastical hierarchy gradually, even imperceptibly, shifted from a position of outward support to acting as the "judge" of government policy. After a while their roles were reversed. The state no longer approved or disapproved of church initiatives; on the contrary, the church became something of a watchdog for government behavior, and the regime, increasingly isolated from society, frequently seemed to be its captive. Government policies of any weight needed ecclesiastic blessing to be accepted. In the 1940s a weakened church had been driven to an implicit pact to shore up its position. By the 1960s, the church's cooperation with the state came from a position of strength and was conditioned on the latter's rapprochement in theory and in practice. From then on the church held a secure position in the social and political chess game of contemporary Mexico. The balance of power shifted substantially, and for the state there was—without provoking a major reaction—no way back.

Notes

1. For this period see Jean Meyer's classic, *La Cristiada* (3 vols.) (Mexico City: Siglo XXI, 1977); Roberto Blancarte, *Historia de la Iglesia católica en México* (Mexico City: Fondo de Cultura Económica-El Colegio Mexiquense, 1992).

2. Victoria Lerner, *La educación socialista* (Mexico City: El Colegio de México, 1979), 15.

3. Episcopado Mexicano, "Carta pastoral colectiva," *Christus* 1, no. 3 (February 1936): 102.

4. *Cultura Cristiana* 2, no. 12 (March 25, 1934): 4.

5. Episcopado mexicano, "Declaraciones del Comité Ejecutivo Episcopal," *Christus* 2, no. 14 (January 1937): 3.

6. Episcopado Mexicano, "Instrucción pastoral del V: Episcopado nacional dirigida a obreros y campesinos de toda la República," *Christus* 1, no. 8 (July 1936): 616.

7. Pius XI, "Carta Encíclica sobre el comunismo ateo," *Christus* 2, no. 18 (May 1937): 401.

8. Luis González, *Los días del Presidente Cárdenas* (Mexico City: Colegio de México, 1981), 62.

9. Cited in William Townsend, *Lázaro Cárdenas, demócrata mexicano* (Mexico City: Biografías Gandesa, 1959), 135.

10. Delegación Apostólica, "Declaraciones del Excmo. y Rmo. Sr. Delegado," *Christus* 1, no. 6 (May 1936): 414.

11. Delegación Apostólica, "Declaraciones del Excmo. Sr. Delegado," *Christus* 1, no. 7 (June 1936): 506.

12. Information from *Hoy*, reproduced in editorial, *Christus* 3, no. 30 (May 1938): 383.

13. Episcopado mexicano, "Los católicos mexicanos y la deuda petrolera," in *Christus* 3, no. 31 (June 1938): 485.

14. *Memorias del Señor Cardenal Miguel Darío Miranda; Arzobispo Primado de México*, vol. 1 (Mexico City: Editorial Progreso, 1987), 252.

15. Luis Javier Garrido, *El partido de la revolución institucionalizada: La formación del nuevo Estado en México (1928–1945)* (Mexico City: Siglo XXI, 1984), 263–85.

16. Eugenio Pacelli, "Instrucción sobre la educación socialista," published as "La voz de Roma," *Cultura Cristiana* 9, no. 8 (February 25, 1940): 4.

17. Episcopado mexicano, "Instrucción del episcopado relativa a la reglamentación del artículo 30," *Cristiana* 9, no. 7 (February 18, 1940): 4.

18. *Excélsior*, January 14, 1940; *Novedades*, June 25, 1940.

19. *Excélsior*, April 17, 1939.

20. *Novedades*, July 10, 1940.

21. *Revista Hoy*, September 31, 1940, 8–9.

22. A. M. "Formación cívico-social; patria y patriotismo," *Cultura Cristiana* 5, no. 46 (November 14, 1937): 4.

23. Episcopado mexicano, "Declaraciones del Excmo. Sr. Arzobispo de México," *Christus* 7, no. 77 (April 1, 1942): 301.

24. "Peligro," ONIR 9, no. 7 (March 1, 1942): 1.

25. President Avila Camacho sent the proposed reform of article 3 to the Chamber of Deputies on December 14. *Novedades*, December 15, 1945. Luis J. de la Peña,

La legislación mexicana en relación con la Iglesia, 3, Cuadernos, Colección Canónica de la Universidad de Navarra (Pamplona: Ediciones Rialp, 1965), 89.

26. *Excélsior*, December 18, 1945.

27. Episcopado mexicano, "Carta pastoral colectiva que el episcopado mexicano dirige a los muy ilustres cabildos . . . ," *Christus* 6, no. 68 (July 1941): 549–64.

28. Carlos Alvear Acevedo, "La Iglesia de México en el período 1900–1962," in *Historia general de la Iglesia en América Latina*, v, México (Mexico City: Ed. Paulinas, 1984), 341.

29. "La Iglesia forjadora de la nacionalidad mexicana," ONIR 15, no. 22 (October 15, 1946): 6.

30. Rodrigo Martínez, "Hay que sostener la idea de patria," *Cultura Cristiana* 10, no. 16 (March 17, 1941): 4.

31. Miguel Alemán, "Discurso del Lic. Miguel Alemán Valdés al protestar como presidente de la República," *Los Presidentes de México ante la Nación, IV, Informes de 1934 a 1966* (Mexico City: Camára de Diputados, 1966), 355.

32. Luis Medina, *Civilismo y modernización del autoritarismo*, in *Historia de la Revolución Mexicana, periodo 1940–1952*, vol. 20 (Mexico City: El Colegio de México, 1979), 94.

33. Medina, *Civilismo y modernización*, 178.

34. *Tiempo* 19, no. 493 (October 12, 1951): 3.

35. In September 1952 President Alemán's daughter entered into a religious marriage in front of the president and with President Avila Camacho serving as godfather. *Tiempo* 21, no. 543 (September 26, 1952), and 544 (October 3, 1952). In contrast, for Ruiz Cortines's stepson's wedding he attended the civil ceremony and then withdrew with his cabinet, leaving the couple to get on with the religious ceremony.

36. ONIR, "Derecho de la asociación profesional a defender los intereses de sus miembros," *Cultura Cristiana* 25, no. 30 (June 17, 1956): 1.

37. José González Torres, "Derecho de los súbditos a ser dirigidos y servidos por la autoridad," *Cultura Cristiana* 25, no. 32 (July 1, 1956): 1.

38. Donald Mabry, *Mexico's Acción Nacional: A Catholic Alternative to Revolution* (Syracuse, NY: Syracuse University Press, 1973), figure 2, 69.

39. *Tiempo* 39, no. 755 (October 22, 1956): 3.

40. Jesús García, "La Iglesia mexicana desde 1962," in *Historia general de la Iglesia en América Latina* (Mexico City: CEHILA-Sigueme-Ed, 1983), vol. v, 365.

41. Olga Pellicer de Brody and José Luis Reyna, *Historia de la Revolución Mexicana, 1952–1960: El afianzamiento de la estabilidad política* (Mexico City: El Colegio de México, 1978), 12.

42. Celam, "Declaración del Consejo Episcopal Latinoamericano a raíz de su IV Reunión," reproduced in *Christus* 25, no. 290 (January 1960): 17.

43. *Excélsior*, April 2, 1959.

44. *Tiempo* 39, no. 977 (June 12, 1961): 22.

45. *Excélsior*, July 2, 1960.

46. Paul Poupard, *Le Concile Vatican II*, Coll. Que sais-je? (París: PUF, 1983), 7.

47. Episcopado mexicano, "Carta pastoral del Episcopado Mexicano sobre el desarrollo e integración del país," reproduced in *Christus* 33, no. 390 (May 1968): 399, 402.

CHAPTER 3 | Thomas Rath

CAMOUFLAGING THE STATE

The Army and the Limits of Hegemony
in PRIísta Mexico, 1940–1960

As the editors of this volume rightly warn, not everything that is difficult to know about the PRI is interesting and important. When it comes to the military, though, the charms of the "seductive episteme of the hidden" can hardly be resisted.[1] The outlines of the postrevolutionary army's history are well known: in the 1920s the army spawned three major rebellions and dominated national politics and the federal budget, and the government implemented a program to tame and professionalize the army, which, with the advent of a civilian president and much slimmer budget by the 1940s, apparently met with success.[2] It has long been, and continues to be, difficult to conduct research that can put empirical flesh on the bones of this familiar institutional narrative.[3] Fortunately, we now have archival sources and a new secondary literature that allow us to challenge conventional interpretations of the army's history and illuminate a central question debated by historians of postrevolutionary Mexico: the degree to which PRI rule rested on consensual mechanisms and enjoyed popular legitimacy.

Synthesizing original archival research with a new secondary literature, this chapter explores what the army's history can tell us about the regime's capacity to extract a degree of support from those it ruled or, at least, to constrain opposition within certain institutional and discursive boundaries.[4] How legitimacy is made and unmade over time is difficult to gauge, particularly in a famously plural nation such as Mexico. This chapter breaks down the problem into separate questions of increasing importance (and difficulty): first, whether the regime had a coherent political and ideological project for the army; second, the degree to which this project enjoyed popular support; and third, whether the regime functioned, and was seen to function, according to its professed ideals.

I argue that by the 1940s the regime succeeded in defining a coherent military policy that was broadly popular but far less successful in matching theory with practice. Although President Manual Avila Camacho (1940–46) was an army officer, as were dozens of others in public office, after 1940 the state claimed to have separated the army from civil government, and this separation indicated the PRI's commitment to stable, consensual rule. In 1948 and 1952 the regime defused serious challenges by dissident officers, securing civilians' dominance of national politics. However, I argue that the pervasive rhetoric of civilianism aimed to camouflage the PRIísta state and the military's continuing autonomy, corruption, and repression; and that, for many people at the time, this discursive camouflage was probably not very convincing. Finally, to conclude, I discuss whether the 1940s and 1950s should be understood as a distinctive period in Mexico's political development.

The Official Image of the Army

In the early 1940s, Mexico's army contained about fifty thousand men, most of them in battalions of infantry and regiments of cavalry stationed around the country in major provincial cities. In most cases each federal state was also a military zone, the commander of which was responsible for the two or three army units typically stationed in the zone, and sent back to the Department of Defense in Mexico City regular reports concerning any disturbances to public order.[5] Mexico's officer corps continued to be distinctly top-heavy and socially heterogeneous: in 1941 the army had 436 generals, about 1 for every 100 soldiers.[6] Most officers were veterans of the revolution's armed phase, although they were increasingly joined by younger graduates of the Military College (reopened in 1925), who were more likely than revolution-era officers to hail from the middle classes and the Federal District. Most officers were stationed in provincial units, although several hundred served in the army's elite assignments: the general staff of the Department of Defense (1943–49), the presidential general staff, a small air force, and, after 1945, an elite presidential guard that took over the most modern, mechanized materiel acquired by Mexico from the United States during World War II.[7] Between 1942 and 1950 troops were a mix of volunteers and conscripts; conscripts were housed in better facilities than the remaining regular troops and kept away from police work in the provinces.[8]

The army was also in charge of the militia of *defensas rurales*, a heterogeneous and controversial legacy of the 1930s. By the end of the 1930s, Cárdenas's efforts to restrict membership in the militia to peasant *ejidatarios* had foundered in the face of resistance by army commanders.[9] On paper, they totaled around sixty thousand men. However, membership turned over frequently, and the actual strength of militia corporations (divided into infantry battalions and cavalry regiments) varied by state and is difficult to gauge: in 1939, a militia battalion in Veracruz and Chiapas contained about four hundred men; in Oaxaca it contained roughly three hundred; in México and the Federal District, only two hundred. It is clear that they were concentrated in areas of old Cristero and Villista mobilization. In 1938, 18 percent of militia units were based in Chihuahua; the states of Jalisco, Durango, Michoacán, and Guanajuato together accounted for 31 percent.[10]

What was the legitimate purpose of Mexico's army? In the 1920s and 1930s, the postrevolutionary government offered varying answers to this question. Military reform was an urgent matter for the Sonoran regime (1920–34) as it clung onto power amid recurrent army plots and rebellions. The Sonorans generally claimed to be molding an apolitical, professional military suitable for a modern, liberal-democratic state, although they generally conceded that this remained a work in progress. In contrast, Cárdenas sought to infuse the army officers and troops with a sense of class solidarity with the working masses and encouraged an active commitment to social reform.[11] As is well known, many military officers moved into open opposition in the face of Cardenismo, including the dissident candidate in the 1940 presidential election, General Juan Andreu Almazán. General Francisco Aguilar cheerfully remembered offering pragmatic advice to some wealthy, conservative military officers who were "scared to death of communism" in the 1930s: "I told them, 'what the hell. If communism comes, be commissars!'"[12] Many commanders mouthed official rhetoric, obstructed the substance of Cardenista reform, and later supported the official candidacy of the moderate Manuel Avila Camacho.

The Avila Camacho administration expunged most of Cárdenas's radical military rhetoric and returned to the Sonorans' ideals of neutrality and professionalism. Free military magazines, lavish photo essays in the national press, and regular radio broadcasts all repeated the idea that the government had modernized the army's materiel and removed it from politics. Indeed, the increased diffusion of propaganda allowed some communities to (sometimes literally) quote official speeches back to the government when complaining about perceived military abuses.[13] The official image of the army as a detached, unified, apolitical institution has not changed much since. At Mexico City's Museo del Ejército, cases of rifles, documents, and uniforms tell a conventional military history from the colony until the 1920s; thereafter, tales of conflict cease, replaced by a video describing the evolving educational institutions and organizational structure of the postrevolutionary army.

In its basic outlines, the idea of government by and for the mass of the civilian population enjoyed broad appeal for quite rational reasons. After all, Mexico's liberal tradition was not some artificial import; liberalism had put down deep and far-reaching roots through the nineteenth century, even as it was subject to local interpretation. Of course, liberal ideas coexisted with the reality of clientelism; the revolution produced many popular military caudillos who mastered an appealing rough-and-ready personal style and delivered material benefits to their followers. For every officer who was fondly remembered thus, it is not hard to find evidence of repressive and reactionary commanders.[14] In any case, clientelism and caciquismo were hardly monopolies of military officers.[15] Mexico was not awash with demands for government by the military as a group. Cárdenas's vision of a military infused with a politicized class consciousness had its supporters among radical teachers, artists, and a handful of CTM leaders. However, there is little evidence that it ignited fierce popular enthusiasm in the way land reform and unionization certainly did.[16] It is not even clear that Cárdenas's project elicited all that much support from the bulk of troops whose benefits and service conditions he improved; observers reported that soldiers probably favored the conservative Almazán in 1940.[17] Cárdenas's radical rhetoric was vague on key points anyway, and he never entirely abandoned the idea of military neutrality in elections. In 1949, the government also replaced its unpopular policy of conscripting thousands of men into the army each year (begun in 1942) with a much less onerous system of weekend military service.[18]

More controversial was the idea that to achieve progress and respectability, Mexico's president must necessarily be a civilian rather than an officer who had left service to enter civilian politics. After the civilian Miguel Alemán became president in 1946, this idea was adopted by the regime. During the 1952 presidential election, General Miguel Henríquez Guzmán's supporters—and other officers involved in dissident politics, such as Octavio Vejar Vázquez—argued for the rights of officers on leave to participate freely in electoral contests. Henríquez also had to fend off jibes about him being less a *militar de carrera* than a parasitic *militar de carretera* addicted to government road contracts, and his campaign de-emphasized his military credentials as it went on.[19]

Adjusting Reality to Rhetoric: Officers and National Politics

It was difficult for Avila Camacho and Alemán to turn Mexican politics into a passable imitation of civilian rhetoric. Above all, they confronted a powerful, ambitious, and sometimes embarrassing corps of officers. The right wing of the army loosely coalesced around Manuel Avila Camacho. Ironically, this included many officers who had sought to counter Cardenista radicalism and offered crucial support for Avila Camacho's presidential run and the return to an official rhetoric of military neutrality. In the process, the Avila Camacho brothers allied with numerous old Callista officers who had been marginalized under Cárdenas, including Generals Donato Bravo Izquierdo, José María Tapia, Rodrigo Quevedo. However, Cárdenas remained a powerful figure in the military; he headed a faction of generally more left-wing, nationalist officers who, U.S. diplomats complained, sought to use Mexico's wartime collaboration with the allies to obtain as much credit and materiel from the U.S. government as possible with a minimum of U.S. control.[20] The immensely wealthy General Abelardo Rodríguez also retained influence over numerous northern officers. In 1936–37, Rodríguez boasted of his continuing influence over the army to U.S. officials, and it was rumored that Cárdenas offered him the job of Secretary of Defense to quiet military discontent. Rodríguez served as a regional commander once more between 1941 and 1943 before running unopposed for Sonora's governorship. He remained Sonora's de facto political boss for decades, was an important influence on the army under Avila Camacho, and reportedly was a close supporter of Generals Gilberto Limón (Secretary of Defense, 1946–52) and Agustín Olachea (Secretary of Defense, 1958–64).[21]

Military commands still afforded lesser officers a host of ways to meddle in regional societies. Officers had a great deal of power over policing: in Guerrero the army command took over the prosecution of homicide cases; in Tlaxcala the officer in charge of the militia worried about their poor discipline and susceptibility to personal feuds and "smooth-talking" agitators but also defended the military's role mediating agrarian disputes, if only for the sake of fomenting order and the militia's morale.[22] Army officers commanded Mexico City's police, and numerous other provincial forces, throughout this period.[23] The army had a set of officers who moved in and out of police and military commands, many of whom specialized in heavy-handed repression. After playing a prominent role fighting cristeros, General Miguel Z. Martínez led gangs of street fighters against Almazanistas during the 1940 election in Mexico City; he intimidated opponents with cries of "give yourselves up *hijos de la chingada*, here comes *huevos de oro!*"[24] He then led Mexico City's police force and numerous military zones until the 1960s, by which point he had acquired a host of landed properties through dubious procedures.[25] While zone commander in Guadalajara in 1945, he summarily executed dozens of petty criminals, dumping their bodies on the edge of the city; his own soldiers developed a line of grim jokes about his brutal character and incongruous high-pitched voice.[26]

Building on this base of judicial autonomy, officers used their posts to enrich themselves and shape government policy and appointments. Complaints about officers selling protection and skimming budgets are legion and are well documented in the few candid military memoirs of the period; commanders also acquired lands, smuggled liquor, owned gambling dens and cantinas, and, of course, obtained construction contracts from the government.[27] Historians' tendency to see these military subordinates as simple conduits of presidential authority in the provinces oversimplifies military politics and, as with other more celebrated (metaphorical) subalterns, elides their agency. After 1937 General Mange built a business empire and sphere of political influence over much of south and central Veracruz.[28] In Durango in 1943 the governorship was disputed between ex-governor General Elpidio Velázquez, who was seeking to impose a puppet civilian successor, and General Blas Coral Martínez, who openly campaigned from his military command, stationed allies in posts across the state, and received payments from the U.S.-based "San Luis" mining company for intimidating and obstructing sectors of the CTM.[29] After General Bonifacio Salinas Leal stepped down from the governorship of Nuevo León in 1943, he rejoined the army and commanded numerous prominent zones but remained a major powerbroker in the state, resisted the Alemán administration's attempts to displace his influence, and was rumored to have influenced the 1958 presidential succession.[30] In 1945 the army charged General Pablo Macías Valenzuela in a military court for planning the assassination of Sinaloa's governor, Colonel Loaiza. Although the hearings were eventually discontinued, they dredged up a range of scandalous details about the army's alliances with local gunmen and political factionalism. Officers were not so influential everywhere; the political machines that controlled the state of Mexico and San Luis Potosí, for example, kept military meddling to a minimum.[31] However, there was no shortage of officers who tried to convert their regional sway into national influence. General Jesús Arias Sánchez became famous in Sinaloa after imposing virtual martial law and conducting bloody campaigns of pacification against bandits and *guardias blancas* in the south of the state in 1942–44; by the late 1940s he had acquired land and business interests across Sinaloa and, like numerous other officers, supported the dissident presidential campaign of General Miguel Henríquez Guzmán.[32]

And yet, by the mid-1950s the demilitarization of national politics had made genuine advances. Mexico would have a civilian president after 1946 and would be free from military rebellions. In the mid-1950s, the British ambassador occasionally heard rumors of planned military uprisings that were told to him by an eccentric, friendly veteran; the ambassador (very reasonably) rejected them as ridiculous fabrications.[33] General Celestino Gasca's 1961 rebellion attracted scattered peasant support but was crushed by the army in a few days.[34] In 1952, the government defeated Henríquez's campaign with a combination of machine politics and repression, aided by Cárdenas's refusal

TABLE 3.1. *Military Expenditure as a Percentage of Gross Domestic Product (GDP) in Mexico and Six Comparatives, 1976*

Country	GDP (%) spent on military in 1976
Mexico	0.6
Costa Rica	0.7
Brazil	1.3
Uruguay	2.2
Argentina	2.4
United States	5.4
Chile	6.1

Source: Alfred Stepan, *Rethinking Military Politics: Brazil and the Southern Cone* (Princeton, NJ: Princeton University Press, 1988), 76–77.

to support his old military ally and Henríquez's limited popular appeal.[35] After the 1940s, apart from the Departments of Defense and the Navy, military officers never occupied more than 4 percent of the cabinet.[36] From the 1940s to the 1970s, the army's share of the federal budget gradually declined and remained small by regional standards. By 1976, Mexico spent less of its gross domestic product on the military than any other country in the Americas (see table 3.1).

Scholars have debated how the government affected these changes. Many historians emphasize a coherent policy of professionalization and depoliticization emanating from the center and focused on national, presidential politics rather than examine the relationship between national and regional military politics.[37] Other scholars have discussed civil-military relations more in terms of a political pact or partnership, although the origins and full dimensions of this pact have long been difficult to access.[38] New research in military, intelligence, and regional archives has clarified the degree to which officers resisted the demilitarization of politics and the extent to which the regime had to respond with political give-and-take and patronage, taking at the national level even as it gave in provincial and operational autonomy.

For example, in the summer of 1948 the Alemán administration confronted a serious crisis in civil-military relations. Alemán had done a number of things to alienate the military. The army had a powerful constituency of officers who simply doubted a civilian could or should govern Mexico and were determined to prevent the drift to civilian power. Zacatecas's General Manuel Contreras told his followers that Mexico should always be governed by a military man; General Mange muttered that Mexico could not be governed by a civilian "*hijo de la chingada pelele*."[39] In the first half of 1948 Alemán removed several long-standing Avilacamachista officers from their posts, including Donato Bravo Izquierdo in Puebla and Rodrigo Quevedo in Mexico City.[40] Discontent in the army was not restricted to a few displaced generals. In February 1948 an agent of the Dirección Federal de Seguridad (Federal Security Directorate, DFS) visited barracks in the state of Hidalgo; in Pachuca, soldiers complained that they were barely paid enough to eat and that a military career "in Mexico is a disgrace"; in Venta Prieta officers openly complained about pay and grumbled to each other that "the future for military officers is black."[41] After Alemán devalued the peso in July, two factions of officers seized their opportunity. Led by Antonio Ríos Zertuche, one group of northern officers demanded Alemán appoint more officers to the government and threatened to found a new military party. General Luis Alamillo and his old patron General Joaquín Amaro also were reported to be plotting Alemán's removal with the support of some younger officers. Behind such machinations lay a threat of force—an entirely plausible one, according to the government's own soldiers and agents.[42]

Although a military "intercession" was "plausibly" rumored through August and September, Alemán survived and went on to nominate and secure the election of a civilian successor.[43] He recovered by boosting army pay, pensions, and benefits.[44] He offered a few dozen young officers an appealing new career as agents in the president's own intelligence service, the DFS.[45] The president's office and the Department of Defense also sold promotions and postings on an unprecedented scale, an old and reliable mechanism of civilian (if not democratic) control. Conversely, some senior officers were paid off; some received funds from the president's own account; other officers remained, or were reinstated, in provincial sinecures. The ten new regional commands created in 1950–51 housed at least four generals who had opposed Alemán in 1948, including Salinas Leal, Quevedo, Mange, and Z. Martínez.[46] In 1948, Cárdenas and Avila Camacho reportedly counseled officers against extreme actions. As the government confronted Henriquismo, the gossipy newsletter *Buro de Investigación Política* noted that "by mere coincidence" the "two most important states flanking the federal district," Michoacán and Puebla, both were governed by military officers and brothers of Cárdenas and Avila Camacho, respectively.[47]

As a consequence, as the PRI entered its heyday of national stability, officers could still expect to lobby and graft in the provinces. The government had long claimed that national civilian rule was achieved by subjecting officers to increasingly regular bureaucratic circulation. The available data show precisely the opposite trend as the circulation of zone commanders slowed between 1934 and 1952. The army is still resistant to releasing a full record of commanders after 1952, stating that such information "does not exist." However, there are numerous examples that suggest the trend continued into the 1960s; commanders' local influence was not restricted to poor, rural backwaters or employed only from the zone command. A faction of Avilacamachista officers moved in and out of military and political posts in Puebla and helped build a *cacicazgo* that controlled state politics from the 1930s to the 1960s.[48] While Salinas remained a fixture in Nuevo León politics, he found a useful ally in neighboring Tamaulipas's redoubtable Tiburcio Garza Zamora. Garza had served under Almazán for decades, owed his ownership of Reynosa's electricity company to the general, and became a key figure in Almazán's 1940 campaign. After 1940, Garza remained a fixture in army posts in the region; he commanded different cavalry, conscript, and militia units in Nuevo León and Tamaulipas before assuming command of Reynosa's eleventh regiment of *defensas rurales* from 1949 to 1957. In 1958–61 he was Tamaulipas's federal deputy, then rejoined the army to command the zones of Chihuahua (1965–67) and Nuevo León (1967–70).[49] Garza used these posts to cement his position as one of the two key military bosses in the state, alongside General Raúl Gárate. He held on to his power company and acquired Reynosa's local paper and most of its nightclubs and cantinas. By 1962, Garza had controlled Reynosa politics, and strongly influenced state politics, "for twenty years."[50]

In the 1950s, officers no longer offered serious challenges to the central government's ideology and presidential authority. The public statements of officers, including those of the military-dominated Partido Auténtico de la Revolución Mexicana, were deliberately "anodyne."[51] However, numerous officers continued to serve as governors, senators, and deputies before moving back into the army. It was perfectly obvious that such officers remained political actors, which is why people continued to meet with them, petition them, and petition the government for certain officers to remain in local commands.[52] In the 1950s zone commanders often accompanied governors and presidents on their electoral campaigns; in Oaxaca, commanders sometimes even gave speeches on politics and rural development on behalf of the state governor.[53] In a pattern reminiscent of Stepan's analysis of mid-century Brazil, military politics under the PRI was enabled by a kind of structural hypocrisy: everyone knew that officers wielded power within the system, particularly in local and regional politics, and that the rules of public discourse prevented people from directly acknowledging it.[54]

Likewise, military corruption was well hidden but remained visible. General Félix Ireta, Michoacán's zone commander from 1954 to 1969, was rumored to be running gangs of cattle ranchers and pistoleros in the 1950s and extracting protection money from municipalities. When complaints about Ireta finally made it into the press, the general threatened to shut down the newspaper for the crime of denigrating the armed forces.[55] This was seen as an unusual case; such explicit threats were usually not necessary. In Reynosa everyone knew General Garza and "saw him as a patriarchal cacique"; he also was known to be using aircraft to run contraband "on a grand scale," although his enemies only ever made such criticisms "with great discretion."[56] Still, if the details of military corruption were difficult to apprehend, the basic fact must have been obvious enough. Jokes about Alemán's sale of promotions were well known in and outside the army.[57] Any business supplying the army would have come across a systematic system of kickbacks; military corruption would likewise not have surprised any of the dozens of businesses who paid protection money to the forty-nine battalions of infantry in Mexico City throughout the 1950s or the thousands who bribed officers every year to exempt their sons from military training on Sunday afternoons.[58]

Repression and Implausible Deniability

Officers retained political power because many were well connected and wealthy, but also because the army remained a crucial instrument of PRIísta rule. Many political scientists argue that civilian control and oversight of the army is generally easier to accomplish when the military does not monopolize necessary specialized knowledge and when civilians can claim some expertise in security. From this perspective, it is perhaps not so surprising that Mexico's officers eventually ceded (loose) control of national politics to civilians.[59] It was difficult for them to claim either a plausible role in external defense or that their policing mission required highly specialized expertise. Nevertheless, the military did possess certain skills, organizational capacity, and knowledge that ensured they remained profoundly necessary to the regime: officers knew the political and social terrain, often a lot better than the over-stretched intelligence services, and they had long experience in organizing a crude, homegrown tradition of counterinsurgency. Moreover, while some officers reportedly found police work demeaning and unpleasant, plenty of others appreciated such work's financial and political benefits; consequently, while military officers headed many police departments, soldiers and police occasionally clashed over control of protection money or local politics.[60]

By the 1950s, the army had shrunk the cavalry and used more infantry and mechanized units; however, soldiers remained dispersed around the country as a police force, much as in the previous two decades. Mexico's regular army was small by regional standards. Between 1951 and 1965, in Latin America only Haiti and Costa Rica had fewer military personnel relative to their population. Mexico's ratio of soldiers to citizens was 1:667, compared with Brazil's 1:400 and Argentina's 1:150.[61] However, unlike armies in the Southern Cone, it was devoted solely to domestic order. In the mid-1950s, zone commanders still stationed policing squads in 20 percent of Mexico's municipalities;[62] soldiers guarded key roads, dams, and power plants, and in 1953 army convoys protected the Acapulco-Mexico City highway from robberies and guarded the Marte R. Gómez dam in Tamaulipas from sabotage by peasant communities.[63] In the 1950s, the army routinely protected rural properties from agraristas and engaged in dozens of petty counterinsurgencies against small forces of frustrated ex-Henriquistas and rebellious indigenous communities in Oaxaca, southwestern Jalisco, and Chiapas. The army's deployment waxed and waned depending on regional political and social dynamics. For example, Puebla politics was rather stable under the governorship of General Rafael Avila Camacho (1951–57). However, this had been achieved only after a spike in military deployments in the 1940s, as the state was crisscrossed by flying columns and the government imposed military officers in municipal governments like latter-day *jefes políticos*.[64]

Defensas rurales also remained numerous and busy, more so in some states than others. Charting changes in the militia over time is challenging. Between 1938 and 1950, the number of militia corporations shrank from 140 to 129. However, Chihuahua alone accounted for 72 percent of the losses. Chihuahua boasted an extraordinary twenty-five militia regiments in 1938; in 1950, its seventeen units were still more than any other state, and other states retained roughly the same proportion of militia as they had in 1938. In Puebla and Morelos, army commanders demobilized militia in suspect areas and recruited elsewhere, keeping overall numbers roughly stable. In 1953, the army demobilized approximately 542 militiamen (22 small platoons and 1 corporation), but enlisted another 742 (2 corporations and 13 platoons).[65]

Despite commanders' increased control over recruitment and training of the militia, their behavior varied. Some defensas rurales served as loyal gangs of pistoleros for local authorities; others were distinctly unreliable agents of rural repression. In Morelos, Jaramillistas regularly picked off the defensas rurales and seized their weapons, facing greater or lesser resistance; in Guerrero, militia consistently joined up with agrarian dissidents.[66] Despite these problems, and repeated complaints and demands that the government disband them, the government evidently still considered militia useful in achieving a loose, crude kind of control in Mexico's distant and poorly integrated countryside. In 1953, the army recorded thirty-seven "notable" incidents policed (in part) by the militia; 30 percent were in Guerrero and 11 percent were in Oaxaca; Morelos, Tamaulipas, and Nuevo León each had 8 percent. The army classified most of these incidents as apolitical missions against bandits or people it vaguely termed "scandalous types" (*escandolosos*); however, some incidents clearly concerned politics and included the militia fighting an "outbreak of political rebellion" in San Cristóbal, Guerrero, and engaging in a "*zafarrancho político*" in Nuevo León. The army also received complaints about militia supporting local caciques and invading lands in Veracruz.[67] In the 1950s, the army happily reported to the president's office how its soldiers and militia shot captured *maleantes* in distant parts of the republic "while they were trying to escape."[68]

To be sure, the PRI tried various ways to conceal the army's involvement in heavy-handed, delegitimizing political repression. After 1939 the army tried to cast itself in a more inclusive, conciliatory light by symbolically recognizing Zapatistas and Villistas, both men and women, as legitimate revolutionary veterans.[69] The government could hardly ignore soldiers scattered around the country but portrayed them as fulfilling a legitimate, constructive policing role under judicial authorities. Communities sometimes viewed military policing of highways and pursuit of criminals as entirely legitimate, despite how (or perhaps because) the army bypassed judicial authorities. Between 1940 and 1957, the federal government received nearly as many petitions from Puebla requesting help from the army in local police work as it did complaints of political repression and corruption.[70] In the 1940s the townspeople of Jamay, Jalisco, knocked on the door of the local garrison and urged soldiers to pursue two men who had kidnapped, raped, and murdered a local woman in the surrounding sierra; the garrison promptly hunted down and executed the men, to the town's satisfaction.[71] In urban areas, the army was probably seen as more reliable and less politicized than the police, although this was something of a backhanded compliment, so poor was the police's reputation; in opinion polls Mexicans ranked the army above the police, and the army garnered more applause during parades than the police.[72]

For controversial, obviously political tasks, the government usually deployed more deniable pistoleros, *porras*, or local police. In Mexico City during the 1940 election, Gonzalo N. Santos recruited paramilitaries for his *grupos de choque* from a floating population of urban gunmen and frustrated veterans; besides deniability, such men offered more initiative and urban savvy than soldiers, many of whom came from rural areas—they were "always ready to serve for these kinds of things," eager to regain favor and perhaps get back on the army payroll at a later date.[73] In 1946 the army's embarrassing massacre of political protesters in León acted as a stimulus for more strategies of deniability, at least in Mexico's cities.[74] During the 1952 election, only two of the sixty-seven incidents of political persecution and murder reported by the Henriquistas were blamed on soldiers.[75] Where paramilitarism was implausible, soldiers simply dressed as civilians. In the backwoods of Michoacán, a squad of soldiers tracked and killed a man suspected of shooting at an officer; they disguised themselves from locals and judicial authorities alike, despite briefly taking off their sombreros and revealing military haircuts.[76] Finally, of course, the government intimidated and censored the press. On the night of July 7, 1952, the police and army violently dispersed a crowd of protesting Henriquistas in Mexico City's Alameda plaza. Journalists at El Universal began excitedly preparing coverage of the massacre and were shocked as they received photographs that appeared to come from a "war zone": tanks in the streets, horses charging at crowds, and soldiers beating up women with sticks. However, the paper's editor soon received a call from the government. Decades later, the journalist Guillermo López Portillo remembered: "The orders were final, we had to rewrite everything, and convert the soldier aggressor into the watchful guardian who was intervening to take from a woman the stone with which she intended to attack him."[77]

Despite these efforts, the sheer depth of the army's involvement in enforcing crude stability was difficult to conceal. In the name of public order, the military violently raided *ejidos* and municipalities; broke strikes; and intimidated, detained, and fined protesters en masse. Some people no doubt viewed it as inevitable, necessary, or desirable, although such sentiments were rarely expressed in public. The generally successful censorship (and self-censorship) of the national press also coexisted with durable local traditions associating the army with repression. In Morelos, villagers derisively referred to federal soldiers as *guachos* and used *gobierno* as a synonym for hostile federal troops; Jaramillistas blamed much local repression on a notorious Captain Martínez, who was stationed in the state throughout the 1940s and 1950s and who was promoted after Jaramillo's murder in 1962.[78] In Puebla, local people complaining about army officers imposed on municipal councils did not mention to the press that such men were members of the army, but they knew that they were; in 1948–51 the denizens of Izúcar de Matamoros could hardly miss this, since the head of the municipal council wore a uniform and boasted of being a member of the presidential guard.[79] In the late 1930s, the denizens of San José de Gracia stopped regarding soldiers as a hostile occupying force and began to see them as generally reliable police. In the east of Michoacán, a shift in attitudes is much harder to detect. José Carmen Soto Correa recently mined a rich vein of local stories about the military's use of torture, collective reprisals, and extrajudicial executions to put down fierce popular resistance to the campaign against *aftosa*, seen as an illegitimate yanqui-backed imposition.[80] Stories from the Triqui region in Oaxaca tell a similar story of politicized brutality. After the government used the army to occupy Mexico City's Instituto Politécnico National in 1955, printmakers made cartoons portraying Secretary of Defense Matías Ramos as a reactionary, yanqui stooge.[81]

While military attempts at secrecy were frequently unconvincing, counter insurgency itself sometimes demanded a blend of national secrecy with spectacular, localized violence. The career of General Agustín Mustieles illustrates the conundrum well. After commanding cavalry regiments across the country in the 1930s, Mustieles became a trusted ally of Manuel Avila Camacho; he was promoted to brigade general in 1939, commanded the army's new third division during World War II, and in 1947 was promoted by Alemán to division general.[82] After Alemán removed the plotting Amaro from Oaxaca's zone command in 1948, Mustieles took over. Mustieles did his best to disguise the military's repression of a popular movement in Oaxaca City against the state governor in 1952; he recruited hundreds of leather-jacketed paramilitaries known as *cuerudos* to beat and disperse protesters. One of the cuerudos remembered being recruited for the job by his old patron General Adrian Castrejón because "the army could do nothing against the strike," whereas he and his friends could because they were no longer members of the army.[83] However, people still blamed Mustieles for organizing the repression; the cuerudos had gathered in the army barracks and been led by Mustieles's personal military aide.[84] When Mustieles took over command of the sixth military region based in Tuxtla Gutiérrez, Chiapas, the local press recalled how he had "trucked in the cuerudos to beat up authentic campesinos" and called for his removal.[85]

In June 1955, Mustieles also organized the army's campaign against a small rebellion of about thirty villagers from La Trinitaria, Chiapas. Explanations of the rebellion vary: the army believed that the men were Henriquistas, while local informants claimed that the rebellion was largely a protest against corn prices and the abuses of the state government and mestizo merchants. After the existing garrison commander took a timid and conciliatory approach, Mustieles sent one of his closest aides, Captain Trujillo Trejo, with clear instructions. Trujillo boosted military forces in the region and captured the men within a few days; he then beheaded five of the remaining twelve men in a village square, leaving the bodies on display, while the heads of the rebels were "taken to Villa Trinitaria passing through the entire settlement before then being put on exhibition on a table in the police station" for the next three days. Mustieles placed army censors in the post offices, systematically cut telegraph lines in the surrounding area, and met the sole local journalist who witnessed the killings and convinced him not to report them. While news of the violence did reach La Prensa, Excélsior, El Universal, and Novedades faithfully reproduced government denials that a massacre, or any important political events at all, had occurred in Chiapas. The display of military terror, mass executions, and beheadings shocked even the intelligence agent sent to investigate; the army, however, insisted it was standard (if secretive) practice.[86]

THE ARMY WAS NOT the government, and its history can only tell us so much about the *dictablanda*'s balance of force and consent. However, soldiers were found all around the country, and the postrevolutionary regime's claim to have fulfilled the revolution's promise to defeat militarism was central to its ideology. By the 1940s, the regime presented a coherent, durable image of the army as an apolitical institution, employed by civilian authorities for occasional legitimate police work. This idea was broadly popular; it was also quite familiar and predated the revolution. Although civilians dominated national politics by the mid-1950s, the Mexican army clung to multiple prerogatives—commanders resisted central policies of rotation and retirement and used their posts to interfere in provincial politics and accrue wealth, and the army remained crucial to policing, particularly in the countryside; people did not always see military policing as political and illegitimate, but many did. Officers and civilian elites reinforced a culture of secrecy around the army's activities and erected formidable barriers to public discussion. The cultural control achieved was real but in many ways superficial. It relied less on the power and appeal of revolutionary symbols and narratives to reshape subjectivities or frame debate than on a proliferation of public secrets and the deliberate fragmentation of the public sphere, particularly the divorce of the national press and political debate from local traditions that viewed the army as a deeply ambiguous, sometimes entirely illegitimate, entity.

This blend of change and continuity marks roughly 1940–60 as a relatively coherent period in the development of the army's relations with state and society, different from the rebellions, experiments in military policy, officer-presidents, and visible military violence of the 1920s and 1930s. This period also left a meaningful legacy. We now know a lot more about the Mexican army's extensive and visible repression of student and guerrilla movements in the 1960s and 1970s. However, the unwritten rules of the political game for the army had largely been established by the mid-1950s—when its core role was the application of force, and sometimes terror, in the service of political and economic domination—and have arguably remained influential throughout Mexico's protracted and uneven democratization. The past twenty years have seen growing demands from many groups in Mexico to open up debate on the military's history and the lack of civilian oversight of defense budgets and military justice.[87] If we understand how the army's politics and institutions were forged historically, we will be in a better position to understand how difficult it will be to foster a meaningful public debate on these matters and the likely costs to Mexican society of not doing so.

Notes

1. Gillingham, preface, this volume.
2. Edwin Lieuwen, *Mexican Militarism: The Political Rise and Fall of the Revolutionary Army* (Albuquerque, NM: University of New Mexico Press, 1968); Jorge Alberto Lozoya, El

Ejército Mexicano (Mexico City: Colegio de México, 1965); William S. Ackroyd, "Military Professionalism, Education, and Political Behavior in Mexico," *Armed Forces and Society* 18, no. 1 (1991): 81–96; Roderic Ai Camp, *Generals in the Palacio: The Military in Modern Mexico* (Oxford: Oxford University Press, 1992).

3. Studies that emphasize the army's political roles after 1940 but that lack detailed research on the topic include Frank Brandenberg, *The Making of Modern Mexico* (Saddle River, NJ: Prentice Hall, 1964); David Ronfeldt, "The Mexican Army and Political Order since 1940," in *The Modern Mexican Military: A Reassessment*, edited by David Ronfeldt, 63–86 (San Diego: Center for U.S.-Mexican Relations, 1984).

4. See Mary Kay Vaughan, *Cultural Politics in Revolution: Teachers, Peasants, and Schools in Mexico, 1930–1940* (Tucson: University of Arizona Press, 1997).

5. Personnel tables, 1941, in AGN/MAC-606.3/91; *Reglamento de las Comandancias de las Zonas Militares* (Mexico City: DAPP, 1937).

6. Author's calculation based on MA to G-2, "Who's Who Army Lists," March 25, 1942, NARA, MIDRF, 2555, "5990.03."

7. Lyle Macalister, "Mexico," in *The Military in Latin American Socio-political Evolution: Four Case Studies*, 197–258 (Washington, DC: Center for Research in Social Systems, 1970); "Mexican Army," 1955, PRO, F0371/120173.

8. Thomas Rath, "Gender and Military Reform in Postrevolutionary Mexico." Paper presented at Latin American Studies Association Conference, October 6–9, 2010, Toronto, Ontario, Canada.

9. Thomas Rath, "Revolutionary Citizenship Versus Institutional Inertia: Cardenismo and the Mexican Army, 1934–1940," in *Forced Marches: Soldiers and Military Caciques in Modern Mexico*, ed. Ben Fallaw and Terry Rugeley (Tucson: University of Arizona Press, 2012), 172–209.

10. "Armed Agrarians," G-2, 1938, NARA/MIDRF-2555/6010.

11. General José Álvarez y Álvarez de la Cardena, *El ejército nacional ante la militarización de obreros y campesino* (Mexico City: American Press, 1938).

12. MA to G-2, May 1944, NARA/MIDRF-2555/"April-June."

13. Ejido "Emiliano Zapata," Tabasco, to MAC, August 24, 1942, AGN/MAC-545.2/14-26.

14. Ann L. Craig, *The First Agraristas: An Oral History of a Mexican Agrarian Movement* (Berkeley, CA: University of California Press, 1983), 78–79; Hans-Werner Tobler, "Las paradojas del ejército revolucionario: su papel social en la reforma agraria mexicana, 1920–1935," *Historia Mexicana* 21, no. 1 (1971), 38–79.

15. Alan Knight and Wil G. Pansters, eds., *Caciquismo in Twentieth-century Mexico* (London: ILAS, 2005).

16. "Lombardo Toledano," in *México visto en el siglo xx*, ed. James Wilkie and Edna Monzón de Wilkie, 105–20 (Mexico City: Instituto Mexicano de Investigaciones Económicas, 1969); Rath, "Revolutionary Citizenship."

17. Lieuwen, *Mexican Militarism*, 135.

18. Thomas Rath, "*Que el cielo un soldado en cada hijo te dio*: Conscription, Recalcitrance, and Resistance in Mexico in the 1940s," *Journal of Latin American Studies* 37, no. 3 (2005): 507–32.

19. Aaron Navarro, *Political Intelligence and the Creation of Modern Mexico, 1938–1954* (University Park: Pennsylvania State University Press, 2010), 248–50.

20. Thomas Rath, *Myths of Demilitarization in Postrevolutionary Mexico, 1920–1960* (Chapel Hill: University of North Carolina Press, 2013), chapter 4.

21. Various reports, 1936–37, MA to G-2, NARA/MIDRF-2512; MA to G-2, May 18, 1944, NARA/MIDRF-2553; "Leading Personalities," May 2, 1947, PRO/F0371/60955; Guillermo J. R. Garduño Valero, "El ejército mexicano, el poder incógnito," *Iztapalapa* 34 (1994): 91–106, 100.

22. *Memorias de la Secretaría de la Defensa Nacional*, September 1941 to August 1942, 170; "Estudio relacionado con el funcionamiento de las defensas rurales," Colonel Toribio Beltrán Pulido, Tlaxcala to Defensa, 1944, AGN/MAC-550/24.

23. Diane Davis, "The Political and Economic Origins of Violence and Insecurity in Contemporary Latin America: Past Trajectories and Future Prospects," in *Violent Democracies in Latin America*, ed. Desmond Arias and Daniel Goldstein, 35–62 (Durham, NC: Duke University Press, 2010).

24. Gonzalo N. Santos, *Memorias* (Mexico City: Grijalbo, 1986), 714.

25. Mario Escobedo to DFS, January 21, 1961, AGN/DFS-63-16-61.

26. Rath, *Myths of Demilitarization*, chapter 5.

27. Arturo Geraldo, *Sobre las Armas* (Tijuana, BC: Impresora Contreras, 1993), 57–60, 80, 129; Fernando García Márquez, February 2, 1948, AGN/DFS-28-8-48/"Versiones públicas: Mustieles Medel, Águstín"; Navarro, *Political Intelligence*, 248–50. See also, Rath, *Myths of Demilitarization*, chapter 4.

28. Paul Gillingham, "Military Caciquismo in the Priísta State: General Mange's Command in Veracruz, 1937–1959," in Fallaw and Rugeley, *Forced Marches*, 210–37.

29. Francisco F. Quezada, Inspector 13, Durango, Durango, to DGIPS, March 14, 1943, AGN, DGIPS, caja 89, 2-1/131/726.

30. Monterrey Consulate to State Department, April 1, 1953, IAMSD-712.00/4-153; Javier Ibarrola, *El ejército y el poder* (Mexico City: Editorial Oceano, 2003), 74–75; Unsigned DFS report 1968, AGN/DFS-"Versiones públicas: Garza Zamora, Tiburcio," 125.

31. Rath, *Myths of Demilitarization*, chapter 4.

32. Consul, Mazatlán, to State Department, April 12, 1944, NARA/MIDRF-2516; Delegado 36, Culiacán, Sinaloa, May 27, 1950, AGN/DGIPS-803/2.

33. Sullivan to FO, July 23, 1954, PRO-F0371/109026, 75–76.

34. Elisa Servín, "Reclaiming Revolution in the Light of the Mexican Miracle: Celestino Gasca and the Federacionistas Leales Insurrection of 1961," *The Americas* 66, no. 4 (2010): 527–57.

35. Elisa Servín, *Ruptura y oposición: El movimiento henriquista, 1945–1954* (Mexico City: Ediciones Cal y Arena, 2001).

36. Camp, *Generals in the Palacio*, 69.

37. Ackroyd, "Military Professionalism." Navarro, while uncovering much new information on dissident officers, also emphasizes (but does not clearly define) the professionalization of the military and intelligence services (Navarro, *Political Intelligence*, 145, 166, 182, 270).

38. Monica Serrano, "The Armed Branch of the State: Civil-Military Relations in Mexico," *Journal of Latin American Studies* 27 (1996): 423–48.

39. Unsigned memo "Zacatecas," May 1950, AGN/DGIPS-803/2; Gillingham, "Military Caciquismo," 211.

40. Personnel tables, AGN/MAV-298/22349.

41. Fernando García Márquez, February 2, 1948, AGN/DFS-28-8-48, "versiones públicas: Mustieles Medel."

42. Rath, *Myths of Demilitarization*, chapter 4.

43. Rapp to FO, August 29, 1950, PRO/F0371/81503, AM1015/16, 27-8.

44. *Alemán y el ejército* (Mexico City: Estado Mayor Presidencial, 1950).

45. Navarro, *Political Intelligence*.

46. Rath, *Myths of Demilitarization*, chapter 4.

47. *Buro de Investigación Política*, January 14, 1952, 24.

48. Personal correspondence, Defensa to author, July 2011; Rath, *Myths of Demilitarization*, chapter 5.

49. Santos, *Memorias*, 733; Report on Tiburcio Garza Zamora, Ríos Thivol, September 26, 1949, AGN/DGIPS-84/2; AHSDN-XI/III/1-476.

50. Memo, Guttiérez Barrios, 1968, AGN/DFS-"versiones públicas: Garza Zamora, Tiburcio."

51. Sullivan to FO, 07/23/1954, PRO/F0371/109026, 75.

52. I discuss these practices in Puebla in *Myths of Demilitarization*, chapter 5.

53. McAlister, "Mexico"; Molina, December 14, 1951, AGN/DFS-00-18-14/"versiones públicas: Mustieles Medel."

54. Alfred Stepan, *The Military in Politics: Changing Patterns in Brazil* (Princeton, NJ: Princeton University Press, 1974).

55. Various correspondence and clippings, 1963–64, AHSDN-XI/III/1-574.

56. DFS memo 1968, and DFS agent, Monterrey, to Gutiérrez Barrios, April 15, 1969, AGN/DFS-"versiones públicas: Garza Zamora, Tiburcio," 125, 152.

57. José Moreno Flores, *Ametrallando! Periodismo humorístico, político, social* (Puebla: El Liberal Poblano, 1966), 140.

58. Juan Veledíaz, *El general sin memoria* (Mexico: Debate, 2010), 119–29. For cartoons criticizing avoidance of military service, see *450 años de lucha: Homenaje al pueblo mexicano* (Mexico City: Taller de Gráfica Popular, 1960), 43.

59. Alfred Stepan, *Rethinking Military Politics* (Princeton, NJ: Princeton University Press, 1988); Harold Trinkunas, *Crafting Civilian Control of the Military in Venezuela* (Chapel Hill: University of North Carolina Press, 2005).

60. Agent, Reynosa to DF, July 28, 1953, AGN/DFS-"versiones públicas: Garza Zamora, Tiburcio."

61. Calculation based on scattergram in Stepan, *The Military in Politics*, 25.

62. Rath, *Myths of Demilitarization*, chapter 5.

63. Agente 129, Tapachula, July 19, 1954, AGN/DFS-"versiones públicas: Mustieles Medle, Agustín"; "Informe relativo a la impartición de garantías," January 9, 1954, AGN/SDN-3/0010.

64. Rath, *Myths of Demilitarization*, chapter 5.

65. Author's calculation based on "Informe relativo a la impartición de garantias," January 9, 1954, AGN/SDN-3/0010.

66. Renato Ravelo Lecuona, *Los jaramillistas: La gesta de Rubén Jaramillo narrada por sus compañeros* (Cuernavaca, Morelos: Editorial la rana del sur, [1978] 2007), 94–97; Alexander Aviña, "Insurgent Guerrero: Genaro Vázquez, Lucio Cabañas, and the Guerrilla Challenge to the Postrevolutionary Mexican State, 1960–1996" (PhD dissertation, University of Southern California, 2009), 319, 328.

67. Author's calculation based on "Informe relativo a la impartición de garantías," January 9, 1954, AGN/SDN-3/0010.

68. "Informe relativo a la impartición de garantías," January 9, 1954, AGN/SDN-3/0010.

69. Rath, *Myths of Demilitarization*, chapter 6.

70. Rath, *Myths of Demilitarization*, chapter 5.

71. Geraldo, *Sobre las Armas*, 52–56.

72. Gabriel Almond and Sidney Verba, *The Civic Culture: Political Attitudes and Democracy in Five Nations* (Princeton, NJ: Princeton University Press, 1989), 68–75; Sullivan to FO, October 1, 1954, PRO/F0371/109026, 102.

73. Santos, *Memorias*, 707.

74. Bateman, "Annual Report, 1946," January 20, 1947, PRO/F0371/60940, AN/397/395/26, 14–15.

75. Enrique Quiles Ponce, *Henríquez y Cárdenas ¡Presentes! Hechos y realidades en la campaña henriquista* (Mexico City: Costa-Amic Editores, 1980), 281–88.

76. Geraldo, *Sobre las Armas*, 107–15.

77. *El Universal*, June 17, 1988.

78. Ravelo, *Los Jaramillistas*, 87–90, 143, 167–69.

79. Rath, *Myths of Demilitarization*, chapter 5.

80. Luis González, *San José de Gracia: Mexican Village in Transition* (Austin: University of Texas Press, 1974), 209; José Carmen Soto Correa, *El rifle sanitario, la fiebre aftosa y la rebelión campesina* (Mexico City: Instituto Politécnico Nacional, 2009), 117–237.

81. *Calacas con su corneta y pelona bayoneta* (Mexico City: Taller de Gráfica Popular, 1956).

82. Reports on military commands, 1934–1941, USMIR, reel 7; AHSDN-XI/III/1-222; Camp, *Generals in the Palacio*, 177.

83. "Entrevista con el Gral. Brigadier Tiburcio Cuellar Montalvo, realizado por Eugenia Meyer, el día 8 de mayo 1973, en la ciudad de México," IM, PHO, 1, no. 45, 61.

84. Iñurreta to DFS, March 23, 1952, AGN/DFS-100-18-14/"versiones públicas: Mustieles Medel." On the strike, see Smith, chapter 11, this volume.

85. Leandro Castillo Venegas, November 7, 1955, AGN/DFS-100-4-1/"versiones públicas: Mustieles Medel."

86. "I.P.S 4," "I.P.S 9," DF to DGIPS, August 24, 1955, AGN/DGIPS-2014-B/31, 8–11.

87. For a useful early analysis, see Martin Edwin Anderson, "Civil-Military Relations and Internal Security in Mexico: the Undone Reform," in *The Challenge of Institutional Reform in Mexico*, ed. Riordan Roett (Boulder, CO: Lynne Rienner, 1995), 167.

CHAPTER 4 | *Rogelio Hernández Rodríguez*

STRONGMEN AND STATE WEAKNESS

The Mexican political system has attracted the attention of many scholars because of its relative political stability. According to these analysts, this stability was the upshot of a process of institutionalization that occurred between the 1920s and 1940s. The resulting system was centered on strong executive power and a single party. This master narrative holds that the institutionalization process developed by abolishing more traditional forms of politics and either eliminating or relegating regional strongmen, thrown up by the revolution, to the margins of provincial power.

A closer look, however, reveals that many strongmen continued exerting their power well into the 1960s and 1970s. Although Lázaro Cárdenas rid the political scene of caciques and caudillos like Tomás Garrido Canabal, Adalberto Tejeda, and Saturnino Cedillo, they were replaced by similar figures who continued to use traditional forms of political control. In fact, the federal government tolerated and even encouraged the persistence of such men to maintain its national predominance. Despite the government's stress on presidential authority and a state-led economic policy, several strongmen dominated their states with just as much arbitrary power as their predecessors. Their continued prevalence and longevity not only questions the capacity of the central government but also the standard narrative of Mexican political development. Even when federal politicians had the opportunity to crush these traditional leaders they often retreated from confrontation, well aware that competent regional powerbrokers were not antithetical but rather essential to the country's stability.[1]

This chapter discusses the coexistence of modern forms of political governance with these state caudillos and seeks to uncover the pragmatic rationale behind the state's continued employment of such figures. In simple terms, strongmen controlled local politics, ensured stability, and kept the peace. In exchange, they were expected to demonstrate loyalty to the center and to offer, when necessary, direct political support. Granted virtual autonomy by federal leaders, they often committed gross abuses of power. In fact, those abuses were the main cause of the downfall of the most noteworthy *cacicazgos*; those who, confident in their power, interfered in sensitive aspects of national politics. With the exception of a single case, the strongmen disappeared because the federal government took advantage of critical situations or citizen protests against regional leaders to force them into extinction. Cacicazgos, in the last instance, fell victim to crises rather than to inexorable bureaucratic expansion.

Central Power and Political Stability

A legitimate government, with authority based on recognized and functional institutions, is crucial in generating both political stability and economic development.[2] Constructing such a government is particularly difficult after a country has experienced a massive, cross-class social movement, as occurred during the Mexican Revolution. The uprising's armed phase destroyed the old regime's political institutions and traditional forms of domination and triggered the emergence of "the generation of the volcano," young, "wild, footloose, and violent" revolutionaries who came of age during the subsequent civil strife.[3] Once the old institutions were eliminated, these new revolutionary leaders asserted their control over regions or, if they crushed the competition, entire states. During the decades immediately after the revolution the federal government coexisted with and even depended on these men for political control. In a vast country bereft of social and economic infrastructure and without political institutions to regulate disputes, these caudillos and caciques guaranteed a rough-and-ready stability. Although armed revolt could occasion their downfall, many adapted to the increasing institutionalization of power and started to form workers' or peasants' organizations or even parties that gradually regulated political relations in their states.

Despite these shifts, administrative, legal, and financial developments slowly but firmly robbed these strongmen of at least part of their role. During the 1920s and 1930s, the government established wide-ranging land distribution and labor regulation programs, which placed at center stage loyalty to the central government rather than the local caudillo. Education, which had been chaotic and decentralized, was gradually brought within the ambit of the federal education ministry. New fiscal laws increased tax revenues, and government-controlled financial institutions like the Banco de México and Nacional Financiera increasingly regulated state economic policy. The army was gradually brought to heel—or at least dissuaded from further rebellions—and the Partido Nacional Revolucionario (PNR) was founded to control both existing and aspirant leaders. These processes removed many of the principal functions of regional strongmen. Yet paradoxically they also left state governors remarkably autonomous in one particular sphere—that of local government. In exchange for compliance, caudillos were granted control of most local political organizations and institutions, including the state congress and the state branch of the local party. The centralization of certain key roles in the hands of the federal bureaucracy opened up space for the decentralization of local politics in the hands of state strongmen.

From the 1930s onward, the federal government intervened in state politics for only two reasons: when a governor attempted to prolong his tenure beyond a reasonable time or threatened federal control. Cárdenas's radical agenda and his spat with Plutarco Elías Calles generated many such conflicts. Garrido Canabal, the Tabasco caudillo, was paid off and removed from power, his influence on Congress nullified.[4] Three years later, the state sent troops to end the rebellion of Saturnino Cedillo, the peasant caudillo of San Luis Potosí, who was tracked down, overpowered, and killed.[5] Yet despite these individual defeats, the state was not sufficiently strong to slough off its collective reliance on such autonomous strongmen, and during the subsequent decades a new generation of younger caudillos came to dominate local politics. They included Gonzalo N. Santos in San Luis Potosí, Maximino Avila Camacho in Puebla, Jorge Rojo Gómez in Hidalgo, Gilberto Flores Muñoz in Nayarit, and Leobardo Reynoso in Zacatecas.

Many of these post-Cárdenas caudillos had developed their political networks during the early decades after the revolution. Santos, for example, replaced Cedillo thanks to the significant services he had provided to the federal government during the 1920s. Between 1928 and 1934 Santos had been elected as federal congressman three times. From this position, he helped build and eventually lead the blocs of representatives and senators who controlled state political groups. Known as a loyal party man, when the president demanded a clear stand regarding first Calles and later Cedillo, Santos did not hesitate to give his allegiance to Cárdenas. He in turn helped nurture the career of Gilberto Flores Muñoz, who started off in politics as an acolyte of Cedillo and went on to become the strongman of Nayarit. In 1935, as federal deputy, Flores Muñoz was entrusted with the task of convincing Cedillo to abandon his rebellion. Moreover, he proposed the strategy of withdrawing the planes that would have been crucial for the upheaval.[6] After such a demonstration of loyalty, Flores Muñoz continued his political career and became governor of Nayarit in 1946, where he built up a power base that ended only when he decided to venture openly onto the national political scene during the administration of Adolfo Ruiz Cortines.

During the same period two further (and longer-lasting) caudillo factions appeared. In 1936 Maximino Avila Camacho was elected governor of Puebla with Cárdenas's support, and two years later he created the so-called Pacto de Honor, which explicitly and ritualistically anointed him as the leader of regional politics.[7] Although Maximino did not survive much beyond the end of his state government's administration, the group he built did survive: another Avila Camacho sibling, Rafael, was governor from 1951 to 1957, and clients and relatives remained important in poblano politics until the early 1970s. In Hidalgo, that "land of caciques," Jorge Rojo Gómez similarly rose to the fore, also with Cárdenas's support. Backed by a network of cacique lieutenants, he effectively ruled the state for at least a decade afterward.[8] Even after his personal fall from power, his family employed these links to control local politics until the 1980s.

These four caudillos (together with many who have not been studied, such as Leobardo Reynoso) altered but did not completely do away with the traditional practices of their predecessors. As Pansters and others have pointed out,[9] after the fall of traditional caudillos, a new kind of strongman appeared in response to the changing face of federal governance. Unlike earlier leaders—who were of rural origin and maintained support in very localized areas through a mix of informal and clientelist practices, strong family ties, and military strength—these "modern strongmen" wielded power by controlling institutions, organizations, and bureaucracies. Men like Santos and Avila Camacho were arbitrary and violent but stayed within the legal and institutional boundaries of formal politics and even respected the figure of the governor, who, although selected and then controlled by them, still exercised a degree of autonomous power. Yet at the same time they also retained much of their predecessors' political style (including paternalism and clientelism), which remained useful for garnering popular support.

This blend of the old and the new, of the institutional and the arbitrary, made these provincial strongmen remarkably resilient in the face of the opposition of the disenchanted peasants, Catholics, and city-dwellers who often contested their rule. Although some ended their political careers by repressing these groups, others, like Rojo Gómez, managed to endure thanks to their reliance on more institutional means of handling conflicts.[10] (It is worth noting that the generational divisions between these traditional and modern strongmen, between Garrido Canabal or Cedillo and Santos, Avila Camacho or Rojo Gómez, are not always immediately clear, particularly because the latter often built their political apparatus and cut their teeth under the protection of the former.) A good example of how these different types of political domain were able to coexist is Emilio Portes Gil, considered by many to be the prototype of the modern caudillo. Despite the fact that he developed his political career during the 1920s, Portes Gil was not a military man and did not participate directly in the armed revolution. Instead he built his career on his loyalty to national leaders like Obregón and Calles, through whom he was elected federal deputy twice, finally becoming governor of Tamaulipas in 1924.[11] Portes Gil effectively controlled state politics—not through armed forces like many of his contemporaries, but rather through organizations and institutions. Just before he came to power he created the Partido Socialista Fronterizo, one of the best-marshaled state parties and a template for the PNR. He also founded a league of agrarian communities and a centralized workers' organization. When Portes Gil left the governorship, he went on to hold a series of prominent national positions (including the most prominent of them all—the presidency), and managed to keep control over the state until 1947. At this point Alemán appointed a governor to dismantle Portes Gil's group, just as he did in Hidalgo to oust Rojo Gómez. Yet despite this defeat, the resources Portes Gil designed and used to maintain local dominance survived him and served as the foundations for their national-level equivalents.

Local Autonomy and Federal Control

Although there were differences between the traditional caudillos and the strongmen who succeeded them, all relied on personalist power, whether exercised directly and without any respect for institutions or through them. During the years immediately after the revolution the federal government was forced to accept caudillos because of their military strength. But in the subsequent decades the government continued to allow their rule because, despite the process of institutionalization, it still lacked the capacity to cope with states' complex local socioeconomic, cultural, and political differences. The pragmatic pact between federal and local powers rested on two implicit understandings. On the one hand, the federal government expected regional strongmen to maintain local stability through control of local institutions. On the other hand, the government also expected caudillos to demonstrate open support for the president and the national regime and guarantee success at the polls.

For example, during the chaotic and bloody presidential elections of 1940, when Juan Andreu Almazán challenged the PRM candidate, Manuel Avila Camacho, the strongmen secured the party victory. In those days, when there was no electoral law that regulated the selection of the polling booth authorities, the followers of each party took over as many booths as possible to guarantee favorable votes. As the PRM were unable to hold the thousands of booths, they gave this responsibility to local leaders, who were charged with mobilizing people to control the polling booths and expelling the Almazanistas.[12] A similar reliance marked elections twelve years later when Henríquez Guzmán's supporters challenged the predominance of the emerging state party. Threatened by left-leaning Cardenistas and other military leaders, once again the government allowed local leaders to repress Henriquista cells and mobilize social groups in support of Ruiz Cortines.[13]

As long as leaders maintained stability and ensured support for the national party, they enjoyed a great deal of local autonomy in what Ruiz Cortines called their "caliphates."[14] In doing so the government did not waste its limited strength attempting to hound out these new strongmen. Rather the regime tolerated and used them, as long as they did not challenge the central power. Far from persecuting them, the government designed control mechanisms to correct excesses and, if needed, eliminate them when they no longer worked. The first mechanism was the removal of administrative and financial support. Tax revenues and public works were centralized by the government so that governors could not develop significant works or programs on their own. In this aspect of local power-building, their reliance on the federal state was almost absolute. The second was the political control of the nomination of federal deputies, senators, and state governors. As has been clearly demonstrated, presidents did not hesitate in removing unwanted governors when they deemed it necessary to restore social stability in the states.[15]

The relationships between the federal government and regional powerbrokers were tense and complex. Subordination undoubtedly existed, but it was always accompanied by a certain autonomy. If—as in the cases of Santos, Flores Muñoz, Rojo Gómez, or Avila Camacho—presidents accepted their suggestions for the election of governors, it was because they still guaranteed the stability of the states. In other states, the federal government was adamant in stopping the continuity and strengthening of local groups, as was the case in Yucatán, Jalisco, and the Estado de México.[16] The institutional arrangement in place for decades involved cooperation, the delegation of power to fulfill certain tasks, and control when there were intolerable excesses. Yet it did not last forever. This pronounced autonomy was bound to clash with aspirations to centralization, and in the 1960s the federal government made its first attempt at a thorough purge of such too-mighty subjects.

Sharing Power with Adolfo Ruiz Cortines

During the 1950s the power of strongmen was remarkable even by the standards of postrevolutionary Mexico. Although no comprehensive studies of the period exist, most authors list at least a dozen major state caudillos. Pablo González Casanova, in his classic *La democracia en México,* claimed that by the 1940s only Santos in San Luis Potosí and Leobardo Reynoso in Zacatecas remained of the revolution's traditional "regional caciques."[17] However, he also recognized that there were forms of rule "similar to caciquismo" in states led by former presidents (such as Cárdenas, Avila Camacho, Abelardo L. Rodríguez, and Alemán) and other strong regional leaders like Rojo Gómez in Hidalgo and Flores Muñoz in Nayarit. Other authors went further, cataloging at least twelve regional strongmen: Abelardo L. Rodríguez and Rodolfo Sánchez Taboada in Baja California; Carlos Sansores Pérez in Campeche; Jorge Rojo Gómez in Hidalgo; Lázaro Cárdenas in Michoacán; Gilberto Flores Muñoz in Nayarit; the Avila Camacho group in Puebla; Margarito Ramírez in Quintana Roo; Gonzalo N. Santos in San Luis Potosí; Emilio Portes Gil and Marte R. Gómez in Tamaulipas; and Leobardo Reynoso in Zacatecas.[18] Unfortunately the lack of specific studies makes it difficult to refine this list. Like Portes Gil, some of the caudillos mentioned had probably seen their local power diminish gradually. Others, like Marte R. Gómez, never possessed a monopoly of state power. Yet both the tentative inventory and González Casanova's circumspect acknowledgment of the "survivals of caciquismo" indicate that during the 1950s strongmen still remained. Furthermore, they controlled entire regions in Mexico with the full knowledge and tolerance of the federal government. In fact, such was the strength of the regional caudillos that by the end of Ruiz Cortines's presidency a handful attempted to influence the presidential succession. Such an explicit infringement of "the rules of the game" went too far. Consequently, in the first years of López Mateos's administration the government clamped down, precipitating the end of two of these traditional figures and the decline of a third.

    Presidential successions were always the result of the personal selection of the outgoing president, who imposed his decision on the rest of the ruling elite. Ruiz Cortines's succession was no exception, yet his rise to power had made him particularly reliant on local strongmen. Both Ruiz Cortines and Santos had served under General Jacinto B. Treviño and they remained close throughout the 1940s.[19] As a result, during the initial jockeying for political office, Santos and other caudillos helped overturn Miguel Alemán's original choice, Fernando Casas Alemán, and chose Ruiz Cortines instead.[20] Furthermore, during the tightly fought election of 1952, this same alliance had managed to repress Henríquez Guzmán's leftist military movement. Santos personally assured Ruiz Cortines of the support of the Huasteca caciques, despite their preference for the Cardenista candidate.[21] At the same time, the Nayarit strongman Flores Muñoz, a close friend of Santos and Ruiz Cortines, was placed in charge of the PRI campaign.[22] Finally, another Santos collaborator, Ignacio Morones Prieto, the governor of Nuevo León, also played a big role in assuring Ruiz Cortines's ascendancy.[23]

Over the next six years all three used their political positions to emerge as major players in national politics. Flores Muñoz and Morones Prieto joined Ruiz Cortines's cabinet as Secretary of Agriculture and Secretary of Health, respectively. As presidential elections approached in 1958, both demanded due recompense. Flores Muñoz had his own power base, founded on both his close personal relationship with Ruiz Cortines and his local influence in Nayarit. As a result, he built his own candidacy without the support of the other strongmen. In contrast, Morones relied on Santos's support for his position, and during pre-election politicking he became the proxy candidate for local caudillos like Santos and Reynoso.[24]

Ruiz Cortines deliberately encouraged the aspirations of both Flores Muñoz and Morones. Subtle hints and recommendations were made on behalf of Flores Muñoz, and the president's wife even came out in support of the Nayarit strongman.[25] At the same time Ruiz Cortines publicly flattered Morones, commended his activity in the department of health, and even suggested that he leave his position to run his presidential campaign full time.[26] Yet it seems that Ruiz Cortines acted in this way to protect his real choice, Adolfo López Mateos. This practice of bluff and counter-bluff would become a political commonplace and be employed repeatedly by his successors.[27] However, it was not only a piece of elaborate political theater but also a pragmatic response to his over-reliance on these regional strongmen.[28] Under these circumstances, Ruiz Cortines decided to encourage these two strong candidates to divide the caudillos' support and protect his chosen candidate from unwanted political pressures.[29]

During the 1950s most political actors acknowledged the power of regional leaders, not only in their specific fiefdoms but also on the national political scene. Santos, for instance, claimed that he had supported Ruiz Cortines as a candidate in 1952 because he had met him some time before, knew his weaknesses, and calculated he could have an influence on him and his government.[30] In turn, Ruiz Cortines was aware of the power of strongmen, not only because of his personal relationships but also because of their demonstrations of support during the struggle against Henriquismo.[31] Yet he did make some efforts to control them. Santos, who expected a major cabinet post, was offered only positions in embassies, a much-used golden handshake for unwanted politicians of the time. By offering Morones the position in the health department he fractured the strongman's support in his home state of Nuevo León.[32] Yet despite these setbacks, Santos and his supporters remained powerful. He appointed the governor of San Luis Potosí with Ruiz Cortines's explicit support, continued to influence Morones in his new position, and directed the health minister toward a presidential candidacy.

Yet the caudillos' involvement in the 1958 presidential elections went too far. By 1959 state tolerance for this kind of overreaching by caudillos had run out. In 1959, in one of the most intense demonstrations against Santos's stranglehold on regional power, the appointed governor was removed and the old strongman forced to leave state politics for good. In 1958, the municipal elections in Zacatecas also witnessed the emergence of powerful opposition groups that were allied against the local caudillo, Reynoso. Lacking presidential support and forced to negotiate with these enemies, the strongman backed down, left the state, and—unlike Santos—acquiesced to being sent abroad as an ambassador.[33] In the case of Flores Muñoz, eliminating his regional power base was even easier. After failing to assure the presidential candidacy, he retired from national politics and in doing so encouraged the rise of Nayarit's opposition parties.[34]

The attempts of Santos, Flores Muñoz, and Morones to influence national politics proved a political windfall for the PRI regime. By overstepping the line between regional predominance and federal influence, the caudillos allowed the government to eliminate their most personalist and arbitrary leaders, those closest in type to the older brand of traditional caudillos. During the succeeding decade, these local strongmen declined even further. Yet they were not extinguished completely. Despite government prejudice, familial cacicazgos lived on in Puebla and Hidalgo throughout the 1960s.

Groups and Families

In the years following Ruiz Cortines's presidency, traditional forms of control persisted, exercised, however, not by any single individual but rather by groups or families. These cacical groups shared with their predecessors both their arbitrariness and their formal respect for the basic institutions of the system. The most illustrative examples of these new networks were Avilacamachismo in Puebla and Rojogomismo in Hidalgo. The former is the best-known case of the formation of a single political group that exerted power without any real competition for thirty-five years. The latter concerns a family that controlled the state intermittently until the 1980s.[35] In Puebla the group's dominance ended when it was incapable of maintaining local stability and caused violent conflicts. But in Hidalgo, a more diffuse case, it managed to survive without major complications and was extinguished more gradually as new generations of family members lost the will to power. Despite their differences, both networks started during the same time, were contemporary to the most traditional groups, and survived in part because of their greater respect for institutional formality.

The Traditional Group

Local predominance in Puebla started because of the influence of one man, Maximino Avila Camacho. Like many other cacicazgos of the 1930s, Maximino's power base had two essential ingredients: the need for an agreed-upon regional authority and the unrestrained support of the federal government. As Pansters argues, Avila Camacho gained exclusive power following the Calles-Cárdenas crisis of 1935. Although his rival, a Callista, won the gubernatorial elections of 1937, Maximino, with the support of the president, was allowed to oust the elected candidate from power and take his place.[36] Once in control of the regional administration, Maximino represented the best possibility of bringing peace to a state that had been racked by power struggles between different local and class interests since the revolution. At the same time, as the stepchild of presidential patronage, Maximino also offered Cárdenas his full support at his most vulnerable political moments.

While the new governor respected institutions, he secured his control by designating friends and relatives in all decision-making positions. With the government and the congress in his hands, Avila Camacho first relied on the existing unions. When these unions sided with his rival for the governorship, he created his own state confederation.[37] With the state under his control, Avila Camacho designed his Pacto de Honor in 1939, through which he forced the state politicians to recognize him as the "exclusive leader" of Puebla. More importantly he also established a sequence of gubernatorial succession. Although Maximino left office in 1941 and died in 1945, the signatories, or "the Avila Camacho group," held the main state office from 1941 to 1973.

The Pacto worked for two main reasons. First, it prevented those born outside the state from influencing regional politics. Second, it distributed political positions fairly equitably among all Puebla's main political groups. Through the Pacto the group controlled municipalities, the local congress, the party, and the government positions and had an influence on the federal legislative nominations. It also ensured local control, prevented internal disputes, and limited the possibility of building a competing local elite. However, with time the group could not adapt to political changes. In its eagerness for self-preservation, the group acted in an increasingly intolerant manner toward opposition factions, which eventually levered the network from power.

Although Maximino often is considered an extreme example of a traditional caudillo, he actually tended to respect institutions more than most of his contemporaries. He created the Pacto to buttress his presidential ambitions. The agreement's political formality and its ordered distribution of political positions held true despite his death. The members of the group not only respected the established sequence of gubernatorial succession but also kept control of institutions, which lent political stability to the state. Few serious disputes and the regular demonstration of regional backing for national authorities brought the Avilacamachista group ample federal support. Only with the election of López Mateos and the moves against Santos in San Luis and Reynoso in Zacatecas did the system start to unravel. Again, the inability of the local governor to deal with regional opposition movements precipitated the group's decline. In 1961 students rose up, demanding changes to the administration of the state university. Three years later, mass mobilizations returned. This time protestors demanded the pasteurization, cheap sale, and improved distribution of milk. On this occasion remonstrations led to the removal of the governor, Antonio Nava Castillo, one of the founding members of Maximino's group and a personal friend of the then Secretary of the Interior Gustavo Díaz Ordaz.

The fall of the governor and the election of Díaz Ordaz as president seemed to offer a respite for the Avilacamachistas, but with the election of his successor, Luis Echeverría, events conspired against this closed state group. There were growing demonstrations, especially by students; a serious confrontation between radical Left and Right groups, during which the governor sided with the latter; and a general shift away from the violent repressive means that had characterized the Díaz Ordaz era. Governors seemed increasingly unable to maintain control. In 1972, Rafael Moreno Valle resigned because he was incapable of solving confrontations within the state university, and one year later his successor, Gonzalo Bautista, was removed after a bloody conflict with students.[38] This decline and fall clearly illustrates the rules of the game that came to govern relations between federal and regional powers. Cacical groups were tolerated because they were deemed to keep the social peace. When they were unable to fulfill this role, either because of inflexibility or mass opposition—often causally related—they were dismissed. In the case of Avilacamachismo, the network was unable to cope with the more sophisticated, diversified, and open political system of the 1970s. As a result, Echeverria allowed the group to fall.

The Ruling Family

Hidalgo has a long history of powerful local caciques distributed among the state's diverse social and ethnic groups.[39] However, during the 1930s, again because of divisions caused by the Cárdenas-Calles conflict, one strongman, Jorge Rojo Gómez, came to the fore. Rojo Gómez had entered politics during the 1920s, but he left the profession in 1928 when he fell out with the governor over the upcoming succession. Six years later, he returned as part of Cardenas's broad coalition. In 1936 he became the official candidate for governor of the state. Like many of the era's governors, he owed his position not to close links to the president or left-wing sympathies, but rather to his perceived ability to contain and control the state's plethora of local caciques.

Hidalgo's fragmented political geography molded Rojo Gómez's approach and, unlike many other strongmen of the period, he did not establish a centralized, personalist regime. Rather he relied on the state's network of rancher and peasant leaders, men like Honorato Austria in Molango and Juvencio Nochebuena in the Huasteca. Nochebuena, a zealous Cardenista, played a particularly important role in solving the region's agrarian problems. During his career, his influence was undisputed, and he held all possible political positions (including local deputy, federal deputy, senator, and municipal president of Pachuca) except governor.[40] Nochebuena's close relationship with the younger politician undergirded Rojo Gómez's rise to power: he helped finance Rojo Gómez's undergraduate studies, introduced him to politics, and pushed him forward as a gubernatorial candidate in 1936.[41]

This paternalist relationship marked Rojo Gómez's political decisions. Although he benefited from the governorship by appointing friends and relatives to positions of local control, the caciques like Nochebuena and Austria had the last say, often hand-picking their own candidates despite Rojo Gómez's complaints.[42] After leaving the government, Rojo Gómez joined the cabinet of Cárdenas's successor, Manuel Avila Camacho. Yet he never gave up his local ties, using his national predominance to secure favorable political outcomes for his former backers. Thus the next governor, Otilio Villegas, was a well-known cacique from the mountain region of Zimapán, and his successor was José Lugo Guerrero, his brother-in-law and former treasurer under his administration.[43]

During the last years of Avila Camacho's reign, Rojo Gómez attempted to secure the presidential candidacy. His failure reduced his influence at both the national and regional levels. Although he managed to shoehorn his personal secretary, Vicente Aguirre, into the governorship from 1945 to 1951, President Alemán overruled his choice of the successor and employed his own appointment, Quintín Rueda, a bureaucrat at the Department of the Interior. In the same year, Alemán completed Rojo Gómez's gradual fall from grace, sending the Hidalgo strongman abroad as ambassador to Japan. Over the next decade he was shunted from one ambassadorial post to another and would never recover his previous influence. Other strongmen, including Alfonso Corona del Rosal (1957–69) and Manuel Sánchez Vite (1969–75), took his place. However, Rojo Gómez's extended family continued to play an important role in state politics.

His son, Jorge Rojo Lugo, who had established a low-profile career in the federal bureaucracy in Mexico City, took advantage of the conflict between Corona del Rosal and Sánchez Vite to once again assert control in the state.[44]

In 1976 President López Portillo appointed Rojo Lugo the Secretary of Agrarian Reform; two years later he resigned his post to take over the running of Hidalgo.[45] Like his father's, Rojo Lugo's governorship was not characterized by strong leadership. In fact, he often was absent from Pachuca, leaving the day-to-day administration to more experienced locals.[46] As a result, Rojo Lugo took little interest in securing a compliant or loyal successor.

However, just as the fortunes of the Rojo Gómez dynasty seemed on the decline, political circumstances revived them. In 1982, Miguel de la Madrid became president and brought with him a new "technocratic" ruling elite. One of this new generation of leaders was Adolfo Lugo Verduzco, a close friend of De la Madrid since university, a cousin of Rojo Lugo, and a nephew of the old strongman Rojo Gómez. Lacking his uncle's political savvy, Lugo Verduzco became governor of Hidalgo on the president's explicit instructions.[47] Like his cousin he spent little time in the state, living instead in Mexico City, where he plotted his return to federal administration.

The narrative of Hidalgo's political history amply demonstrates how traditional power survived well into the modern "technocratic" era of the 1980s. The Rojo Gómez family's protracted regional influence is perhaps exceptional, a function of the state's long-standing reliance on the politics of cacique and family rule.[48] Yet it also demonstrates how traditional leaders adapted extremely successfully to new institutions and new rules of the game. Rojo Gómez's shift into the bureaucratic elite allowed space for other groups, surrounding Corona del Rosal and Sánchez Vite, to coexist with the state's first family. Decades later, it allowed his family members to establish contacts with key policymakers and take charge of the state once again.

Final Thoughts

The construction of the modern Mexican political system has its roots in the revolution and the proliferation of caudillos and caciques generated by the civil wars. The centralization process that started with the end of the armed struggle transferred some of the powers of these local strongmen to the federal government. Yet it was never complete, and in reality the Mexican state continued to rely on these figures to maintain stability in all but a few states.

Revisionist historians interpret the turbulent and often contradictory process of centralization as proof of the official party's supremacy and its ability to reduce opposition in a short time. Arnaldo Córdova described how the government built mass organizations, created self-serving laws, eliminated local powers, and created an all-powerful state, or what he termed the Mexican Leviathan.[49] This state then took advantage of the country's political stability to put in place a program of capitalist economic development. Córdova and other revisionist thinkers assumed that the essential condition for the success of this project was the elimination of revolutionary caudillos and the traditional ways of exerting power. Recent studies have demonstrated that local caciques and strongmen continued to exert influence within their local fiefdoms long after the 1930s, yet few were deemed sufficiently powerful to control states or play leading roles in national politics.

The system was, in reality, more complex than either the revisionist model of the Leviathan state or the recent model of prolonged local power structures allow. The federal government often delegated faculties and autonomy to local governments and state leaders in return for keeping the peace. This tolerance fostered arbitrary acts. Only when those acts—the shooting of an opposition politician, the imposition of unpopular municipal presidents, the invention of a new tax—threatened to generate serious conflicts did the federal government intervene. As a result, the stability of Mexico's dictablanda was less a product of the wholesale elimination of caudillos and more a result of their redirection and regimentation. Regional strongmen, traditional groups, and cacique families survived well into the final decades of the twentieth century, even when more democratic political processes were on the rise.

Caudillos were particularly strong in predominantly agricultural states such as San Luis Potosí, Puebla, Nayarit, Zacatecas, or Hidalgo.[50] There they could dominate economic and political resources and act as the exclusive intermediaries between local groups and the state. At the same time, extremely fragmented socioeconomic, political, and cultural geographies necessitated local leaders able to understand and balance competing interests. Strongmen survived because Mexico was not the completely powerful, centralized state that earlier scholarship described and because it seems questionable that the years between 1940 and 1968 constituted a coherent, relatively conflict-free period.

Yet even Mexico's strongmen eventually surpassed their utility. Entrusting political stability to local caudillos was always a risk. Strongmen disappeared when that risk came to outweigh their worth, as they threatened political stability in two ways: through a dialectic of protest and repression and through their patent intention to meddle in the most sensitive arena of national politics, the presidential succession. The "wild men" of the party gave way to new men, less flamboyant and personalist, more respectful of the country's institutions. Some kept their influence until the 1950s and 1960s, but by then the rhythm of regional disputes combined with their political ambitions to exhaust government tolerance. Only a few groups of caudillo "juniors" stumbled into the 1980s before finally falling from the political scene.

Since then, the strongmen and their traditional ways of exerting power have dissipated but not entirely vanished. Cacicazgos survive in certain areas and union organizations: Elba Esther Gordillo's power as a national cacique exceeded that of all but a handful of her twentieth-century forebears. Governors have, ironically, actually benefited from the fall of the PRI. Without the presidentialism of the previous system, state governors have recovered the political autonomy granted to them by the constitution. With large financial resources—state governments are now permitted to raise funds through bond issues—and new administrative responsibilities, local governments now enjoy a freedom that often runs counter to national interests and that promotes the resurgence of more traditional ways of exercising power.

Notes

1. Jeffrey Rubin was one of the first to point out the weakness of the state and its ongoing tolerance for *caciques* until at least the late 1950s. Yet his point needs more empirical underpinning because the assumption remains that Heliodoro Charis was an exception and that few caciques survived so long. Jeffrey W. Rubin, "Decentering the Regime: Cultural and Regional Politics in Mexico," *Latin American Research Review* 31, no. 3 (1996): 85–126.

2. Samuel P. Huntington, *Political Order in Changing Societies* (New Haven, CT: Yale University Press, 1968).

3. Luis González y González, *Pueblo en vilo* (Mexico City: SEP, 1995), 136–37; Alan Knight, *The Mexican Revolution* (2 vols.) (Cambridge: Cambridge University Press, 1986), vol. 2, 520.

4. Alicia Hernández, *La mecánica cardenista*, Historia de la Revolución Mexicana, no. 16, (Mexico City: El Colegio de México, 1979).

5. Romana Falcón, *Revolución y caciquismo: San Luis Potosí, 1910–1938* (Mexico City: El Colegio de México, 1984), 273–75.

6. Vicente Leñero, *Asesinato: El doble crimen de los Flores Muñoz* (Mexico City: Plaza y Valdés, 1997), 68.

7. Wil Pansters, *Política y poder en Puebla: Formación y ocaso del cacicazgo avilacamachista, 1937–1987* (México City: FCE, 1998), 111–17.

8. Matthew Richards, "The Elite of Hidalgo State, Mexico: The Grupo Huichapan, 1937–2005" (PhD thesis, University of Wales, Swansea, 2006), chapter 4; Frans Schryer, *Ethnicity and Class Conflict in Rural Mexico* (Princeton, NJ: Princeton University Press, 1980), chapter 7.

9. Pansters, *Política y poder en Puebla*, 98–100; and "Goodbye to the Caciques? Definition, the State, and the Dynamics of Caciquismo in Twentieth-century Mexico," in *Caciquismo in Twentieth-Century Mexico*, ed. Alan Knight and Wil Pansters (London: ILAS, 2005); Dudley Ankerson, "Saturnino Cedillo, a Traditional Caudillo in San Luis Potosí, 1890–1938," in *Caudillo and Peasant in the Mexican Revolution*, ed. David A. Brading (Cambridge: Cambridge University Press, 1980); Raymond Buve, "Peasant Movements, Caudillos, and Land Reform During the Revolution (1910–1917) in Tlaxcala, Mexico," *Boletín de Estudios Latinoamericanos y del Caribe*, no. 18 (1975).

10. I prefer the term *strongman* to distinguish these more institutional figures from the caciques and caudillos of the 1930s. The terms *caudillos* and *caciques* have very clear connotations regarding the personal, informal, and clientelist control of resources and politics, and they are most commonly applied to postrevolutionary leaders. How-

ever, I am forced to use the terms *caudillos* and *caciques* at times to avoid repetition. For discussion of the terms *caudillos* and *caciques*, see the works of Brading, *Caudillo and Peasant*, and Knight and Pansters, *Caciquismo in Twentieth-Century Mexico*.

11. Arturo Alvarado, *El portesgilismo en Tamaulipas: Estudio de la constitución de la autoridad pública en México posrevolucionario* (Mexico City: El Colegio de México, 1992).

12. Gonzalo N. Santos, *Memorias* (México City: Grijalbo, 1986), 685, 707–29; Ariel José Contreras, *México 1940: Industrialización y crisis política* (Mexico City: Siglo XXX, 1977); Luis Medina, *Del cardenismo al avilacamachismo: Historia de la Revolución Mexicana*, no. 18 (Mexico City: El Colegio de México, 1978).

13. Elisa Servín, *Ruptura y oposición: El movimiento henriquista, 1945–1954* (Mexico City: Cal y Arena, 2001).

14. Santos, *Memorias*, 908.

15. A senator's nomination was a presidential appointment, not only because the chamber has important federal prerogatives but also because the senate was a real counterbalance to the power of governors. Presidents often selected senators who came from rival political groups to the incumbent governor. Roger Ch. Anderson, "The Functional Role of the Governors and their States in the Political Development of Mexico, 1940–1964" (PhD thesis, University of Wisconsin, 1971); and Rogelio Hernández Rodríguez, *El centro dividido: La nueva autonomía de los gobernadores* (Mexico City: El Colegio de México, 2008).

16. Jolle Demmers, *Friends and Bitter Enemies: Politics and Neoliberal Reform in Yucatan, Mexico*. Thela Latin America series, vol. 14 (Utrecht, The Netherlands: Thela, 1998); Javier Hurtado, *Familias, política y parentesco: Jalisco, 1919–1991* (Mexico City: FCE, 1993); and Rogelio Hernández Rodríguez, *Amistades, compromisos y lealtades. Líderes y grupos políticos en el Estado de México, 1942–1993* (Mexico City: El Colegio de México, 1998).

17. Pablo González Casanova, *La democracia en México* (Mexico City: Era, 1975), 46–47.

18. Arturo Sánchez Gutiérrez, "La política en el México rural de los años cincuenta," in *The Evolution of the Mexican Political System*, ed. Jaime E. Rodriguez (Berkeley: University of California Press, 1993), 222; and Ariel Rodríguez Kuri, "Los años maravillosos: Adolfo Ruiz Cortines," in *Gobernantes mexicanos*, ed. Wil Fowler (Mexico City: FCE, 2008), vol. II, 275.

19. Santos, *Memorias*, 766.

20. Lázaro Cárdenas, *Apuntes* (Mexico City: UNAM, 1986), vol. II, 441.

21. Cárdenas, *Apuntes*, vol. II, 823–26.

22. Cárdenas, *Apuntes*, vol. II, 768.

23. Santos, *Memorias*, 874–80.

24. Santos, *Memorias*, 911; Juan José Rodríguez Prats, *El poder presidencial: Adolfo Ruiz Cortines* (Mexico City: Porrúa, 1992), 233.

25. Leñero, *Asesinato*, 77–78; Rodríguez Prats, *El poder presidencial*, 233.

26. Santos, *Memorias*, 900, 909.

27. Daniel Cosío Villegas, *La sucesión presidencial* (Mexico City: Joaquín Mortiz, 1975).

28. The PRI's Head of Press during the last years of Ruiz Cortines's administration, presumably Moisés Ochoa Campos, would remember a talk that Agustín Olachea, PRI's president, had with Ruiz Cortines in which both examined the presidential candidates. Olachea claimed the strongest were Flores Muñoz and Morones, followed by Angel Carvajal and Ernesto Uruchurtu, Secretary of the Interior and Regente of the

Federal District, respectively. Ruiz Cortines brought up López Mateos, and Olachea replied he was too young and inexperienced. Given the comments made by Ruiz Cortines, Olachea concluded that the chosen one would be Morones (interview with Jorge Hernández Campos, quoted in Rodríguez Prats, El poder presidencial, 232–33). A similar account is presented by Gilberto Loyo, the Minister of the Economy during Ruiz Cortines's administration. Again, López Mateos was not mentioned at all until Ruiz Cortines proposed him. Like Olachea, Loyo concluded that Morones would be nominated (Leñero, Asesinato, 78). Both accounts indicate that López Mateos was not viewed as a strong aspirant and that many saw Morones as the successor of Ruiz Cortines.

29. According to Santos, this was the explanation given by Ruiz Cortines when he questioned him about having selected someone as inexperienced and lacking in firm support as López Mateos. The president argued that Flores Muñoz and Morones had divided the groups and that López Mateos would be able to reconcile them (Santos, Memorias, 910).

30. Santos, Memorias, 889.

31. Henríquez Guzmán had the support of Marcelino García Barragán, former governor of Jalisco, who still had some influence over the area, as well as that of the former governors of Nayarit, Juventino Espinosa, and Francisco Parra. Despite all of this, they could not do much in Nayarit because the governor was Flores Muñoz and he used all his power to nullify them and favor his friend Ruiz Cortines (Servín, Ruptura y oposición, 236–37).

32. Santos, Memorias, 899–900.

33. A. Rodríguez Kuri et al., "Un retrato actual: 1940–1991," in Historia mínima de Zacatecas: La fragua de una leyenda, ed. Jesús Flores Olague (Mexico City: Noriega editores, 2002).

34. Flores Muñoz rejected heading a dissident political movement organized by some of his supporters and accepted Ruiz Cortines's selection. With that decision Flores Muñoz ended the long history of internal rebellions that had marked earlier successions (Leñero, Asesinato, 80).

35. When these cases are mentioned one can easily think of the political elites of the Estado de México, widely known as the Grupo Atlacomulco. That elite, however, is an example of professionalism, similar to the national elite that ruled the country until the 1980s. Far from being a single group, the Grupo Atlacomulco consisted of several groups that maintained a carapace of apparent unity to prevent federal intervention. This case study far exceeds the scope of the present chapter; for a detailed treatment, see Hernández Rodríguez, Amistades.

36. Pansters, Política y poder en Puebla, 111–14.

37. Pansters, Política y poder en Puebla, 114, 121–24.

38. Pansters, Política y poder en Puebla, chapter VI.

39. Frans Schryer has written two noteworthy studies on Hidalgo's political history: Ethnicity and Class and The Rancheros of Pisaflores: The History of a Peasant Bourgeoisie in Twentieth-Century Mexico (Toronto: University of Toronto Press, 1980).

40. Schryer, Ethnicity and Class, 128.

41. When Rojo Gómez got married, Nochebuena lent him his own suit. Schryer, Ethnicity and Class, 129. Richards, The Elite of Hidalgo State, 89.

42. Richards, *The Elite of Hidalgo State*, 97–100.

43. Schryer, *Ethnicity and Class*, 30–31; Richards, *The Elite of Hidalgo State*, 102.

44. Richards, *The Elite of Hidalgo State*, 111–16.

45. Rojo Lugo's appointment recognized the family's importance in Hidalgo; as with Carlos Hank, Oscar Flores, and Jesús Reyes Heroles, López Portillo included him in his cabinet as the representative of a strong state group. José López Portillo, *Mis tiempos* (Mexico City: Fernández Editores, 1988), table 1, 473.

46. As Richards notes, Rojo Lugo used to spend more time in Pachuca's red light zone than in the state government; his governorship was really conducted by his general secretary, Jesús Murillo Karam (Richards, *The Elite of Hidalgo State*, 152, 166).

47. Richards, *The Elite of Hidalgo State*, 154.

48. Richards, *The Elite of Hidalgo State*, 176.

49. Arnaldo Córdova, *La ideología de la Revolución Mexicana: La formación del nuevo régimen* (Mexico City: Era, 1973).

50. The point is interesting but outside the scope of this chapter. See Rogelio Hernández Rodríguez, "Challenging Caciquismo: An Analysis of Leadership of Carlos Hank González," and Wil Pansters, "Goodbye to the Caciques," both in Knight and Pansters, *Caciquismo*, 249–71, 349–76, respectively.

CHAPTER 5 | *Wil G. Pansters*

TROPICAL PASSION IN THE DESERT

Gonzalo N. Santos and Local Elections in Northern
San Luis Potosí, 1943–1958

The day after Manuel Alvarez became governor of San Luis Potosí on September 26, 1955, the political elite of the state gathered in Gonzalo N. Santos's house in the capital, aptly known as La Quinta Tamuin after his official place of residence in the warm lowlands of the Huasteca. During this meeting, which was "neither secret nor public," the strongman of San Luis Potosí gave a speech. With his typical, florid combination of irony, humor, and self-confidence, Santos talked about the political situation in the state. Portraying himself as a man a little older than four hundred years, with centuries of political experience, and as *"Jefe del grupo,"* he claimed the right to give those present some advice. First, he pointed out the political hierarchy in the state: Manuel Alvarez is the governor and those present will have to respect and obey him. However, there is an important caveat: ". . . when it comes to me, although it is not necessary to say so, I am responsible for the politics of the state, because this is what you have decided." Second, Santos sent out a message to aspiring young members of the group:

> A political somebody isn't made overnight, political prestige can't be built up in a few weeks munching gruyère sandwiches and sipping asparagus soup, to make it as a political somebody takes many years, sacrifices, dangers, some courage and perhaps no little skill . . . the experience of my four hundred years, I repeat, gives me the right to talk to you like this. It is not a good idea to get ahead of yourselves in Mexico City or in San Luis Potosí; undue and untimely initiatives don't lead anywhere . . . I want to remind you that in this political group there is a ladder,

that in this political group there are hierarchies and that he who today didn't get exactly whatever it was they wanted and deserved may just get it later on . . .

Santos believed that with coordination and loyalty his group could "aspire to greater things."[1] He was wrong. Three years later, his brother-in-law Manuel Alvarez was ousted from power and his political group disbanded. Santos's 1955 assessment placing hierarchy and loyalty above talent and aspiration proved mistaken. However, at the time of his speech to the "general staff of the Revolutionary Element" of San Luis Potosí he was still strongly in command of "the archetypical single-cacique state of the 1940s."[2] Ambitious members of the group were reminded that Santos had picked Alvarez and would continue to be the kingmaker.

Gonzalo N. Santos is often viewed as the prototypical regional cacique of postrevolutionary Mexico. This is as much because of his genuine control of the state during most of the 1940s and 1950s as to his flamboyant behavior and speech, which became widely known after the publication of his *Memorias* in 1984. While people who knew Santos personally call attention to his willpower, "*ojos de tigre*," political savvy, sangfroid, and rhetorical ability, it is worth probing whether the narrative voice of the *Memorias*—with its bluster of power, seeming candor, and bluff—overstates his dominance in a grab for prominence in national history.[3] After all, he was smart enough to understand the performative dimension of narration, something that might apply more generally to PRIísta rule.[4]

Gonzalo Santos hailed from an important ranchero family in the lower part of the predominantly Indian Huasteca. Members of mestizo and criollo local elites spoke Indian languages and were firmly integrated in local Huasteca society, so different from the highly stratified society of highland San Luis Potosí. Drawn into the revolution through factional politics, it was not until the 1920s that the Santos family achieved the upper hand. By then Gonzalo had become the family's most prominent member, emerging in the 1920s as an important leader in Congress, where he learned the new rules of the game and became one of the great political fixers of the period. Santos was actively involved in building the new institutions of the postrevolutionary order, although sometimes against his own convictions, as when he bowed to Calles's 1932 law banning re-election of federal deputies, who had hitherto operated as an extension of gubernatorial power at the national level.[5] The world of congressional and factional politics, unions, bureaucracy, and national press was deeply distinct from life and politics in his native Tampamolón.

During his astonishing career he acquired skills that would make him the Big Man of San Luis Potosí: a combination of *Wille zur Macht* and the ability to rule with different "language games." The American vice-consul described him as "a highly cultured person, who is a forceful speaker" but also "blunt at times."[6] Santos drew on a ranchero way of doing politics in his role of urban politician. He was proactive, impulsive, and *"tropicalmente pasional,"* as Díaz Soto y Gama once portrayed him.[7] Lomnitz also stressed the tactical utility of Santos's ranchero machismo in the corridors of power in Mexico City and the potosino capital.[8] But the reverse is also true: knowledge of the national political and bureaucratic labyrinth was crucial for establishing control over his home state. That command of two political cultural codes enabled him to extend his rule from the Huasteca, via Mexico City, to the governor's mansion in 1943. Santos remained the dominant force in San Luis for the next fifteen years, his *cacicazgo* a showcase of personal power with institutional underpinnings.[9] In the second half of the 1950s, the enduring grip of Santismo on politics and society provoked the emergence of opposition groups both within and outside the PRI.[10] In the run-up to the 1958 municipal elections these groups joined forces, an opposition subsequently and decisively backed by President López Mateos. The last Santista governor, Manuel Alvarez, was forced to resign in January 1959.[11] Santos himself, however, remained influential in his native Huasteca until his death in 1979.

Studying Caciquismo and Elections in Post-Cardenista Mexico

The study of the rule of Gonzalo N. Santos in San Luis Potosí is a complex matter. The cacicazgo lasted across almost three state *sexenios*, during which it dealt with four presidents. Moreover, San Luis Potosí had a troubled recent history but also an extremely varied socioeconomic and cultural geography. The state has been described as a huge and broad stairway that moves upward from east to west, from the humid and warm coastal plains and slopes of the Sierra Madre Oriental (the Huasteca), through the wide valleys of Rioverde and Ciudad del Maíz, two subsequent "steps" at fifteen hundred and seventeen hundred meters above sea level, reaching the dry, thinly populated western highland, the upper floor of the state, at twenty-two hundred meters.[12] Each of these regions has its own distinctive social, economic, and political interest groups. Governing such an ecologically and socially diverse state requires meeting two conditions: federal political and budgetary support for social and economic policies and durable political alliances with key local actors and power brokers.[13] This chapter examines the latter element through the lens of local political processes and electoral practices under the Santos cacicazgo. In such circumstances, are local actors forced into political submission, or can they successfully engage in negotiations? What does the Santos cacicazgo look like when viewed from below? Which strategies, means, and arguments did local groups and elites employ to gain access to office, and how did state authorities deal with them? What was the balance of forces between local actors and the regional cacique, and how did it shift over time?

Three observations are germane here. First, the examination of local elections helps us to understand broader issues such as power and state-making during the transition from revolutionary to PRIísta Mexico. The standard account of elections during the heydays of PRIísmo argues that they were "safe and predictable" affairs that provided opportunities for ambitious politicians to gain access to public office and for communication between local populations and rulers. Moreover, elections during the PRI's "golden age" rested on an electoral system that restricted the number of parties with official recognition, contained laws that favored the largest party and privileged it with access to financial resources and the media, and guaranteed PRI control of electoral institutions.[14] While all this is true, this account misses the point about the nature of elections during the 1940s and 1950s on two accounts. First, it looks primarily at elections and the PRI in a wider electoral field, where indeed not much was going on, thereby underestimating the importance of (pre-)electoral competition *within* the party. Intrapartisan strife was often the only game in town. Second, the study of electoral politics is often limited to the national arena (Almazanismo, Padillismo, Henriquismo), which ignores the fact that local elections constituted a major political battleground since the nineteenth century.[15] Fortunately, historians have started to unravel the significance of local elections in this period. Newcomer has written a cultural history of the violent 1945 elections in León, whereas Gillingham's work on "unseen elections" finds that the ruling party's primaries permitted "extensive contestation and participation."[16] This chapter contributes to this line of research.

Second, the examination of local electoral practices during the 1940s is particularly important and interesting in the case of San Luis Potosí, since they constituted a major battleground for the reconstitution of rule and stability after the collapse of the Saturnino Cedillo cacicazgo.[17] After all, then as now, it is one thing to bring in the army and hunt down an already debilitated strongman but quite another to reconstruct power and stability from below. This is what the three governors who ruled San Luis Potosí immediately after Cedillo's revolt discovered. The rise of the Santos cacicazgo can be fully understood only against the background of the developments between 1938 and 1943; consequently, the next section focuses on the bitter political battles in the state's towns and villages during those years. Interestingly, in the second half of the 1950s opposition against the Santos cacicazgo also arose to a great degree from below, which points to the enduring importance of local political arenas as sources of political change (and stability).

Third, to understand the local workings and social basis of the state-wide cacicazgo Santista, it seems instructive to examine an area outside Santos's home terrain, the Huasteca, where his family had acquired influence and power since the middle of the nineteenth century.[18] I therefore look at the northern part of the state, a region geographically, economically, and culturally distinct from that of the Huasteca. Moreover, the north is generally considered to have been the Achilles heel of the Cedillo cacicazgo.[19] My definition of this region is pragmatic: at the end of 1944 Santos issued a decree that reduced the number of electoral districts from fifteen to nine, two of which constitute the north of the state.[20] The third electoral district lies entirely on the highest level of the potosino highland in the northwestern (and rather isolated) part of the state, bordering Zacatecas, and comprises the municipalities of Salinas, Villa de Ramos, Santo Domingo, Charcas, Venado, and Moctezuma. Most of these are large but sparsely populated. The fourth district is in the northeastern part of the state along the railway and highway to Saltillo and Monterrey, situated on the second and third "steps" of San Luis Potosí's geological stairway. It contains the municipalities of Matehuala, Cedral, Catorce, Vanegas, Villa de Guadalupe, and Villa de la Paz. Water is scarce across the north, and the region was generally considered the poorest of the state. In 1950 it contained 160,000 people, almost one-fifth of the population of the state; the most important city was Matehuala, with thirty-five thousand inhabitants.

In the mid-twentieth century, San Luis Potosí was an overwhelmingly agricultural state but had stark differences between its ecological zones. The highlands have poor salty soils that are not very apt for agriculture. Of the four products that made up more than 70 percent of the state's agricultural production in 1955—maize, coffee, sugar cane, and oranges—the latter three are not grown in the north at all, and maize is grown only insufficiently (in relation to population).[21] Instead, the distinctive dry land forestry products of the region are *lechuguilla* and *palma*, fiber plants that grow spontaneously in the semi-deserts of northern San Luis Potosí. These plants are used to produce *ixtle*, a raw material used in the manufacture of textiles. Harvesting lechuguilla and palma, an extremely arduous task, constituted a complementary though scant source of income for the peasantry in the *zona ixtlera* around Matehuala. Cattle and goats supported another important rural livelihood, again centering on the city of Matehuala. What modest industry existed was in the main extractive, centering on minerals in the northeast and salt in the northwest. Some towns—Charcas, Villa de la Paz, Catorce—were practically built around the significant but declining mining industry; others, such as Salinas, were built around salt production.

The most important social groups in the area during the 1940s and 1950s thus were impoverished peasants, many eking out a living with the harvest of ixtle or as cattle ranchers or miners; there were some pockets of railroad and industrial workers and a small urban professional middle class. Most of these groups were integrated into the corporatist institutions of the PRM/PRI, and as such they battled out their conflicts within the confines of the ruling party and the state-wide cacicazgo of Gonzalo N. Santos.

Politics and the Military in the Shadow of Cedillo: San Luis Potosí, 1938–1943

When Saturnino Cedillo was killed in January 1939 the state of San Luis Potosí was in disarray. The federal government appointed General Rivas Guillén as interim governor until new elections brought to power General Reynaldo Pérez Gallardo in September 1939, with the "unyielding support of General Rivas Guillén and his influence with President Cárdenas."[22] His task was to rearrange political and social relations in the state; he failed dramatically and was removed from office in late 1941. As a result, the state went through another two years of political jockeying. It was not until Gonzalo N. Santos assumed power in 1943 that stability returned.

Upon his appointment Rivas Guillén began purging cedillistas from local office, often replacing them with local labor leaders who had participated in the downfall of Cedillo.[23] To restore the constitutional order, elections for governor, local congress, and mayors were planned for 1939. From the beginning two candidates for the gubernatorial elections came forward: General Reynaldo Pérez Gallardo, who had led the armed pursuit of Cedillo, and federal deputy and former electricity worker León García, who, alongside Gonzalo N. Santos and Gilberto Flores Muñoz, had played a crucial role in the political downfall of Cedillo. While Pérez Gallardo enjoyed the support of provisional governor Rivas Guillén, García was supported by *agraristas* and organized labor.[24] Both men engaged in a bitter struggle for the PRM nomination, leading to pre-electoral violence, riots, and political instability during most of 1939.[25] After tumultuous primaries, in May García was declared the winner by the National Executive Committee.

Similar disputes within the PRM developed around the municipal elections, which were to take place almost two months before the gubernatorial strife. Whoever gained control of the municipalities would be in a favorable position for the gubernatorial contest. Shortly before the elections, the PRM secretary general instructed the San Luis Potosí party leader to back the León García candidates.[26] When he refused, he was dismissed, but even then part of the potosino PRM refused to comply.[27] In what was perceived as an anti-PRM rebellion, Pérez Gallardo put *brigadas de choque* in place to force the outcome in his favor.[28] With two PRM committees operating simultaneously, directing contradictory instructions to municipal authorities, the elections on June 11, 1939, took place in the midst of confusion, disturbances, violence, and the intervention by army and police. Afterward, each faction installed their own *juntas computadoras*. The disturbances and irregularities were amply documented by Gobernación, which concluded that ". . . state authorities, most municipal authorities, as well as the army violated the electoral law by exercising pressure and acting in favor of the Pérez Gallardo slates."[29]

Thus the municipal elections deeply divided the military group of General Rivas Guillén, which threw its weight behind fellow general Pérez Gallardo, and the more radical civilian group of León García and party organizations. The stalemate in San Luis became complete when, at the end of June, parallel administrations took office in nearly all municipalities.[30] The explosive political situation at the local level took a dramatic turn when President Cárdenas momentarily ended the power struggle between the army and the party machine by forcing León García out of the gubernatorial contest. This unusual decision was most likely driven by the president's wish to appease the army in the light of the Almazanista challenge in the upcoming presidential race.[31] With León García out of the gubernatorial race, his local followers also lost out, and Pérez Gallardo easily won the gubernatorial elections in August 1939.[32]

However, the imposition alienated potosinos and the local PRM. The relationship between governor and unions only worsened, and in Mexico City León García was plotting revenge.[33] On top of that, Pérez Gallardo found the state treasury empty. His response—an extraordinary urban property tax, a failed attempt to raise income taxes, and the suspension of public sector salary payments—created additional popular resentment. New municipal elections, scheduled for December 1940, drew rival PRM factions once again into a conflict "in which money and government force did more than the will of the people"; in Matehuala, for example, Pérez Gallardo sent in the military to oust opponents.[34] He was nevertheless forced to surrender seventeen municipal governments.[35] Problems for the beleaguered governor peaked on April 15, 1941, when nine local congressmen removed him from office with the help of federal zone commander General Eulogio Ortiz, who occupied the governor's palace, disarmed the police, and installed Deputy Manuel Alvarez as interim governor. When Pérez Gallardo resisted, Secretary of the Interior Miguel Alemán brokered a deal by which Pérez Gallardo reassumed power only to request a four-month leave of absence. General Ortiz was transferred. Yet the conflict continued; new problems arose and the opposition to Pérez Gallardo became increasingly national.[36] After a government-sponsored police attack on the legislature and the Justice Tribunal, deputies and magistrates fled to Ciudad Valles and formed a parallel government.[37] Then news broke that in the town of Cárdenas a judge had been murdered and that the governor was allegedly involved. In these circumstances, the Permanent Commission of Congress observed the administrative situation in San Luis Potosí as anarchy as "none of the three powers exercise their legal functions properly."[38] A few days later, President Avila Camacho declared the state powers nonexistent and Congress appointed Colonel Ramón Jiménez Delgado as provisional governor.[39]

1943: New *Reglas del Juego*

Since the *desaparición de poderes* in August 1941, the state was practically run by the provisional governor alone because the state congress did not operate and popularly elected municipal authorities did not exist. Re-instituting constitutional order hence required local and state congressional elections in 1943. In addition, federal and gubernatorial elections were scheduled for July 1943. Interestingly, the date of the local congressional elections was decided upon only after it became clear who would be *el bueno*, the center's favored candidate, in the gubernatorial contest. When, shortly before Christmas 1942, Gonzalo Santos officially announced he would run for governor, he knew that San Luis Potosí could be turned into an entirely new playing field—his playing field.

"We are in full political activity in the State of San Luis Potosí. The labor and agrarian organizations of the State have commenced to work for the candidacy of the old revolutionary and friend of the people, Gonzalo N. Santos," senator León García declared in January 1943 in Mexico City.[40] Senator Gilberto Flores Muñoz was to lead the Santista campaign. Santos's only potential opponent, former interim governor Rivas Guillén, who enjoyed considerable support in the state, dropped out of the race a month after he had entered the fray.[41] With the political and organizational weight of the corporatist machine of the PRM and that of his *"compadre"* President Avila Camacho behind him, it was Santos who called the shots. A key issue was how to make the most of the complex electoral agenda of San Luis Potosí. In January 1943, the national PRM president considered that, given the absence of a constitutional order, elections for local deputies and mayors were to be held first.[42] As it turned out, the mayors were not elected until the end of the year. This gave Santos the opportunity to establish himself before confronting local societies.

The first move on the emerging playing field was the election of local deputies. On February 1, 1943, provisional governor Jiménez decreed that these elections were to take place at the beginning of April, leaving little time for all necessary legal steps. The candidates put forward by Santos unanimously won the PRM primaries, and even before they were properly elected they threw him a party and shouted *"Viva el jefe!"*[43] Several of these fifteen deputies (such as Eugenio Quintero) would play key roles as Santista brokers in their respective districts during the years to come. In May, a few days after the first local congress since 1941 met, the deputies decided to extend the gubernatorial term to six years in accordance with a federal initiative.[44]

The second move was the selection and election of federal deputies, which proved more difficult. In Matehuala, Santos was violently confronted by an angry labor leader who claimed a larger following than his preferred candidate, Pablo Aldrett, and in Tamazunchale the Santista candidate and his pistoleros seriously beat up the candidate of the Frente Electoral Revolucionario Nacional Campesino.[45] The recently founded PAN fielded three candidates in San Luis Potosí.[46] On election day, July 4, 1943, the Santistas indulged in a whole range of election "tactics," ranging from moving polling booths to tampering with ballots and the use of force.[47] Unsurprisingly, Santos's six candidates won and became key cadres in his subsequent power group. Luis Jiménez Delgado, brother of the provisional governor, was apparently paid off for his support; he was unimportant in the coming years, but his substitute, the young lawyer Antonio Rocha, became Santos's attorney general and eventually governor in the late 1960s. Pablo Aldrett was Santos's comrade in arms in the struggle against Cedillo; Fernando Moctezuma, another highly educated protégé of Santos, would occupy several high administrative positions; Ismael Salas became his secretary of finance and then his successor as governor; Santos's brother-in-law, Manuel Alvarez, would become governor in 1955. The gubernatorial elections coincided with those of federal deputies and Santos duly assumed office at the end of September 1943. Immediately after the elections, he put a team to work on reforming the state constitution and the civil and penal law codes.

Constitutional reform constituted a third move that turned the potosino political and legal playing field into a dominion of Santos. After only six weeks in power Santos issued a new state constitution that significantly enhanced the governor's political control of the state. Article 90 of the new constitution established that the state attorney general—a gubernatorial appointee—would sanction the outcome of municipal elections, a faculty previously held by the local congress.[48] Municipal elections thus came under executive control, legally buttressing the process of political centralization already under way. (Santos also tried and failed to give the attorney general authority over local congressional elections.[49]) With the new constitution in hand, local elections were scheduled for December 12, 1943. However, six weeks before the elections there were still no PRM candidates, which the local media attributed to the "rigorous political control the Gonzalo N. Santos administration wants to impose."[50] Then, within a week, the PRM held primaries across the state, selected Santista slates, and oversaw their subsequent election.

Thus in only one year, Gonzalo Santos assembled the building blocks of a lasting cacicazgo. He had done so by carefully shaping the electoral and political agenda. Helped by the provisional governor, he packed the local congress with loyalists and had the gubernatorial period extended to six years. He then had himself elected governor, with his most trusted cronies—some old allies, others talented young lawyers—as federal deputies. With local and federal deputies in place he had sufficient time and organizational capacity to broker the candidates for the municipal elections, at the same time transferring their validation to the executive. In view of the profound instability of San Luis Potosí in previous years, this was a remarkable accomplishment, albeit not for Santos himself. Before he or any of his followers were officially elected, he self-assuredly affirmed that "here in San Luis, in our *patria chica*, I'm coming to deliver my body and soul and I'm the skipper."[51]

Santismo, Local Politics, and Electoral Practice in Northern San Luis Potosí

More than fifty years ago, Vincent Padgett criticized the view that the PRI was "nothing more nor less than an instrument of presidential domination."[52] In his view, the realities of the Mexican political system and the workings of the ruling party could not be reduced to monolithic, top-down, authoritarian control mechanisms. A key element in his argument concerned the party's weakness at the municipal level, which obliged party leaders to negotiate the outcomes of local elections with local factions. The major objective of these informal negotiations was to construct some consensus between rival factions and "create an arrangement acceptable to the community as a whole," thereby guaranteeing broad electoral support.[53] However, Padgett readily suggested that things did not always work out that way and that the single most important reason was local caciques attempting to control municipal office. It is interesting to investigate whether, and to what degree, ruling party elites were forced into such negotiations when they enjoyed a strong, state-wide cacicazgo backed from Mexico City. In other words, do the relationships between local and regional political actors acquire a distinct modality because of the Santos factor? The study of local politics in San Luis Potosí during the 1940s and 1950s constitutes a litmus test—a least-likely case study—of popular agency in elections.

In Charcas, local elections were characterized by the struggle between a dominant coalition of business interests and union bosses from the mining town itself and *ejidatarios* from the rural hinterland. A key figure in the former group was Genaro Mendoza, a wealthy businessman who acted as the local agent for major companies such as Cervercería Cuauhtémoc, PEMEX, and Pepsi Cola.[54] He also held several political positions, such as president of the local PRI after 1945, mayor, and federal deputy in the 1950s, and he enjoyed a key ally in José Rodríguez, leader of the local miners' union and mayor between 1956 and 1959. The Mendoza clan was continuously opposed by agrarista interests from the local *ejido* communities. Although it seems that some of the leaders of the latter group were occasionally offered secondary positions in municipal government, the dominance of the Mendoza clan and its close links to the Santos machine were impressive. Already in 1943 they successfully called in the army to prevent the "agitation" of dissidents on election day. As a consequence, in the 1950s the excluded group, which drew on old-time agraristas and veterans of the revolution, sought refuge in the Partido Político General Félix U. Gómez and later in political organizations that played a role in the downfall of the Santos cacicazgo. At the end of 1958, numerous ejidos suspended paying taxes to voice their opposition. During his visit to Charcas on February 16, 1959, interim Governor Martínez de la Vega, who had just replaced the last Santista governor Manuel Alvarez, was besieged by an angry crowd that stormed the town hall, shouted *"Muera el cacique Genaro Mendoza,"* and demanded an immediate ousting of the Mendoza/miners group. The next day the mayor resigned and a municipal council was formed.[55]

Whereas in Charcas Santos had to reckon with urban business and union interests, in adjacent Santo Domingo he had to deal with cattle ranchers who owned large tracts of semi-desert lands, especially in the western part of the municipality, an area previously dominated by the hacienda of Yllescas.[56] The hacienda owner, Hermenegildo Gutiérrez, had managed to cling to some property through his excellent relations with Cedillo.[57] It would not prove difficult to sustain his privileged position with the new strongman of the state, fellow cattle rancher Gonzalo Santos, with whom common economic interests translated into a political deal. For years, Gutiérrez had acted as the spokesman of the highlands' former cattle *hacendados*, whose properties had largely been partitioned in favor of ejidos. He had strong opinions concerning what he considered twenty years of "unsound experiments, anarchy and disorder," which had led to agrarian destruction.[58] His key argument was that the arid highlands of San Luis Potosí could sustain only extensive cattle ranching and that large landholdings were the only viable economic units. For Gutiérrez, the problem of the struggle for land in Mexico could be resolved only by the "redistribution of population, not of land."[59] In reference to what remained of his own hacienda of Yllescas, he noted the drastic decline of the number of cattle since 1910 and hence the loss of a source of wealth. The numbers are indeed impressive: of the 132,000 head of livestock (predominantly sheep) held by Gutiérrez and his tenants in 1910, only 27,000 remained in 1942 (of which a third belonged to Gutiérrez and the rest to ejidatarios).[60] In the heyday of Cardenista reform, "real disaster" had come upon the hacienda, which lost twenty-eight thousand hectares to ejidal grants, forcing the sale of most of Gutiérrez's livestock. Gutiérrez believed that the ejidatarios would eventually face the same fate as a result of a combination of deficient know-how and technology, water shortages, mismanagement, governmental inefficiency, and what he called their "moral bankruptcy, an inate defect of their class."[61]

The ejido leader of Yllescas was certainly astute enough to see that Hermenegildo Gutiérrez was behind the candidacy of Francisco Moreira for mayor of Santo Domingo in 1943, as well as behind Julián Loera, the former *apoderado* of the hacienda, who became mayor in 1947 and 1956 and who local ejidatarios saw as "*el ejecutor de las voluntades de los terratenientes.*"[62] The ejidatarios rightly believed that decisions about candidates for local office were made in Santos's offices and not in Santo Domingo. The coming to power of Santos opened up opportunities for local cattle ranchers to regain control of the municipality, but the outgoing mayor had other ideas, a situation that gave rise to a spectacular electoral fraud. The day after the elections in December 1943, the outgoing mayor informed Santos that the elections had not taken place, arguing that the ballots had arrived too late.[63] However, the representative of Francisco Moreira (who would become mayor himself in 1950) argued that thirty-five hundred ballots of the Moreira slate had arrived on time but were never used. Hence, no elections took place.[64] Then, a few weeks later, a stunning verdict by Attorney General Antonio Rocha concluded that no irregularities had taken place and that Moreira had won the elections with thirty-five hundred votes. To appease the ejidatarios of Yllescas, Santos sent local deputy Olivo Monsiváis to Santo Domingo; Monsiváis ordered the Moreira slate to include an ejidatario, a decision that was perceived as pure window dressing.[65] The *carro completo* victory of Moreira sent out a clear signal about who would be in charge during the coming years.

Electoral fraud also was used in the village of Moctezuma, where an influential local faction headed by Higinio Flores managed to maintain control of the municipality, causing problems for the state authorities throughout the 1940s. At the end of 1943, mayor Basilio García, belonging to the Flores clan, attempted to impose a crony as the next PRM candidate for mayor. However, peasant groups put forward alternative candidates and protested against the enduring dominance of the Flores clan, not only in local political office but also over water resources. The dissident groups persistently demanded that governor Santos reject the machinations of the Flores clan, referring to a speech in which Santos promised that "the caciques would cease to exist because they have a dark record of undermining liberty."[66] To gain the upper hand the Flores clan forced *comisariados ejidales* to turn over their ejido seals, allowing them to fabricate documents testifying to massive peasant support. A few years later, during the 1946 primaries, voter credentials were withheld from the dissident group. The latter remained unsuccessful throughout the 1940s, as the state authorities sided with the dominant clan and offered dissidents only secondary positions in municipal government.

It was not always possible for state authorities to side with an influential local faction against peasant interests. Some municipalities were so divided that Santos's only option was to impose a trusted outsider. This was the case in Salinas, the salt-producing rural municipio in the northwest. Across the 1940s ejidatarios, small cattle ranchers, salt-workers—themselves divided between the CTM and the Sindicato de Trabajadores de Sales (FROC)—and the *cabecera*'s middle classes battled against each other to such a degree that Santos was repeatedly forced to dissolve an existing administration, annul elections, and install a compromise municipal council with representatives from all competing factions. In 1943, the elected mayor was fired and replaced by former local deputy Colonel Eugenio Quintero, who headed a municipal council. But even then tensions remained and Santos was compelled to send in the chief of the state police with armed men to secure a peaceful transmission of power and support Quintero's administration. At the end of 1946, ejidatarios were pitted against the FROC, and although special envoy Pérez Cerillo made it clear to Santos that the ejidatarios outnumbered the workers and their middle-class allies, the governor backed the latter group.[67] The dissident peasants from the villages surrounding Salinas were prevented from registering candidates for the upcoming elections but refused to give up.[68] The elections were consequently rigged, provoking widespread protest and forcing Santos to annul the elections and reappoint Quintero. The members of the municipal council then were summoned to the capital, where they were admonished by Santos to put their differences behind them, but to no avail: the competing factions' apparent acquiescence to the cacique's decision was betrayed by the Department of Interior protests landing on the desks of Gobernación in Mexico City. Albeit with central backing, Santos was only able to rule in Salinas through Colonel Quintero, a situation that persisted until 1949, when three groups fiercely competed for the PRI nomination, leading one group to leave the party and found a local front—the Comité Político Salinense—the only one in the entire state to compete against the PRI. Despite the attempts by trusted Santista officials to have the PRI candidate (of the salt workers' union) elected, the electoral results were again annulled, and a third consecutive council was appointed by governor Salas. Only in the 1950s were the new subregional strongmen of the area—local deputy Major José Garcia Zamora and especially Pablo Aldrett, president of the PRI and leader of the regional Liga de Comunidades Agrarias (LCA)— able to impose their candidates without difficult postelectoral negotiations.

Unsurprisingly, when pressure against the Santos cacicazgo mounted at the end of the 1950s, Salinas became an attractive hunting ground for the opposition. The case of Salinas clearly shows the limits of cacique rule and the consequent recourse to drastic measures. Moreover, Salinas, like Charcas, represents a microcosm of developmentalist Mexico, which benefited urban economies and societies and transferred the costs to the rural hinterland.[69]

The enduring instability in Salinas stands in stark contrast to developments in the municipality of Catorce. Notwithstanding some minor rivalries between the inhabitants of the old mining town of Catorce and the low-lying surrounding villages, the municipality was controlled by a faction with good connections to regional and state-level political leaders.[70] The group of cacique and local deputy Agapito Beltrán maintained firm control throughout the 1940s and 1950s, weathering first his support for Cedillo against Cárdenas and later the deep political crisis that brought down the Santos cacicazgo in 1958–59. When interim governor Martínez de la Vega intervened in favor of an opposition group, he was unable to undo the Beltrán clan's enduring influence, and in the 1960s they regained control of the municipality.[71]

The most important city in northeastern San Luis Potosí was Matehuala, the center of the mining and industrial area (the American Smelting and Refining Corporation—ASARCO—operated here) that also encompasses the districts of Catorce and Villa de la Paz. As such, political control of the area was key for any ambitious leader intent on constructing a state-wide power structure. Key social players in the area were miners, capital, urban middle classes, and *ixtlero* peasants. Throughout the 1940s and 1950s, Santos was able to access the political potential of this entire area through his most important subregional power broker, Pablo Aldrett. Aldrett was already an influential labor leader and politician in Matehuala during the 1930s. A mechanic at the ASARCO plant and secretary general of the local miners' union, he had been mayor during Cedillo's rule, but—in contrast to Agapito Beltrán in Catorce—he had switched sides to the anti-Cedillistas in 1937.[72] From that moment on, Aldrett was heavily involved in the struggle against Cedellismo, as was Santos. After the Cedillo rebellion, he first fought with General Pérez Gallardo against León García in the gubernatorial race of 1939 and then turned against the incompetent military governor.

In the following decades, he would become a key player of what I call the intermediate layer of the Santista cacicazgo, someone to whom Santos and later Salas and Alvarez delegated political and organizational responsibilities. So when an interim mayor complained to Santos in 1945 that he had been ordered by Aldrett to resign to make room for someone of the latter's picking, Santos answered: "I kindly ask you to follow the orders of the federal deputy for the district Aldrett."[73] While at that time Aldrett was federal deputy, he would also become local deputy (twice), president of the state PRI, leader of the regional Liga de Comunidades Agrarias, and senator at the end of the 1950s. He kept Matehuala firmly under control of the Santos clan until the mid-1950s, when a local doctor attempted to gain access to Aldrett's political group and, when denied, ran as an independent candidate in the local elections. The parallels with developments in the potosino capital—where the Nava brothers, also doctors, struggled against Santos at the same time—are striking. In Matehuala, Dr. Zumacarregui would become secretary general of the Alianza Cívica Potosina that emerged in 1958 from the ashes of Cedillismo and revolutionary veterans and that would become a key local player in the struggle against Santos.[74]

The authority of Aldrett, whom Santos described as "my loyal friend," reached far beyond the municipality of Matehuala.[75] A dissident group of peasants from Catorce identified him as the "*gran elector*" behind the local cacicazgo of Agapito Beltrán, and discontented ejidatarios and railroad workers from Vanegas saw the enduring dominance of the clan of Gregorio Zamora as the product of "Pablo Aldrett and Agapito Beltrán . . . the spokesmen of Gonzalo Santos." Dissidents in Cedral called him the man behind cacique Porfirio Mata Lara.[76] In the latter town, Aldrett originally worked together with the heavy-handed Ramírez family, which was so utterly uncompromising that it eventually caused problems. In 1943 local deputy José Santos Ramírez pushed forward his brother, a miner, as mayor against a competing group. During the elections armed men forced citizens to vote for Ramírez, apparently leading to almost fifteen hundred votes for the PRM candidate and a mere five for the opposition, less than the number of candidates on the slate itself. (The Ramírez brothers were later accused of having organized the "elections" in their own house, since no polling stations were installed and no electoral credentials were handed out.) However, this time they went too far. In a letter to Santos, the marginalized group referred to a written agreement, probably brokered by Aldrett and Santos, not to pursue protests in exchange for a coalition slate. However, on election day, the Ramírez brothers distributed ballots that excluded the rivaling group, something that was later confirmed by the attorney general's report on the elections in Cedral. In a curious legal argument, the victory was still rewarded to the candidate of the Ramírez clan but with the slate of the original political bargain.[77] While Santos had sought to secure a broad electoral base by proposing a compromise slate, much along the lines noted by Padgett, the Ramírez brothers went for a *carro completo*. In the end they were left with nothing. It was not that they had used the whole tool kit of electoral sabotage against their rivals, as did so many local Santista henchmen, but rather their disloyalty to a deal approved by Santos that left them in the cold. Interestingly, during the 1950s they joined forces with the opposition against what was then the privileged Santista faction in Cedral. They did so successfully because in 1964, after the dismantlement of the cacicazgo Santista, José Santos Ramírez would be the PRI candidate for mayor again.

The attempts by Aldrett and Santos to reconcile personalist politics with corporatist interests sometimes caused problems. In 1947 serious problems occurred in the most northern municipality of Vanegas, when the local administration, selected by Aldrett, confronted a protest movement of ejidatarios and railroad workers. Santos first sent the chief of the state police, who incarcerated the dissident workers on charges of disarming the local police and organizing a protest meeting. When tensions persisted, he abandoned the repressive option and commissioned the *oficial mayor* of the state government to broker a deal between two rival groups of railroad workers, a rivalry linked to a national leadership conflict in the railworkers' union.[78] In 1959, the railworkers' union would join the bandwagon of the movement against Santos and Aldrett, a movement that coincided with the national railworkers' conflict.[79]

IN MANY, IF NOT most, municipalities, elections came with intense factional disputes and conflicts, the overwhelming majority of which were within the ruling party itself. How did Santos and members of his regional clan deal with these persistent challenges?

The first evident conclusion is that the interactions between Santos and local factions were mediated by specific local circumstances, actors, and balances of power. Across the north, Santos and his successors had to resolve the tensions between corporatist (and hence party) interests and personalist, cacical constellations of power. Unilaterally siding with local caciques to the detriment of miners or railroad workers generally created political problems, since the marginalized groups belonged to powerful national unions with a voice in Mexico City. However, in many cases local strongmen like Pablo Aldrett had their roots precisely in those corporatist organizations, which created the need for continuous negotiations with other corporate interests within the party, mostly peasants. This indicates not only the colonization of corporatist organizations by cacique interests but also that corporatist labor, which had functioned as a key instrument in the hands of national elites in the struggle against Cedillismo and Perezgallardismo, became part of the modernized cacicazgo of Santos. Building a sustainable cacicazgo *outside* the corporatist structures of the ruling party was no longer an option.

The second conclusion about Santos's engagement with local electoral disputes was that its overall objective seems to have been negotiation with dissident groups and their incorporation, in some form, in local administrations. Although in most cases the dissidents were offered only one option—and a secondary one at that (and even then promises were not always kept)—the general Santista strategy could be termed *inclusive subordination*.[80] This strategy clearly differed from the uncompromising course followed by Pérez Gallardo (and León García for that matter), who had been unwilling or unable to broker agreements with competing local factions and interest groups, exacerbating political conflicts and forcing his eventual resignation. If Santos understood one thing from the failures of Pérez Gallardo, whom he called "an absolutely irrelevant and discredited madman," it was that pragmatic and goal-oriented negotiations (even with a token outcome) constituted a better route to power and domination than short-sighted intransigence.[81] Santos understood, as Enrique Márquez once observed, that "his personal course [was] intertwined with the broad and complex political metamorphosis of caciquismo . . . and with another phenomenon . . . : the genesis and consolidation of the *pragmatism* that defines *traditional Mexican politics*, within which the case of Santos seems paradigmatic."[82] In this sense, there seems to be no significant difference with practices found by Padgett in other regions. Governing local power domains demanded a pragmatic approach, even for eminent caciques.

The third conclusion concerns the fact that Santos used a number of his political lieutenants to deal with local elections, sometimes after he or his successors had personally discussed matters with dissidents.[83] These were the men put in place by Santos in 1943 through the "guided elections" of local and federal deputies and, after the gubernatorial elections, in his own administration. If we leave aside the Huasteca for a moment, it is thus fair to conclude that the cacicazgo was built from above, through the formation of a relatively small clique of Santistas that was subsequently instrumental in taking control of local political and electoral arenas. In 1943, local deputy Agustín Olivo Monsiváis was in charge of the negotiations with dissident groups in Moctezuma. On behalf of Santos himself, Oliva first put the front men of the dissident group in their place and then offered them a secondary position on the candidate list. In 1946, Santos sent the former municipal president of the capital, Ignacio Gómez del Campo, to Moctezuma with the sole purpose of ensuring that the fraudulent primaries received the backing of the state authorities, and in 1949 Ismael Salas confided this task to the president of the state PRI. The key figure in the northeast, and probably in the entire north, was Pablo Aldrett, who was awarded with a prestigious political career for his loyalty and brokerage. However, when things became more complicated and disturbances and violence were likely outcomes of enduring political stalemates, Santos would dispatch the chief of the state police with a contingent of armed men and appoint a member of the military to control the situation, as happened in Salinas throughout the 1940s. In the potosino north, more than pistoleros operating in the gray zone of the state, it seems that Santos drew on official law enforcement agencies to impose order upon restless communities.

Fourth, negotiations aimed at the inclusive subordination of dissidents were mostly a response to the employment of instruments of electoral coercion by dominant factions. The documents are scattered with examples of manipulation and fraud by local caciques, particularly during the run-up to elections. These practices were tolerated by the state authorities, but when they endangered the electoral process itself or incited dissidents to break away from the ruling party, Santos and his political lieutenants would intervene to broker an agreement between rival factions and interest groups. If, as I have shown for the case of Cedral, local strongmen persisted in blatant fraud despite a previously brokered agreement, they would lose out. If electoral coercion and fraud were widespread, references to the use of violence were surprisingly absent from the documents. Although Santos was not alien to "the health-giving properties of vaccination by cordite," it seems not to have been the main instrument of political control in northern San Luis Potosí.[84] It is likely that the situation in the Huasteca, where Santos had important business interests, was different.

Finally, while the numerous attempts of dissident groups in the villages and towns of northern San Luis Potosí to gain access to local office could be interpreted as expressions of popular agency and resistance, the complaints about local caciques and their fraudulent practices often contain expressions of acquiescence and (forced) submission to the powers that be. After dissident Tomás Campos, a pardoned Cedillista rebel, was offered a secondary position in the administration of Moctezuma in 1943, he wrote to Santos that he willingly honored party discipline "with the aim not to create any conflicts or worries for your government."[85] Six years later, Francisco Saucedo informed governor Salas that, when ordered to play the second violin, "I am disposed to discipline myself according to the demands of the PRI and take the position of second regidor."[86] In 1943, the dissatisfied political group in Cedral confronted Gonzalo Santos with the machinations of Pablo Aldrett to impose the local deputy's brother as mayor, which was said to contradict the governor's campaign promise to respect majority preferences. While the group feared nepotism and corruption, it added that if this decision "has been approved and sanctioned by you, we do not wish to act against your wishes."[87] The ultimate basis for the effectiveness of the politics of inclusive subordination was the popular recognition, perhaps begrudging, that Santos was the undisputed strongman of the state. Again, this strongly contrasts with the ill-fated governorship of Pérez Gallardo. Then, local dissident groups did not recognize the authority of the governor (despite the support he enjoyed from the federal authorities), and hence the space for oppositional politics and destabilizing antagonisms expanded considerably.

Notes

1. *Versión taquigráfica de la charla del señor Gonzalo N. Santos, 27 de septiembre de 1955 en La Quinta Tamuín, San Luis Potosí*, Archivo General del Estado de San Luis Potosí (AGESLP), 171.1. For a similar cacical yet orderly (and "fairly equitable") carve-up of political positions in Puebla, see Hernández Rodríguez, chapter 4, this volume.

2. Paul Gillingham, "Force and Consent in Mexican Provincial Politics. Guerrero and Veracruz, 1945–1953" (PhD thesis, Oxford University, 2005), 192.

3. I thank Paul Gillingham for suggesting the idea of the politics of narrative voice. During my research I interviewed several former politicians (friends and foes) and others, and most would express their views on the persona of Santos along these lines.

4. Pieter de Vries, "The Performance and Imagination of the Cacique: Some Ethnographic Reflections from Western Mexico," in *Caciquismo in Twentieth-Century Mexico*, ed. Alan Knight and Wil Pansters, 327–46 (London: Institute for the Study of the Americas, 2005).

5. Rogelio Hernández Rodríguez, *El centro dividido: La nueva autonomía de los gobernadores* (Mexico City: El Colegio de México, 2008), 29.

6. Shields to Thurston, October 10, 1949, in National Archives Record Group (NARG) 84, file 350 San Luis Potosí, 1949.

7. *El Heraldo. Diario independiente*, October 7, 1943.

8. Claudio Lomnitz-Adler, *Exits from the Labyrinth: Culture and Ideology in the Mexican National Space* (Berkeley: University of California Press, 1992), 195–204, 299–302.

9. For interesting parallels with the cacicazgo of Maximino Avila Camacho in Puebla, see Wil G. Pansters, *Política y poder en Puebla. Formación y ocaso del avilacamachismo en Puebla, 1937–1987* (Mexico City: Fondo de Cultura Económica, 1998).

10. As early as 1952 the press was reporting the existence of *Insurgencia Cívica*, which rallied against the climate of political repression. *Excélsior*, September 5, 1952.

11. For a more detailed analysis see Wil G. Pansters, "Citizens with Dignity: Opposition and Government in San Luis Potosí, 1938–1993," in *Dismantling the Mexican State?*, ed. Rob Aitken, Nikki Craske, Gareth A. Jones, and David E. Standsfield, 248–54 (Basingstoke, U.K.: MacMillan Press, 1996). See also, Tomás Calvillo Unna, "San Luis Potosí 1958" (MA thesis, El Colegio de México, 1981).

12. Octaviano Cabrera Ypiña, *San Luis Potosí: Monografía del Estado*, 3rd ed. (3 vols.) (San Luis Potosí: n.p., 1968).

13. Hernández Rodríguez, *El centro divido*, 21–54.

14. Daniel C. Levy and Kathleen Bruhn, *Mexico: The Struggle for Democratic Development*. 2nd ed. (Berkeley University of California Press, 2006), 87–88.

15. See the revisionist work of Alicia Hernández Chávez concerning the municipio in Mexico's political development since the late eighteenth century, in Hernández Chávez, *Mexico: A Brief History* (Berkeley: University of California Press, 2006).

16. Daniel Newcomer, *Reconciling Modernity: Urban State Formation in 1940s León*,

Mexico (Lincoln: University of Nebraska Press, 2004); Gillingham, chapter 6, this volume.

17. For the collapse of the cacicazgo, Dudley Ankerson, *El caudillo agrarista: Saturnino Cedillo y la revolución Mexicana en San Luis Potosí* (Mexico City: INHERM, [1984] 1994), 151–97.

18. Enrique Márquez Jaramillo, "La casa de los señores Santos (un cacicazgo en la Huasteca Potosina, 1876–1910)" (MA thesis, El Colegio de México, 1979).

19. Enrique Márquez, "Gonzalo N. Santos o la naturaleza del 'tanteómetro político,'" in *Estadistas, caciques y caudillos*, ed. Carlos Martínez Assad (Mexico City: UNAM, 1988), 390.

20. Decree 142, AGN/DGIPS-797/2-1/48/392, and *El Heraldo*, November 12, 1944.

21. Almacenes Nacionales de Depósito S.A., *Estado de San Luis Potosí: Esquema Social y Económico* (Mexico City: Almacenes Nacionales de Depósito S.A., 1955), 32.

22. Consular report, November 30, 1940, NARG-812.00/59/SLP/162.

23. Consular reports, July 2, 1938, and August 3, 1938, NARG-812.00/59/SLP/125, 126.

24. Pérez Gallardo to Cárdenas, February 12, 1939, AGN/LC-711/304.

25. For example, García's campaign manager was murdered. Consular reports, January 3, 1939, and April 3, 1939, NARG-59-812.00/134, 137.

26. Frente Popular Electoral Pro-León García to García Tellez, May 22, 1939; García de Alba to Cerda, June 6, 1939, AGN/DGG-2/311-M-20-37742.

27. Cerda to Consejo Nacional PRM, June 9, 1939, AGN/DG-2/311-M-20-37742.

28. Salas to Cárdenas, June 10, 1939, AGN/LC-544.5/1048.

29. Elecciones municipales verificadas el domingo 11 de junio de 1939 en el estado de San Luis Potosí, June 21, 1939, AGN/DGG-2/311-M-20-37742, 21–22.

30. Telegrams Salas to Cárdenas, June 15, 1939, and June 16, 1939, AGN/LC-544.5/1048, Consular reports, June 2, 1939, and June 28, 1939, NARG-59-812.00/141, 142.

31. Unusual because at the last minute the president went against the PRM and against Gobernación's devastating report, causing the dismissal of national PRM president Luis I. Rodríguez, who disagreed with the decision. Interview with the son of León García, Lic. León García Soler, March 24, 1993, Mexico City.

32. Consular reports, July 5, 1939, and August 1, 1939, NARG-59-812.00/143, 144.

33. Consular reports, February 3, 1940; February 29, 1940; August 31, 1940; and September 30, 1940, NARG-54/812.00 SLP/152.

34. FTESLP to Ávila Camacho, January 2, 1941; FESP-PRM to Ávila Camacho, January 6, 1941, AGN/MAC-543.21/1-1 leg. 1. See *El Luchador*, October 3, 1940; October 17, 1940; October 24, 1940; October 31, 1940; November 15, 1940; November 22, 1940; and December 20, 1940; *Nuevo Día*, October 6, 1940; November 17, 1940; December 29, 1940; and January 2, 1941; *La Voz del Pueblo*, December 16, 1940.

35. The anti-Pérez Gallardo group further consisted of Juan Lozano, Pablo Aldrett of the district of Matehuala, Pedro S. Alvarez, and Adolfo M. Sandoval. Letter from local deputies Manuel Alvarez and others to Ávila Camacho, January 1, 1941, AGN/MAC-543.21/1-3 leg. 2 (copied to Gonzalo N. Santos; Consular report, February 28, 1941, NARG-59/812.00 SLP/166; *El Nacional*, February 27, 1941). The governor was pushed into a deal with the León García group and to hand over various municipalities, among them Matehuala. *Nuevo Día*, March 2, 1941; Consular report, March 31, 1941, NARG-59/812.00 SLP/167. See also *La Voz del Pueblo*, March 5, 1941.

36. Deputies from San Luis Potosí used the platform of the *Primer Congreso Nacional de Legislaturas* to accuse the governor of aggression against deputies, dividing labor and peasant movements, and forming *guardias blancas*. Primer Congreso Nacional de Legislaturas to Ávila Camacho, July 27, 1941, AGN/MAC-543.21/1; *Excélsior*, August 7, 1941.

37. Telegram from local deputies to Avila Camacho, August 12, 1941; telegram from Avila Camacho to local deputies, August 13, 1941; telegram from local deputies to Avila Camacho, August 14, 1941, AGN/MAC-543.21/1-3 leg. 2; telegram from magistrates González et al. to Avila Camacho, September 13, 1941, AGN/MAC-543.21/1-3 leg. 3.

38. Comisión Permanente del Congreso de la Unión to Avila Camacho, August 15, 1941, AGN-DGG-2/314.1(20)1; *Excélsior*, August 16, 1941.

39. Avila Camacho to Secretarios de la H. Comisión Permanente del Congreso de la Unión, August 18, 1941, AGN/DGG-2/314.1(20)1; Consular reports, August 21, 1941, and August 30, 1941, NARG-59/812.00 SLP/177, 178; *Excélsior*, August 20, 1941.

40. Quoted in Jordan to Secretary of State, January 30, 1943, NARG-812.00/San Luis Potosí/194.

41. Jordan to Secretary of State, December 31, 1942, NARG-812.00/San Luis Potosí/193. Santos lived up to his pledge to president Avila Camacho that Rivas Guillén "will not withstand me for more than fifteen days." See Gonzalo N. Santos, *Memorias* (Mexico City: Grijalbo, 1986), 765, 767.

42. Jordan to Secretary of State, January 30, 1943, NARG-812.00/San Luis Potosí/194.

43. Jordan to Secretary of State, April 30, 1943, NARG-812.00/San Luis Potosí/197; *El Heraldo. Diario Independiente*, March 24, 1943.

44. *El Heraldo. Diario Independiente*, May 4, 1943.

45. *El Heraldo. Diario Independiente*, June 1, 1943; Corona y Navarro to Avila Camacho, July 6, 1943, AGN/MAC-544.4/23, see also AGN-DGG 2.311 (20)-2. The Frente Electoral Revolucionario Nacional Campesino was a short-lived organization that fielded thirty-one candidates in the federal elections of 1943. See Luis Medina, *Del cardenismo al avilacamachismo: Historia de la revolución mexicana, 1940–1952*. Vol. 18 (Mexico City: El Colegio de México, 1978), 202.

46. The PAN participated in twenty-one districts. See Medina, *Del cardenismo al avilacamachismo*, 200. Apparently, one of the PAN candidates in San Luis Potosí was a local *sinarquista* leader (Jordan to Secretary of State, June 30, 1943, NARG-812.00/San Luis Potosí/199).

47. AGN-DGG 2.311 (20)-2.

48. *Constitución política del estado de San Luis Potosí*, suplemento al número 93 del Periódico Oficial, November 4, 1943.

49. *El Heraldo. Diario Independiente*, December 16, 1944; Jordan to Secretary of State, December 30, 1944, NARG-812.00/San Luis Potosí 12-3044.

50. *El Heraldo. Diario Independiente*, October 25, 1943.

51. *El Heraldo. Diario Independiente*, March 24, 1943.

52. L. Vincent Padgett, "Mexico's One-Party System: A Re-Evaluation," *The American Political Science Review* 51, no. 4 (1957): 995.

53. Padgett, "Mexico's One-Party System," 1003.

54. Mendoza to Salas, December 19, 1949, AGESLP-173/1(15).

55. *El Heraldo*, February 17 and 18, 1959. The opposition to the Mendoza clan won a battle but not the war; the Mendoza's financial and political backing from the miners' union enabled them to make life miserable for the municipal council "*por el solo hecho que aún no les quita el dolor que les ha causado el derrocamiento que tuvieron por el Pueblo a sus largos años de fatal Casicasgo* [sic]." The clan later regained local control (letter from a group of women to Martínez de la Vega, December 12, 1959).

56. Ankerson discusses the extension of the hacienda of Yllescas but speaks about almost 246,000 hectares at the time of the 1918 presidential decree that granted land for ejidos (see *El caudillo agrarista*, 209–10). More generally, until the 1920s Santo Domingo had been home to San Luis Potosí's largest haciendas.

57. Romana Falcón, *Revolución y caciquismo: San Luis Potosí, 1910–1938* (Mexico City: El Colegio de México, 1984), 205.

58. Hermenegildo Gutiérrez, *La reconstrucción de México: El problema de la ganadería* (Mexico City: Editorial Polis, 1943), 25.

59. Gutiérrez, *La reconstrucción de México*, 41.

60. Gutiérrez, *La reconstrucción de México*, 75.

61. Gutiérrez, *La reconstrucción de México*, 23.

62. Ejidatarios to Alvarez López, October 1, 1955, AGESLP-173/1 (33).

63. Navarro to Santos, December 13, 1943, AGESLP-173/1 (33).

64. Orozco to Santos, December 15, 1943, AGESLP-173/1 (33).

65. Assorted documents, AGESLP-173/1 (33).

66. Unión Municipal de Agricultores en Pequeño del Municipio de Moctezuma to Santos, November 4, 1943, AGESLP-173/1(21).

67. Report from Pérez Cerrillo to Santos, November 28, 1946, AGESLP-173/1 26.

68. Canizales a.o. to Santos, December 26, 1946, AGESLP-173/1 (26).

69. I thank Paul Gillingham for pointing out this parallel.

70. Aguayo to Alvarez, September 26, 1955, AGESLP-173/1(07).

71. Arrellano Belloc to Cárdenas, June 26, 1937, AGN/LC-544.4/23 leg. 2.

72. Agent V-2 to Oficina de Información Política y Social, December 13, 1937, AGN/DG-2/311/M-20/28263/22.

73. Nava to Santos, June 6, 1945, and Santos to Nava, May 8, 1945, AGESLP-10.1/1(19), Cambio de poderes, Matehuala.

74. José E. de la Cerda, *Contra el Cacicazgo Santista nació la Alianza Cívica Potosina* (San Luis Potosí: n.p., 1958), 33.

75. Santos, *Memorias*, 772.

76. For Catorce see AGESLP-173/1(07), and about Cedral, Gutiérrez to Alvarez, n.d., AGESLP-173/1(08).

77. Coronado and others to Santos, December 4, 1946, and report by attorney general, December 20, 1946, AGESLP-173/1(08).

78. The workers group not represented in the municipal administration feared persecution and demanded protection. Several authors to Santos, January 23, 1947, and the report of Pérez Cerrillo to Santos, February 14, 1947, both AGESLP-173/1(44).

79. FFCC de la República Mexicana in Vanegas and Presidente Comisariado Ejidal de la V. Vanegas to Martínez de la Vega, November 7, 1959, AGESLP-10.2/1(44), Conflicto de Poderes.

80. Díaz to Salas, December 7, 1949, AGESLP-173/I(21), recounts that two *regidores* were promised to the dissident group, but on election day the promise was not kept.

81. Santos, *Memorias*, 728.

82. Márquez, "Gonzalo N. Santos," 385, emphasis in the original.

83. Lomnitz-Adler noted something similar for the Huasteca, *Exits from the Labyrinth*, 341n12.

84. Márquez, "Gonzalo N. Santos," 392.

85. Lista parcial de candidatos a presidentes municipales, June 18, 1939, AGN/DGG-2/311 M(20) 37742; Campos Pérez to Santos, November 3, 1943, AGESLP-173/I (21).

86. Saucedo to Salas, October 13, 1949, AGESLP-173/I (21).

87. Pablo Hipólito, chairman of the Partido Político Acción Revolucionaria, to Santos, December 5, 1943, AGESLP-173/I (08).

CHAPTER 6 | *Paul Gillingham*

"WE DON'T HAVE ARMS, BUT WE DO HAVE BALLS"

Fraud, Violence, and Popular Agency in Elections

Unseen Elections

This chapter analyzes elections from the perspective of the people who queued up to vote in PRIísta Mexico's numerous elections. It makes four arguments: (1) election-rigging was endemic; (2) despite institutional and informal electoral manipulation, the second half of the 1940s was a period of democratization centered on the primary elections of the Partido Revolucionario Institucional (PRI); (3) party leaders shut down what ambiguous democracy there was in the early 1950s, replacing it with a more clearly defined competitive authoritarianism; and (4) the practices developed during this period remained salient, municipal elections in many places remained competitive, and they continued to channel popular inputs into the selection of policies and personnel, "shaping, in turn, the dictablanda."

Some of these arguments may be unexpected, as elections in modern Mexico, until the PRI began to lose or barter them away, have not been taken seriously. Even PRIístas were tempted more to satirize than analyze them: Rubén Pabello Acosta, a journalist and state deputy, began his coverage of the 1952 presidential elections with "the story . . . [of] a gringo who, wanting to boast to a poor Mexican of how in his country everything was done with mathematical precision, told him: 'In the US the winner is definitively known the day after the elections are done.' Our rustic fellow countryman immediately replied: 'That's nothing, mister. In Mexico we know who's going to win a year before the election is held.'"[1] Such electoral nihilism was nothing new; similar world-weary sketches of democratic failure cropped up in Porfirian newspapers. "Effective suffrage," wrote another journalist in 1893, "does not exist in Mexico."[2] Corporatist scholars agreed, portraying postrevolutionary elections as little more than celebrations of patronage and legitimizing political theater. Even their role in elite recruitment was seen as minor; Peter Smith rated the postrevolutionary "electoral network" as less influential than "administrative" or "executive" paths to the cabinet.[3] That the few elections to have been studied in detail were also the most clumsily rigged presidential contests only reinforced the assumption—still current among North American political scientists, more *matizado* by Mexican scholars such as Pablo González Casanova and Rogelio Hernández Rodríguez—that Mexico lacked "meaningful electoral competition" until the 1980s.[4]

Yet the *leyenda negra* of Mexican elections as perennially irrelevant is unsustainable. Peasants competed vigorously in the municipal elections of Guerrero and Oaxaca after independence; Santa Anna repeatedly failed to rig congressional elections.[5] To Daniel Cosío Villegas the narrow margins that characterized two of Benito Juárez's victories demonstrated the competitiveness of even some presidential elections.[6] After what José Yves Limantour described as the "complete electoral inertia" of the Porfiriato, the 1920s and 1930s saw a return to more representative contests in which local and regional parties won elections in the teeth of fierce opposition from traditional and national elites.[7] The Partido Nacional Revolucionario (PNR), and after it the Partido de la Revolución Mexicana (PRM), did not walk into central dominance but rather struggled—often failing—to impose its diktat in regional elections of all levels. The Partido Revolucionario Chihuahuense, a PNR affiliate, ran candidates against the PNR's men; during the 1930s governors across the country defied Mexico City's instructions and rigged state elections at all levels, from municipal to gubernatorial, against the national party.[8] It was not until the mid-1940s that party cadres sidelined their regional competitors, such as Veracruz's Partido Socialista de las Izquierdas. With their passing a provincial multiparty system ended.

Electoral competition, however, did not. It was displaced inside the newborn PRI, whose internal elections became ferocious contests between hugely diverse politicians: peasant radicals, communist workers, right-wing ranchers, crypto-Catholics, labor caciques, and crony capitalists.[9] Such men competed among themselves, one dissident complained, as though they "weren't *compañeros* and members of the same party."[10] It was "very rare" for a party slate to lose because the party's backing was "a guarantee of triumph," and the party elections were the "ones that count, without a doubt," "the important political fight[s]," whose results—sometimes—were an "expression of the people."[11] Primary campaigns generally took up three-quarters of the electoral season, and turnouts regularly eclipsed those of the later constitutional elections.[12] These contests made the 1940s a key transition period, during which a party leadership of authoritarian ambition coexisted with an eclectic membership and a tradition of popular mobilization. It ended in February 1950, when the PRI's National Assembly quietly changed the party statutes and abolished primaries.[13]

Election Rigging and Popular Representation

An election began with the *convocatoria*, the party's call for candidates, which constituted the starting gun for a complex, two-phase campaign race. The first phase of that race centered on candidate selection: the convocatoria triggered the registration of contenders and the revision of the electoral rolls, and candidate selection then followed. Before 1945 and after 1950 party rules specified voting in corporate conventions, while the PRI initially ran primary elections with individual voting at polling stations distributed on a geographical basis. A result was determined within a week of election day by a counting committee, the *junta computadora*, whose decision then required confirmation by regional and national party leadership. Because party slates generally won the constitutional elections, the primaries that decided those slates were the main battleground. In disputed elections competition spilled outside the party as losing PRIístas seceded to run at the head of independent, fly-by-night parties. The second phase of constitutional elections and the recognition of results ended contests at all bar municipal levels, where postelectoral haggling was endemic. An election was a long haul: the 1946 party statutes specified six months' advance notice for state and legislative elections and nine months for presidential elections.[14]

Mexicans frequently depicted elections as rites of appointment, predetermined by coteries of the influential clustered around presidents, governors, or regional strongmen, the *"grandes electores."*[15] At the highest level, an "informal senate" composed of ex-presidents decisively influenced the incumbent president's choice of successor.[16] At a gubernatorial and senatorial level, the presidential inner circle was believed to decide most contests in advance. Congressional elections were more of a grey zone, their outcomes a barometer of the relative influence of regional and national elites. Mayoral elections, finally, were swayed in major towns and cities by federal powerbrokers and governors, whereas in lesser towns and villages local deputies often were seen as kingmakers. Widespread popular belief in such straightforward powers of appointment shines through the begging letters sent to the prominent. "My backers esteem me," begins one of the many such missives President Alemán received from long-lost relatives in the Veracruz backwoods, and proposed me for the presidency of this village of San Juan Evangelista I want as a poor man you to recommend me to all those who surround you ... I was very close to your father and I helped him in what I could and you are my blood and he always said that if he could he would give me a *chamba* ... I always saw you as family and for that reason I want you with your power to give me [the mayor's job] ... you don't know me but I love you and please answer favourably and forgive me my spelling.[17]

Six similar letters to Alemán wangled another distant relative, Juan Matías Valdés, a town councilor's job; across the border in Loma Bonita, Oaxaca, an Alemán cousin running for mayor was described as "behaving honourably ... despite this relationship." Clientelist faith in kinship was well founded.[18]

Yet the apparent simplicity of central control was belied by the intense effort that elites invested in managing elections. It was not haphazard that PRIístas conceptualized elections as problems; the *problema electoral* offered a complex series of interests to be reconciled and conflicts to be resolved, and in that process the machinations of rival factions and the levers of popular mobilization all counted. Behind the problem lay a long-standing fixation with the *municipio libre* and the rhetoric of revolutionary democracy, immovably lodged in public discourse. Voluminous correspondence aggressively compared central speechifying with local fraud: "even if we are peasants," wrote one group of ejidatarios to the Department of the Interior, "we know our obligations to the right to vote and be voted for, and we hate dirty tricks and professional politicians."[19] Ordinary Mexicans complained bitterly about corrupt or authoritarian practices, and state authorities sometimes reacted and sacked *ayuntamientos* installed through flawed or imaginary elections.[20] For elites, elections were a necessary evil, their manipulation a vital black art.

That manipulation was exercised at four sites: the convocatoria, the primaries, the constitutional elections, and, finally, the vote count and recognition of a winner. In some races foreknowledge of official preference was enough to suppress competition: of the four gubernatorial elections held in Veracruz and Guerrero between 1944 and 1951, three were single-candidate beauty parades. Other elections required more intensive management. "Undesirable" candidates for town councils were sometimes straightforwardly denied the chance to register, their disenfranchisement enforced by "the terrorism often exercised by municipal bodies."[21] Where such blunt measures were impossible, those rigging the election could go to the opposite extreme and flood the registry with spurious candidacies, allowing a *patrón* to control more than his share of the polling stations and lending his victory a cosmetic touch of competition. Once rivalries were demarcated, the next step was the mustering of support from the party sectors; for municipal and legislative elections this stemmed from individual *ejidos*, union chapters, and *organizaciones populares*, whereas gubernatorial and presidential elections required the candidate to be anointed at state- or nationwide conventions. Well-engineered conventions covered top-down manipulation with a façade of popular democracy, and they were frequently held without warning. *Madrugando* (literally, "waking up before") the opposition allowed party leaders to flood a provincial cinema or sports ground with stooge delegates and impose candidates before dissidents could muster their own delegates. When surprise was lost, convention-fixers took to more labor-intensive methods: the creation of phony collective organizations, the intimidation of what unions and peasant leagues actually existed, the forgery of nominations from far-off ejidos. Finally, the police could always physically bar stubborn dissidents from the convention hall.[22] These public demonstrations of elite preference notably thinned the ranks of candidates; the absence of such clear signaling in lower-level elections helped make these messier and more competitive.

When primaries were competitive the electoral alchemy of mobilization, demobilization, and fraud became highly significant. Deputies, mayors, bureaucrats, peasant and union leaders, *corrido* singers, and reporters were all deployed to guide—*orientar*—the electorate. Campaign rallies were fleshed out by *acarreados*, "the peasants and the unemployed who lend themselves to come to any [political] event in favour of any candidate under the incentive of a Sunday out, to drink copiously and to earn themselves one or two pesos to animate any of these farces."[23]

Acarreados were more than a rural lumpenproletariat, though; they included bureaucrats, teachers, and unionized workers whose participation as muralist backdrops was often coerced by the menace of unemployment. Regional leaders reviewed the party municipal committees, weeding out less reliable election-riggers, and attempted to deny dissidents their quota of polling station representatives.[24] As the party cadres arranged the institutional conditions for official victory, they disrupted the day-to-day operations of their opponents. Campaign offices were raided, their banners, posters, and records stolen.[25] The trucks that were essential to campaigning were denied by dint of fining drivers who transported dissidents.[26] Public notaries, required under some electoral laws to certify the assemblies that constituted parties, were generally prominent in the local PRI and often refused to certify their opponents.[27] While only a minority of elections were ever seriously violent—during the most contested local elections of the 1940s only 17 percent of *municipios* in Guerrero and 5 percent of those in Veracruz actually reported violence threats, beatings, and stabbings were common enough; the 1950 Veracruz gubernatorial election was singled out as unprecedented precisely because it never made the crime pages.[28]

When the outcome was still in question on election day, rigging peaked. Ayuntamientos "lost" electoral rolls, party agents refused to distribute ballot papers or voter credentials, and those dissidents who were not disenfranchised could always be outnumbered by squads of hired voters who voted early and often. In Taxco's 1948 primaries, for example, the bulk of the electorate was formed by four hundred fifty acarreados who "went from polling booth to polling booth . . . there were those who voted up to three times in a single booth."[29] Policemen, soldiers, and pistoleros could arrest dissidents or drive voters away in clashes that were only occasionally lethal.[30] The violent theft of ballot boxes was less risky and more commonplace: during Coatepec's 1949 municipal primary, for example, Elías Forzan, "seeing himself lost," had the ballot boxes stolen by a gang armed with knives and clubs.[31] He then won.

When primaries were close enough to end in such open, delegitimizing fraud, the losers often seceded and ran against the party in the ensuing constitutional elections. In such cases the electoral engineering of the primary season was repeated and intensified. *Orientaciones* became more frequent and categorical and ran increasingly through the conduits of the state. In June 1946 Mexico's mayors were instructed to "cooperate, as much as is possible, so that all the inhabitants of your municipio, registered or not, go to the ballot boxes to deposit their vote in favour of our candidate, señor Licenciado don Miguel Alemán."[32] The repression of "undesirable" campaigns became more authoritarian once these left the party fold. Voters received threats of dismissal for supporting the opposition. In 1947 Culiacán's public transport workers were warned that they would lose their concession if they did not switch sides; three councilors who failed to do so were fired.[33] (Inside the PRI, ballot papers recorded individual voter's decisions, requiring their names as well as those of their chosen candidates.[34]) Perhaps the greatest change was the increase in the frequency and intensity of violence between primary and constitutional elections. Violence could erupt in an unplanned escalation of polling day rivalries, or it could be a more deliberate phenomenon; in extremis party gunmen undertook the purposive, theatrically violent occupation of public space for the entire day, something that happened once in Mexico City in 1940 and many times in the unsung streets and squares of the provinces.[35]

Such blanket clampdowns were not always rational, for even after polling day there remained assorted bureaucratic ways to alter unwelcome results. Local officials, seeing the voting run against the official candidate, could refuse to install the junta computadora.[36] The party delegate collecting the vote packets could insert votes for the official candidate before they came anywhere near the junta; during Coatepec's 1947 primaries for local deputy, a federal agent watched as Ferrer Galván's 74 votes in polling booth 1 were inflated by the party representative to 269.[37] If the balance of local forces left dissidents controlling both vote packets and the junta computadora, then electoral fixers could conjure up a second junta computadora, complete with a second set of votes, party documentation, and photos to prove their physical existence. Finally, "undesirable" victories could always be vetoed by the legislature or, in the case of municipalities, nullified—along with the elections—by gubernatorial decree: in 1944 nearly one in five of the winning slates in Guerrero's municipal elections were replaced by appointed councils.[38] There were, in short, multiple procedural safety nets to protect party brokers from unwanted election results.

So far, so top-down. This broad panoply of methods to manipulate elections chimes with the stereotypical image of swaggering PRIísta domination—an image turned literature by Fuentes, cartoon by Quezada, memoirs by Santos, film by *La ley de héroes*, and political science by Brandenburg. Yet the lack of grassroots agency in such depictions does not square with the intensity with which elites invested in rigging elections. In reality popular mobilization threatened to alter the outcome of an election at three stages: during the cognitive/managerial process of *auscultación*, across the long haul of a contested campaign, and inside the games of bluff and barter that began when election day ended.

For a start, the preferences established higher up the political ladder were not plucked from thin air, clientelism, or rent-seeking alone. The detailed biographies that spies and party agents drew up on precandidates and the painstaking tours of governor's representatives and local deputies give substance to the notion of auscultación, the selection of genuinely popular candidates.[39] Before a convocatoria was issued, the ambitious encouraged their supporters to write to central government and promote them as men (and increasingly women) of the people. Guerrero's teachers' union suggested that its members write "a little letter or a simple note to the diverse organs of the Party . . . as well as to the Secretary of the Interior, with a copy to the person whom you are supporting, in which you make clear your recognition of him whose work has earned it . . . One must have faith in the zeal of our National Government which in a shrewd way gauges the mood of the people."[40]

The ensuing letters were phrased in terms of an explicit quid pro quo: the promotion of would-be candidates in exchange for their track record of accessing state benefits—development projects, land grants, soft loans—for their would-be constituents. The center's spies and state powerbrokers applied similar litmus tests of popularity in their attempts to make sense of provincial politics. "My aim," wrote one of San Andrés Tuxtla's local worthies to the governor, introducing his recommendations for municipal slates, "is to procure that the Ayuntamientos be represented as well as possible, by honest people, who have the backing of the municipality's inhabitants to the end of getting some public work done."[41] Department of the Interior reports on candidates came to conclude with a section headed Popular Acceptance.[42] Auscultación was perceived as a basic civil right: in 1964 the townsmen of Perote, Veracruz, complained that their mayor, who had been branded a charlatan doctor, arms smuggler, and looter of archaeological sites, had been imposed "without any prior auscultación."[43] Revolutionary orthodoxy, enduring even as it was betrayed, held that elected officials should have some record of satisfying popular goals.

Some did. Elections were frequent; the states ran an average of more than one election a year, and the more frequent elections are the more difficult they are to rig. Grassroots resistance exercised decisive influence over municipal elections in particular. In this respect PRIísta Mexico might be compared to the Kuomintang's regime in Taiwan, where single-party national dictatorship—leavened with a token opposition dubbed the *dangwai*, or outsiders—coexisted with competitive local primary elections, or to Kenya under the Kenya African National Union (KANU), who leavened one party rule with intra-party competition for parliamentary seats.[44] From a federal perspective, the insignificance of most municipal governments made what Dahl termed "the cost of toleration" of defeats lower than the "cost of suppression"; meanwhile, for most voters, municipal contests counted more and were more verifiable than state or federal elections.[45] Popular election-monitoring worked: "the irregularities in the voting for deputies," noted Gobernación during Taxco's 1948 primaries, "were the greater, as more attention was paid to the municipal elections."[46] Nor were electoral managers invariably powerful enough to impose the party's solutions. During the 1946 Veracruz municipal elections, for example, two of the governor's fixers toured sixteen southern municipios in an attempt to manage the forthcoming contests. They were seemingly successful in 38 percent of the municipios, where local politicians agreed to follow the party line. In 44 percent of cases, however, local PRIístas either continued fighting among factions or rejected the suggested candidates.[47] In the aftermath of the elections, moreover, the governor's men faced further disappointment: half the municipal committees that had agreed to follow the party line reneged and returned dissident slates. Electoral outcomes matched the goals of the party operators in less than a quarter of cases.

The party elites accordingly approached the 1949 municipal elections with wary caution: they issued the convocatoria one rather than the statutory six months in advance and held public meetings with local deputies "to end the campaigns of diatribe and insults prevalent on other occasions."[48] Yet a sample of twenty-two results from these elections reinforces the impression of the partial, patchwork, and negotiated nature of provincial electoral control. Here six cases were strongly contested, with rival factions claiming victory.[49] While none of the dissidents were allowed to win outright, frantic backstage negotiations ensued; in this case, the party's list of winning slates was delayed three times, and when released (three weeks late) it identified only the *presidentes municipales* since "the pulling and pushing of electoral accommodation was still underway."[50] Popular leaders, or, indeed, caciques—discerning the two is difficult, at times semantic—who "got in line" stood to earn compensatory electoral posts, bureaucratic jobs, the promise of outright victory next time. The losers of the 1947 congressional primaries for Orizaba and Córdoba were generously rewarded for accepting rigged defeats: within a couple of years one had become federal deputy, the other workers' leader of the PRI's regional committee.[51] Guerrero's teachers, having backed a particularly detested official candidate for governor, wrote to Mexico City to announce that they "had determined that two of our most zealous and hardworking leaders should take part in the next Government."[52] Embracing cooptation could be a self-serving sell out; it could also be a roundabout but effective path to popular representation.

The other path was to continue resistance after the elections. Protests to the Department of the Interior and the presidency commonly marked both the immediate aftermath of polling day and the formal transfer of power. Local traditions and national precedents of popular violence in response to electoral fraud underwrote such letters. Two postelectoral massacres—in León, Guanajuato, and Tapachula, Chiapas—marked the acceptable limits of hardball provincial practice. The foreknowledge that central government would fire politicians who used massacres to manage local politics lent ordinary Mexicans a powerful lever for postelectoral haggling. Such brinkmanship signals were directed horizontally at local rivals as well as vertically to state and national governments, and they were made flesh in the crowds that physically denied imposed ayuntamientos access to town halls. In 1947 the newly elected ayuntamientos of Apaxtla, Coahuayutla, Cocula, and Tixtla, Guerrero, all met with enough popular resentment to dissuade their members from turning up to take power; in Guasave, Sinaloa, a shoot-out achieved the same end.[53] When such controversial ayuntamientos did move into the town hall, dissidents could form a parallel government and appeal for investigation and recognition from Mexico City. In 1939 there were parallel ayuntamientos in nearly all of San Luis Potosí's municipios; in 1948 excluded *agraristas* formed parallel ayuntamientos in nearly a quarter of Guerrero's municipios.[54] Sometimes the two phenomena coalesced, and dissidents would seize the town hall to install their own government. In Ajuchitlán, Guerrero, gunmen in the town hall opened fire on agraristas protesting the rigged 1948 elections, and "the indignation of the Pueblo provoked, they hurled themselves through the doors and windows with sticks, stones, machetes, billhooks, daggers, pistols, shotguns and other arms and stormed the hall."[55] Such popular violence could be read as revolt and repressed: the Ajuchitlán agraristas, who had formed a similar parallel ayuntamiento four years earlier, ended up languishing in jail for months without trial.[56] In December 1962 soldiers bloodily shut down Genaro Vázquez's protest outside (and perhaps projected seizure of) Iguala's city hall, driving him into the mountains.[57] Yet violence could also be recognized by authorities as collective bargaining by riot and a compromise negotiated. The strategy worked often enough to be prevalent across Mexico during the rest of the twentieth century: in 1982 alone there were at least thirty-five town hall occupations in states as disparate as Chiapas, Guanajuato, Jalisco, San Luis Potosí, and Tlaxcala.[58] Postelectoral resistance was a risky strategy, but one with three realistic aims: an immediate veto of opponents' entry to government, seats on a compromise municipal council, and a greater sensitivity to future demands.

The critical questions are how frequently were elections competitive and how frequently did popular mobilization decisively influence their outcome. Both are difficult to answer. By the mid-1940s the inevitability of party triumph in federal elections was so ingrained that when one PRM candidate lost he stepped up to the podium of Congress, complained that trying to change the party's decision was "as futile as trying to melt the snow from the top of Popocatépetl with a single match," and blew his brains out in protest.[59] The (sometimes literally) warring factions of earlier state congresses had vanished, replaced by the homogeneity of the *carro completo*. Of the ten legislatures elected in Guerrero and Veracruz between 1940 and 1952, only one, Guerrero's 1942–44 Congress, was overtly divided. In such contexts it is a fair assumption that the auscultación stage was the main point at which public opinion could influence results. But local contests were a different matter. "Municipal elections," fretted a leading PRIísta in Veracruz, "excite the citizens too much and in many places give rise to fights and divisions."[60] Such fights, divisions, and protests were logical only if Mexicans entered these elections believing that they might somehow win.[61] The high rates of protests across the 1940s and early 1950s—when on average a fifth but in some years as many as half of the elections examined were protested—suggest that a lot of Mexicans voted for their mayors and councilors in the belief that these elections were competitive (see tables 6.1 and 6.2).

Were they right? Some municipal elections were indeed won by dissident or opposition candidates. In 1952 the leftist Partido Popular (PP) was awarded Cuetzala del Progreso, Guerrero, the state police evicting local PRIístas from

TABLE 6.1. Municipal Election Protests in Guerrero, 1944–1952

Year	Primary elections/ conventions subject to protest (%)	Constitutional elections subject to protest (%)	Municipalities reporting violence (%)	Protested elections overall (%)
1944	11	47	17	49
1946	1	8	0	8
1948	19	33	8	36
1950	—	8	1	8
1952	—	13	1	13

Source: AGN/DGG-2.311M(9) series.

TABLE 6.2. Municipal Election Protests in Veracruz, 1943–1952

Year	Primary elections/ conventions subject to protest (%)	Constitutional elections subject to protest (%)	Municipalities reporting violence (%)	Protested elections overall (%)
1943	5	9	0.5	12
1946	3	13	1	13
1949	18	24	4.5	31
1952	—	17	1	17

Source: AGN/DGG-2.311M(26) series.

the town hall, while independent slates won three ayuntamientos in Veracruz. During the 1950s, state governments in Oaxaca faced the stark choice of sending in troops or acknowledging Partido Acción Nacional (PAN) victories across much of the Mixteca.[62] Yet overt upsets were comparatively rare.[63] By far the most common result of popular mobilization was a more subtle exercise of power, as dissidents became veto players who barred the unpopular from power.[64] As Adolfo López Mateos put it, "caciques remain in power as long as the community tolerates them."[65] He may have been a bit overoptimistic; just how frequently such blackballing worked is difficult to quantify. The most historically visible mechanisms of veto are annulled elections and/or the gubernatorial appointment of a municipal council. Yet these can signify radically different outcomes. Annulled elections could represent a successful popular veto; they could also mean a popular victory being overturned. Municipal councils could be vehicles for compromise; in Atzacán,

Veracruz, a council smoothed over the violent competition between the Liga and local union chapters for peasant recruits.[66] They could, on the other hand, be petty, often enough military, dictatorships installed to override local representation: agrarista strongholds such as Ursulo Galván and Villa Cardel, Veracruz, or San Jerónimo, Guerrero, were repeatedly ruled by appointed councils.[67] Between 1943 and 1949 Salinas, San Luis Potosí, was ruled by one Colonel Quintero; at one point or another during the 1940s the state government of Puebla appointed military officers to head such councils in every major town outside the capital.[68] Such equifinality muddies the interpretive waters.

Yet it is clear that while state and national elites aspired to thorough electoral control, they found it too costly to establish universally. Veracruz authorities struggled for a decade to root out municipal clients of the Aguilarista cacicazgo; in Guerrero the campaign against local agraristas was abandoned half-finished, the attempt almost costing the governor his job. In Guanajuato the sinarquista merchants of San Luis de la Paz straightforwardly defied the governor's representative, a Gobernación agent, and the garrison commander and rigged the 1947 election against a PRIísta popular front spanning rival sinarquistas, agraristas, miners, teachers, and a lonely communist.[69] As Pansters shows, even Gonzalo N. Santos was incapable of foolproof electoral domination. Moreover, the repression Santos employed to defend his electoral preeminence was unsustainable. In 1952 his arrest of a PAN/Unión Nacional Sinarquista (UNS) candidate detonated a "civic insurgency"; in 1959 his bitter enemy Salvador Nava, a right-wing Catholic, became mayor of the state capital.[70] The widespread efficacy of local mobilization—whether to install the genuinely popular or to veto the genuinely unpopular—was demonstrated by the opposition's focus on local elections. As early as 1948 the PAN ran several hundred municipal campaigns; the municipio, Efraín González Luna told the PAN convention, was Mexico's "political wellspring."[71]

That belief eventually paid off. The end-of-century democratic transition began in villages and towns: between 1979 and 1987 opposition parties won more than half of Mexico's 236 most important municipios, foreshadowing and helping drive later victories at gubernatorial and senatorial levels.[72] Yet those victories did not come out of the blue. From the late 1950s on the PAN won in major cities such as San Luis Potosí, Hermosillo, Monclova, and Mérida and in minor, generally *serrano*, villages. Elsewhere the PRI was a fig leaf covering autonomous parties, such as the *charistas* who dominated Juchitán, Oaxaca, from the 1940s to the mid-1960s or the popular representatives who ran Zinacantán, Chiapas, until the 1970s.[73] (Even the PANista Nava was a member of the PRI's Sector Popular.)[74] Both party and people knew that such representation was underpinned by the threat of collective bargaining by riot, the sort of large-scale, widespread riots that broke out in the municipios of Zacatecas in 1958 and Chihuahua and Baja California in 1959 (where someone upped the ante by planting a time bomb in the governor-elect's office[75]). The commonplace that competitive elections were absent from Mexico's towns and villages until the early 1980s is, in short, inaccurate. More accurate is the national division of power advanced by Adolfo Ruiz Cortines: federal legislators and governors for the presidency, local legislators for the governors, and municipal governments for the *pueblo*.[76]

Taking Mexicans Away from Elections and Elections Away from Mexicans
Alemán came to office promising democratization. President Avila Camacho had invoked wartime necessity to justify the suppression of political competition ("in the face of the war to which Nazi-fascist aggression has driven us, internal controversies—no matter how respectable—must go silent"[77]). As the war came to an end a pent-up demand for reform emerged. In September 1944 the leader of Congress "made a frontal attack on the PRM," criticizing "the one-party system in Mexico, and the gangster methods used at election times, which make democracy a farce."[78] By the end of 1945 the PAN was demanding electoral reform while persistent rumors predicted a comprehensive liberalization of the political system.[79] The tipping point came in January 1946 at León, Guanajuato, when the army used machine guns on a crowd of Catholic militants who were protesting fraudulent elections; the PRM hastily convoked a national convention, abolished itself, and arose from the ashes as the PRI.[80] That party's founding statement declared in the opening sentence that it "accepted absolutely and without reservation the democratic system of government" (the revolution came in second); Alemán, taking the oath as the PRI's candidate, vowed "to struggle in the polls for a democratic triumph, without deals, tricks or violence, respecting the verdict of the *pueblo* even if this is adverse."[81]

This rhetoric was read in the remotest villages as an offer ". . . to change with the new Party the hateful procedures of electing Representatives by naming between *camarillas*."[82] In the cities "public opinion [was] marked by optimism and confidence" as a regime that playwright Rodolfo Usigli called a "manufacturer and salesman of wholesale hope" took power; the hope was, Cándido Aguilar remembered, that "democracy would take root" under Alemán.[83] Early developments seemed to substantiate the rhetoric. The PAN won their first municipio in Michoacán and four seats in Congress. Alemán fired the governors of Chiapas and Oaxaca for postelectoral violence during his second month in office. These were, the British ambassador wrote, "milestone[s] on Mexico's march to democracy." Manuel Gómez Morín was "very hopeful" about the new government; at its 1947 convention his party expressed support for President Alemán.[84] There was an *apertura democrática* across Latin America in the mid-1940s that left all major countries as formal—if ill-defined—democracies; Mexico was an exemplar.[85]

As in the rest of Latin America, however, Mexico's was a brief, quickly reversed transition. By the early 1950s belief in Alemán's promises of reform had faded across Mexico, the opposition—dissident PRIístas, the PAN, the PP, and the Sinarquistas—disenchanted by the combination of promises of reform, primaries, presidential denunciations of *caciquismo*, and tightening central control of elections. In Otatitlán, Veracruz, less than 10 percent of the villagers voted in the 1949 municipal elections, and the winner received thirty votes, representing 1 percent of the population.[86] In Matamoros, Tamaulipas, a Gobernación agent made three tours of the 1951 municipal elections and counted a total of fifty-five voters at the only four polling booths (of more than twenty) that had any voters at all.[87] In Morelos the Partido Agrario-Obrero Morelense did not run gubernatorial candidates after Jaramillo's defeats in 1946 and 1952, concluding that *"por las buenas no se puede."*[88] Municipal election protests in Guerrero declined in the early 1950s. Shifting elite practices catalyzed popular disenchantment, with press statements phrased as communiqués transmuting elections into "political cases" to be "resolved" from on high: pro-government newspapers in Guerrero and Veracruz announced the results of the 1950 and 1951 gubernatorial elections before the campaign season even began.[89] There always had been cyclical and geographical variation in the intensity of election rigging, popular mobilization, and popular representation. Yet the changes in the practice of Mexican elections in the late 1940s went beyond cyclical variation. A handful of far-reaching institutional changes made elections abruptly less competitive, for all the façade of a tolerated opposition and a Federal Electoral Commission, and made Mexicans more cynical about the value of their vote.

The central change was the end of primary elections. Primaries are a universal demand of dissidents fighting party fixers. In the United States Theodore Roosevelt instituted them in his 1912 presidential run; in "safe" congressional districts of the 1940s they were "not a successful alternative to two-party competition," but they were nonetheless "real election[s]," two-thirds of them close calls.[90] In Mexico, primaries were introduced by centrist party leaders desperate for legitimacy in a struggle against popular dissatisfaction, elite reformism, and looming military subversion. They briefly fostered intense and overt competition in provincial politics. But PRI leaders got more grassroots democracy than they had bargained for and might well have abolished primaries sooner had the devaluation of 1948 not profoundly shaken the government. Instead, severely weakened, Alemán promised further reform; "most unusually" Congress held an extraordinary session in

January 1949 to draw up a new electoral law mandating primaries for all parties. Ten months later the government had made a remarkable recovery, and in December Alemán felt strong enough to launch a "systematic anti-Communist campaign" and to pass legislation banning primaries.[91] The PRI then changed its statutes in the national convention of February 2–3, 1950, which sat for two brief mornings and acclaimed the return to bloc convention voting as "new waves of light, principles of the purest democracy."[92] This was something of a U-turn: five years earlier, founding the party, they had condemned the same procedures as "antidemocratic."[93]

The new level of central control went far beyond bloc voting; during the late 1940s and 1950s PRIísta elites placed further procedural restrictions on internal and external electoral competition.[94] Party regulations were progressively tightened to decrease the length of electoral seasons.[95] Legal obstacles to opposition campaigning increased while checks on fraud decreased: in Guerrero, Governor Gómez Maganda increased the state police budget and authorized policemen to break up unlicensed political meetings while simultaneously instructing his *presidentes municipales* to use cardboard boxes as ballot boxes.[96] Detailed, questionable results were no longer made public: the *Diario de Xalapa*, which had traditionally printed vote tallies for congressional elections, ceased doing so in 1950.[97] Outside the PRI key parties were banned under the provisions of the 1946 electoral law, which gave Gobernación the power to register and deregister parties, placing them on or taking them off the ballot. They used it in 1948 to deregister the Sinarquistas and in 1949 the communists. Subsequent reforms in 1951 and 1954 raised the bar for obtaining or keeping the registry, requiring that parties have seventy-five thousand certified members, construct civic centers, and maintain a substantial presence in at least two-thirds of the states.[98] In February 1954 Gobernación used the new law to abolish General Henríquez Guzmán's left-leaning Federación Popular del Pueblo Mexicano (FPPM).[99] With its passing went the only significant national opposition for a generation; until the 1980s the PAN never got beyond 10 percent in a presidential election. At a national level, at least, the British embassy was right: the PRI had become "the steamroller in Mexican politics."[100]

The token space allotted to the surviving opposition parties of the 1950s was no substitute for the disorderly competitiveness of primaries. In some places such parties may have paradoxically reduced the effective choices of voters, siphoning internal competition out of the PRI and legitimizing a party monoculture without establishing a competitive external alternative. In Veracruz 75 percent of the (unusually hard fought) 1964 municipal elections were multiparty affairs: the opposition won all of 3 percent of them. Inside the PRI, on the other hand, popular inputs clearly counted in those same elections, even in the absence of primaries: 9 percent of candidates were publically vetoed before polling day, and a further 7 percent of eventual victories were annulled.[101] The electoral reforms of 1963, which offered the PAN a handful of congressional seats through proportional representation, were table scraps designed to check disturbing levels of abstentions. (Notably fewer Mexicans in the north, Mexico City, and the center-west bothered voting; the PAN's deputies themselves abstained from taking their congressional seats in 1958.) However, in the long run—a very long run, if a week is a long time in politics—those seats grew into real power as opposition parties capitalized on a persistent democratic culture and governments incrementally upped their numbers.[102]

In the interim, what endured? The diverse noncompetitive functions of elections remained highly significant. Elite aspirations to legitimacy made campaign seasons times of opportunity and social mobility for strategic sectors of the ruled, who could negotiate political or material gains in exchange for collaboration in mounting the spectacle of an election. Campaigns simultaneously remained essential channels of communication between villagers and their distant rulers, many of whom appeared only in the run-up to an election. Brief and stage-managed as tour visits were, they undoubtedly served the interests of both sides as politicians broadened their local knowledge and tried to gauge the hegemonic minimum of services that they could deliver. Elections remained, as they had been even in Porfirian times, conjunctures when elites could be temporarily generous—with benefits ranging from barbecues to land grants—in purchasing some grudging compliance from the ruled.

And PRIísta elections remained a lot more than *costumbrista* reruns of the old Porfirian plays. The "largely democratic culture" identified by Fagen and Tuohy in 1960s Xalapa and by Booth and Seligson in northern industrial towns of the late 1970s persisted.[103] It translated into a handful of overt opposition wins in three types of municipio: northern cities, strongly Catholic cities, and serrano villages. It was expressed in the reduced, but still noteworthy, tradition of electoral protests, particularly strong at the municipal level, where the return of the bloc vote in the early 1950s—in which small groups of centrally marshaled PRIístas barred themselves in cinemas, theaters, and other public spaces forcibly excluded dissidents and declared themselves representative party conventions—provoked "a flood of protests."[104] It shines through Gobernación's potted biographies of PRIísta mayors; while some had lurid entries in the "criminal record" and "popular acceptance" rubrics, others would undoubtedly have won free and fair elections.[105] It was expressed in the vigorous participation of newly enfranchised women, whether in the ranks of the PP, whose women aggressively demanded the right to vote against the PRI in Paso del Macho, or inside the PAN, whose women took over the majority of Iguala's polling stations in 1948 and managed the (disallowed) victory of a PANista woman as presidente municipal.[106] The prospect of such difficult-to-manage mobilization—doubling the electorate overnight—may even, Jolie Olcott suggests, have been one more good reason to abolish primaries.[107] Finally, a long-term belief in the benefits of elections emerged repeatedly in the work of provincial journalists, ranging from the sly asides of the *Diario de Xalapa* to the straightforward *Trinchera de Culiacán*, which described the presidente municipal as "a dagger to the hopes of democracy," to the irate *Guerrerense* columnist who demanded that "a real vote" be removed from government correspondence.[108]

Above all, primaries were eloquent of what endured—that electoral culture—and what had been lost: much, but not all, of the practice. They became totemic to reform-minded PRIístas, such as Carlos Madrazo, Jesús Reyes Heroles, and Luis Donaldo Colosio. In 1957 Cárdenas proposed their resurrection as part of democratizing the PRI.[109] When primaries were fleetingly reintroduced for mayoral elections—in Sonora in 1961, in ten states in 1965—dissidents formed new parties within the PRI and long-term abstainers turned out to vote, believing that these were genuinely unpredictable, representative contests; many voters were not even party members.[110] Madrazo gambled his tenure at the head of the PRI on that enthusiasm and on the assorted locally popular candidates who won open elections; but the gamble failed and he was ousted on November 17, 1965, within a year of taking over, after the final straw of a struggle with Governor Leopoldo Sánchez Celis over municipal elections in Culiacán. Hardline PRIístas were unusually forthcoming in their postmortems of the "chaos," "*desorientación*," "divisions," and "vulgar squabbles" into which this "wrong direction" had plunged the party. Primaries had not only divided party members; they had opened the door for opposition wins in major towns such as Santa Barbara, Chihuahua, and Taxco, Guerrero, and they had been subject to wholesale cancellations in Oaxca. They were, Senator Carlos Loret de Mola judged, "good in theory, a disaster in practice"; their abolition, *Excélsior* tentatively criticized, meant more "directed democracy."[111]

In the second half of the 1940s Mexico went through what our contemporaries would dub a democratic transition. For four years Mexicans experienced genuine if flawed elections. Notwithstanding the ubiquity of election rigging, they went to the ballot boxes to choose between slates of highly diverse PRI candidates; their choices were sometimes influential and occasionally decisive in determining the results. Primaries reflected popular agency in three ways: the election of dissidents; the veto, more commonly, of unacceptable official candidates; and the exchange of electoral discipline in the most important contests for representation in secondary positions. The radically opposed factions inside the early revolutionary party exemplified Gramsci's dictum: "even if no other legal parties exist, other parties do in fact always exist."[112] The representation obtained by such "organic parties" through the primaries of a heterodox PRI, whose electoral managers were at times clearly out of their depth, was sometimes comparable to that of a (corrupt and unbalanced) multiparty system. The democratic functions of the PRI's primaries should not be exaggerated. They did not provide direct popular representation at any level beyond the municipal. Dissidents, moreover, were not perforce democrats: Nabor Ojeda, Cándido Aguilar, and Vidal Díaz Muñoz, to name but a few, were election-fixers of considerable experience. In Chihuahua in 1965, fifty-four of a total of sixty-six local party presidents resigned to compete in the primaries, and in Ciudad Juárez the ex-party leader Armando González Soto won, benefiting along the way from bribes, acarreados, and bureaucratic obstructionism.[113] Yet primaries did provide unpredictable results and official defeats. Even the black farce of the 1948 Taxco election had some representative effect, causing the party to quietly replace the official candidate for mayor.[114] Primaries, for all their flaws, permitted the inclusion and participation that underpin a Dahlian polyarchy.[115]

Like many recent transitions, Mexico's provoked heady optimism, subsequent confusion, and the eventual disillusionment of a competitive authoritarian ending. Between the 1950s and the late 1970s Mexico was a country in which numerous elections gave almost uniform results: victories for the PRI and—unlike predominant-party democracies like Japan or India—the requisite supermajorities, rooted in both formal and informal electoral manipulation, to block all but glacially incremental institutional change. As in contemporary competitive authoritarian states, elections remained "arenas of contestation through which oppositions [could] legally—and legitimately—challenge incumbents," who "[were] forced to sweat."[116] Independent local majorities running campaigns as PRIístas in name alone quite often did not have to sweat to have their power rubber-stamped (though just how often this occurred needs more research at the intersection of the qualitative and the quantitative). Overt opponents, though, had to sweat blood to win a minority of local contests and, more feasibly, to veto the winners of others. Yet even at the PRI's peak, mobilizations mattered. As one village protester put it, "We don't have arms, but we do have balls." That didn't help him much: soldiers beat him with rifle butts, his *compañeros* retreated sullenly to the general store, and the election stayed stolen.[117] But enough others had the same attributes to form jostling, angry crowds beneath a soft authoritarian surface. Their efforts and their memories constituted a recessive gene in the Mexican body politic; one that was sporadically expressed across the entire period of the dictablanda, and one that reemerged critically in the protracted transition of the late twentieth century.

Notes

1. *Diario de Xalapa*, July 7, 1952.
2. *Diario del Hogar*, August 15, 1893.
3. Peter H. Smith, *Labyrinths of Power: Political Recruitment in Twentieth-Century Mexico* (Princeton, NJ: Princeton University Press, 1979), 144–58.
4. Caroline C. Beer, *Electoral Competition and Institutional Change in Mexico* (Notre Dame, IN: University of Notre Dame Press, 2003), 11; see also Todd A. Eisenstadt, *Courting Democracy in Mexico: Party Strategies and Electoral Institutions* (Cambridge: Cambridge University Press, 2004), 94. Pablo González Casanova's later work stressed the long-term "democratic meaning" of elections. Pablo González Casanova, "Democracia en tiempos de crisis," in *Las elecciones en México: Evolución y perspectiva*, ed. Pablo González Casanova (Mexico City: FCE, 1985), 17–18; Rogelio Hernández Rodríguez, *El centro dividido: La nueva autonomía de los gobernadores* (Mexico City: El Colegio de México, 2009), 38–47.
5. Peter Guardino, *Peasants, Politics and the Formation of Mexico's National State: Guerrero, 1800–1857* (Palo Alto, CA: Stanford University Press, 1996), 86–100; Peter Guardino, *The Time of Liberty: Popular Political Culture in Oaxaca, 1750–1850* (Durham, NC: Duke University Press, 2005); Michael Costeloe, "Generals versus Politicians: Santa Anna and the 1842 Congressional Elections in Mexico," *Bulletin of Latin American Research* 01.8, no. 0.2 (1989), 257–58.
6. Daniel Cosío Villegas, *La Constitución de 1857 y sus críticos* (Mexico City: Secretaría de Educación Pública, 1973), 130–35.
7. Alan Knight, *The Mexican Revolution* (2 vols.) (Lincoln: University of Nebraska, 1990), vol. 1, 53.
8. Mark Wasserman, *Persistent Oligarchs: Elites and Politics in Chihuahua, Mexico, 1910–1940* (Durham, NC: Duke University Press, 1993), 56; assorted election reports AGN/DGG-2.311M(9)/5B, 6B; *Excélsior*, January 18, 1939, Adrian Bantjes, *As If Jesus Walked on Earth: Cardenismo, Sonora, and the Mexican Revolution* (Wilmington, DE: Scholarly Resources, 1998), 66; Ben Fallaw, *Cárdenas Compromised: The Failure of Reform in Postrevolutionary Yucatan* (Durham, NC: Duke University Press, 2001), 132.
9. Ugalde to Gobernación, August 11, 1947, AGN/DGIPS-90/F. Ugalde.
10. Ojeda to Avila Camacho, September 21, 1944, AGN/DGG-2/311G(9)2/241/V.IV.
11. *Trópico*, January 7, 1945; Ojeda to Alemán, October 18, 1944, AGN/DGG-2/311G(9)/239/2 vol. II; Massey to State Department, March 30, 1949, NARG-812.00/3-3049; *Excélsior*, January 20, 1946; *Diario de Xalapa*, August 29, 1949.
12. "Calendario de Elecciones Internas del PRI," San Luis Potosí, 1948, AGN/DGIPS-797/2-1/48/392.
13. Laidlaw to State Department, February 17, 1950, NARG-712.00/2-175.
14. PRI statutes 1946, chapter IV, articles 56, 71, 74, in various authors, *Historia Documental del Partido de la Revolución, toma V: PRM-PRI, 1945–1950* (Mexico City: Institución de Capacitación Política, 1982), 189–90, 276–79.
15. Pavón Silva to Gobernación, May 6, 1948, AGN/DGIPS-797/2-1/48/392, Ricardo

Corzo Ramírez et al., *Nunca un desleal: Cándido Aguilar* (Mexico City: Fondo de Cultura Económica, 1986), 300.

16. Burrows to State Department, April 18, 1950, NARG-712.00/4-1850; Taylor to Eden, November 21, 1952, F0371/97540; "Mexico: Annual Review for 1950," February 6, 1951, Foreign Office 371/90819.

17. Martínez Gómez Alemán to Alemán, May 16, 1952, AGN/DGG-2.311M(26)/79.

18. J. M. Valdés to Alemán, October 10, 1949; Comité Político José Azueta to Gobernación, July 9, 1955, AGN/DGG-2.311M(26)/78/6; PS-8 to Gobernación, July 12, 1948, AGN/DGIPS-90/2-1/131/737.

19. Ejidatarios of Mamadi, Azoyú, to Gobernación, December 12, 1948, AGN/DGG-2.311M(9)/3B/7.

20. As occurred in Ayahualulco, Veracruz, in 1945, or in Olinalá and San Marcos, Guerrero, in 1949. Election summary, AHEV-1412/549/0, Leyva Mancilla report 1949, AP-175/352.072.073ETN.

21. Liga to Avila Camacho, November 28, 1944, AGN/DGG-2.311M(9)/5B/75; Gobernación to Ruiz Cortines, June 19, 1947, AHEV-1507/548/57; Pavón to Alemán, September 20, 1949, AGN/DGG-2.311M(26)/77/2l Bateman to Bevin, December 6, 1945, F0371/44478.

22. Ojeda to Avila Camacho, November 22, 1944, AGN/DGG-2/311G(9)/239/2.

23. Agent I-85 to Gobernación, March 30, 1936, AGN/DGIPS-171/7.

24. Ojeda to Alemán, November 7, 1944, AGN/DGG-2.311M(9)/5B/63; Reza Sotelo to Gobernación, October 26, 1948, AGN/DGG-2.311M(9)/6.

25. Catalán Calvo to Liga Guerrero, August 1, 1944, AGN/DGG-2/311G(9)2/239/v.I.

26. PS-2 to Gobernación, March 2, 1940, AGN/DGIPS-78/5; Ojeda to Alemán, November 11, 1944, AGN/DGG-2/311G(9)2/239v.II.

27. Ortega to Gobernación, February 13, 1946, AGN/DGG-2/311P(26)/I/107.

28. Author's analysis, AGN/DGG-2.311 M(9) AND M(26) series, *Diario de Xalapa*, July 10, 1950.

29. J. N. M. to Gobernación, October 11, 1948, AGN/DGIPS-102/JNM; CNC/CNOP Paso del Macho to Gobernación, October 9, 1952, AGN/DGG-2.311M(26)/78/8.

30. Ojeda to Gobernación, December 17, 1948, AGN/DGG-2.311M(9)/4B/80; Reivindicación Social to Gobernación, October 26, 1948, AGN/DGG-2.311M(9)/3B/8.

31. Alemán Celestino to Alemán, August 12, 1949, AGN/DGG-2.311M(26)/77/45; *Diario de Xalapa*, September 13, 1949.

32. Confederación Nacional de Ayuntamientos de la República circular, no. 13, June 7, 1946, AMI-1946.

33. Pavón Silva to Gobernación, August 22, 1947; Acedo Cárdenas to state legislature, November 11, 1947, AGN/DGIPS-794/180.

34. Party statutes of 1946, chapter IV, article 61, in various authors, *Historia Documental del Partido*, 277.

35. Delgado Cruz Grande, Guerrero, to Alemán, December 5, 1944, AGN/DGG-2.311M(9)/5B/71; Román, Ajuchitlán, to Sánchez Taboada, October 19, 1948, AGN/DGG-2.311M(9)/3/122; ejidatarios Cuetzala del Progreso to Ruiz Cortines, January 1, 1953, AGN/DGG-2.311M(9)/3B/23.

36. Nava to Gobernación, December 8, 1944; acta, junta computadora Mochitlán, December 7, 1944, AGN/DGG-2.311M(9)/4B/14, 6.

37. PS-37 to Gobernación, May 5, 1947, AGN/DGIPS-796/2-1/47/424.
38. Catalán Calvo to Gobernación, January 2, 1945, AGN/DGG-2.311M(9)/5B/75.
39. For examples, see AGN/DGIPS cajas 78, 129, 767, 797.
40. Circular, SNTE Guerrero February 5, 1950, AGN/DGIPS-800/2-1/49/444.
41. Turrent to Carvajal, August 16, 1949, AHEV-1696/549/01.
42. "Estado de Veracruz: Aspirantes a Presidentes Municipales" series (1964), AGN/DGIPS-1997A/2-1/010(18)"64"/52.
43. *Excélsior*, September 18, 1964.
44. Joy Langston, "Elite Ruptures: When Do Ruling Parties Split?," in *Electoral Authoritarianism: The Dynamics of Unfree Competition*, ed. Andreas Schedler (Boulder, CO: Lynne Rienner, 2006), 62–64.
45. Robert Dahl, *Polyarchy: Participation and Opposition* (New Haven, CT: Yale University Press, 1971), 15.
46. J. N. M. to Gobernación, October 11, 1948, AGN/DGIPS-102/JNM.
47. Absalón Pérez to Ruiz Cortines, August 22, 1946; Contreras to Ruiz Cortines, October 7, 1946, AHEV-1412/549/0.
48. *Diario de Xalapa*, August 3, 12, and 28, 1949.
49. Partial list of results of 1950 Veracruz municipal elections, AGN/DGG-2.311M(26)/79/8.
50. *Diario de Xalapa*, September 12, 22, and 23, 1949.
51. PS-5, PS-9 to Gobernación, May 6, 1947, AGN/DGIPS-796/2-1/47/424; list of federal deputies 1952, AGN/DGIPS-791/2-1/46/67; *Diario de Xalapa*, August 3, 1949.
52. SNTE Guerrero to Ruiz Cortines, August 15, 1950, AGN/DGG-2.311G(9)3/242/Nov. 1948.
53. Secretario de Gobierno Guerrero to Gobernación, January 16, 1947, AGN/DGG-2.311M(9)/4B/66; Leyva Mancilla report 1947, AP-175/352.072.073ETN; *El Universal*, January 2, 1948.
54. Pansters, chapter 5, this volume; *La Verdad*, January 4, 1949.
55. Comité Democrático Independiente Ajuchitlán to Gobernación, January 1, 1949, AGN/DGG-2.311 M(9)/3/122.
56. Nieto to Gobernación, January 1, 1945, AGN/DGG-5B/2.311M(9)69; Leyva Mancilla to Gobernación, June 27, 1949, AGN/DGG-2.311M(9)/3/122.
57. Armando Bartra, *Guerrero bronco: Campesinos, ciudadanos y guerrilleros en la Costa Grande* (Mexico City: Ediciones Era, 2000), 96–97.
58. Alvaro Arreola Ayala, "Elecciones municipales," in González, *Las elecciones en México*, 337.
59. Benjamin T. Smith, *Pistoleros and Popular Movements: The Politics of State Formation in Postrevolutionary Oaxaca* (Lincoln: University of Nebraska Press, 2009), 266.
60. Regional Committee to Central Committee PRI, May 29, 1946, AHEV-1412/549/0.
61. A reasoning shared by Beatriz Magaloni, *Voting for Autocracy: Hegemonic Party Survival and Its Demise in Mexico* (Cambridge: Cambridge University Press, 2006), 6.
62. Smith, *Pistoleros and Popular Movements*, 229.
63. *El Universal*, November 1, 1952, and January 9, 1953.
64. For veto players, see George Tsebelis, "Decision Making in Political Systems: Veto Players in Presidentialism, Parliamentarism, Multicameralism and Mutipartyism," *British Journal of Political Science* 25 (July 1995): 289.

65. Cited in Alexander Aviña, "Seizing hold of memories in moments of danger: guerrillas and revolution in Guerrero, Mexico," in *Challenging Authoritarianism in Mexico: Revolutionary Struggles and the Dirty War, 1964–1982*, ed. Fernando Herrera Calderón and Adela Cedillo (New York: Routledge, 2012), 48.

66. Galaviz to Ruiz Cortines, November 29, 1946, AHEV-1412/549/0.

67. Román to Alemán, December 3, 1947, AGN/DGG-2.311M(9)/4B/59; *Novedades*, January 21, 1948; Sedena to twenty-sixth military zone, July 21, 1942, AGN/DGG-2/317.4(26)/64/24; Román to Alemán, December 3, 1947, AGN/DGG-2.311M(9)/4B/59.

68. Rath, chapter 3, and Pansters chapter 5, this volume.

69. PS-8 to Gobernación, December 27, 1947, AGN/DGIPS-90/2-1/131/737.

70. *Excélsior*, September 5, 1952; *Novedades*, August 6, 1952; September 9, 1952; October 4, 1952.

71. PS-20 to Gobernación, February 6, 1947, AGN/DGIPS-79/2-1/130/633; Dickinson to State Department, April 2, 1948, NARG-812.00/4.248.

72. Hernández Rodríguez, *El centro dividido*, 151.

73. Jeffrey Rubin, *Decentering the Regime: Ethnicity, Radicalism, and Democracy in Juchitán, Mexico* (Durham, NC: Duke University Press, 1997), 52–54; Frank Cancian, *The Decline of Community in Zinacantán: Economy, Public Life, and Social Stratification, 1960–1987* (Palo Alto, CA: Stanford University Press, 1992), 129–30.

74. Enrique Riveron Fragoso to DFS, September 12, 1958, AGN/DFS-Salvador Nava/VP/LI, 1.

75. Memo "Actividades del Gral. Cuenca Diaz," March 22, 1965, AGN/DGIPS-1294/1.

76. Hernández Rodríguez, *El centro dividido*, 41–42.

77. Quoted in Alberto J. Pani, *El retroceso democrático del nuevo regimen* (Mexico City: A. J. Pani, 1947), 10.

78. Annual report for Mexico 1944, January 22, 1945, F0371/44478.

79. Bateman to Bevin, November 21, 1945, F0371/44478.

80. For the massacre see Daniel Newcomer, *Reconciling Modernity: Urban State Formation in 1940s León, Mexico* (Lincoln: University of Nebraska Press, 2004), 143–76.

81. Declaration of Principles in various authors, *Historia Documental del Partido*, 254; *El Nacional*, January 21, 1946.

82. Martínez to Gobernación, October 22, 1946, AGN/DGG-2.311M(26)/74/8.

83. Bateman to Bevin, February 24, 1947, F0371/60940; Rodolfo Usigli, "El caso de 'El Gesticulador' in Usigli," *Teatro Completo* (4 vols.) (Mexico City: Fondo de Cultura Económica, 1966–1996), vol. II, 541; Aguilar speech, Fortín, October 11, 1951, AGN/DGIPS-19/13.

84. Bateman to Bevin, January 21, 1947, F0371/60940; Washington to State Department, June 7, 1948, NARG-812.00/6-748; Dickinson to State Department, April 2, 1948, NARG-812.00/4.248.

85. Leslie Bethell and Ian Roxborough, "Latin America between the Second World War and the Cold War: Some Reflections on the 1945–1948 Conjuncture," *Journal of Latin American Studies* 20, no. 1 (1988): 167–89.

86. Torres to Carbajal, November 30, 1949, AHEV-1702/549/115; INEGI, *Censo del estado de Veracruz 1950* (Mexico City: Instituto Nacional de Estadística y Geografía, 1953), 28.

87. Rios Thivol to Gobernación, November 5, 1951, AGN/DGIPS-84/2-1/131/655/v.IV.

88. Tanalís Padilla, *Rural Resistance in the Land of Zapata: The Jaramillista Movement and the Myth of the Pax Priísta, 1940–1962* (Durham, NC: Duke University Press, 2009), 108–38.

89. *Diario de Xalapa*, July 24, 1949; *Diario de Guerrero*, June 27, 1950.

90. Admittedly when incumbents failed to run, but this was, of course, universal in Mexico. Julius Turner, "Primary Elections as the Alternative to Party Competition in 'Safe' Districts," *The Journal of Politics* 15, no. 2 (May 1953): 198, 206–7, 210.

91. Foreign Office, "Annual Report on Mexico for 1948," FO371/74076; *Diario Oficial*, February 21, 1949; "Annual Political Report for Mexico, 1949," FO371/81501; "Political and Economic Developments in Mexico, December 1949," NARG 712.00/2; Laidlaw to State Department, February 17, 1950, NARG-712.00/2-1750.

92. J.N.M. and J. G. V. to Gobernación, February 2, 1950, and February 3, 1950, AGN/DGIPS-19/12.

93. Various authors, *Historia Documental del Partido*, 213.

94. "Recent Political Events in Mexico," March 4, 1950, FO371/81503/AM1015/1.

95. Various authors, *Historia Documental del Partido*, 187, 279, 669–70.

96. Marcial Rodríguez Saldaña, *La desaparición de poderes en el estado de Guerrero* (Chilpancingo: Universidad Autónoma de Guerrero, 1992), 125; Gómez Maganda to presidentes municipales, July 3, 1952, AMI-1952/104.

97. *Diario de Xalapa*, September 13, 1950.

98. A method of excluding regional parties followed in Putin's Russia, where parliamentary parties must have members in all eighty-nine regions. Steven Levitsky and Lucan A. Way, *Competitive Authoritarianism: Hybrid Regimes After the Cold War* (Cambridge: Cambridge University Press, 2010), 197.

99. Francisco José Paoli Bolio, "Legislación electoral y proceso político, 1917–1982," in González, *Las elecciones en México*, 146–52.

100. "Recent Political Events in Mexico," April 3, 1950, FO371/81503/AM1015/1.

101. Author's analysis, "Presidentes Municipales del Estado de Veracruz" series, AGN/DGIPS-1997A/2-1/010(18)"64"/52.

102. Paoli Bolio, "Legislación y proceso político, 1917–1982," and Rogelio Ramos Oranday, "Oposición y abstencionismo en las elecciones presidenciales, 1964–1982," both in González, *Las elecciones en México*, 148–61, 163–94, respectively.

103. John A. Booth and Mitchell A. Seligson, "The Political Culture of Authoritarianism in Mexico: a Reexamination," *Latin American Research Review* 19, no. 1 (1984): 106–24; Richard R. Fagen and William S. Tuohy, *Politics and Privilege in a Mexican City* (Palo Alto: Stanford University Press, 1972).

104. Coatzacoalcos cólonos to Alemán, September 2, 1952, AGN/DGG 2.311P(26)/2/107; Centro Político Acción Cívica Acapulco to Gobernación, November 21, 1952, AGN/DGG-2.311M(9)/4B/74; Vecinos Metlatonoc to Alemán, November 15, 1952, AGN/DGG-2.311M(9)/2B/155; *El Universal*, September 6, 1952.

105. For examples from the 1960s, see AGN/DGIPS-1320.

106. Ortíz to Liga, November 9, 1949, AGN/DGG-2.311M(26)/78/8; Pavón Silva to Gobernación, September 5, 1948, AGN/DGIPS-800/2-1/49/444.

107. Jolie Olcott, personal communication, November 15, 2011.

108. *Trinchera de Culiacán*, January 3, 1967; *Acapulco Gráfico*, November 30, 1952.

109. Rogelio Hernández Rodríguez, *La formación del politico mexicano: el caso de Carlos A. Madrazo* (Mexico City: El Colegio de México, 1991), 132–35.

110. Namely Aguascalientes, Baja California, Chihuahua, Durango, Guerrero, Michoacán, Oaxaca, Puebla, Sinaloa, and Tamaulipas. Hernández Rodríguez, *La formación del político mexicano*, 149–50; memo, DGIPS to Gobernación, April 11, 1965; Bustamante Díaz and De la Peña Hernandez to DFS, April 11, 1965, AGN/DGIPS-1303/1.

111. *Excélsior*, November 19, 1965.

112. Antonio Gramsci, *Selections from the Prison Notebooks* (London: Lawrence and Wishart, 1996), 149–52.

113. W. V. D'Antonio and Richard Suter, "Elecciones preliminares en un municipio mexicano: nuevas tendencias en la lucha de México hacia la democracia," *Revista Mexicana de Sociología* 29, no. 1 (January–March 1967): 96–101.

114. PS-34 to Gobernación, October 11, 1948, and December 7, 1948, AGN/DGIPS-102/JNM, AGN/DGIPS-91/2-1/131/748/CMC.

115. Robert Dahl, *On Democracy* (New Haven, CT: Yale University Press, 2000), 91.

116. Levitsky and Way, *Competitive Authoritarianism*, 12, 30.

117. PS-16 to Gobernación, January 11, 1949, AGN/DGIPS-94/2-1/131/802.

WORK AND RESOURCE REGULATION

CHAPTER 7 | *Michael Snodgrass*

THE GOLDEN AGE OF CHARRISMO
Workers, Braceros, and the Political Machinery
of Postrevolutionary Mexico

Winter was setting in on the northern desert plains when the coal miners of Nueva Rosita elected to become Mexico's protagonists in a postwar conflict sweeping through the Americas. From Appalachia to Chile, the labor struggle pitted embattled mining communities against an emergent alliance of multinational capital, the Cold War state, and anticommunist union bosses. The miners' heroic, if quixotic, movement would conclude a transitional chapter in Mexican labor history. Sixteen years earlier, in 1934, labor activists from the same Coahuila coal fields—then the biggest in Latin America—helped found Mexico's Mine and Metallurgical Workers Union, which quickly organized smelters and steel mills as well. Like the oil and railroad unions, the miners elected communist leaders (locally and nationally) well into the 1940s, an era of unprecedented strikes. This sustained militancy in strategic industry threatened the state's industrialization policy. Mining generated 30 percent of federal revenues, and it fed steel and electric power industries vital for development. Moreover, unions that once rallied behind President Cárdenas were now divided in their allegiance to the Partido Revolucionario Institucional (PRI). In a swift, eighteen-month campaign, labor authorities orchestrated the takeover of key unions by party loyalists willing to restrain industrial militancy for perks and power. In May 1950 the miners' union was last to fall. Its dissident locals then proved hardest to control, especially in Coahuila and Nuevo León, home to one-third of the union's members, men who mined the lead, zinc, and coal that fed the region's steel mills and smelters. At the miners' national convention, the locals had supported Antonio García Moreno, a Monterrey steel worker whose blatantly fraudulent defeat provoked widespread dissent. García's victorious rivals hastily sent "anti-communist delegates to re-organize" the northern locals, a brazen assault on the union's democratic traditions. Nueva Rosita's Local 14 was among the first to feel the force of the intervention.[1]

Nueva Rosita was a company town, founded by ASARCO. The American company's historic dominance of Mexican mining made it an early target of miners' organizers. Once achieved, unionization altered the balance of power within the community and in the pits. Mine workers sat on the city council. Their collective contract gave them a voice down in their subterranean workplace. Then, just as the state and ASARCO expected, the compliant leaders imposed on Local 14 conceded to a mine modernization plan, one that intensified labor conflict because new drilling and cutting machines threatened jobs and exacerbated occupational hazards. But the miners of Nueva Rosita were now on their own. Labor authorities declared a June 1950 protest strike illegal, forcing workers back to the mine to save their jobs. Local 14 then was "sanctioned"—its elected officials deposed and the union hall closed—because these miners insisted that García Moreno was still their legitimate national leader. So when five thousand workers gathered in Nueva Rosita's plaza that October and elected to strike "what was really at stake was the defense of union democracy and local autonomy in the Miners Union."[2]

The ensuing showdown lasted four months and drew international attention to a struggle that matched the miners against ASARCO, the government, and union bosses in Mexico City. Great hardship befell the strikers' families. Their kids were expelled from school. ASARCO cut water and electric power supplies. Labor authorities froze strike funds and closed Local 14's health clinic and cooperative store. Their parish priest even threatened to excommunicate militant workers.[3] For a time, solidarity funds arrived from miners abroad. The region's steel workers and cotton *ejidos* donated food and clothing. But weeks passed, the winter cold set in, and children died of hunger and disease. Rank-and-file unity weakened when federal mediators declared the strike illegal, permitting ASARCO to hire replacements. Nearly one thousand strikers returned to the mine. Then the military arrived. Soldiers blockaded highways, expelled journalists, and patrolled city streets to enforce a prohibition against the right to assemble. Isolated and desperate, their community an armed camp, the miners of Nueva Rosita set out on an eight-hundred-mile march on Mexico City to petition the president directly.

Journalists called it the "Caravan of Hunger." The fifty-day journey took four thousand miners—with their families and supporters—to a city that few had seen. They defined their struggle as one "for a free and democratic Mexico, where the law is enforced, and Mexicans treated with dignity and respect." Authorities played along. The miners marched to the heart of the nation, paying their respects at the Monument to the Revolution, attending mass at the Basilica of Guadalupe, holding a protest rally before the National Palace. Mexico City officials then herded the marchers into a guarded encampment at a local park. The press demonized the strikers as dupes of their communist leaders, who were reportedly hanging out at the "swankiest hotels, where they uncork the most aromatic cognac and toast the proletariat."[4] President Alemán simply ignored them. After a week, Mexico's Labor Minister reaffirmed the strike settlement, placed the miners on a train, and sent them home with vague promises of being rehired. Fewer than eight hundred got their jobs back. Some returned to their rural villages. Many, being second-generation miners, followed the crowded migrant trail to booming Monterrey. Others joined Mexico's growing exodus of braceros to the United States. Back at the mine, mechanization proceeded, the work force shrank, and coal output ascended to record levels within two years. The mine workers who stayed on experienced the setback of union democracy. But in exchange they became working-class beneficiaries of a system that rewarded labor peace with a package of union rights and welfare benefits that cemented the PRI's social pact with industrial workers.

The coal miners' defeat concluded an era of confrontation that transformed labor relations and made the union a permanent and effective presence in the workplaces and blue-collar communities of Mexico. In many ways, Nueva Rosita symbolized the transition from progressive Cardenismo to Mexico's "institutionalized revolution." As a truly postrevolutionary period began, policy shifted emphasis from social justice to development, resulting in new means of achieving old revolutionary goals, from industrialization to rural pacification to securing union loyalty to the new regime. This labor-state alliance famously became "one of the historical foundations of Mexican political stability." As schoolchildren all learned, it was a 1906 miners' strike at Cananea "that formed the prelude to the Revolution."[5] So revolutionary leaders, from Madero to Cárdenas, all balanced efforts to restrain worker militancy with concessions, both piecemeal and dramatic, from labor legislation to the nationalization of Mexican oil. Through its support of labor bosses and concessions to union workers, the state maintained "political loyalty . . . labor tranquility . . . [and] its revolutionary credentials." Union leaders boasted of this "well-oiled machine," and political analysts attributed the pax PRIísta to the corporatist structures and patron-client networks upon which it ran.[6] No unions concerned authorities more than the "petroleum, railroad, mining and sugar workers." The labor minister, who orchestrated their coercive takeover, lauded these industrial unions as "the strongest pillars" of the newly christened PRI.[7] No sectors were more strategic to state economic policy and few unions had longer histories of workplace militancy and political autonomy. This chapter examines how state policymakers tamed their militant traditions and cultivated the loyalty of compliant union bosses known as *charros*. It analyzes how a mix of punitive sanctions and beneficial concessions—a system known as *charrismo*—secured rank-and-file quiescence in the mining and steel industries of the north. It then shifts to Jalisco to illustrate how a bracero program meant to alleviate rural poverty became a perk delivered to rank-and-file members by the sugar workers' union. Union bosses' capacity to deliver the proverbial goods to workers, and the vote for the PRI, with minimal recourse to intimidation or violence, made this a golden age of charrismo.

Labor's Institutionalized Revolution

Workers cemented their alliance with the state during the presidency of General Lázaro Cárdenas, who resolved to unionize workers and secure their constitutional rights by confronting powerful business interests, both foreign and national. A three-year period (1933–36) saw the unification of nearly all workers in the railway, oil, mining, and metallurgical industries, as well as sugar mill workers, in what became Mexico's dominant agro-industrial sector. The state's aggressively pro-labor policy proved brief, exceptional, and deeply polarizing. But the consequences were great and enduring. By the late 1940s, when the labor insurgency cooled, unions represented 10 percent of Mexican workers, a figure that improved slightly thereafter.[8] But organized labor represented workers in every key industry and region of Mexico, from Gulf Coast oil to northern mines to industrial cities both old (Puebla, Torreón) and new (Monclova). Even Monterrey, once depicted as a bastion of nonunion industry, actually hosted four miner/metalworker locals and the largest section of the rail workers' union.[9] Such geographic range and strategic muscle explains labor's coming political clout and thus state efforts to appease workers, court leaders' loyalty, and regulate their unions.

Postrevolutionary Mexico faced a policymaking dilemma—social justice versus national development—that confronted every revolutionary and populist regime in Latin America. Mexico's relative success at balancing labor demands with economic policy helps explain the durability of the PRI. So does the state's institutional ties to unions. The majority of organized workers belonged to "official" unions affiliated with the Confederation of Mexican Workers (CTM). To these the state extended jurisdictional monopolies and the closed shop, thus impeding independent union challenges. In 1938, labor became a formal sector of the ruling party, which then apportioned political posts to union leaders. These "quotas of power" extended labor's voice—and the PRI's power—from city hall to the federal senate.[10] So, with union membership came party membership (virtual or mandatory) and, for the next sixty years, unions dutifully mobilized the ranks to vote for the PRI. Mexico thus pioneered the corporatist style of labor-state relations that became common in Latin America.[11] It endured longer than in Brazil or Argentina. But the corporatist pact still remained tenuous into the late 1940s, a transitional moment in Mexico's labor history.

The post-Cardenista state hinged Mexico's future not on economic redistribution but development and production. Poverty remained endemic and industry was the cure. Since the earliest days of the revolution, policymakers and union leaders had advocated industrialization as the key to national reconstruction and economic independence. Three decades of revolutionary violence and instability left Mexican industry—from mines to railway lines to textile mills—in a state of disrepair. The government put rhetoric to effect with protective tariffs, tax concessions, and a labor policy designed to enhance the investment climate by curtailing strikes and restraining wage demands. The state even promoted its new health and social insurance system, the Instituto Mexicano del Seguro Social (IMSS), not as a revolutionary project for which unions had lobbied, but as a social policy to serve industrial development.[12] Wartime conditions spurred industrialization, and import substitution policy put Mexico on the road to self-sufficiency in manufacturing. Even the Marxist opposition endorsed a project that promised to liberate Mexico from the clutches of backwardness and dependency. Unionists also recognized the need for industrial modernization, which promised safer working conditions. But it also generated massive job losses, as Puebla textile operatives and Coahuila coal miners learned in the 1950s. Workers demanded development on their terms; rather than accept salary and job cuts in the name of patriotic sacrifice, for example, railway union leaders lobbied for higher freight charges to modernize infrastructure and finance benefits.[13] Unions now had the organizational muscle to resist, and confrontation escalated as wartime hardship and state industrialization policy threatened workers' earlier conquests.

The early years of the Mexican miracle were hardly golden for working-class Mexicans. Wartime inflation, peso devaluations, and state policies to restrain wages more than wiped out the gains of the Cárdenas years. Social inequalities grew. Emigration to the United States soared as well, now under the tutelary hand of a bracero program that some perceived as a state-sponsored "safety valve" to release rural discontent. Migrants' earnings actually helped finance industrialization.[14] But industrial peace remained elusive as contract disputes and material hardships fueled strikes and galvanized support for militant communist leadership in the oil, railway, and mining/steel unions into the late 1940s. Times changed quickly under President Alemán, a onetime labor lawyer who specialized in accident claims for railwaymen and miners. Once in office the underdogs' former defender launched an industrialization-at-all-costs strategy and warned in his inaugural address that "the union must not become a threat to the project of development."[15] The state blamed communist agitators for the industrial unrest. Its labor allies offered a solution. By then, the CTM had a new leader, Fidel Velázquez, a staunch anticommunist with a practiced disregard for democratic unionism. Velázquez would dominate organized labor until his death in 1997. But the CTM's future seemed uncertain in 1948, when the industrial unions disaffiliated, organized a rival bloc, and declared their unions' political independence from the PRI. Miners and railwaymen had traditions of union autonomy dating to the 1920s. But now such dissidence threatened the corporatist foundation of the ruling party itself.

Mexico's Labor Ministry employed its legal authority and coercive powers to replace leftist militants with their more compliant and deferential rivals. The railroad union succumbed first and, in a most dramatic fashion, Jesús Díaz de León led five hundred workers in the takeover of union headquarters. Díaz was in fact retaking the union, having been voted out one day earlier for soliciting a government investigation of union finances. His subsequent "moralization" campaign against communists and corruption earned him a brief measure of rank-and-file support.[16] And his love of the Mexican rodeo, whose horsemen are called *charros*, earned Diaz a nickname ("*El Charro*") that entered the lexicon of Mexican labor as a generic (and derisive) term for state-approved labor bosses. Their enduring style of unionism—nonconfrontational, anticommunist, corrupt, and sometimes violent—became known as charrismo. The takeover of Mexico's largest union also set a precedent as the state exploited rifts in the historically fractious oil and mine unions to orchestrate the overthrow of militant leadership. When, in late 1949, rival factions of petroleum workers staged competing conventions, the Labor Ministry arbitrated the outcome to install pro-government leaders. Six months later, the miners convened, and authorities simply decertified delegates representing thirty-nine thousand of fifty-two thousand members, thus sanctioning the communist Antonio García Moreno's fraudulent defeat by Jesús Carrasco (alias "*El Charrasco*"). Protest always ensued. But military deployments subdued dissidence in old communist strongholds, from the railway shops of Monterrey to the Gulf Coast oil refineries. Newly installed charros then intervened among dissident locals, as at Nueva Rosita, and employed a statutory "exclusion clause" to purge their rivals. The "Caravan of Hunger" that opened this chapter thus marked "the last gasp of the militant unionism of the 1940s."[17]

These union takeovers achieved their intended effects. Charro leaders quickly herded their tamed unions back into the corporatist corral, breaking the last viable labor opposition bloc in twentieth-century Mexico. They also acquiesced to the very industrial modernization schemes that helped spark labor unrest. The oil workers union relinquished its dream of managerial control. Mechanization proceeded in Coahuila's mines. The railwaymen's new leaders sowed the seeds of rank-and-file rebellion by conceding wage freezes, layoffs, and modified work rules.[18] Dissent was now contained by statutory revisions that strengthened executive leadership to authorize strikes, negotiate collective contracts, control union funds, and sanction rebellious sections or dissident leaders. New statutes also certified the holding of political and union office simultaneously and established punitive sanctions against opposition political activism. From then on, labor's became a reliable vote and charrismo "a more effective way of regulating workers' political behavior than the complex business of election-rigging."[19]

Mexican labor history followed a pattern prevailing throughout the Americas, from Peronist Argentina to the postwar United States, as combative union movements "were transformed into relatively docile, compliant, bureaucratic organizations . . . under the watchful regulatory eye of the state." Under this system of business-friendly unionism, organized labor "joined management in disciplining the work force . . . and containing industrial conflict."[20] Hallmarks of the transition were purges of leftist militants, restrictions on the right to strike, and the skillful manipulation of nationalist and anticommunist discourses by both authoritarian *and* democratic regimes. In Chile during the early Cold War, for example, the state brought a draconian end to the "Popular Front" coalition by breaking strikes, jailing militants, and banning the communist party. It did so because "labor militancy in the copper mines . . . threatened their entire program of economic development." To Mexico's north, in another model democracy, American radicals were purged and entire unions expelled from the Congress of Industrialized Organizations (CIO) as federal legislation curtailed industrial militancy and banned communists from elected union offices.[21] The Mexicans cited this Taft-Hartley Act (1947) to legitimize their own Cold War labor policy. Meanwhile, during the 1950s, a re-unified American Federation of Labor-CIO signed on to the U.S. State Department's foreign labor policy in Mexico. Operating directly or through allies like the United Mine Workers, the State Department subsidized Mexican union elections, invited charros to labor education programs in the United States, and screened films on business-labor cooperation at miners' union locals. The extent to which this foreign policy "shaped the development and direction" of Mexico's labor movement remains unclear.[22] While they relished the perks, charros needed no cajoling from the gringos to purge their fractious unions of radical dissent. Nonetheless, Mexico's labor-left ascribed great agency to U.S. officials and business executives, whose guiding hand and deep pockets were allegedly behind the state's repression of the ASARCO mine workers and the big railway strikes of 1958–59.[23] What is certain is that the aura of labor peace ushered in by charrismo bolstered the U.S. capital flows crucial to Mexico's ongoing industrialization.

Across the Americas, the conservative drift of union leadership and state labor policy paralleled a progressive development of social welfare reforms and, in Mexico, notable improvements in working-class living standards. To the extent that workers did experience a golden age—one reflected in wages, benefits, or consumption patterns—it began in the 1950s and extended through the 1970s. Restrictive wage policies held earnings shamefully far behind productivity gains. But industrial union workers fared better—and sooner—than studies of real wage indices reflect.[24] Workers in mining, steel, and oil earned significant production bonuses and their belated wage recovery "was more than compensated by an increase in benefits."[25] Consumer prices stabilized, too, as cost-of-living increases fell from an astounding average of 22 percent annually (1940–46) to less than 5 percent (1954–72).[26] Mexico's State Food Agency (later CONASUPO) offered further relief to urban working-class consumers, expanding its price-controlled inventories from basic staples in the 1940s to clothing, shoes, toys, and other nonfood items.[27] Working-class families also benefited greatly from increased state spending on education, public health, and social security. From its founding, the IMSS offered benefits beyond what most union workers then enjoyed, covering their dependents, maternity care, disability, and old-age pensions. By the mid-1960s, IMSS covered more than six million dependents, and its modernist complexes, designed by Mexico's leading architects, showcased the state's new commitment to public health.[28] State spending on health and education produced results: average life expectancy leaped from forty to sixty years and literacy rates climbed from 44 to 66 percent (1940–70), trends suggestive of improved living standards for working-class families, who also enjoyed greater job security than any generation before 1950 and since 1982. Economic development and educational opportunity made possible the generational mobility that propelled the workers' children into an urban middle class, a development in which their blue-collar parents took great pride.[29]

This is not to downplay the tarnished underside of Mexico's "miracle." For all the benefits that came with a union job, workers who challenged the charros faced punitive firings or a visit from union thugs. Collective action begot greater consequences. The state struck back when the influential yet fractious railroad workers' union paralyzed that industry three times in 1958–59. The military seized railway facilities and sequestered union halls. Police raided strikers' homes. In the end, four workers died, sixty union leaders were arrested, and several thousand workers were fired. Strike leaders Demetrio Vallejo and Valentín Campa got eleven years in Lecumberri prison for the crime of "social dissolution," a wartime anti-sedition law that criminalized dissent.[30] In a country known as a haven for political refugees from Spain and Latin America, the jailing of union activists gave Mexico its first renowned political prisoners, labor martyrs who would symbolize the repressive face of the pax PRIísta for student activists of the 1960s or the neo-Zapatistas of the 1990s.

For many scholars, a complex movement that begs further research exemplifies the use of "state terror" to stifle democratic aspirations. Yet the railway strikes also illustrated just how tenuous labor co-optation might be. After all, the first strikes pressured the Labor Ministry to certify the election of Vallejo's dissident slate of reformers. A second walkout in early 1959 secured wage hikes and extended welfare benefits for workers on Mexico's principal railway lines. Authorities thus bent to popular pressures, despite opposition from a hostile press, the U.S. government, and charro leaders of other unions. Then came a third strike, meant to extend the collective contract to several small regional lines by paralyzing the nation's railways during the Easter holidays. Even Vallejo's own reformist allies opposed a strategic blunder that angered public opinion and exposed the railwaymen to the state's draconian crackdown.[31] However, as it had done before and did again, the state followed this *palo* with a lot more *pan*. Over the next five years, the state doubled its social insurance (IMSS) program to cover 20 percent of Mexican workers. Railway workers recall the years following the strike less for their coming estrangement from a bureaucratized union hierarchy than for the significant wage gains, medical benefits, and housing subsidies that improved their families' living standards.[32] By then, charro leaders in Mexico's mining, steel, and sugar industries also had forged a culture of rank-and-file quiescence as charrismo entered into its golden age of relative legitimacy and consent.

Rethinking Charrismo

By the time of the railway strikes, charrismo had evolved into a "cozy old system whereby union leaders cooperate with the government and in turn get cushy government jobs."[33] Cooperation meant limiting strikes and delivering the vote. It could entail the creation of "ghost unions" and the sale of "protection contracts." Labor racketeering satisfied legal niceties, but the period's most enduring legacy effectively stymied independent unions and delivered compliant labor to industrialists. Such employers—foreign and Mexican alike—profited immensely from charrismo. Nor were pseudo-unions limited to smaller enterprises, staffed by recent rural migrants who associated the revolution more with Pancho Villa than article 123. There was the auto industry, in the heart of Mexico City, where union leaders at Ford and General Motors were "company-paid overseers . . . [drawn] almost entirely from outside the workforce." Like the charros caricatured in the novels of Paco Ignacio Taibo II, these paternalistic and violent bosses drove luxury cars, drank with the managers, and collected dues but held few union assemblies.[34] But not all charros deserved the corrupt and thuggish reputation that so many earned. Some who were branded as traitors were honest unionists whose rivals opposed them for their political (PRIísta) loyalties or their preference for bargaining over confrontation. One suspects that General Cárdenas—who had insisted that workers choose "nationalism over class warfare"—took pride in union pragmatists who restrained militancy to promote economic development.[35] Union leaders also operated within the parameters of a post-Cardenista Mexico, where powerful business lobbies, U.S. foreign policymakers, and a red-baiting press all clamored for labor restraints. The state's legal controls and coercive arm further limited strategic options. So charrismo endured. Yet "despite its importance to the political life of Mexico," few labor historians have examined "the nature and characteristics" of a system that, "after being imposed by force created mechanisms which, in one form or another acquired a certain consensus among workers . . . or at least their passive acquiescence."[36]

No charro dominated his union longer than Napoleón Gómez Sada, the smelter worker who rose through the rough-and-tumble world of Monterrey labor politics to become the miners' national leader in 1960. He revised the statutory prohibition against union re-election, and remained in office the next forty years.[37] The union claimed big gains under his early watch. Wages and production bonuses grew steadily, as did the miners' political clout. Policymakers bolstered his nationalist credentials further when the state "Mexicanized" mining, developing new sites and acquiring old enclaves like Cananea copper. Nationalizing this "cradle of the revolution" was a union goal since the 1930s. Mexico's industrialization spurred heavy investments in both mining—where employment soared from 60,000 to 150,000 (1960–77)—and steel, whose production doubled each *sexenio* from 1940 to 1970. Industrial expansion produced union jobs and unprecedented levels of occupational security and mobility.[38] Gómez Sada could thus boast sincerely of "defending my hard-working comrades, their jobs, and the nation, so that we don't become victims of indiscriminate plunder by foreign capital."[39] Their *corridos* and history through oral interviews suggest that workers shared his ideals of economic nationalism. The fact that Gómez walked with a pronounced limp, the result of a smelter accident that killed two workmates, further bolstered his macho reputation among workers who took pride in the dangers they encountered in Mexico's mines and mills.[40]

Union propaganda commemorated the miners' radical history of struggle, from Guanajuato in 1810, where "the fire of revolutionary justice emerged from the mines," to Cananea, where the 1906 copper strike "set the labor movement in motion." But union leaders also cautioned the ranks that, "a responsible working class, [is] one that fights for its rights, but also contributes to national progress."[41] That discourse reflected a marked decline in militancy. Strikes were rarely authorized after 1950, and that restraint led to charges of betrayal. Salvador Castañeda, who led a Monterrey steel local in the 1950s, later acknowledged that "those of us chosen to lead the union in those years were called *charros* by the people that opposed us, and *charro* in our language means servile, being the company's errand boy." The leaders were so labeled for practicing "honorable" and "disciplined unionism." Come each contract revision, they studied production, costs, and earnings, and "the union never asked for a wage increase that was not justified by the profits." Its early years of confrontation, and the collective contracts that resulted, locked in benefits and transformed workplace relations. Charrismo did not turn back the clock. Rather, as a review of collective contracts at Fundidora Steel illustrates, biannual negotiations improved pension plans, accident compensation rates, and production bonuses. Shop-floor delegates defended work rules related to job security, promotions, grievance procedures, and occupational safety standards. They also upheld "contractual vices" that employers abhorred, such as seniority rights, limits on subcontracting, and a controversial "admission clause" that reserved new or vacated jobs for union nominees.[42]

Union hiring certainly underpinned corrupt charrismo, as in the oil workers' union, where charros sold part-time jobs to enrich themselves, weave webs of dependency, and augment union funds. The practice also generated resentment from local job seekers when unions transferred skilled members to fill positions in newly opened mines, refineries, or sugar mills.[43] But union statutes reserved full-time posts for sons, brothers, or fellow unionists. For example, Miners Local 67, in Monterrey, reserved 75 percent of vacancies for steel workers' sons or brothers. Nominating rights were earned by seniority. The rest went to activists blacklisted by nonunion employers or to workers laid off from other union plants. There were many jobs to fill. In Monterrey, the number of steel and smelter workers climbed from seven thousand (1946) to fifteen thousand (1970), meaning that around fifty thousand *regiomontanos* resided in unionized miners' households. Union hiring sustained tight-knit occupational communities by transferring high-paying jobs from father to son. The admission clause also protected families from discriminatory hiring policies that kept children from steel worker households or "radical PEMEX families" out of nonunion plants.[44] While charrismo established a degree of political co-optation and labor control, rank-and-file workers retained militant reputations that dogged their families throughout the twentieth century.

Meanwhile, as labor forces grew in mining and steel, charro leaders effectively negotiated the ongoing expansion of benefits. Well before the state launched its worker housing program (INFONAVIT, 1972), miners' locals secured new residential tracts in Monterrey, a city beset by chronic housing shortages. In Cananea and Nueva Rosita, the union negotiated the sale of company housing directly to mine workers. The advent of IMSS met initial opposition from workers who already enjoyed health and pension benefits. But union leaders pressured employers to cover rank-and-file contributions (3 percent of earnings) and, in Monterrey, the miners' influential locals lobbied IMSS to construct a specialized clinic for workers confronting occupational hazards unique to metallurgical plants.[45] Union-run cooperative stores, which supplied thousands of families with meat, work boots, or appliances, received tax exemptions from the state and subsidies from employers. Monterrey's Cooperativa Acero claimed prices 30 percent below local retail levels. Blue-collar families thus experienced an evolution of consumption patterns from the later 1940s (beer, shoes, radios) to the mid-1960s, when union households could spend greater earnings on automobiles, appliances (gas stoves, blenders, TVs), and their children's education.[46] Miners' locals also administered savings and loan programs, operated bus companies and funeral homes, and negotiated the companies' financing of everything from sports to technical training to schools for their children. Of course, other employers in Mexico, from Monterrey's big nonunion brewing, glass, and cement firms to the auto plants of Mexico City, offered labor similar perks. But for mine and metal workers, benefits once bestowed as "privileges" had become contractual "rights" secured by the union. Indeed the Monterrey Group's renowned system of company paternalism, designed after the revolution to stem unionization, grew in rhythm with the gains in wages and benefits secured by the city's miners' locals.[47]

Charro leaders proved equally effective—and more influential—beyond urban centers like Monterrey. Their quotas of power ensured labor the political representation needed "to defend the interests of the union and the Mexican working class," as the oil workers claimed. The PRI allocated these posts of "popular representation" to unions based on their respective weight in a given state or municipality.[48] The quotas thus dealt political appointments to oil union charros in Gulf Coast states and to the sugar workers' union in Jalisco. By 1968, the miners boasted three federal deputies, eight state congressmen, ten mayors, and eighty city council members. Napoleón Gómez Sada served twice in the federal senate. On the one hand, given the limits to congressional power, such appointments merely offered a "symbolic confirmation of labor's inclusion in Mexico's governing coalition."[49] Political appointments rewarded a charro with additional salary, local status, and access to patronage, explaining why dissidents stigmatized them "as politicians and job seekers rather than dedicated trade union members."[50] But, on the other hand, charros proved effective at the municipal level, in industrial enclaves where political office became a union monopoly.

Here is where effective charros—flush with union funds and privileged access to state patronage—could deliver the goods. None did so more exceptionally than the oil workers, whose fantastically rich Local 1 became an autonomous political machine, doling out jobs, financing schools, and distributing charity throughout the central Gulf Coast region.[51] In the miners' case, locals in single-company towns dominated city halls across the north, from the mining communities of Sonora to the steel city of Monclova. Under union watch, the older mineral enclaves experienced a process of "urban emancipation" as foreign companies transferred ownership of basic infrastructure (buildings, streets, schools) and control of city services to union-run municipalities. The charro leadership imposed in 1950 mobilized their influence to pave streets, build parks, and add street lights, securing both funding and construction equipment from employers. The process forged a direct clientelistic link between union and community. But leaders also defended other constitutional and contractual rights, from maintaining the article 123 schools to the provisioning of free water and electric power to workers' homes.[52] "Urban emancipation" built on a history of paternalism and union struggle in these classic mining enclaves. But in the new mining towns developed through the Mexicanization program, workers credited Napoleón Gómez himself for the modern housing, sports facilities, and medical clinics that arrived to their communities.[53] It was these new locals, staffed by Gómez's cronies and more dependent on Mexico City's patronage, that became the legitimizing foundation of charro rule. As one dissident Monterrey steel worker recalled, Gómez's dominance built upon his "iron control" over dozens of small locals whose "interests were advanced due only to Napoleón's influence."[54] From the 1950s onward, union leadership brought its rewards, as evinced by the intra-union struggles among rival charro *grupos*. Their capacity to dispense patronage—city jobs, loans, and licenses—"permitted the charros to broaden their political clientele."[55]

The advent of *charrismo* concluded struggles for power between leftists and pro-government leaders in Mexico City. But if the miners' union offers a representative case, it did little to diminish the battles for supremacy within industrial union locals. Out in the provinces, the internal democracy for which the union was once renowned survived, albeit in a fashion that mirrored Mexico's own system of one-party rule. The union locals held regular elections and enforced the principle of no re-election, but union posts alternated between competing charro groups. Dissidents called this system by which rival PRI factions alternated in power "charrismo disguised as democracy." Their own resistance mainly expressed itself in union assemblies, where they took leaders to task for abuses of power that ranged from mismanaging union cooperatives to "tampering with politics and forgetting about the workers' problems." From their perspective, it was their rivals' ongoing competition for the "quotas of power" and the "booty" they skimmed from the cooperative that divided their locals. From Monterrey to Cananea, leftists regularly put forth their own slates during union elections. Their opponents labeled them "divisionists." But charros rarely silenced the reformers "because that way they could claim that we had democracy in the union." Napoleón Gómez even welcomed the dissent, boasting of "the vast range of ideologies . . . from moderation to radicalism within our union locals." So the dissidents persisted, struggling as much against charrismo as rank-and-file passivity.[56] Indeed, charro leaders endured no meaningful challenges for almost thirty years, until mounting workplace grievances fuelled a rank-and-file movement to depose Napoleón and democratize the union. In the meantime, a union's political influence brought tangible returns to blue-collar communities.

"We Began to Open Our Eyes"

Far from the rugged mining towns and gritty urban neighborhoods of the north, in the semitropical valleys south of Guadalajara, charro leaders of the sugar workers' union dispensed another form of patronage. Consistent with a region deep in Mexico's emigrant sending heartland, Jalisco's charros offered rank-and-file workers the right to migrate north each season as braceros. Few policies received more sustained criticism than the bracero program (1942–64), the bilateral accord through which the U.S. government issued 4.6 million guest-worker contracts to migrant farm workers. Its effects were particularly notable in west-central states like Jalisco, which received disproportionate shares of bracero quotas.[57] Mass migration posed an embarrassing dilemma for the postrevolutionary state. For its critics, the braceros became a source of shame, symbolic of a failed revolution and another reminder of Mexico's growing dependence on the United States. Policymakers countered that the money earned and skills learned would promote development in the countryside, where demographic pressures were mounting. Federal spending—on health, education, and infrastructure—now went to the cities, not small farmers. So scholars of rural development argue that "migration, not the ejido, proved to be Mexico's 'way out' of its development crisis . . . For the government, encouraging migration meant rural peace through American agriculture." Noting the disproportionate share of braceros from the west-central strongholds of Cristeros and Sinarquistas, they conclude that migration offered an escape valve against political discontent, unemployment, or social service demands.[58]

Not surprisingly, Mexican officials never discussed the bracero program in terms of the safety-valve thesis. While rural peace did prevail in the states that sent the most workers north, neither suspicion nor outcome proves intentionality. To the extent that the bracero program served political ends, it did so by offering the prized contracts to friends of the PRI as it extended its nationwide political machine. Despite the controversy it generated, no policy proved more popular among urban workers and the rural poor. Never in the program's history was there a shortage of aspiring braceros. That demand underpinned a thriving black market in bracero permits, which quickly became a form of patronage that state party bosses and small-town mayors often rewarded or sold to their constituents. But the bracero program functioned differently in the sugar-producing valleys of Jalisco.

By the late 1930s, the state's mill workers had succeeded in their own hard-fought battle for union recognition. In a region where low-intensity political violence was endemic, organizing drives and then inter-union battles proved fatal. As in the other fractious industrial unions, radicals were purged in the 1940s. State policy also snared the sugar workers in the same developmental trap as the railwaymen. That is, just as state-imposed restraints on railroad wages helped to subsidize freight costs, so too did price ceilings on sugar limit earnings for mill workers, all to satisfy urban demand in one of the world's greatest sugar-consuming nations.[59] Like other members of Mexico's big industrial unions, the mill workers conceded wage restrictions but secured significant benefits from the 1940s onward: eight-hour days, health benefits, company housing, and schools for their children. Their union locals also dominated municipal politics (and some still do). The leader of the sugar worker union during these years was "Chema" Martínez, a mechanic from Jalisco's Tamazula mill. After organizing Local 80 in 1941, Martínez became a state congressional deputy and the leader of the Jalisco Workers Federation (1943–46). By the mid-1950s, when the bracero program reached its apogee, he was elected secretary general of the national union. Under his watch, the wide swatch of sugar-growing municipalities south of Guadalajara received more bracero contracts per capita than any region in the state, despite official prohibitions on the contracting of industrial workers.[60]

That favoritism became evident in 1945. Men from Jalisco were still prohibited from migrating north as braceros by a governor fearful of labor shortages. So at the union's behest, the federal Labor Department intervened to secure the governor's approval to contract sugar workers. Union leaders wrote to the governor, informing him that mills then were inactive for the season and that "the departure of these compañeros will in no way harm the state's economy." The prime bracero contracting months of May through October coincided perfectly with the sugar industry's *tiempo muerto*, the down season when the region's mills laid off all but small crews of maintenance men. The governor approved and more than three thousand mill workers and truck drivers from nine locals were contracted in Guadalajara. Whatever one's rank in the occupational hierarchy, nearly all departed as braceros, for pay rates in the fields of California far surpassed what the relatively high-paid mill workers earned. So it was that mill workers became braceros, and privileged ones at that. In contrast to most braceros from Jalisco, they never paid for a permit, and their union chartered buses to transport them to the contracting center in Sonora, alleviating another financial burden that most hard-pressed families shouldered themselves. So while the state's critics frequently asserted the safety-valve thesis during the 1950s and 1960s, it seems that in fact the program sought to achieve distinct political ends: rewarding the PRI's allies in the labor movement.

The "reward" consisted of months of hard work in the fields of the American southwest, time once spent idly during sugar's "dead season." But the real payoff came in the dollars earned (which spiked with each peso devaluation), the money saved, and the lessons learned. Braceros returned home with radios, bicycles, sewing machines, and tools, items often unattainable for semirural Mexicans of their class. Some invested in cargo trucks. Others purchased land and became cane farmers themselves. There were some, of course, for whom seasonal migration was simply a youthful adventure, who squandered their earnings in the cantinas, brothels, and gambling halls that surrounded farm labor camps. Others skipped their contracts, migrated to American cities, and gave up the mill life for good. Whatever the individual outcome, emigration and return migration brought positive material change to the mill towns of Jalisco. The experience produced new cultural outlooks as well, much as policymakers intended. Nearly all sugar workers, living in urban outposts in the shadows of the mills, invested their savings in home renovation, inspired by living conditions they observed up north. "We began to open our eyes a little more" recalled Manolo Zavala, a former mill worker from Tala who labored and traveled through California's Central Valley. "We all wanted concrete houses after we saw how they lived up there." "That is what *cultura* is," added his colleague, "having a bathroom, a real roof, and a tile floor." "It was a real learning experience," concluded a worker from nearby Ameca, a mill town that "escaped from its stagnation" because of the money and insights that return migrants brought home.[61]

Sugar mill workers in Jalisco saw considerable improvements in their lives with unionization in the early 1940s. In a region and industry with no union tradition, they perhaps felt less remorse than the mine or steel workers of the north over the sudden emergence of charrismo. Mill work continued to sustain their families and communities, but the considerable savings earned through bracero stints brought measurable improvements to the material lives and opened their eyes to a world beyond the rural mill towns. The benefits they gained from that experience, and the lessons it taught to their children, helped to institutionalize the culture of migration for which western Mexico is so renowned today.

Conclusion and Postscript

The last braceros returned to Mexico when the 1964 harvest concluded. More than twenty years had passed since the bilateral program of state-sanctioned migration began. A generation later, migrants returned to a nation living through a "Mexican miracle" of economic dynamism and political stability. Urban Mexico, with its industrial jobs, was therefore exerting a greater pull on rural migrants than the promise of El Norte. The newcomers settled into sprawling shantytowns and industrial suburbs, where PRI operatives astutely extended social services to further expand the party's political machine beyond its base of industrial workers, peasant leagues, and public-sector unions. Those migrants who secured jobs in booming industries like steel or automobiles discovered that the golden age of charrismo was starting to unravel by the mid-1970s. How the mechanics of that era of consensus operated across Mexico's industrial landscape begs for further study. But for three decades, a system demonized by dissident workers and labor scholars alike delivered considerable benefits to rank-and-file workers. Therefore they forsook their unions' militant traditions and accommodated themselves to a style of labor relations that brought greater job security and material progress than any generation of Mexican workers experienced before or since.

The longer it endured, it seems, the more venal and corrupt charrismo became. In the early 1970s, renewed efforts to modernize plants and speed up production sparked a worker insurgency of veteran dissidents and militant youngsters. The "new unionism" movement erupted in industries both old (railways, electric power) and new (automobiles, electronics). It illustrated the historic fragility of labor control. The struggle elicited the greatest response from Mexico's rank-and-file mining and steel workers. Angered by a sharp spike in fatal accidents—169 dead in a Coahuila mine blast, 17 at Monterrey's Fundidora Steel—reformers and militants capitalized on the miners' tradition of internal democracy to oust charro leaders from locals across the north. Arguing of Napoleón Gómez that "a good leader has become a union traitor," newly elected activists pledged to "wipe out charrismo once and for all."[62] They almost succeeded. Yet at the miners' national convention in 1978, federal labor officials deployed their legal authority to decertify union dissidents and renew Gómez's hold on the reins of charro rule.

Napoleón Gómez thus guided the miners' union through the coming two decades of boom, bust, and the historic fall of the PRI. Consistent with its *pan y palo* approach, Mexico's Labor Ministry followed the quelling of union dissent with record wage hikes and the hiring of thousands of part-time workers into full-time jobs. Then came the debt crisis and the state's neoliberal decision to downsize and privatize the mines and mills. Loyal to the end, Gomez acquiesced to a policy that cost his union more than fifty thousand jobs and destabilized the communities that charrismo once so effectively served. No wonder that veteran unionists interviewed in the 1990s looked back with such nostalgia on a golden age of charrismo.[63] For by then, former steel workers from Monterrey and coal miners from Coahuila had joined the sons of Jalisco sugar workers as they headed north from Mexico once again.

Notes

1. Kan to State Department, August 4, 1950, NARG-59/812.00/8-450.

2. Luis Reygadas, *Proceso de trabajo y acción obrera: Historia sindical de los mineros de Nueva Rosita (1929–1979)* (Mexico City: Instituto Nacional de Antropología e Historia, 1988), 111. See also Victoria Novelo, "De huelgas, movilizaciones y otras acciones de los mineros del carbón de Coahuila," *Revista Mexicana de Sociología* 42, no. 4 (1980): 1355–77; Mario Gill, ed., *La huelga de Nueva Rosita* (Mexico City: MAPRI, 1959).

3. A local example of what Blancarte describes as broader church efforts "to temper workers' demands" (chapter 2, this volume).

4. Reygadas, *Proceso de trabajo*, 125; John Mraz, "Today, Tomorrow, and Always," in *Fragments of a Golden Age: The Politics of Culture in Mexico Since 1940*, ed. Gilbert M. Joseph, Anne Rubenstein, Eric Zolov, 116–58, 127–29 (Durham, NC: Duke University Press, 2001).

5. Hector Aguilar Camín and Lorenzo Meyer, *In the Shadow of the Mexican Revolution: Contemporary Mexican History, 1910–1989*, trans. by Luis Alberto Fierro (Austin: University of Texas Press, 1993), 184; Viviane Brachet-Márquez, *The Dynamics of Domination: State, Class, and Social Reform in Mexico, 1910–1990* (Pittsburgh: University of Pittsburgh Press, 1994), 8.

6. Alan Riding, *Distant Neighbors: A Portrait of the Mexicans* (New York: Vintage, 1984), 83–84.

7. Labor Minister Ramírez Vásquez in the *New York Times*, January 4, 1950.

8. The figure climbed to 15 percent by 1970. Kevin Middlebrook, *The Paradox of Revolution: Labor, the State, and Authoritarianism in Mexico* (Baltimore: Johns Hopkins University Press, 1995), 154.

9. Michael Snodgrass, *Deference and Defiance in Monterrey: Workers, Paternalism, and Revolution in Mexico, 1890–1950* (New York: Cambridge University Press, 2003); Alex Saragoza, *The Monterrey Elite and the Mexican State, 1890–1940* (Austin: University of Texas Press, 1988) suggests that labor "made no inroads" in the northern industrial capital.

10. Middlebrook, *The Paradox of Revolution*, 72–106.

11. Howard Wiarda, ed., *Authoritarianism and Corporatism in Latin America—Revisited* (Gainesville: University Press of Florida, 2004).

12. "Poor health," the labor minister proclaimed, "keeps the people's vitality and the individual's productivity at their low levels." Rosalina Estrada Urroz, *Del telar a la cadena: La condición obrera en Puebla, 1940–1976* (Puebla: Benemérita Universidad Autónoma de Puebla, 1997), 254; Michelle Dion, *Workers and Welfare: Comparative Institutional Change in Twentieth-Century Mexico* (Pittsburgh: University of Pittsburgh Press, 2010).

13. Estrada Urroz, *Del telar a la cadena*, 143–68; Valentín Campa, *Mi testimonio: Memorias de un comunista mexicano* (Mexico City: Cultura Popular, 1978).

14. Remittances trailed only tourism and mining as a source of foreign exchange, so bracero remittances helped stabilize the peso and offset the costs of foreign credit and capital goods imports.

15. Jorge Basurto, *Del avilacamachismo al Alemanismo (1940–1952)* (Mexico City: Siglo XXI, 1984), 97.

16. Middlebrook, *The Paradox of Revolution*, 135–46; Antonio Alonso, *El movimiento ferrocarrilero en Mexico, 1958–1959* (Mexico City: Era, 1972), 87–89.

17. Ian Roxborough, "Mexico," in *Latin America Between the Second World War and the Cold War, 1944–1948*, ed. Leslie Bethell and Ian Roxborough, 190–216 (Cambridge: Cambridge University Press, 1992), 213.

18. Middlebrook, *The Paradox of Revolution*, 135–40, 144–46.

19. Paul Gillingham, "Force and Consent in Mexican Provincial Politics: Guerrero and Veracruz, 1945–1953" (DPhil thesis, University of Oxford, 2005), 207.

20. Charles Bergquist, *Labor in Latin America: Comparative Essays on Chile, Argentina, Venezuela, and Colombia* (Palo Alto, CA: Stanford University Press, 1986), 4–5.

21. Thomas Klubbock, *Contested Communities: Class, Gender, and Politics in Chile's El Teniente Copper Mine, 1904–1951* (Durham, NC: Duke University Press, 1998), 272; Robert Zieger, *The CIO, 1935–1955* (Chapel Hill: University of North Carolina Press, 1995), 253–93.

22. Norman Caulfield, "Mexican State Development Policy and Labor Internationalism, 1945–1958," *International Review of Social History* 42, no. 1 (1997): 45–66 (quoted).

23. Gil, *La huelga de Nueva Rosita*; Campa, *Mi testimonio*, 246, 252–53.

24. Jeffrey Bortz and Marcos Aguila, "Earning a Living: A History of Real Wage Studies in Twentieth-Century Mexico," *Latin American Research Review* 41, no. 2 (June 2006): 112–38.

25. Isidro Morales, "The Consolidation and Expansion of PEMEX, 1947–1958," in *The Mexican Petroleum Industry in the Twentieth Century*, ed. Jonathan C. Brown and Alan Knight (Austin: University of Texas Press, 1992), 226–27; Reygadas, *Proceso de trabajo*, 168.

26. Estrada Urroz, *Del telar a la cadena*, 295–97.

27. Enrique Ochoa, *Feeding Mexico: The Political Uses of Food Since 1910* (Wilmington, DE: Scholarly Resources, 2000), 177–94; Marvin Alisky, "CONASUPO: A Mexican Agency Which Makes Low Income Workers Feel Their Government Cares," *Inter-American Economic Affairs* 27, no. 3 (winter 1973): 47–59.

28. Estrada, *Del telar a la cadena*, 251–72; Ana-Maria Wahl, "Economic development and social security in Mexico, 1945–1985," *International Journal of Comparative Sociology* 35, no. 1/2 (1994), 59–81; Irene Nicholson, *The X in Mexico: Growth Within Tradition* (New

York: Doubleday, 1966), 239–42. The IMSS still covered only 17 percent of the population in the mid-1960s, restricting these reforms to urban beneficiaries, but by the 1980s Mexico's was among the highest rates of coverage (65 percent) in Latin America, Wahl, "Economic development and social security in Mexico."

29. See interviews in Snodgrass, *Deference and Defiance*, 301–6.

30. Salvador Corro and José Revele, *La Quina: El lado oscuro del poder* (Mexico City: Planeta, 1989); Alonso, *El movimiento ferrocarrilero*.

31. Luciano Cedillo Vasquez, *De Juan Soldado a Juan Rielero* (Mexico City: Publicaciones Mexicanas, 1963), 88–92.

32. Dion, *Workers and Welfare*, 154; John Mraz, "Made on Rails in Mexico," *Jump Cut: A Review of Contemporary Media* 39 (June 1994): 113–21.

33. *Time*, April 13, 1959.

34. As late as the 1960s, the majority of Ford workers were unaware of their own union membership. Stephen Bachelor, "Miracle on Ice: Industrial Workers and the Promise of Americanization in Cold War Mexico," in *In from the Cold: Latin America's New Encounter with the Cold War*, ed. Gilbert M. Joseph and Daniela Spenser (Durham, NC: Duke University Press, 2008), 257–58; Paco Ignacio Taibo II, *Cosa Fácil* (1977), *Cuatro Manos* (1997).

35. Snodgrass, *Deference and Defiance*, 189, 307–8: Cárdenas's 1940 speech to CTM, quoted by Myrna I. Santiago, *The Ecology of Oil: Environment, Labor, and the Mexican Revolution, 1910–1938* (New York: Cambridge University Press, 2006), 335.

36. Reygadas, *Proceso de trabajo*, 12–13, 96.

37. Roderic Ai Camp, *Mexican Political Biographies, 1935–1993*, 3rd ed. (Austin: University of Texas Press, 1995), 291; Rossana Cassigoli, *Liderazgo sindical y cultura minera en Mexico: Napoleón Gómez Sada* (Mexico City: Porrua, 2004).

38. Raúl Delgado Wise and Rubén Del Pozo Mendoza, "Mexicanization, Privatization, and Large Mining Capital in Mexico," *Latin American Perspectives* 32, no. 4: 70–73; Michael Snodgrass, "'New Rules for the Unions': Mexico's Steel Workers Confront Privatization and the Neoliberal Challenge," *Labor: Working-Class History of the Americas* 4 (fall 2007): 81–103.

39. "Don Napoleón Gómez Sada: Una vida al servicio de los trabajadores mineros mexicanos," *Boletín del Sindicato Minero Mexicano*, December 29, 2009.

40. Snodgrass, *Deference and Defiance*, 275–80.

41. "Don Napoleón Gómez Sada."

42. Castañeda interviews in Snodgrass, *Deference and Defiance*, 178–90, 265–81; collective contracts of Local 67 in Archivo Histórico Fundidora Monterrey (AHFM), Monterrey, Mexico; Reygadas, *Proceso de trabajo*, 87–88; Juan Luis Sariego, *Enclaves y minerales en el Norte de México: Historia social de los mineros de Cananea y Nueva Rosita, 1900–1970* (Mexico City: Ediciones de la casa chata 26, 1988), 373–89.

43. The policy explains why sugar mills in Morelos hired out-of-state workers from Tamaulipas or Veracruz rather than local farmers' sons, as seen in McCormick's chapter 8 in this volume.

44. Cases of blacklisting in Snodgrass, *Deference and Defiance*, 273–74, 293.

45. Sariego, *Enclaves y Minerales*; AHFM: *Informe*, March 14, 1945; Juan Manuel Elizondo, *De historia y política* (Monterrey: UANL, 2000), 33–34.

46. Ochoa, *Feeding Mexico*, 85; Estrada Urroz, *Del telar a la cadena*, 303–17.

47. Bachelor, "Miracle on Ice"; Snodgrass, *Deference and Defiance*, 254–55.

48. Guadalupe Pacheco Mendez, "Los sectores del PRI en las elecciones de 1988," *Mexican Studies/Estudios Mexicanos* 7, no. 2; oil union statutes in V. Novelo, "Las fuentes de poder de la dirigencia sindical en Pemex," *El Cotidiano* 28 (March–April 1989).

49. Middlebrook, *The Paradox of Revolution*, 102.

50. Mexico City Embassy to State Department, August 28–29, 1958, in *Foreign Relations of the United States, 1958–1960: American Republics, Vol. V (1958–1960)*, ed. John P. Glennon (Washington, DC: United States Government Printing Office, 1991), 840–42.

51. Fernando Arce Gaxiola, "El caciquismo obrero: Joaquín Hernández Galicia en Ciudad Madero," in *Partido Revolucionario Institucional, 1946–2000: Ascenso y caída del partido hegemónico* (Mexico City: Siglo XXI, 2006), 94–97.

52. Sariego, *Enclaves y minerales*, 330–50.

53. Archivo General de la Nación: Dirección General de Investigaciones Políticas y Sociales (AGN/DGIPS), Sindicatos, 1525C/14, December 1980; *Excélsior*, May 21, 1981.

54. Aurelio Arenas interview in Sandra Arenal, *Fundidora: Diez años después* (Monterrey: UANL, 1996), 180–81.

55. Reygadas, *Proceso de trabajo*, 141–42.

56. AGN/DGIPS, Sindicatos, 1524A/3, 1524B/6; interviews with Manuel Domínguez, Rafael Duéñez, and Jesús Medellín in Arenal, *Fundidora*, 35–37, 113–17, 136–38.

57. For the program's implementation in Jalisco see Michael Snodgrass, "Patronage and Progress: The Bracero Program from the Perspective of Mexico," in *Workers Across the Americas: The Transnational Turn in Labor History*, ed. Leon Fink, 245–66 (New York: Oxford University Press, 2011).

58. James Sandos and Harry Cross, *Across the Border: Rural Development in Mexico and Recent Migration to the United States* (Berkeley, CA: Institute of Governmental Studies, 1981), 35, 42–43.

59. Susan Kaufman Purcell, "Business-Government Relations in Mexico: The Case of the Sugar Industry," *Comparative Politics* 13, no. 2 (January 1981): 211–33.

60. Camp, *Mexican Political Biographies*, 448; contracting figures in Archivo Histórico de Jalisco-Gobernación, 1951 (caja 3), 1952 (caja 17), 1958 (caja 7).

61. Author's interviews with Manolo Zavala Salazar, June 28, 2007, Tala, Jalisco; Francisco Gónzalez Núñez, May 16, 2007, Ameca, Jalisco; Javier Salazar Areola, May 14, 2007, Ameca, Jalisco.

62. AGN/DGIPS, Información de estados, Nuevo León, July–November 1978, 1203A.

63. Snodgrass, "'New Rules for the Unions.'"

CHAPTER 8 | *Gladys McCormick*

THE FORGOTTEN JARAMILLO

Building a Social Base of Support for Authoritarianism in Rural Mexico

The figure of Rubén Jaramillo dominates the story of peasant activism in midcentury Mexico. Not only did he help found Zacatepec, a giant sugar cooperative in southern Morelos, he also went on to run for governor and to spearhead two armed risings against the state government. The fact that this story ends in tragedy—his 1962 assassination, alongside most of his family—makes it all the more compelling.[1] Morelos is, after all, the heartland of the agrarian revolution, witness to another such betrayal in 1919: the assassination of Emiliano Zapata. Yet together with a legacy of autonomous communal struggle, the region also housed a critical base of support for the PRI. The majority of rural peoples there voted for the PRI, depended on the political order for their livelihoods, and rallied on its behalf in moments of crisis. To create this social base, the postrevolutionary regime implemented a capitalist industrial development model that frustrated peasant communities and turned them into a subordinated and supportive group.[2]

This contradiction between support and resistance is personified in the biographies of Rubén and his three brothers. Rubén's two younger brothers, Reyes and Porfirio, joined him in his struggles against the political order; Porfirio went on to organize peasants at the Atencingo cooperative in neighboring Puebla.[3] But Antonio, the eldest, never took up arms against the state and worked diligently for the Zacatepec cooperative. He nevertheless endured constant harassment from government officials. As Antonio's son recalls, "he was always being threatened . . . they watched his every move in case Rubén contacted him."[4] Antonio buried the remains of Porfirio after his assassination in 1955, and subsequently those of Rubén,

Rubén's wife, and his three stepsons. Though Antonio is remembered as the one brother who never engaged in political action, in reality he led protests in the late 1940s against corrupt and violent general managers. That Antonio's actions during these years have been forgotten reflects both the more compelling stories of his younger brothers and the fact that Antonio went on to collaborate with the governing order in the 1950s.

To explore this contradiction and to understand why so many supported the PRI, this chapter focuses on the Jaramillo brothers and analyzes two distinct moments of mobilization in Zacatepec: 1942–43 and 1947–48. Rubén and Porfirio figured prominently in the first mobilization. The second brings into play lesser-known peasant leaders, including Antonio, who remained around Zacatepec once Rubén and Porfirio left to pursue other avenues of political action. Studying these two moments allows us to take a capacious view of local forms of negotiation and adaptation as an authoritarian state took shape and shows how peasant activism evolved in response to deliberate neglect, a modicum of concessions, clientelism, and repression. We see the limits of older languages and practices of radicalism, whether of armed revolution or Cardenista populism. We see the routinization of forms of protest in moments of peace, including writing to government officials or joining caravans to Mexico City to try and personally meet them. We also see peasant leaders rejecting radical options and adamantly attempting to stay within legal channels while pressing their demands. And we see those channels narrowing across the 1940s, forcing peasant leaders to opt for more creative strategies or, as became commonplace in the 1950s, to simply give up.

The failures and limited successes that peasants experienced in these two mobilizations discouraged them from subsequent radicalism. After the first they learned that they risked being stripped of cooperative membership, threatening their families' already tenuous livelihoods. The second underlined the ease with which cooperative officials resorted to repression. Rural peoples in southern Morelos thus became acutely aware of the heavy costs exacted for speaking out—costs that became unbearable as violence grew more prominent in the 1950s. Their reluctance was all the more apparent with the resurgence of popular mobilization in urban and rural settings. While rural peoples in Nayarit, Sonora, and Sinaloa mobilized after 1958, members of Zacatepec's peasant cooperative remained decidedly quiet. Patronage and co-option, on the one hand, and repression and violence, on the other, had acted in tandem to solidify a base of support for the emerging political order. The apparent backing of some Morelos peasants for the state during its crisis in the late 1950s came after two decades of enduring disappointment, increasing dependence on clientelism, and suffering repression for speaking out.

Tanalís Padilla's recent work on Rubén Jaramillo focuses on the ideology and praxis of the dissidents who went into the mountains. My work explores the ideology and praxis of those who stayed behind and worked with mill, party, and government. This allows us to consider how three phenomena—the routinization of protest and repression; patronage and co-option; and the twin role of memory in structuring political action then and the representations of that action now—nurtured a social base of support for authoritarian rule. Finally, weighing the limits of peasant autonomy across the period reveals the origins of state power and the learning process by which both peasants and state actors discerned the limits of each other's power and tolerance, establishing in the process the *reglas no escritas* that structured state/society relations in the coming decades.

Production, Protest, and Disenchantment

Between 1934 and 1940, President Lázaro Cárdenas inaugurated a range of collective enterprises across Mexico's countryside. Not only did he seek to modernize long-neglected rural areas but he also involved many of the two-thirds of Mexicans then residing in the countryside in the project of state formation. The president intended these enterprises to strengthen the communal land tenure system of *ejidos* and channel popular mobilizations into a new, more enlightened and inclusive postrevolutionary political economy. Collective agricultural ventures ranged from cotton in the Laguna, henequen in Yucatán, to, most notably, large sugar cooperatives in Veracruz, Tamaulipas, Puebla, Sinaloa, and Morelos. In contrast to crops such as coffee, which afforded producers some autonomy, sugar production tied growers and mill workers, along with their families, into joint and heavily dependent ventures to modernize the countryside under the close supervision of government officials.[5] Sugar production took up the largest share of the more than nine hundred cooperatives that Cárdenas created while in office, making sugar one of the nation's most important agricultural crops by the 1950s.[6] By the mid-twentieth century, Mexico had become one of the largest producers (and consumers) of sugar in the western hemisphere, surpassed only by Brazil and Cuba.[7]

Among the cooperatives set up by Cárdenas, the Emiliano Zapata Sugar Production Cooperative of Peasants and Workers in Zacatepec, Morelos, was one of the biggest. Founded in 1938, Zacatepec quickly became the single largest employer in Morelos, with a budget double that of the state's government.[8] The millions of pesos financing this budget came from the sale of sugar to the government's clearinghouse for national distribution and, to a lesser extent, from federal subsidies. Not only did the cooperative's budget cover the salaries of hundreds of white- and blue-collar workers operating its offices and sugar mill, it also financed local hospitals, schools, a technical college, roadways, and other regional development projects. The cooperative's main expenditure, however, was buying the sugar cane delivered to its doors by thousands of peasants across the region. The cooperative produced approximately twenty-one thousand tons of sugar in 1938–39; by the early 1950s this had increased to more than sixty thousand tons a year.[9] The production of this much sugar involved enormous effort from the surrounding communities. By the late 1940s fifty-six ejidos from across Morelos, including the towns of Zapata and Jaramillo, delivered sugar cane to the Zacatepec mill.

The sheer size of Zacatepec's membership roster—approximately four thousand peasants, one thousand industrial workers, and several hundred white-collar workers, along with their respective families—conveys the vision government planners had when building the large-scale sugar production cooperative to develop a region devastated during the revolution. On the surface, the fact that both peasants and workers were equally invested in the cooperative suggested they would work together for their collective well-being. Yet tense relations between the two groups quickly disabused them of any hope of disinterested collaboration. Peasant disillusionment arose in large part from the state's adoption of a two-pronged approach to negotiation with the cooperative's members. The sugar mill's workers held a privileged position inside the cooperative, whereas those who labored in the fields producing sugar cane to sell to the cooperative found their concerns consistently ignored. While the government pushed peasants into organizations that tended to be chaotic, politically compromised, and ineffectual, such as the Confederación Nacional Campesina (CNC), the workers' unions of the Confederación de Trabajadores de México (CTM) accrued substantial benefits for their members. Government officials had used this strategy of divide and rule among popular groups for several years by the time it was implemented in Zacatepec.[10] Although peasant and worker members of the cooperative resisted this strategy early on, its long track record assured it would eventually weaken independent popular mobilizations.

The first step in implementing this strategy was to create a two-tier system, both politically and economically, among cooperative members. By permitting the Sindicato de Trabajadores de la Industria Azucarera, the branch of the CTM representing sugar industry workers, to gain a foothold inside the cooperative, officials established a double standard. Workers were able to forward their demands through the effective, politically sanctioned body of the union's Section 72. Peasants, on the other hand, were left with the often ineffectual CNC, searching for different ways to elicit a response from inattentive government officials.[11] After initially organizing themselves against the CTM and fighting for the removal of Section 72, a strategy they quickly realized was fruitless, peasant leaders sought an alliance with the increasingly powerful union.[12] Section 72 had proven its mettle by repeatedly challenging cooperative authorities and established a precedent for effectively representing its constituents—a representation peasants hoped would extend to them. Rubén Jaramillo, one of the principal peasant leaders, had the advantage of having two close allies among the workers active in Section 72: his younger brother, Porfirio, and Mónico Rodríguez, an acknowledged supporter of worker-peasant alliances. In 1942 together they began to support direct action methods, including calls for a general strike.

The appeal of such tactics only increased when, on February 11, 1942, President Avila Camacho issued the first of his two sugar cane decrees.[13] Spurred by the fear of wartime food shortages, this sought to ensure that Mexico's sugar mills could provide a reliable and plentiful source of domestic sugar. It centralized control of cane cultivation in the hands of the cooperative's general manager by giving him power over credit disbursement and access to irrigation. The decree ordered peasant cooperative members to exclusively grow sugar cane and penalized the cultivation of other plants, including those necessary for subsistence and crop rotation. Peasants interpreted this as betrayal, viewing the decree as antithetical to Avila Camacho's democratic rhetoric. Not only did the decree limit peasants' autonomy, it also tied their livelihoods to the general manager and provided no recourse for peasants to contest his power. That Avila Camacho issued the decree and continued to ignore peasants' calls to raise the price of sugar cane proved their disenfranchisement in modern Mexico. It became obvious to Rubén Jaramillo and other peasant leaders that writing to the president, as they had in the weeks leading up to the announcement of the decree, was futile.[14]

In April 1942, two months after the sugar cane decree went into effect, Zacatepec peasants and workers responded by organizing a joint strike. Peasants mobilized with the mounting evidence that the government and the cooperative's general manager systematically marginalized their concerns. In stark contrast, workers struck for more concrete reasons. Foremost among them, the general manager refused to grant them the 15 percent pay raise the president ordered for all sugar industry workers in January 1942 to stave off threats of a national strike.[15] Not only was this going to be the first large-scale strike by cooperative members, it also marked the first test of the new worker-peasant alliance. With the threat of a strike on the table, Zacatepec workers and peasants compiled a list of thirty-five demands they sent to Severino Carrera Peña, the cooperative's general manager, on April 8, 1942.[16] The order of the demands revealed the hierarchy of workers' and peasants' interests. The first fourteen demands dealt primarily with workers' concerns, such as reinstating the twenty-six workers fired in April for protesting against the manager. The fifteenth demand finally addressed peasants' issues, demanding increased and timely payment for sugar cane as well as transparent representation on the cooperative's governing bodies. Of the thirty-five demands, seven addressed peasants' issues, four dealt with joint concerns, and the remaining twenty-seven reflected workers' demands.

Since the general manager refused to negotiate with the strikers, some four thousand workers and peasants halted production at Zacatepec. Workers shut down the refinery's machines and peasants refused to cut or deliver cane. The general manager, backed by the Department of the Economy, immediately ordered all the strikers suspended. In a strategy employed in other sugar-growing regions (and in other strategic industries, such as oil and railroad), government officials sent in soldiers from the nearby headquarters of the twenty-fourth military zone to surround the sugar mill and, by the following morning, take over the refinery.[17] Along with arresting six strike leaders (and releasing them three days later), soldiers harassed peasants to resume delivering sugar cane to the mill and workers to return to their posts.[18] Such swift retaliation made it clear to the strikers that neither government officials nor the general manager was willing to negotiate: as one of the arrested put it, "[the] government sent soldiers, sent the army, to force peasants to allow their sugar cane to be cut without any chance of dialoguing."[19] In explaining the government's actions, Francisco Javier Gaxiola, the Secretary of Economy, argued that the strikers' actions were illegal and deserved to be repressed.[20]

Whatever they thought before the strike, the peasants of Zacatepec now understood that national leaders would not intervene on their behalf or personally side with them; the era of Cárdenas and his empowering of rural peoples was over. While Cárdenas named his brother-in-law, Antonio Solórzano, as the cooperative's first general manager to ensure the success of the enterprise and his close oversight, subsequent presidents used their ability to designate the general manager to reward political supporters.[21] Peasants' feelings of betrayal are evident in a letter Rubén Jaramillo sent to Avila Camacho on June 22, 1942, the same day he was expelled from the cooperative.[22] For the first time, Jaramillo linked federal officials with the general manager and labeled them "compromised" leaders. He called their actions in Zacatepec "criminal" and asked the president to form a tribunal to look into their "shameful maneuvers" inside the cooperative. Such a statement suggests nostalgia for the time of Cárdenas, when peasants felt political leaders cared about the cooperative and genuinely wanted to improve the lives of rural peoples. The result of the first strike at Zacatepec brought with it an additional lesson: officials exacted a high price for collaboration between workers and peasants. If it was the government's intent to use its violent response to teach this lesson, it worked. The general manager stripped Rubén Jaramillo and twenty-six other leaders of membership in the cooperative, effectively ending Jaramillo's livelihood as a *cañero*; a tactic of punitive firing also employed in the industrial disputes explored by Michael Snodgrass in chapter 7. This, in combination with military repression, ended the worker-peasant alliance.[23] With their leaders gone and the CNC still ineffective, peasants could not organize as a constituency inside a clientelistic system built on corporate bodies.

Even though Rubén Jaramillo was no longer a member of the cooperative, government officials feared his ability to mobilize the area's rural peoples and continued to dissuade him from organizing against them. Their intimidation became increasingly violent as the peasant leader resisted attempts to bribe him into submission, first by the cooperative's general manager and later by government officials. By February 1943, according to Jaramillo, judicial police officers had tried three times to capture and kill him. Jaramillo, along with some of his supporters, fled to the nearby mountains to escape government authorities. Over the next months, they had several skirmishes with judicial police and gunmen hired by the cooperative's general manager. On June 13, 1944, Rubén Jaramillo and his supporters met with President Avila Camacho in Mexico City to discuss their reasons for taking up arms. In return for laying down weapons, the president promised the Jaramillistas they would not be prosecuted for taking up arms and offered Rubén a job as an administrator of a small market in Mexico City. He accepted.[24]

With the first Jaramillista revolt over, the peasant leader joined the ranks of bureaucrats the government employed in the rapidly expanding capital city.[25] Perhaps this was a pragmatic decision from a peasant leader weary of hiding in the mountains, fearing for his life. He had tried to articulate effectively a broader popular movement by appealing to rural communities and looking for allies among workers and inside the government. Instead of finding interlocutors, as he had under Cárdenas, Jaramillo now dealt with government officials who ignored his demands and readily resorted to violence. His acceptance of the official job thus signaled the government's success at frustrating a popular mobilization that could have posed a serious threat to its power. That Rubén Jaramillo now lived in the city, far away from his base in southern Morelos, signaled the extent of the government's victory: it had taken and tamed—albeit temporarily—the purported heir of Emiliano Zapata.

Development, Clientelism, and Co-option in the Making of a Social Base

To understand why this first example of peasant activism fizzled out, especially so soon after thousands engaged in a general strike, it is necessary to return to the Zacatepec cooperative to see what was taking place while Jaramillo led his armed uprising. After the general manager defeated the strikers, the collaboration between peasants and workers fell apart. Porfirio Jaramillo, Mónico Rodríguez, and several others who originally supported the alliance between workers and peasants continued to be active in Section 72 during 1943.[26] However, they did so under difficult conditions. As the general manager fought to roll back the union's power inside the cooperative, Section 72 leaders now focused exclusively on protecting their members.[27] Far from collaborating with peasant members of the cooperative, new labor leaders adhered to a strict economistic strategy that promoted piecemeal improvements without large-scale challenges.[28] Much to Porfirio's dismay, Section 72 leaders deliberately pitted workers against peasants inside the cooperative. Within a short time he left to organize *ejidatarios* in nearby Atencingo.

Some long-standing peasant leaders left the cooperative out of fear for their lives, having been stripped of their membership and frustrated by repeated failures to negotiate with authorities. Others ceased being activists and joined the ranks of the cooperative's bureaucrats, accepting the status quo and compromising their ability to press for change. Pablo and Davíd Serdán, for example, both participated in the 1942 strike; Davíd had been temporarily stripped of his membership status. In the aftermath of the strike, however, Pablo accepted an offer to become mayor of Zacatepec and Davíd became a white-collar worker inside the cooperative's administrative offices.[29] Whether out of fear or co-optation, the sudden departure of these leaders left a vacuum in the ability of the local communities to organize, stripping peasants of representation before federal and cooperative authorities. That vacuum was all the more evident because national organizations representing peasants remained weak. Unfettered intimidation, co-option, and exile of grassroots peasant leaders—long-standing practices in rural Mexico—announced their arrival at the Zacatepec cooperative following the strike.[30] In contrast to earlier moments, however, these practices were couched in the language of developmentalism, coupled with the perception—although not the practice—that peasants had an actual say in the cooperative by virtue of their membership status. Officials thus accommodated the strategy of divide and rule to the logic of modernization emerging in the 1940s.

Five years after the cooperative's inauguration, the CNC's dismal record rendered it an unattractive option for peasants seeking redress of their grievances. Instead, peasants opted for smaller-scale lobbying from their respective communities.[31] Much as they had under Lázaro Cárdenas, peasants wrote directly to the sitting president to intercede on their behalf. Peasants organized caravans to Mexico City in an attempt to meet with presidents directly, caravans so commonplace that they followed a set routine. After the president's personal secretary ushered them away with a promise that the president would look at their petition, they proceeded to visit other governmental offices, where they received receptions similar to that at the president's office. While on the caravan, peasants often remained in the capital city for several days, setting up tents outside government offices and hanging banners listing their demands. The caravans' trajectory represented an attempt to extract a promise from a government official to look into their cause. Such a promise, even if illusory, allowed peasants to avoid returning emptyhanded to their communities.[32]

The frequency and the ritualized nature of the letter-writing campaigns and caravans show that rural peoples saw them as among the few ways to lobby government officials other than taking up arms. Because they were nonthreatening, such tactics also allowed rural peoples to circumvent violent reprisals. Using these "safe" tactics, peasants projected themselves onto the national stage—in a written or physical form—by lobbying national leaders instead of local or regional officials. Individuals appealed to officials as part of a shared revolutionary culture, appeals reinforced by the status of many as Zapatista veterans and by their direct connection to Cárdenas's personalistic legacy.[33] Given that other options had failed, falling back on reifying a shared revolutionary culture—with all its patriarchal affects–was one of the few available actions for people determined to stay within the confines of legality and avoid repression. Rural peoples increasingly (and particularly in the 1947–48 mobilization) adopted a language of modernization to support and legitimize their demands. Setting aside revolutionary in favor of developmentalist rhetoric marked a profound shift in the most frequently used form of rural activism of the time.

The relationship between peasant cooperative members and government officials remained locked in a status quo that lasted until the enterprise was dismantled in the early 1990s. The only exception occurred between 1947 and 1948 and involved the eldest of the Jaramillo brothers, Antonio. Politically moderate local leaders failed to go beyond these ritualized, often fruitless, protests—even in the face of damning evidence of corruption that threatened the cooperative's very existence—because of the general manager's overwhelming power. In early 1947 peasants' complaints of abuses, ranging from the rigging of scales used to weigh sugar cane to unreliable transportation of the cane to the factory, increased significantly. General Manager Severino Carrera Peña responded by forming a security force—referred to as the *guardias blancas*—to support his illegal activities and repress protestors. If a member of the peasant cooperative questioned the reading on the rigged scale when delivering his cane, the guardias blancas beat him. This already tenuous situation worsened dramatically in June 1947 when Rodrigo Ampudia del Valle replaced Carrera Peña. Chaos inside the cooperative (fed by unbridled corruption), the activities of the guardias blancas, and a new general manager intent on continuing the same abuses all combined to push peasants down new paths to make their voices heard.[34]

Area peasants resorted to new strategies to petition officials to intervene and correct the problems that threatened their personal and collective economic well-being. With earlier peasant activists gone, communities had to turn to new representatives to articulate their demands. These individuals, including Antonio Jaramillo, had remained on the sidelines during earlier mobilizations, thus escaping the waves of expulsions and repressions that had forced previous leaders to flee. They tended to hold local leadership positions: Antonio, for example, was the leader of the Tlaquiltenango ejido and had a long track record of supporting the cooperative in a variety of administrative capacities. Instead of using the CNC or allying with Section 72 workers, these new leaders formed their own committees and appealed to officials directly and through public media. These actions marked a watershed, constituting a new type of (direct but legal) peasant mobilization as an alternative to either radical action or the CNC. Moreover, their demands were nowhere near as ambitious as those of 1942 and tended to conform to the more economistic and clientelistic norms of the late 1940s. They wanted the cooperative to succeed, and they saw excessively corrupt and ill-equipped general managers as standing in the way of this goal; instead of fighting for a greater say in the cooperative's affairs, they pressed for an end to the endemic mismanagement they saw as jeopardizing the financial health of the enterprise.

This new wave of mobilizations officially began on March 30, 1947, with the publication in *Novedades* of an open letter to President Miguel Alemán. Cane growers complained of rampant irregularities in production, including unreliable transportation and corrupt field inspectors, and the virtual absence of any leadership from the vigilance and administrative councils. Even more worrisome, the petitioners noted the increasing presence on the cooperative's payroll of guardias blancas, who routinely harassed members for complaining. Such a public airing of the cooperative's problems elicited an immediate official response, and in April a government representative came to investigate.[35] The individuals whose names appeared in the open letter fearfully denied giving permission to include their names. Only Mateo Torres Ortiz, an ejidatario from Acatlipa and a founding member of the cooperative, acknowledged signing the petition. Finding little explanation from the protestors, the investigator relied on the opinion of Juan Nieto, a representative of the cooperative's administrative council, when forming his conclusions. Nieto accused the Confederación General de Trabajadores (CGT), an independent leftist organization, of being behind the letter in a blatant challenge to the CTM's and CNC's authority in Zacatepec. The investigator confirmed the existence of guardias blancas, yet he did not attribute individuals' reluctance to claim credit for the open letter to possible persecution by them.

Although fear of retribution seemingly stopped almost all of the petitioners from speaking up to the investigator, they grew more vocal in the following months. In May, thirty *comisariados ejidales* signed letters to the president and other government officials following up on the earlier accusations.[36] The clamor finally elicited a reaction—not from the CNC, but from other bureaucratic agencies that suggested some form of state responsiveness. Over the course of three weeks, investigators from the Department of the Economy and Department of Agriculture went to the area and confirmed the substance of the allegations, with one investigator going so far as to call the situation a "Porfirian dictatorship."[37] The investigator from the Department of the Economy noted the overwhelming prevalence of accounting irregularities, ranging from rampant theft in the cooperative's general store to the payout of hundreds of thousands of pesos to supporters of the general manager.[38] The reports all agree on one significant fact: cooperative members did not trust management because they saw the leaders as only interested in their own personal profit.

Mateo Torres Ortiz, Timoteo Montes de Oca, Andrés Rueda, and Antonio Jaramillo appeared at the helm of this mobilization and claimed to represent all cooperative members. Besides writing as members and as heads of their respective ejidos, they wrote under the banner of local organizations with names such as the Frente Obrero Morelense and the Comisión de Orientación y Unidad de Ejidatarios y Obreros de la Sociedad Cooperativa del Ingenio de Emiliano Zapata. They claimed to have the support of the CGT.[39] Although the CGT may have afforded them some ideological support early on, it was not until much later in the sequence of mobilizations that a national leader of the CGT arrived in Zacatepec to help peasant activists. Until then, emerging local leaders chose to highlight their identity, not as peasants or as veterans of the Zapatista forces, but as rural workers. Although they repeatedly used the moniker of workers, none of these letter writers in fact worked in the factory.

When Ampudia del Valle arrived in June 1947, this new wave of organizers set out to ensure that the new general manager recognized their authority. While earlier petitions called for government intervention into the cooperative's affairs to restore order, they now included targeted demands. In particular, a letter dated July 1 illustrates this sea change, including numerous examples of the relatively new language of "integral development," "intensive cultivation systems," and "systematic analysis of land quality" and organizing its recommendations into four subsections detailing technical upgrades to irrigation systems and land management.[40] In August the organizers held an extraordinary general assembly with the support of 3,597 cooperative members to unanimously reject as inept the representatives currently sitting on the administrative and vigilance councils and, instead, to elect their own leaders to sit on parallel councils.[41]

Far from threatening to take extralegal routes to press their demands, new peasant activists made a concerted effort to stay within legal channels, even while trying new strategies such as electing parallel councils. Moreover, they expressed their support for the government's vision of rural modernization, couched in the language of developmentalism, and made no mention of a shared revolutionary culture or their status as former Zapatistas. This change in rhetoric and adherence to legal strategies of direct action suggest that such a culture and, for that matter, the Cardenista legacy in the area no longer carried as much currency within the communities. Furthermore, their overt appeal to integral development shows that these leaders wanted to remind government officials that peasants should play a role in modernizing Mexico. As part of a reminder that peasants were still there, these leaders also sought to showcase their ability to understand and deploy developmentalist ideas—in other words, peasants could be modern too.

The conflict came to a head in October 1948, when peasants and workers, acting independent of one another, accused Ampudia del Valle of being even more corrupt than Carrera Peña.[42] Mateo Torres Ortiz, Antonio Jaramillo, and others complained (under the letterhead of the Unión Campesina Obrera Morelense) that "the planting of sugar cane has stopped as a result of persecution, bad treatment, and the lack of payment."[43] Section 72 ordered work stoppages; the general manager called in troops to harass the striking workers.[44] By the end of the month, however, the general manager publicly agreed to consider changes, and news articles immediately announced an end to the conflict. One, however, noted that Mateo Torres Ortiz had gone to the president's residence in Mexico City to complain that the general manager had not kept his promise.[45]

Torres's story shows what happened to those who continued to press for autonomous political action. In early 1948, cooperative officials had (falsely) accused Torres of attempting to agitate ejidatarios against a local credit society and terminated his membership.[46] Barred from entering the cooperative or from lobbying as a member, Torres had two choices: to continue radicalizing within the CGT or withdraw from political activity. He chose the former, and the CGT figured prominently in the October 1948 mobilization, but such radicalization further diminished his legitimacy among local communities because officials (successfully) labeled him an outside agitator. After 1949, Torres ceased to write letters to officials and disappeared from the public record. Those peasant leaders who, in contrast to Torres, backed down and resumed their positions inside the local political order managed to escape unscathed and, in some cases, even benefited from their renewed quiescence.

After Ampudia del Valle died in a mysterious plane crash in 1949, Eugenio Prado took over the reins of the Zacatepec cooperative in 1950. Prado, originally from Chihuahua, arrived with considerably more experience in sugar production than the preceding two general managers and remained at the helm for a decade. The naming of Prado as general manager could be interpreted as a concession to peasant demands. It could also be a pragmatic decision recognizing that those peasants were, in fact, right: the crisis inside the enterprise was spiraling out of control, threatening the entire economy of Morelos. Although created under Cardenista plans for rural modernization, the Zacatepec cooperative was too big and too much a symbol of government intervention in the heartland to be allowed to go bankrupt.

The Politics of Memory and Demobilization

Mateo Torres Ortiz was quickly and comprehensively forgotten. None of the individuals from Morelos whom I interviewed recalled hearing of him. Some were supporters of the Jaramillistas, others opposed or even informed on the movement's activities, and still others never participated in any political activity. All remembered events in the 1940s and clearly identified historical markers of the decade, yet Mateo Torres Ortiz did not register in their memories. Although his voice resonates loudly in the written historical record and he was partly responsible for the government appointing a much more moderate and capable general manager in 1950, half a century later his activities seem to have barely registered in the historical memory of the people for whom he fought.

The memory of Antonio Jaramillo met a fate similar to that of Torres Ortiz. Antonio Jaramillo, who continued for several months as treasurer for the Unión Campesina Obrera Morelense, eventually stepped out of the political limelight in 1949. As his son explained, "even if you were organized, what did you do? . . . [My father] did not want to get involved in those things because he already had us—his family and my mother."[47] As the eldest, he took care of his siblings' families when they sought refuge in the mountains and after their assassinations. He was also the one who endured interrogations and constant surveillance because of his surname and the one who collected the bodies of his two murdered siblings. As his son and widow explained, Antonio never talked about those years and quietly went about his life in the aftermath of the violence that robbed him of his brothers.[48] He died in 1970 of health complications and, according to his son and widow, from unresolved grief. However, when I asked the two of them if they remembered Antonio participating in political mobilizations when he was the leader of the Tlaquiltenango ejido, they said that they did not. They instead talked about the close relationship between Antonio and Eugenio Prado, the general manager after 1950.

In spite of more than two years of ardent political activism through legal channels, Antonio Jaramillo and Mateo Torres Ortiz have been forgotten. Perhaps the story of Rubén Jaramillo masked the political activism of others who went after him. Perhaps because their stories did not conclude with taking up arms, or being murdered and subsequently exalted by Carlos Fuentes, there was no place for Antonio Jaramillo and Mateo Torres Ortiz in the heroic rendering of mid-twentieth century rural mobilizations. Even today in southern Morelos, Manichaean collective memories exalt local heroes and demonize villains, such as Ampudia del Valle, to explain ongoing problems afflicting the region, including high poverty rates, labor unrest, and the difficulty of depending on sugar cane in a globalized economy. In a context imbued with continuities from earlier decades and exacerbated by the problems of a modernized world, community members are reluctant to remember forms of popular support of an authoritarian political order.

The deterioration of the peasants' position inside the Zacatepec cooperative illustrates the overall change in the political balance of forces and the lessons peasants drew from it. In contrast to earlier efforts, this new strategy of calling on integral development to justify their protests netted results. Although Eugenio Prado continued many of the same corrupt practices that had become the norm at the cooperative, he nevertheless ushered in a variety of social welfare programs and instituted the modernization of sugar production that garnered him considerable support from all cooperative members. Government officials learned they could not entirely discount peasant members in their plans for the cooperative, registering the need for a modicum of social welfare programs to ensure against peasant reaction.

If anything, these programs further demobilized the peasantry and tied local leaders to clientelistic networks. As one informant recalled, "it made peasants lazy because they conformed."[49] Antonio Jaramillo became a close ally of Prado and took advantage of the general manager's invitation to visit him personally when at the cooperative's offices. Through Prado's generosity, Antonio Jaramillo found employment for his young nephew, Enrique, as a mechanic inside the cooperative. As Enrique Jaramillo explained, the cooperative was nicknamed "La Engorda" during Prado's tenure as general manager because "there was a lot of money in it . . . there were rolls of bills they would take because of the corruption."[50]

That Prado successfully co-opted this new generation of local leaders and ushered in a system of production nicknamed "La Engorda" marked the culmination of a strategy to divide and rule that had demobilized the majority of the peasantry in southern Morelos. Throughout the 1950s, Zacatepec peasants did not mount a concerted mobilization to protest their marginalization as they had in the 1940s. Peasant leaders, including Antonio Jaramillo, stayed quiet even against the backdrop of popular mobilizations throughout Mexico after 1958, including those in rural areas in Coahuila, Sonora, Sinaloa, and Nayarit.[51] The silence of these peasant leaders, however, is not surprising considering their experiences mobilizing in the 1940s, their heavy dependence on clientelism, and ongoing repression in the area. We have to remember that Antonio buried Porfirio in 1955 and endured considerable harassment from police and military officers searching for Rubén. The costs of breaking the status quo and joining these popular movements were just too high.

Protests from peasant cooperative members gathered momentum against Prado, whom they accused of excessive corruption, as the 1950s came to a close. Some dissidents were long-term supporters of Rubén Jaramillo, including Félix Serdán, while others were representatives of the Vieja Guardia Agrarista, including Emiliano Zapata's son, Nicolás.[52] Government investigators subsequently confirmed their accusations, including one who listed a series of financial anomalies to illustrate the "ease with which ejidatarios' money is spilled."[53] Although not deliberately linked to the protests, Prado left the cooperative in 1960. What stands out about this wave of protests, especially in comparison with the ones from the 1940s, is the limited scope of demands (replace the general manager) and the use of the same strategies (letter-writing campaigns and caravans to Mexico City) to press their cause. Although it involved many, this mobilization is an example of the routinization of protest that emerged after the 1942 strike. That peasant activists did not expand their demands or look to new strategies, including linking up with the broader popular mobilizations emerging after 1958, and immediately backed down after Prado's departure suggests the limited scope of their activism. Instead of a challenge, this movement triggered a corrective measure from the government to once again align the status quo.

Perhaps the most important reason why the peasant leaders of the 1947–48 mobilization have been forgotten is because many went on to support La Engorda in the 1950s, thus losing the heroic sheen of their earlier actions. As one informant stated, "it was a cooperative on paper and nobody wanted things to change."[54] In the dichotomous recollections of good versus bad, or revolutionary versus antirevolutionary, little room remains for those who straddled both camps at different moments. This was, however, the most common and most influential model of peasant political participation in the period. Such participation—critical in cementing a social base of support from the revolutionary heartland—helped the government deflect threats from popular mobilizations elsewhere after 1958. It begs restating, however, that this social base was forged after years of peasants negotiating the limits of their marginalization, and based on their need to tap into clientelistic networks for their own and their families' survival, and the ever-present threat of violence.

THE DELIBERATE TRANSFER of resources to booming industrial centers—exacerbated by demographic shifts from rural to urban areas—contributed to the PRIísta state shifting attention away from rural development.[55] Yet policymakers could not entirely favor industry over agriculture, considering what came before 1940 in rural Mexico, including the violent *cristiadas* and militant agrarian movements in north-central Mexico. In addition to mobilizations before 1940, periodic outbursts of peasant protest, such as the two cases studied in this chapter, showed that the government had to give some concessions to the peasantry in the making of Mexico after *Cardenismo*. Southern Morelos, symbolically central and home to a flagship cooperative, represented a critical testing ground for the sustainability of clientelism and for how far government officials could disregard peasants in their plans for modernization.

Through a combination of co-option, divide and rule among popular groups, the narrowing of protest channels, and the strategic deployment of repression, the PRIísta state secured a cadre of loyal supporters among local leaders. That allegiance could be temporary or long term but succeeded in demobilizing peasant leaders at critical moments of protest. Such leaders were systematically offered sinecures—from Rubén Jaramillo's job as a market administrator in 1944 to Porfirio taking the helm of the ejidal cooperative in nearby Atencingo in 1947 and Antonio Jaramillo's nephew's place as a mill mechanic—to temper their radicalism. Thus we see how the family most associated with radical resistance in mid-twentieth-century Mexico periodically collaborated with the political order. This was also the family that showed what happened to those who refused these overtures; by the 1960s two of the brothers had been assassinated. The regime successfully shut down grassroots organizing in communities with a long track record of protecting their autonomy and encouraged these same communities to forget the historical memory of such a legacy.

Antonio's story proves that, far from being irrelevant, the countryside was essential to the emerging authoritarian state. Not only did the exploitation of rural communities afford policymakers the surplus necessary to redirect profits to fund industrialization elsewhere in Mexico, it also cemented the social base of support that would go on to bolster the regime's authority throughout the remainder of the twentieth century. If there was ever a golden age for peasants at Zacatepec, it came early and was short-lived: between 1938 and 1941. In the context of the communities dependent on the cooperative, including Jojutla, Tlaquiltenango, Tehuixtla, Galeana, Puente de Ixtla, and many others, local forms of authoritarianism announced their arrival early in the process of consolidating the political order at the national level. After the two moments of mobilization in the 1940s, authoritarianism was very much a fixture of the landscape of southern Morelos, so much so that previously active peasants chose to sit out the broader mobilizations emerging after 1958.

The postrevolutionary regime did not invent the strategies of divide and rule, clientelism, and selective repression as means to control popular classes. The history of state formation in Latin America and beyond has many examples of such a strategy employed to secure control of different social groups across distinct regions.[56] Yet the Mexican case stands out for the degree to which this division succeeded at quelling opposition from popular groups in regions with a long-standing tradition of defending their autonomy, such as those in southern Morelos. Peasant organizing in the 1940s, in particular, helped government leaders learn how to tackle challenges from popular groups—challenges that gathered momentum as state-led industrialization stumbled after 1952, as popular mobilizations surged after 1958, and as the political order's authoritarian bent became increasingly evident in the 1960s. To understand these processes, we thus need to comprehend how this political order was constructed, identify its building blocks, and consider what it looked like from the vantage point of the rural communities on which it was imposed.[57] Doing so shows that parts of the Mexican countryside witnessed a different—and more violent—experience with the emergence of an authoritarian political order than urban areas.

Notes

1. For a comprehensive analysis see Tanalís Padilla, *Rural Resistance in the Land of Zapata: The Jaramillista Movement and the Myth of the Pax Priísta, 1940–1962* (Durham, NC: Duke University Press, 2008).

2. Arturo Warman, *Y venimos a contradecir: Los campesinos de Morelos y el estado nacional*. 2nd edition (Mexico City: Casa Chata, 1978). Others who studied these issues in Morelos include Armando Bartra, *Los herederos de Zapata: Movimientos campesinos posrevolucionarios en México, 1920–1980* (Mexico City: Ediciones Era, 1985); Guillermo de la Peña, *A Legacy of Promises: Agriculture, Politics, and Ritual in the Morelos Highlands of Mexico* (Manchester, UK: Manchester University Press, 1982); and Claudio Lomnitz, *Exits from the Labyrinth: Culture and Ideology in a Mexican National Space* (Berkeley: University of California Press, 1993).

3. For details see David Ronfeldt, *Atencingo: Politics of Agrarian Struggle in a Mexican Ejido* (Palo Alto, CA: Stanford University Press, 1973).

4. Interview with Tito Jaramillo, July 19, 2009, Tlaquiltenango, Morelos.

5. Fulgencio Batista announced this strategy in Cuba at the same time. Robert Whitney, "The Architect of the Cuban State: Fulgencio Batista and Populism in Cuba, 1937–1940," *Journal of Latin American Studies* 32, no. 2 (May 2000), 444–45, 454.

6. Between the 1920s and 1960s, sugar production roughly doubled each decade. Horacio Crespo and Enrique Villanueva, *Estadísticas históricas del azúcar en México* (Mexico City: Azúcar S.A., 1988), 795–98.

7. Juan M. Aurrecoeche, Armando Bartra et al., eds., *De haciendas, cañeros, y paraestatales: Cien años de historia de la agroindustria cañero-azucarera en México, 1880–1980* (Mexico City: Escuela Nacional de Estudios Profesionales Acatlan, Universidad Nacional Autónoma de México, 1993); Horacio Crespo, ed., *Historia del azúcar en México*. 2 vols. (Mexico City: Editorial del Fondo de Cultura Económica, 1988); and Sergio de la Peña and Marcel Morales Ibarra, *El agrarismo y la industrialización de México, 1940–1950: Historia de la cuestión agraria mexicana*. Vol. 6 (Mexico City: Singlo Veintiuno Editores, 1989).

8. Padilla, *Rural Resistance*, 67.

9. Crespo and Villanueva, *Estadísticas históricas del azúcar*, 30–32.

10. Romana Falcón (*La semilla en el surco: Adalberto Tejeda y el radicalismo en Veracrúz (1883–1960)* [Mexico City: Gobierno del Estado de Veracruz, 1986]) discusses earlier manifestations of this strategy.

11. See AGN Secretaría de Trabajo y Previsión Social—Sociedades Cooperativas/Zacatepec (AGN/STPS-SC/Zac) Caja 1 Leg (September 1, 1941).

12. AGN/STPS-SC/Zac-1/1 (August 6, 1941).

13. *Diario Oficial de Morelos*, February 11, 1942.

14. AGN/Ramo Presidentes/Manuel Avila Camacho (AGN/RP/MAC) vol. 596 Exp 523.1/13-1 H 312 (January 3, 1942); AGN-RP/MAC-943 Exp 565.4/117 H13; AGN-STPS-SC/Zac Caja 1 Leg 1 (January 20, 1942).

15. AGN/STPS/RG-3/1/100/53-1 H134–144 (January 21, 1942).

16. AGN-RP/MAC-596/523.1/13-1 H174–180 (April 4, 1942).

17. For similar events in Atencingo, see Ronfeldt, *Atencingo*, 105–45.

18. Renato Ravelo Lecuona, *Los Jaramillistas: La gesta de Rubén Jaramillo narrada por sus compañeros* (Mexico City: Editorial Nuestro Tiempo, [1978] 2007), 26–27; interview with Félix Sérdan Najera, April 14, 2004, Tehuixtla, Morelos.

19. Author's interview with Félix Serdán Najera, April 14, 2004, Tehuixtla, Morelos.

20. *El Nacional*, June 11, 1942.

21. For further discussion of Solórzano, see Padilla, *Rural Resistance*, 61, 65; Gisela D. Espinosa, "La reforma agraria y el nuevo modelo agroindustrial, 1935–1947," in *De haciendas, cañeros y paraestatales: Cien años de historia de la agroindustria cañero-azucarera en México, 1880–1980*, ed. Armando Bartra (Mexico City: UNAM, 1993), 132; and Rubén Jaramillo, *Rubén Jaramillo: Autobiografía y Asesinato* (Mexico City: Editorial Nuestro Tiempo, 1967), 33–34.

22. AGN-RP/MAC-596/523.1/13-2 H547 (June 22, 1942).

23. AGN/STPS-SC/Zac-1/2 (June 22, 1942).

24. Jaramillo, *Rubén Jaramillo*, 48, 51, 93, 98.

25. Jaramillo, *Rubén Jaramillo*, 94–106.

26. AGN-STPS-SC/Zac-1/2 (January 20, 1943), AGN-RP/MAC-596/523.1/13-2 H391–393 (January 21, 1943).

27. AGN/STPS-SC/Zac-1/3 (January 27, 1944). For similar battles at Atencingo, see Ronfeldt, *Atencingo*, 48–50.

28. For more on this strategy, see Kevin Middlebrook, *The Paradox of Revolution: Labor, the State, and Authoritarianism in Mexico* (Baltimore: Johns Hopkins University Press, 1995); and Susan Gauss, *Made in Mexico: Regions, Nation, and the State in the Rise of Industrialism, 1920s–1940s* (University Park: Pennsylvania State University Press, 2010).

29. Interview with Félix Serdán Najera, April 14, 2004, Tehuixtla, Morelos.

30. Heather Fowler-Salamini provides an example of these earlier practices (*Agrarian Radicalism in Veracruz, 1920–1938* [Lincoln: University of Nebraska Press, 1978]).

31. AGN/RP/MAC-596/523.1/13-2 H378 (January 16, 1943); AGN-RP/MAC Vol N/A Exp 565.4/374 H 49–51 (March 10, 1943).

32. AGN-RP/MAC-596/523.1/13-2 H378 (January 16, 1943); AGN-RP/MAC Vol N/A Exp 565.4/374 H49–51 (March 10, 1943). See also the numerous reports from federal agents who infiltrated these caravans, e.g., AGN/DFS Exp 32-1 (CNC) Leg 2 H1118–119 (March 5, 1955).

33. For shared revolutionary culture, see Gilbert M. Joseph and Daniel Nugent, eds., *Everyday Forms of State Formation: Revolution and the Negotiation of Rule in Modern Mexico* (Durham, NC: Duke University Press, 1994).

34. A simultaneous opening took place in Atencingo, when Porfirio Jaramillo took over the cooperative (Ronfeldt, *Atencingo*, 76–104).

35. AGN/STPS-SC/Zac-2/9 (May 2, 1947).

36. AGN/STPS-SC/Zac-2/8 (May 27, 1947).

37. AGN/STPS-SC/Zac-2/9 (July 27, 1947).

38. AGN/STPS-SC/Zac-2/9 (July 27, 1947).

39. For example, AGN/STPS-SC/Zac-2/8 (April 12, 1947).

40. AGN/STPS-SC/Zac-2/9 (July 1, 1947).

41. AGN/STPS-SC/Zac-2/8 (August 13, 1947).

42. AGN/STPS-SC/Zac-3/13 (October 21, 1948).

43. AGN/RP/MAV-473/523.1/18-4 H67–67 v (October 2, 1948) and Exp 523.1/18-5 H 61–70 (November 2, 1948).

44. Interview with Beta Galarza, June 10, 2004, Chiconcuac, Morelos.

45. *Excelsior*, October 29 and November 1, 1948; *La Prensa*, October 29, 1948.

46. AGN/STPS-SC/Zac-3/11 (January 19, 1948); AGN/STPS-SC/Zac-2/9 (February 14 and February 20, 1948).

47. Interview with Tito Jaramillo, July 19, 2009, Tlaquiltenango, Morelos.

48. Interviews with Elizabeth Vásquez, July 3, 2004, and Tito Jaramillo, July 19, 2009, Tlaquiltenango, Morelos.

49. Interview with Sergio Estrada Cajigal, August 24, 2004, Cuernavaca, Morelos.

50. Interview with Enrique Jaramillo, April 12, 2004, Tlaquiltenango, Morelos.

51. Marco Bellingeri, *Del agrarismo armado a la guerra de los pobres, 1940–1974* (Mexico City: Ediciones Casa Juan Pablos, 2003); and Francisco A. Gómez-Jara, *El movimiento campesino en México* (Mexico City: Editorial campesina, 1970).

52. Interview with Félix Serdán Najera, April 14, 2004, Tehuixtla, Morelos; AGN/RP/Adolfo López Mateos-940-2, Exp 703.4/15, H29–34 (December 1958); AGN/STPS-SC/Zac-6/23 and AGN/STPS-SC/Zac-6/28 (August 24, 1959).

53. AGN/RP/ALM-579/521.8/8, H13–15 (February 1960).

54. Interview with Sergio Estrada Cajigal, August 24, 2004, Cuernavaca, Morelos.

55. See Bartra, *Los herederos de Zapata*; de la Peña, *Legacy of Promises*; Nora Hamilton, *The Limits of State Autonomy: Post-revolutionary Mexico* (Princeton, NJ: Princeton University Press, 1982); de la Peña and Morales Ibarra, *El agrarismo y la industrialización*; Stephen R. Niblo, *Mexico in the 1940s: Modernity, Politics, and Corruption* (Wilmington, DE: Scholarly Resources, 1999).

56. See, for example, Gillian McGillivray, *Blazing Cane: Sugar Communities, Class, and State Formation in Cuba, 1868–1959* (Durham, NC: Duke University Press, 2009); Laura Gotkowitz, *A Revolution for Our Rights: Indigenous Struggles for Land and Justice in Bolivia, 1880–1952* (Durham, NC: Duke University Press, 2007); and Greg Grandin, *The Blood of Guatemala: A History of Race and Nation in Guatemala* (Durham, NC: Duke University Press, 2000).

57. I thus build on the analyses of Florencia Mallon, *Peasant and Nation: The Making of Postcolonial Mexico and Peru* (Berkeley: University of California Press, 1995); Middlebrook, *Paradox of Revolution*; Alan Knight and Wil Pansters, eds., *Caciquismo in Twentieth-Century Mexico* (London: Institute for Latin American Studies Press, 2006); and Jeffrey W. Rubin, *Decentering the Regime: Ethnicity, Radicalism, and Democracy in Juchitán, Mexico* (Durham, NC: Duke University Press, 1997).

CHAPTER 9 | Christopher R. Boyer

COMMUNITY, CRONY CAPITALISM, AND FORTRESS CONSERVATION IN MEXICAN FORESTS

Late in the winter of 1954, a group of *ejidatarios* from the Heredia y Anexos, Chihuahua, signed their name to a plaintive letter describing the desperate straits in which they found themselves. They told the secretary of agriculture that their community had "no means of subsistence other than our sawmill and woods, since we do not have much cropland."[1] The problem, from the *ejido* leaders' perspective, was that the federal government had declared an indefinite ban (*veda*) on logging in most parts of Chihuahua, purportedly to give its forest ecosystems time to recover from decades of mismanagement and overuse. The peasant leaders did not say whether their woods had escaped the onslaught of commercial logging, although they suggested as much a few months later, when they wrote that forests covered more than 70 percent of their land grant and constituted the community's most important asset. Even so, they did not challenge the ecological rationale for declaring the logging ban; instead, they questioned whether forestry experts understood the social costs of doing so. "We believe that in making a Decree of *veda* that includes our lands," they wrote, "no one considered that we had taken advantage of the benefits that General [Lázaro] Cárdenas had offered us and formed a [producers'] Cooperative that was our only means of survival." By ignoring that the forestry cooperative represented the only source of regular work, the villagers argued that forestry bureaucrats had in essence cut off the ejido from its own land and forced its residents to choose between hunger and migration.[2]

Conflicts over woodlands have been a flashpoint between rural communities and forestry authorities since 1917, when the postrevolutionary agrarian reform began to turn over land, including forests, to rural communities. By the 1950s, Mexican management policies had shifted away from a brief experiment in community-based forestry that peaked during the 1934–40 Cárdenas administration in favor of a new and more rigid form of resource management associated with the presidencies of Manuel Avila Camacho (1940–46) and Miguel Alemán (1946–52). The Cardenista model had required the beneficiaries of land reform to form producers' cooperatives and log their own land under the close scrutiny of the Forest Service.³ Cárdenas also had expanded access to forests and all other types of rural land by vastly broadening the scope of land reform and distributing eighteen million hectares, or around 10 percent of the nation's agricultural and forest land, to eight hundred thousand families. These initiatives were part of a still broader set of development policies that could be described as "social landscaping," that is, the attempt by Cárdenas and his supporters to modernize the landscape by building roads, expanding irrigation, and promoting forestry. While undeniably a paternalist undertaking, social landscaping sought to both "rationalize" the use of natural resources and transform rural people's relationship with the natural world in a way that anticipated key aspects of what is now known as community-based conservation.⁴

The Cardenista project of social landscaping was undermined by the intensive and virtually unregulated extraction of natural resources to support the allied effort during World War II. As the war came to a close and the economy began growing at a breakneck pace during the "Mexican Miracle," natural resource policy became increasingly didactic, rigid, and, in some instances, overtly exclusionary. The Mexican state increasingly sought to assert sovereignty over natural resources, usually by making reference to economic nationalism. Yet many of these ostensibly nationalist (and rationalizing) policies masked an increasingly sharp form of crony capitalism in which regional and national politicians used regulation to arbitrate access to the nation's natural resources.

Forests are a case in point. Presidents signed a series of decrees granting timber interests, paper companies, and favored conglomerates special timber concessions (known as Forest Industry Management Units, or UIEFS), while revisions to the forest code barred most locally managed logging operations. Equally as important, logging bans emerged as a key component of the government's effort to manage forests. The bans themselves were not new—the first ones were enacted in the 1920s, and Cárdenas put several more in place—but these early bans had targeted small areas in a bid to preserve municipal woodlands for tourism or to clamp down on particularly egregious cases of over-logging by timber companies. In contrast, Cárdenas's successors used them for very different purposes.⁵

In the wake of World War II, the Avila Camacho and Alemán administrations sought to revitalize the private sector and move the nation down the path of development and modernization by shifting natural resource policies away from the community-based, albeit paternalist, footing of Cardenista social landscaping in favor of the more business-friendly schema of "preserving" forests. The two presidents issued fifteen decrees that collectively curbed logging in some or all of twenty states, accounting for around half of the nation's forests. Yet these "bans" were not intended to halt logging completely; instead, they carved out exceptions for favored corporations such as timber companies and paper mills, which often became the sole legal consumers of forest products in areas subject to a veda. Peasant organizations and small landowners could also request such an exemption, particularly if the Forest Service placed them in special districts known as Forest Management Units, or UOFs. As a practical matter, however, few of them had the administrative capacity or political ties to earn such exemptions. The result was a discriminatory regime of conservation that barred rural people from using their own land while opening it to other uses. Similar episodes of "fortress conservation" in the United States' Yellowstone National Park and nature reserves in Africa have denied the native peoples and rural poor who live within their boundaries the right to hunt animals, log forests, or in some cases even continue to live in their homelands.[6] Unlike Africa and North America, Mexico did not displace the people who lived in protected areas; indeed, national parks (created for the most part during the Cárdenas years) even contemplated ways for local populations to continue using the land.[7] Nevertheless, the postwar logging bans did create an exclusionary regime perhaps best described as a creole version of fortress conservation that effectively stripped some communities of the right to use their land while simultaneously opening a backdoor for commercial interests to get at ejidal forests.

Forestry was big business. According to one estimate, the timber industry made 500 million pesos in the mid-1950s—paper production made another 466 million—making it a larger part of the economy than the steel or beer industries and only slightly smaller than textiles; in addition, it employed around fifty thousand people, making it one of the nation's principal sources of employment.[8] Most states had some form of timber industry, but it developed most fully in the temperate forests brimming with valuable softwoods such as pine in northern states such as Chihuahua and Durango and in south-central states such as Mexico, Guerrero, Michoacán, Oaxaca, and Veracruz. The bans did succeed in capping the growth of all this commercial logging, yet they did little or nothing to stem the destruction of forests themselves. In some cases, they actually encouraged deforestation. How can we account for this apparent contradiction? First, the state lacked the capacity and in many cases the will to fully enforce its own regulations. Forestry officials could police legitimate forestry operations and aboveboard trade in forest products, but there was little they could do to clamp down on "pirate" logging operations, much less on peasant communities that made unauthorized cuts or sold timber on the thriving black market. In addition, forest wardens' widespread reputation for corruption casts doubt on their effectiveness, and the bans sometimes became just one more administrative layer in an already confusing tangle of federal forestry regulation. As one observer put it in the late 1950s, "there are some zones or regions that have double or triple protection because they are protected by a general ban as well as designated as a watershed, forest reserve, or national park."[9] Even forestry officials sometimes lost track of which particular communities, companies, species of trees, and regions were subject to a ban.[10] More fundamentally, Mexico's regime of creole fortress conservation sparked widespread resentment among the people who lived and worked in the woods. Most small-time logging outfits had no more pull with the federal government (and in some cases far less) than ejidos did, and neither group had any real alternative to guarantee their survival.

Almost overnight, Mexican policy had shifted from the redistribution, paternalism, and social landscaping of the Cárdenas years to an exclusionary form of natural resource management. The roots of this change can be traced to an antipopulist line of reasoning that forestry experts had developed over the previous decades. This identified peasants' use of the forests as the primary threat to forest ecosystems (a secondary threat being unregulated logging by "irresponsible" timber companies). The increasingly bureaucratized and technocratic state that evolved in the wake of World War II gave these experts a platform on which to put their theories into practice, although not necessarily with the results they had anticipated. Throughout the 1950s and into the following decades, forestry experts became increasingly aware of the limits of managing the landscape by simply decreeing the forests off-limits, although many of the bans themselves endured until the early 1970s.[11]

A Genealogy of Conservation Management in Mexico

Unlike most parts of the developing world, where colonial states or foreign environmentalists encouraged the development of national parks and other protected areas, fortress conservation in Mexico was a homegrown and in this sense creole product, the brainchild of forestry experts inspired by revolutionary nationalism yet disturbed by the idea that postrevolutionary agrarian reform committed forest ecosystems to the care of ejido communities. Mexican leaders faced the task of rebuilding government, economy, and infrastructure and refashioning society along "revolutionary" lines in the wake of the revolution. Yet most of these leaders had no intention of overturning their prerevolutionary social hierarchy. As the new generation of bureaucrats and conservation-minded intellectuals turned their attention to managing the nation's public resources, they found it necessary to walk a thin line between the desire to rein in foreigners and major landowners who logged indiscriminately in states like Michoacán and Chihuahua and the impulse to increase their own control of the rural population's use of forests.

In the 1920s it seemed that conservationists would make the regulation of timber companies their primary concern. In newspaper articles and public speeches, forestry experts rejected their predecessors' preference for powerful, foreign-dominated enterprises that extracted Mexico's natural wealth but left little in return. Miguel Angel de Quevedo, Mexico's foremost naturalist of the early twentieth century, blamed most deforestation on nineteenth-century liberal regimes that allowed for the "ruination of very large portions" of forestlands. Rapacious outsiders gained control of communally held property (as well as lands that had belonged to the Catholic Church) and logged them, as Quevedo wrote, "usually without producing any benefit for villagers themselves."[12] Another analyst more succinctly characterized the Porfirian timbering regimen as a period of "unjust pillage."[13] By posing the problem in these terms, conservationists placed the blame for deforestation not only upon the overly solicitous Porfirian regime but also upon the foreign-dominated forest industry itself.

Nationalism drove not only conservationists' criticisms of past mistakes but also their proposals for postrevolutionary Mexico's management of natural resources. Again, Quevedo figured among the leading voices. Speaking at Arbor Day festivities in 1924, he asserted that educators could best fulfill their "aspirations for the effective progress of the Nation (Patria)" by cultivating children's love for trees.[14] By the 1940s and 1950s it became commonplace for scientists, industrialists, and political leaders to equate forests with the nation itself. In a 1951 speech President Miguel Alemán described forests as one of the most important national patrimonies and urged "all Mexicans—and the foreigners who live among us—not only to preserve [forestlands] but to expand them." Alemán told his listeners that they should consider trees to be, like their children, "part of our national integrity."[15] Business leaders with an interest in forest products also adopted the rhetoric of nationalism. A few years later, newspaper magnate José García Valseca averred without a hint of irony that "to plant and care for trees should be as obligatory as the paying of taxes" and worried that "in but a few years, we will bequeath our children a desert instead of a patria."[16] Even the directors of lumber companies, who had every reason to dislike postrevolutionary forestry laws, declared themselves prepared to collaborate with the government's "campaign of protection and conservation of Mexico's natural resources."[17]

Most observers recognized that powerful timber interests and pliant public officials had outlived the Díaz regime and continued unpatriotically to overuse forests without regard for the environmental (and political) consequences. In 1940 an editorialist from La Prensa decried the collusion between the Forest Service and businessmen in terms that clearly recalled earlier critiques of Porfirian perfidy. The paper blamed deforestation on the unscrupulousness of "influential politicians, small-time rural bosses, and venal [government] employees," all of whom paved the way for avaricious timber companies to cut at will in the nation's forestlands.[18] Anxieties about commercial logging did not diminish over time. Two decades later, a former head of the forest service objected to "these 'industrialists'" who indeed deserve the scathing appellation of "*rapamontes*" [ravagers of the forest], often acting in collusion with "'accessible' public functionaries" to deforest ever-larger swaths of land.[19] Like Quevedo, these observers believed that the large forest companies routinely suborned government regulators to achieve their ultimate goal of pillaging Mexico's forests.

Yet if conservationists worried that bureaucrats and lumber companies could not be counted on to responsibly manage the nation's forests, they did not hold out much more hope for the peasantry. Writing in 1916 as delegates began to formulate a new constitution, Quevedo warned that a wrong-headed land reform program might "sacrifice the remaining forests" if it proposed to give a land grant to each indigenous family without taking proper measures to ensure that they would act as good stewards of the land.[20] Instead of simply turning over plots of land to rural people wholesale, Quevedo recommended that the government guarantee a decent wage for rural workers. He further warned that beneficiaries of land reform should not be given title to the parcels they worked because "fee simple ownership would put [rural folk] in a position to give up their lands at the first opportunity."[21] Such concerns led politicians to structure the land reform in such a way that ejidal communities received usufruct of land grants rather than direct ownership. Moreover, the logging of ejido lands was technically forbidden until 1948 unless ejidatarios formally incorporated themselves in lumbering cooperatives and filed forestry plans with the appropriate officials, a legal requirement that beneficiaries of land reform ignored with near unanimity until the mid-1930s. For Quevedo and his followers, a regime of enlightened instruction and paternalist land tenure arrangements held the best promise of improving the consciousness of rural people. They believed that without such measures beneficiaries of land reform would sell out to predatory entrepreneurs or deforest vast tracts of their ejido parcels to plant crops in soil that was ill suited for agriculture.

Even during the administration of Lázaro Cárdenas—arguably Mexico's most populist and progressive postrevolutionary president—forestry experts expressed deep misgivings about the ability of popular classes to use the forests in a sustainable manner. In a 1940 press release the administration intimated that much of the harm to the nation's forests came from forest fires caused by the "lack of education of those people who live in the countryside."[22] Such official misgivings did not diminish over time. In a 1967 speech to a national congress of timber industry representatives, the subsecretary of forests and fauna explained that the chief threat to the nation's forestlands were "the destructive and irrational actions of man, when his conduct is governed by the blind impulses of ignorance, misery, and avarice."[23] Like many others at the time, this official had begun to suspect that an enlightened and patriotic industrial sector might function as a more responsible steward of the forests than the ignorant, impoverished, and avaricious masses.

Not everyone agreed. Enrique Beltrán, a distinguished zoologist who held a doctorate from Columbia University and directed the Forest Service during the 1958–64 administration of Adolfo López Mateos, laid much of the blame for deforestation on discriminatory conservation policies. Beltrán argued that even though rural people often obtained woodlands as part of ejido land grants, the government's "absurd restrictive forest policy" functioned to erect "all sorts of barriers against the use of forest resources, with the idea that the lack of utilization [of the forest] was the best guarantee of its conservation."[24] He argued that restricting ejido beneficiaries' access to stands of timber on their lands would only lead to an increase in deforestation because "the *campesino* who owns forest—and who is kept from utilizing timber—has ended up regarding trees not only as useless but as veritable enemies that impede him from cultivating his little parcel of land and harvesting . . . a few more ears of corn to satisfy his family's hunger or to sell. Any method of destroying the forest has seemed good to him as long as it served to open up a bit of land to farm."[25] Beltrán took issue with his predecessors' conclusion that ignorance and avarice alone drove rural people to overexploit the forest. For him the problem lay not in peasant consciousness but in policies that rewarded some practices and penalized others.

Restrictive measures such as logging bans seemed to be an ideologically attractive way to protect the national patrimony. The bans responded to conservationists' concerns by functioning as a catch-all that promised to safeguard the forest ecosystems from whoever threatened them without imposing the political imperative of actually determining the exact causes of over-logging. Rather than identify and impose sanctions on particular groups—whether timber companies or members of the popular classes—the bans indiscriminately clamped down on everyone. In this way, large areas could be declared protected zones through a one-size-fits-all decree that provided the semblance of governmental responsiveness to deforestation.

Enacting the Bans

Bans on timber extraction derived their juridical basis from article 27 of the 1917 Constitution. Although that article is best known as the constitutional foundation for Mexico's massive land reform project and for Lázaro Cárdenas's dramatic expropriation of petroleum reserves in 1938, it also contains a conservationist plank that allowed for the state to "impose on" property to safeguard its conservation.[26] The nation's first forest code, passed in 1926, expanded on this environmentalist ideal and declared "the conservation and propagation of forest vegetation in the National Territory" to be in the public interest (*de utilidad pública*). The code implored citizens to "cooperate with the Government in the conservation and regeneration" of forests.[27] Realizing that such cooperation might not arise spontaneously, the authors of the code authorized the president "to conserve or restore forest vegetation" by prohibiting "some or all utilization or harvesting of forest lands," including land held by private individuals, that is, declaring a veda.[28] Armed with this law and the essentially similar ones that succeeded it, presidents could unilaterally prohibit the harvesting of specific species of flora or declare outright bans on timbering in any given area.[29]

Even before the 1926 law specifically authorized logging bans, President Álvaro Obregón (1920–24) made some modest stabs at curbing the overuse of forests by declaring moratoria. As railroad companies made frenzied efforts to rebuild track devastated by revolutionary fighting, Obregón fired off angry telegrams prohibiting the use of exotic hardwoods for railroad ties and condemning the "alarming cutting of woods" in the state of Hidalgo.[30] Toward the end of his term he also established small, protective forest reserves in central Mexico and in the states of Jalisco and Veracruz.[31] His successor, Plutarco Elías Calles (1924–28), declared few bans. When he did do so, however, he was not afraid to challenge powerful industrial interests. For example, in 1928 Calles banned the felling of *oyamel* (a species of pine) in Mexico State. Although this region had been over-logged for centuries, it seems that the Department of Agriculture aimed this ban specifically at the Lorento y Peña Pobre paper mill, which had repeatedly invaded the lands of nearby villages to harvest wood for pulp.[32]

The tenor of conservationist projects changed during the Cárdenas presidency, when Quevedo headed the newly established Department of Forestry, Fish, and Wildlife.[33] In 1936 alone, the first year that the department functioned normally, Cárdenas declared thirteen bans in nine different states.[34] Throughout his presidency, no fewer than fifty-four bans and protected forest zones were established.[35] The Cárdenas bans normally covered no more than a few thousand hectares and rarely covered more than an entire municipality. Not until the Avila Camacho and Alemán administrations did bans and other measures begin to erect a true regime of fortress conservation. In addition to eleven major bans, these presidents created five forest preserves in river basins encompassing another more than ten million hectares.[36]

Yet none of these measures proposed to halt all logging in protected areas. It was commonplace for one privileged organization or another to gain special exemptions, particularly during the Avila Camacho and Alemán administrations. These presidents often issued decrees for the "partial suspension" of a timbering ban to allow specific businesses or, more commonly, companies that enjoyed a UIEF concession to harvest timber; indeed, some of the original veda decrees included language that exempted concession holders from the very outset of the ban.[37] UIEFs were intended to harness the forests to Mexico's industrial expansion by giving highly capitalized timber product companies (such as paper mills) access to forests regardless of whether a ban was in place. The law directed UIEF concessionaires to cooperate with private landowners, indigenous communities, and the ejidal communities to decide where logging would occur and set fair prices for any wood extracted. In practice most concession holders operated with little government oversight and failed to pay market value for timber or offer jobs to locals.[38] Even when timber companies failed to win presidential dispensation to keep operating, Forest Service officials known as "heads of veda zones" could grant permission for businesses, individuals, and ejidos to continue their operations.[39] Local politicians also gave members of their political clientele privileged access to the forest from time to time, although strictly speaking they did not have the authority to do so. Regardless of the legal technicalities, however, governors and congressmen had the political influence to ensure that "their" people received special licenses to log in areas subject to bans. On at least one occasion a congressman was accused of using hired guns to remove clandestine loggers from a region subject to a ban to make way for his own clientele of clandestine loggers.[40]

A typical example of the way that bans functioned can be gleaned from the case of the El Perote region of central Veracruz. In the waning days of the Cárdenas administration, a twenty-year ban on all timber extraction was placed on twenty municipalities of western Veracruz, including El Perote.[41] Within weeks, the campesinos who worked as lumberjacks for small-time regional lumber companies mobilized under the leadership of Fidencio González, a local leader of the CTM labor union. Timber workers originally directed their complaints to local officials, but they soon chose to address Cárdenas himself. González and a delegation traveled to Mexico City to register their request to continue timbering the forests "with the understanding that [the workers] are prepared to satisfy all the pertinent requirements regarding the need to reforest the zones to be exploited and the manner in which to do so."[42]

The federal government stood firm. The ban remained in place, and El Perote was soon declared a forest preserve since it fell within the watershed of the Laguna de Alchichica.[43] In fact, the area had been declared a national park three years earlier. On that occasion, however, forestry officials got their signals mixed when they discovered that the department of land reform had granted an ejido to a peasant community inside the territory of the proposed park. Logging companies took advantage of the jurisdictional confusion and hired ejidatarios to log as many trees as possible before the government could unsnarl the bureaucratic mess.[44] According to one of the landowners whose property was nationalized and turned over to the ejidatarios of Jalacingo, a village near El Perote, peasant leaders in collusion with the owners of pirate lumber mills clear-cut several hundred hectares of forestland to open up new fields. The ex-landowner said that the agrarians had nearly "finished off" the forests on the land grant. The depletion of woods on the original ejido led the lumber companies to "incite" the peasants to request an expansion of their ejido, which it then logged before turning it over to the peasants.[45]

Local forest officials typically treated the ongoing logging in El Perote with a knowing wink. In 1946 peasant organizations charged that logging companies took advantage of a drought-induced subsistence crisis in the woodlands to pay villagers a pittance for wood that they converted into charcoal and sold for huge profits in Tampico.[46] Adolfo Ruiz Cortines, the governor of Veracruz, sent a steady stream of letters to the secretary of agriculture, accusing forest wardens of collaborating in the "interminable current" of contraband timber flowing out of El Perote, which, he said, had not only aggravated the already serious problem of erosion and threatened to the last remaining stands of American sweet gum (*liquidambar*) and sycamore (*haya*).[47] The Forest Service made a surprise inspection in 1949 that discovered nine sawmills operating illegally in the municipalities covered by the timbering ban. In an uncommonly direct press release, it noted that the ban "has unfortunately been broken quite frequently, especially in the region of Perote, where criminal loggers, occasionally in collusion with corrupt officials (*malos elementos*) in the Forest Service, have caused enormous destruction."[48] Even this inquiry had little long-term effect. Loggers simply relocated their clandestine operations to the nearby Tuxtlas region and began harvesting tropical cedar (*cedro*) and tulipwood (*palo rosa*) on ejido lands there. As for El Perote, some of the terrain had become so denuded by then that sheet erosion set in, and foresters concluded that trees would never grow there again.[49] The government declared a new ban on the El Perote area in 1952, but this one had no greater impact than the previous one. It was not lifted until the 1970s in light of what one observer called the bans' "obvious failure."[50]

Several factors undermined the El Perote bans, but the corruption of forestry officials clearly stood somewhere near the top of the list. The Forest Service may have ranked among the most corrupt branches of the government in the postrevolutionary years. As early as 1929, a special commission of experts empaneled by a group of congressmen determined that the Forest Service constituted a "blight" (lunar) on the Department of Agriculture. The commission found that forest wardens "are accustomed to traffic with forest concessions . . . and protect [illicit] forest shipments." Indeed, the venality of some wardens was said to reach such heights that they demanded "miniscule" bribes of fifty centavos to look the other way as peasants trucked individual loads of charcoal out of forests where any use of the wood was theoretically prohibited.[51] The culture of corruption did not change much during the Cárdenas years. One expert working in the Forest Service during the late 1930s (who may have had a personal grudge against Quevedo) documented "numerous errors and abuses of authority, extortion, and graft on the part of Overseers and secondary employees, particularly Forest Wardens."[52] Allegations of graft surfaced again in 1940, this time from an internal audit in the Department of Agriculture that revealed graft on a massive scale, particularly (and politically conveniently) located in the lower strata of Forest Service personnel. Responding to this news, El Universal, Mexico City's leading daily at the time, heaped opprobrium upon the Forest Service and characterized it as the main cause of deforestation in Mexico.[53]

Racketeering riddled the Forest Service to such a point that in 1950 the Department of Agriculture took a drastic step. In May of that year it fired all members of the Federal Forest Police who had been hired before January of that year and threatened to arrest anyone who improperly posed as a forest warden.[54] It is possible that this initiative led to a temporary redoubling of vigilance of forest regulations, but there is little to indicate that corruption entirely disappeared from the Forest Service. When forest wardens or even the army did crack down on clandestine logging, it was sometimes because powerful local timber interests hoped to cut villagers out of local markets. For example, in 1947 Governor of Guerrero Baltazar Leyva Mancilla claimed jurisdiction over ejido woods and sold the rights out from under the land reform beneficiaries, leading to armed clashes between timber companies and fifteen peasant communities.[55] In another case a decade later, a local forest warden organized his own workforce and sent them into the forests outside Uruapan to cut trees (despite a logging ban) that belonged to the indigenous community of San Lorenzo. The villagers rallied in defense of their property and attacked the woodcutters, killing at least one.[56] By then, three or four forest wardens died every year trying to carry out such "conservation" measures.[57]

Ejidatarios, indigenous people, and other rural groups also tried to bring their troubles to the attention of national leaders. Communities sent plaintive letters to presidents describing the economic burdens that a sudden loss of timber revenues caused them. Typical of such missives, representatives of loggers in the largely indigenous town of Quiroga, Michoacán, wrote President Alemán to explain "the situation that we and our families are suffering through here, so we come lamenting that here in this town there is no other work other than the wood."[58] Most business interests showed no more enthusiasm for the bans than lower-class rural folk did. For example, a 1949 ban against timbering in a multimillion-hectare zone covering large parts of Chihuahua, Durango, Sonora, and Sinaloa raised the hackles of some of the most important Chihuahuan industrialists. The Chihuahuan chamber of commerce sent the president a list of the individuals and companies that the ban would harm and implored him to avoid the "grave prejudice that the total inactivity [of timber companies] will cause."[59] Another group of timber magnates put the matter a bit more bluntly. They published an open letter to condemn the "abrupt and drastic" nature of such acts and to charge that the government unreasonably declared bans at the drop of a hat.[60]

Rural violence and the deep-seated corruption of the Forest Service were not the only systematic problems engendered by the bans. Even when the bans somehow could be enforced with some degree of success, they often created unanticipated problems because officials did little to remedy the sudden lack of wood. When the Cárdenas administration established a ban on logging in the region around Veracruz City, for example, it failed to provide for an alternative source of cooking fuel. In this case, the ban simply created a black market for charcoal cut from the few remaining nearby forests. One observer explained that "if immoderate logging is going on, it is because there are people who make up to three trips during the middle of the night" to cut enough wood to meet the city's demand for cooking fuel. In this particular case the ban also provoked a schism between two nearby peasant communities when one group of politically connected peasants invaded a protected area inside their neighbors' community in a bid to gain control of timber they hoped to use for charcoal.[61]

A similar situation arose a dozen years later in Michoacán. In 1950, a fruit growers' union wrote the president to complain that the scarcity of wood created by a recently declared ban had driven up the price of packaging for produce. A representative of the growers declared that his colleagues might have to cancel their fruit production contracts for the year if they could not find inexpensive crates. He then gamely asked if the government would kindly "indicate how to acquire containers for the same price that we had been paying."[62] Clearly, the bans could spark resentment not only among those who made their livelihoods in the forests but also among consumers of wood products.

Few people supported the bans. Apart from conservationists (who mostly hailed from the urban intelligentsia),[63] small-town businessmen constituted the only other major constituency for banning logging. Civic boosters hoped that bans would protect the woodlands to which tourists might flock. In 1940 this idea took hold in a sector of the business community in the mining town of Angangueo, Michoacán. The entrepreneurs who hoped to tap into the tourist trade stated that the recently declared ban on logging "will greatly benefit the people of Michoacán, for whom we have been laboring with so much energy."[64] Their hopes for a tourist boom apparently went unfulfilled. Even the late twentieth-century tourist potential of the nearby monarch butterfly reserve has failed to produce enough revenue to stem the economic logic that has driven deforestation in the region.[65]

Taking the Measure of the Bans

It is tempting to argue that vedas were little more than bureaucratic sleights of hand intended to give favored entrepreneurs a monopoly on legal access to forest resources. They contained exceptions that often allowed logging in banned areas to continue unabated, and corruption was entrenched among the forest wardens who were supposed to enforce them. Even so, it would be a mistake to assume that the bans were enacted *only* as a means to grant politically connected timbering interests some sort of special access to forest lands. In other words, the bans did serve to some extent as the conservationists had intended: as a means of protecting the nation's ecological patrimony.

Indeed, it seems that logging bans slowed commercial logging in the early 1950s and restrained it for nearly two decades thereafter; however, it is difficult to establish exactly what this rate was. Official statistics that purport to reflect the rate and location of timbering probably drastically misrepresent the scale and location of logging because they derived from forest wardens' unreliable reports, and in any case there were not enough to police timber operations on a national scale. A more reliable way to assess the extent of commercial logging is to assess the amount of lumber shipped by rail. Trains transported most industrial timber until at least the late 1950s, when road construction made trucking an increasingly cost-effective alternative. The data shown in figure 1 do not purport to represent the actual amount of logging going on in temperate forests (many people cut wood for their own use,

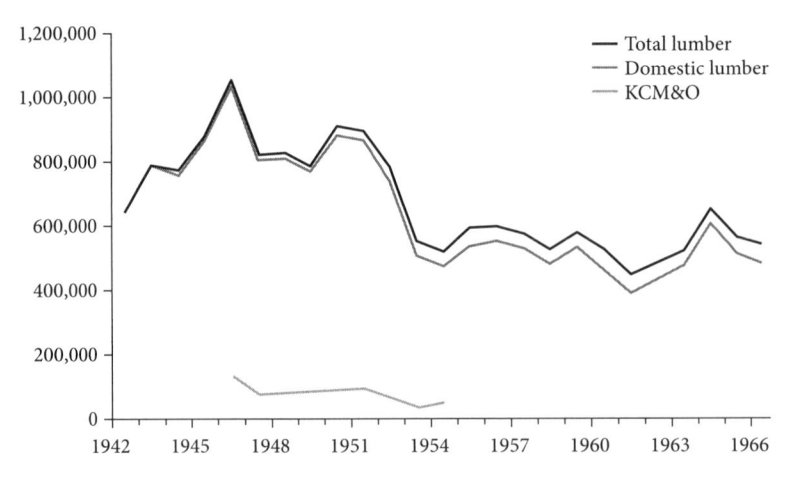

FIGURE 9.1. Metric Tons of Lumber Transported via Rail, 1942–1966
Sources: Mexico, Secretaría de Comunicaciones y Obras Públicas, Departamento de Comunicaciones Terrestres (various labels), *Estadísticas de Ferrocarriles de concesión federal* (Mexico City: various publishers, 1942–66); Mexico, Secretaría de Economía, Dirección General de Estadística, *Anuario estadístico de los Estados Unidos Mexicanos* (Mexico City: Talleres Gráficos de la Nación, 1942–66).

made it into charcoal, or transported it to market without using railways), and there is probably a small but progressive bias in the amount of commercial timber not reflected by these data, thanks to the ever-increasing use of heavy trucks. Still, it is safe to say that the broad trends the data represent do reflect medium-term dynamics of commercial wood transportation in temperate forests.

The lines showing the trends suggest that the amount of timber transported via rail declined sharply between 1949 and 1955. This contrasts with government statistics of lumber production, which indicate that the overall level of roundwood production remained steady during this period.[66] Taken together, these data—insofar as it corresponds to reality—suggest that there may have been a decline in the amount of commercial logging. Such a decline seems plausible, at least in the first years the bans were in place. As we have seen, most of the major bans in central Mexico and the northern Sierra Madre Occidental were declared between 1949 and 1952, around the same time that the Forest Service tried to purge unreliable forest wardens; these initiatives clearly seem to have put the brakes on the virtually unregulated logging during World War II and its aftermath. Such a decline is further supported by the trend line for the Kansas City, México y Oriente railroad (KCM&O), which was dedicated nearly exclusively to transporting timber in the sierras of Chihuahua to a handful of large sawmills and experienced a similar precipitous decline in lumber freight when a ban was declared on logging Chihuahuan forests. Despite popular resistance, industrialists' bluster, corruption, and inside deals, it would seem that the bans did in fact have a dampening effect on industrial logging.

Fortress conservation also took a major toll on the Mexican ecosystem. By making it difficult for woodland communities and small-scale operators to use the forest legally, the bans pushed many of them in the direction of clandestine logging. While large timber companies that bought wood from small-scale "pirate" timbering operations and peasant communities directly or indirectly contributed to much of this *clandestinaje*, it was probably more common for peasants and local woodcutters to creep into woods to make charcoal, cut wood for lumber (or roof shingles), and clear fields for agriculture. Such clandestine operations probably did more harm to the ecosystem than commercial logging because woodsmen had to move quickly and avoid the prying eyes of forest wardens who might demand bribes or charge them with infractions. The twin imperatives of speed and stealth made clandestine loggers cut indiscriminately and, in some cases, leave behind everything but the most valuable timber; if crops or cattle moved onto the land they cleared, there was virtually no possibility of reforestation. Clearly, the bans did not so much halt unauthorized logging as drive it into the shadows.

LOGGING BANS DID TEMPER the expansion of Mexico's notoriously inefficient industrial logging regime during their heyday, although their main function seems to have been to convert UIEF concession holders and other major timber interests into the sole legal markets for forest products in their respective zones. Despite their dubious record of success, the Forest Service did not propose to end logging bans until 1971, when it announced that they had the "completely negative" effect of stymieing rural development and encouraging the destruction of the forests.[67] Two years later, the Department of Agriculture formally began to phase out vedas on a national scale. By the end of the decade, no major statewide bans were still in effect, although a few new small-scale ones were established in particularly hard-hit areas.

Ironically, Forest Service policies echoed ideas—initially developed by Enrique Beltrán in the mid-1960s—that sought to strengthen the role of rural communities in the management of natural resources. In place of the bans, the government intended to promote greater industrialization, rationalization, and "participation of the campesino sector in the benefits of all activities associated with the use and industrialization of the forest."[68] To this end, the Forest Service recommended the abrogation of logging bans that had been in effect for at least twenty-one years (and in some cases much longer) in thirteen states and the federal district.[69] The epoch of unquestioned support for fortress conservation had come to an end; it was replaced by a renewed interest in community-based conservation that in some ways resembled the old Cárdenas model of social landscaping.

Mexico's creole regime of fortress conservation also had been undermined by lack of a cross-class and indeed cross-cultural consensus among timber companies, rural peoples, and the Forest Service. Even though some corporations earned exceptions from the bans, many others did not, and the timber industry generally regarded them with hostility. People who lived in the forestlands, of course, tended to flout them whenever possible. The top-down implementation of fortress conservation developed in the postwar years nevertheless remained a central part of the Forest Service's strategies of resource management, virtually guaranteeing that official conservation would not develop a strong constituency in rural Mexico. Despite some half-hearted gestures to teach rural communities more sustainable forestry techniques and raise public awareness of environmentalism through spectacles such as Arbor Day, conservationists did little to galvanize support for their policies. Efforts to engage industrialists were only slightly more successful. Nor did fortress conservation ever disappear altogether; as recently as 2003, forestry officials backed by troops attempted to remove Zapatista rebels from the Montes Azules Biosphere (created in 1978), allegedly to protect its rainforest ecosystem.[70] Yet its decline in the 1970s corresponded with a rise in environmentalism among the popular classes. Some communities in Michoacán, Guerrero, Oaxaca, Quintana Roo, and elsewhere demanded greater control over how forests were used in a bid to manage their land in ways that simultaneously fit with regional plans created by the Forest Service and local needs. While the success of such community-based strategies is still very much in doubt, they already seem to have done more to create a sustainable future for forests (not to mention the people who depend upon them) than a quarter-century's worth of fortress conservation ever accomplished.[71]

Notes

1. Archivo General de la Nación, Mexico City, Documentos de la Secretaría de Agricultura y Recursos Hidráulicos (AGN-SARH), Caja 1575, exp. 2/28, leg. 3, Ramos Tores et al. to Secretaría de Agricultura y Ganadería, February 7, 1954.

2. On the "wealth" (*riqueza*) of ejido forests, see Ramos Torres to Adolfo Ruiz Cortines, November 13, 1954, AGN/SARH-1575/2/28-3.

3. In a bid to avoid confusion, I use the Americanized term *forest service* to refer to the federal bureau charged with managing the nation's forests, even though its official name changed five times during the period covered by this chapter.

4. Christopher R. Boyer and Emily Wakild, "Social Landscaping in the Forests of Mexico: An Environmental Interpretation of Cardenismo, 1934–1940," *Hispanic*

American Historical Review 92, no. 1 (February 2012): 73–106. For an overview of community-based conservation, see Fikret Berkes, "Rethinking Community Based Conservation," *Conservation Biology* 18, no. 3 (2004): 621–30.

5. Christopher R. Boyer, "La segunda Guerra Mundial y la crisis de producción en los bosques mexicanos," *Historia Ambiental Latinoamericana y Caribeña* 2, no. 1 (September 2012–February 2013): 7–23.

6. Dan Brockington, *Fortress Conservation: The Preservation of the Mkomazi Game Reserve* (Bloomington: University of Indiana Press, 2002).

7. Emily Wakild, *An Unexpected Environment: National Park Creation, Resource Custodianship, and the Mexican Revolution* (Tucson: University of Arizona Press, 2011).

8. Manuel Hinojosa Ortiz, *Los bosques de México: Relato de un dispilfarro y una injusticia* (Mexico City: Instituto Mexicano de Investigaciones Económicas, 1958), 12.

9. Hinojosa Ortiz, *Los bosques*, 45.

10. For example, "Visita del Sr. Subsecretario . . ." *Boletín Forestal* (Chihuahua), May 1951, 15; assorted correspondence, Villa Coss of Durango and various lawyers and government officials, AGN, Miguel Alemán Valdés (MAV), 351.1/7257.

11. Dan Klooster, "Campesinos and Mexican Forest Policy during the Twentieth Century." *Latin American Research Review* 38, no. 2 (2003): 94–126.

12. Miguel Ángel de Quevedo, "El problema de la deforestación en México: Solución práctica del mismo," *México Forestal* 2, no. 7–8 (1924): 64–69, 65.

13. Hinojosa Ortiz, *Los bosques*, 66.

14. Miguel Ángel de Quevedo, "Alocución del Señor Ing. M. A. de Quevedo . . . ," *México Forestal* 2, no. 3–4 (1924): 30–32, 31.

15. Miguel Alemán, *Los Arboles: Patrimonio de la Nación*. Collección Popular 15 (Mexico City: Editorial Ruta, 1951), 3.

16. Cited in *Novedades*, October 30, 1958, 1.

17. *Boletín Forestal*, October 1949, 15.

18. *La Prensa*, April 22, 1940.

19. Enrique Beltrán, *La batalla forestal: Lo hecho, lo no hecho, lo por hacer* (Mexico City: Editorial Cultura, 1964), 40; Lane Simonian, *Defending the Land of the Jaguar: A History of Conservation in Mexico* (Austin: University of Texas Press, 1995), 133–40.

20. Miguel Ángel de Quevedo, *Algunas consideraciones sobre nuestro problema agrario* (Mexico City: Imprenta Victoria, 1916), 15.

21. De Quevedo, *Algunas consideraciones*, 69 and in general 47–98. Fee simple ownership is the strongest form of ownership; an absolute and unconditional title.

22. Cited in *El Universal*, April 23, 1940.

23. Noé Palomares Navarro, "Palabras," in *Memoria de la III Convención Nacional Forestal* (Mexico City: Talleres de Imprenta y Offset "Policromía," 1967), 46.

24. Beltrán, *La batalla forestal*, 82.

25. Beltrán, *La batalla forestal*, 83.

26. Simonian, *Defending the Land*, 79.

27. Secretaría de Agricultura y Fomento, Dirección Forestal y de Caza y Pesca, *Ley forestal y su reglamento* (Mexico City: Talleres Gráficos de la Secretaría de Agricultura y Fomento, 1930), 6, emphasis in original deleted; Christopher R. Boyer, "Revolución y paternalismo ecológico: Miguel Ángel de Quevedo y la política forestal, 1926–1940," *Historia Mexicana* 57, no. 1 (2007): 91–138.

28. Secretaría de Agricultura y Fomento, *Ley forestal*, 57.

29. Marvin D. Crocker, "The Evolution of Mexican Forest Policy and Its Influence upon Forest Resources" (PhD dissertation, Oregon State University, 1973).

30. Obregón to Negri, June 2, 1922, quoted in Gobernador del Estado to Obregón, May 11, 1921, AGN, Álvaro Obregón (O.C.), 121-A-B-3.

31. Cited in José Luis Calva Téllez, *Economía política de la explotación forestal en México: Bibliografía comentada, 1930–1984* (Mexico City: Universidad Autónoma Capingo/Universidad Nacional Autónoma de México, 1989), 411.

32. See Agustín Salvia Spratte, *Los laberintos de Loreto y Peña Pobre* (Mexico City: Ediciones el Caballito, 1989), 61.

33. On Quevedo and the department, see Simonian, *Defending the Land*, chapter 5.

34. *Boletín del Departamento Forestal y de Caza y Pesca*, vols. 3 and 4 (1936–37).

35. Calva Téllez, *Economía Política*, Appendix IV.

36. For a list, see Secretaría de Agricultura, Ganadaría y Desarrollo Rural, Subsecretaría de Planeación, *Anuario estadístico de la producción forestal* (Mexico City: Tallares de la Dirección General de Información Agropecuaria, Forestal y de Fauna Silvestre, 1996), 815, tables 212 and 213.

37. For example, see the partial suspensions declared in 1952 in favor of Triplay Maderas de Durango, Montes, Industrias y Minas (Mexico State and Michoacán), Telefonía (Chihuahua), and Maderas Campechanas, all in AGN-MAV, 111/42114.

38. Salvia Spratte, *Los laberintos*, 73.

39. See the indirect allusion to this phenomenon in Escarcega D. and Ornelas to Alemán, Chihuahua, April 20, 1951, AGN/MAV-351.1/18644.

40. Meyer to Avila Camacho, October 1, 1944. AGN, Manuel Avila Camacho (MAC), 501.1/104,

41. *El Universal*, December 5, 1939.

42. *El Universal*, March 13, 1940. See also *El Nacional*, March 12, 1940. González was Secretario de Acción Campesina de la Federación de Trabajadores del Estado de Veracruz.

43. Coquet to Director General de Información, July 15, 1946, AGN/MAC-545.22/573.

44. Patricia Gerez Fernández, "¿Qué pasa en el Cofre de Perote?," in *Desarrollo y Medio Ambiente en Veracruz*, ed. Eckart Boege and Hopólito Rodríguez (Mexico City: CIESAS/Fundación Friedrich Ebert, 1992), 152.

45. Banda to Avila Camacho, November 5, 1944, AGN/MAC-501.1/5.

46. Report of Rubén Martínez, contained in Calderón to Secretario de Agricultura, December 30, 1946, Archivo Histórico del Estado de Veracruz (AHEV), caja 1339, exp. 3220.

47. Adolfo Ruiz Cortines to Secretaría de Agricultura y Fomento, November 13, 1946, and February 10, 1947, AHEV-1339/3220.

48. *Excélsior*, April 25, 1959.

49. *Novedades*, November 3, 1952.

50. Gerez Fernández, "¿Qué pasa en el Cofre de Perote?," 152.

51. *El Gráfico*, August 17, 1929.

52. Sánchez to C. Presidente de la República, January 31, 1939, AGN, Lázaro Cárdenas del Río (L.C.R.), 502/12.

53. *El Universal*, April 22, 1940.

54. *El Universal*, May 18, 1950.

55. Gómez Galeana to Alemán, April 25, 1947, and February 3, 1948, AGN/DGIPS-12/2/380(9)38.

56. González Nava to Dip. Raymundo Flores Fuentes, July 31, 1957, AGN/SARH-753/2333/2.

57. *Excélsior*, May 9, 1957.

58. Diego Guzmán et al. to Presidente Constitucional de los Estadosunidos [sic] Mexicanos, September 23, 1950, AGN/MAV-351.1/5210.

59. Escarcega D. and Ornelas to Alemán, Chihuahua, April 20, 1951, AGN/MAV-351.1/18644.

60. *Boletín Forestal*, May 1951, 15.

61. Carlos García to Miguel Angel de Quevedo, Veracruz, April 23, 1939, AGN/LCR-501.1/56.

62. Director Gerente de la Unión Citricultores Michoacanos to Presidente de la República, September 4, 1950, AGN/MAV-351.1/5210.

63. For a collection of letters written to the president by educated urbanites requesting limits on timbering, see AGN/MAC-501.1/5. See also Comisión Permanente del Primer Congreso Nacional Deportivo Pro-Reforestación to Presidente de la República, August 22, 1950, AGN/MAV-351.1/6216.

64. Asociación de los Hijos y Amigos de Angangueo to Lázaro Cárdenas, November 19, 1940. See also *Boletín de la Asociación de los Hijos y Amigos de Angangueo*, no. 3, November 15, 1940, AGN/LCR-501.2/375.

65. Joel Simon, *Endangered Mexico: An Environment on the Edge* (San Francisco: Sierra Club Books, 1997), 242–44.

66. See the *Anuario Estadístico*, 1950–60.

67. Cuauhtémoc González Pacheco, *Los bosques de México y la banca internacional* (Mexico City: Instituto de Investigaciones Económicas, Universidad Nacional Autónoma de México, 1995), 26–52, 2.

68. Secretaría de Agricultura y Ganadería, Subsecretaría Forestal y de la Fauna, "Levantamiento de vedas Forestales," typescript, 1973; Calva Téllez, *Economía Política*, 438–41, 91.

69. Statewide or nearly statewide bans were lifted in Aguascalientes, Baja California Norte, Chihuahua, Colima, Guanajuato, Hidalgo, Jalisco, Michoacán, Morelos, Puebla, Querétaro, Sinaloa, Sonora, Veracruz, and the Federal District.

70. Bill Weinberg, "Mexico: Lacandón Selva Conflict Grows," NACLA *Report on the Americas* 36, no. 6 (2003): 26–47.

71. For case studies on these experiments in community forestry, see David Barton Bray, Leticia Merino Pérez, and Deborah Barry, eds., *The Community Forests of Mexico: Managing for Sustainable Landscapes* (Austin: University of Texas Press, 2005).

CHAPTER 10 | *María Teresa Fernández Aceves*

ADVOCATE OR *CACICA*?

Guadalupe Urzúa Flores: Modernizer and Peasant
Political Leader in Jalisco

On December 7, 2004, a Jalisco congressman announced to the state legislature that María Guadalupe Urzúa Flores (1912–2004) had died. According to the state representative, Urzúa Flores was an outstanding and well-known Jalisco PRIísta at the national, regional, and local levels. He stated that Urzúa Flores "was an intelligent advocate of the outcasts, who always shared her knowledge and fought for educational issues."[1] He finished by lauding her promotion of public works and asked his fellow members of Congress to observe a minute of silence. Her long and successful political career, which included stints as a councilwoman, congresswoman, and mayor, shows that she was more an advocate, or *gestora*, than a *cacica*, or local strongwoman. More selflessly than most, she exercised power to modernize rural Jalisco. From the 1940s onward she promoted health and educational programs, pushed for land reform, and tried to influence the implementation of public works, including the construction of an asylum, dams, an electrical power system, and highways as well as the introduction of drinking water, postal service, telephones, wells, and waterholes.

The story of Urzúa Flores helps us explore how individual experiences in rural Mexico intertwined with broader processes such as the sanitation of Mexican society, the modernization of patriarchy, the execution of land reform, the building of modern political corporatist institutions, and the incorporation of women in public posts.[2] Urzúa Flores is indeed an excellent example of the nuances of how Mexican social policy was built at competing and contrasting levels, from the top down and the bottom up, by *caciques* and rural advocates. In this chapter I explore how Urzúa Flores emerged as a rural leader, enjoyed a long political career, and, by representing male and female peasants, became a political and cultural intermediary between local, state, and federal groups. To do this she had to negotiate the shifting dynamics of power among these different factions. She initially remained at the margins of the local political structures, subordinate to a raft of authoritarian rural caciques. Yet empowered by both agrarian reform and full female suffrage, Urzúa Flores became more familiar with the legal codes and political networks necessary to lobby on behalf of her constituency. In doing so she shifted from being a subordinate of various caciques to a rural advocate in her own right.

The first section discusses the conceptual differences between cacique and advocate. The second section examines Urzúa Flores's family background; the village politics of her hometown, San Martín Hidalgo; and the changing political forces of the various ruling caciques. The third section looks at Guadalupe's campaign to build a local hospital and illustrates how she became a local leader and advocate. In the fourth section I discuss her ideas on the role of women, women's needs, and her proposal for land reform aimed specifically at peasant women. Finally, I briefly trace her role as a congresswoman and municipal president. I argue that the case of Urzúa Flores helps us think about what it meant to be a charismatic and influential woman in rural Mexico after the 1940s, and I contend that feminist scholars need to think more about this kind of women and how to name them: cacicas or advocates?

Caciques versus Advocates

To understand Urzúa Flores's long and successful political career as an advocate, it is necessary to highlight the differences between the terms *cacique* and *advocate* by shedding light on their modus operandi. Most scholars agree that the term *cacique* refers to local leaders who employed arbitrary, personal, informal, and violent means of exercising power.[3] "Resistant to formal laws and regulations," they used different methods, including verbal persuasion, intrigue, clientelism, and violence.[4] Such practices could elicit respect but also vehement opposition. As Alan Knight argues, caciques were "flesh-and-blood local bigwigs, who were known, feared, respected or hated."[5] As a result, many followed distinct career arcs, rising up during periods of crisis, maturing, and then perishing at the hands of their opponents.[6]

During the twentieth century, most Mexican governments relied on caciques to mediate between the state and particular territories. Although they often officially represented the state, their local standing depended on traditional forms of patrimonial and clientelist authority. As such, they can "be seen as products of the incongruous union of 'modern' politics with 'traditional' society . . . [with its unequal] bonds of reciprocity and patronage."[7]

Caciques were particularly common in the period immediately after the revolution. Although some were throwbacks to the Porfirian era, many were popular leaders who defied local landlords, priests, and elites. However, during the following decades, they became increasingly institutionalized, adapting to a stronger government apparatus and "facilitat[ing] and condition[ing] state intervention."[8]

In addition to being connected to a distinct way of doing politics, caciques also have been identified with traditional notions of Mexican masculinity and feted for their sexual prowess, propensity to violence, and hard drinking.[9] According to Heather Fowler-Salamini, caciques' methods—including "the use of violence, the manipulation of power, nepotism and physical and psychological intimidation"—have been conceived as "distinctly male mechanisms."[10] Although some feminist historians have rethought the relationship between *caciquismo* and gender and unearthed a variety of female *cacicazgos*, they often have concluded that cacicas often used the same methods as their male counterparts.[11]

Urzúa Flores was not a cacica. She was what I call an advocate. Advocates differed from traditional caciques in two ways. On the one hand, rather than instrumentally using state patronage to build up personal clientelist links, they were more altruistic, solving local problems to benefit communities. On the other hand, they also eschewed the threat or use of violence.[12] Such an approach necessitated three interlinking qualities: an intimate knowledge of the needs of the local communities, an understanding of the state's political and bureaucratic power structure, and a talent for the rhetorical and written demands of lobbying.[13] Although the favorable solution of local problems contributed to advocates' local prestige, unlike caciques they were not the driving force behind those demands.

Thus, although advocates often had to work from within state organizations, they were not simply modern, airbrushed, media-savvy versions of traditional revolutionary caciques. Instead they could trace their descent from turn of the century social Catholics, who strove to carve out positions as local intermediaries and activists within the patriarchal hierarchy of the Catholic church. In mid-century Mexico they were most closely related to the middle-class social workers described by Nichole Sanders. Like the social workers who struggled on behalf of poor mothers and orphans in Mexico City, rural advocates sought solutions to distinct local problems and in doing so shaped the state's social policy.[14] By the 1940s, such approaches had forced "policymakers [to] believe that the state would succeed by working in partnership with women."[15]

At times, advocates and caciques could appear similar. They shared certain roles, as intermediaries within a paternalist and clientelist political system.

Both received compensations for their loyalty as well as political protection. Both participated in electoral processes and both gathered political information because it was crucial to know the changing power relations within their communities. As a result, advocates like Urzúa Flores often were accused of being caciques. Yet they never pursued power for power's sake nor employed violent means to do so. As we shall see, some caciques, like General Marcelino García Barragán, were also advocates. However, not all advocates were cacicas.

Family Background

María Guadalupe Urzúa Flores was born in Jocotepec, Jalisco, on the Chapala Riviera on December 12, 1912. She grew up in a liberal family who were, in general, professionals, probably from the incipient rural middle class. Her father's family comprised musicians who had been based in Jocotepec for some time. In contrast, her maternal grandfather was a more recent arrival; he had served as a physician in Benito Juárez's guards.[16] In 1896 the families came together when the musician married the doctor's daughter and schoolteacher, Rosario Flores Monroy.[17] They had two children: Manuel and Guadalupe. Rosario Flores Monroy died after giving birth to Guadalupe, and her death shaped Guadalupe's life. Guadalupe's father decided to keep and raise Manuel in Jocotepec, while three-day-old Guadalupe went to live with her aunts in San Martín Hidalgo.

During the revolution, local leaders in San Martín Hidalgo became *agraristas*, taking advantage of the 1915 agrarian law to demand the restitution of their properties. Venustiano Carranza visited the village in 1916 and publicly recognized these leaders; three years later they received their lands.[18] Over the next decade the village became divided between those who had benefitted from government largesse and those who had not. During the Cristiada (1926–29) these divisions ossified, and the village split between pro-state agraristas and anti-state Cristeros. During the 1930s, Alfonso G. Ceballos, a classic agrarian cacique of the Cárdenas era, ruled the village, using force and electoral imposition to maintain control and removing both Callistas and Cristeros from power. Ceballos's local dominance generated greater political rewards: in 1936 he was made a senator's deputy and in 1943 a federal congressman.[19] Political power also brought economic returns, and by the 1940s Ceballos had become owner of one of the largest ranches in the region.[20]

Guadalupe's uncles and aunts hailed from the rural middle class. Most worked as teachers, but Julia was a pharmacist who owned a drugstore in San Martín Hidalgo.[21] According to interviews with those who knew Guadalupe, her relationship with Julia taught her many of the lessons she later would employ in political life. First, it taught her to sympathize with, respect, and help society's outcasts. Many of her aunt's clients visited the drugstore to receive treatment for leprosy, a disease that automatically led to poverty, marginalization, and exclusion. For Guadalupe, it was only a small step from empathizing with the village lepers to commiserating with the community's wider underclass. In fact, it proved especially easy in an era when poor peasants represented the diseased social body[22] and were instructed to "be sanitized—[their] drinking, gambling, playing, womanizing, and violence curtailed."[23]

Beyond this moral lesson, Guadalupe's relationship with Julia also taught her more explicit political rules. According to those I interviewed, these included the value of hard work, the importance of honesty in public service, the avoidance of politicking, and a profound distrust of men. The last rule was probably the result of Julia's rape by the municipal president during the Cristiada.[24] Guadalupe did not pursue all this advice; instead she began her own process of individualization,[25] giving these values and practices another meaning and reconfiguring them to answer immediate popular demands. Perhaps her aunt's distrust of men affected Guadalupe in another way. She certainly used her beauty to attract, manipulate, and work with men in the political sphere but always kept her romantic and intimate relations with men entirely separate.

At the same time, Guadalupe also displayed an interest in politics from an early age.[26] In 1922 Guadalupe skipped school and went to the kiosk to hear José Guadalupe Zuno's progressive speeches about land reform and workers' rights during his gubernatorial campaign.[27] Impressed by the young schoolgirl, after finishing his speech Zuno reached down and introduced himself to Guadalupe. They would remain firm friends. Besides listening to the speeches of regional leaders, Guadalupe also paid attention to local agrarista Silvestre Coracero's stories about the agrarian movement in San Martín Hidalgo. According to a rather romanticized biography by one of her followers, as a child Guadalupe asked Coracero if he could show her his plot of land. He replied with tears in his eyes that it had been taken away. Guadalupe promised to return it when she grew up.[28]

Unlike many other girls growing up in Catholic Jalisco, Guadalupe received a liberal state education. She started her studies at the Josefa Ortiz de Domínguez School in San Martín Hidalgo and finished her primary education at the school attached to the teacher training college in Zacoalco de Torres.[29] In Guadalajara she attended a middle school and studied accounting for three years.[30] At the *Academia Comercial "Vizcarra"* in Guadalajara she received training in commercial law and shorthand with the aim of becoming a secretary. Here she acquired the rudiments of written culture needed to send letters and petitions on behalf of her constituents.

Yet Guadalupe's teenage years were not simply about education. By the end of the 1920s Guadalupe had become an attractive young woman who took part in the new rhythm of rural festivities. She organized the mariachi band of the *Flecherros'* barrio, and during Lent in 1931 she was elected the princess of the carnival of San Martín Hidalgo.[31] (The beauty competition acted as a secular, government-sponsored counterpoint to the staid Catholic practices that dominated earlier Lenten rituals.) Because of her beauty and cheerful character, Guadalupe had several suitors vying for her attention. San Martín Hidalgo still maintained a racial hierarchy of beauty, and as an educated white woman surrounded by mestizo peasants, she probably reveled in displaying her sexuality to these devoted men. However, despite the fact that she attracted attention, she eschewed marriage, maintaining throughout her life that married women always suffered.[32] Instead she resolved to take charge of her sexuality and became another type of woman: one who promoted the modernization of patriarchy and sought to transform traditional gender roles through civic, labor, and agrarian reforms.[33] At the same time, her health and social programs concurred with the "rationalization of domesticity" promoted by the Department of Education (SEP) and other state agencies that supported "'modern' notions of health, hygiene, medicine, household organization, and child development."[34]

In the 1930s Guadalupe started her involvement in public works. In 1933 she met Lázaro Cárdenas during his campaign tour of San Martín Hidalgo. As a trained teacher, she also worked at the Centro Cultural Deportivo "Hidalgo" and organized the *Academia de Capacitación Femenil Municipal*, a workshop that gave instruction in cooking, embroidery, shorthand, and English. She formed a theater group called "Hidalgo," which raised funds for a basketball court, participated in a program of planting trees, and helped build a road between the town's cemetery and its main street. Two years later she started her career as an advocate, allying with the regional military chief Marcelino García Barragán to construct a highway between Guadalajara and Barra de Navidad. She visited local communities, collected signatures, and sent their petitions to federal authorities, while General García Barragán met with entrepreneurs, governors, and federal bureaucrats.[35] By the mid-1930s such projects had generated clear agrarian and political affiliations. In 1936 she joined the female branch of the Regional Agrarian Committee, and in 1938 she became the secretary of feminine action for the peasant wing of the national party and a founding member of the Confederación Nacional Campesina (CNC).[36]

By her mid-twenties, Guadalupe had made it clear that she identified herself with the community's outcasts. She soon became known as *voluntariosa*—meaning both keen and/or stubborn—someone who refused to give up her work on behalf of the poor. Her interest and commitment to eliminate leprosy and improve her own town's living conditions and health, educational, and communication services distinguished her as a social fighter. For Guadalupe, the search for social justice was important. At the entrance of her house, she had a mural that said: "if you love liberty and fight against injustice, you may come in, since you are at home."

Although Guadalupe was close to local *ejidatarios*, she did not advocate for the complete elimination of rural inequality. Rather, like the governing party after 1940, she sought a rise in the living standards of peasants. Yet despite this ideological confluence, many rival politicians sought to explain her ascent in sexual terms. One rumor claimed that Guadalupe enchanted men and bent them to her will, linking the advocate's beauty to the nineteenth-century image of the femme fatale, the siren who attracted, manipulated, and destroyed men.[37] Another rumor—which gained popular purchase—suggested that Guadalupe, by entering politics, had sacrificed her femininity and sense of honor.[38]

Social Work and Advocacy

To understand how Urzúa Flores managed to manipulate official bureaucracies to fulfill local demands, it is worth focusing on a specific case study, namely the construction of the hospital in San Martín Hidalgo. Although the federal state had dabbled in linking healthcare to agrarian reform, by the 1940s the government had focused its efforts on providing medical care to the urban poor.[39] Despite this shift, a mixture of bottom-up local fundraising and effective advocacy by intermediaries like Urzúa Flores could still bring results.[40] In the early 1940s, Urzúa Flores used her experience as Secretary of Social Affairs and Health for the Ejido Committee[41] to begin public fundraising for a hospital in San Martín Hidalgo.[42] In this year, Guadalupe sent several letters to the Treasury, the governor of Jalisco, and Chicago-based *braceros* to request a plot on which to build the proposed institution. She suggested a piece of land next to the Calvary Church. She also requested financial help for the construction of the hospital, arguing that the project was "in fulfillment of a humanitarian and patriotic responsibility."[43] By 1944 she had been made president of the village's pro-hospital committee and had put together a budget for the costs of its construction. In the same year the government granted the requested location for building the hospital and the committee began work.

Nevertheless, such local advocacy had its limits. Funds were not forthcoming, and in mid-1945 Guadalupe went to Mexico City to talk with Gustavo Baz, the Health Minister, about the public health problem in San Martín Hidalgo. She paid particular attention to the ostracized peasants with leprosy. A picture in her personal archive indicates that she had an interview with Baz as well as representatives from the National Federation of Technical Schools.[44]

Because Urzúa Flores had attended a school attached to one of the teacher training colleges, she probably sympathized with their demands for better accommodation, rations, and stipends.[45] During the interview with Baz, she asked if he could grant her funds to finish the building of the hospital and provide doctors and nurses to run it. According to the male elders of San Martín Hidalgo, her beauty impressed the minister so much that she was able to obtain what she solicited. However, her personal archive indicates that this face-to-face meeting was not enough, and she had to continue her work despite Baz's promise.

During the last half of 1945 the committee worked hard at the fundraising campaign by sending letters to federal, state, and local representatives of state agencies and braceros in the United States. They also sponsored bullfights, sold drinks at local *cantinas*, sold bread and flowers, and organized a series of fundraising parties. By 1946 the committee received a letter notifying them that they would be given ten thousand dollars from the Department of Health. However, they received only five thousand. Guadalupe wrote again to Baz to inform him of their progress, detail the precarious economic condition of her hometown, and request more funding. Two years later the committee agreed to use the five thousand dollars for "a septic tank, plaster, floors, two bathrooms, and a main entrance." In 1949 the committee received another twenty-five hundred dollars. At that point, Urzúa Flores sought greater state support and approached Beatriz Velasco de Alemán, the wife of President Miguel Alemán, to ask for help.

Velasco not only represented an alternative route to the president; as the wife of an important political leader, she often was deemed duty-bound to show interest in "soft issues" of health. Access to the president's wife seemed to open doors, and the following year Urzúa Flores wrote to President Alemán, explaining that "with a lot of sacrifices" they had been able "to build part of a hospital in San Martín Hidalgo" but that "many things" remained before its "final completion."[46] By 1952 the state provided a monthly stipend of 250 pesos to cover expenses. By 1953 the hospital had evolved significantly and Urzúa Flores estimated that it had cost nearly ninety thousand dollars in total. Yet the institution still required local input. To run the hospital, the committee proposed that the town's doctors train young local women to attend the sick. Women would receive a three-month training in inoculations, the use of medical tools, preventive medicine, and hygiene. With this training, these women could work in the hospital, receive a modest salary, and aid both their families and society at large. Aping contemporary state pronouncements that emphasized women's maternal roles and linking this to ideas of Christian duty, the committee advertised the posts as follows: "To serve others is a duty that is imposed by God. Prepare yourself to supply relief to the humble homes of the suffering with your knowledge and experience. Don't throw away the opportunity that has presented itself. If you are not a mother, think that every woman is potentially a mother and that you should prepare yourself for maternal love as well as for more sublime experiences."[47] Individual women like Urzúa Flores may have shaped public policy, but popular perceptions of gender roles remained firmly intact.

From Health and Public Works to Women's Issues in the 1950s

Mexican women had campaigned for women's suffrage since the 1910s. In the late 1930s the *Frente Único Pro Derechos de la Mujer* failed to get women the vote. In the second half of the 1940s this issue gained force once more as different women's associations mobilized and pushed for female suffrage. The debate focused on issues of social equality. According to Gabriela Cano, "in the mindset of the Ruiz Cortines administration women had no social relevance by themselves, as individuals with their own rights. They were important as long as they supported their man in his daily struggle and as long as they carried out their role as a mother. Only then were they recognized as possessing specific moral virtues."[48]

During Adolfo Ruiz Cortines's 1952 presidential campaign, Urzúa Flores organized a group of women who waited for him on the highway and forced the presidential bus to stop. When Ruiz Cortines asked who Urzúa Flores was, some local people pointed out that she was "a *voluntariosa* woman" who worked very hard for her community and an elected councilwoman from San Martín Hidalgo. Ruiz Cortines allowed her to get on the bus. In so doing Urzúa Flores made the dramatic shift onto the national political scene. She would become Jalisco's first federal congresswoman and was one of the first five federal congresswomen in Mexico.[49] She benefited from Ruiz Cortines's policy of sharing power between the presidency and other local leaders.[50]

In April 1953 the Partido Revolucionario Institucional (PRI) held the First National Women's Congress. As a councilwoman, Urzúa Flores presented a paper entitled "Women's Issues." This was a turning point in Guadalupe's agenda, as she expanded beyond health and public works to more general problems of gender inequality. The shift resembled a move toward what Temma Kaplan has termed *female consciousness*. While Guadalupe still accepted "the gender system of [her] society," with its stress on home life and motherhood, her defense of these ideals pushed her toward gradual politicization.[51] In her paper, Guadalupe asserted that a woman was the foundation of the household. As a result, the state had a duty to respect her, protect her, and maintain her dignity. Until now, she claimed, the Mexican legislature had done little to fulfill these duties, and so she demanded that the legislature introduce a body of regulations designed to do just that. She argued that women must receive a just wage that satisfies their needs and should not be forced to work more than nine hours as stated by the Labor Code. It is also necessary to establish training centers, where women can be properly instructed and to stop the influence of fanaticism that atrophies their mind . . . In a poor home, women lack everything, because of the meager wage of their husbands or their own salaries, and are unable to produce strong and well-nourished children. Because their feeding is inadequate and is often not sufficient to feed them and their children, there is a high rate of infant mortality, and [in this case] the child, society and the Patria lose.[52]

Guadalupe demanded the punishment of medical doctors who gave health certificates to people with venereal diseases; the extension of health services to prostitutes; the increase of inoculations against diphtheria, smallpox, and typhus; the donation of corn mills and sewing machines; and the intensification of programs designed to give women an idea of "civic culture."[53]

During this period, Urzúa Flores not only lobbied for social programs for San Martín Hidalgo but also started linking up with other councilwomen to press for wider regional campaigns. In May 1953 a group of councilwomen from the municipalities of Guadalajara, Tamazula de Gordiano, Puerto Vallarta, Ahualulco de Mercado, and San Martín Hidalgo proposed to the state's first congress of municipalities that they work on the problems outlined by Urzúa Flores.[54] The prominence of these female politicians illustrates that by the early 1950s women were seen as key to the co-option of a large section of the voting public. In Jalisco, female elected leaders moved from running as councilwomen, state congresswomen, and federal congresswomen during the 1950s to mayors in the 1960s and deputy senators in the 1970s.[55]

In July 1953 Urzúa Flores presented a paper at the First Women's National Congress about the reforms needed in the agrarian code to grant equal rights to women. Like Concha Michel, a teacher and Communist in the 1930s, Urzúa Flores demanded that peasant women enjoy the same right to receive land as men.[56] She argued that Mexican peasant women had worked in the fields, participated actively in peasant movements, and been involved in community efforts to demand equal rights for men and women. For Urzúa Flores, though, the principal role of the peasant women was that of moderator, not agitator. She believed that the "peasant woman" would be "an example of courage, patience, and perseverance," concluding that the revolution owed a debt to the Mexican peasant woman and that this debt had yet to be paid.

After the closing of the First National Women's Congress, Guadalupe became the national representative of peasant women in the CNC, expanding her role from advocate and councilwoman to policymaker. On August 9, 1953,

Guadalupe proposed that the president implement the following policies: organize peasant women into Female Leagues; inform them of the president's proposals for solving their economic and agrarian problems; and promote their involvement in boards of moral, civic and material improvement. During her three-year tenure as a CNC leader, she followed this plan, privileging material advancements such as schools, childcare centers, school breakfasts, and maternity centers for mothers and children. She programmed a three-week educational and technical training course for female peasants about Mexican history, political economy, civic education, child rearing, hygiene, crops, law, literacy, rural tourism, sports, and physical education. In these workshops women received "scientific" instruction laden with middle-class values and assumptions of political obedience, which taught them how to be good mothers and wives and how to engage in civic and political life through the CNC and the PRI.[57]

How did Urzúa Flores conceive of the peasant women she was appointed to serve? Like many urban teachers and policymakers, Guadalupe had a deeply naturalizing view of the *campesina*. In some of her personal writings she laid out her ideas in full. She envisioned the peasant woman as loving her patria, her land, and her school. She stated that as a political leader she desired that the peasant household achieve both unity and prosperity and argued that a commitment to social justice could achieve these aims. She concluded: "In this way, I will fight against all resistance that opposes the ideal that lives and grows more each day in my female consciousness."[58] Guadalupe's ideas of peasant women were not only gender constructions; they also intertwined with class and race issues. Guadalupe was far whiter than most of the peasants she helped. Her formal suits contrasted sharply with campesinas' more practical costumes. Thus, although she attempted to help these peasant women, she failed to undermine established social hierarchies or the normal expectations of poor women. In fact, her actions probably reinforced the paternalist nature of the system. Her sole publication, *Decálogo para nuestras voluntarias del ejército femenino protector de la infancia y de la salud*, focused on women's roles as mothers and rearers of healthy children.

The 1955 Federal Elections for Congress

Although the president backed Urzúa Flores's shift from local to national prominence, her political ascendance was not without controversy. Her campaign for state deputy in 1955 provoked a heated debate. Editorials in the state newspaper El *Informador* questioned electoral transparency, criticized the exclusion of the Partido Acción Nacional (PAN), disapproved of the president's absolute control of the selection process granted by the Electoral Code of 1946, satirized the meaning and function of these federal state representatives, pointed out the role of violent and repressive caciques in local politics, and cast doubt on the real emergence of women as voters and elected officials.[59] In Jalisco the most contentious electoral district was Autlán. The town became a kind of electoral laboratory that tested the strength of local caciques backed by the PRI, the regional force of the PAN, and women's power to shape local politics. The town had particular significance because it was the birthplace of Efraín González Luna, the leader of the PAN's Catholic faction, as well as the center of PRIísta General Marcelino García Barragán's cacicazgo.[60] During the electoral campaign, six hundred conservative women of Autlán protested to El Informador that PRI politicians were going to place voting booths far out of town.[61] They claimed that it was only possible to get there by horse. Yet despite these complaints, Urzúa Flores won. Fraud might have played a part, but so did her reputation for delivering social justice and, as a "strong-willed woman," for getting things done. After her victory, Carlos Pineda Flores, a PANista congressman, denounced the election of Urzúa Flores as an example of PRI fraud. Urzúa Flores replied that she had traveled through 19 of the region's towns and had won with a clear majority of 22,476 votes to Pineda Flores's 5,471.[62] She also sought to embarrass the PANista by claiming that he failed to follow the civic and moral duties which she, a woman, so dutifully obeyed.[63]

As a congresswoman, Urzúa Flores visited her electoral district frequently and pursued the same policy of pressing the government hard for the introduction of infrastructure and public works. During her term she successfully lobbied for a hospital, mobile health brigades, the construction of schools, more federal teachers, the introduction of drinking water in Tecolotlán, and the paving of the streets of San Martín Hidalgo. In doing so she demonstrated that when women were elected to public posts they were just as capable of fulfilling social programs as their male counterparts. The tensions between her accomplishments and the stereotypes of Mexican women, which still pervaded politics in the region, were expressed in pieces in the local newspapers. On the one hand, many articles lauded her efforts at bringing "modernization" and "progress" to the area.[64] On the other hand, others were less adulatory, mocking the presumptuous and immoral attitude of political women. In one cartoon a man is shown on his knees praying that his wife would not become a congresswoman.[65] In another the first congresswomen are depicted as mermaids on the shore, the congressmen armed and ready to hunt them.[66]

Despite these slights, Urzúa Flores continued. She was federal congresswoman four times (1955–58, 1964–67, 1970–73, and 1976–79) and represented the central and coastal regions of Jalisco in the CNC.[67] She was also head of the female sector of the CNC at the federal and state levels.[68] The position of federal congresswoman suited her goals. Such a position offered her space to maneuver and a certain degree of autonomy in challenging authoritarian local caciques, as the following example illustrates. In 1957, as a federal congresswoman representing the electoral district of Autlán, she co-opted the presidential candidate Adolfo López Mateos's campaign slogan, "Caciques last only as long as the people want," to present a diagnosis of the region's problems.[69] Claiming that local caciques still influenced politics in the region and abused, made death threats against, and falsely imprisoned peasant protestors, she demanded that the government offer women economic autonomy, build more irrigation projects, and fund more rural schools.

The complaint coincided with articles in El Informador that attacked the continued involvement of caciques in local politics and the threat they presented to the lives and livelihoods of peasants.[70] These attacks on cacique control seem to have focused on the local strongman, General García Barragán, whose support of Miguel Henríquez Guzman's electoral campaign in 1952 had sidelined him from the national party.[71] Was Urzúa Flores turning on her old ally, trying to escape from the tutelage of the men who still dominated the region?[72] Perhaps, in which case this attempt to cross the gendered boundaries of Mexican politics was less successful than her other, less contentious campaigns. López Mateos rehabilitated García Barragán, reinstating him to lead the military zone in Guadalajara and in 1964 appointing him defense minister.[73] The PRI, it turned out, was unwilling to let a woman take control of an entire region.

Los Lupistas

So far I have described Urzúa Flores's relations with politicians further up the political hierarchy. However, to maintain local control, Guadalupe also created a network of followers in Jalisco's towns and villages, popularly known as the "*lupistas*." Her most loyal and faithful followers were Tomás García Tadeo, a mailman; Jesús Camacho Barreto, a teacher and mayor of San Martín Hidalgo; and Juan Díaz. She also allied with local agrarian leaders in the neighboring villages. Beyond these figures her supporters were predominantly peasants and ejidatarios. Her female base was organized around the female section of the *ejido*. However, these campesinas were not as visible as her male supporters, perhaps because of the violence, both symbolic and physical, that female politicking could incur.[74]

After the death of the revolutionary agrarian cacique Alfonso Ceballos in 1950, she used this network of lupistas to put in place supportive municipal authorities. To do this, she built strong links with federal and state political networks. According to local elders, she proposed candidates directly. Almost all came from the CNC, and on most occasions her suggestions were taken up by the local PRI. However, during the 1970s the CNC started to lose ground to the middle-class catch all sector of the party, the Confederación Nacional de Organizaciones Populares (CNOP). According to Jaime Sánchez Susarrey, by this stage the CNC was the weakest sector of the official party in Jalisco, controlling only a single electoral district.[75] This shift caused considerable problems for Guadalupe. Local agrarian businessmen dedicated to the production of maize allied with the CNOP leader, Guillermo Cosío Vidaurri, and displaced lupistas in municipal governments from the 1970s through the 1990s.

Only Urzúa Flores escaped the cull. She was municipal president twice: first in her native town of Jocotepec (1983–86) and second in San Martín Hidalgo (1997–2001). By the late 1990s she was in her eighties, had diabetes, and was easily disoriented. Yet she still possessed considerable popular legitimacy. During the same decade the PRI had suffered two defeats in San Martín Hidalgo. In response, a few savvy PRI operators noticed that when Urzúa Flores attended public events, many people reached out and greeted her with affection, gratitude, and respect. This faction harnessed her popularity, put her up for election, and recovered political ground. Many people knew that Guadalupe was being used, but nobody did anything. Because of her age and the onset of Alzheimer's disease, she was unable to realize that her time had passed. The minutes of the municipal council in San Martín recorded what she suggested when the council was in session. Several times she proposed getting a plot on which to build the hospital that she had managed to construct in the 1940s. She had lost her sense of space, time, and memory. Younger PRIístas took advantage and sequestered municipal funds for their own use. Guadalupe eventually died in an old people's home in Jocotepec in 2004, ninety-one years old and alone.

Final Considerations

By adopting a long-term, biographical perspective, this case study helps to personalize and explain key shifts in Mexico's twentieth-century politics—from the construction of the new revolutionary state to the building of modern corporatist institutions to their eventual collapse. At the same time, Guadalupe's life history lays out the changing place of women in Mexican politics, from organizing specifically female-oriented groups to joining state agencies to running for electoral office.

Guadalupe did not belong to a political family or one linked to the region's cacicazgos, and she first entered politics because of her pity for the village outcasts. This sense of commitment marked her career, and she continued to lobby for the construction of hospitals, schools, libraries, dams, highways, and social welfare centers until her death. At the same time, she was never a radical feminist; instead she promoted the modernization of patriarchy and the rationalization of domesticity through her bottom-up advocacy and her female consciousness. The length of her political career contrasted markedly with the fairly short career span of most women of her generation, like Hermila Galindo (who asked the constitutionalist deputies to include women's suffrage in the 1917 Constitution) or Elvia Carrillo Puerto. These women played important roles at certain times in certain spaces and often relied on the patronage of important (male) relatives. Urzúa Flores may not have been such a vocal proponent of radical change, but as an advocate she contributed significantly to expanding the role of peasants, rural communities, and women within the PRI after the electoral changes of the late 1940s and early 1950s.

After the foundation of the PRI in 1946 and the recognition of women's municipal suffrage in 1947, the party's newly enfranchised women supported its daily construction of hegemony. Women expanded the PRI's base, mobilized when they were required, and contributed to offsetting dissident movements during the administrations of Miguel Alemán, Adolfo Ruiz Cortines, and Adolfo López Mateos. After the recognition of women's suffrage at the federal level in 1953, the PRI promoted the gradual incorporation of women through female branches at all levels. These branches were designed to ensure, discipline, and make permanent women's political loyalty.[76] However, there were contentious relationships within the PRI because of the gap between policy and practice. After the federal elections of 1958, women protested bitterly that party unity was still lacking because many male members still perceived women as "unfit for politics." PRIísta women requested a real program and demanded that the male leadership of the PRI recognize the civil participation of women.

Despite the discrepancies between men and women within the PRI, during the 1950s PRIísta women focused mainly on social policies, which often concerned their role as mothers. Women became key reformers in communities and in the party, often co-opting their expected role as mother and caregiver to push the "softer" social benefits of state reform. Thus the entry of women into the political sphere reconfigured the PRI's aims. There was a move away from land and labor reform and toward welfare, hospitals, schools, and childcare, areas in which women played key roles. More money was now spent on appeasing these key voters through workshops (sewing, food, vegetable gardens) especially because they were perceived as instinctively pro-church conservatives. In the long run the presence of women within the PRI made the party more inclusive of distinct political cultures, ranging from macho revolutionary cacique posturing (like Gonzalo N. Santos) to these rather altruistic advocates, in doing so marginalizing an earlier generation of powerful conservatives: the women of Acción Católica Mexicana.

Women like Urzúa Flores, with her legacy of hospitals, free medical services, schools, and kindergartens and her legions of male and female followers, were crucial to the renovation of PRI strength during the 1950s and 1960s, especially during the political conflicts with both the left and right. These women were undoubtedly extremely powerful, and by allowing Urzúa Flores to run for federal office, the PRI acknowledged this fact. Yet they did not act as traditional caciques, with their martial heritage, network of supportive kin, and small-town demagogy. Rather, they seem closer to advocates, pushing for social change within the system and, in so doing, maintaining it.

Notes

1. Archivo del Congreso del Estado de Jalisco (ACEJ), *Diario de Debates*, 1:XI, no. 76, "Tiene la palabra el diputado Armando Pérez Oliva."

2. *Diario Oficial*, February 12, 1947, 3–4; Enriqueta Tuñón Pablos, *¡Por fin . . . ya podemos elegir y ser electas!* (Mexico City: CONACULTA, 2002), 75; Partido Revolucionario Institucional, *Presencia de la mujer en la vida cívica de México* (Mexico City: PRI, 1952), 7–8.

3. For a complete bibliography and discussion of the extensive literature on caciquismo see Alan Knight and Wil G. Pansters, eds., *Caciquismo in Twentieth-Century Mexico* (London: ILAS, 2005).

4. Paul Friedrich, "A Mexican Cacicazgo," *Ethnology* 4, no. 2 (April 1965): 190, 204–5; Alan Knight, "Caciquismo in Twentieth-Century Mexico," in Knight and Pansters, *Caciquismo*, 3.

5. Knight, "Caciquismo," 11.

6. Friedrich, "A Mexican Cacicazgo," 191; Knight, "Caciquismo," 18; Wil Pansters, "Goodbye to the Caciques? Definition, the State and the Dynamics of Caciquismo in Twentieth-century Mexico," in Knight and Pansters, *Caciquismo*, 363.

7. Knight, "Caciquismo," 11, 17, 13.

8. Knight, "Caciquismo," 30; Pansters, "Goodbye to the Caciques," 363.

9. Knight, "Caciquismo," 40; Pieter de Vries, "The Performance and Imagination of the Cacique: Some Ethnographic Reflections from Western Mexico," in Knight and Pansters, *Caciquismo*, 327–49; Friedrich, "A Mexican Cacicazgo"; Claudio Lomnitz-Adler, *Exits from the Labyrinth: Culture and Ideology in the Mexican National Space* (Berkeley: University of California Press, 1992).

10. Heather Fowler-Salamini, "Caciquismo, sindicalismo y género en la agroindustria cafetalera de Córdoba, Veracruz, 1925–1945," in *Integrados y marginados en el México posrevolucionario: Los juegos de poder local y sus nexos con la política nacional*, ed. Nicolás Cárdenas García and Enrique Guerra Manzo (Mexico City: UAM-Xochimilco, 2009), 210.

11. Francie Chassen-López, "A Patron of Progress: Juana Catarina Romero, the Nineteenth-Century Cacica of Tehuantepec," *Hispanic American Historical Review* 88, no. 3 (2008): 393–426; Fowler-Salamini, "Caciquismo, sindicalismo"; María Teresa Fernández Aceves, "Engendering Caciquismo: Guadalupe Martínez, Heliodoro Hernández Loza and the Politics of Organized Labor in Jalisco," in Knight and Pansters, *Caciquismo*, 201–27.

12. I prefer to use the word *advocate* instead of *lobbyist*. For a discussion of the term *lobbying* in Mexico see Sebastián Lerdo de Tejada C. and Antonio Godina, El lobbying en México (Mexico City: Miguel Ángel de Porrúa, 2004).

13. Antonio Castillo Gómez, "Cultura escrita y sociedad," *Cultura Escrita and Sociedad* 1 (2005): 11.

14. Nichole Sanders, *Gender and Welfare in Mexico: The Consolidation of a Posrevolutionary State* (University Park: Pennsylvania State University Press, 2011), 2, 88.

15. Sanders, *Gender and Welfare*, 28.

16. Author's interview with Manuel Urzúa, April 24, 2008, Ajijic, Jalisco.

17. Asociación de Maestros Egresados de la Escuela Normal de Jalisco, *La Escuela Normal de Jalisco: Galería de generaciones de maestros egresados de ella, 1894–1958* (Guadalajara: s.e., 1958), 4.

18. Armando Méndez Zárate, "La reforma agraria en San Martín de Hidalgo, Jalisco 1915–1935" (BA thesis, Universidad de Guadalajara, 2010).

19. El Informador, March 12, 1950.

20. Jorge Alonso, *El rito electoral en Jalisco, 1940–1992* (Guadalajara: Centro de Investigaciones y Estudios Superiores en Antropología Social, 1993), 28; Guillermo de la Peña Topete, "Populism, Regional Power, and Political Mediation: Southern Jalisco, 1900–1980," in *Mexico's Regions: Comparative History and Development*, ed. Eric Van Young (San Diego: University of California, 1992), 203.

21. Author's interview with Manuel Urzúa, April 24, 2008, Ajijic, Jalisco.

22. Mary Kay Vaughan, "Modernizing Patriarchy: State Policies, Rural Households, and Women in Mexico, 1930–1940," in *Hidden Histories of Gender and State in Latin America*, ed. Maxine Molyneux and Elizabeth Dore, 194–214 (Durham, NC: Duke University Press, 2000), 197.

23. Vaughan, "Modernizing Patriarchy," 200.

24. Cited in Méndez Zárate, "La reforma agraria." Accounts differ. According to Tomás García Tadeo, her aunt Julia was raped (interview with Tomás García Tadeo, December 8, 2006, San Martín Hidalgo, Jalisco). According to Francisco Francillard it was an attempted rape (interview with Francisco Francillard Chalves, April 18, 2008, Tepehuaje, Jalisco).

25. See Norbert Elias's ideas about individualization. Dennis Smith, "The Civilizing Process and the History of Sexuality: Comparing Norbert Elias and Michel Foucault," *Theory and Society* 28, no. 1 (February 1999): 79–80.

26. Like the seven agrarian leaders in Naranja studied by Paul Friedrich, Guadalupe also lost a parent during early childhood and was in contact with contentious local politics that produced a desire to change political life, struggle for land reform, and expand the use of and access to power. Paul Friedrich, *The Princes of Naranja: An Essay in Anthrohistorical Method* (Austin: University of Texas Press, 1986).

27. Author's interview with María Guadalupe Urzúa Flores, December 12, 2002, San Martín Hidalgo, Jalisco.

28. Profesor Pepe Camacho, "Manuscrito sobre la biografía de Guadalupe Urzúa," sin publicar.

29. Found in her personal archive, a certificate from a superior primary school for girls under the name of Guadalupe Urzúa contradicts Camp's short biography. Camp reconstructed political biographies based on replies to a questionnaire that he had

sent to selected politicians. Why did she claim she had studied in a rural normal school? CMGUF-BCCG-CIESAS-Occidente, certificado de escuela primaria superior para niñas, Zacoalco de Torres, May 15, 1931.

30. Roderic Ai Camp, "Women and Political Leadership in Mexico: A Comparative Study of Female and Male Political Elites," *Journal of Politics* 41, no. 2 (May 1979): 578.

31. CMGUF-BCCG-CIESAS-Occidente, carpeta 1930s.

32. Author's interview with Guadalupe Urzúa Flores, December 7, 2002, San Martín Hidalgo.

33. Mary Kay Vaughan, "Cultural Approaches to Peasant Politics in the Mexican Revolution," *Hispanic American Historical Review* 79, no. 2 (1999): 194, 197, 200.

34. Vaughan, "Cultural Approaches," 300.

35. Ileana Cristina Gómez Ortega, "La participación política en Jalisco. Las primeras diputadas en Jalisco" (BA thesis, Universidad de Guadalajara, 2007), 62; *El Informador*, August 25, 1930, and August 13, 1931.

36. Camp, "Women and Political Leadership," 579.

37. For a detailed analysis of this image see Gabriela Cano, *Se llamaba Elena Arizmendi* (Mexico City: Tusquets Editores, 2010), 22.

38. See María Teresa Fernández Aceves, "Voto femenino," in *Enciclopedia de Época. Política*, ed. Jorge Alonso (Guadalajara: Universidad de Guadalajara, in press).

39. Ana María Kapelusz-Poppi, "Physician Activists and the Development of Rural Health Postrevolutionary Mexico," *Radical History Review* 80 (spring 2001): 45–46; Manuel Quijano, "La medicina en México de 1940–2000," *Revista de la Facultad de Medicina de la UNAM* 46, no. 6 (2003): 215–16.

40. Sanders, *Gender and Welfare in Mexico*, 15–16, 92, 102.

41. Camp, "Women and Political Leadership," 438.

42. CMGUF-BCCG-CIESAS-Occidente, carpeta hospital, 1940s.

43. CMGUF-BCCG-CIESAS-Occidente, carpeta hospital, 1940s, Carta, June 2, 1941.

44. Guadalupe Urzúa's papers, June 19, 1945; personal unclassified archive of Jesús Camacho Barreto.

45. Antonio Gómez Nashiki, "El movimiento estudiantil mexicano. Notas históricas de las organizaciones políticas, 1910–1971," *Revista Mexicana de Investigación Educativa* 8, no. 27 (2003): 194.

46. CMGUF-BCCG-CIESAS-Occidente, carpeta hospital, 1950s.

47. CMGUF-BCCG-CIESAS-Occidente, carpeta hospital, 1950s.

48. Gabriela Cano, "Ciudadanía y sufragio femenino: El discurso igualitario de Lázaro Cárdenas," in *Miradas feministas sobre las mexicanas del siglo XX*, ed. Marta Lamas (Mexico City: FCE, 2007), 185.

49. In 1954, Aurora Jiménez Palacios became the first Mexican congresswoman, representing Baja California.

50. Rogelio Hernández Rodríguez, *El centro dividido: La nueva autonomía de los gobernadores* (Mexico City: El Colegio de México, 2008), 41.

51. Temma Kaplan, "Female Consciousness and Collective Action: The Case of Barcelona, 1910–1918," *Signs* 7, no. 3 (1982): 545–66, 545; Andrew Grant Wood, *Revolution in the Street: Women, Workers, and Urban Protest in Veracruz, 1870–1927* (Wilmington, DE: Scholarly Resources, 2001), 228.

52. CMGUF-BCCG-CIESAS-Occidente, carpeta sufragio femenino, 1953.

53. CMGUF-BCCG-CIESAS-Occidente, carpeta sufragio femenino, April 31, 1953.

54. Gómez Galeana to Alemán, April 25, 1947, and February 3, 1948, AGN/DGIPS-12/2/380(9)38.

55. Fernández Aceves, "Voto femenino."

56. Jocelyn Olcott, *Revolutionary Women in Postrevolutionary Mexico* (Durham, NC: Duke University Press, 2005), 93–94.

57. CMGUF-BCCG-CIESAS-Occidente, Carpeta Plan de Trabajo, 1953–56, 1953.

58. CMGUF-BCCG-CIESAS-Occidente, Carpeta sufragio femenino, n.d., 1953.

59. *El Informador*, July 7, March 16, March 2, February 28, February 1, January 19, and January 7, 1955.

60. See Héctor C. Castañeda Jiménez, *Marcelino García Barragán. Una vida al servicio de México* (Guadalajara: UNED, 1987); Gregorio Rivera Morán, "La cultura política de los maestros de Autlán: prácticas docentes, valores democráticos y formas de hacer política" (PhD diss., CIESAS-Occidente, 2002).

61. *Diario de Debates*, Periodo ordinario, August 24, 1955; *El Informador*, April 12, June 25, and June 27, 1955.

62. Archivo del Congreso de la Unión, Diario de Debates de la H. Cámara de Diputados, Legislatura XLIII, Año Legislativo I, no. 6, August 24, 1955.

63. Fernández Aceves, "Voto femenino."

64. *El Informador*, February 8, February 15, June 1, August 15, September 15, and December 2, 1956, and July 17, 1957.

65. *El Informador*, July 25, 1957.

66. *La mujer*, [1961].

67. Roderic Ai Camp, *Biografías de políticos mexicanos, 1935–1985* (Mexico City: FCE, 1992), 578; Jaime Sánchez Susarrey, "Mecanismos de negociación y concertación política," in *Historia política, 1940–1975: Jalisco desde la revolución*, ed. Ignacio Medina and Jaime Sánchez Susarrey (Guadalajara: Gobierno del Estado de Jalisco, 1987), 233; Camp, "Women and Political Leadership," 438.

68. Miguel González Compeán and Leonardo Lomelí, eds., *El partido de la revolución: Institución y conflicto (1928–1999)* (Mexico City: FCE, 2002).

69. CMGUF-BCCG-CIESAS-Occidente, ponencia, 1957; Hernández Rodríguez, *El centro dividido*, 30.

70. *El Informador*, January 5, 1955.

71. Elisa Servín, *Ruptura y oposición. El movimiento henriquista, 1945–1954* (Mexico City: Cal y Arena, 2001), 165–325.

72. *El Informador*, July 17, 1942.

73. Javier Hurtado, *Familias, política y parentesco: Jalisco, 1919–1991* (Mexico City: FCE, 1993), 85.

74. Author's interview with Guadalupe Urzúa Flores, December 7, 2002, San Martín Hidalgo.

75. Sánchez Susarrey, "Mecanismos de negociación," 215–17.

76. Gisela Zaremberg, *Mujeres, votos y asistencia social en el México priísta y la Argentina peronista* (Mexico City: FLACSO, 2009), 273.

CHAPTER 11 | *Benjamin T. Smith*

BUILDING A STATE ON THE CHEAP
Taxation, Social Movements, and Politics

In September 1960 the Mexican minister of finance Antonio Ortiz Mena welcomed the Cambridge economist Nicholas Kaldor to write a report on the state of Mexico's tax system. The task was so sensitive that Kaldor was forced to work incognito in a "hotel in the hills outside Mexico City." His recommendations, which simply aimed to introduce "an effective and impartial system of progressive taxation, which would ensure that the burden of taxation [was] equitably shared between rich and poor" were so radical that he feared their realization would provoke "a change . . . little short of a social revolution, comparable in nature to that caused by the land reform which followed the Revolution of 1910."[1] The Keynesian intellectual was not alone. A few years earlier, Oscar Lewis's informant, Manuel Sánchez, compared life in the United States to life in Mexico and concluded that if the Mexican "government tried that tax business here, . . . it might even cause a revolution."[2] State bureaucrats were similarly realistic. After a series of meetings between the finance minister and eminent business leaders, the report's suggestions were watered down. The tax reforms of 1962 and 1964 left taxation "with its various schedules, classifications, omissions, and discriminations" not only "exceedingly complex and inequitable" but also "incredibly low."[3]

Throughout the postwar period, both federal and state administrations attempted to extract greater tax revenue from the Mexican population. Yet, as the stories above suggest, resistance was widespread and vociferous. Not only business leaders and industrialists but also merchants, artisans, market sellers, workers, and peasants evaded payment, sent letters of complaint to the government, and came together to form powerful social movements to protest real or perceived increases in fiscal demands. The local tax collector became a figure of fear, mistrust, and hatred who was depicted as ill-educated, exploitative, and inveterately corrupt.[4] Although the federal government succeeded in constructing a functional tax base, taxes remained extremely low, and certain interest groups avoided fiscal charges. Furthermore, as the federal government gradually centralized the gathering of certain taxes, state and local governments were left to collect the most controversial and difficult taxes. This combination of consensual and coercive tax regimes forged after the war shaped the paradoxes of the Mexican state, centralizing power but leaving the federal state poorly financed and weak; opening a dialogue with the urban poor but at the same time institutionalizing inequality and low-level corruption.

Despite an intense and ongoing interest in the formation of the Mexican state, few historians have examined the role of taxation in this process.[5] Yet as economists and political scientists have argued, "the history of state revenue production is the history of the evolution of the state."[6] On the one hand, taxes underwrite the capacity of the state to carry out goals and describe the balance between accumulation and redistribution that gives states their political and social character. On the other hand, taxation forms a central arena for the conduct of state-society relations, shaping the social contract between rulers and ruled.[7] In Mexico, the establishment of a functioning tax system played both roles. Fiscal policies introduced during the 1940s and early 1950s increased the centralization of revenue collection in the hands of the federal government, stripping states and municipalities of political autonomy. Yet, at the same time, by allowing certain salient exceptions, the federal government also made taxation both heavily regressive and extremely low. This not only accelerated inequality, it also limited the state's capacity for authoritarianism, corporatism, or even cultural hegemony. In the most prosaic terms, the state often remained unable to fund the necessities of military intervention, party regimentation, political co-option, or cultural negotiation. Furthermore, underfunded local governments were compelled to employ forced labor to complete ambitious infrastructure projects and small bribes, or *mordidas*, to fund functionaries. Disputes over taxation, which swept through the country's provincial cities during the 1940s and 1950s, also shaped the political rules of the game, both generating large, cross-class, often female-led social movements and channeling state resources to these conurbations.

Federal Taxation

After the revolution, the cash-strapped state attempted to regularize Mexico's tax system. Revolutionaries baulked at the Porfirian scheme, which depended on both unstable external markets and a bewildering array of individual, overlapping local taxes.[8] During the 1920s and 1930s, successive presidents pushed for reform, with little success.[9] However, during the 1940s, presidents Avila Camacho and Alemán capitalized on the growth of the wartime economy to make fiscal gains. First, Avila Camacho decreed increases in federal income tax on diverse occupations, including commerce, farming, and law. At the same time, federal tax inspectors sought to apply the tax to a greater proportion of the workforce. As a result, over the next decade, income tax jumped from 12 to 26 percent of federal income.[10] Second, the state sought to centralize taxes on commerce and industry.[11] By 1947 Alemán claimed that there were "more taxes, and these [were] more complicated and less harmonious than ever before."[12] As a result, in February 1947 he held the Third Fiscal Congress, which cancelled the costly, cumbersome, and ineffective *impuesto del timbre* and replaced it with the *impuesto de ingresos mercantiles*, which directly charged the income of commercial companies.[13]

The reforms went a long way toward centralizing tax collection in the hands of the federal state. Between 1910 and 1949 federal taxes increased sevenfold, state taxes threefold, and municipal taxes by barely 50 percent. As Luis Aboites Aguilar argues, the 1940s was "the true point of inflection" for this "fiscal centralization." During the decade, federal taxes rose 9.5 percent year after year, whereas state taxes increased by only 2.3 percent annually.[14] Municipalities lagged even further behind, stripped of the power to tax those private properties that had been turned into *ejidos*. During the next decade, municipal coffers declined even further, as President López Mateos transferred communal lands to federal control. By the 1960s federal income dwarfed state and municipal incomes. Under López Mateos, municipalities received just 3 percent of total treasury contributions. This inequity had profound political consequences, increasing the power of the central state and limiting both state and municipal autonomy. Both now relied on the whims of the Treasury for most funding.[15] Furthermore, federal handouts were seriously unequal. Whereas industrialized Nuevo León gained 4.5 percent of spending, rural Oaxaca received only 1.1 percent.[16] Dissent could now provoke serious fiscal penalties.

Despite this general shift toward fiscal centralization, Mexico's federal taxation system remained disorganized, inefficient, and subject to omission and evasion. State governors were particularly reluctant to sacrifice the certainty of regular income in return for the promise of future federal support. The federalization of taxation on beer, introduced in 1939, was initially recognized by thirteen states.[17] As governors discovered that the new system lowered their tax revenue, however, many backed out of the agreement. In 1942 the governor of Tlaxcala explained that the federal system halved state income from the sale of beer, led to late payment of state officials, and was impossible to implement effectively. Later that year, Tlaxcala left the system.[18] Other states resisted the federalization of taxation on gasoline. In six states, governments continued to charge property taxes on PEMEX lands long into the 1950s.[19] The 1947 Fiscal Convention demonstrated the limits of federal power as state and municipal authorities refused to allow a modification of the constitution delineating each administrative tier's fiscal role. Even the tax on commercial income, which was introduced only after a period of prolonged negotiation, was refused by ten governors when they returned to their states. Some rejected the system outright. Others deliberately dragged their feet to delay its implementation. In 1948 the governor of Chihuahua argued that he would have to "consider the subject with calm and make a precise study . . . in order to avoid any trouble." The state only joined the system six years later.[20]

Despite Avila Camacho and Alemán's aims, reforms not only failed to centralize revenue collection but also permitted nonpayment of taxes on a massive scale. In some cases, omission was deliberate. As Aboites Aguilar argues, the federal government used exceptions and privileges to manage its relationship with certain interest groups. On the one hand, the Alemán government made key concessions to industrialists and merchants to encourage private investment and ensure political compliance. New enterprises and those deemed necessary for the development of manufacturing were granted exemptions of five to ten years.[21] After provincial industrialists complained about the state's harsh new tax evasion law, Alemán backed away from the legislation.[22] Six years later, Adolfo Ruiz Cortines made similar concessions to the business elite, retreating from a plan to increase income tax and reverting to the debt financing of public programs.[23] On the other hand, this system of omissions also extended to the lower classes. The postrevolutionary governments, cognizant of the unpopularity and inefficiency of rural tax collection, continued to exempt *ejidatarios* from direct federal taxation, leaving the job to local administrations.

If the federal state's unwillingness to enforce taxation was often deliberate, this system of omissions also encouraged a culture of illegal evasion. The underfunded government lacked the institutional capacity, technology, knowledge, or legal backing to impose any tax effectively. According to González Casanova, by the 1960s federal tax collectors failed to receive as much as 75 percent of their fiscal dues.[24] In fact, tax evasion was both so prevalent and so socially acceptable that the British ambassador claimed that elites treated the process as "an acquired right rather than merely a sport."[25] The evasion of income tax was particularly prevalent. For example, in 1940 Jesús Cienfuegos, a Spanish citizen, owned at least twelve *pulquerías*, a cinema, and a bullring in downtown Puebla. According to a government agent, all these properties were registered under false names. When federal tax inspectors came to collect income tax, the supposed owner was nowhere to be found. By November 1940 the agent estimated that Cienfuegos owed at least 12,800 pesos in back taxes.[26] Similarly, Manuel Parra Mata, leader of the notorious Veracruz anti-*agraristas*, la Mano Negra, never paid taxes on his *aguardiente* business, paying off the Xalapa tax collector every year.[27] Evasion also was pervasive further down the economic hierarchy, among the ranchers, small merchants, transient salesmen, and urban artisans. Federal tax inspectors repeatedly complained that poorer citizens involved in various small-scale household industries lacked even the basic accounting materials necessary for taxation. The federal tax inspector for Coahuila grumbled that he could tax less than "one percent of the city's population and no one in the countryside."[28]

Deliberate omissions and systematic evasion meant that, despite attempts to increase federal taxation, fiscal income remained extraordinarily low. As Kaldor concluded, the Mexican tax system, "owing to both legislative provisions and administrative defects," was "too small not only absolutely but relative to its stage of underdevelopment."[29] Although the Mexican economy grew between 1939 to 1945, taxes as a proportion of gross domestic product (GDP) actually dropped from 11.4 to 8.3 percent.[30] By 1965 the proportion had reached 10.4 percent, but Mexico still ranked last among other Latin American countries in terms of tax collected as a percentage of GDP. Whereas other populist, industrializing states like Argentina and Brazil had harnessed growth to increase tax revenue, Mexico remained among the lowest fiscal performers in the Americas, around the level of post-*violencia* Colombia or civil war era Guatemala (table 11.1).

Low fiscal income and the accompanying system of omissions and evasions had profound economic and political consequences. First, because the government was forced to spend most of its paltry income on infrastructure and administrative costs, state social spending was severely curtailed. According to James Wilkie, between 1940 and 1958 state administrations spent only an average of 14.8 percent on education, social security, health, welfare, and housing.[31] During the 1950s, the state's much vaunted education campaign absorbed a pitiful 1.4 percent of state expenditure, as opposed to 2.5 percent in Argentina, 2.6 percent in Brazil, and 4.1 percent in Argentina. Social security, which covered 8.4 percent of the population in Peru and a heady 24.9 percent in Argentina, reached only 6.6 percent of the population in Mexico.[32]

Second, the tax system also served to widen the gap between the rich and poor. To finance ambitious projects on a minimal budget, the Banco de México was forced to print money. This "inflationary financing" helped increase inflation and the cost of living, exacerbating the decline of real wages.[33] Even after the state introduced new stabilization policies from the mid-1950s

TABLE 11.1. Taxation as a percentage of GDP in Latin America, 1965

Country	Taxation as a percentage of GDP, 1965
Brazil	30.4
Chile	25.4
Venezuela	23
Ecuador	22.9
Uruguay	22.5
Peru	19.9
Argentina	18.9
Panama	18.6
Costa Rica	16.9
Bolivia	14.7
Nicaragua	14.3
El Salvador	14.3
Honduras	14.3
Dominican Republic	14.3
Colombia	13.4
Paraguay	13
Guatemala	10.7
Mexico	10.4

Source: Roger D. Hansen, *The Politics of Mexican Development* (Baltimore: Johns Hopkins University Press, 1971), 84.

onward, taxation still caused inequality. Exemptions and evasions favored the wealthy and regressive taxes stripped the poor of their cash at a higher rate than their richer compatriots.[34] As Kaldor argued, "there can be little doubt that the proportion of income effectively paid in taxation is lower in the high income ranges ... than in the case of average incomes."[35] Without effective redistribution, inequality in Mexico remained extremely high. By 1958, Ifigenia M. Navarrete estimated that the poorest 70 percent of Mexicans earned just 28.5 percent of the national wealth, a drop of more than 2 percent since 1950. In comparison, the top 5 percent earned 49.3 percent of the country's income.[36]

Third, low fiscal income hamstrung political capacity, or what Alan Knight has called "the weight of the state." At the most prosaic level, the federal government was able to pay only a very limited number of employees. Spending on the army was lower than any other country in Latin America.[37] The ratio of one bureaucrat per 176 citizens remained the same from 1940 to the mid-1960s.[38] According to Roger Hansen, the ratio of "agricultural extension agents" (e.g., engineers, representatives of state banks) to peasants in Mexico was around 1:10,000 as opposed to 1:1600 in Costa Rica, 1:1900 in Nicaragua, and 1:3200 in El Salvador. Only Guatemala after Arbenz had fewer contacts between the state and the agrarian workforce.[39]

Fourth, and perhaps less tangibly, the predominance of tax evasion shaped how Mexicans assessed their social contract with the state. Rather than conceiving of the relationship as one of broadly shared mutual obligations, many viewed it either in crudely exploitative or darkly humorous terms. Elites treated taxation "as an impertinence," peasants "as another feudal burden."[40] When a local tax inspector demanded Oaxaca market sellers pay their due, most "mocked" the man, claimed that "no one paid," and asked whether the proceeds would go toward "another house for the governor."[41] Those who did pay not only resented their misfortune but also saw the lack of state investment as clear proof of government corruption. If most Mexicans learned to speak the state's language of mutual responsibility, they often did so under duress or with a bitter, knowing smile.

Even this brief overview of the development of federal taxation undermines our understanding of how the post-1940 state worked. Fiscal policy certainly fed into greater centralization and favored the business elite, as revisionists argued. Yet the fiscal dependence of the state and municipalities was neither as prevalent or all-encompassing as many revisionists claimed. More importantly, low taxation severely reduced both the coercive and the co-optive powers of the federal state. Mexican presidents after 1940, unlike their populist Brazilian or Argentine peers, were much less well equipped to impose either an authoritarian or a corporative system with any degree of efficacy. Oil revenue made up some of the shortfall, but in general rule was by necessity *blanda*. Yet neither do contemporary historians, with their emphasis on everyday negotiations over cultural practice, entirely explain the state's relative stability and longevity. Negotiations between the state and citizens necessitate at least some state actors. How did this work in a region like Oaxaca, where federal bureaucrats numbered barely one for every four hundred inhabitants?[42] Furthermore, how did these negotiations function with only limited socioeconomic give, financial redistribution, and social mobility? Finally, how profound were these agreements over nation, memory, or state power if the mutual obligations over taxation were barely skin deep? I suggest that to understand how this system persisted, it is necessary to go beyond the rarefied condemnations of Keynesians like Kaldor and toward the black (fiscal) economy of Mexico's provincial towns and villages.

Local Taxation and Popular Resistance

If the federal state forged a concessionary tax policy to avoid conflict, most state governments were less perspicacious. During the 1940s, federal fiscal centralization placed increasing pressure on state treasuries. As a result, governors turned to increasingly coercive means to extract revenue. However, they found little success. In the countryside, tax inspectors tried to prey on ranchers and ejidatarios but returned empty handed. In the cities, local authorities confronted powerful cross-class coalitions of traditional elites and recent urban immigrants, which turned nonpayment strikes into referenda on governors' terms.

During the postrevolutionary period, state governments reluctantly relinquished two major sources of income. First, states lost the steady revenue from the property tax on haciendas, which had been transformed into ejidos. Second, states gradually renounced the ability to tax industry and commerce directly.[43] At the same time, states came under mounting pressure to implement ambitious modernization schemes, including roads, dams, and irrigation projects.[44] Under attack for his tardy implementation of public works, the Zacatecas governor, Leobardo Reynoso, objected that without these old taxes, state budgets barely covered half of his proposed schemes.[45]

To meet this demand, state governors published a host of new fiscal laws. Between 1950 and 1952, *Excélsior* reported that authorities had issued at least eighteen laws.[46] Without their traditional sources of income, administrations now relied on two sources: increased property taxes and *alcabalas*. In 1940 the governor of San Luis Potosí, on finding the state treasury empty, introduced a one-off urban property tax.[47] A decade later the governor of Sonora complained that "urban properties [were] valued at the same rate as during the Porfiriato."[48] The following year, the state congress passed a new fiscal law that doubled rates on urban properties and expanded urban rates into growing semi-urban *barrios* that were previously classified as rural.[49]

State governments also increased their reliance on alcabalas, or irregular charges on commercial transactions.[50] These were the states' last resort and the most invasive, coercive, and despised form of taxation. They were gathered by hundreds of state tax collectors who were stationed in towns' commercial plazas and would charge merchants, peasants, and ranchers for the entrance and exit of agricultural goods. According to Moisés de la Peña, Mexico's great ethnographic economist, Guerrero inspectors practiced "nocturnal fiscal vigilance," creeping around the roads at night in search of trucks, carts, and mules loaded with market produce. He concluded that "because of the unpopularity of the tax, the *alcabala* needs a system of systematic inspection and watchfulness, like that employed by detectives."[51] Moreover, because collection was so difficult, states often enforced commercial monopolies to reduce costs. In return for fixed rates, rich merchants were allowed to monopolize the sale of certain products. In Oaxaca City during the late 1940s, favored traders held monopolies of mescal, eggs, chicken, livestock, and coffee.[52] Although the federal government had banned alcabalas repeatedly since the Porfiriato, desperate state treasuries continued to include them in fiscal legislation. As De la Peña observed, "when they ban alcabalas, local treasuries assume a sardonic smile, fall silent and continue nonetheless." During the 1940s and 1950s, almost all the new fiscal laws increased the rate and ambit of alcabalas. Between 1941 and 1944, the governor of Guerrero added sixteen new alcabalas to the existing fourteen charges. At the same time, he raised taxes on dried skins from 20 to 60 pesos, those on coconut oil from 5 to 10 pesos, and those on peanuts from 0.5 to 5 pesos per kilo.[53]

Because rising property taxes and alcabalas demanded direct intervention and affected the broad mass of society, they generated ample resistance in both the countryside and the cities. In the rural areas of the south, evasion was particularly widespread. Between 1943 and 1947 ejidatarios in Guerrero paid less than 20 percent of estimated taxes. In Ometepec three ejidos owed four years, four owed three years, and five owed two years of back taxes; one had never paid. According to De la Peña, most tax inspectors had given up the thankless task of collection, instead devoting their time to private business.[54] Although most rural tax evasion was isolated and disorganized, there is evidence of systematic tax evasion in certain regions. In Oaxaca's Costa Chica, village-level contrition became mass acts of civil disobedience as almost all the ejidos refused to pay the state taxes on their lands. Many maintained a classic discourse of moral economy. Demanding "justice," they argued that although they were "prepared to pay" a certain amount that they believed to be "in accord with the law and the production of our lands," anything above this was deemed extortionate. By 1948 the peasants had started what the tax collector called a "tax strike." "Some agrarian communities, in a systematic manner are denying their contribution, sure that if they continue waiting it will all be forgiven by the Treasury of the State." As the tax collector from the Costa Chica indicated, there was very little state authorities could do to enforce compliance. Because ejidos were federal properties, they could not be embargoed and because they were communal enterprises, the state could not prosecute individual members. Many peasants rejected any connections to the Ejido Bank, so the threat of removing funding was often ineffective.

In fact, because rural taxation was so unproductive many state authorities turned toward taxing Mexico's provincial cities with their growing populations and concentrations of industrial and commercial enterprises. Yet these were equally reluctant to foot the fiscal bill. Although provincial cities contained a growing population of workers linked to increasingly obedient unions like the CTM, they also comprised considerable informal sectors. According to Clark Reynolds, the number of Mexicans working in the urban "service sector" (retail trades, construction, and household service) increased from 796,000 in 1930 to more than 3 million by 1960. By this point they comprised nearly 20 percent of the cities' working populations.[55] These service sector employees, especially small merchants and petty street vendors, became the foci of urban resistance to state fiscal increases throughout the postwar period. As new arrivals, informal workers, and women they remained relatively unattached to the increasingly regimented government unions. Furthermore, as commercial employees, carrying agricultural produce in and out of mercantile centers, they were highly sensitive to increases in alcabalas. Finally, working in the streets and markets of provincial capitals—within earshot of the cries of newspaper vendors, in sight of the governor's palace, and in contact with rural and urban customers from all social classes—they were politically savvy. As one government agent argued, the market in Oaxaca City was "the vital nerve of the politics of the state. . . . Any Oaxacan knows that before the governor can govern with the Congress, he must first come to an accord with the plaza or the market. When the market approves all is well, when it reproves, nothing can be done. The market of the city of Oaxaca City represents the public opinion of all the state."[56]

As a result, when desperate governors sought to increase revenue from the provincial cities, they often confronted major resistance. Beyond the incessant rumble of individual complaints, this confluence of political and social factors prompted at least eighteen large-scale mobilizations against tax increases between 1940 and 1952. These were spread throughout the country and across the duration of two presidencies, but there were some common geographical and temporal patterns. Most protests originated in state capitals, where people inverted the "law of fiscal distance" by observing up close the systematic siphoning off of state funds and consequently refusing attempts to collect revenue. There were mobilizations in Querétaro in 1942, in Aguascalientes in 1942 and 1948, in Villahermosa in 1941 and 1955, in Oaxaca City in 1947 and 1952, and in San Luis Potosí in 1950. Others originated in provincial commercial centers like León, Matamoros, Orizaba, and Iguala. Finally, there were smaller, less cogent mobilizations in towns on state borders, which were particularly affected by intrastate charges. Movements concentrated in the less wealthy central and southern states; here industry and federal contributions provided less income for local treasuries. As a result, they tended to rely on informal, invasive taxes. Although most movements followed new fiscal laws or informal tax raises, there were seven mobilizations between 1946 and 1948. During these years social groups took advan-

TABLE 11.2. Anti-tax protests, 1940–1955

Date	City
1940	Orizaba
1940	Colima
1941	Matamoros
1941	Saltillo
1941, 1955	Villahermosa
1942	Queretaro
1942, 1948	Aguascalientes
1946, 1948	León
1947	Tlaxco
1947	Iguala
1947	Amecameca
1947, 1952	Oaxaca
1947	Tapachula
1950	San Luis Potosí

Sources: Archivo General de la Nación, Dirección General de Gobierno (AGN, DGG), 2.314.1(1) 1; AGN, DGG, 2/314 1 (3) 1; AGN, DGG, 2/314 1 (18) /1; Archivo General de la Nación, Manuel Avila Camacho, 564.1/57; *Diario de Guerrero*, 07/27/1947; Archivo General de la Nación, Migual Alemán Valdés (AGN, MAV), 564.1/174; AGN, MAV, 564.1/306; Benjamin T. Smith, *Pistoleros and Popular Movements: The Politics of State Formation in Postrevolutionary Oaxaca* (Lincoln: University of Nebraska Press, 2009), chapters 7, 8, 10; Archivo General de la Nación, Dirección General de Investigaciones Políticas y Sociales (AGN, DGIPS), 102.9; AGN, IPS, 764.1; AGN, DGIPS, 798.8; Wil Pansters in this volume; Rogelio Hernández Rodríguez, *El centro dividido, La nueva autonomía de los gobernadores* (Mexico City: El Colegio de México, 2008), 88–89.

tage of the political opportunity offered by the presidential elections to lever unpopular governors from power (table 11.2).

Most historians, following the government line, have portrayed these antitax mobilizations as attempted right-wing coups, orchestrated from the topdown by a resurgent bourgeoisie.[57] However, growing evidence suggests that they were, in fact, ideologically flexible, popular, organic, and cross-class. First, local political opportunity and not ideological commitment shaped political alliances and discourses of nonpayment. At times, protesters linked with conservative organizations like the PAN or the Chamber of Commerce and spouted the language of free commerce. Tax protesters in Aguascalientes backed the right-wing candidate for municipal president, Humberto Brand Sánchez, and claimed that high taxes "destroyed business."[58] But in other regions, lobbyists collaborated with broadly left-wing movements to protest regressive tax structures, which penalized the poor. In 1947 the Comité de

Propietarios Pobres of Iguala allied with a radical faction of the CNC to lower property taxes on semi-urban properties.⁵⁹ In fact, in most regions these social movements forged links with supporters on both the left and right. Both PANistas and Henriquistas supported the anti-tax mobilization in Oaxaca City in 1952.⁶⁰

Second, these movements involved, and were often controlled by, members of the urban lower classes. The 1948 Aguascalientes movement comprised the city's association of water users and disenfranchised members of the local branch of the railway union and numbered more than six thousand protesters.⁶¹ A similar alliance of laborers, petty traders, and market vendors also organized protests in Oaxaca City in 1947 and 1952.⁶² Furthermore, urban women dominated many of these mobilizations. Although Nabor Ojeda, the CNC leader, formally directed the complaints in the city of Iguala, the organization that directed demonstrations, the Comité de Propietarios Pobres, was largely female. Nearly half of the 513 signatories were female, and 3 of the 6 leaders of the committee's board were women.⁶³ In Aguascalientes in 1948, a phalanx of more than six hundred women led the protests on June 3, 1948, holding up signs that read, "We women demand honourable government."⁶⁴

Third, these urban movements often broke from their wealthy supporters to express their discontent and push for more radical, popular demands. For example, the official leaders of the 1948 Aguascalientes strike were Edmundo Ortega, an ambitious PANista; Caterino Solaña, the head of the railway workers; and Raymundo Carillo, the director of another radical union. These politicians attempted to direct their lower-class supporters, but regimentation was extremely difficult. Railway workers resisted union instructions and started a succession of train stoppages. Protesters turned a silent march into a loud and defiant expression of popular anger.⁶⁵ Similarly, despite attempted control by the elite, women in Oaxaca City used the movement to demand a political voice. In 1952 Patricia Leal Cienfuegos, a market vendor, wrote articles in the local press that lamented women's long period of political oppression: "For a long time, you have supported the yoke of slavery on your backs." Now, however, Oaxaca's women were "defending [their] dignity and [their] rights." One of these rights was what she described as democracy, or "the right to choose elected representatives." She contrasted the women "who [believed] in democracy and dignity" and had showed that they were "worthy of protesting with dignified men" with the governor's barbarity.⁶⁶ Other popular groups also betrayed their elite backers and used the political opportunity to protest continuing economic exploitation. In 1948 the tax protestors of León, Guanajuato, complained that "the large merchants [continued to] exploit the people of the city, charging prices which most humble people cannot afford."⁶⁷

The Paradoxes of the New Social Contract

Although such vociferous, widespread opposition left state treasuries cash poor, the solutions paradoxically bolstered the power of the federal government. Opposition movements in the cities generated a proliferation of social programs as successive governments concentrated on funneling their limited funds toward urban groups, lowering food prices, providing free housing, and concentrating hospitals and schools. Meanwhile in the countryside, desperate local governments relied on the church, forced labor, and low-level corruption to provide social services, build infrastructure, and fund administration. Both strategies played into federal hands. In urban areas, the federal state could also harness support by backing ready-made networks of anti-tax protestors against provincial governors. At the same time, rural efforts supported a degree of state presence without sullying federal authority. In fact, by periodically dismissing a particularly exacting tax collector or targeting a vicious cacique, the national government could co-opt popular rural groups. The fiscal weakness of the 1940s fed into the relative political stability of the dictablanda in the 1950s.

Despite numerous instances of police brutality, illegal imprisonment, and political assassination, the urban anti-tax protests were remarkably successful. To curry favor and diminish state autonomy, the federal government often backed protestors. Federal pressure compelled the governor of Aguascalientes to reduce taxes and fire his treasurer and minister of the interior in 1942.[68] An unfavorable senate committee report on finances in Coahuila, which claimed that tax increases had "been absorbed by a corrupted bureaucratic system," forced the local governor to ban alcabalas.[69] As protesters realized that they could expect a fairly favorable response from the government, they pushed for greater gains. Especially after the massacre at León in 1946, activists pressed not only for tax reductions but also for the dismissal of unpopular state administrations. In 1947 and 1952 tax mobilizations in Oaxaca City successfully levered governors Edmundo Sánchez Cano and Manuel Mayoral Heredia from power.[70] In 1955, tax strikers got rid of Tabasco governor Manuel Bartlett Bautista.[71]

At the same time, by highlighting dissatisfaction in the cities, anti-tax protests also cemented the state's shift toward favoring urban demands. Provincial campaigns, which introduced controls on the price of food, subsidized housing, the construction of infrastructure, and social services, often directly followed these attempts at collective bargaining by riot.[72] In the immediate aftermath of Oaxaca City's 1947 tax protests, the federal government floated loans to the state authorities; these loans paid for improved water provision, sewage, paving, price controls, and carefully conceived pieces of populist theater. The city's market vendors, who had resisted state co-option for more than a decade, joined the local branch of the CNOP. The opposition newspaper, El Chapulín, hailed the new PRI governor as "one of the best in Oaxaca's history."[73]

The frequency, popularity, and virulence of urban anti-tax mobilizations not only promoted urban services but also molded rural policies for the succeeding decades. Unable to harness the tax base of the provincial cities, state governors and municipal councils turned toward less formal means of funding administration. First, they shifted from tax collection to low-level corruption, effectively replacing the unpopular and illegal alcabalas with off-the-books mordidas, what González Casanova called "the small proceeds from fines and licenses."[74] A government agent sent to southern Guerrero in April 1952 to inspect the tax system explained the change in full. He admitted that because of the introduction of a new state fiscal code "there [was] not strictly a tax of persons or vehicles that [traversed] the state that could be officially called the alcabala." However, state and municipal police stationed outside the cities of Taxco, Chilpancingo, Tierra Colorado, and Acapulco and the towns bordering the surrounding states now charged motorists, truckers, and merchants fifty- to one hundred-peso fines for spurious infractions of the transit regulations. As he concluded, "perhaps not in a direct manner, nonetheless the authorities are still charging large quantities of money for crossing the state."[75]

Second, local authorities also turned away from funding entirely, increasingly relying on forced labor to complete infrastructure projects. Central authorities had always relied on communal labor (*faenas* in Central Mexico or *tequios* in Oaxaca and Chiapas) to complete regional projects. In the 1930s Ralph Beals recounted at length how a local *cacique* from north of Oaxaca City forced peasant villagers to carry a large Chevrolet van over the sierra to his hometown, where he would spend his days driving the vehicle round the plaza.[76] Yet with the central government's renewed emphasis on infrastructure construction, local leaders shifted communal labor from fairly acceptable village projects (like churches, chapels, and schools) toward less locally specific operations (like irrigation channels, telegraph poles, and roads). Supported by military authorities and backed by the threat of fines or jail, local authorities tailored this custom to the demands of central government, reinventing tradition by force. In Chihuahua, state authorities "with a blind faith in indigenous communalism" imposed the Mesoamerican tradition on Tarahumara villages where such labor practices had never existed.[77] In Oaxaca, the Tequixtepec council, backed by the local garrison, coerced peasants to work for a month on the Huajuapan-Tehuacán highway, even though government engineers had deliberately bypassed the community to punish villagers "for trying to vote for the PAN."[78] North in Huachinango, Puebla, a cacique forced laborers into opening a road for the Compañía Mexicana de Luz y Fuerza Motriz. In Tamiahua, Veracruz, the soldiers of the nineteenth military zone dragooned villagers into working without pay on the Tuxpan-Tampico highway. Resistance to these informal working practices was common. Peasants refused to work, fled to their *jacales* in the hills, and wrote long letters to the president, quoting article 5 of the 1917 Constitution, which outlawed labor without remuneration.[79] But without a secure fiscal base, local government built the Mexican miracle by shanghaiing this unwilling agrarian labor force.[80]

Third, regional and local authorities aped the statistical inventiveness of their federal masters, and lied. In 1947, Génaro Ramos, the cacique of Miahuatlán, Oaxaca, claimed that he had helped in the construction of more than one hundred kilometers of the Miahuatlán-Puerto Angel road. Yet when the local military commander turned up to inspect the project, he found that "barely 20 km of road" had been laid.[81] Five years later, Manuel Mayoral Heredia, the governor of Oaxaca, made a similar assertion, arguing that state taxes had been used to fund the construction of the Huajuapan-Pinotepa highway. Local opposition leaders pointed out that after two years of alleged work, "not one single stone had been set down."[82] Other strongmen operated sophisticated facades designed to appease the occasional federal visitors. Throughout the 1940s and 1950s Luis Rodríguez, the cacique of the Region Mixe, emblazoned his private coffee warehouse with the words "School Cooperative" to prove to dignitaries his progressive credentials.[83] For combative local journalists who bothered to make the trek to the provinces, annual governors' reports merely listed a succession of "illusions" and "Potemkin villages."[84]

Fourth, local governments started to harness the social efforts of the church. Building on the rapprochement between federal authorities and the ecclesiastical hierarchy, municipal authorities increasingly ignored the anticlerical dictates of the constitution and allowed churches to run schools and own property, effectively farming out social services to private institutions.[85] During the 1940s, priests and members of the ACM in Guadalajara established orphanages, clinics, and parish schools throughout the new barrios of the city "in the absence of any other type of labour or political organizations."[86] Even in the comparatively under-churched south, state authorities encouraged church social programs. In 1944 in Oaxaca City, the local branch of the ACM purchased a building in the city center and established a charity hospital. For seven centavos a month, lay worshippers could purchase full health coverage for their family.[87] Four years later, a local priest, with the support of the Department of Health, collected more than three hundred thousand pesos from local churchgoers to establish a similar hospital to the north in Huajuapan, Oaxaca.[88] Local governments engineered a similar agreement with Protestant churches. In 1954 the president of Guadalajara allowed the evangelical La Luz del Mundo congregation to purchase municipal lands. In return, the church provided schools, social services, and jobs.[89]

BY THE 1950S this black fiscal economy, which forsook serious urban taxation and instead embraced corruption and forced rural labor, was firmly in place. Both strategies permitted the extension of dictablanda without serious investment or prolonged confrontation. Administrators earned a living wage, schools were built, and roads were laid. At the same time, both national and local authorities could now focus their thin funds on the country's cities, co-opting the vocal informal workforce into the CNOP through the provision of cheap food, schools, water, electricity, and—perhaps most important—land. This highly decentralized funding system not only encouraged economic modernization but also permitted the central government to maintain a populist veneer, building a broad (if conditional) coalition of support on the cheap. Forced to bear the weight of the state modernization effort, both the urban poor and increasingly the peasant masses focused their ire on local bosses, corrupt policemen, and incompetent tax collectors.[90] The central state, by occasionally removing or sidelining these figures, seemed to support their cause. In many ways, the state's fiscal administration mirrored its political system. Looking down from the apex of presidential power, the system appeared to be centralized and strong. During the period after 1940, federal funds rose and outstripped state and municipal collections by far. Yet beneath these figures operations remained disorganized and yielded little. Because successive federal administrations had bargained away a fiscal base for stability, local leaders were forced to pull in the slack. In the countryside caciques not only maintained political discipline behind the optical illusion of bureaucratic rule, they also operated as the government's informal fiscal enforcers, forgoing systematic taxation and instead relying on forced labor, small-time corruption, church services, and fictionalized accounts of completed projects.

The Mexican government's tax system, established during the 1940s and 1950s, remained important well into the last days of the PRI regime. Although Luis Echeverria attempted to institutionalize Kaldor's suggested reforms for a second time in 1972, opposition from the private sector again undermined the effort. As Echeverria sought to increase social spending to appease both urban and rural discontent, public revenues still lagged behind expenditures. Returning to the "inflationary growth" model of the 1940s, monetary expansion and foreign debt funded the rise, at least in part precipitating the crash of 1976.[91] Although two years later major tax reforms ironed out some of the inequalities of the tax system, over recent years the proportion of tax to GDP has again slipped to between 11 and 12 percent—and again is the lowest in Latin America. As President Enrique Peña Nieto has discovered, "the low tax burden implies that the fiscal accounts continue to be highly vulnerable," especially when oil fields start to dry up.[92]

Notes

1. Nicholas Kaldor, *Reports on Taxation II* (New York: Holmes and Meirer, 1980), 218–19; Sarah Babb, *Managing Mexico: Economists from Nationalism to Neoliberalism* (Princeton, NJ: Princeton University Press, 2001), 86; Anthony P. Thirlwall, *Nicholas Kaldor* (New York: New York University Press, 1987), 140–42.

2. Oscar Lewis, *The Children of Sánchez: Autobiography of a Mexican Family* (New York: Random House, 1961), 338.

3. Morris Singer, *Growth, Equality and the Mexican Experience* (Austin: University of Texas Press, 1970), 231; Roberto Anguiano Equihua, *Las Finanzas del Sector Público en México* (Mexico City: UNAM, 1968), 167–69, 180–82; Rafael Izquierdo, *Política hacendaria del desarrollo establizador, 1958–1970* (Mexico City: El Colegio de México, 1995), 41–54; Leopoldo Solís, *Economic Policy Reform in Mexico: A Case Study for Developing Countries* (New York: Pergamon Press, 1981).

4. For example, Aldous Huxley, *Beyond the Mexique Bay* (New York: Harper and Brothers, 1934), 140.

5. Exceptions include Luis Aboites Aguilar, *Excepciones y privilegios: Modernización tributaria y centralización en Mexico, 1922–1972* (Mexico City: El Colegio de México, 2003); Peter Guardino, *Peasants, Politics, and the Formation of Mexico's National State: Guerrero, 1800–1857* (Palo Alto, CA: Stanford University Press, 1996); Barbara A. Tannenbaum, *The Politics of Penury: Debts and Taxes in Mexico, 1821–1856* (Albuquerque: University of New Mexico Press, 1986); Marcello Carmagnani, "El liberalismo, los impuestos internos y el estado federal mexicano, 1857–1911," *Historia Mexicana* 38, no. 3 (1989): 471–96.

6. Margaret Levi, *Of Rule and Revenue* (Berkeley: University of California Press, 1988), 1; Kenneth L. Sokoloff and Eric M. Zolt, "Inequality and the Evolution of Taxation, in *Economic Development in the Americas since 1500: Endowments and Institutions*, ed. Stanley L. Engerman and Kenneth L. Sokoloff (Cambridge: Cambridge University Press, 2012), 168–69.

7. Deborah A. Brautigam, "Introduction, Taxation and State-Building in Developing Countries," in *Taxation and State-Building in Developing Countries, Capacity and Consent*, ed. Deborah A. Brautigam, Odd-Helge Fjeldstad and Mick Moore, 1–33 (Cambridge: Cambridge University Press, 2008).

8. Carlos Marichal and Steven Topik, "The State and Economic Growth in Latin America: Brazil and Mexico, Nineteenth and Early Twentieth Centuries," in *Nation, State and the Economy in History*, ed. Alicia Teichova and Herbert Matis, 349–72 (Cambridge: Cambridge University Press, 2009).

9. Alberto J. Pani, *La política hacendaria y la Revolución* (Mexico City: Cultura, 1926), 73–82; José Iturriaga de la Fuente, *La revolución hacendaria: La hacienda pública con el presidente Calles* (Mexico City: SEP, 1976); Susan M. Gauss, *Made in Mexico: Regions, Nation,*

and the State in the Rise of Mexican Industry (University Park: Pennsylvania State University Press, 2010), 34–45.

10. Aboites Aguilar, *Excepciones y privilegios*, 193.

11. In 1940 Mexico still had 250 different taxes, comprising 57 federal, 131 state, and 62 municipal charges. There were eighty on commerce and industry alone (Aboites Aguilar, *Excepciones y privelegios*, 191).

12. Secretaría de Hacienda y Crédito Público, *Tercera convención nacional fiscal: Memoria 1947* (3 vols.) (Mexico City: Secretaría de Hacienda y Crédito Público, 1947), vol. I, 7.

13. Secretaría de Hacienda y Credito Público, *Tercera convención nacional fiscal*; Aboites Aguilar, *Excepciones y privilegios*, 206–16.

14. Aboites Aguilar, *Excepciones y privilegios*, 42.

15. Pablo González Casanova, *Democracy in Mexico*, trans. Danielle Salti (Oxford: Oxford University Press, 1970), 24–30.

16. Anguiano Equihua, *Las Finanzas*, 367.

17. Aboites Aguilar, *Excepciones y privilegios*, 172.

18. Santilla to Avila Camacho, January 5, 1942, Archivo General de la Nación, Manuel Avila Camacho (AGN/MAC) 564.1/45.

19. Aboites Aguilar, *Excepciones y privilegios*, 186.

20. Secretario Particular del Gobernador to President Alemán, February 4, 1948, AGN/MAV-564.1/588.

21. Kaldor, *Reports on Taxation II*, 244.

22. Aboites Aguilar, *Excepciones y privilegios*, 217.

23. Olga Pellicer de Brody and José Luis Reyna, *Historia de la Revolución Mexicana, 1952–1960: El afianzamiento de la estabilidad política* (Mexico City: El Colegio de México, 1978), 157. Even cinema owners managed to get the federal government to back down on proposed taxes. See Paxman, chapter 13, this volume.

24. González Casanova, *Democracy in Mexico*, 139. The figure, which is without citation, closely matches Hugo G. Nutini and Barry Isaac's estimation of 60 percent (*Social Stratification in Central Mexico, 1500–2000* [Austin: University of Texas Press, 2010], 131–32).

25. Alan Knight, "Cárdenas and Echeverría: Two 'Populist' Presidents Compared," in *Populism in Twentieth Century Mexico: The Presidencies of Lázaro Cárdenas and Luis Echeverría*, ed. María L. O. Muñoz and Amelia M. Kiddle (Tucson: University of Arizona Press, 2010), 30n74.

26. AGN, Dirección General de Investigaciones Políticas y Sociales (AGN/DGIPS) 76.4, Agent PS 6 to Secretaría de Gobierno, March 18, 1940.

27. Antonio Santoya, *La Mano Negra, Poder Regional y estado en México (Veracruz, 1928–1943)* (Mexico City: Consejo Nacional para la Cultura y Las Artes, 1995), 59.

28. Antonio Covarrubias to Miguel Alemán, September 12, 1948, AGN/MAC-564.1/876.

29. Kaldor, *Reports on Taxation II*, 215–17.

30. Enrique Cárdenas, *La hacienda pública y la política económica, 1929–1958* (Mexico City: Fondo de Cultura Económica, 1994), 113–14.

31. James W. Wilkie, *The Mexican Revolution: Federal Expenditure and Social Change since 1910* (Berkeley: University of California Press, 1970), 83, 85, 87.

32. Roger D. Hansen, *The Politics of Mexican Development* (Baltimore: Johns Hopkins University Press, 1971), 85–86.

33. Barry Siegel, *Inflación y desarrollo: Las experiencias de México* (Mexico City: Centro de Estudios Monetarios Latinoamericanos, 1960), 179–87.

34. Centro de Estudios Contables, "Es Justo Nuestro Sistema de Impuestos?," in *La economica Mexicana*, ed. Leopoldo Solís, vol. 2 (Mexico City: Fondo de Cultura Económica, 1973), 62.

35. Kaldor, *Reports on Taxation II*, 217; Anguiano Equihua, *Las finanzas*, 144–205.

36. Ifigenia Navarrete, "La distribución del ingreso en México, tendencias y perspectivas," in *El perfil de México en 1980* (Mexico City: Siglo XXI, 1977), 15–71, 37.

37. Wilkie, *The Mexican Revolution*, 77.

38. Alan Knight, "The Weight of the State in Modern Mexico," in *Studies in the Formation of the Nation-State in Latin America*, ed. James Dunkerley (London: ILAS, 2002), 216–17.

39. Hansen, *The Politics*, 86.

40. Knight "Cárdenas and Echeverría," 30n74; Moisés de la Peña, *Guerrero Económico* (Chilpancingo: Gobierno del Estado de Guerrero, 1949), 626.

41. *El Chapulín*, January 4, 1947.

42. Benjamin T. Smith, *Pistoleros and Popular Movements: The Politics of State Formation in Postrevolutionary Oaxaca* (Lincoln: University of Nebraska Press, 2009), 1–2.

43. Moisés de la Peña argued in his economic profile of Chihuahua that the federalization of taxes on logging, mining, gasoline, matches, phosphorus, electric energy, and beer had halved annual revenue (*Chihuahua Económico* [Mexico City: s.e., 1948], 341).

44. Daniel Newcomer, *Reconciling Modernity: Urban State Formation in 1940s Leon, Mexico* (Lincoln: University of Nebraska Press, 2004), 35.

45. Leobardo Reynoso report, March 21, 1947, AGN-MAC-564.1/134.

46. *Excélsior*, July 23, 1952.

47. See Pansters, chapter 5, this volume.

48. *Informe del Gobernador de Sonora a la legislatura local* (Hermosillo: Gobierno del Estado de Sonora, 1951).

49. *Informe del Gobernador de Sonora a la legislatura local* (Hermosillo: Gobierno del Estado de Sonora, 1952).

50. Luis Aboites Aguilar, "Alcabalas posporfirianas: Modernización Tributaria y Soberanía Estatal," *Historia Mexicana* 51, no. 2 (2002): 381.

51. De la Peña, *Guerrero Económico*, 628.

52. *El Momento*, November 25, 1945; *La Voz de Oaxaca*, February 27, 1945.

53. De la Peña, *Guerrero Económico*, 667, 659.

54. De la Peña, *Guerrero Económico*, 650–51.

55. Clark W. Reynolds, *The Mexican Economy: Twentieth-Century Structure and Growth* (New Haven, CT: Yale University Press, 1970), 386.

56. *Buro de Investigación Política*, March 31, 1952.

57. Newcomer, *Reconciling Modernity*, 10; Luis Medina, *Historia de la Revolución Mexicana, periodo 1940–1952. Vol. 20, Civilismo y modernización del autoritarismo* (Mexico City: Colegio de México, 1979), 98–108.

58. Negri Baeza to Secretaría de Gobierno, October 29, 1947, AGN/DGIPS-102/9.

59. Ojeda to Secretaría de Gobierno, November 2, 1947, AGN, Miguel Alemán Valdés (MAV)-564.1/57.

60. Smith, Pistoleros, 381–85.

61. Informe Jesús Díaz, June 17, 1948, AGN/DGIPS-102.9.

62. Smith, Pistoleros, 310–24, 376–94.

63. Ojeda to Secretaría de Gobierno, November 2, 1947, AGN/MAV-564.1/57.

64. Informe Jesús Díaz, June 17, 1948, AGN/DGIPS-102.9.

65. Ortega Romero to Secretaría de Gobierno, May 15, 1948, AGN/DGIPS-798.8.

66. El Chapulín, March 27, 1952.

67. Carlos Martínez Assad, Los sentimientos de la región: Del Viejo centralismo a la nueva pluralidad (Mexico City: INEHRM, 2001), 182–84.

68. Dr. Alberto Valle to Gobernación, July 7, 1942, AGN, Dirección General de Gobierno (AGN/DGG)-2.314.1(1)1.

69. Informe de la Comisión del Senado, September 27, 1941, AGN/DGG-2.314.1(1)1.

70. Smith, Pistoleros, 310–27, 376–401.

71. Rogelio Hernández Rodriguez, El centro dividido: La nueva autonomia de los gobernadores (Mexico City: El Colegio de México, 2008), 88–89.

72. Enrique Ochoa, Feeding Mexico: The Political Uses of Food Since 1910 (Wilmington, DE: Scholarly Resources, 2000), 71–156; Diane Davis, Urban Leviathan: Mexico City in the Twentieth Century (Philadelphia: Temple University Press, 1994); John C. Cross, Informal Politics, Street Vendors and the State in Mexico City (Palo Alto CA: Stanford University Press, 1998), 160–87; Manuel Perlo Cohen, "Política y vivienda en México, 1910–1952," Revista Mexicana de Sociologia 41, no. 3 (1979): 816–20.

73. Smith, Pistoleros, 335–47.

74. González Casanova, Democracy in Mexico, 29.

75. Informe, June 11, 1952, AGN/DGIPS-104-2-1/131/1074.

76. Ralph L. Beals, "Ethnology of the Western Mixe," University of California Publications in American Archaeology and Ethnology 52 (1951): 36.

77. Juan Luis Sariego Rodriguez, El Indigenismo en la Tarahumara: Identidad, comunidad, relaciones interetnicas y desarrollo en la Sierra de Chihuahua (Mexico City: INAH, 2001), 16.

78. Archivo del Municipio de Tequixtepec, Gobernación, Luis Vasquez to secretario particular del Gobernador, September 6, 1956.

79. Paul Gillingham, "Force and Consent in Mexican Provincial Politics: Guerrero and Veracruz, 1945–1953" (PhD dissertation, Oxford University, 2005), 270–71.

80. There is a debate to be had concerning just how willing/unwilling such labor was; for a more positive appreciation, see De la Peña, chapter 12, this volume.

81. Ramos to Governor Vasconcelos, April 4, 1947, Archivo General del Poder Ejecutivo del Estado de Oaxaca (AGPEO), Gobernacíon, 1947.

82. Smith, Pistoleros, 370.

83. Luis Rodríguez to SEP, June 8, 1950, Archivo del Municipio de Tlahuitoltepec.

84. El Chapulín, April 3, 1954.

85. Nicole Sanders, "Gender, welfare, and the 'Mexican miracle': The politics of modernization in postrevolutionary Mexico, 1937–1958" (PhD dissertation, University of California, Irvine, 2003), 123–25. See also Blancarte, chapter 2, this volume.

86. Guillermo de la Peña and Renée de la Torre, "Microhistoria de un barrio tapa-

tio: Santa Teresita (1930–1980)," in *Vivir en Guadalajara: La ciudad y sus funciones*, ed. Carmen Castañeda, 119–38 (Guadalajara: Ayuntamiento de Guadalajara, 1992), 126.

87. Smith, *Pistoleros*, 276–77.

88. Luis de Guadalupe Martínez, *La lucha electoral del PAN en Oaxaca, Tomo I (1939–1971)* (Mexico City: n.p., 2002). For an example of church involvement in health provision in Mexico City, see Larissa Lomnitz, *Networks and Marginality: Life in a Mexican Shanty Town* (New York: Academic Press, 1977), 185.

89. Jason Dormady, "'Not just a Better Mexico': Intentional Religious Community and the Mexican State, 1940–1964" (PhD dissertation, University of California, Santa Barbara, 2007).

90. See Hernández Rodríguez, chapter 4, this volume.

91. Solís, *Economic Policy Reform*, 119–20.

92. Juan Carlos Moreno-Brid and Jaime Ros, *Development and Growth in the Mexican Economy: A Historical Perspective* (Oxford: Oxford University Press, 2009), 203–5.

CULTURE AND IDEOLOGY

CHAPTER 12 | Guillermo de la Peña

THE END OF REVOLUTIONARY ANTHROPOLOGY?
Notes on *Indigenismo*

The historical elaboration of the concept of culture in nineteenth-century Europe implied a basic and perhaps inevitable ambiguity. On the one hand it appealed to the universality of the human spirit; on the other it referred to the particular beliefs, symbols, and practices of a given human collectivity.[1] Discourses on the protection and promotion of national culture—first developed in Europe and then, recurrently, in postcolonial countries—added to the concept a dimension of power: the state became responsible for defining the object of its protection. *Indigenismo*, first coined in Mexico at the beginning of the twentieth century, has always been tainted by similar ambiguities and political connotations. In Mexican usage, indigenismo means the institutionalized state action aimed at improving the lot of the indigenous population while converting them into full participants in national society and culture. While the existence of indigenous peoples and cultures is recognized, it also is regarded as something that has to be radically transformed in order to construct a full-fledged Mexican society—to "forge the Fatherland," to use Manuel Gamio's expression.[2]

Mexican *indigenista* policies, however, have varied considerably since their launch by Gamio in 1917. Although these variations have received contrasting assessments from different authors and critics, most of them speak of three successive periods—roughly speaking, the revolutionary, the bureaucratic-corporatist, and the postmodern-neoliberal. The first (1917–40) often is eulogized as a period of social activism and mobilization; the second (1940 to the late 1970s) covers the years of institutional consolidation and focuses on party hegemony and capitalist expansion. The third stage, which overlaps with the major crises of the party and the protectionist economic model, corresponds to the emergence of political pluralism and the establishment of militant ethnic organizations in search of new ideas of the nation.

In this chapter I am primarily concerned with the second period. During those years, blanket social activism came to an end. But neither radical indigenistas nor indigenous groups saw their voices completely quashed. The indigenista apparatus was not a monolithic authoritarian machine: it included researchers and field officers with diverse—even contradictory—political perspectives and strategies. In turn, the indigenous population was not a passive, submissive clientele. Cultural promoters and teachers recruited from the communities may have served the interests of the PRI, but they also represented indigenous claims. Indigenista discourses, policies, and actions not only expressed state authoritarianism but also laid bare contradictions within the government and the ongoing inputs of indigenous peoples. In addition, since indigenismo was closely intertwined with professional anthropology, I shall refer to the political connotations and transformations of this discipline, both within Mexico and in the context of the global order of the period. I suggest that Mexican/Mexicanist anthropology can be best analyzed as—to use Mary Louise Pratt's expression—a "contact zone": a point of convergence for multilateral scientific thought influenced by nationalist experience, political interests, indigenous agency, and European/U.S. neocolonial ideology.[3]

"Revolutionary Indigenismo"

Gamio's Directorate of Anthropology started a program for interdisciplinary, applied research, aimed at social development and nation building, to be carried out in different regions of the country. This program was primarily conceived to benefit the indigenous population, which at the time numbered about four million (one-third of the total population).[4] Many aspects of indigenous culture and society had to be obliterated, but other "positive" aspects would become part and parcel of national culture, conceived as revolutionary and *mestizo*, that is, a mixture of (reconverted) traditional/Indian and modern/European elements.[5] Concomitantly, the Department of Education, under the leadership of José Vasconcelos, created the Department of Indigenous Education in 1923 and launched the program of Cultural Missions, aimed primarily at improving the lot of indigenous groups.[6] In 1924 the Directorate of Anthropology became dependent on the Ministry of Education and worked in connection with rural schools. In fact, several prominent anthropologists started their careers as teachers.

Moisés Sáenz, a pedagogue and anthropologist who, as undersecretary of education, had visited many remote indigenous villages in 1927 and 1928, documented the deep breaches that existed between rural schools and local people born with differences in language, beliefs, and culture.[7] In 1932 Sáenz organized a team of anthropologists and social scientists, in the fashion of Gamio's program, to study the Purépecha region known as *La Cañada de los Once Pueblos* in Michoacán to improve official development strategies and communication techniques. Here, he was met by a deeply divided population and by open aggression from the local agrarian leaders, who had become powerful and feared *caciques*.[8] The study of La Cañada could not be completed. From the perspective of Sáenz and other members of the Mexican intelligentsia, the ideals of revolutionary social transformation required not only intense interdisciplinary research and social planning but also an adequate transmission of innovative ideas, designed to induce widespread grassroots support.

With Cárdenas's election, indigenista intellectuals founded the Departamento Autónomo de Asuntos Indígenas (DAAI). Its priorities were a respectful dialogue between indigenous and mestizo cultures and the promotion of genuine democratic grassroots organizations based on local political traditions.[9] One of its first projects was the *Projecto Tarasco* in Michoacán, which intended to revitalize local culture and recover the Purépecha language as an instrument of learning and communication. In addition, the DAAI impelled regional congresses where indigenous representatives publicly presented their economic, social, and cultural demands.[10] During the 1930s, a number of intellectuals and academics, including anthropologists, sympathized with the Soviet theory of nationalities and wrote about Mexican Indians as "oppressed nationalities."[11] In particular, anthropologist Alfonso Fabila used his groundbreaking ethnohistoric and ethnographic research among the rebellious Yaquis of Sonora to argue in favor of indigenous political self-determination. For him, "the Yaqui nationality" had fought against Spanish colonization and then against military aggression from Mexican authorities and settlers to preserve their egalitarian and admirable way of life.[12]

In 1938 the right of historical indigenous communities to their communal lands was explicitly included in the constitution. In 1940 a presidential decree partially returned their ancestral territory to the Yaquis and recognized a limited jurisdiction of ethnic authorities in local affairs.[13] Concomitantly, in the Sierra Tarahumara, a commission formed by the DAAI, the Department of Labor and other government agencies recommended the same policy of recognition of territorial and political autonomy for "the Tarahumara race."[14] Other anthropologists linked to the DAAI, such as Carlos Basauri and Miguel Othón de Mendizábal, focused attention on the economic and health issues of indigenous groups and on strategies to solve these problems.[15] Prominent among such strategies was the transformation of the production of traditional arts and crafts into prosperous cooperatives. Mendizábal also contributed to the creation of the Instituto Politécnico Nacional, where he participated in the school of rural medicine and the school of anthropology. Both Mendizábal and Sáenz struggled to create a branch of applied anthropology, which was open to European ideas on social dynamics, currently exemplified in Mexico by the work of Robert Redfield.[16] Social problems, however, were not simply those inherited from the prerevolutionary regime: the emergent revolutionary elites also created new conflicts and contradictions.

The Pátzcuaro Congress and the Emergence of the Instituto Nacional Indigenista

With the approval of President Cárdenas, the DAAI convened the First Inter-American Indigenista Congress, which took place in Pátzcuaro, Michoacán, in 1940. This congress was attended by government officers, intellectuals, and indigenous representatives from the majority of the American countries. In the inaugural address, Cárdenas pronounced his famous dictum: "Our indigenous problem is not to keep the Indian Indian, nor to indigenize Mexico, but to mexicanize the Indian."[17] One of the leaders of the Mexican delegation was Vicente Lombardo Toledano, who had written in favor of the recognition of "indigenous nationalities." In his speech to the congress, however, he adopted a different line and spoke of integration and national unity. Other delegates, including those identified with the Communist Party, followed this line. Many had made a pact with Cárdenas's government on the matter, prioritizing national unity over ideological consistency and indigenous rights.

The support of Latin American delegates for the ideas of integration and acculturation contrasted with the policy of reserves advocated by the U.S. delegate, John D. Collier.[18] The delegates also discussed the benefits of agrarian reform, public health programs, agricultural extension, promotion of small-scale local industries, and bilingual education, but they did not touch the polemical issue of the recognition of ethnic territories and authorities. At the end of the congress, they unanimously approved the creation of an Indigenista Inter-American Institute, and all governments agreed to create in their respective countries an institution with ministerial rank in charge of indigenous affairs.[19]

Despite this noble declaration, the DAAI lost importance and autonomy at the end of Cárdenas's presidency. The new president, Manuel Avila Camacho (1940–46), appointed a moderate minister of education, who lasted less than a year and was followed by an outright conservative. There were no more regional congresses, activism in favor of agrarian reform, or state-sponsored discourses on ethnic autonomy. The Tarascan Project was dismantled, and the U.S Protestant group, the Summer Institute of Languages, was put in charge of producing leaflets for bilingual education. The program of Cultural Missions continued but without its political overtones. At the same time, the program of land distribution lost its impetus.[20] Many leftist anthropologists accepted that "to favor the transition from caste to class" indigenous interests should not be considered separate from the interests of the working class in general.[21] They also agreed on the need for national unity, especially since in 1942 the Mexican government had declared war on the Axis powers. Anthropological research became more academically oriented, carried out now mainly by the Universidad Nacional Autónoma de México (UNAM) and the Instituto Nacional de Antropología e Historia (INAH).[22] At the Escuela Nacional de Antropología e Historia (INAH's teaching branch), students received some Marxist influences from teachers such as Paul Kirchhoff, but their intellectual categories mainly came from German historicism and the Anglo-Saxon structural-functionalist school.[23] From 1940 onward, U.S. collaboration became the norm for Mexican anthropologists. Between 1942 and 1944 the University of Chicago sponsored a vast research project in the Chiapas Highlands under the direction of Sol Tax and Alfonso Villa Rojas. The latter had previously worked with Robert Redfield in Yucatán. This project recruited several students from the institute, including Ricardo Pozas, Fernando Cámara, and Calixta Guiteras-Holmes. According to Pozas, he had to argue for the inclusion of the study of indigenous exploitation by the dominant *ladino* class.[24] Also in the 1940s, Bronislaw Malinowski and Julio de la Fuente undertook research on the regional market system in Oaxaca under the auspices of Yale University. The Institute of Social Anthropology of the Smithsonian Institution sponsored a new Tarascan Project, directed by George Foster, as well as one of the Tajín Totonac of Veracruz, conducted by Isabel Kelly and Ángel Palerm. These projects produced detailed ethnographies; they also explored the adaptive ability of the indigenous population. Although the presence of U.S.-sponsored projects had been strongly felt since the turn of the century, those of the 1940s set the tone for anthropological work in Mexico for the next twenty or thirty years. (This work was reflected in the volumes of the *Handbook of Middle American Indians*, published throughout the 1960s and 1970s.) This was connected to the U.S. government's global promotion of "area studies" and the attempt to construct what David Nugent has termed "a new geography of knowledge."[25]

During the late 1940s, President Miguel Alemán (1946–52), reshaped the ruling party, which was now rebaptized the Partido Revolucionario Institucional (PRI). The DAAI was replaced by a Directorate of Indigenous Education, which had a much more limited scope. Gonzalo Aguirre Beltrán, a medical doctor who had done graduate work in anthropology at Northwestern University, was the first director. He had previously worked with Manuel Gamio and was the author of a pioneering book on the ethnohistory of the black population in Mexico.[26] In 1948 the National Congress approved the creation of the Instituto Nacional Indigenista (INI). Alfonso Caso, a prominent archeologist, lawyer, and PRI politician, was appointed director, and Aguirre Beltrán became sub-director. Caso articulated a definition of the indigenous peoples in terms of culture and community affiliation rather than "race." As a result, indigenista action was aimed at cultural change and community development, which were conceived as steps on the path toward national unity. In turn, Aguirre Beltrán and his close collaborator Julio de la Fuente—one of the radical delegates to the Pátzcuaro Congress—coined the concept of intercultural regions to refer to the fact that indigenous communities could be understood only in the spatial context inside which they interacted with and were subordinate to nonindigenous groups and settlements. In so doing, they recovered both Gamio's idea of regional studies and Sáenz's concern with political domination.[27]

Following Alemán's vision for national development, the government entrusted the INI with missions related to the large-scale development of infrastructure in support of capitalist modernization. Thus, in 1949 Aguirre Beltrán carried out field research among the Purépecha of the Tarascan Plateau in Michoacán, an area that would be affected by the hydraulic works of the Tepalcatepec Commission.[28] Then he was sent to the Chiapas Highlands, where the Pan-American Highway was provoking changes in the indigenous communities. In turn, Moisés T. de la Peña, a professional economist and self-trained social anthropologist working with the INI, undertook a vast study of the Mixteca Sierra, which had been similarly bisected by the Pan-American Highway.[29] Aguirre Beltrán's idea of the *Centros Coordinadores Indigenistas* (CCIs)—public institutions of applied research—was taking shape. And in 1951 he founded the first one in San Cristóbal de las Casas, Chiapas. It was designed to guide and accelerate "the process of acculturation."[30] In the following five years other CCIs were created for the Tarahumara Sierra of Chihuahua, the Tarascan Sierra, and the Papaloapan Basin in Oaxaca. The Patrimonio Indígena del Valle del Mezquital, which did not depend directly on the INI but followed the CCI model, was founded in 1952.

Indigenismo and "the Process of Acculturation"

Aguirre Beltrán's critics later reproached his supposed "betrayal" of the radical indigenista spirit. Ricardo Pozas complained that INI policies wanted to substitute individualist market values for indigenous communalism. Aguirre Beltrán answered that he was in fact returning to the progressive ideas of Manuel Gamio.[31] Gamio had been a disciple of Franz Boas. In the context of the early years of Mexico's social revolution, Gamio wanted to combine Boas's respect and appreciation for native cultures with the revolutionary ideal of a new egalitarian and modern society. This new society could not be created without the decisive intervention of a progressive state. In contrast, Moisés Sáenz, who died a premature death in 1940, wanted an integrated society, but he came to believe that the process of integration had to start from below. Sáenz was extremely critical of the concept of "incorporation," which had been central to Gamio's indigenista theory. Instead, he proposed "not to incorporate the Indian but to integrate Mexico." This would mean "not only for the Indians to become more Mexican but also for the Mexicans to become more Indian."[32] Sáenz wrote in the context of deep religious conflicts and factional rivalry. The new ruling class included political bosses—caciques—who often were violent and corrupt.[33] As a consequence, Sáenz believed that the only way to prevent their emergence and the privileges of their clientele was to foster grassroots democracy. In the case of the indigenous communities this meant respect for their political traditions and values. In contrast, Aguirre Beltrán explicitly assumed an antirelativist, pro-Western position as the best antidote to exploitation and oppression. Nevertheless, he also contended that acculturation did not mean the destruction of the vernacular cultures but their adaptation to, and fusion with, the vigorous national—mestizo—culture.[34]

Like Gamio, Aguirre Beltrán's intellectual influences included a blend of Porfirian and U.S.-inflected cultural historicism. His first major theoretical book was *Formas de Gobierno Indígena*, published in 1953, in which he developed his central ideas on the necessary relationship between acculturation, national modernity, and citizenship.[35] His argument was based on his interpretations of (1) ethnohistorical research on the social and political organization of indigenous groups during the pre-Hispanic, colonial, and early independence periods, and (2) the comparative ethnography of three different intercultural regions: the Sierra Tarahumara, the Chiapas Highlands, and the Tarascan Plateau. In the ethnohistorical section, he concluded that before the Spanish conquest there was nothing that could be deemed "a nation" and that during the following centuries indigenous groups never had the opportunity to construct a national project. Only the Mexican Revolution had provided ideas and policies for both national integration and acculturation. Integration referred to social linkages among people from different localities, regions, and classes, which had multiplied in the context of large-scale mobilizations against Porfirio Díaz's dictatorship and were further enhanced by the expansion of markets and communications. Acculturation—at the time a fashionable term in U.S. anthropology—was the process of the production of common idioms and customs resulting from frequent contact between groups with different cultures. Aguirre Beltrán argued that, during the colonial period and the nineteenth century, integration had been partially impeded by caste segregation and acculturation had been distorted and hindered by asymmetrical power relations. In modern Mexico, segregation and subordination could be dismantled by the expansion of class consciousness and the struggle for legal and social equality.

In the ethnographic section of *Formas de Gobierno Indígena*, the comparison of the three groups led to the conclusion that the Purépecha or Tarascan people of Michoacán, being more acculturated, were more capable of democratic participation in national institutions through membership in or support for political parties that competed in municipal, state, and federal elections. In contrast, both the Tzotzil and Tseltal communities of the Chiapas Highlands, and in a more drastic manner the Tarahumara people, could only participate in subordinate communal ("tribal") institutions. Because of cultural limitations, the relationships of the Tzotzil, Tseltal, and Tarahumara peoples with the nation were dominated by mestizos, ladinos, or "whites" who monopolized economic resources, prestige, and power. Consequently, the raison d'être of indigenismo was to favor complete integration and acculturation. The colonial distinction between Indians and non-Indians had to disappear, This would only be made possible by weakening the domain of those non-Indian groups, which maintained and made the most of such distinctions. The indigenista agencies—the CCIs—would be located at the site of regional power, generally a town or city, because their first mission was to chart not just the problems of the indigenous population but also the power mechanisms that created those problems. The ensuing diagnoses would lead to master programs of transformation that would be carried out by other specialized government agencies. Such programs should include the building of basic infrastructure, sanitation campaigns, access to health services, land distribution, free markets of products and labor, organizations of producers and laborers, schools with programs of bilingual education, and the consolidation of modern republican institutions, particularly the *municipio libre* ruled by a democratic council. This last point was extremely important: it implied the disappearance of the ethnic traditional corporative structures and systems of authority, which, in Aguirre Beltrán's opinion, were a major hindrance to the emergence of individual citizenship based on universal legal principles. To implement all these changes gradually and without provoking conflicts within the communities, the intermediation of bicultural promoters recruited and trained by the INI would be crucial.

Indigenista Contradictions

When the INI was created, Ricardo Pozas and Gonzalo Aguirre Beltrán became friends and close collaborators. Pozas had previously worked in Chiapas, so he helped with the preparatory research for the first CCI. Together they wrote an influential article on indigenous institutions and state policies in the twentieth century.³⁶ But when Pozas began to organize cooperatives and encourage communal organization in San Cristóbal de las Casas, he became estranged from the increasingly disapproving INI authorities. To compound his position, he also denounced the maneuvers of the PRIísta governor of Chiapas, who had engineered a maize shortage through shady deals with Guatemalan importers.³⁷ As a consequence of his critical attitude, the INI took Pozas out of Chiapas and exiled him to a research position in the Papaloapan basin. His successor in the Chiapas CCI was a man who—again, according to Pozas—had the task of dismantling the cooperatives because "[those Indians] already knew how to do commercial activities and exploit their fellow Indians [so they didn't need cooperatives any longer]."³⁸

However, despite Pozas's complaints, the CCI did start to gain the trust of the Highland Indians through the training of bilingual cultural promoters and the foundation of schools and health posts. In fact, CCI initiatives were so successful that the state government accused the anthropologists of subversive activism.³⁹ One of the main causes of contention was the INI's opposition to the damaging influence of the regional liquor monopoly, which operated under the protection of powerful local politicians. In 1954, Julio de la Fuente, who directed the CCI after Aguirre Beltrán, led an investigation of the monopoly and the problem of alcoholism in the communities. The report of this investigation remained unpublished until 2009, and the power of the monopolists and alcohol dealers stayed largely unchallenged.⁴⁰

The participation of the INI in the Papaloapan Commission had started in 1949, when Alfonso Villa Rojas and a handful of collaborators assumed the complicated task of researching an area inhabited by more than twenty thousand Mazatec Indians and then organizing and monitoring their resettlement. Many Mazatec families did not speak Spanish and were ill-equipped to challenge a modernizing bureaucratic machine designed to shift them from their villages, habitats and customs. They also had to adjust to the presence of hundreds of non-Indian laborers from urban and industrial environments, who arrived in the region to build the dam. In the book that documents the process, Villa Rojas made an honest presentation of the complexities and challenges involved. But he only briefly mentioned the discontent and political agitation generated by the dam and the flooding of the Mazatec territory. Tension reached a peak in late 1952 when certain groups of Mazatecs took up arms and rebelled. This movement, officially imputed to supporters of the oppositional presidential candidate, Miguel Henríquez Guzmán, was—like so many other petty insurgencies—cut short by brutal repression and removed from the public record.⁴¹ Furthermore, in Villa Rojas's account there was no mention of the fact that—whether by mistake or carelessness—the populations of several of the new towns did not coincide with those of the flooded villages. This implied the awkward mixing of villagers who spoke different dialects of Mazatec (there were five of them) and created problems of communication in schools.[42] Neither did he mention that most of the recommendations made by the INI team were not fully implemented by the state or the federal authorities. At the same time, Villa Rojas suggested that resettlement implied a jump in the acculturation process, since the new towns had urban characteristics and modern facilities, but he made no analysis of the pernicious implications of this new type of forceful and distorted acculturation.[43]

Throughout the following decades, similar macro-projects were carried out in the basins of the Fuerte River in the state of Sinaloa and of the Usumacinta and Grijalva Rivers, which run through the states of Tabasco and Chiapas. In 1958 Aguirre Beltrán wrote about the "disastrous cultural shock" and "acute social disorganization" provoked by the relocation of indigenous peoples in the absence of an integrated development project.[44] He mentioned the Papaloapan project as an example of the difficulties of resettlement, and in a 1975 article he recognized that there were major disagreements between the INI anthropologists and the commission's administration. However, he still supported the building of the dam as a nationalistic effort that generated hydraulic energy for the benefit of the whole Mexican nation. In a similar vein he defended the works of the Tepalcatepec Commission, which became part of the Balsas Commission in 1961.[45] Like the Mazatecs of the Papaloapan basin, the indigenous inhabitants of Tepalcatepec suffered radical transformations in their landscape and environment. These transformations affected landholding arrangements and the organization of agricultural production. The dams allowed for the control of flooding as well as an enormous expansion of irrigation. The provision of hydraulic energy benefited vast areas and stimulated the creation of industries. Modern roads and airports were built, schools and hospitals were created, and there was a major increase in literacy and the control of endemic illnesses.[46] Yet for many critics, negative environmental effects, the deepening of social inequality, cultural conflicts, and continuing peasant dependency and subordination outweighed these selective benefits.[47]

The dismantling of traditional forms of rule and the imposition of municipal governments as the only legal system of local political organization and representation also provoked indigenous discontent and resistance. Aguirre Beltrán wrote disapprovingly about the emergence of the "*Consejo Supremo Tarahumara*" (Tarahumara Supreme Council), which was never officially recognized but had a determining influence on the region. The story of the council began in the Cárdenas years, with the regional congresses organized by the DAAI, leftist schoolmasters, and bilingual Tarahumara teachers. Even though the DAAI did not participate after 1940, the congresses continued, culminating in the creation of the representative council. Until this point, indigenous communities in the region lacked proper representation. Furthermore, local mestizos blocked the participation of Tarahumaras in municipal councils.[48] In this context, a new type of regional corporative representation seemed a good solution. But the INI national authorities and particularly Aguirre Beltrán were vehemently opposed, arguing that this type of "tribal government" violated the Mexican Constitution. In spite of this opposition, the *Consejo Supremo* played a leading if unofficial role in the negotiations for the creation of a CCI in the Sierra Tarahumara. Moreover, Francisco Plancarte, the founding and long-time director of the CCI, frequently resorted to the council for advice and negotiations with the communities and their ethnic authorities.[49]

The rigid opposition of the upper echelons of the INI to the recognition of ethnic authorities contradicted official discourse which stressed the need for the democratic participation of underrepresented indigenous peoples. In addition, it was common knowledge that the state and federal authorities often failed to respect municipal representation but rather favored local caciques or the members of agrarian reform institutions like the *Comisariados Ejidales* and *Comisariados de Bienes Comunales*. Such organizations usually eschewed democratic methods and instead rested on clientelistic, often illegal mixtures of rewards and punishments. In his book on indigenous politics, Aguirre Beltrán expressed his enthusiasm for the disappearance of traditional authorities among the Tarascans and the increasing dominance of municipal councils. But in the same text he documents how the composition of municipal councils reflected the interplay of informal interest groups, irrespective of their nominal party affiliations. In the 1950s all *municipios* in the Tarascan Plateau were in the hands of the PRI, but to be a party member meant different things in different places. A frequent cause of disagreement was the local application of agrarian reform legislation. This legislation recognized two types of social property: *comunal*, for those tracts of land that had been the property of an indigenous community during the colonial period, and *ejidal*, for land granted by the government to landless petitioners. Usually *ejido* terrains were expropriated from large, private haciendas. The PRI apparatus favored the formation of ejidos because they allowed for the vertical organization of petitioners and a more active presence of the party in the communities. But in those Tarascan municipalities where the best land had not been channeled into haciendas, ejidos were instead created on old communal lands. This provoked anger among local dwellers, who rejected official control of these lands. As a result, the winners of municipal elections were often bitter critics of agrarian reform. But they still belonged to the PRI, even though they sympathized with the rightist critiques of the Unión Nacional Sinarquista.[50]

Despite Aguirre Beltrán's influence, even within the INI, prominent anthropologists followed Alfonso Fabila's work on the Yaqui and continued to praise autonomous indigenous political systems. Both Julio de la Fuente, in his monograph on the Zapotec community of Yalalag, and Moisés T. de la Peña, in his vast and careful study of the Mixteca, recognized the linkage between communal work (*tequio*) and traditional authority. In the case of Yalalag, de la Fuente described the baroque hierarchical system (inherited from the colonial period) in which political and religious offices were intertwined. As an adult male climbed the hierarchy he gained prestige and power—but both prestige and power depended on his capacity to serve the community throughout his life.[51] "After all," wrote de la Peña, reflecting on his own research, "the service of authority is a [type of] *tequio*." He noticed that where the tequio had disappeared there was "neither authority nor organization, neither public order nor useful services." In his view, indigenista policies should reinforce the institution of *tequixtlato* (the organization of communal work) as well as the councils of elders.[52] De la Fuente agreed and added that the hasty substitution of modern cooperatives for traditional forms of cooperation could have disruptive effects and hindered "progress" in the communities.[53]

The Paradoxes of Indigenous Resistance and Indigenista Action

There has been little research done on the subject of open indigenous opposition to indigenista policies during the 1940s and the 1950s. It is well known that members of some indigenous groups participated in two massive peasant opposition movements—the *Unión General de Obreros y Campesinos Mexicanos* and the *Partido Agrario Obrero Morelense*. Their protest, however, was against a lack of economic opportunities for small rural producers, corruption in the agrarian reform apparatus, and the repression of political dissidents. Their demands did not include the recognition of cultural rights nor political autonomy for indigenous peoples.[54] Ethnic resistance was manifested in the stubborn persistence of local corporate institutions, which combined the maintenance of the social order with the organization of both communal work and religious festivals. Such institutions coexisted with official republican councils in different manners—as rivals or collaborators.[55] In some cases—the Tarahumara Sierra; the Yaqui Valley; the Zapotec, Mixe, and Mixtec Sierras; and the Isthmus of Tehuantepec—communal bodies were interconnected through pan-ethnic or multiethnic organizations and social movements,[56] but they usually had a complicated relationship with the cultural promoters and bilingual teachers of the INI. Elders and other communal authorities often saw promoters as subversive agents who threatened to destroy tradition; however, they also recognized them as political mediators among disjointed structures of authority.[57] In turn these mediators often participated in and sometimes manipulated communal institutions in favor of the ruling party. In a provocative article on the Tzotzil municipality of Chamula in the Chiapas Highlands, Jan Rus documents the emergence and continuity of what he ironically calls "the *Comunidad Revolucionaria Institucional*," which was dominated since the years of President Cárdenas by a new political elite of bilingual teachers who assumed the role of guardians of tradition, ensured control over local elections, and discouraged—even repressed—any type of protest or conflict. Marco Calderón has described similar processes in the Purépecha municipalities of Michoacán.[58]

But the function of intermediation suffered other transformations throughout the years. Two decades after the first printing of *Formas de Gobierno Indígena*, many of the indigenous teachers and professionals recruited by the INI had become outspoken critics of indigenista policies. They were joined in their critiques by a new generation of anthropologists, intellectuals, and students in search of a concept of national unity and social justice that did not exclude cultural diversity or political and legal pluralism.[59] The accusations against the INI included bureaucratic inefficiency and corruption, which determined that the indigenous population was still the poorest in the country. During the period of President Echeverría (1970–76) the response of the government was to multiply the number of CCIs and (against the advice of Aguirre Beltrán) improvise *consejos supremos*—like the one in the Tarahumara Sierra—for every ethnolinguistic group, supposedly to reinforce indigenous representation in each region. The legal status of the consejos, however, was not within the official structure of government. Instead, they became parts of the PRI apparatus (through the peasant sector of the party). Such "tribal" organisms created from above had little significance, and most of them quietly disappeared *sin pena ni gloria*.[60]

The third period of Mexican indigenismo really began in the 1980s with the collapse of economic protectionism, the weakening of the PRI, and the resurgence of social movements and a civil society, which pressed for democratization and respect for cultural rights. During the next two decades, the constitution was changed to recognize the multicultural nature of the nation and the rights of indigenous peoples to autonomy, while the federal government substituted the INI for the National Commission for the Development of Indigenous Peoples, created the National Institute for Indigenous Languages, dismantled the agrarian reform program, and redefined its development policies. But that is another story.

MEXICO'S INDIGENOUS GROUPS have undergone a long and slippery transition: from legal subjection under Spanish rule to legal inexistence under liberal legislation to—with the development of indigenista ideologies—candidacy for mestizo citizenship. In the period between 1920 and 1940 the revolutionary government and its indigenista agencies advanced a definition of citizenship in connection with large-scale, vertically organized mobilizations in favor of certain social reforms. Overall these contributed to the empowerment of a new political elite entrenched in a dominant party. From 1940 to 1980, however, the meaning of mestizo citizenship changed. The new emphasis was on capitalist industrial modernization and national unity, always under the leadership of the (now "institutionalized") revolutionary party. Politicians on both left and right hailed industrial growth as the indispensable key to the nation's prosperity. The mission of the peasantry was defined as the provision of both cheap foodstuffs and labor surpluses for the expanding urban and industrial areas. The role of the INI was to facilitate this mission. What remained constant was the hegemonic project, which attempted to mold everyday life in indigenous communities to definitions and categories (such as nation, national culture, integration, and acculturation) concocted at the top of the political system.[61] Yet such a strategy necessitated the active participation of indigenista functionaries and indigenous intermediaries, who often had diverging views on priorities and strategies. The intellectual and political evolution of both anthropologists and ethnic brokers often contributed to a radical critique of government actions. In turn, indigenous communities developed their own "everyday forms of resistance," which after 1980 became manifest in important, sometimes radical, social movements that defended an alternative definition of national formation and citizenship. Such movements succeeded insofar as the government not only modified certain laws and discourses concerning indigenous peoples but also declared the explicit intention to reinvent indigenismo–an intention still unfulfilled.

The revolutionary regime fostered a type of nationalistic anthropology that had a privileged expression in the theory and practice of indigenismo. The study of *los indios mexicanos* and their habitats exerted a strong academic and humanistic attraction for a number of major intellectual figures. The state channeled such industry to acquire information about largely unknown groups and regions, a plan that suited its own plans for their appeasement and control. From 1940 to 1960, government policies toward indigenous peoples included their reorganization, and often their resettlement, as part of a national plan for socioeconomic and ideological transformation. Promotion and funding by U.S. academics and institutions fed into these policies.[62] In Mexico the presence of American institutions and scholars as well as the availability of American grants for students and researchers helped the development of cultural and social anthropology.[63] Such U.S. influence probably favored the analytical focus on the peculiarities of ethnic cultures and the conditions of their absorption by the dominant national and international cultures. It was fortunate that many Mexican anthropologists, like the people they studied, were able to resist "acculturation."

Mexican indigenismo had a strong and lasting influence in Latin American anthropology and social policies. After the 1940 Pátzcuaro Congress, several governments in the region created indigenista institutions, and most of them passed protective legislation and launched educational and sanitary programs modeled after the experience of Mexico. Professionals from this country broadcasted their ideas in the journal *América Indígena* and in the Indigenista Inter-American Congresses, which met every four years. The National School of Anthropology and History in Mexico City received Latin American students and visiting scholars. The work of Gamio, Sáenz, Aguirre Beltrán, and others was well known by their Latin American colleagues, and the latter's theory of acculturation became a sort of official doctrine for the Indigenista Inter-American Institute, as the CCIs were visited by Latin American delegates who profited from Mexico's experience.[64] Since the 1960s the concept of acculturation was strongly rejected by certain postcolonial anthropologists and ethnic organizations. Aguirre Beltrán stressed that the specific tempo of acculturation in a given situation was determined by the nature of power relationships, but he maintained that the ultimate direction of change toward cultural homogeneity and national identity could not be altered. Anthropologists like Darcy Ribeiro and Roberto Cardoso de Oliveira in Brazil and Guillermo Bonfil in Mexico challenged this thesis. These authors argued that, given the strength and aggressiveness of the dominant culture, the real alternatives for indigenous peoples were disappearance or resistance. Furthermore, cultural change could be construed as a resistant strategy to preserve indigenous identity and distinctiveness. Acculturation really meant "cultural transfiguration."[65] At the same time, ethnic movements throughout the continent rejected acculturation as an insidious form of racism and ethnocide.[66] Against this accusation, apologists for the INI as well as certain independent academics cited the real actions of the INI, in many regions, as being in favor of education and health and against land invasion and exploitation from ranchers, miners, and commercial lumbering.[67] Between the triumphal preaching in favor of official indigenismo in the 1950s and the dark and pessimistic accounts of its critics a few decades later, more serious research and reappraisal of such an important social and cultural policy is still needed.

Notes

1. Zygmunt Bauman, Culture as Praxis (London: Sage Publications, 1999), 1–2.
2. Manuel Gamio, Forjando patria: Pro-nacionalismo (Mexico City: Porrúa, 1916).
3. See Mary Louise Pratt, Imperial Eyes: Travel Writing and Transculturation (London: Routledge, 1992).
4. Luz María Valdés, Los indíos en los censos de población (Mexico City: UNAM, 1995).
5. Manuel Gamio, La población del Valle de Teotihuacán (3 vols.) (Mexico City: Talleres Gráficos de la Nación, 1922).
6. Guillermo de la Peña, "Educación y cultura en el México del siglo XX," in Un siglo de educación en México, ed. Pablo Latapí, vol. I, 43–83 (Mexico City: Fondo de Cultura Económica/Consejo Nacional para la Cultura y las Artes, 1998).
7. Moisés Sáenz, "Sierra de Puebla" (unpublished manuscript, 1927) and México íntegro (Lima, Peru: Imprenta Torres Aguirre, 1939).
8. Moisés Sáenz, Carapan: Bosquejo de una experiencia (Lima, Peru: Librería e Imprenta Gil, 1936); Jaime Loyola Rocha, "La visión integral de la sociedad nacional, 1920–1934," in Carlos García Mora, ed., La antropología en México: Panorama histórico. 2. Los hechos y los dichos (Mexico City: Instituto Nacional de Antropología e Historia, 1987), 171–75.
9. Sáenz, Carapan; Sáenz, México íntegro.
10. Luis Vázquez León, "La práctica de la antropología social durante el cardenismo," Cuicuilco. Revista de la Escuela Nacional de Antropología e Historia 2, no. 5 (1981): 8–17.
11. Vicente Lombardo Toledano, "Geografía de las lenguas de la Sierra de Puebla, con algunas observaciones sobre sus primeros y sus actuales pobladores," Universidad de México 3, no. 13 (1931): 14–96; Miguel Othón de Mendizábal, "Problemas indígenas y su más urgente tratamiento" [c. 1936], Obras Completas, vol. 5 (Mexico City: n.p., 1946), 7; cf. Gonzalo Aguirre Beltrán, Lenguas vernáculas: Su uso y desuso en la enseñanza: la experiencia de México (Mexico City: CIESAS, Ediciones de la Casa Chata, 1983), 177–200.
12. Alfonso Fabila, Las tribus yaquis de Sonora: Su cultura y anhelada autodeterminación (Mexico City: DAAI, 1940)
13. Adrian Bantjes, As if Jesus Walked the Earth: Cardenismo, Sonora, and the Mexican Revolution (Wilmington, DE: Scholarly Resources, 1997).
14. Juan Luis Sariego, El indigenismo en la Tarahumara (Mexico City: Instituto Nacional Indigenista, 2002), esp. 91–97.
15. Carlos Basauri, La población indígena de México (3 vols.) (Mexico City: Departamento de Asuntos Indígenas, 1940).
16. For more on Mendizábal and Basauri, see Arturo España Caballero, "La práctica social y el populismo nacionalista, 1935–1940," in García Mora, La antropología en México, 246–52; Robert Redfield, Tepoztlán (Chicago: University of Chicago Press, 1930); Robert Redfield and Alfonso Villa Rojas, Chan Kom: A Maya Village (Washing-

ton, DC: Carnegie Institution, 1934); Robert Redfield, *The Folk Culture of Yucatán* (Chicago: University of Chicago Press, 1940).

17. Lázaro Cárdenas, "Los indígenas, factor de progreso," *Educación. Revista Mensual de Pedagogía y Acción Sindical*, IV (Número Dedicado al Primer Congreso Indigenista Interamericano; June 1940), 10.

18. Collier had been appointed by Franklin D. Roosevelt to head the U.S. Bureau of Indian Affairs and take charge of "the Indian New Deal."

19. Guillermo de la Peña, "Social and cultural policies towards indigenous peoples: Perspectives from Latin America," *Annual Review of Anthropology* 34 (2005): 717–39.

20. See Jesús Silva Herzog, *El agrarismo mexicano y la reforma agraria* (Mexico City: Fondo de Cultura Económica, 1985), chapter 11.

21. Julio de la Fuente, "Cambios raciales y culturales en un grupo indígena," *Acta Anthropológica* 3 (1948): 48–67.

22. The INAH was founded in 1938 as a comprehensive federal institution that gradually incorporated museums, the restoration and maintenance of pre-Hispanic and colonial monuments, and anthropological research at large.

23. Carlos García Mora, "Paul Kirchhoff, el instigador," *Antropología y marxismo* I (1979): 7–10.

24. Luis Vázquez León, "El investigador en acción: Entrevista a Ricardo Pozas," in Jorge Durand and Luis Vázquez, eds., *Caminos de la antropología: Entrevistas a cinco antropólogos* (Mexico City: Instituto Nacional Indigenista, 1990), 143–45.

25. David Nugent, ed., *Locating Capitalism in Time and Space: Global Restructuring, Politics, and Identity* (Palo Alto, CA: Stanford University Press, 2002).

26. Gonzalo Aguirre Beltrán, *La población negra de México* (Mexico City: Fondo de Cultura Económica, 1972 [1946]).

27. Gonzalo Aguirre Beltrán, *El pensar y el quehacer antropológico en México* (Puebla: Benemérita Universidad Autónoma de Puebla, 1994), 142–44.

28. See Gonzalo Aguirre Beltrán, *Problemas de la población indígena en la cuenca del Tepalcatepec* (Mexico City: Instituto Nacional Indigenista, 1952); David Barkin and Timothy King, *Regional Economic Development: The River Basin Approach in Mexico* (Cambridge: Cambridge Latin American Studies, 1970).

29. Moisés T. de la Peña, *Problemas sociales y económicos de las Mixtecas* (Mexico City: Instituto Nacional Indigenista, 1950).

30. Gonzalo Aguirre Beltrán, *El proceso de aculturación y el cambio sociocultural en México* (Mexico City: Universidad Iberoamericana, 1970 [1958]).

31. See Aguirre Beltrán's introduction to *Arqueología e indigenismo* (Mexico City: Secretaría de Educación Pública, 1972); Manuel Gamio, "Aculturación espontánea," in *Homenaje al Dr. Alfonso Caso* (Mexico City: n.p., 1951), 175–79.

32. Moisés Sáenz, *México íntegro*, 232; Alexander Scott Dawson, *Indian and Nation in Revolutionary Mexico* (Tucson: University of Arizona Press, 2004), 68–70.

33. Paul Friedrich, *Princes of Naranja: An Essay in Anthrohistorical Method* (Austin: University of Texas Press, 1986); Guillermo de la Peña, "Poder local, poder regional: Perspectivas socio-antropológicas," in *Poder local, poder regional*, ed. Jorge Padua and Alain Vanneph (Mexico City: El Colegio de México/Centre d'Etudes Mexicaines et Centramericaines, 1986).

34. Aguirre Beltrán, *El proceso de aculturación*.

35. Aguirre Beltrán, *Formas de gobierno indígena* (Mexico City: Imprenta Universitaria/UNAM, 1953).

36. Gonzalo Aguirre Beltrán and Ricardo Pozas, "Instituciones indígenas en el siglo XX," in *Métodos y resultados de la política indigenista en México*, ed. Alfonso Caso et al. (Mexico City: Instituto Nacional Indigenista, 1954).

37. Vázquez León, "El investigador en acción," 159.

38. Vázquez León, "El investigador en acción," 152.

39. Aguirre Beltrán, *El pensar y el quehacer antropológico*, 150.

40. Julio de la Fuente, *Monopolio de aguardiente y alcoholismo en los Altos de Chiapas*, with an introduction by Stephen E. Lewis (Mexico City: Comisión Nacional para el Desarrollo de los Pueblos Indígenas, 2009). See also Stephen E. Lewis, *The Ambivalent Revolution: Forging State and Nation in Chiapas, 1910–1945* (Albuquerque: University of New Mexico Press, 2005); Stephen E. Lewis, "The National Indigenist Institute and the Negotiation of Applied Anthropology in Highland Chiapas, Mexico, 1951–1955," *Ethnohistory* 55, no. 4 (2008): 609–32.

41. Benjamin T. Smith, *Pistoleros and Popular Movements: The Politics of State Formation in Postrevolutionary Oaxaca* (Lincoln: University of Nebraska Press, 2009), 371–72.

42. Isabel Horcasitas de Pozas and Ricardo Pozas, "Del monolingüismo en lengua indígena al bilingüismo en lengua indígena y nacional," in *Pensamiento antropológico e indigenista de Julio de la Fuente*, ed. Félix Báez-Jorge et al. (Mexico City: Instituto Nacional Indigenista, 1980), 145–95, 154–55.

43. Alfonso Villa Rojas, *Los mazatecos y el problema indígena de la cuenca del Papaloapan* (Mexico City: Instituto Nacional Indigenista, 1955), esp. chapters 9 and 10.

44. Aguirre Beltrán, *El proceso de aculturación*, 52.

45. Gonzalo Aguirre Beltrán, "Etnocidio en México: Una denuncia irresponsable," *América Indígena* 35 (1975): 405–18. This article was written in response to denouncements of the "ethnocidal" actions of the INI and the Mexican government; cf. Alicia M. Barabas and Miguel A. Bartolomé, *Hydraulic Development and Ethnocide: The Mazatec and Chinantec People of Oaxaca* (Copenhagen: International Working Group for Indigenous Affairs, 1973).

46. Aguirre Beltrán, *Problemas de la población indígena*; Villa Rojas, *Los mazatecos*; William L. Partridge, Antoinette Brown, and Jeffrey Nugent, "The Papaloapan Dam and Resettlement Project: Human Ecology and Health Impacts," in *Involuntary Migration and Resettlement: The Problems and Responses of Dislocated Peoples*, ed. Art Hansen and Anthony Oliver-Smith (Boulder, CO: Westview Press, 1982), 245–63; William L. Partridge and Antoinette Brown, "Desarrollo indígena entre los mazatecos reacomodados," *América Indígena* 43 (1983): 343–62.

47. Miguel A. Bartolomé and Alicia M. Barabas, *La presa Cerro del Oro y el Ingeniero Gran Dios: Relocalización y etnocidio chinanteco* (Mexico City: Instituto Nacional Indigenista, 1990); Eckart Boege, *Los mazatecos ante la nación: Contradicciones de la identidad étnica en el México actual* (Mexico City: Siglo Veintiuno Editores, 1988); Marco A. Calderón Mólgora, "Desarrollo integral en las cuencas del Tepalcatepec y el Balsas," in Juan Ortiz Escamilla, *Transformaciones de los paisajes culturales en la cuenca del Tepalcatepec* (Zamora: El Colegio de Michoacán, 2011).

48. Sariego, *El indigenismo*, 104–16.

49. Francisco M. Plancarte, *El problema indígena tarahumara* (Mexico City: Instituto Nacional Indigenista, 1954), 86, 90, 96.

50. Aguirre Beltrán, *Formas de gobierno indígena*, 201–6.

51. Julio de la Fuente, *Yalálag: Una villa zapoteca serrana* (Mexico City: Museo Nacional de Antropología, 1949).

52. De la Peña, *Problemas sociales*, 136–38; Enrique Ochoa, "Lic. Moisés T. de la Peña: The Economist on Horseback," in *The Human Tradition in Mexico*, ed. Jeffrey Pilcher (Wilmington, DE: Scholarly Resources, 2003).

53. Julio de la Fuente, "Cooperación indígena y cooperativismo moderno" [1944], in Julio de la Fuente, *Educación, antropología y desarrollo de la comunidad* (Mexico City: Instituto Nacional Indigenista, 1964), 167–82.

54. Guillermo de la Peña, "Civil Society and Popular Resistance: Mexico at the End of the Twentieth Century," in *Cycles of Conflict, Centuries of Change: Crisis, Reform, and Revolution in Mexico*, ed. Elisa Servín, Leticia Reina, and John Tutino, 305–45 (Durham, NC: Duke University Press, 2007).

55. Even today, in many villages a man has to participate in corporate bodies to gain legitimacy as a viable candidate for the *ayuntamiento*. See Guillermo de la Peña, *A Legacy of Promises: Agriculture, Politics and Ritual in the Morelos Highlands of Mexico* (Austin: University of Texas Press, 1981), chapters 7 and 8.

56. Juan Luis Sariego, *El indigenismo en la Tarahumara*; Alejandro Figueroa, *Por la tierra y por los santos* (Mexico City: Consejo Nacional para la Cultura y las Artes, 1994); Smith, *Pistoleros*, 370; Salomón Nahmad, *Fuentes etnológicas para el estudio de los pueblos ayuuk (mixe) del Estado de Oaxaca* (Mexico City: CIESAS, 1987); Howard Campbell, *Zapotec Renaissance: Ethnic Politics and Cultural Revivalism in Southern Mexico* (Albuquerque: University of New Mexico Press, 1994).

57. Eric Wolf was among the first anthropologists who drew attention to the crucial importance of cultural and political brokers in Mexico in his classic article "Aspects of Group Relations in Complex Societies: Mexico," *American Anthropologist* 58 (1956): 1065–78.

58. Jan Rus, "The Comunidad Revolucionaria Institucional: The Subversion of Native Government in Highland Chiapas," in *Everyday Forms of State Formation: Revolution and the Negotiation of Rule in Modern Mexico*, ed. Gilbert Joseph and Daniel Nugent (Durham, NC: Duke University Press, 1994); Marco Antonio Calderón Mólgora, *Historias, procesos políticos y cardenismos: Cherán y la Sierra Purépecha* (Zamora: El Colegio de Michoacán, 2004).

59. Arturo Warman et al., *De eso que llaman antropología mexicana* (Mexico City: Nuestro Tiempo, 1970).

60. Félix Báez-Jorge, *¿Líderes indios o intermediarios indigenistas?* (Mexico City: Escuela Nacional de Antropología e Historia, 1984).

61. In Slavoj Žižek's words, "the operation of hegemony 'sutures' the empty universal to a particular content" (*The Ticklish Subject: The Absent Centre of Political Ontology* [London: Verso, 1999], 205fn).

62. David Nugent, *Locating Capitalism in Time and Space*.

63. Juan Comas, "La enseñanza de la antropología y la utilización de antropólogos en Hispanoamérica," in *Homenaje al Dr. Alfonso Caso* (Mexico City: n.p., 1951), 112.

64. De la Peña, "Social and Cultural Policies"; Marco Calderón Mólgora and José Luis Escalona Victoria, "Indigenismo populista en México: Del maestro misionero al Instituto Nacional Indigenista," in *Caras y Máscaras del México étnico: La participación indígena en las formaciones del Estado mexicano*, ed. Andrew Roth Seneff (vol. 2) (Zamora: El Colegio de Michoacán, 2011).

65. Darcy Ribeiro, *Fronteras indígenas de la civilización* (Mexico City: Siglo Veintiuno Editores, 1971).

66. Guillermo Bonfil Batalla, ed., *Utopía y revolución: El pensamiento político de los indios latinoamericanos* (Mexico City: Siglo Veintiuno Editores, 1981).

67. Ralph Beals, "Anthropology in Contemporary Mexico," in *Contemporary Mexico: Papers of IV International Congress of Mexican History*, ed. James W. Wilkie, Michael C. Meyer, and Edna Monzón de Wilkie (Berkeley: University of California Press for the UCLA Latin American Center/El Colegio de México, 1976).

CHAPTER 13 | *Andrew Paxman*

COOLING TO CINEMA AND WARMING TO TELEVISION
State Mass Media Policy, 1940–1964

Convention holds that the media policy of the postrevolutionary Mexican state prioritized the spreading of a particular social glue: nationalism. Federal authorities sought to inculcate fealty to the nation, at the expense of loyalties toward local, municipal, and state-level powers. They sought to unite the people around a mythologized history, which borrowed from regional stereotypes but possessed a common sense of the "authentic" and "traditional." In implementing this policy, the state advanced twin aims: to suppress the country's regional *caudillo* culture and to substitute affection for one's visible community with appreciation for something more abstract: *mexicanidad*. Most scholars have tended to argue (or assume) that this hegemonic cultivation of nationalism was largely successful.[1]

This chapter, however, is less interested in the persuasiveness of media than in the design and impact of media policy. While recognizing the important role of state-backed nationalism, I argue that policy from 1940 to 1964 was driven as much if not more by two other goals: the political and social containment of the urban "masses" and the uniting of the populace in support of the PRI. We can see that this trio of aims was not always one and the same when we consider that the majority of films exhibited during the so-called golden age of Mexican cinema were foreign, a trend facilitated by the state's refusal to enact screen quotas for native product.[2] While these decisions in favor of the free market did not serve nationalism, they did serve the continued expansion of mass entertainment, which was deemed effective in containing the proletariat. Furthermore, whether an evening's feature hailed from Mexico or elsewhere, it always followed a newsreel that extolled the president and his ministers, so the free market also served the propaganda aims of the PRI.

Two further factors influenced mass media policy, both of them financial. One was industry economics. Film production was always an expensive business, with high operating costs; these were both visible (from film stock to actors' fees) and hidden (from the rake-off that producers made from inflated budgets to bribes paid to union chiefs). Producers also had to compete with the Hollywood machine and Europe's revived industries. The available evidence strongly suggests that most Mexican features of the 1940s and 1950s lost money, so state and private banks probably recouped only a fraction of their loans. Television, in contrast, required high fixed costs (broadcast facilities, repeater stations, actor contracts) but low operating costs, not least because many shows in the early years were produced by advertisers and broadcast live. Overseas production was not a threat but an ally; with foreigners prohibited from owning Mexican stations, local channels could cherry-pick the best shows from the U.S. and Europe. Once the state had helped television expand its reach nationwide by letting its chief broadcasters unite as a monopoly and building a microwave network for signal relay, there was little need to further subsidize the industry. Television's greater economic efficiency contributed to the state's gradual neglect of the film industry.

The other financial factor shaping media policy was, for lack of a better term, "crony capitalism." The bullion produced during cinema's golden age largely ended up in the hands of exhibitors, and here the main players were well connected and protected. In addition, politicians also probably held covert stakes in premier theaters. Hence the state's refusal to implement screen quotas served exhibitors (and their pals) at the expense of producers. Later, the favoritism afforded television was in part due to the fact that President Alemán held a sizeable covert stake in one of Mexico's three foundational networks.

This study has several broader purposes. First, it relates the decline of golden age cinema and the ascent of television as Mexico's dominant mass medium. It offers an analytical narrative that—in contrast to most existing scholarship—examines media policy in holistic fashion: film, radio, and television.[3] Recasting nationalism as just one of several policy aims helps explain cinema's qualitative demise during the late 1940s and 1950s. Bringing economics into the equation—a factor underemphasized in most media histories—helps explain why television enjoyed more lasting state favor than did film.

Discussion of economics requires attention to economic actors, a second broad purpose here. Paul Gillingham's preface to this text mentions "additional phenomena . . . previously hidden" that expand our understanding of power within Mexico's *dictablanda*, and these should include the influence of the business elite; this sector, I argue elsewhere, constituted the forgotten pillar of the modern Mexican state.[4] Unlike labor, *campesinos*, and the middle sectors, big business went unincorporated as an official arm of the PRI, yet its influence was arguably greater. As evidence from the mass media shows, industrialists and the state operated in symbiosis, a relationship characterized by mutual reinforcement of monopoly power yet sometimes marked by disagreement, divergent priorities, and subterfuge. The state did not always have its way.

Finally, this chapter's long-term approach inevitably raises the question of a causal link between Mexico's high usage of mass media and the durability of the *pax* PRIísta. The existence of such a link, long an article of faith of both the Mexican state and its leftist critics, remains open to debate.[5] But this survey may at least help future researchers explore the link in a manner based less on ideological conviction and more on evidence.

The Avila Camacho Years: Rapid Expansion, Laissez-Faire Nationalism

The administration of Manuel Avila Camacho (1940–46) is typically described as an era of high nationalism. Some of the most enduring emblems of *mexicanidad* date from it: María Félix as *Doña Bárbara*, launching herself as "La Doña," an icon of indomitable beauty; Jorge Negrete as the singing *charro* in *¡Ay Jalisco, no te rajes!*; *María Candelaria*, a prizewinner at Cannes that starred Dolores del Río as a Xochimilco maiden; *¡Mexicanos al grito de guerra!*, a flag-waving period piece with Pedro Infante; and a series of nine hit comedies from Cantinflas, cementing his image as the epitome of working-class irrepressibility. There is some consensus that these six years witnessed the qualitative zenith of film's golden age.[6] Meanwhile, a rapid expansion in radio coverage—sets in use more than doubled from 450,000 to over a million—brought to a growing public the culturally resonant boleros of Agustín Lara and Pedro Vargas.[7]

Michael Nelson Miller writes: "*Avilacamachismo* was an attempt on the part of the state to create a mass media-based cultural nationalism. . . . [It] was constructed at popular and high cultural levels, ranging from radio, popular music, dance, musical theater, posters, film, and cartoon magazines to art, architecture, ballet, and classical music."[8] While there was more to Avila Camacho's political philosophy than a cultural program, this summary encapsulates usual perceptions of the era. But how much did such manifestations of nationalism owe to the regime itself, and to what extent were they its overarching mission? The fundamental flaw in Miller's analysis (and he is not alone in this) lies in an assumption of a "juggernaut" state and a relegation of the private sector to the status of a bit player.[9] Holistic examination of the

Avila Camacho years reveals a cultural policy inherited from the 1930s, shaped by negotiation with Mexican and U.S. business elites, and somewhat constrained in its nationalistic goals by a laissez-faire decision making that favored those elites.

The era of Lázaro Cárdenas (1934–40) set the tone for media policy under Avila Camacho, but less in its general commitment to nation building than in the pragmatic willingness to compromise seen in its last two years. Initially, Cardenismo promised concerted intervention. In 1935 the state subsidized the building of the CLASA film studio and lent logistical support to its first feature, the stirring but nuanced *Vámonos con Pancho Villa*. It created an Autonomous Department of Press and Publicity (DAPP) to generate content for radio and newspapers and regulate all media. It bankrolled propagandistic newsreels for movie theaters, first via subsidies for CLASA's fortnightly *Noticiario* then directly via the DAPP. It revised laws to increase state access to commercial stations from 10 to 30 minutes per day and demand that "typical Mexican music" constitute a minimum 25 percent of each radio show. The Cárdenas regime also encouraged the unionization of the film industry, and in 1937 it introduced a minimum screen quota for Mexican films at theaters.[10]

Yet, as Alan Knight argues, the high nationalism of the middle Cárdenas years petered out from mid-1938. Massive capital flight forced a more accommodating stance toward national and foreign investors. The media landscape underwent a parallel change: radical measures that sought to subordinate mass media to the will of the state were shelved or reversed. Plans by the left-wing Communications Minister Francisco Múgica to create a radio network funded by BBC-style license fees, or even to nationalize the industry, were scrapped. In 1939 ruling party radio station XEFO (formerly XE-PNR) switched to a commercial format, and six of the fourteen state-owned stations ceased operations. Two months before Cárdenas left office, the screen quota was dropped because local output was still unfeasibly small. In both cases, radio and film, the reversals owed in part to concerted lobbying by the private sector.[11]

Like policy, media content of the 1940s would echo that of the 1930s. Under Cárdenas, radio stations, most of them privately owned, pioneered a diet of popular (chiefly Mexican) music. They promoted artists (e.g., Lara, Vargas, and Toña la Negra) whose popularity would later translate to film and television. Much of the music was regionally distinctive—mariachi from Jalisco, huapango from Veracruz—but via radio it came to be "urbanized" for mass consumption and beamed nationwide, thus serving state goals of national unification.[12] In film, a flirtation with social realism gave way to a preponderance of rural musical comedies, following the huge success at home and abroad of *Allá en el Rancho Grande* (1936). So great was the rush to cash in on this *comedia ranchera* that producers churned out twenty more in 1937 alone.[13] Anticipating the conservative, paternalistic, and nostalgic strain of nationalism that became a mass media staple from the 1940s, *Rancho Grande* celebrates a mythical, neo-Porfirian era in which landowners ruled as benign patriarchs and peasants knew their place. In a dig against Cardenista radicals, the hero's stepfather is a self-declared communist and a buffoonish drunk.

Avila Camacho trod the same moderate path as the latter-day Cárdenas. He limited state intervention, doing less to protect and subsidize national media than is often assumed. With regard to radio, his government liberalized rules about foreign content.[14] With regard to film, while it formalized the system of censorship,[15] it resisted recurrent calls for screen quotas in 1943 and 1946, despite the fact that a now-healthy rate of production (an annual average of sixty-four films) improved the case for them. Avila Camacho fulfilled the promise of a Film Bank. But whereas Cárdenas had mooted an institution capitalized at 2.8 million pesos, with the state contributing half, what emerged in 1942 was a largely private-sector bank, capitalized at 2.5 million pesos, the state committing a mere 10 percent.[16] Even the films themselves were arguably less nationalistic than often thought. An internationalist or pro-U.S. agenda pervaded some. According to Seth Fein, "ideologically, Mexican cinema of the 1940s produced a national, but not nationalistic, discourse that supported the regime's main domestic projects: political incorporation and capitalist accumulation."[17]

The rather laissez-faire policies were in part due to wartime priorities. Mexico's May 1942 alliance with the United States, its reliance on U.S. suppliers for film stock, and its desire to reciprocate Rooseveltian good neighborliness, which included technological assistance to the film and radio industries, all militated against protectionism.[18] The state's minimal support for the Film Bank also reflected the wealth of Mexico's captains of industry. Those disposed to dabble in film—such as Luis Legorreta, president of the Banco Nacional de México; politician-turned-industrialist Alberto J. Pani; Auto-Mex/Chrysler founder Gastón Azcárraga; and the ubiquitous sugar planter-turned-venture capitalist William O. Jenkins—were wealthy conservatives who had little need for either subsidies or ideological supervision.[19] Following the logic of post-1938 pragmatism and Avila Camacho's pro-business leanings, the state continued to surrender cultural production to the private sector.

In addition, Avila Camacho permitted the cultivation of what were clearly monopolies in the making: the movie-theater empire of William Jenkins and the radio kingdom of Emilio Azcárraga Vidaurreta. The president's hands-off treatment of Jenkins was especially egregious. It ignored the 1934 Monopolies Law inasmuch as by 1946 Jenkins and his partners owned twenty-five of the roughly seventy-five venues operating in Mexico City.[20] What made their clout monopolistic was the fact that rival chains were all much smaller. This disparity enabled the Jenkins group to secure superior rental terms with film distributors. It also gave them the muscle to bully those distributors into withholding their best product from competitors, most of whom would sell out to Jenkins in the 1950s.[21] Furthermore, the government refrained from forcing Jenkins to comply with the "51 percent law" of June 1944, a decree restricting foreigners to a minority stake in any business; while regulations allowed the Department of Foreign Affairs to issue waivers, several sectors, including film, were declared inadmissible.[22]

Avila Camacho's generosity to the Jenkins group owed to a multilevel symbiotic relationship.[23] Jenkins prepared the ground for interdependence by contributing more than anyone to the Puebla gubernatorial war chest of the president's brother Maximino in 1936, following up with a four hundred thousand-dollar loan to Manuel's campaign in 1940.[24] The president repaid the favor by turning a blind eye to Jenkins's illicit investments and business practices (chiefly in film, but also in land purchases, newspaper ownership, and tax evasion). His rejection of screen quotas, if chiefly the result of U.S. pressure, benefited Jenkins by allowing him to program his venues entirely according to public demand, which in Mexico City still preferred foreign fare. At the same time, the president responded to pressure from the unions, which were railing against wartime inflation, by favoring labor in disputes at two of Jenkins's other businesses: a textile mill and a sugar plantation. Such high-profile acts afforded Avila Camacho a semblance of revolutionary good standing and signaled to cabinet leftists that he was not entirely in thrall to Jenkins.

The exchange of favors in the film industry, which was fast becoming Jenkins's principal profit center, served not only the president but also the wider purposes of the state, which under both Avila Camacho and Alemán faced the dual challenge of rapid urbanization and a drastic decline in the purchasing power of the poor.[25] Jenkins's freedom to profiteer in film exhibition encouraged him to build more theaters, each offering a wide range of ticket prices, which facilitated—in the view of the state—the containment and patriotic consolidation of the urban millions. The expansion also brought greater numbers within the reach of the state-subsidized newsreels that accompanied every feature.[26]

A similarly reciprocal arrangement underpinned Azcárraga's dominance in radio. Due in great part to his programming savvy, along with his technology links to NBC and CBS, Azcárraga's flagship stations, XEW and XEQ, rapidly developed networks of affiliates. His umbrella conglomerate, Radio Programas de México, grew from 6 stations to 60 (nearly half the national total of 132) within a year of its founding in 1941. As commercial operations, these outlets gave the people what they wanted: Mexican music suffused with nationalism, machismo, the nobility of poverty, and other strains of social conservatism. Such content chimed happily with state goals of unification and pacification. The networks' great popularity ensured that millions of Mexicans heard the party-line newscasts and bulletins that punctuated their daily schedules, along with the weekly state-sponsored cultural magazine, *La hora nacional*, begun in the Cárdenas years.[27]

The Azcárraga operation was a highly effective conduit for propaganda and it cost the government little; allowing it to develop a near monopoly satisfied both parties. This is not to say that Azcárraga and the state acted in lockstep. Disdainful of Cardenista radicalism, the mogul had bet on the wrong horse in the 1940 election, backing Juan Andreu Almazán, and there were signs that the Avila Camacho brothers harbored resentment. In 1943 Maximino (as Communications Minister) moved XEQ's transmission frequency up the dial, giving its preferred location to a station owned by a political ally; this station, XEX, was partly backed by the state and possibly co-owned by the Avila Camachos themselves. In 1946 Manuel refused Azcárraga's entreaties for a television concession.[28] Overall, however, political pragmatism carried the day.

The Alemán Years: Nationalism Compromised

The Alemán years (1946–52) were as much a high point of cultural nationalism as the Avila Camacho era. This was the period that saw film output climb above one hundred features per year. Highlights included *Río Escondido*, a maudlin hymn to education and selfless patriotism, and Pedro Infante's "Pepe el Toro" trilogy, which mixed melodrama with hummable tunes and a soothing subtext about the nobility inherent in being Mexican and poor. The era saw radio set ownership double again to more than two million and yielded the stardom of José Alfredo Jiménez, whose songs—a staple on Azcárraga's XEW—conveyed a confessional style of amorous, alcohol-fuelled lament, coming to typify a characteristic of Mexican machismo. It was on Alemán's watch that television was born, Mexico pipping Brazil and Cuba to become the first Latin American nation with a daily TV service. The musical artists of radio and the melodramatic style of film translated easily to small-screen genres; bullfighting and wrestling joined the mix. In a foreshadowing of television's future role as propaganda ministry for the PRI, no sooner had Channel 4 debuted as Mexico's first station than it trained its cameras on Alemán, airing his 1950 *informe*.[29]

These cultural achievements, however, tended to mask the true nature of Alemanismo. In practice, media policy during these years was unprecedentedly laissez-faire. The goal of cultural nationalism—in terms of healthy local output and protection from foreign product—was partly compromised in favor of free-market forces, from which Hollywood, the president, and his cronies stood to benefit. As was the case under Avila Camacho, the content of film and TV programming (newsreels and newscasts aside) was less important to the state than the proliferation of movie theaters and radios or TV sets. Both film and television presented test cases of state commitment to cultural nationalism, and in both cases the state backed down.

Trouble was brewing for Mexican cinema as early as 1946. After World War II, Hollywood ramped up production and the British, French, and Italians revived their war-damaged industries, all of which intensified competition for screens. The growing muscle of the Jenkins group allowed it to dictate terms. As exhibitors, they could offer to distributors a lower percentage of the box office pesos. As financiers they could force leaner budgets on producers. These producers and distributors were often the same people, and as they found themselves squeezed at both ends of their business, they clamored for protection. They wanted greater subsidy support and guaranteed screen time. They demanded the state get serious about what they deemed an anticonstitutional monopoly.[30]

In 1947 Alemán threw the producers a bone by nationalizing the Film Bank—renamed the Banco Nacional Cinematográfico (BNC)—and upping its capitalization to ten million pesos. This failed to alter the fundamentals of the industry; Jenkins's theater chains remained dominant, both as exhibitors and the funders of producers.[31] Then the National Association of Cinema Impresarios (ANEC), once formed as a buffer to Jenkins's expansion, succumbed to his control.[32] ANEC illustrated its muscle when it protested a 10 percent tax on box office receipts in Torreón by shuttering the city's five theaters. Within two weeks the Torreón city hall backed down. Next Jenkins captured the Rodríguez Brothers Circuit, the largest exhibitor in Monterrey. Northern theater owners lobbied Alemán, claiming that Jenkins was hurting them through monopolistic practices, such as pressing BNC-backed Películas Nacionales, the main distributor of local pictures, to withhold product. Lack of access to Mexican films, which were very popular in the provinces, threatened to bankrupt their theaters. The capital's exhibitors made similar protests.[33]

Alemán had little choice but to act. After all, there was his own image to protect. The president had projected himself as a patron of the nation's arts: he liked to be seen with movie stars and to trot them out for public relations purposes; he had even appeared in *Río Escondido*, playing himself.[34] That autumn, Congress wrote Mexico's first cinema legislation, which promised a variety of boosts and protections, including the long-sought screen quotas.[35] But the Film Industry Law of December 1949 was less than half the battle; it needed to be complemented by regulating legislation and then by enforcement. In August 1951 the state finally issued the regulations: a 50 percent screen quota would apply across the nation; one clause threatened noncompliant exhibitors with nationalization.[36]

Hollywood was prepared for such a battle. Its studios had experienced resisting quotas elsewhere. Allied with the Jenkins group, they adopted a twin strategy. Having consulted with the U.S. State Department, the studios let it be known that protectionist limits would be met with restrictions on Mexican films in the United States; this was a tough counterpunch, for Mexico's producers reaped a far higher fraction of their revenues north of the Rio Grande than did Hollywood south of it.[37] At the same time, fifty theater owners requested an injunction against the quota on grounds that it was unconstitutional. The injunction was granted. Alemán knew Hollywood well enough to have predicted this outcome all along. He had made his nationalistic stand. Now, for appearance's sake, he let the quota remain on the books without attempting to enforce it. In late 1952 Congress approved a revised version of the 1949 law with the quota incorporated; after all, the supreme court had yet to rule on the matter. It would be up to Alemán's successor to decide whether he wanted to enforce it.[38]

As for television, Alemán made the most important decision ever to shape Mexican broadcasting: that it should be run privately, not by the government.[39] A state-run, license-supported industry had begun in the United Kingdom in 1936; the United States had followed in 1939 with a private, commercially supported model. Both the British and U.S. structures followed local precedent in radio, and since Mexican radio was a mostly private industry, television could have been expected to follow suit. But a group of intellectuals headed by the composer Carlos Chávez demanded that television be a public medium. They faced intense opposition from the private sector, especially Azcárraga. Looking to resolve the debate with the pretense of impartiality, Alemán asked Chávez to form a commission to evaluate private versus public television. Chávez appointed the writer Salvador Novo and Mexico's top TV expert, inventor Guillermo González Camarena, to head the investigation. A year later, in 1948, the so-called Novo Report emerged. Not surprisingly, it conveyed a split decision: Novo favored a public TV format akin to the BBC, whereas González Camarena, a friend of Azcárraga, proposed a U.S.-style industry of private networks. Alemán opted to back the latter.

Alemán's decision reflected both his capitalist convictions and personal motives. Azcárraga had to wait four years to gain a concession, while Puebla auto-dealer Rómulo O'Farrill, a friend of Alemán, was awarded a concession within a year of applying. Stalling Azcárraga and favoring O'Farrill was retribution for Azcárraga's support of Almazán in 1940.[40] When in 1947 Alemán commissioned the Novo Report, he also awarded O'Farrill the concession for radio station XEX. The license gave O'Farrill the chance to learn about broadcast operations, while Novo's research project bought him time to plan his entry into television. Ignoring Azcárraga's renewed pleas for a TV concession, the president waited another year after the Novo Report before setting up a commission that would define the regulations for television, affording O'Farrill yet more time. Azcárraga's expertise and the support for his project from other industrialists meant Alemán could not ignore him altogether, but he waited until July 1950—when O'Farrill's Channel 4 was in test transmissions—to hand the radio magnate a license. It would take Azcárraga until spring 1951 to launch Channel 2.

Alex Saragoza argues that Alemán was betting O'Farrill's head start and state support would soon prompt Azcárraga to beg for a merger. Such a deal would give O'Farrill access to Azcárraga's technical and programming resources and allow Azcárraga access to the political protection of Alemán; it would put O'Farrill in majority control, but it would allow Azcárraga to remain dominant in radio.[41] The sum of Alemán's machinations strongly suggest that the president held a covert stake in Channel 4.[42] Five years before he died, O'Farrill's son and deputy in the TV business, Rómulo Jr., would confirm that Alemán and O'Farrill had been partners in television from the start.[43]

By approving a commercial model for television, Alemán compromised the state's commitment to cultural nationalism in two ways. First, a private industry would rely on sponsors, which in turn would mean that Mexico's TV screens promoted all kinds of foreign products, as was already the case with radio. Since major advertisers bought blocks of airtime for which they produced their own shows, the broadcast slate was soon packed with titles like *Revista Musical Nescafé* (1952–73) and dramas produced by Proctor & Gamble and Colgate-Palmolive, often using radio scripts from Cuba. Second, this commercially driven industry would later seek to save costs and increase viewership by screening truckloads of Hollywood films and imported series. As Carlos Monsiváis once wrote of the Alemán years: "Nationalism becomes a noble sentiment, supported every so often, while the country's economy is denationalized, gradually and systematically."[44]

The Ruiz Cortines Years: Cooling to Cinema

That the regime of Adolfo Ruiz Cortines (1952–58) cooled toward cinema may seem odd. It was, after all, in 1958 that the industry achieved its highest ever output: a spectacular 135 films.[45] But there is critical consensus that, continuing a trend of the Alemán years, quantitative increase paralleled qualitative decline. As Eduardo de la Vega has argued, the high yield of the 1950s gave an impression of a continued golden age that was quite deceptive. He cites the example of "El Indio" Fernández, the most acclaimed director of the 1940s. Fernández followed four lyrical classics, from La perla (1945) to Maclovia (1948), with a string of low-budget features that caused his reputation to wane, "and it was not long before this process of decadence brought down with it the prestige of . . . Mexican cinema." Under Alemán and Ruiz Cortines, the industry tended to assemble formulaic B-pictures—churros—for mass consumption: family melodramas, urban comedies, tearjerkers about fallen women in cabarets. Innovative work by two superior talents, Roberto Gavaldón and Luis Buñuel, only partially disguised the rot.[46]

Ruiz Cortines's term began with a barrage of criticism against the Jenkins group. A wave of front-page articles focused on its monopolistic practices in exhibition, its intimidation of distributors, and its growing control of film finance, which allegedly forced producers to deliver cheap genre pictures.[47] The state responded with a seemingly bold initiative to revive industry fortunes and curtail Jenkins. Conceived by BNC chief Eduardo Garduño, the plan raised the credit ceiling, allowed producers control of distributor Películas Nacionales, mooted an annual import quota of 150 films, and loosened the rules on what a local film could depict.[48] In some respects, Mexico began to close the "gloss gap" with Hollywood, shooting in color and even widescreen formats. But the "Plan Garduño" failed on two fronts. Most producers persisted in making the cheap flicks that appealed to lower-income audiences and failed to interest the more lucrative theaters, and they continued to receive state support for doing so. The favored genres multiplied to include horror, Westerns, and melodramas featuring masked wrestlers, but these films were just as shoddy as the formulaic pictures of before, a deficit of creativity exacerbated by the reluctance of the directors' union to admit new talent.[49] Second, to bolster Películas Nacionales, Garduño issued new shares in the distributor, but most of these were snapped up by Jenkins's allies. By the end of 1953, producers affiliated with Jenkins were again enjoying BNC credit and it was clear that Garduño's strategy to bolster production quality was compromised. A cartoon in El Universal captured the paradox: identifying Jenkins as the "film monopoly," it showed him as the recipient of both stern rebuke and a bagful of cash from Garduño.[50]

The Plan Garduño proved to be little more than symbolic. Through lack of political will it achieved the reverse of some objectives and otherwise had no effect. Imports averaged 340 films per year for the sexenio.[51] One of the major structural blocks to the plan was the four-peso cap on ticket prices in the capital. The cap upheld the high frequency of moviegoing but deepened the inclination of producers to shoot on a shoestring. Once again, cultural policy privileged containing the masses over support for native artistry and desire for international acclaim.[52] The decision by the supreme court that year not to enforce the screen quota—the 50 percent guarantee signed into law by Alemán—tended to confirm this set of priorities.[53]

In 1957 former president Abelardo Rodríguez, who had built a theater circuit stronghold in the northwest and then tried to combat the Jenkins group on its home turf (Mexico City, Puebla, Veracruz), threw in the towel and sold out to the American.[54] There were no longer grounds for pretense that the Jenkins group was anything other than an exhibition monopoly, and still Ruiz Cortines did nothing. After Rodríguez surrendered, other independents were evidently inspired to give up, too, because a *Variety* profile of the Jenkins group in December 1958 elucidated just how large their empire had grown: between venues owned and affiliated, they controlled sixteen hundred or so theaters, nearly 80 percent of the national total.[55]

Ruiz Cortines's reluctance to move against the film monopoly presumably followed the reasoning of his predecessors. Jenkins was providing a public service and doing so efficiently. His hundreds of theaters entertained the urban millions, and thanks to price caps they did so cheaply. Overall, Jenkins and his partners were aiding a huge boom in moviegoing. In Mexico City the number of venues doubled from 67 in 1938 to 133 in 1958; nationwide, those years saw the total grow from 863 (with less than half in regular operation) to 2,100.[56] Furthermore, restriction of such a high-profile U.S. businessman would have sent the wrong message at a time when the state, with its program of Import Substitution Industrialization, was urging foreign manufacturers to set up plants. Besides these factors, and the possibility that senior politicians held covert stakes in Jenkins's holdings, the American's controversial profile made for a useful lightning rod for leftist and nationalist discontent.[57]

In his tolerance of monopoly, the president proved consistent. In 1955 he gave Mexico's three infant TV networks permission to merge, giving rise to TeleSistema Mexicano (TSM), the forerunner of today's Televisa.[58] Competition had taken a high financial toll on both Azcárraga and the O'Farrill-Alemán partnership. Programming initially proved expensive; it was said that even sports broadcasts were unprofitable. Yet more costly was the expansion of television's reach through repeater stations. Another problem was the modest size of the middle class, which meant that sales of TV sets proceeded slowly. Because of low penetration, in 1955 fewer than 5 percent of homes had a TV.[59]

Still, Azcárraga had much the stronger hand: the larger stable of talent, drawn from his radio networks; a better assembly of technicians; longer-standing relationships with advertisers; and lengthier experience in broadcasting. His hand only grew stronger. In 1953 O'Farrill lost a key advantage when Ruiz Cortines initiated an anticorruption drive, targeting much of the cronyism initiated by Alemán; Channel 4 began to lose its favored status. In 1954 Azcárraga convinced González Camarena to transfer to him his poorly performing Channel 5. Finally, in January 1955, in a reversal of the result on which Alemán had betted, it was O'Farrill who turned to Azcárraga seeking a merger. Ruiz Cortines approved the union. Costly competition was delaying the geographical roll out of the medium, and the government wanted another nationwide means of drawing Mexicans into the revolutionary family. Some months earlier, under pressure to raise workers' salaries, the president had begun a custom of delivering messages to the nation via radio and television, and he had capped his initial address with a prototype TV sound bite: "¡México al trabajo fecundo y creador!"[60]

The foundation of TSM was finalized in March, with Azcárraga in charge. It was clearly anti-constitutional. In a circumvention of the 1934 Monopolies Law, the concessions for Channels 2, 4, and 5 continued to be held by three distinct companies, not by TSM. Yet these three companies no longer existed as separate entities. Administration, sales, and technical operations became centralized. As a monopoly, TSM posed legal and ethical problems. Competition among broadcasters can spur programming creativity, raise salaries for employees, foster fairer prices for advertisers, and discourage newscasts from pro-government rigidity. Even Azcárraga admitted there was an issue. In a 1961 press conference he declared that, once Mexican television had taken another year or two to mature: "we ought to divide the O'Farrill interests and ours so as to discontinue the appearance [sic] of a monopoly."[61]

Yet the merger served the state's larger purposes. Costs would shrink and expansion plans consolidate. The deal also facilitated an overall symbiosis, similar to precedents in radio and cinema. This involved a commitment to socially conservative entertainment and pro-government news programming in exchange for a de facto license to build a monopolistic empire. Even better, Azcárraga was an entrepreneur with a proven record for producing mass entertainment without need for long-term subsidy. The U.S. precedent, where by 1956 more than 70 percent of households owned a TV, showed that television was the industry of the future.[62] It also was evincing superior potential as a showcase for politics: TV news had already supplanted theater newsreels, and, in the Democratic primary contest that year, the telegenic Estes Kefauver nearly defeated the early front-runner, Adlai Stevenson, because of his savvy TV appearances; these included the first televised debate between presidential contenders.[63] As for the viability of film, the jury (on both sides of the border) was out.

The López Mateos Years: Warming to Television

After his suppression of the dissident railworkers in 1959, the left-ward, statist swing of Adolfo López Mateos (1958–64) found echo in the media landscape. In 1960 the president made two apparently bold moves, introducing the first-ever comprehensive law to address the medium of television and nationalizing the theater circuits at the heart of the Jenkins group's operations, COTSA and Cadena de Oro. Despite the headlines generated by these acts, neither proved to be of paradigm-shifting importance.

The move against Jenkins occurred at year's end, after another barrage of bad press directed against the American.[64] How much this slew of criticism motivated the president is hard to say; certainly it gave López Mateos a sense of how popular the move would be, which in turn raises the possibility that he actively encouraged the flak to build public expectation, so to reap greater political capital. In all, 365 theaters were taken over at a cost of twenty-six million dollars. Those cinemas were only a quarter of what Jenkins controlled, but they were the wholly owned theaters, the cream of the crop. Even before closing the deal, López Mateos garnered plaudits. The governor of Campeche said the move would prevent unjust delays in the release of Mexican films and so it demonstrated the president's "pure patriotism."[65]

Yet the expropriation was an anticlimax. State control of the best theaters—as well as the famous Churubusco film studio, bought two years before—did little to alter the trajectory of Mexican cinema. It failed to improve its market position at home and suffered a near-collapse in Central and South America.[66] Talk of an industry in crisis continued. The same creatively atrophied corps of directors whose union had admitted few new members since 1944 dominated output, producers continued to inflate their budgets and take few risks, and the contrast between Mexican and foreign cinema was never so great. Formulaic melodramas, cheap farces, and masked-wrestler flicks (most in black and white) vied with literate epics, Hitchcock thrillers, and big-budget musicals (most of which were in color).[67] Nationalizing the film industry was ultimately a symbolic act, putting it in a category similar to the other major seizure of 1960: that of the electricity sector.[68] Still, the cinema move was the more purely symbolic because it was the less economically rational: unlike the foreign power companies, Jenkins had not been repatriating profits.[69] And while those firms belonged to faceless investors, this American was infamous.

The 1960 Federal Radio and TV Law proved similarly symbolic. Chiefly conceived as a nationalistic effort to preserve the Mexican-ness of content, its formulation fell subject to the lobbying of broadcasters. Attempts by left-wing lawmakers to limit per-hour advertising minutes and include an overall public service definition proved in vain; daily educational and cultural programming was mandated, but only "up to 30 minutes." The law generously defined broadcast licenses as lasting up to thirty years. As for ideology, while encouraging the promotion of family ties, national traditions, "Mexican values," and "democratic convictions" and forbidding content contrary to "*bue-*

nas costumbres," the law left censorship to the broadcasters. Later it emerged that TV industry lawyers had helped to write the legislation; Fátima Fernández Christlieb calls this fact "unsurprising, if we bear in mind that there have been federal deputies who are also commercial-station concession holders or executives."[70]

More influential was the state's commitment in 1959 to the expansion of its National Microwave Network (initially designed for telephony) for the relay of TV signals. This network would consist of transmitters across the vast tracts of often mountainous territory where TSM's stations could not reach. In the era before satellites, microwave retransmission was the most practical way of relaying a TV signal. Microwave constituted a massive subsidy to TSM, which had been spending large amounts of capital on provincial expansion. Indeed, in 1961 Azcárraga sold most of his stake in Radio Programas de México, funneling the proceeds into TSM. This was a bold move because radio was still king: sets totaled more than three million, four times the number of TV sets; radio scooped 36 percent of that year's $120 million in advertising spending, compared with just 6 percent for television. So it was a combination of Azcárraga's capital realignment and the indirect subsidy of microwave that ensured that by 1968, when the network was completed and the Olympics came to Mexico, television would overtake radio as the most lucrative medium.[71]

The consolidation of a monolithic TV broadcaster—renamed Televisa in 1973—would be cast by the Azcárraga family in proudly nationalistic terms and with some good reason. From the early 1960s, its telenovelas became popular exports. In 1969 it established a variety show, Siempre en domingo, as the country's premier forum for musical talent; an in-house prohibition against performing in English helped cement its image as a patriotic showcase. In the 1980s Azcárraga's son, Emilio Azcárraga Milmo, would launch the international news network ECO as a pan-Hispanic answer to CNN.[72]

At the same time, TSM/Televisa functioned as a Ministry of Information for the PRI. This had been evident in the 1952 election, when TSM kept opposition candidate Henríquez Guzmán out of its newscasts, a precedent followed for decades. The company's long-running chief news anchor, Jacobo Zabludovsky, doubled as a radio and TV consultant for both López Mateos and Gustavo Díaz Ordaz. TSM's coverage of the 1958 railworkers' action painted the strikers as extremists or criminals; its coverage of the 1968 protest movement ignored the students' demands, gave exclusive voice to officialdom, and downplayed the body count of the Tlatelolco massacre.[73] TSM/Televisa came to be perceived as having a dual function: a conduit of propaganda and an apparatus for containing the masses.[74] This was not just the view of the firm's many critics; it was also that of the family that ran it.

Azcárraga Milmo spoke frankly of his dedication to those twin missions: "This company sides with Mexico, with the President of the Republic, and with the PRI," and "Mexico is a country with a working class that's really screwed, and that's not going to stop being screwed. Television has the obligation to bring entertainment to those people, to free them from their sad reality and their difficult future."[75]

BY THE TIME López Mateos left office in 1964, cinema's golden age was long past. Pedro Infante and Jorge Negrete were dead, and the popularity of María Félix was waning. There were new stars, like Silvia Pinal, Ignacio López Tarso, and Mauricio Garcés, but few creative and committed directors to coax them beyond the banal. The origins of the malaise dated from the 1940s. The Mexican government could have forced the hands of the directors, producers, and the Jenkins group, obliging them to desist from monopolistic and profiteering practices, as the U.S. government often did with Hollywood.[76] The state could have shown greater creativity with its quotas and vigilance with its subsidies, policies successfully pursued by France and Italy.[77] By allowing the film industry to slide into mediocrity and cultivating an increasingly interdependent relationship with television, the state not only opted for what promised to be the more effective propaganda vehicle, it also seemed to apply a cost-benefit analysis. Few Mexican films, even during the "golden" 1940s, had made money; many if not most bank loans were never repaid.[78] Television, as the U.S. experience suggested, could generate handsome profits without a long-term need for handouts.[79]

As for policy rationale, the state always valued the media for their seductive possibilities. Inaugurating XE-PNR radio in 1931, PNR propaganda chief Manuel Jasso promised that the station would effect "the spiritual incorporation of the proletarian masses, by means of art, literature and music; understanding and solidarity between all the inhabitants of the country."[80] In 1943, when honoring Walt Disney and Louis B. Mayer for their services to bilateral relations, Foreign Minister Ezequiel Padilla declared that film was able to penetrate "directly into the heart of the masses."[81] In 1946 Avila Camacho submitted a bill proposing a commission to promote the film industry, and his preamble noted the ability of Mexico's cinema to promote "feelings of unity and cohesion."[82] Similarly, article 5 of 1960's broadcasting law stated that "radio and television have the social function of contributing to the strengthening of national integration and the bettering of human coexistence."[83]

Gauging the efficacy of such policies lies beyond the scope of this chapter. But whether Mexico's media functioned effectively as escape valves, cathartic salves, and drivers of national unity, their viewing involved great amounts of time, hours that might otherwise have been spent, for example, expressing discontent. In the 1960s, thanks in part to price controls, Mexico had the joint highest per-capita rate of film attendance in the world. A *Variety* correspondent noted: "cheap film entertainment for the masses is deemed a must to offset inequities of income. . . . The analogy to 'bread and circuses' has often been made."[84] In recent decades, thanks in great part to the *telenovela* factory of the Azcárragas, Mexico has exhibited one of the world's highest leisure-time quotients of TV watching.[85] The possibility of a causal link, however partial, between high mass media usage and the pax PRIísta—relative to the modern history of other developing nations—surely merits some probing.

Examination of media policy from 1940 to 1964 enhances our understanding of nation building as a negotiated process. At the level of reception, contestation and rejection of hegemonic messages certainly occurred, as scholarship has fragmentarily shown. At the level of policy, however, negotiation occurred chiefly between state actors and business elites and between the remarkably divergent goals of *nacionalismo*, PRIísmo, and profit. Media policy was shaped as much by William Jenkins and Emilio Azcárraga as by the federal government. At the meeting of private and public interests we find major compromises over the state's nation-building agenda. Diffusion of nationalism remained a key policy goal but not the transcendent one, for it often jostled with the federal aims of popular containment and PRI self-promotion and with the economic realities of production costs and elite profiteering. In the end, it mattered little to Los Pinos that Mexicans were abandoning Jorge Negrete for John Wayne or large screen for small, just as long as they had access to cheap entertainment and news from loyal sources.

Notes

1. See Carlos Monsiváis, "Vino todo el pueblo y no cupo en la pantalla," in *A través del espejo: El cine mexicano y su público*, ed. C. Monsiváis and C. Bonfil (Mexico City: El Milagro, 1994); Michael Nelson Miller, *Red, White, and Green: The Maturing of Mexicanidad, 1940–1946* (El Paso: Texas Western Press, 1998), chapters 4 and 5; Andrea Noble, *Mexican National Cinema* (London: Routledge, 2005), chapter 3; Fernando Mejía Barquera, *La industria de la radio y la televisión y la política del estado mexicano (1920–1960)* (Mexico City: Fundación Manuel Buendía, 1989), chapters 2–7; Joy Hayes, *Radio Nation: Communication, Popular Culture, and Nationalism in Mexico, 1920–1950* (Tucson: University of Arizona Press, 2000); Claudia Fernández and Andrew Paxman, *El Tigre: Emilio Azcárraga y su imperio Televisa*, rev. ed. (Mexico City: Grijalbo, 2013]), chapters 3 and 5; Celestine González de Bustamante, "*Tele-Visiones* (Tele-Visions): The Making of Mexican TV News, 1950–1970" (PhD dissertation, University of Arizona, 2006); Alex Saragoza, "Behind the Scenes: Media Ownership, Politics, and Popular Culture in Mexico (1930–1958)," in *Los intelectuales y el poder en México*, ed. Roderic Ai Camp (Mexico City: Colegio de México, 1991); Anne Rubenstein, "Mass Media and Popular Culture in the

Postrevolutionary Era," in *Oxford History of Mexico*, ed. Michael Meyer and William H. Beezley (New York: Oxford University Press, 2010).

2. During the 1940s, just 15 percent of films released were Mexican; during the 1950s, 20 percent. María Luisa Amador and Jorge Ayala Blanco, *Cartelera cinematográfica, 1940–1949* (Mexico City: UNAM, 1982), 378; María Luisa Amador and Jorge Ayala Blanco, *Cartelera cinematográfica, 1950–1959* (Mexico City: UNAM, 1985), 364.

3. I omit print media since (except for comic books) they had small circulations. Chappell Lawson, *Building the Fourth Estate: Democratization and the Rise of a Free Press in Mexico* (Berkeley: University of California Press, 2002), 61.

4. Andrew Paxman, "William Jenkins, Business Elites, and the Evolution of the Mexican State: 1910–1960" (PhD dissertation, University of Texas at Austin, 2008), 4–9.

5. On the belief of critics, see, for example, Raúl Trejo Delarbre, ed., *Televisa, el quinto poder* (Mexico City: Claves Latinoamericanas, 1985).

6. Emilio García Riera, *Breve historia del cine mexicano* (Zapopan, Jalisco: Mapa, 1998), 120; Eduardo de la Vega, "Origins, Development and Crisis of the Sound Cinema," in *Mexican Cinema*, ed. P. A. Paranaguá (London: British Film Institute, 1995), 79–93, 89; John King, *Magical Reels* (London: Verso, 2000), 47. Carl Mora differs, equating the golden age with the Alemán *sexenio*, his definition privileging quantity of output over quality (*Mexican Cinema: Reflections of a Society, 1896–1980* [Berkeley: University of California Press, 1982], 75).

7. Hayes, *Radio Nation*, 32f, 74f.

8. Miller, *Red, White, and Green*, 1.

9. Miller, *Red, White and Green*, chapters 4, 5; cf. Mora, *Mexican Cinema*, 52, 59.

10. Mora, *Mexican Cinema*, 43, 49; Seth Fein, "Hollywood and United States–Mexican Relations in the Golden Age of Mexican Cinema" (PhD dissertation, University of Texas, Austin, 1996), 152–58, 192–204; Hayes, *Radio Nation*, 66f.

11. Hayes, *Radio Nation*, 77f; *Variety* (New York), October 9, 1940, 13. For a study of Cardenista policy toward radio, see Mejía Barquera, *La industria*, chapter 3.

12. Hayes, *Radio Nation*, 32f, 73–75.

13. Mora, *Mexican Cinema*, 36–49.

14. Hayes, *Radio Nation*, 120.

15. From 1941, Gobernación reviewed all films and certified them for appropriate audiences; Emilio García Riera, *Historia documental del cine mexicano*, 2nd ed. (Guadalajara: University de Guadalajara, 1992), vol. 2, 182.

16. *Variety*, March 16, 1938, 12; October 20, 1943, 25; October 23, 1946, 18; and March 23, 1947, 19; *Anuario Financiero de México, 1942* (Mexico City: Associacíon de Banqueros de México, 1943), 381; García Riera, *Historia documental*, vol. 2, 236–38.

17. Fein, "Hollywood," 298f.

18. See Fein, "Hollywood," chapters 5, 6.

19. *Anuario Financiero 1942*, 381; *Variety*, January 6, 1943, 178; García Riera, *Historia documental*, vol. 2, 237f; interview with Salvador Elizondo, Instituto Mora, Mexico City, Archivo de la Palabra (hereafter Mora-Palabra), PH02/27, 6f, 14f.

20. *Variety*, December 18, 1946, 23; July 17, 1946, 12; Paxman, "William Jenkins," 298–300.

21. *El Universal*, September 13, 1944; *Hoy*, October 29, 1949.

22. Stephen Niblo, *War, Diplomacy, and Development: The United States and Mexico, 1938–1954* (Wilmington, DE: Scholarly Resources, 1995), 215. Jenkins protected himself against foreign ownership limitations through the use of *prestanombres*; Paxman, "William Jenkins," 281–83.

23. See Paxman, "William Jenkins," chapter 7.

24. Maximino is held to have partnered in some of Jenkins's businesses (Stephen Niblo, *Mexico in the 1940s: Modernity, Politics, and Corruption* [Wilmington, DE: Scholarly Resources, 2000], 283–87); email to author from Manuel Avila Camacho López (Maximino's youngest son), September 11, 2006.

25. Mexico City alone grew 74 percent, from 1.75 to 3.05 million, between 1940 and 1950, while the real (inflation-adjusted) minimum daily wage for the capital declined by 56 percent between 1939 and 1951; Niblo, *Mexico in the 1940s*, 1; Kevin Middlebrook, *The Paradox of Revolution: Labor, the State, and Authoritarianism in Mexico* (Baltimore: Johns Hopkins University Press, 1995), 214, table 6.1.

26. Ricardo Pérez Montfort, "El discurso moral en los noticieros fílmicos de 1940 a 1960," in *Los archivos de la memoria*, ed. Alicia Olivera de Bonfil (Mexico City: INAH, 1999), 147–63.

27. Mejía Barquera, *La industria*, 129–31; Hayes, *Radio Nation*, 67–79; Alex M. Saragoza, *The State and the Media in Mexico: The Origins of Televisa* (forthcoming), cf. Saragoza, "Behind the Scenes," 758–60.

28. Hayes, *Radio Nation*, 117f; Mejía Barquera, *La industria*, 140–42.

29. García Riera, *Breve historia*, 150, 185; Mora, *Mexican Cinema*, 75–80; Hayes, *Radio Nation*, 33, 74f; William Gradante, "'El Hijo del Pueblo': José Alfredo Jiménez and the Mexican Canción Ranchera," *Latin American Music Review* 3, no. 1 (1982): 36–59; Fernández and Paxman, *El Tigre*, 75.

30. José Revueltas in *Hoy*, October 29, 1949; assorted correspondence to Alemán, 1949, AGN/MAV-523.3/54. In fact, the group owned just 15 percent of the nation's theaters (*Variety*, October 4, 1950, 15; February 18, 1948, 54), not the 80 percent claimed by Revueltas; however, this 15 percent included most of the first-run screens in the big cities, and the group had leasing arrangements with others, so Jenkins indeed operated a monopoly in a de facto sense.

31. García Riera, *Historia documental*, vol. 4, 105–9; *Anuario Financiero de México, 1947* (Mexico City: Associación de Banqueros de México, 1948), 135; *Variety*, June 28, 1950, 13; December 20, 1950, 53; *Siempre!*, August 8, 1953, 14.

32. Assorted correspondence to Alemán, 1949, AGN/MAV-523.3/54; *Variety*, January 9, 1946, 240; Rafael Rojas Loa (ANEC) to Alemán, February 11, 1950, AGN/MAV-437.3/227; Fein, "Hollywood," 352f.

33. *Variety*, January 15, 1947, 19; January 29, 1947, 17; March 12, 1947, 25; assorted correspondence, February 17 to May 21, 1949, AGN/MAV-523.3/54.

34. Niblo, *Mexico in the 1940s*, 49f, 160; Mora, *Mexican Cinema*, 78.

35. Fein, "Hollywood," 600–604.

36. Fein, "Hollywood," 607f.

37. In 1944 Hollywood made only 2 percent of its revenues in Mexico, while Mexican producers relied on U.S. distribution for 15 to 25 percent of their budgets. Guy Ray, Mexico City, to State Department, October 6, 1944, records of the U.S. Department of State (NARG 59), 812.4061-MP/10-644, 4f.

38. Fein, "Hollywood," 608–15. On Hollywood quota battles with Europe, see Thomas Guback, *The International Film Industry: Western Europe and America since 1945* (Bloomington: Univeristy of Indiana Press, 1969), chapter 2.

39. Except where noted, my discussion of TV under Alemán draws from Fernández and Paxman, *El Tigre*, 72–78. See also Mejía Barquera, *La industria*, chapter 4; Alex Saragoza, "Television," in *Encyclopedia of Mexico: History, Society, and Culture*, ed. M. Werner (Chicago: Fitzroy Dearborn, 1997), 1397f.

40. Saragoza, *The State and the Media*.

41. Saragoza, *The State and the Media*.

42. For evidence the Alemán family held a stake in TV since around 1955, if not before, see the stock market prospectus *Grupo Televisa, S.A. de C.V.* (New York: Goldman Sachs International, December 9, 1991), 10, 60.

43. Interview with Rómulo O'Farrill Jr., June 29, 2001, Mexico City.

44. Fernández and Paxman, *El Tigre*, 99–102, 118f, 172f; *Variety*, November 29, 1961, 34; Monsiváis, "Alto Contraste," in *Amor perdido* (Mexico City: Era, 1977), 35.

45. García Riera, *Breve historia*, 211.

46. Eduardo de la Vega, "The Decline of the Golden Age," in *Mexico's Cinema: A Century of Film and Filmmakers*, ed. J. Hershfield and D. Maciel (Wilmington, DE: Scholarly Resources, 1999), 171–74, 186–89.

47. *El Universal*, February 2, 9, 15, 16, 1953; *Excélsior*, February 4–7, 1953. Criticisms were also leveled by the senator Gen. Jacinto B. Treviño, former president Abelardo Rodríguez, and BNC chief Garduño himself; *Excélsior*, February 8, 9, 14, 1953; *El Universal*, February 14, 1953; *Tiempo*, February 13, 1953, 45; February 27, 1953, 42.

48. *El Universal*, August 29, 1953; García Riera, *Historia documental*, vol. 7, 7–10; De la Vega, "Decline of the Golden Age," 177–79.

49. García Riera, *Historia documental*, vol. 3, 109f, 220; Charles Ramírez Berg, *Cinema of Solitude: A Critical Study of Mexican Film, 1967–1983* (Austin: University of Texas Press, 1992), 5f, 41.

50. *El Universal*, December 3, 1953.

51. Amador and Ayala Blanco, *Cartelera cinematográfica, 1950–1959*, 357–62.

52. García Riera, *Breve historia*, 255, 279; Fein, "From Collaboration to Containment," in *Mexico's Cinema* [NB: 2nd ref.; cf. fn46], 155. That the cap was chiefly a "mass containment" tactic rather than an anti-inflation initiative is affirmed by the fact that during the three *sexenios* in which it persisted (c. 1953–70), inflation remained generally low while real wages in Mexico City more than doubled; see Middlebrook, *The Paradox of Revolution*, 215, table 6.1.

53. Fein, "Hollywood," 617.

54. *Variety*, October 4, 1950, 15; Gabriel Ramírez, *Miguel Contreras Torres, 1899–1981* (Guadalajara: Universidad de Guadalajara, 1994), 106; Fideicomiso Calles Torreblanca, Archivo Abelardo L. Rodríguez, Empresas.

55. *Variety*, December 3, 1958, 11.

56. *Variety*, August 17, 1938, 25; November 13, 1938, 123; December 1958, 11.

57. For an allegation of Ruiz Cortines's interest in Jenkins's exhibition business, see AGN/ALM-136.3/831, Don Verdades, *Corrido del cine mexicano* (Mexico City: n.p., [1959]). For Jenkins as a whipping-boy of the nationalist Left, see Paxman, "William Jenkins," 376–81, 411–24.

58. The following section is based on Fernández and Paxman, El Tigre, 76–80. See also Francisco Hernández Lomelí, "Obstáculos para el establecimiento de la televisión comercial en México (1950–1955)," Comunicación y Sociedad 28 (September–December 1996): 147–71.

59. González de Bustamante, "Tele-Visiones," 41, 300.

60. José Agustín, Tragicomedia mexicana 1: La vida en México de 1940 a 1970 (Mexico City: Planeta, 1998), 128.

61. Variety, March 8, 1961, 38.

62. Tim Brooks, "A Short History of Network Television," in The Complete Dictionary to Prime Time Network and Cable TV Shows, 1946–Present, ed. T. Brooks and E. Marsh (New York: Ballantine, 1995 [6th ed.]), x–xxi.

63. Erik Barnouw, Tube of Plenty: The Evolution of American Television (New York: Oxford University Press, 1977), 168–71; Craig Allen, Eisenhower and the Mass Media (Chapel Hill: University of North Carolina Press, 1993), 105–7.

64. See for example Excélsior, June 8, 1960; Política, June 1, 1960, 27–29; Miguel Contreras Torres, El libro negro del cine mexicano (Mexico City: n.p., 1960).

65. Excélsior, November 21 and December 1, 1960; El Universal, November 30, 1960; Time, December 26, 1960, 25f; Trueba Urbina, Campeche, to López Mateos, November 18, 1960, AGN/ALM-705.1/26; Paxman, "William Jenkins," chapter 9.

66. In the capital, screen time for Mexican films failed to improve: 40 percent in 1960, 39 percent in 1970. Alejandro Flores García, Cinecompendio 1971–1972 (Mexico City: A Posta, 1972), 27; María Luisa Amador and Jorge Ayala Blanco, Cartelera cinematográfica, 1960–1969 (Mexico City: UNAM, 1986), 425–39. Central and South American revenue fell by 40 percent between 1955 and 1970, and the European market also waned; only U.S. revenues remained healthy, because of Latino immigration; Flores García, Cinecompendio, 38–43.

67. Salvador Elizondo, "El cine mexicano y la crisis," in Hojas de cine (Mexico City: SEP, 1988), II: 37–46; Mora, Mexican Cinema, 101–10; García Riera, Breve historia, 234f, 247f.

68. Enrique Krauze, Mexico: Biography of Power (New York: Harper Perennial, 1998), 657.

69. Manuel Gómez Morín, quoted in James Wilkie and Edna Monzón de Wilkie, México visto en el siglo XX: Entrevistas de historia oral (Mexico City: Instituto Mexicano de Investigaciones Económicas, 1969), 209.

70. El Universal, December 27, 1959; Diario Oficial, January 19, 1960, 1–8; Fatima Fernández Christlieb, Los medios de difusión masiva en México (Mexico City: Juan Pablo, 1996 [1982]), 156–61; Hayes, Radio Nation, 120f.

71. Fernández and Paxman, El Tigre, 116–18; Fernando Mejía Barquera, "50 años de televisión comercial en México," in Televisa, el quinto poder, 29.

72. Fernández and Paxman, El Tigre, 170–76, 192f, 397–99.

73. González de Bustamante, "Tele-Visiones," 70f, 74f, 101–11, 150, 237–55; Fernández and Paxman, El Tigre, 117f, 178–82.

74. Lawson, Building the Fourth Estate, 29; Florence Toussaint, "Televisa: una semana de programación," in Televisa, el quinto poder.

75. Proceso, March 20, 1990; El Nacional, February 11–12, 1993. See also Fernández and Paxman, El Tigre, 381–97, 465–68.

76. Most famously, in 1948 the Supreme Court forced the studios to sell their theater chains and desist from "block booking"; for this and other antitrust rulings, see

Harold Vogel, *Entertainment Industry Economics* (New York: Cambridge University Press, 2007), 67–69.

77. Guback, *The International Film Industry*, 21–27, 150–52, 156–59.

78. An economic history of the industry is lacking, but reports of box office travails surfaced often. See, e.g., *Variety*, June 19, 1940, 12; January 8, 1947, 179; and December 27, 1950, 12.

79. It has not yet come to light when TSM reached an operational break-even point. Production Chief Luis de Llano Palmer estimated that TSM broke even around 1965 (interview with author, 1998, Mexico City).

80. Quoted in Mejía Barquera, *La industria*, 55.

81. Quoted in Miller, *Red, White, and Green*, 97.

82. Avila Camacho to Congress, "Ley que crea la Comisión para el Fomento de la Cinematografía Nacional," January 17, 1946, AGN/MAC-201.1/5.

83. *Diario Oficial*, January 19, 1960.

84. *Variety*, June 1, 1966, 21.

85. In a 2006 survey of 18 members of the Organisation for Economic Co-operation and Development, Mexico ranked no. 1 in the percentage of leisure time spent watching TV, with 48 percent (*Pocket World in Figures* [London: The Economist, 2009], 95).

CHAPTER 14 | *Pablo Piccato*

PISTOLEROS, *LEY FUGA*, AND UNCERTAINTY IN PUBLIC DEBATES ABOUT MURDER IN TWENTIETH-CENTURY MEXICO

Murder is one of the central themes in the public sphere in contemporary Mexico. We think of murder as an act of violence from which detectives extract an explanation and, when they can, a suspect. During the middle decades of the twentieth century, the public gave criminal violence a clear political meaning. The figures of the police detective and the pistolero were key characters in these interpretations, although there were multiple voices involved. Some murders were hard to explain or revealed inconvenient truths. In these cases, instead of seeking justice, state representatives simply sought a viable explanation, preferably from suspects, who obliged because of coercion or because they wanted to tell their story. In some difficult cases, the police would close the case through the *ley fuga*.

Such uncertainty remains clear today, especially in the many unsolved, drug-related killings. According to a police officer in Culiacán, Sinaloa, as soon as local detectives see any sign that a homicide is connected to the cartels they close the investigation. Recent academic and official reports confirm this.[1] Elmer Mendoza's novels have used this fact to give new intensity and verisimilitude to the murder genre. His homicide cops in *Balas de plata* and other novels are robbed of the very questions they are trying to answer by their more powerful narcotics counterparts. The causes of and responsibility for these crimes remain clouded by suspicions of corruption and internal business disputes among gangs. The same cloud extends to any murder when responsibility is not immediately established. In the fourth part of his novel 2666, Roberto Bolaño writes about the remains of women found dead in a Mexican border city. Page after page Bolaño describes clothes, details from the place of the finding, bones. There is little else: only the traces of the victims' identities. There is no unfolding resolution of a mystery and no detective able to find the murderer. The problem with murder, Bolaño suggests, is not discovering the truth behind it, but making sense of it. Indeed, unlike other predatory crimes, murder excludes the victim from any subsequent exchange about its consequences, whether they involve punishment or forgiveness. The living are left to deal with it. Yet such uncertainty is not simply a construction of the globalized, modern age; it is a well-established aspect of crime and policing in Mexico. The practical rules that made it acceptable were established in the middle years of the twentieth century and have only been exacerbated and amplified by the drug violence of recent years.

Homicide has been a key theme in the relationship between civil society and the state, the definition of victim's rights and authorities' obligations, and public discussions about justice and transgression. Viewing murder in Mexico from a historical perspective provides a necessary distance from the Weberian notion that the state had any serious claim to the monopoly of the legitimate use of force. If anything, it had the monopoly of suspicious behavior. *Caciques*, pistoleros, policemen, or soldiers got away with murder because somebody protected them. Everybody knew that truth and justice existed, but were not always causally connected. Instead, stories that made sense of the daily use of violence permeated much of public life during the years after the revolution.

Murder should be viewed not only as a means to an end or a problem of public health or public order but as a communicative act to be received and decoded by an audience. When people talked about murder in twentieth-century Mexico, and sometimes when they committed it, they engaged in critical exchanges with the state. Famous and common homicides created a field of public discussion, captivated audiences, and transformed the rules for participation in the public sphere. Not only the educated and powerful could speak to public opinion and victims and criminals became the object of the attention of the press. The distinction between political assassinations and crimes motivated by greed, passion, or other causes is not essential; all were political in that they tested institutions and confirmed the irrelevance of the judiciary.[2] The all-powerful president seemed weaker when he could not guarantee justice and protection, particularly against some of his wayward subordinates. Impunity, which was more tangible in everyday life than presidential power, magnetized the interest of diverse audiences, turning them into one public united by the idea that justice was a right and that the state was obligated to provide it. This public judged the performance of authorities with theoretical unanimity given the clear moral value of homicide. Furthermore, in spite of the political violence documented in this volume, these critical exchanges would become a key aspect of the process of political incorporation and democratization initiated in the last quarter of the twentieth century.³

This politicization of homicide began around the 1930s and was clearly established by the 1950s. Two interconnected processes defined this transformation. On the one hand, the regime that emerged from the revolution sought to "institutionalize" coercion by replacing the personal and rough order of revolutionaries and caciques with overlapping groups of professional police and loyal pistoleros. On the other hand, newspapers, radio, and movies incorporated more Mexicans into public debates. Even as the PRI regime controlled the industrial press, murder became the object of open debates about the limits of the rule of law. I attempt to illustrate these points through a few famous cases examined by the press and the recently opened archives of the Mexico City Police Department Secret Service. Finally I examine pistoleros, detectives, and the ley fuga.

Murder and the Public Sphere

The most famous Mexican murder case, already studied in depth by several scholars, is that of Francisco "Goyo" Cárdenas, who strangled and buried four women in his Mexico City house in 1942. He sexually assaulted his victims but also claimed to have performed experiments with their bodies. Everyone knew and discussed the story: housewives and female prisoners wrote to the president and newspapers demanding protection and justice; congressmen and editors proposed the reinstatement of the death penalty; police detectives gave their own views; reporters and doctors treated Cárdenas like a celebrity.⁴ Cárdenas was declared mentally unfit to stand trial in spite of his intelligence and education; yet he was only released from prison in 1976, later receiving applause in Congress as an example of a regenerated criminal.⁵

Cárdenas was tracked down and arrested by agent Ana María Dorantes, although her bosses took all the credit. (Female investigators were put in charge of murder cases where the victims were prostitutes or when young women disappeared.⁶) As soon as the bodies were found, everyone recognized that Cárdenas was different from the average murderer. He was willing to describe his gruesome crimes, talk about his relationship with the victims, or discuss his life. Journalists interviewed him at length in his cell with the authorization of the judge.⁷ He was, in the opinion of Alfonso Langel, leader of the lawyers' union, "not [the] butcher [who] can kill with great calmness, . . . as is the best defined type of born criminal . . . the pistolero."⁸ Cárdenas, in contrast, was an articulate murderer who explained his crimes. Other serial killers of the time received little attention or were granted little expertise because they lacked his eloquence. This was the case, for example, of "La descuartizadora" of Colonia Roma, Felícitas Sánchez Aguillón, who was accused of killing several children, including her own, and disposing of their dismembered bodies in trash cans and empty lots. In 1941 she was arrested, indicted on charges of illegal burial, then released. She committed suicide two months later.[9]

Another example of a murderer willing to make articulate explanations was Ema Martínez. On March 6, 1959, she shot and killed senator Rafael Altamirano at his office, in front of multiple witnesses. She was arrested on the spot and immediately began to make statements to the press. With tears in her eyes she claimed, "he sank me. . . . He finished my life and left me on the streets!" The scandal made the front pages for a few days and then died out, just as most crime stories in Mexican newspapers did once a suspect had been arrested. Even if brief, the scandal allowed Martínez to uncover corruption in the federal bureaucracy. She told reporters that she had been a victim of the Federal Pensions Office's culture of sexual debauchery. As Altamirano's secretary, she had been coerced into having a relationship with him. When they broke up, she was fired. Then Altamirano had her detained by agents of the Federal Security Directorate and taken to a psychiatrist's clinic to be declared mentally ill. The Federal Pensions Office refused to return her savings to her. A subordinate of Altamirano, Rafael Aréchiga, brought Martínez to his own apartment, drugged her, took pictures of her in "inconvenient positions," and circulated them among her female coworkers. Although she sued Aréchiga and Altamirano for defamation, the case was dismissed. Fearing for her security, she had to leave for Chiapas and then went to Guatemala. She returned to Mexico City in 1959 to finally collect her money, which she used to buy back the gun she used to kill Altamirano.

Ema Martínez's decision to kill the senator was, in her words, an attempt to clear her name. After her arrest she refused to argue that she was mentally ill or had acted in self-defense: she simply laid out her accusations. Her claims fueled comments in the press about the corruption reigning among bureaucrats. Altamirano, it was suggested, was an example of politicians who moved from obscure jobs to elected office because of their personal connections and who used their positions to get rich and have sexual adventures with female subordinates. The implication was so subversive that the judge in charge of the case halted Martínez's interviews with reporters. To avoid the taint of possible complicity, President López Mateos did not attend Altamirano's wake, but rather sent a then-obscure bureaucrat, Luis Echeverría.

Press coverage of Martínez's case shows how murder offered opportunities to present a critical yet ostensibly apolitical view of the regime. One of the main dailies in Mexico City, El Universal, rarely had more than one page of police news and devoted ample space to classified ads and social news. Although the newspaper displayed little sympathy toward the murder, its reporters faithfully reproduced and confirmed Martínez's statements while editors hinted that other bureaucrats were involved in the scandal and criticized the judge for limiting access to the suspect after she had promised to name them. Even *Amanecer*, a newspaper from Altamirano's home state of Querétaro, began the coverage calling her "*una loca guatemalteca*" but eventually reproduced a lengthy interview with her and accepted her argument by characterizing the assassination as a "crime of passion."[10]

La Prensa, the newspaper with the highest circulation in the country for many years, gave the story a different tone. *La Prensa* centered on police news, running gruesome photos and large, sensational headliners on the front and back pages. The tabloid gave the murder extensive coverage. Although journalists condemned her and repeated the usual pleas to reinstate the death penalty, they also embraced her narrative. Editorials and caricatures denounced the corruption and immorality exposed by her case. In doing so, *La Prensa* amplified a story that was critical of the government yet acceptable in the context of police news, where events were defined by personal passion rather than ideological conflict. Police stories went into great detail in describing the lives of upper-class victims or suspects who would otherwise be protected from the public eye, blurring the borders between public and private in ways that were not possible elsewhere in the media. Ema Martínez knew this. Her crime was not perfect but worked because it allowed her to put her story at the forefront of public opinion.

During the weeks Ema's case unfolded, López Mateos's government confronted the independent railroad workers' union in a process that lead to the arrest of hundreds, police searches of union and Communist Party offices, and charges against labor leaders that resulted in lengthy prison terms. Both *El Universal* and *La Prensa* reproduced the government's anticommunist rhetoric against workers and adhered to the line of "national unity." But they continued reporting sensational crimes, reproducing the words of suspects, and hinting at immorality at the higher echelons of the regime.

The Cárdenas and Martínez stories were only two of the scandalous narratives that since the 1920s had made a deep impact on public culture. Murders recounted and photographed in gory detail, stories of corruption and impunity, and the exploration of criminal minds revealed areas rarely dealt with in the political or social pages of newspapers. The postrevolutionary regime controlled the press with little violence, relying instead on advertising, loans, paper subsidies, and envelopes thick with cash or job offers. Histories of the press in the twentieth century stress presidential control and corrupt self-censorship, but they are based only on the first section of morning national newspapers, the one that would usually include the names of high officials.

Scholars ignore the police section, the second edition of the main newspapers, and publications focused on crime news, such as Alarma! and La Prensa, where corruption was routinely denounced and the contradictions among authorities could emerge.[11] The police news or nota roja was a guide to navigate the dangers of everyday life, and even murderers, according to the testimony of one suspect, read them aloud and with great care.[12] The constant game of crime and justice (who got caught and who did not, who became a helpless victim, and who was able to retaliate) framed the reading of police news and the exercise of citizenship. As they had been doing since colonial times, most people dealt with government representatives through the roles of victims or suspects. The difference in the twentieth century was that those interactions found a powerful amplifier in police news, which made individual stories the object of public interest.

Burying the Dead

Not all murders were the object of such detailed stories and explanations as those committed by Goyo Cárdenas and Ema Martínez. Many, the majority in fact, remained unsolved and only succinctly reported in the press because they did not involve famous victims or suspects. Although this remained true throughout the century, the numbers and practices associated with homicide changed over time. According to official government statistics, since the 1920s homicide declined steadily in Mexico. Figure 14.1 shows a stable total number of persons indicted for homicide contrasting with growth in the total number of crimes during the period for which we have consistent figures. Figure 14.2, which shows national rates per total population for the most important crimes, demonstrates a decline in homicide during most of the twentieth century. Although rates are high in recent years, particularly in certain regions, they are lower than in the years before and immediately after the revolution. In the capital, the rate of homicide sentenced per 100,000 inhabitants averaged 46 between 1885 and 1871, was 31 in 1909 and climbed to 37 in 1930 before decreasing thereafter.

These statistics do not register the "dark figure" of homicides, which did not lead to prosecutions. The numbers of people deceased because of foul play according to public health sources is consistently larger than the number of those indicted (figure 14.3), explaining why even though homicide was probably decreasing in relative numbers, it grew as a concern for public opinion. The number of deaths reported as homicide by forensic sources was consistently higher than that of judicial statistics. The difference in the years where both numbers are available—an average of 65 percent for the country between 1926 and 2005, and 91 percent for the Federal District—confirms that justice only reached a limited number of cases.

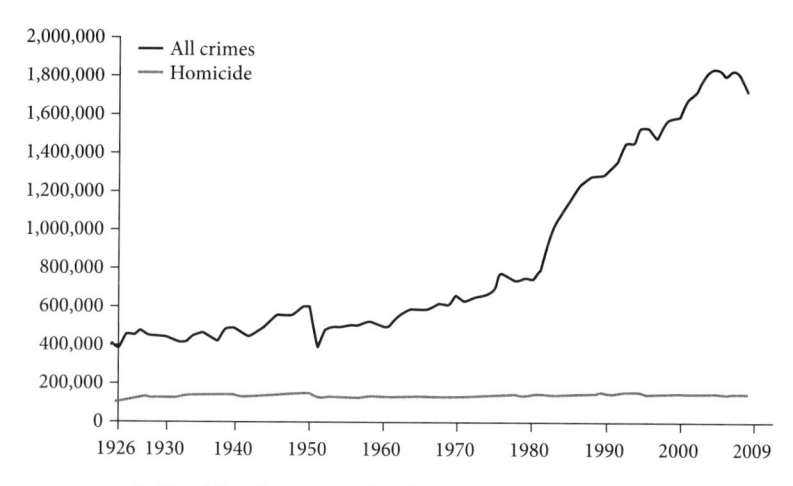

FIGURE 14.1. Indicted for all crimes and for homicide in Mexico, 1926–2009

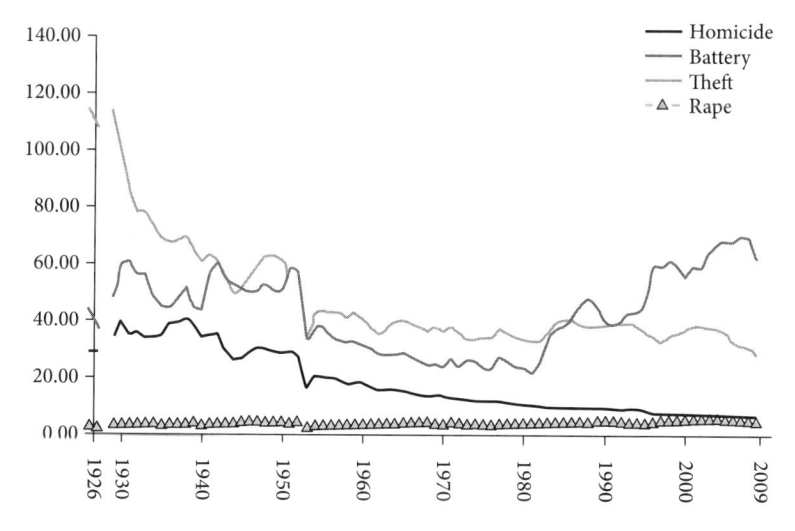

FIGURE 14.2. Indicted per 100,000 for selected crimes in Mexico, 1926–2009

Pistoleros and Politics

The ways in which homicide was committed begins to explain both the apparent decrease and the statistical gaps. Street corner brawls were the most visible form of homicidal violence early in the century, before guns increased the occurrence of violent crime. As practices changed the meanings of murder also evolved. A knife fight between two men expressed the honor of both rivals, provided that certain basic rules were followed. Guns made it more difficult

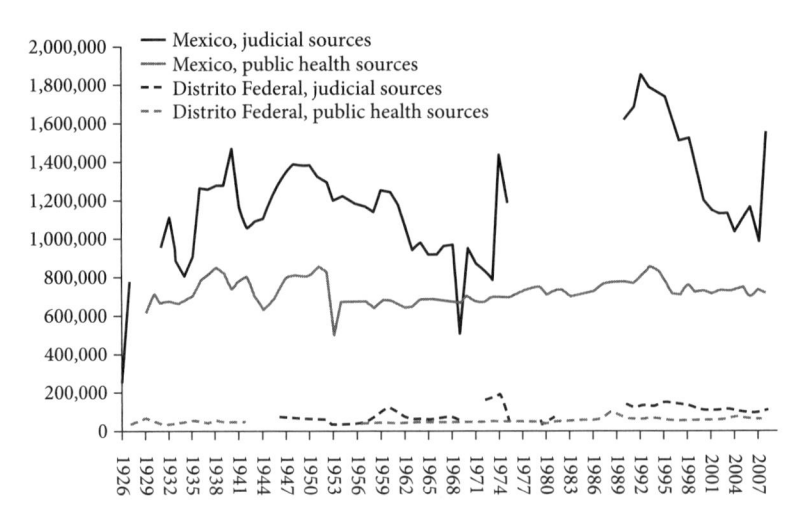

FIGURE. 14.3. Homicide rates from judicial versus public health records, 1926–2009
Sources: "Estadísticas del crimen en México: Series históricas, 1901–2001"; Anuario Estadístico de la República Mexicana, various years. The number of homicides from judicial totals was calculated from indictments for homicide; public health totals are calculated from homicides reported as cause of death.

to express equality or even the appearance that fighters were abiding by honorable forms. As former revolutionaries obtained respectable official positions or *cacicazgos*, the image of the pistolero came to be associated with the growth in inexplicable homicides.

Even as they became increasingly common, few people owned guns, so their use in homicide was not necessarily meaningless. The pistoleros of the mid-century used their revolvers to demonstrate political clout without any pretense of fair play, often bragging about the power of their employers. The gun in the waistband was part of their outfit, a symbol of power they flaunted like a badge—and they also flaunted official badges.[13] They dressed in a clearly identifiable way. Dr. Joaquín Maass Patiño had a traffic incident with one man in 1948 but decided to let it go because the man in the other car was "tall and slender, with [a] thin black mustache, dressed with turn-up cuff blue jeans, a Texan hat and a white shirt, so he seemed to me the bodyguard pistolero of a politician."[14] The man was, in fact, on his way to a hit.

The pistolero was the bodyguard and enforcer for a politician, a criminal, or both; he was close to—if not a member of—the police, an expert in violence always beyond the reach of punishment. Pistoleros were easy to find in places linked with "*turbios negocios*" (prostitution, drug trafficking, extortion) in which their connections gave them a competitive advantage.[15] They mixed the criminal with the political: they operated against opposition or independent union leaders, students, or electoral rivals like Gonzalo N. Santos and his Thompson-wielding *gargaleotes*. Although their violence was private in that pistoleros responded to their bosses rather than to any state policy, they were also highly visible to the public and the press. Their crimes expressed the state's limited monopoly of legitimate violence and the ample impunity of those associated with powerful actors. Langel, cited above, defined the pistolero as a born criminal whose "role is to kill . . . when his boss tells him to eliminate [a] certain person, he goes and does it with great calm; and he repeats the crime when he is ordered to again." Pistoleros were a necessity of political life. Even president Miguel Alemán's driver was suggestively nicknamed "El Asesino."[16]

The category of the pistolero did not exist in criminological taxonomies, but he became a ubiquitous figure in the realm of crime, police, and politics.[17] In 1939, commenting on the murder of agrarian leader Eduardo Guichard in a Mexico City café by Armando Armenta Barradas, a member of a rival Veracruz clan, *Excélsior* saw the case as a rural atavism in an urban, modern polity. The crime revealed "an environment of decomposition and insecurity that causes fear, precisely indicated by the frequency of murders committed with premeditation, cruelty and advantage, by individuals of certain local reputation, pals or accomplices of leaders or officials, or at least their pistoleros."[18] In subsequent years pistoleros were condemned from different ideological positions as a dying but resilient breed.[19] Recent scholarship confirms the rural roots of *pistolerismo*. "Entrepreneurial caciquismo" used violence by "*hombres de confianza*" to maximize the benefits of access to public office.[20] By 1968, however, Rafael Bernal's hard-boiled novel *El complot mongol* centered on an aging, nostalgic pistolero, Filiberto García, who remembered those times when his trade was more appreciated, Now it was all "lots of law and . . . lots of order"; "before one needed balls and today one needs a degree."[21] García's ironic reference to a "school of pistoleros" echoed a facetious announcement in 1943 by *El Momento*, from Oaxaca, about the "*Primer Congreso de Pistolerismo*" held in that city.[22] Both referred to the institutionalization of pistoleros and the *pistolerización* of politics.

It is not surprising, then, that people explained unsolved murders as the result of hidden interests and that representatives of the state were usually at the receiving end of suspicion. National and Mexico City archives contain copious anonymous letters from citizens denouncing suspects and revealing their dark pasts. One premise of these letters was that the triggermen were seldom the actual culprits or intellectual authors. In 1948 Luis Saldívar Martínez wrote from the Tlaxcala prison to President Alemán, stating that he had been led on to kill Aurelio León Alvarez but that the responsibility rested with "the intellectuals Eustaquio Sánchez and Baltazar Maldonado." In what can be read both as an accusation and a suggestive critique of certain philosophical ideas, Saldívar Martínez reflected, "you will very well know that there are many intellectuals who utilize material elements to get rid of whoever hinders their ideals."[23]

The archives suggest that there was, at least in the middle decades of the century, an active demand for the services of "material elements." They could be paid ten thousand pesos or more for pulling the trigger, although the middlemen could bag up to ten times that much. To kill movie industry union leader Alfonso Mascarúa, the intermediary Alejandro Ponce de León hired Alfonso Trujeque García, a former boxer with a reputation as a mean fighter who would slam the heads of adversaries against the pavement during street brawls. Trujeque asked for five thousand pesos but was offered ten thousand. José Antonio Arredondo had refused to take twenty thousand for the same job, explaining to Ponce de León that "if I did not do it when I was screwed [jodido] much less now that I do not need it."[24]

Hired guns could be part of networks of family or friends before becoming stable pistoleros, ready to do any job "when his boss tells him to eliminate a certain person." Loyalty was the key virtue. Marciano Armenta, accused of ordering the murder of senator Mauro Angulo in 1948, bragged that he would never be incriminated, even if they arrested one of his men, because "my boys do what I order because I have disciplined people and we all work in coordination." The Armenta clan, based in Plan de las Hayas, Veracruz, had the political muscle and reach into Tlaxcala. When a detective told him that there was indeed a confession, Armenta refused to believe it, protesting that the man in custody "is too much of a man and also knows our code, because in our family whoever speaks or confesses and endangers our lives, will die."[25]

Crimes committed by pistoleros were seldom solved in an acceptable way. Citizens writing to the president saw pistoleros as "well-situated abnormal, inveterate assassins," about whom little could be done because of their political clout.[26] Given the weakness of the justice system in assigning blame and providing good explanations, it seemed logical, from the point of view of the public, to explain any murder as the product of hired guns. As pistoleros became the most visible expression of the new practices of murder, public opinion inevitably interpreted murders as political—either because of their motives or because of the impunity that surrounded most of them.

Detectives were the missing link between murder's uncertainty and its resolution. Although there were many, and several private schools taught forensic science, detectives never achieved the cultural and legal authority they had in other countries. Famous real-life detectives like Valente Quintana or competent criminologists like Alfonso Quiróz Cuarón were exceptional, and they often were considered to be corrupt. Regular police detectives were far from this glamorous prototype: they had little education or prestige, and whatever achievements they claimed were mainly products of their close association with criminals.[27] The detective fiction emerging in Mexico during the period exemplified these perceptions. Dumb street cops antagonized the poor and thievish detective Péter Pérez in the short stories of José Martínez De la Vega. Antonio Helú's detective Maximo Roldán (an acronym of *ladrón*) was another criminal turned detective. In Rodolfo Usigli's *Ensayo de un crimen*—the first and probably the best novel of the genre in Mexico—inspector Herrera was a corrupt policeman who became a private investigator.[28] Chucho Cárdenas, the hero of Leo D'Olmo's weekly stories in *La Prensa*, was a reporter who solved cases against the police thanks to his ability to mingle with prisoners and the support of his bosses at the newspaper. This perception of the justice system and the police as corrupt and reliably unreliable was not compatible with the classics of the genre. American pulp fiction does not always flatter the law, but even there we find detectives who, however cynical about the system, see their job as an obligation of honor.[29]

In Mexico, on the other hand, police detectives were not guides to the truth but rather obstacles to its emergence. The capital's Secret Service archives document the police work that caused such distrust. For detectives who had competing loyalties and little concern about method, gathering evidence from the crime scene was not a priority. In a few cases physical evidence could yield results, as in the case of Senator Angulo. Agents were proud to inform the press that "through modern scientific means" it was possible to ascertain that the same gun had killed another Tlaxcalan politician months earlier—yet, as we will see later in this chapter, the political implications of the case led to a frustrating resolution.[30] Police detectives cited newspaper reports as often as forensics as sources of evidence. In the case of Angulo, they referred to information that "was known" publicly or among unspecified circles. Detectives, witnesses, even suspects read the police news carefully because it contained valuable information about the context and actors of a case: the names of those involved, links with previous cases, and political battles within unions or at the state or local levels, *cacicazgos*, or other informal organizations. In provincial newspapers, reports of crimes often contained the names of perpetrators before they were even mentioned by authorities. The press synthesized the public knowledge that led the police to the suspects.[31]

Once suspects were arrested, police agents made their mark on the case by subjecting them to difficult interrogations. The documents produced by mid-century Mexican authorities do not speak of torture but some *amparos* presented by suspects' lawyers and relatives do. The wife of Ponce de León, the intermediary, denounced the authorities for the "savage physical and moral torture" of her husband. The police replied to the judge denying the charges in the standard form they used to reject such requests, yet the final report of the Secret Service itself stated that Ponce de León had provided information after "severe interrogations."[32] Confessions constituted sufficient evidence to close a case, thus also explaining the lack of interest for physical evidence.

The *Ley Fuga*

In contrast, a suspect's failure to confess could have dire consequences. Several cases in the Secret Service archives document the death of suspects during investigations and, if we believe the press, extrajudicial executions were an open secret. There is a long tradition of the use of ley fuga since the nineteenth century. Killing the suspect before the end of a case prevented additional information about "intellectuals" from becoming public, providing some form of closure to the story but leaving many questions unanswered. The ley fuga also was defended as a means of direct justice. Even if the practice was sanctioned by custom, it was illegal, and Secret Service agents went to considerable lengths to explain the circumstances in which suspects died while in custody.[33]

Santiago Rodríguez Silva, for example, was suspected of killing three women in a barbershop in Tacubaya in 1934. Even though circumstantial evidence incriminated him, he refused to confess. He underwent long interrogations and eventually admitted to killing the women only in self-defense. He was taken to the crime scene to reconstruct the events—a common practice during investigations that, if anything else, yielded pictures of suspects holding the gun or grabbing the neck of a stand-in for the victim.[34] But things took a different course in Tacubaya. In a letter to the press that accounted for the subsequent events, the chief of police of the Federal District explained that the reconstruction was performed at 11 P.M. to avoid the hostile crowds that had surrounded earlier proceedings. Not surprisingly, as the reconstruction was held in a barbershop, there were razor blades all over the place. The chief informed that, "unfortunately," in a moment of distraction, Rodríguez Silva grabbed one and swung it at an agent. He was shot dead by another agent, and the case was closed. The press reported on the conclusion of the story in a way that made it seem logical rather than irregular, including editorials in favor of the death penalty and even a statement from Rodríguez Silva's mother acknowledging that his crime was so great that he expected his death.[35]

The Politics and Perception of Murder: A Case Study

The investigation, public discussion, and resolution of Mauro Angulo's assassination, mentioned earlier, provides a fitting example of the ways in which crime narratives shaped public perceptions and the shifting lines between common and political crime. Looking at places and characters, this example also suggests the continuity between rural and urban crime that both histories of crime and agrarian struggle often fail to observe.

The murder of Senator Angulo as he was coming out of his morning visit to the bathhouse was performed with professional efficiency: four shots to the head; another round at the only witness, who survived; and a rapid escape in a car that was waiting around the corner. The news spread rapidly from the sidewalk in Insurgentes where Angulo lay. Two fellow senators came to the scene and then reported to President Alemán; Tlaxcala governor Rafael Avila Bretón arrived in the capital the same morning. Indignant, Alemán instructed "all the police agencies" to participate in the investigation. In statements to the press, several of Angulo's eight grown children expressed surprise and grief, as did the peasants who came to his burial after the wake in the senate. Linked from the start to Tlaxcalan affairs, the case confirmed that politics bred crime. In an editorial entitled "No hay justicia," La Prensa concluded that, along with its usual apologia for the death penalty, "in countries like ours, crime becomes a dynastic hierarchy, a political lineage of the darkest and proudest descent."[36]

The presidential order that "all the police" spring into action reflected the pressures exerted by these opinions. The variegated structure of police institutions usually led to competition. Multiple police agencies rushed to the scene of high-profile crimes, starting parallel investigations, in doing so diluting responsibilities and making explanations less convincing. Agents of the State Prosecutor were in charge of preparing indictments, but the Secret Service (among other agencies) also conducted investigations and chased suspects. Rather than collaborating, in some circumstances men from different agencies fought each other.[37] Alemán's order was meaningful because all of these bodies were ultimately subordinated to the president, since he appointed high-ranking judicial, army, and Federal District officials.[38]

Immediately after the crime, Alemán received telegrams demanding a thorough investigation, some of them citing links between this case and the 1947 murder of former Tlaxcala deputy Aurelio León. Petitions and suggestions came from army officers, unions, students associations, professionals, and workers and peasants from Tlaxcala and elsewhere. Both Angulo and León were likely candidates to the governorship of the state, so petitioners interpreted the crime as an attack on the "civic rights" of Tlaxcala inhabitants. Since "it is already known" who killed León, argued four signatories from Apizaco, Angulo's case, if not solved, could become another example of authorities' protection of the same "intellectual author."[39] Don Roque, a combative weekly from Apizaco, saw León's case as another example of the rampant pistolerismo that governor Rafael Avila Bretón seemed too lenient to curtail. Angulo's assassination was a confirmation of the same problems. Failure to act would have caused "*pistolerismo* [and] racketeering. . . . The swindlers of public ballots and all the anti-social pests would have seized power, holding honest people in a reign of terror for many years." *Don Roque* reported that Marciano Armenta, the main suspect as the "intellectual author," was preparing a rebellion against the government with other caciques.[40]

During the investigation, Secret Service officers also received letters volunteering information about the political background of the case. One referred to the surviving Tlaxcala senator, Gerzayn Ugarte; another implicated governor Rafael Avila Bretón, whereas others referred to Puebla, Guerrero, and Veracruz politics. Investigators discarded at the outset romantic or economic motives and focused instead on the infrapolitics of Tlaxcala. A military commander in Veracruz reported to his superiors that he decided to look for Angulo's murderers because he read that they might be hiding in his region.[41] Soon both political and police interpretations led in the same direction. The jeep used in the murder (although now in a different color and without wheels) belonged to Armenta; according to the forensics experts, the gun used to kill León was the same as that used against Angulo, and that also pointed to Armenta.[42] With the collaboration of Tlaxcala state prosecutors, the agents went so far as to bring together in a meeting Armenta, the remaining Tlaxcala senator, Gerzayn Ugarte; the state's governor, Avila Bretón; the owner of a brothel in Apizaco, Eustaquio Sánchez; and other local authorities. According to the agents' report, Armenta challenged them to get any of his men to confess and officially maintained his innocence, yet he told Ugarte and others that he had Angulo killed because he wanted to be governor and because Angulo had killed "by crucifixion" his brother Teodoro Armenta after accusing him of supporting Almazán.[43]

Once the detective work was over the case moved toward a resolution, which was concerned more with public perception than the rule of law. When Armenta and his accomplices were finally arrested, letters, telegrams, and press statements from his lawyers and relatives protested against their irregular detention and torture; Armenta's lawyer accused the Federal District's police chief of ignoring an amparo.[44] A letter to Alemán signed by Manuela López declared that her husband was involved in both León and Angulo's cases under the duress of Apizaco's political authorities, including the future governor Felipe Mazarrasa. The policemen and pistoleros who forced her husband to become involved—the same men who beat and raped her when she tried to rescue him—claimed to have orders from Alemán himself.[45]

Marciano Armenta and his suspected accomplices Armando Armenta Barrados and José López Hernández were taken from Mexico City to the state of Veracruz to help arrest brothers Hugo and Arturo Izquierdo Ebrard. The trip took place even though the former three had not been charged and their lawyers had presented amparos to keep them in Mexico City. The convoy of suspects and agents stopped in a lonely and foggy area near Magueyitos, Veracruz, so the suspects could attend to their bodily needs. Instead they ran in different directions and were shot as they disappeared into the fog. The image of Marciano Armenta's body was on the front page of La Prensa two days later.[46]

The apparent use of ley fuga in this case was slightly more contentious than in the case of the Tacubaya barbershop. Relatives of the dead suspects, like Gloria Flores, wrote to Alemán. She accepted the idea that it was an execution designed to make some people pay for the deaths of León and Angulo, but she complained about the ruthless arithmetic of the revenge killings, arguing that making three men pay for the death of only two was unfair.[47] In the press, the episode of Magueyitos meant that justice, if not the law, had been served, although with some rough edges that the establishment of the death penalty could smooth out.[48] The afternoon edition of Excélsior, Últimas Noticias, always ready to voice opinions deemed lowbrow and more extreme than the morning edition, claimed that the ley fuga could be understood as a "defensive reaction of society" that involved "the collective subconscious."[49] La Prensa described the scene in Magueyitos as the epilogue of "a long career of crimes and professional pistolerismo, when everything had finished and senator Angulo's blood, among others, had been revenged."[50] It entitled the description of the events by General Pedro J. Castro, chief of the Federal District's Secret Service, "The executioner's version."[51]

The use of the ley fuga could not be recognized openly because it impinged on the rule of law and the reputation of officials. When news of the Magueyitos shooting reached Mexico City, the attorney general, Franco Sodi, declared that the suspects had been taken on the trip without his authorization and implied that the ley fuga had been applied. After General Castro paid a visit to his house, Sodi published a letter in the following days explaining that he had never doubted Castro's honor.[52] To the press, Castro declared that he was not "un matón" and that the death of the suspects under his direct custody was "very embarrassing" because he was a member of the army and had a clean record. He explained that he did not apply the ley fuga because that would go against his honor as a military man but that if he had allowed Armenta to vanish, suspicion would have fallen on him because of the suspect's wealth; thus he had no choice but to kill him.[53] He had public supporters despite such flimsy logic. A Veracruz organization in the capital wrote to Alemán, denouncing journalistic attempts to "distort" the circumstances of the death of "the pistoleros Armenta," and praising Castro. While Armenta was the prototype of the *cacique pistoleril*, Castro was an honorable man who had in previous years helped rid the state of Veracruz of criminals.[54]

The case was as much about Tlaxcala as it was about Veracruz. The shooting took place in that state, and Castro went directly to Xalapa to notify the governor and future president Adolfo Ruiz Cortines.[55] Ruiz Cortines congratulated the agency, saying that "he wholeheartedly agrees with the events and states that he wishes that would be the way to end the era of terror that those subjects have imposed on the state, and he also told us that public opinion agreed with what had happened."[56]

THE ASSASSINATION OF Angulo is an example, perhaps starker in its political implications, of how murder created a field of public discourse, a space of debate that was open to diverse voices and not dominated by any one particular authoritative perspective. Relatives of victims and suspects, policemen and politicians, journalists and anonymous tipsters all took part. It was inherently critical of state institutions and agents, even as it could indirectly lead to justifying extrajudicial executions. Through press, literature, and the radio it attracted broad audiences and constituted them into vocal publics that addressed the media and political authorities.

The contemporary use of violence and the media by drug traffickers is a product of the role that crime has played in the public sphere since the mid-twentieth century. The cruelty and the numbers today might seem to be on a different scale, but they are depicted and discussed with the same logic. According to that logic, police investigation of drug-related murders is less relevant than the perceptions of public opinion. Detectives, prosecutors, and judges seem corrupt or weak and lack the authority to build convincing accounts and explanations of crime; impunity remains the most common consequence of murder. Today, as in 1948 or 1959, when senators Angulo and Altamirano were killed, politics could not be clearly separated from the criminal use of violence, and there was a consensus in favor of bending of the rule of law to achieve swift justice. Against a Weberian view of sovereignty, most of the actors cited here believed that it was acceptable, and perhaps useful, to balance the supremacy of the law against other established, if irregular, practices of violence as long as they lead to something that resembled order and peace.

From this perspective, politics is no longer a self-contained field of public life or historical study. The evidence examined here at least suggests the need to open the register of themes and voices usually deemed politically relevant. Although the central role of violence in postrevolutionary politics has been established, we still have much to learn about how caciquismo was constructed—what the practices and meanings of violence actually were. The evidence shown here suggests that the divide between rural and urban and traditional and modern is not so useful in that regard. While scholars have not been very good at reading the second section of newspapers, criminals have continued to produce stories that challenge political order. Their narratives could come in the shape of romantic stories about honor, as in the case of Ema Martínez, or in the form of mere press releases, as in today's executions by drug cartels. We fail to read them at our own peril.

Notes

1. Personal communication, April 2008; "*Muertes del narco ya no se investigan: Miles de casos quedan en un limbo entre autoridades locales y federales,*" El Universal, February 23, 2009.

2. A similar argument could be made of homicides committed in rural as opposed to urban contexts. The evidence I analyze does not contain enough of the former to build a good comparison.

3. Pablo Piccato, "Altibajos de la esfera pública en México, de la dictadura republicana a la democracia corporativa: La era de la prensa," in *Independencia y Revolución: Pasado, presente y futuro*, ed. Gustavo Leyva et al. (Mexico City: Fondo de Cultura Económica-Universidad Autónoma Metropolitana, 2010), 240–91; Jürgen Habermas, *The Structural Transformation of the Public Sphere: An Inquiry into a Category of Bourgeois Society* (Cambridge, MA: MIT, 1991). On unanimity as a trait of politicized public spheres in Spanish America see François-Xavier Guerra, *Modernidad e independencias: Ensayos sobre las revoluciones hispánicas* (Mexico City: Editorial MAPFRE, Fondo de Cultura Económica, 2000), 271. On politics and crime narratives in contemporary Mexico see Robert Buffington and Pablo Piccato, "Introduction," in *Mexican Crime Stories: Case Studies, Causes Célèbres, and Other True-to-Life Adventures in the Social Construction of Deviance*, ed. Robert Buffington and Pablo Piccato (Albuquerque: University of New Mexico Press, 2009).

4. Experts and lay people joined in a true "interpretive feast," to use Carlos Monsiváis's apt words (*Los mil y un velorios: Crónica de la nota roja* [Mexico City: Consejo Nacional para la Cultura y las Artes, Alianza Editorial, 1994], 26). Everard Kidder Meade, "Anatomies of Justice and Chaos: Capital Punishment and the Public in Mexico, 1917–1945" (PhD dissertation, University of Chicago, 2005).

5. Andrés Ríos Molina, *Memorias de un loco anormal: El caso de Goyo Cárdenas* (Mexico: Editorial Debate, 2010). See Reinalda Salgado, Cuernavaca, to Manuel Avila Camacho, September 8, 1942, Archivo General de la Nación, Manuel Avila Camacho (AGN, MAC), 541/630. The telegram was added to the investigation proceedings and excerpted by *Novedades*, October 2, 1942, 9. Prisoners expressed their views in *El Universal Gráfico*, September 25, 1942.

6. *El Universal Gráfico*, September 11, 1942; *Ultimas Noticias*, September 11 and 15, 1942. For a man who killed a prostitute he exploited out of jealousy, *Novedades*, October 1, 1942.

7. *El Universal Gráfico*, September 19, 1942.

8. *Ultimas Noticias*, September 22, 1942.

9. Ana Luisa Luna, *La Crónica Policíaca en México: Nota Roja 40s* (Mexico City: Diana, 1993), 57; *La Prensa*, April 9, April 29, and July 17, 1941.

10. *Amanecer*, March 6–8, 1959.

11. See Julio Scherer García and Carlos Monsiváis, *Tiempo de saber: Prensa y poder en México* (Mexico City: Aguilar, 2003); Piccato, "Altibajos de la esfera pública." For an interesting new reading of the nota roja see J. M. Servín, *D.F. Confidencial, crónicas de delincuentes, vagos y demás gente sin futuro* (Mexico City: Almadía, 2010); *El Universal*, March 9 and 10, 1959.

12. Declaración del detenido Rafael Barradas Osorio, February 23, 1948, Archivo Histórico del Distrito Federal, Sección Jefatura de Policía, Serie Investigación y Seguridad, Servicio Secreto (AHDF/JP/ISSS) c.10 exp. 65, 1948.

13. Lic. Javier Torres Pérez, Mexico City, to Ruiz Cortines, August 28, 1958, AGN, Adolfo Ruiz Cortines (AGN, ARC), 541/1003; Jorge Vélez to Alemán, Port Isabel, September 26, 1948, AGN, Miguel Alemán Valdés (MAV), 541/50; Paul Gillingham, "Who killed Crispín Aguilar? Violence and Order in the Postrevolutionary Countryside," in *Violence, Coercion, and State-Making in Twentieth-Century Mexico: The Other Half of the Centaur*, ed. Wil Pansters, 91–111 (Palo Alto, CA: Stanford University Press, 2012).

14. AHDF/JP/ISSS-10/65, 1948, f. 125. Other descriptions in AHDF/JP/ISSS-4/30, legajos I y II, 1936; Roberto Blanco Moheno, *Memorias de un Reportero* (Zacatecas: Litografía Zacatecana, 1966), 96.

15. *Policía Internacional*, año 1948, no. 7, vol. 1, table 1. Other examples in *Excélsior*, October 1; AJ-RS, 23196, 1; *Detectives* 1, no. 17: 5; AHDF/JP/ISSS-4/30, legajos I y II, 1936.

16. Paul Gillingham, "Force and Consent in Mexican Provincial Politics: Guerrero and Veracruz, 1945–1953" (PhD dissertation, Oxford University, 2005), 242.

17. *Ultimas Noticias*, September 22, 1942, 1. The term was first registered in the debates of the Chamber of Deputies in 1940 against Almazanistas, Mexico, "Diario de los Debates de la Cámara de Diputados del Congreso de los Estados Unidos Mexicanos," electronic database, http://cronica.diputados.gob.mx/.

18. "La ola de sangre," editorial, *Excélsior*, August 2, 1939.

19. Orantes Arnoldo Telegramas, November 15, 1954, AGN/ARC-541/458, Firma Héctor R. Cobar, por la Secretaría de Relaciones P. de la Alianza Juvenil Anticomunista, Guatemala.

20. Stephen E. Lewis, "Dead-end Caudillismo and Entrepreneurial Caciquismo in Chiapas, 1910–1955," in *Caciquismo in Twentieth-Century Mexico*, ed. Alan Knight and Wil G. Pansters, 151–68 (London: Institute for the Study of the Americas, 2005).

21. Rafael Bernal, *El complot mongol* (Mexico City: Joaquín Mortiz, 1969), 9, 11.

22. Bernal, *El complot mongol*, 187; *El Momento*, May 23, 1943, quoted in Benjamin Smith, *Pistoleros and Popular Movements: The Politics of State Formation in Postrevolutionary Oaxaca* (Lincoln: University of Nebraska Press, 2009), 217; AHDF/JP/ISSS-10/65, 1948.

23. AHDF/JP/ISSS-10/65, 1948, f. 1.

24. AHDF/JP/ISSS-11/75, 1954.

25. AHDF/JP/ISSS-10/65, 1948. Thanks to Paul Gillingham for the reference to the Armentas. The origins of the clan as *guardias blancas* for cacique Manuel Parra and the massive violence in 1920s and early 1930s Veracruz are well explained in Antonio Santoyo, *La Mano Negra: Poder regional y estado en México: Veracruz, 1928–1943* (Mexico City: Consejo Nacional para la Cultura y las Artes, 1995).

26. Javier Torres Pérez, Mexico, to the President, August 28, 1958, AGN/ARC-541/1003.

27. See AHDF/JP/ISSS-12/88, 1959. *Novedades*, October 11, 1942, 10.

28. Antonio Helú, *La obligación de asesinar* (Mexico City: CNCA, 1991); Ilan Stavans, *Antihéroes: México y su novela policial* (Mexico City: Joaquín Mortiz, 1993), 90–93, 108. On Valente Quintana Monsiváis, *Los mil y un velorios*, 20; Stavans, *Antihéroes*, 67, 69, 79–83, 155–57. See also Glen S. Close, *Contemporary Hispanic Crime Fiction: A Transatlantic Discourse on Urban Violence* (New York: Palgrave Macmillan, 2008); Persephone Braham, *Crimes against the State, Crimes against Persons: Detective Fiction in Cuba and Mexico* (Minneapolis: University of Minnesota Press, 2004).

29. Leo D'Olmo, *El otro. Aventuras de Chucho Cárdenas, El gran reportero-detective Mexicano (Serie Escrita Especialmente Para "La Prensa")* (Mexico City: La Prensa, 1947); Pepe Martínez de la Vega, *Aventuras del detective Péter Pérez* (Mexico City: Plaza y Valdez, 1987). For the detective as "a man of honor" see Raymond Chandler, *The Simple Art of Murder* (New York: Vintage Books, 1988), 18.

30. AHDF/JP/ISSS-10/65, 1948.

31. *La Prensa*, February 19, 1948. On criminals named, *Amanecer* (Querétaro, Querétaro), March 1, 1959; *Don Roque* (Apizaco, Tlaxcala), 1:19, June 23, 1946, 1.

32. AHDF/JP/ISSS-11/75, 1954.

33. Meade, "Anatomies of Justice and Chaos"; Paul J. Vanderwood, *Juan Soldado: Rapist, Murderer, Martyr, Saint* (Durham, NC: Duke University Press, 2004), 48, 55.

34. Jesse Lerner, *The Shock of Modernity: Crime Photography in Mexico City* (Mexico City: Turner, 2007).

35. AHDF/JP/ISSS-3/20, N/522/1204; *La Prensa*, May 3, 1934.

36. *La Prensa*, February 18, 1948.

37. An episode in a cantina in *La Prensa*, February 26, 1948.

38. Diane Davis, "Policing and Mexican Regime Change: From Post-Authoritarianism to Populism to Neo-Liberalism," *Crisis States Working Papers Series No. 2*, 2007.

39. AGN/MAV-541/347.

40. *Don Roque*, December 7, 1947, 1:19, 2; February 29, 1948, 1:31, 2; and April 11, 1948, 1:37, 1.

41. José María Islas to Comandante Jesús Galindo, Mexico, February 21, 1947 (1948), letter to Jefe Comisiones de Seguridad y Jefe Policía Judicial, f. 65, AHDF/JP/ISSS-10/65, 1948.

42. AHDF/JP/ISSS-10/65, 1948.

43. Agents Pedro C. Balderas Salinas and Gonzalo Balderas Castelazo to Gral Brig Jefe Servicio Secreto, February 26, 1948, AHDF/JP/ISSS-10/65, 1948; *La Prensa*, February 26, 1948.

44. Fernando Novoa to Alemán, Federal District, February 21, 1948, AGN/MAV-541/347.

45. AGN/MAV-541/347.

46. *La Prensa*, February 28, 1948.

47. AGN/MAV-541/347.

48. Clippings, n.d., AHDF/JP/ISSS-10/65, 1948.

49. Recorte de Ultimas Noticias de Excélsior, February 27, 1948, AHDF/JP/ISSS-10/65, 1948.

50. *La Prensa*, February 28, 1948.

51. *La Prensa*, February 28, 1948.

52. *La Prensa* February 29, 1948.

53. *La Prensa*, February 28, 1948.

54. Telegram from José de la Mora, Comité Estatal de la Sociedad Revolucionarios Mártires de Rio Blanco, DF, to Alemán, February 27, 1948, AGN/MAV-541/347.

55. *La Prensa*, February 28, 1948.

56. Another agent went days later to survey Veracruzano public opinion and found widespread support (AHDF/JP/ISSS-10/65, 1948).

CHAPTER 15 | *Tanalís Padilla*

RURAL EDUCATION, POLITICAL RADICALISM, AND *NORMALISTA* IDENTITY IN MEXICO AFTER 1940

In December 1951, Jesús Robles Martínez, one of the leaders of Mexico's official teachers' union, declared that the *leyenda negra*, portraying teachers as the perpetual seeds of social disruption, had finally been laid to rest.[1] Robles and other *charro* leaders were referring to the hostility of right-wing sectors of society to the revolutionary state's educational endeavors. But Robles's statement was not a critique of the revolution's antagonists; rather, it indicated how the government had sought to tame teachers' penchant for political mobilization. Teachers and their union leaders had been at the heart of the radical process of educating the rural masses since the 1920s. But as the state moved rightward after 1940 this role became increasingly inconvenient. As a result, the SEP tried to rein in the radical tendencies it had previously instilled in its army of civil missionaries.

Efforts to pacify educators produced mixed results. On one hand, the social ascendancy promised by a career in education led ambitious teachers to fall dutifully in line with official dictates. Moreover, teachers could be remarkably adept at inserting themselves into local power structures. Their reputation as the "anti-*cacique*" notwithstanding, "the potential of [the] educational project for colonization by caciques old and new has not always been recognized."[2] Caciques were key to the PRI's rule, and teachers often successfully played this role of power broker by appropriating the revolution's emancipatory rhetoric to establish their own spheres of influence.[3] On the other hand, teachers also represented an important and durable component of opposition to the PRI regime. From the formation of independent union movements, such as the Movimiento

Revolucionario del Magisterio (MRM) in the 1950s and the Coordinadora Nacional de Trabajadores de la Educación (CNTE) in the 1970s, to dramatic actions such as the 2006 Oaxaca rebellion, teachers continue to be at the heart of grassroots resistance in Mexico. Just as significant are the numerous instances of educators acting as progressive community organizers and guerrilla leaders that provide iconic examples of the radical nature of Mexico's *normalistas*. In fact, few institutions within the educational system have had as strong a reputation for political radicalism as the *normales rurales*, the rural teacher training colleges.

This chapter analyzes the political radicalism of the normales rurales during the 1960s, when student activism was particularly strong. The Cuban Revolution emerged as an important reference point for *normalista* militancy, but their politicized identity also was rooted in Mexico's own educational policy. The early emphasis on socialist education, the poverty from which students originated, the state's abandonment of the countryside after 1940, and the experience of these teachers in the communities where they taught all imbued rural educators with a righteousness that fueled involvement in political struggles.[4] Together, these factors helped construct a specific normalista identity that acquired mythic proportions in both popular and official circles.

The tension between the state and the normales rurales highlights that steady progression toward authoritarianism or a mid-century *dictablanda* elucidated by this volume. Politically, rural teacher training colleges demonstrate the contradiction beneath the revolution's institutionalization: socialist ideals both survived and formed the basis of new forms of radicalism. Materially, the schools gave children of humble origin a path to social mobility, an especially important escape valve for the countryside given the lack of rural development. On the cultural front, the normales rurales upheld the image of Mexico as a nation possessing a rural soul, an essence that would justly and progressively be transformed into a modern one. That was the ideal at least, for when students attempted to make this vision a reality, state repression was not long in coming.

Rural Education and the Mexican Revolution

In the years after the revolution rural education became a central concern of Mexico's reformers. Although priorities shifted over time, three major aims stood out. First, teachers often helped communities with the logistical details involved in gaining *ejido* lands. In this way they linked the abstract ideals of nationhood taught in their classrooms with more material benefits. Teachers thus personified the social justice promised by the revolutionary government. At the same time, the SEP was also one of the primary instruments of national integration. Although Mexican intellectuals could blur the lines between *campesinos* and *indígenas*, they were adamant that they would not institute a U.S.-style system of reservations or segregation. Moisés Sáenz, an anthropologist who became the undersecretary of education, affirmed that the two goals of rural education were "the incorporation of the great mass of indigenous people into the Mexican family, [and] the formation of a rural spirit."[5] Finally, teachers were expected to instruct communities on the best farming methods. The centrality of agriculture to the educational endeavor is perhaps best expressed by the head of the cultural missions, Rafael Ramírez, who proclaimed that since "it is agriculture that is one of the main concerns in the lives of campesinos, rural education needed to capture that interest and become *agricultural by nature*."[6]

To train these teachers, the government established the first state normal school in 1922 in Tacámbaro, Michoacán. The normales rurales subsequently underwent several structural transformations, and individual schools often changed locations. In the 1920s there were three main institutions charged with rural education: the cultural missions, the regional normales, and the central agricultural schools. These latter institutions, built during the administration of Plutarco Elías Calles (1924–28), were designed to modernize agricultural production. Built as cooperatives of between one and two hundred students, the central agricultural schools were equipped with modern farming machinery and given large estates to cultivate. In the 1930s, the SEP fused these institutions into regional schools for campesinos, where in four years students could become either agricultural technicians or rural schoolteachers. The schools were coeducational, structured as cooperatives, placed a strong emphasis on self-sufficiency and self-governance, and adopted a socialist educational philosophy that emphasized teachers as both cultural and political leaders. At their peak during Cárdenas's presidency, there were thirty-five such regional schools. When Avila Camacho became president, however, rural education was restructured once again. The new government cut funding, closed several institutions, separated the training of agricultural technicians and teachers, eliminated socialist education, standardized the curriculum to match that of urban normales, and returned to training men and women in separate rather than coeducational institutions.[7] By the end of Avila Camacho's term, normales had declined from twenty-six to eighteen.[8] In the 1950s the number of normales rebounded before suffering a drastic reduction in 1969, when President Gustavo Díaz Ordaz (1964–70) closed fourteen of the twenty-nine institutions. This move elicited widespread protests among normalistas, who saw the president's actions as a deliberate attack on student militancy.

Designed specifically for the sons and daughters of campesinos (although the children of rural schoolteachers could also attend), the normales provided both avenues for upward social mobility and a willing army of missionaries trained to bring modernity and civilization to Mexico's remotest corners. Given the agrarian mission of rural schools, the architects of the new educational system argued that it was campesinos who would constitute the most committed apostles. The philosophy behind the normales thus encapsulated the new revolutionary order brought about by the revolution: the breakdown of a rigid social hierarchy and the incorporation of peasants into a nation-state concerned with social justice.

Life at the Normales

The importance of their educational and redemptive mission emerges as a consistent theme in the life stories of normalistas. The journey to the normal typically began in a poor and remote community. Here the young adolescent, thanks to the initiative of a teacher or family member, was encouraged to enter one of the normales, often against the desires of his or her parents. Once admitted, life at the boarding school was austere and rigid. Far away from their families, students turned to their peers for solace and company, forming a bond that sometimes lasted a lifetime. On graduation, the journey began anew. The young teacher was dispatched to a faraway town. There, with only the most basic infrastructure and in hostile conditions fomented by the church's opposition to secular education, the young instructor taught the basics to children and adults alike. Equally important, the teacher also attempted to inculcate modern cultural practices, replacing superstitious and religious beliefs with rational, scientific thought, adopting new hygiene rituals and moderating alcohol consumption.

Individual student background and experiences varied, but the memories of the normalistas shared a common structure and epic quality. Although trained decades later, their narratives bore the imprint of the postrevolutionary golden age of the SEP. Ironically, given the state's use of education to counteract the church's power, the teachers' missions were shrouded in religious language and imagery. Vasconcelos, for example, declared in 1920, "let us initiate a crusade of public education, let us inspire a cultural enthusiasm akin to the fervor our ancestors instilled in the enterprises of religion and conquest."[9] Rural education was in essence part of the revolutionary state's official narrative.[10] In their protests normalistas consistently reminded the government of the normal's noble origins.

The government had quite deliberately established some normales on expropriated haciendas, giving the schools an air of poetic justice. To drive the point home, even those that were not built on old estates were constructed to resemble haciendas. While persistent underfunding made for an austere existence, the facilities themselves were extensive and included dormitories, dining halls, theaters, adjacent housing for teachers, farmlands, barns, silos, metal and carpentry workshops, as well as sports facilities that often included swimming pools. To twelve-year-olds arriving from communities where the elementary school often consisted of a one-room shack in which students of all grades learned together, these institutions made a powerful impression and opened a world of possibilities.

Central to memories of life in the normales are the rigorous nature of the scheduled responsibilities, the rustic infrastructure, and the adoption of a self-sacrificing missionary attitude. Yet most emphasize that despite the meager setting and scant food, conditions were preferable to the poverty of the countryside. José Ángel Aguirre, a normalista from Chihuahua, claims that,

> when I studied at Salaices we had to do without a lot. The food was meager. I was placed in a dorm where there was no bed, nothing. I had only the pair of sheets we had been asked to bring and we all slept on the floor. Of the four dormitories in the school, two had no beds and those were for the newly arrived. So we slept on the floor, on a bit of cardboard, and it was very cold, but would you believe it? I was in heaven! Because even if the food was meager, it was at least assured and where I was from, sometimes we had nothing to eat. But there was something else: I knew that studying was the only chance I had to escape the miserable condition in which we lived.[11]

Francisco Casimiro echoes this sentiment: "The school dorms had what my home didn't. For me it was something wonderful to be able to sleep alone in a bed, to have blankets, the fact that I was given clothes and food. It would have been hard to have that in my house. . . . We were even given an allowance!"[12] Manuel Arias tells a poignant story to illustrate the same point: "In my house there was a wicker basket that is known by different names in different regions. Here in the Tarahumara it is a 'chiquihuite,' 'huure,' or tortilla basket. Well that basket, even though it had been there for many years, was practically new. There was never a tortilla that fell into it because between the comal [griddle] and the basket, there were nine pairs of hands fighting for it and whoever caught it ate it." Even though Manuel remembers missing his family, he was thrilled to be at the normal. "A full belly makes for a happy heart! There were some who didn't last and returned to their homes. Not me, because I knew that if I went back I was going to be hungry but not at the normal, even if it was just beans and tortillas."[13]

The normales were bustling centers of activity. "Seen from above," reflected a former student, "they must have looked like beehives with teachers and students all engaged in multiple activities."[14] The rigorous schedule began at 5:30 A.M., when a military-style band sounded the wake-up call.

Five minutes later students had to be out in the courtyard of the school for roll call. Once completed, they had twenty minutes to wash up and make their bed. Their first class began at 6 A.M. An hour later students were to clean their assigned area, which could include yards, gardens, or classrooms. Breakfast was at 8 A.M. and, as with all meals, specific groups were in charge of serving the food or washing dishes afterward. Classes resumed at 9 A.M. and lasted until 1 P.M., after which the normalistas had the main meal of the day and could rest until 3 P.M., when a diverse set of activities began anew. These included tending to the school's crops and animals and taking workshops that ranged from carpentry to the use of agricultural machinery. This was also the time when students would rehearse dance, music, and poetry for their weekly Friday gatherings. Sports teams would also practice during this time, and special commissions in charge of making bread, tortillas, or clothing would tend to their tasks. Students were again free from 5 to 7 P.M., at which point they had a light meal before a mandatory hour of studying. A no noise call was issued at 10 P.M., when roll was taken to ensure that each student was in bed. Pupils had the weekend off, time they could use to take care of any pending personal issues or visit nearby towns.[15] Given the distance from their home communities, most students stayed in the normales throughout the school year.

To promote the ideal of democracy, the normales had a self-governing structure in which a student committee was in charge of enforcing adherence to the rules. This design was in accordance with the ideas of John Dewey, who argued that discipline must come from among the pupils so that they understood the logic of the regulations. Contrasting with this democratic ideal was the military-like quality of the school's daily function and a points system that penalized students through deductions if they neglected their duties or broke the rules. The number of points depended on the severity of the infraction and could eventually lead to expulsion.

Such structured discipline coupled with their educational mission gave the normales a redemptive quality reminiscent of Russia's 1930s Gorky colony. Anton Makarenko had created the colony for war orphans and sought to instill in them a strong work ethic and emphasize the collective as a means of liberating the individual.[16] In Mexico, this quality can be seen in the schools' very design: their self-sufficiency, discipline, and attention to matters such as personal hygiene. In fact, normalistas frequently refer to Makarenco's *The Pedagogical Poem* to describe the environment at the training colleges. Arias reflects that

> it was a place in the style of Makarenco where we the students were the teachers, in which the trumpet sound was the signal to begin or conclude

the day, where we had to do work in the field and in the kitchen. Without knowing it, we were, from the pedagogical point of view, a Montessori center. The Montessori method places the child, or the student in a certain environment and says, "Leave him. Give him the necessary elements and leave him. Don't even explain the issues. He himself will see the issues at stake, find them and resolve them."[17]

As well as looking back fondly on the daily hardships at the normales, former students also focus on the generation of strong bonds with their fellow students. Older students took it upon themselves to develop a mentoring relationship with incoming children. Herminia Gómez, who attended the normal in Saucillo, Chihuahua, remembers, "There was a way in which the students from the higher grades would adopt and teach us . . . I was placed on the committee in charge of food. 'Why me?' I asked. They said I was too skinny and they wanted to see if that would help me gain some weight."[18] Likewise, Belén Cuevas remembers, "When it was cold and we had to wash our face and brush our teeth we had to crack the ice with our toothbrush because sometimes the tubs of water were covered with ice. . . . The bathrooms were large and a bunch of us fit in. And sometimes there was no hot water, so with cold, cold water we had to shower. But I think, because of our youth, we didn't even feel it."[19] Moreover, these shared experiences created a tight connection among the students. Manuel Arias, recalls, "Our idols during our first, second and third year in the normal were the students in the higher grades. I don't completely remember the names of my teachers. But I remember exactly the names of my fellow students who were role models: the best orator, the one who could best recite poetry, the best conversationalist, the best debater."[20] Likewise, César Navarro, from the normal of San Marcos in the state of Zacatecas, relates:

> Five hundred students living together, interacting every day, well, that provides a special type of relationship, not necessarily idyllic, but by the nature of the normal's structure we were a tight-knit community where older students would care for the younger ones. . . . It was they who emphasized the importance of the normales, why they had been created. It was something they instilled in us very early on. . . . One of the many things I learned, because you have to share everything, is that a very special sense of solidarity is established in the life of a boarding school.[21]

The normales opened up a universe for these young students. In *Saltando la cerca*, a self-published autobiographical novel, Arias provides an important glimpse into how normalistas conceived their experience: "In that tiny universe kids from urbanized towns and mining towns and large agricultural towns such as the Laguna region interacted. This cultural mix would be . . . one of the first and most important sources of knowledge about other customs and paradigms that would fuel a sense of universal brotherhood and tolerance for that which was different."[22] Arias' narrative demonstrates the process by which students developed an awareness and eventually a progressive consciousness. "For despite our different origins," he continues, "there was a common denominator, that is a class-consciousness, a thirst to fix things because economically and even racially, [our] families were in the most difficult position."[23]

"The Teacher Had to Be Politicized"

Avila Camacho's right-ward shift reverberated through all levels of Mexico's educational establishment. One by one the tenets of socialist education were overturned, first by substituting scientific socialism with Mexican revolutionary socialism and eventually by eliminating references to socialism all together. Instead, education would now be guided by the principles of national and spiritual unity. Moreover, SEP officials increasingly spoke of tighter cooperation with the private sector. Unsurprisingly, overturning socialist education meant purging the education establishment of those suspected of being communist sympathizers. This included the abolition of normales' mixed dormitories, which had been supported by communists since the 1920s.[24]

Beyond reforming sleeping arrangements, the SEP also implemented other measures to reduce the autonomy of the normales. First, they isolated normales from surrounding communities by restricting the control they had over nearby rural schools, diminishing agricultural activities and eliminating the schools' cooperatives. Moreover, to tighten control over individual schools, SEP authorities began to demand detailed accounts of their internal workings.[25] A further attack came as the SEP imposed a uniform curriculum between urban and teacher training colleges. This measure was justified as a way to address the inferiority attributed to the education at rural normales. However, a significant sector of the normalistas identified this move as a way of undermining an educational system that had devoted special attention to the countryside.[26]

Yet such moves seemed to reinforce rather than diminish normalistas' identification with social justice. Two and a half decades after it had been overturned, students still identified strongly with socialist education and its underpinnings of social justice. As one normalista stated, "We felt part of that [Cardenista] mission and we defended it, not just as an educational project but in terms of what the teacher's role should be in the community. We read Rafael Ramírez, Moisés Sáenz, those preeminent figures of Mexican pedagogy. . . . There was a sense of belonging to the rural education project and to the normal rural. . . . So there was an academic commitment but also a social and political one that found expression in militant activism."[27] As it evolved, normalista activism would combine the principles of the 1910 revolution with the principles of the anti-imperialist struggles of the 1960s. But the revolutionary language of national construction continued to frame these ideals. For example, a 1967 student proclamation stated that the rural teacher "has not just been the professional locked inside the four walls of the classroom. He has been and continues to be a social promoter, a community organizer and a tireless defender of the principles that guided the Revolution."[28]

The preeminence of the Federación de Estudiantes Campesinos Socialistas de México (FECSM) was key to this dynamic. Formed in 1935, the FECSM had committees in every rural normal. But while the FECSM appears again and again in normalista demonstrations, government intelligence documents, and student testimonies, there are next to no studies of Mexico's oldest student organization. Like other leftist groups, it suffered numerous fractures, was plagued with factionalism, and, especially after 1969, had to operate as a semi-clandestine organization. Its internal documentation remains jealously guarded by a few of its veterans.

The FECSM's significance lay in its ability to foster a specific socialist identity that linked students and peasants. Moreover, the organization logistically could organize and coordinate mobilizations in training colleges across the country. José Luis Aguayo, who headed the FECSM in 1965, stated that this society was key to forging "the normalista way of thinking." He characterized the rational for the organization in the following way: "The student society was to contribute to the socialization, democratization and politicization of the new teachers. The Club of Political and Ideological Orientation (COPI) was an affiliate to the FECSM and existed in every normal, contributing to our political consciousness because we considered political formation one of the most important qualities in teachers. This simple concept, that the teacher should be politicized, is very hard to understand nowadays. But we were formed with it because to be a good citizen at the service of the fatherland, one had to be politically informed." This notion, at one time key to Mexico's revolutionary educational system, had virtually disappeared by the early 1960s, according to Aguayo. He concludes that "only in the normales rurales was it preserved."

Aguayo attributes the persistence of this distinct normalista identity to the FECSM, which remained loyal to the revolution's original educational philosophy. "That is what allowed this thought to stay alive, and permitted the formation of teachers that had the same political and ideological substance." Aguayo terms this spirit "the normalista self."[29] Moreover, it is clear that the FECSM's labors created an environment in which political organizing flourished. César Navarro, for example, recalls that it was at a FECSM assembly in the normal of San Marcos where he first heard the Second Declaration of Havana. "I assure you I didn't understand a thing! I was too young." But its significance became etched in his mind. "The declaration was on a 33 record that was guarded like a great treasure among the students." It was also through the FECSM that Navarro found out about guerrilla leaders such as Arturo Gámiz and Lucio Cabañas, both of whom gave speeches at the organization's assemblies. "It was a formative process," Navarro explains, "after five or six years attending such assemblies you're bound to pick up *something*, even how to organize an assembly, how to put an agenda together, how to come to an agreement. We would vote and end by singing the Federation's anthem, the International Union of Students' . . . anthem and we would always close with the Internationale. Still today they sing the Internationale at the normales' assemblies."[30]

"The Cuban Revolution Invigorates Us"

During the 1960s, the normales were characterized by extensive student activism. Although this normalista identity suggested means of political mobilization, local political and socioeconomic problems channeled and focused discontent. Aguayo, a student from Salaices, reflects on this process:

> Because we lived in such precarious conditions and due to the great difficulties that we had in obtaining any material improvements, we were rebels, and very sensitive to social problems. The political thought of normalistas evolved in accordance with the country's situation. During the first stage the hope was that students would participate alongside communities and that the school would reach out technically, culturally and organizationally toward the communities. As the problems in the towns became more complicated, the type of leadership of teachers and future teachers also changed. They went from protest to rebellion to the aspiration of a new society for all of Mexico.[31]

Normalistas never had to look far to put their ideals of social justice into practice. Engagement with the surrounding community had been an ideal that lay at the very heart of the normales rurales since their origins. Herminia Gómez, a student at the normal of Saucillo, relates that "the people would themselves ask us to participate, to show our solidarity with them. For example, when they closed down this plywood factory the workers organized a march from Parral to Chihuahua and they would come to the normales to invite us and ask for our support. Of course we supported them! We supported workers, students at other schools and campesinos."[32] As Lucio Cabañas,

Guerrero's famed guerrilla leader, recalled, "those of us from Ayotzinapa, from the normal rural, would go into all the tiny little hamlets, have demonstrations and organize campesinos. In fact, as student leaders in Ayotzinapa we'd collect clothes for the poor campesinos who didn't even have anything to wear and would approach us at Ayotzinapa."[33] Raúl Álvarez Garín, a leader in the 1968 student movement in Mexico City, recalls that in Saucillo it was the female "normalistas who headed the land invasion precisely because the *guardias blancas* and the army, hesitated a little before shooting them. It was harder for them to first hurt the young students. These were not spontaneous actions, we had rehearsed them."[34]

Across the country Mexico's normalistas participated in land takeovers alongside campesinos, aided striking workers, and formed an important part of Mexico's student movement. In Chihuahua, normalistas were especially active within the Unión General de Obreros y Campesinos Mexicanos (UGOCM). Government agents noted that teachers as well as students sympathized with the land squatters, and the director of Saucillo was replaced due to such sympathies.[35] In some cases, students even led invasions and, they emphasized, female students would dress up as men and mingle among the ranks of campesinos.[36] Other reports more explicitly condemned such gender transgressions, noting that the thirteen girls from Salaices who led land invasions "slept in the open field alongside campesinos, undermining the honor that lady students should preserve."[37] When the leaders of one invasion were detained in February 1964, almost the entire student body of Saucillo and a significant number of those from Salaices demonstrated outside the municipal jail to demand their freedom.[38]

The political mobilization in Chihuahua's two rural training colleges is especially significant because of the 1965 guerrilla assault on the military headquarters of Ciudad Madera. Led by Arturo Gámiz, a rural schoolteacher, and Pablo Gómez, a young medical doctor (who was also a normal rural teacher), the strategy resembled Fidel Castro's attack on La Moncada barracks and is often cited as inaugurating Mexico's era of guerrilla movements. The attacks failed and eight of the dozen or so participants were killed. Such dramatic actions resulted from the government's refusal to heed more moderate measures taken in previous years by the UGOCM. The attacks reverberated in the normales of Salaices and Saucillo where, with proclamations such as, "Let us continue the revolutionary movement in Madera" and "They buried their bodies but not their ideas," students defended guerrilla actions and protested against the government's retaliation.[39]

Even outside Chihuahua, the Madera attack sparked debate within normales about the strategy deemed necessary to achieve change. Lucio Cabañas, head of the FECSM from 1961 to 1963, spoke of the need to make a revolutionary jump from peaceful protest to armed revolt. Navarro's memories are telling:

> I first met Lucio and Arturo at one of the concert-like assemblies we had at the normal. This gives you an idea of the type of environment at the normales. The following year we heard what happened in Ciudad Madera. We sent letters, telegrams, fliers, because, well, they had been our *compañeros*. . . . That environment makes it so that you find out what's happening in other normales . . . the fact that we had known Arturo and now he was dead and the action itself was amazing, incredible. But it also led us to ask "What is happening here?"[40]

Answering such questions led normalistas to reflect on their own life histories and begin to place the poverty of their own families in the context of Mexico's highly skewed socioeconomic hierarchy. For example, Manuel Arias's father died of silicosis after years of working for an American-owned mine in Chihuahua. Arias himself had taken odd jobs that ranged from shining shoes to selling tamales. Before entering the normal, he even worked as a gardener in an American neighborhood in Chihuahua. "That's when I found out how the *gringos* lived. Their kids appeared straight out of a Gerber commercial. . . . They had bikes that they just left lying on the grass. They had grass! In my neighborhood there were only rocks. They had swimming pools. We didn't even have drinking water. . . . I was the example of poverty in the middle of insulting abundance. And that had an impact on me. That, and the way my father and his fellow co-workers were treated at the mine."[41]

"In Chihuahua," wrote Jesús Santos Valdés, general inspector of northern Mexico's normales rurales, "everything is grand, even the injustice."[42] Entitled *Madera: razón de un martiriologio*, his text presents a detailed account of Chihuahua's land tenure structure, socioeconomic indicators, and government repression. He concludes with photographs of the funeral for the six fallen soldiers—given full military honors—juxtaposed to the grizzly images of Madera's eight slain guerrillas whose bodies were thrown into a common grave. Playing on the double meaning of *tierra* as both land and dirt, the governor of Chihuahua, Práxedes Giner Durán, is said to have instructed: "Since it was tierra they fought for, give them tierra until they've had enough."[43]

Before Gámiz met his demise, he had spoken about his motivations, claiming that "nothing has infused the oppressed of the Americas with so much hope, confidence in the future and the certainty of victory, as the Cuban Revolution."[44] His words suggest yet another layer of normalista political consciousness. While students at the teacher training colleges became radicalized by immediate conditions rather than the triumph of the Cuban Revolution itself, the island's revolution lent a framework of legitimacy and sense of righteousness to their struggle. As it had during the last few years of the Jaramillista struggle in Morelos, and as it would become in Lucio Cabañas' insurrection in Guerrero, the Cuban Revolution provided a dynamic new frame of reference.[45] Not only was Cuba important for those who debated the possibilities of armed struggle, it also sparked intense discussion about the nature of Mexico's own revolutionary heritage. As Eric Zolov states, the island's example "exacerbated and ultimately helped crystallize ideological tensions" in Mexico itself.[46] Cuba's socialist reforms, especially in the realm of education and land distribution, vividly exposed the limitations of Mexico's institutionalized revolution. Finally, Cuba's ability to resist U.S. aggression further propelled a David and Goliath sense of possibility to popular struggles across the globe. In Mexico, official nationalist rhetoric notwithstanding, elites had long partnered with their northern neighbors. UGOCM peasant squatters used to take over U.S.-owned lands by raising the Mexican flag and symbolically reclaiming that territory for Mexico.[47]

It is not surprising that the Cuban Revolution became a constant reference for normalistas. Alma Gómez, daughter of Pablo Gómez, one of the leaders of the Madera attack, and herself a normalista, provides a vivid picture of how the Cuban Revolution shaped life at the normales rurales. "In the normal, on May 23, 'Student's Day' there were a series of activities, among them a parade with various floats. And there is a picture—which must have been taken in 1961—where, on one of those floats, the girls are dressed with beards and in olive green clothing. That was the influence of the Cuban Revolution, and how it came all the way over there." In her own house, remembers Alma, "my dad listened to Radio Habana Libre on a short-wave radio . . . every day at dawn when I awoke my dad was listening to Radio Habana. We would hear the speeches of Fidel, of Che, all of that. And well, then there was also a campaign with people on the left of solidarity and support for the Cuban Revolution."[48] In 1967 the graduating class of Saucillo voted to call themselves the "Castro Ruz Class" and wanted this name explicitly printed on their diplomas.[49] So strong was the aura created by the Cuban Revolution in the normales that even relatively apolitical students absorbed some of the rhetoric. When Belén Cuevas studied at Saucillo, for example, she "was never really aware of politics . . . I was very sociable. I was always on the social events or recreational committee, organizing tributes to the flag." Yet when Belén was assigned to her first job in a remote community and one of the family members with whom she stayed asked if she was Catholic, she felt at a loss because, she narrated, "in those times we were so filled with the ideas of Fidel Castro that, very clandestinely, we would listen, sometimes from one of our teachers' radios, we would listen to Radio Habana. So we were filled with socialist ideas, of protest, of socialism."[50]

Harnessing the state-backed sense of mission to new demands, students carried their ideas of socialist transformation and international solidarity to the communities where they taught. José Luis Aguayo, for example, was teaching in Guadalupe Hidalgo, a small community in Mexico's northern sierra, when he received the news of Che Guevara's assassination. "So we had a vigil for Che, right there in the middle of the sierra. I pronounced a few words, badly interwoven, about the figure of Che, and someone else sang something, and that's how we did the vigil. That shows the kinds of preoccupations we had, in a really rustic and difficult place where we couldn't do much socially but we'd do these things."[51]

Given such political activities, it is no wonder that the rural teacher training colleges gained notoriety in official circles in which they were frequently deemed nests of communists. One government report, for example, stated that Saucillo and Salaices "are graduating educators who deform their social and educational duties and who as teachers constitute real problems in the communities where they are assigned. Their anarchist attitudes provoke confusion and disorientation especially among campesinos."[52] In March 1968 the newspaper El Universal published a declaration from Mexico's Youth Confederation (an organization linked to the PRI) that read, "The rural teacher training schools, today diseased with anti-patriotic sentiments, should be closed. . . . They have become centers purely of political agitation [and] it's too expensive to sustain these parasitic institutions."[53]

An attack on the normales rurales was not long in coming. In 1969 the SEP implemented an overhaul of the system, an act students interpreted as retaliation for the 1968 student movement in general and a strike against normalista organizing in particular. In a move protested throughout the training colleges, the government shut down fourteen of the country's twenty-nine normales rurales, turning them into technical agricultural schools. The remaining fifteen suffered a further blow: the elimination of the first three years of study in which students completed their secondary education. Rather than entering the normal rural after completing elementary school, students now had to finish junior high before enrolling. This measure considerably undermined the spirit and practice behind the normales rurales, for if in many areas students barely had access to primary education in their home communities, secondary education was next to impossible. Aside from the structural limitations this now imposed on potential students, normalistas argued that this measure was the government's way of avoiding the politicization of younger students by their older peers.

The measure elicited a wave of protest. The FECSM denounced the reforms, stating that they aimed at "repressing the independent struggle of the young and working masses of our country." They claimed the move "[represented] one more link in the long chain of retaliations against those who participated in the popular student movement begun on July 26 of last year."[54] Normalistas and campesinos employed two distinct arguments to defend the schools. On the one hand, they claimed they had their roots in the 1910 revolution. "The normales rurales were born from the revolutionary struggle," stated a letter from graduates of the normal rural of Roque, Guanajuato. Implementing the proposed reform, it continued, "means going backwards on the ideals that [are] crystallized in the Mexican Constitution."[55] Similarly, campesinos from Comalillo, Guanajuato, declared that the normales rurales were "the only living legacies left from the revolution fought by Villa and Zapata."[56] On the other hand, they also argued that they offered valuable opportunities to the poor. Mixing a clear sense of history, class consciousness, and the apposite appropriation of official discourse, another community protested: "Since we're always hearing talk about cultural progress don't make us think that we continue to live in the era of *Porfirismo* when only the children of the bourgeoisie had access to education."[57] Another letter to President Díaz Ordaz drove this point home: "It is you who are always going on about how there shouldn't be illiteracy, that there should be education in Mexico. In what way, if you now want to eliminate the normales rurales, the only hope of the campesino?"[58]

Reflecting on the closure of half of the rural teacher training colleges, Navarro states, "I find a direct correlation with the links between the student community, the teachers and the popular movements, since in the end you can't explain rural movements, especially insurrectional ones, without understanding the presence of the graduates of normales rurales."[59] It is unclear how the government determined which schools to close. Notably, some of the normales with strong traditions of organizing—Ayotzinapa, El Mexe, and Saucillo—were preserved. Perhaps the government feared that targeting them would elicit such a militant response that the protest would be too difficult to contain.[60] As it was, the 1969–70 academic year began with the normales rurales under a virtual state of siege.[61]

On the most prosaic level, halving the normales rurales was consistent with the policy of most administrations after Cárdenas, which devoted less attention and less financial support to the countryside. That the closures came so soon after the 1968 Tlatelolco massacre gave the measure a heightened political charge. Given the long tradition of student militancy at the normales rurales, it was difficult not to interpret it as an attack on popular organizing. Writing a history of the normal of Salaices—which was shut down in 1969—Aguayo, a graduate from that school, concluded that, "as a result of the bloody 1968 attack, the government unleashed an assault on the normales."⁶² Navarro sees it as a longer-term process: "Since General Cárdenas left office we were always at the brink of a precipice. That is, since the normales rurales were created they had to row upstream. Subsequent administrations always saw them as something that corresponded to a different era or a different project. For this reason, any resources, means of subsistence or support that the normales had was attained thanks to the struggle of its students. . . . It was an eternal fight for survival."⁶³

Conclusion

The political consciousness forged in the normales rurales stands as an important testament to the enduring legacies of Mexico's own rural educational project. It is also an example of the militant resistance generated by the abandonment of social reforms and the PRI's increasing authoritarianism. Despite the official party's claim to embody the revolution, it continuously reneged on the social tenets of the 1917 Constitution. In so doing it led many social groups, especially Mexico's youth, to search outside an increasingly repressive official party for a vision of social justice. Although the government played down its authoritarian interventions in a generally well-controlled national media, left-wing networks spread news of the crushing of schoolteachers and telegraph and oil workers's mobilizations in 1958, the curtailing of the railway workers's strike in 1959, the murder of Rubén Jaramillo in 1962, and the arrest of land invaders throughout the period. When the government massacred students peacefully demonstrating in Tlatelolco's plaza in 1968, the party lost any pretense of revolutionary justice.

"The Cuban Revolution invigorates us," normalistas declared at a 1961 FECSM gathering in Michoacán. There is a "need to establish a constant and collective dialogue that seeks to find methods and forms so our ideas reach the government of Mexico," continued the proclamation.⁶⁴ Because of their history, design, and student body, the normales rurales became a natural place to link student and campesino grievances. The political consciousness forged in such an environment drew on a series of factors that crystallized in radical action with such frequency that these institutions became famed—and maligned—for their militancy. That emblematic guerrilla figures such as Arturo Gámiz, Pablo Gómez, and Lucio Cabañas were intimately linked to the rural teacher training colleges is somewhat ironic: the very schools the revolutionary government had once designed to create a loyal citizenry were now producing its most militant foes. In a sense, however, the architects of Mexico's rural education succeeded in creating the apostles of the revolutionary state: as subsequent administrations abandoned those ideals, it was rural schoolteachers who most militantly raised their voices in protest.

Notes

1. Luis Hernández, "Misael Núñez Acosta: Relato de una infamia," *La Cultura en México/Suplemento de Siempre!* 1471 (September 2, 1981): 7–8. I am grateful to Paul Gillingham and Benjamin Smith for their thoughtful suggestions on this article. Likewise, I thank Heather Fowler-Salamini for her comments on the conference paper upon which this piece is based. I undertook some of the revisions while a fellow at the Institute for Historical Studies at the University of Texas at Austin.

2. Paul Gillingham, "Ambiguous Missionaries: Rural Teachers and State Façades in Guerrero, 1930–1950," *Mexican Studies* 22, no. 2 (summer 2006): 336.

3. See, for example, Benjamin Smith, "Inventing Tradition at Gunpoint: Culture, Caciquismo and State Formation in the Región Mixe, Oaxaca (1930–1959)," *Bulletin of Latin American Research* 27, no. 2 (2008): 215–34.

4. In this sense my study is consistent with recent works that privilege local historical dynamics to explain grassroots struggles in Latin America during the Cold War. See Gilbert Joseph and Daniela Spenser, eds., *In from the Cold: Latin America's New Encounter with the Cold War* (Durham, NC: Duke University Press, 2008).

5. Engracia Loyo, ed., *Casa del pueblo y el maestro rural mexicano* (Mexico City: SEP, 1985), 25.

6. Loyo, *Casa del pueblo*, 34 (emphasis in original).

7. This background description is based on Alicia Civera Cerecedo, "La legitimación de las Esculas Normales Rurales," *Documentos de Investigación*, no. 86 (Zinacantepec: Colegio Mexiquense, 2004), 5–7.

8. Alicia Civera Cerecedo, *La escuela como opción de vida: La formación de maestros normalistas rurales en México, 1921–1945* (Zinacantepec: Colegio Mexiquense, 2008), 327–28, 376–78.

9. Alicia Molina, ed., *José Vasconcelos: Textos sobre educación* (Mexico City: SEP, 1981), 208.

10. *Los maestros y la cultura en nacional, 1920–1952*, vols. 1–5 (Mexico City: Museo Nacional de Culturas Populares/Dirección General de Culturas Populares, 1987).

11. Author's interview with José Angel Aguirre Romero, February 12, 2008, Chihuahua, Chihuahua.

12. Author's interview with José Francisco Casimiro Barrera, September 12, 2008, Morelia, Michoacán. Casimiro refers here to the "Partida de Recreación Educativa" (Educational Recreation Contribution, or PRE), a small sum of money for personal expenses that each student received every week.

13. Author's interview with Manuel Arias Delgado, February 13, 2008, Chihuahua, Chihuahua.

14. José Luis Aguayo Alvarez, *Salaices: Escuela normal rural formadora de maestros* (Chihuahua: Ediciones del Azar, 2002), 105.

15. José Luis Agayo Alvarez, ed. *Un paseo por los recuerdos* (Chihuahua: La Asociación Civil de Exalumnos de Salaices, 2007), 41–42.

16. See Anton Makarenko, *Poema Pedagógico* (Mexico City: Ediciones de Cultura Popular, 1975).

17. Author's interview with Manuel Arias Delgado, February 13, 2008, Chihuahua, Chihuahua.

18. Author's interview with Herminia Gómez, February 13, 2008, Chihuahua, Chihuahua.

19. Author's interview with Belén Cuevas, February 12, 2008, Chihuahua, Chihuahua.

20. Author's interview with Manuel Arias Delgado, February 12, 2008, Chihuahua, Chihuahua.

21. Author's interview with César Navarro, September 5, 2009, Mexico City.

22. Manuel Arias Delgado, *Saltando la cerca* (Chihuahua: self-published, 2007), 44–45.

23. Author's interview with Manuel Arias Delgado, February 13, 2008, Chihuahua, Chihuahua.

24. Civera Cerecedo, *La escuela*, 359–80.

25. Civera Cerecedo, *La escuela*, 399, 413–14, 393.

26. Greaves, *Del radicalismo a la unidad nacional*, 182.

27. Author's interview with César Navarro, September 5, 2009, Mexico City.

28. "Estado de Morelos," July 1, 1967, AGN/DFS-63-19-67/L2/H202-204.

29. Author's interview with José Luis Aguayo Alvarez, February 10, 2008, Chihuahua, Chihuahua.

30. Author's interview with César Navarro, September 5, 2009, Mexico City.

31. Aguayo Álvarez, *Un paseo por los recuerdos*, 71–72.

32. Author's interview with Herminia Gómez, February 13, 2008, Chihuahua, Chihuahua.

33. Luis Suárez, ed., *Lucio Cabañas, el guerrillero sin esperanza* (Mexico City: Roca, 1976), 53.

34. "Los años de la gran tentación," interview with Raúl Álvarez Garín, in Hermann Bellinghausen, ed., *Pensar el 68* (Mexico City: Cal y Arena, 2008), 30.

35. "Memorandum," June 6, 1963, AGN/DFS-100–5–1–63/L6/H 307; AGN/DFS-100–5–1–964/L2/H110–11108/24/1964.

36. "Memorandum," February 20, 1964, AGN/DFS-100–5–3–64/L1/H 413–416.

37. "Memorandum: Antecedentes sobre los distintos problemas que presentan las escuelas normales rurales en el estado," April 15, 1964, AGN/DFS-100–5–1–64/L8/H52–54.

38. "Memorandum," February 19, 1964, AGN/DFS-100–5–3–64/L1/H-406–407; "Memorandum," February 20, 1964, AGN/DFS-100–5–3–64/L1/H-413–416; "Memorandum," February 24, 1964, AGN/DFS-100–5–3–64/L1/H424–425.

39. "Estado de Chihuahua," October 12, 1965, AGN/DFS-100–5–1/L14/H206–210; "Estado de Chihuahua," October 5, 1965, AGN/DFS-100–5–1–65/L14/H160–162.

40. Author's interview with César Navarro, September 5, 2009, Mexico City.

41. Author's interview with Manuel Arias, February 13, 2008, Chihuahua, Chihuahua.

42. *Madera: Razón de un martirologio* (Mexico City: n.p., 1968), 12.

43. Laura Castellano, *México Armado, 1943–1981* (Mexico City: Ediciones Era, 2007), 80.

44. Castellano, *México Armado*, 69.

45. See Tanalís Padilla, *Rural Resistance in the Land of Zapata: The Jaramillista Movement*

and the Myth of the Pax-Priísta, 1940–1962 (Durham, NC: Duke University Press, 2008); Alexander Aviña, Spectres of Revolution: Peasant Guerrillas in the Cold War Mexican Countryside (Oxford: Oxford University Press, forthcoming). For a different view see O'Neill Blacker, "Cold War in the Countryside: Conflict in Guerrero, Mexico," The Americas 66, no. 2 (2009): 181–210. She sees a starker separation between local histories and international events. The latter, she argues, were the domain of urban activists.

46. Eric Zolov, "¡Cuba sí, Yanquis no! The Sacking of the Instituto Cultural México-Norteamericano in Morelia, Michoacán, 1961," in In from the Cold: Latin America's New Encounter with the Cold War, ed. Gilbert M. Joseph and Daniela Spenser (Durham, NC: Duke University Press, 2008), 214.

47. Hubert C. De Grammont, "La Unión General de Obreros y Campesinos," in Historia de la Cuestión Agraria Mexicana: Política estatal y conflictos agrarios 1950–1970 (Mexico City: Siglo Veintiuno Editores, 1989), vol. 8, 244.

48. Author's interview with Alma Gómez, February 3, 2008, Mexico City.

49. "Estado de Chihuahua," June 15, 1967, AGN/DFS-100–5–1–67/L20/H391.

50. Author's interview, Belén Cuevas, February 12, 2008, Chihuahua, Chihuahua.

51. Author's interview, José Luis Aguayo Alvarez, February 10, 2008, Chihuahua, Chihuahua.

52. "Memorandum: Antecedentes sobre los distintos problemas que presentan las escuelas normales rurales en el estado," April 15, 1964, AGN/DFS-100–5–1–64/L8/H52–54.

53. El Universal, March 14, 1968.

54. "En Defensa de las Normales Rurales Contra la Reforma Antipopular y Reaccionaria," August 8, 1969, AGN/DFS-63–19–69/L7/H59–66. The FECSM went on to criticize the 1956 closure of the Politécnico's internado. For that struggle see Pensado, chapter 16, this volume.

55. Comité de la Sociedad de Ex-Alumnos de Roque to President Gustavo Díaz Ordaz, July 16, 1969, Archivo Histórico de la Secretaría de Educación Pública-Consejo Nacional Técnico de la Educación (hereafter AH/SEP-CONALTE), Caja 101, exp. 1341, leg. 1.

56. Mauricio Alvarado and six other signatories to Luis Alvarez, President of the Consejo Nacional Técnico de la Educación, n.d., AH/SEP-CONALTE-101/1341/1.

57. Roberto Jiménez and twenty-six other signatories to Luis Alvarez, President of the Consejo Nacional Técnico de la Educación, July 18, 1969, AH/SEP-CONALTE-101/1341/1.

58. Antonio García to Luis Alvarez, July 17, 1969, AH/SEP-CONALTE-10/1341/1.

59. Author's interview with César Navarro, September 5, 2009, Mexico City.

60. La Jornada, February 20, 2000.

61. AGN/DFS-63–19–69/L5/H 26–33, July 29, 1969.

62. Aguayo Alvares, Salaices, 161.

63. Author's interview with César Navarro, September 5, 2009, Mexico City.

64. "Se informa en relación con las Escuelas Normales Rurales," April 29, 1961, AGN/DFS-63–3–61/L7/H108.

CHAPTER 16 | *Jaime M. Pensado*

THE RISE OF A "NATIONAL STUDENT PROBLEM" IN 1956

On September 27, 1956, a violent student brawl erupted on the streets of Mexico City. According to the newspapers, the fighting began when Augusto Velasco, president of the student-run university cafeteria, and fellow-student Luis Muñoz "violently attacked" another group of students. Muñoz, along with his "shock brigade," was quoted as saying before the attack: "We don't want any more agitation. [What] we want is to study." As "proof" of this alleged student attack, the conservative newspaper *Excélsior* printed a large photograph on its front page with the following description:

> The battle between students unfolded with great fury. Castillo Mota is shown giving . . . Luis Muñoz a phenomenal beating. The picture speaks for itself: Mota demonstrates his fighting abilities while Muñoz falls to the ground. It all occurred as a result of a division [within the Comedor] between students from the Universidad, those from the Politécnico, and those from the Normal School.[1]

Students were outraged at this and other coverage of the event by what they identified as the "mercenary media," and they began to circulate a variety of accounts that differed greatly from that of *Excélsior*, which, along with *El Universal*, *Novedades*, and the magazine *Tiempo*, had remained loyal to the government throughout this period.[2] To begin with, they rejected the newspaper's assertion that a "division between students" had led to the altercation. In fact, students in the cafeteria were more likely divided by regional differences than any rigid divisions based on their schools of origin.[3] More important was that they contended that the student brawl did not, in fact, take place. What actually happened was that a group of *pistoleros* (agent provocateurs) led by Castillo made a well-planned attack on a group of bona fide students who were protesting the closing of various Cárdenas-era projects designed to benefit low-income students. *Excélsior* documents this, but the accompanying narrative of the photo completely distorts the actual event. A student newspaper angrily asked, "Exactly which students was *Excélsior* referring to?" It couldn't be the individuals referenced in its front page, it remarked, "because we all know that they are hired thugs." According to the student newspaper, Castillo was part of the so-called Gorillas gang and had a lucrative career as a pistolero for the Department of the Interior. Some students went as far as to say that Nabor Carillo, the rector of the National Autonomous University of Mexico (UNAM), had paid for the attack.[4] Similarly outraged by the twisting of the facts by right-leaning journalists, another student newspaper noted, "It is inconceivable to think that [provocateurs] . . . are employed by our schools . . . But the fact that they are portrayed in the media as the defenders of real students is even more inconceivable."[5]

Despite the students' claims government authorities moved quickly to arrest all the "communist agitators" who they claimed had been involved in the protest, including Nicandro Mendoza, the president of the Frente Nacional de Estudiantes Técnicos (FNET), and a dozen more young people who were picked up by the police for having organized the student strike at the Instituto Politécnico Nacional (IPN) earlier that year.[6] Following these arrests, and specifically responding to the increasing magnitude of the 1956 strike, District Attorney Julio Ramírez remarked: "The harm to the Politécnico and its students caused by Nicandro Mendoza and the other agitators is so extensive and serious that they all deserve to be indicted under the Law of Social Dissolution."[7]

This chapter argues that the 1956 student movement at the Politécnico was a defining moment in the history of Mexican student politics and resistance. More than 1968, this event signaled the end of one era of student activism and the beginning of a new one. The 1956 movement was the last in a series of public demonstrations demanding a return to Cardenista "popular politics." Yet, as the first sizeable student uprising of the Cold War era, this movement also marked the beginning of a new rhythm of student militancy and authoritarian reaction that would come to characterize the "long sixties."[8] Throughout this period, the government and conservative voices in the media challenged earlier, favorable interpretations of Mexico's youth by stressing the "unpatriotic" elements associated with the rise of the country's student problem.[9]

As a result, this chapter also proposes that the events of 1968 should be understood in the context of a series of continuities with 1956. As a handful of studies have demonstrated, this broader history of student activism reached its initial climax during the Morelia Congress of 1963, when young activists tried to bring the various leftist student organizations together under the umbrella of the new *Central Nacional de Estudiantes Democráticos* (CNED); returned with greater intensity between 1965 and 1968, when the Díaz Ordaz administration made it clear that it would not tolerate militant students or rebellious youths; and ended in the early to mid-1970s, when student unrest was channeled toward urban and rural guerrilla warfare.[10] In fact, as early as 1956 students not only started to articulate an incipient notion of democracy that aimed to challenge the authoritarian hierarchical structure and corruption of their schools (and the labor sector) but also began developing many of the repertoires of collective action that would be wheeled out by their successors across the 1960s.

Despite the longer history of student activism that took place within the broader context of the long sixties, the scholarship continues to see 1968 as a "watershed moment."[11] Indeed, middle-class students "woke up" during this crucial year to further challenge the state in a more confrontational and successful fashion. As stressed in this chapter, however, working-class students had been awake far longer. The omission of their history in the scholarship can be largely attributed to the crucial role that protagonists of the 1968 movement (*sesentaocheros*) have played in creating a mythology of 1968.[12] This group of elite leftists has not only been in charge of cultural production in Mexico for the last fifty years but also has published most of the history of student activism. Primarily interested in stressing the protagonist roles of their leading voices, they have, in general, minimized the important role students played in advancing new and revised ideas of democracy during the periods before and after 1968.[13] The student activism described here would grow in both intensity and sophistication in the aftermath of the 1956 strike. The same would prove true regarding the multiple legal and extralegal mechanisms of control put into place throughout this period by the state to contain young *revoltosos* (troublemakers). Besides the implementation of the Law of Social Dissolution and the use of *granaderos* (riot police), the state would also continue to rely on the illegitimate use of surgical violence and provocation at the hands of corrupt school authorities and thugs for hire.

The Founding of the Politécnico

The IPN was founded in 1936–37.[14] Its main goal was to serve the nation by educating the children of the working class in the latest technological advances.[15] Unlike UNAM, it was to enjoy an official relationship with the state that precluded institutional autonomy. The government designated its directors while its budget was to be drawn up with the exclusive goal of meeting the nation's greatest needs.

For decades, the link between the state and the institution hamstrung student independence. Students were encouraged to unite into a single organization representing all *politécnicos* (IPN students). In 1937 this coalition took the name the Federación Nacional de Estudiantes Técnicos or FNET. In return for student compliance, the government was to ensure that the schools were equipped with the latest technology and guarantee that students received practical training that would help meet the needs of the nation; it was charged with providing an education for all members of the popular sectors of society through the provision of full and partial scholarships, subsidized meals and dormitories, and committed to budget increases that would support the growing student population. This increased significantly in the nation's capital from 8,026 in 1942 to 37,429 in 1966.[16]

The quid pro quo established during the administration of Lázaro Cárdenas resembled many of the social contracts of the years following the revolution. And, at least initially, young politécnicos enthusiastically embraced the state's declared causes of social justice, anticlericalism, and anti-imperialism.[17] Soon, however, calls for a less authoritarian model of schooling would impinge on an already entrenched structure of state corporatism and alter the relationship between politécnicos and the state.

The Abandonment of Popular Education

In the aftermath of World War II, Mexico began to experience the tremendous economic growth of the "Mexican miracle," and between 1940 and 1966 gross domestic product grew 368 percent.[18] However, a closer look at other statistics reveals that this boom came at a high price. In particular, the "miracle" did not benefit all sectors of society equally. Roger Hansen noted, for example, that economic growth during this period did not imply a reduction of social and economic inequalities. He concluded that the cost of living index for working class families in the nation's capital grew from 21.3 in 1940 to 75.3 in 1950 (the index was 100 in 1954) and "real wages fell by perhaps as much as one-third between 1940 and 1950."[19] The situation did not improve during the next decade for the poorest 30 percent of families: they experienced a decline in their monthly incomes from an average monthly salary of 302 pesos in 1950 to 241 in 1963.[20] In contrast, the richest 30 percent of families saw an average increase in their monthly incomes from 1,132 pesos in 1950 to 2,156 in 1963.[21]

Economic disparities had an important effect on the composition of schools. Initially, more than 80 percent of students enrolled in the IPN came from the working, public, and peasant sectors.[22] Only a small fraction of politécnicos (4.7 percent) came from households in which their parents had a professional career.[23] A student enrolled in the Politécnico during the 1950s later noted during an interview that little had changed in the wake of the 1956 student protest: "the fact that we were students certainly put us in a privileged position; but in reality, the overwhelming majority of politécnicos were from the working class."[24]

The socioeconomic circumstances of the politécnicos differed from the overwhelming majority of students enrolled at UNAM during the same period. The first census taken at UNAM in 1949, for example, indicated that 29 percent came from parents who were described as merchants, 20.64 percent as public employees, and 10.58 percent as professionals. Unlike the majority of working class politécnicos, a total of 70 percent of all students enrolled at UNAM in the late 1940s could be broadly defined as members of the middle class.[25] David E. Lorey noted that little had changed over a decade later.[26]

The class differences between politécnicos and universitarios would influence the distinct political trajectories that these two groups of students would take during the following decades. Politécnicos, for example, became the principal critics of the amendment of article 3 of the constitution, which under President Cárdenas had declared that all elementary schools should follow a socialist pedagogical plan.[27] The changes to the constitution stated that education would be scientific, secular, democratic, compulsory, and national. Moreover, as part of what would be an ongoing effort to depoliticize students, the authorities declared that education would be free of any political bias.[28] The original announcement in 1941 was immediately followed by the removal of key proponents of popular education.[29] (In the countryside these included, as Padilla points out, entire institutions; nearly a third of the normales rurales were shut down.[30]) During the same period, debates over the trajectory of popular education dovetailed with other pressing internal issues. Government attacks against the so-called reds in the IPN gained substantial support in the business sector through influential members of the Confederation of Chambers of Manufacturing (CONCAMIN), which hoped to weaken public seats of power in the Politécnico to achieve privatization.[31]

Politécnicos did not take long to resist the conservative policies of the postrevolutionary state. The first signs of mass student discontent appeared inside the IPN in March 1942, after government authorities (supported by wealthy industrialists of the CONCAMIN group) announced that the IPN would be divided into trade schools. Student disgruntlement coalesced into a strike once again in April 1950, when President Miguel Alemán threatened to further weaken the IPN by depriving it of the vocational schools. Conciliatory efforts on the part of the government were enough for the student leaders to end the two strikes. Nevertheless, political grievances and socioeconomic frustrations among politécnicos would reach a boiling point during the 1956 protest and subsequently in 1968, when IPN students and their younger counterparts from the secondary schools (*vocacionales* and *preparatorias*) would create the most militant brigades of the movement and successfully expose the weakness of the infamous *granaderos* and the state.³²

The 1956 Student Protest and Conservative Reactions Published in the Press

On April 11, 1956, what began as a unanimous IPN strike soon exploded into one of the largest student uprisings in Mexico's history. Although the movement started in the politécnicos with twenty-five thousand students, it soon spread to students at the National Teachers' School, the Normal School, the School of Physical Education, and some thirty-three Rural Normal and Practical Agricultural Schools. By the first week of May, the movement had become national in scope and more than one hundred thousand students strong.³³

The two most important political demands made by the politécnicos were the immediate dismissal of Rodolfo Hernández Corso, the director of the IPN, and the implementation of a New Organic Law that would guarantee students autonomy and participation in the governance of the IPN.³⁴ From the standpoint of the politécnicos, Hernández Corso epitomized the insidious influence of the United States and its Cold War policies of international development. His education in the United States (he earned his MA at Northwestern University and his PhD at Stanford University) raised suspicion among students of pro-gringo bias.³⁵ But it was the director's support for one particular U.S. initiative that established his status among students as a symbol of "Yankee imperialism" and its "corrupt infiltration" of popular education. The initiative, known as Plan Columbia, was a project carried out under contract by Columbia Teachers College of New York to survey the needs of Mexican industry for technically trained workers and personnel and the facilities available in Mexico for such training.³⁶ Plan Columbia, in other words, had little to do with student politics. For politécnicos, however, it represented the initial and most egregious attempt by U.S. investors to promote the privatization of Mexican industries and eventually to replace Mexican workers and teachers with foreigners.³⁷ As a student who witnessed the strike remembered, "In this emerging environment of the Cold War, we saw everything with suspicion. Many of us were convinced that 'Uncle Sam' wanted to privatize our schools, our oil industry, and our lands."³⁸ A former IPN teacher similarly recalled that "the teachers of Columbia were going to indoctrinate our young students to the 'American way of life,' and to protest the potential replacement of our nationalist teachers with gringos, the working class youth of the Politécnico took their dissatisfaction to the streets."³⁹

In addition to representing Yankee dominance, Hernández Corso also came to represent the corrupt and abusive management typical of many government authorities. In a student newspaper, politécnicos accused him and his close associates of funding their own political campaigns by deliberate manipulation of the school budget.[40] Equating the director with corrupt union leaders, students rejected Hernández Corso's "politics of *charrismo*" as a mechanism for the blatant abuse of power inside the schools.[41] Students labeled him and his cronies "academic charros" who threatened to take away scholarships if students dared to vote for the "wrong" student representative.[42] For young politécnicos, there was little perceptible distinction between the corruption of both the unions and the universities.

Yet it also was clear to students that the IPN director was merely a representative of deeper structural problems and that the authoritarian character of the Politécnico was embedded in its very constitution. It was found, for instance, in the way the president handpicked directors with close ties to the government, without any consultation with the student population. To democratize the schools of the IPN, FNET representatives looked to a legal tool that would officially institute a different balance of power. They proposed a New Organic Law to create a Mixed Commission composed equally of school authorities and students.[43]

Students recognized that their cause could not succeed without taking their grievances to the streets in a more public and confrontational fashion. To this end, and without waiting for the blessing of the older generation of leftists (such as Vicente Lombardo Toledano, who had played an important supporting role in earlier student revolts and who unsuccessfully attempted to do likewise in 1956), they devised a number of innovative strategies of collective action that would be used by their successors in 1968, namely, informational brigades, hit-and-run political rallies, and the physical occupation of public space.[44]

Politécnicos organized information brigades to educate the public about their cause through organized off-campus sessions. With names that aimed to take back the symbols of the revolution from the state, such as the *Brigada Emiliano Zapata* and the *Brigada Lázaro Cárdenas*, these brigades traveled to other schools and nearby pueblos to inform the public about the importance of their movement.[45] Members of these brigades also traveled to factories (albeit with limited success) to link their struggle with an increasingly disgruntled working class, which two years later would attempt to break the control of *charro* leaders by launching another more organized wave of massive public uprisings to demand increased salaries and independent unions.[46]

Politécnicos also adopted a more spontaneous and confrontational tactic that came to be known as the "*mitin relámpago*," or "lightning rally." These comprised three or four students who, without prior permission, quickly organized political meetings at factory gates, street corners, markets stalls, and schools. These rallies had to be organized "in small numbers" and "performed rather quickly" because, as one of the leaders noted later in an interview, "gangs of [provocateurs] were always on our backs." Their primary goals were—as they would be again in 1968 and throughout the 1970s—to raise funds for the movement and denounce the "false accusations made daily against the students in the mercenary newspapers."[47] In particular, they accused journalists of *Excélsior* and *El Universal* of aligning themselves with the "reactionary" government that, in collaboration with powerful members of the business sector and leaders of the conservative opposition, wanted to eliminate the populist character of the Politécnico.[48]

For some of the more radical students, direct action also meant taking over property and spaces. At first this took the form of hijacking school buses, but as the uprising continued and the stance of the authorities hardened, a group of students began to apply more pressure by taking over classrooms, cafeterias, dormitories, and administrative offices. Once in physical possession of the buildings, politécnicos organized "self-defense guards" that future generations of students would continue to use to defend their "liberated territories" from government-sponsored provocateurs and granaderos.[49]

Efforts to liberate spaces temporarily gave politécnicos a number of minor victories, including a broader awareness on the part of a new generation of disgruntled and more militant students, who launched similar protests in other parts of the country, such as in Michoacán, where a movement also had acquired critical mass.[50] However, this increasingly confrontational stance against the government served as a double-edged sword. Negative press combined with the propaganda distributed by provocateurs not only distorted student aims but, as happened throughout the sixties, also portrayed young activists as "foreign" elements of "subversion."[51] Unable to accept the violence as a symptom of genuine social protest and incapable of seeing the students themselves as deliberate, reasoned, and adult dissenters, the conservative media attributed the students' violence to their immaturity and vulnerability to dangerous "outside influences."[52] Just a few days after the student strike erupted, one reporter for *Tiempo*, referring to the social subsidies politécnicos received from the government, angrily condemned the young students as "egotistical brats ... who had neglected to appreciate what the pueblo had given to them."[53] "What can we expect from this generation, which prefers subversion and anarchy?" an editorial in *Excélsior* asked.[54] A political attitude embraced by female students in the streets, others angrily lamented, contradicted Mexican (and thus appropriate) notions of femininity.[55] In short, the politécnicos were no longer mere "ungrateful children of the Revolution," as the media had insisted during previous student uprisings;

rather, by their association with communism they were "dangerous agents of unpatriotic forces."

Since the root cause of student unrest was the lack of respect for patriotic authority, the conservative press saw discipline as the only proper response. As throughout the Cold War era, it began to demand a more authoritarian stance on the part of the government to control the "increasingly dangerous" students. In the opinion of a growing number of journalists, sanctions needed to come from the top. To meet this national "crisis of authority," as one editorial commentator of *El Tiempo* put it, the legal apparatus of government could be applied in the form of a strict constitutional law that spoke directly about "obligations," just as laws existed that spelled out "constitutional rights."[56] Claiming to represent the sentiments of many private citizens, some wrote to newspapers and magazines imploring the president "to discipline" the "little Red demagogues," with "force if necessary," if they continued to "refuse to obey orders from their older authorities."[57] As would happen in 1968, others took their concern a step further by insisting that the "indecent" and "politically foreign" behavior of the students had become so "out of control" that vigilantism was necessary.[58] The implication was that the government, like an overindulgent parent, had been too soft with the revoltosos and that ordinary citizens needed to confront the students more directly to "reestablish order."[59] School authorities agreed, and they too would play an important role in pressuring the government to seek viable solutions to end the strike.

Alejo Peralta and the Employment of Agent Provocateurs

FNET representatives officially called off the seventy-two-day strike on June 21, 1956. The decision was made after President Ruíz Cortines sent to Congress a New Organic Law that aimed to answer some of the students' demands. The law guaranteed greater investments in the infrastructure of the Politécnico and called for the creation of a mixed commission, comprising equal numbers of students and professors, that would study the main technical, academic, and social problems of the Politécnico. Yet these and additional accords included in the law failed to resolve the fate of Hernández Corso, whose immediate removal from the Politécnico had been one of the strikers' central demands.[60] Fearing for his safety, Hernández Corso never set foot inside the Politécnico again.[61] In mid-August he was replaced by Alejo Peralta, who rapidly turned out to be a much more authoritarian figure. Echoing the concerns stressed in numerous newspapers, the new director lamented that "delinquent activism" had spread to other schools in Mexico, including a number of nearby secondary schools affiliated with UNAM as well as other provincial universities.[62] Peralta and the press demanded that the activists be stopped. Like "the rojillos" at the Politécnico, they stressed, these students also had begun to challenge their respective school authorities through public confrontations.[63] With a background as a wealthy businessman, the self-made millionaire believed that all the IPN's problems could be solved if it was run like a private enterprise.[64] Key to this shift was the depoliticization of the revoltosos who had been implicated in fomenting "disorder" at the Politécnico since the 1940s. The head of the Mexico City Police Department agreed with the new director's plan and promised to initiate a much harsher campaign against the rebellious students.[65]

The repression at the various schools initially came in the form of a series of systematic acts of violence and provocation against the students. School and government authorities financed pistoleros to discredit all student activists, encouraged a more aggressive effort on the part of the government to put down the revoltosos, and approved the arrest of the leading figures of the 1956 strike under the Law of Social Dissolution. For example, on one occasion preceding the imprisonment of Nicandro Mendoza, newspapers reported that a group of students wearing Politécnico sweaters had vandalized a movie house.[66] However, a closer look at student accounts reveals that these so-called students had nothing to do with the politécnicos. Following the vandalizing of the movie house, a group of protesters wrote the following declaration on a blackboard outside the main school of the Politécnico for all to read: "People of Mexico: [The politécnicos] would never dare assault the pueblo simply because we are part of it. It is the enemies of popular education who defame our glorious IPN through malicious and evil tricks. [It is they] who finance gangs of criminals . . . who create chaos in various parts of the city wearing sweaters with the colors of our school [white and maroon]."[67]

This and similar incidents denounced by strikers provided further evidence for a phenomenon whereby authorities hired professional thugs (later known as "porros") to intimidate student activists and discourage potential sympathizers. Nonetheless, these methods proved only partially effective, and the Mexican state, like other contemporary Latin American countries, resorted to military repression. This "last resort" to solve the nation's student problem would be repeated in 1968, when porros and riot police proved to be ineffective once more.[68]

Operation P and the "Celebrated" Reestablishment of Authority

On August 10, 1956, the Department of Education (SEP) announced that it was barring access to the boarding school and suspending all assistance (such as scholarships) to the students there. According to the school authorities, targeting dormitory residents was a "necessary" step at this point to protect the "real" students from the political "agitators" who had taken over the institution since 1950.⁶⁹ Police chief Molinar agreed. Echoing the conservative sentiments published in the press, he contended that student activists should be prosecuted as "enemies of the nation," in accordance with the most rigorous statutes of the law.⁷⁰ To this end, Molinar issued specific instructions to the motorized battalion, the new body of granaderos, and members of the Secret Service to "put a definite stop to all disorderly behavior" promoted by the politécnicos by arresting all "subversive students" who refused "to cooperate" with the authorities.⁷¹

The clampdown soon reached new heights. On September 23, 1956, President Ruíz Cortines called in the Federal Army to occupy the schools of the IPN. The Secretary of Defense, Matías Ramos, led the operation, which was labeled "Operation P," and involved eighteen hundred soldiers, more than three hundred granaderos, more than a hundred officers from the Judicial Police, and an indeterminate number of agents from the Federal Security Directorate (DFS). Once the IPN was occupied, the government ordered the battalion to arrest all "troublemakers" who refused to cooperate with the school and local authorities.⁷² Following the temporary arrests of more than three hundred interns, Peralta told a reporter that "the boarding school would be transformed into permanent barracks for the military" until order was fully restored. "If the FNET was found to be involved in a single act of protest that endangered the lives of the students," Peralta added, "we will ask the federal troops to use all necessary force."⁷³

According to various press accounts, the public was extremely satisfied with the actions. "At last," a number of individuals who wrote to the newspapers earnestly proclaimed, "the strike had ended" and "the nest of revoltosos had been shut down."⁷⁴ A number of politicians hastened to join the chorus of approval, including PANistas, who had historically been quite critical of the government but who, on this occasion, simply deemed "necessary" the closing of the boarding school.⁷⁵ Government officials voiced their support for the action in the newspapers and made sure to single out Alejo Peralta for praise. In *Novedades*, the deputy of the Federal District offered his congratulations to both President Ruíz Cortines and Alejo Peralta.⁷⁶ Even a handful of key Cardenistas, who had kept their distance from the strike, praised the military occupation of the IPN. For example, Lázaro Cárdenas's former secretary, Luis I. Rodríguez, claimed the repression was "a necessary measure" and announced that, "the behavior of the students of the Politécnico had gone too far." "They had trampled the most vital rights of the people," others insisted, and "the government only did what should have been done a long time ago."⁷⁷ State department officials in Mexico voiced comparable sentiments of approval.⁷⁸ Peralta supposedly received in "just two days . . . more than five hundred telegrams of support, sympathy, gratitude, and admiration from local neighbors, politicians, state officials, businessmen, teachers, and private individuals." In turn, Peralta declared the occupation of the IPN a "glorious victory" for the nation.[79]

It did not take long for student factionalism to set in after the military occupation of the Politécnico as groups with various political affiliations vied for power in the FNET's new order. New leaders of FNET were to be elected during the congress of technical students in late October 1956. Several factions supported by different school authorities and politicians put forward candidates for the presidency. As competing shock brigades intervened by intimidating young voters, the "Ramiristas" emerged as the most important faction. The group was sponsored by Enrique Ramírez y Ramírez, a former member of the Partido Popular. They had triumphed over followers of Vicente Lombardo Toledano as well as various anticommunist groups. Ramirista control of the Politécnico would last until 1964.[80] In exchange for loyalty to the government of Adolfo López Mateos (1958–64), the Ramiristas, amidst unprecedented levels of corruption, acquired substantial political power and immunity to attack from other FNET leaders.[81] In short, in the aftermath of the 1956 strike, the FNET became another charro organization at the service of the government, and its nominal association with the Left remained but a hollow artifact of history.

AFTER THE IPN strike of 1956 was prematurely called off by President Ruíz Cortines in mid-June, a number of competing political powerbrokers began to fund more aggressive mechanisms of control to repress the most politicized students. These involved both provocation and the manipulation of student-centered violence. These methods would be consolidated throughout the long sixties as "student charrismo" and eventually "porrismo." But, it became increasingly evident that such provocation was failing to contain the forces of student protest. Student charrismo strained to resolve its own "crisis of authority."

By responding with direct force, the government demonstrated that the Mexican state, when pushed, could be as repressive as any other Latin American regime. In answer to mounting pressure, school and government authorities called for the closing of the boarding school, which was flagged as the place where major political and social problems of the Politécnico originated. President Adolfo Ruíz Cortines ordered the military occupation of the IPN and the imprisonment of the principal political activists. They would be charged variously with "treason," "terrorism," and a variety of other crimes covered by the catchall Law of Social Dissolution. The leaders of the student protest were imprisoned, the boarding school was closed, and the IPN was occupied by the Federal Army.

Following the 1956 student protest, the state proceeded to dismantle the progressive and popular student organization, the FNET, and convert it into a charro student federation. The organization retained the name and leftist rhetoric of its predecessor but was controlled by loyal supporters of the government. In 1964 the Ramirista era would end, only to be followed by a time dominated by an even more authoritarian and corrupt group of leaders who were financed by a number of influential politicians close to Gustavo Díaz Ordaz. Among these leaders were Alfonso Corona del Rosal and Jesús Robles Martínez, who developed close ties with the new president.[82] They used all their power with the National Union of Educational Workers and the Federation of Government Employees' Union to manipulate the FNET. Dominant porro leaders, such as Alfonso Torres Saavedra, aka "El Johnny," would work in opposition to the leaders of the 1968 student protest.[83] By then it also was clear that the FNET could not hold its own in this conflict; it completely vanished from the IPN that same year.

Thus, for politécnicos, it was 1956 and not 1968 that marked a watershed in the history of student activism. Following this critical event, the IPN would witness a gradual transformation in its student body, shifting from a working-class institution in the 1940s and early 1950s to a more middle-class institution in the late 1950s and 1960s, a shift that would coincide with physical improvements to the schools of the IPN and a change in politécnicos' demands. In the earlier period, they asked for basic needs such as the creation of dormitories inside their schools and the construction of communal cafeterias with subsidized meals. In the wake of the 1956 strike their requests became more directly political and sweeping, calling for freedom for all political prisoners and greater participatory democracy in schools and labor unions. These incipient demands for a more democratic Mexico, the innovative repertoires of collective action (including the use of mítines relámpagos and informational brigades) and the state reactions they provoked would set the political tone and the trajectory of the 1968 student movement.

Notes

1. *Excélsior*, September 28, 1956. The *Comedor Universitario*, or university cafeteria, was a publicly and privately financed downtown cafeteria that since its creation in the 1930s had subsidized and served free meals to hundreds of low-income students from the National Autonomous University of Mexico (*universitarios*), the National Polytechnic Institute (*politécnicos*), and the Normal School (*normalistas*).

2. "UNAM," in *Fondo Reservado del Instituto de Investigaciones Bibliográficas* (hereafter FRIIB), vol. 1, exp. 73, n.d. On state-press relations, see Evelyn P. Stevens, *Protest and Response in Mexico* (Boston: MIT Press, 1974); and Chappell H. Lawson, *Building the Fourth Estate: Democratization and the Rise of a Free Press in Mexico* (Berkeley: University of California Press, 2002). On the limits of this relationship, see Alberto del Castillo

Troncoso, "El movimiento estudiantil de 1968 narrado en imágenes," *Sociológica* 23, no. 68 (September–December 2008): 63–114; and Celeste González Bustamante, "1968 Olympic, Dreams and Tlatelolco Nightmares: Imagining and Imaging Modernity on Television," *Mexican Studies/Estudios Mexicanos* 26, no. 1 (winter 2010): 1–30.

3. "¿Rectitud o vandalismo?," in FRIIB, 1/24, June 1956.

4. *Cometa Universitario*, no. 3 (October–November 1956) in FRIIB, 1/91; Archivo General de la Nación, Dirección Federal de Seguridad (hereafter AGN, DFS), exp. 63-4-953, L-1, H-26

5. *Cometa Universitario*, no. 3 (October–November 1956), in FRIIB, 1/91.

6. *Excélsior*, September 29 and 30, 1956; *El Universal*, September 28, 1956.

7. *Excélsior*, September 29, 1956.

8. On the "long sixties," see Arthur Marwick, *The Sixties: Cultural Revolution in Britain, France, Italy, and the United States, c. 1958–c. 1974* (Oxford: Oxford University Press, 1998); Diana Sorensen, *A Turbulent Decade Remembered: Scenes from the Latin American Sixties* (Palo Alto, CA: Stanford University Press, 2007); René O. Rivas, *La izquierda estudiantil en la* UNAM: *Organizaciones, movilizaciones y liderazgos (1958–1972)* (Mexico City: UNAM, 2007); Jaime Pensado, *Rebel Mexico: Student Unrest and Authoritarian Political Culture during the Long Sixties* (Palo Alto, CA: Stanford University Press, 2013).

9. On competing yet relatively positive interpretations of Mexico's youth before the 1950s, see Jaime Pensado, "Between Cultured Young Men and Mischievous Children: Youth, Transgression, and Protest in Late Nineteenth-Century Mexico," *Journal of the History of Childhood and Youth* 4, no. 1 (2011): 26–57; José A. Pérez Islas et al., eds., *Historias de los Jóvenes en Mexico City: Su presencia en el siglo XX* (Mexico City: INJ, 2004).

10. See, for example, Enrique de la Garza, Tomás Ejea León, and Luis Fernando Macías, *El otro movimiento estudiantil* (Mexico City: Extemporáneos, 1986); Antonio Gómez Nashiki, "El Movimiento y la Violencia Institucional: La Universidad Michoacana de San Nicolás de Hidalgo, 1956–1966," *Revista de Investigaciones Educativa* 12, no. 35 (October–December 2007): 1179–208; Eric Zolov, "¡Cuba sí, Yanquis no! The Sacking of the Instituto Cultural México-Norteamericano in Morelia, Michoacán, 1961," in *In from the Cold: Latin America's New Encounter with the Cold War*, ed. Gilbert M. Joseph and Daniela Spenser, 214–52 (Durham, NC: Duke University Press, 2008); Rivas, *La izquierda estudiantil en la* UNAM; Lucio Rangel Hernández, *La Universidad de Michoacana y el movimiento estudiantil, 1966–1989* (Morelia: IIH, 2009); Elizabeth Henson, "Madera 1965: Primeros Vientos," and Alexander Aviña, "Seizing Hold of Memories in Moments of Danger: Guerrillas and Revolution in Guerrero, Mexico," in *Challenging Authoritarianism in Mexico: Revolutionary Struggles and the Dirty War, 1964–1982*, ed. Herrera Calderón Fernando and Adela Cedillo, 19–39, 40–59 (London: Routledge, 2011); Wil G. Pansters, *Politics and Power in Puebla: The Political History of a Mexican State, 1937–1987* (Amsterdam: CEDLA Edita, 1990).

11. Gilberto Guevara Niebla, *La libertad nunca se olvida: Memoria del 68* (Mexico City: Cal y Arena, 2004); Arnulfo Aquino Casas and Jorge Perezvega, *Imágenes y símbolos del 68: Fotografía y gráfica del movimiento estudiantil* (Mexico City: UNAM, 2004); Alvaro Vázquez Mantecón and Sergio Raúl Arroyo, *Memorial del 68* (Mexico City: UNAM, Dirección General de Publicaciones y Fomento Editorial, 2007); Consejo Nacional para la Cultura y las Artes, *1968: Un archivo inédito* (Mexico City: Consejo Nacional para la Cultura y las Artes, 2008); Eduardo Valle, *El año de la rebelión por la democracia: Con una*

cierta mirada (Mexico City: Oceano, 2008); Carlos Monsiváis, *El 68: La tradición de la resistencia* (Mexico City: Ediciones Era, 2008); Pablo Gómez, *1968: La historia también está hecha de derrotas* (Mexico City: Porrúa, 2008); *Memorial del 68*, documentary directed by Nicolás Echeverría (Mexico City: TV UNAM, 2008); Salvador Martínez della Rocca, ed., *Voces y ecos del 68* (Mexico City: Porrúa, 2009).

12. For additional critiques of the sesentaocheros see Barry Carr, "The Many Meanings of 1968: The Student-Popular Movement Thirty Years After." http://www.latrobe.edu.au/history/news/digital/carr1.htm.1; Herbert Braun, "Protest of Engagement: Dignity, False Love, and Self-Love in Mexico during 1968," *Comparative Studies in Sociology and History* 39, no. 3 (1997); Vania Markarian, "El movimiento estudiantil mexicano de 1968: Treinta años de debates públicos," *Anuario de Espacios Urbanos, Historia, Cultura, Diseño* (2001): 239–64; Jaime Pensado, "The (forgotten) Sixties in Mexico," *The Sixties: A Journal of History, Politics and Culture* 1, no. 1 (June 2008): 83–90.

13. This is particularly evident in the multiple accounts written by Gilberto Guevara Niebla, Elena Poniatowska, Carlos Monsiváis, Raúl Alvarez Garín, and Luis González de Alba.

14. The foundation of the IPN relied on the conglomeration of the existing technological and vocational schools, including six *prevocacionales*, four *vocacionales*, and seven professional schools. See Eusebio Mendoza Avila, *La educación tecnológica en México* (Mexico City: IPN, 1980).

15. Carlos Ornelas Navarro, "La educación técnica y la ideología de la Revolución Mexicana," in *Ideología de la Revolución Mexicana*, ed. Graciela Lechuga (Mexico City: UAM, 1984), 33–60, 36.

16. Mendoza Ávila, *La educación tecnológica*; María de los Angeles Rodríguez Alvarez et al., *IPN: 50 años en la historia de la educación tecnológica* (Mexico City: IPN, 1988), 161; Joaquín B. Sánchez Hidalgo, *Trazos y mitos de una utopía: La Institución Politécnica* (Mexico City: SAIPN, 2000), 190.

17. *Excélsior*, May 1, 1937; Roberto Brito Lemus, "Cambio generacional y participación juvenil durante el Cardenismo," in *Historias de los Jóvenes en Mexico City: Su presencia en el siglo XX*, ed. José A. Pérez Islas et al., 233–80 (Mexico City: INJ, 2004).

18. Dan Hofstadter, *Mexico, 1946–1973* (New York: Facts on File, 1974), 23–24; Howard F. Cline, *Mexico: Revolution to Evolution, 1940–1960* (New York: Oxford University Press, 1962).

19. Roger D. Hansen, *The Politics of Mexican Development* (Baltimore: Johns Hopkins University Press, 1971), 72–73.

20. Jeffrey Bortz, "Wages and Economic Crisis in Mexico," in *The Mexican Left, the Popular Movements, and the Politics of Austerity*, ed. Barry Carr and Ricardo Anzaldúa Montoya (San Diego: Center for U.S.–Mexican Studies, 1986), 41–46, 45.

21. These numbers exclude the top 4.8 percent of families.

22. Rodríguez Álvarez et al., *IPN: 50 años*, 63.

23. Or 14.2 percent if one was to include those students whose head of the families were "housewives."

24. Author's interview with Jorge Oceguera (head of the IPN cheerleading team, 1950–57), February 5, 2005, Mexico City. Jesús Flores Palafox, student and teacher of the IPN, 1952–58, expressed comments similar to those of the author.

25. The remaining 30 percent were from the lower and upper class sectors. Lucio

Mendieta y Nuñez, "La clase media en Mexico City," *Revista Mexicana de Sociología* 17, no. 2/3 (May–December 1955): 527–28.

26. David E. Lorey, *The University System and Economic Development in Mexico since 1929* (Palo Alto, CA: Standford University Press, 1993), 148–49, 197.

27. Student activism at UNAM during this period was rather restricted. Donald Mabry, *The Mexican University and the State: Student Conflict, 1917–1971* (College Station: Texas A&M University Press, 1982). On the amendment of article 3, see Ornelas Navarro, "La educación técnica," 48.

28. Cline, *Mexico: Revolution*, 194–96.

29. Luis Medina, *Del cardenismo al avilacamachismo: Historia de la Revolución Mexicana*, no. 18 (Mexico City: El Colegio de México, 1978).

30. Padilla, chapter 15, this volume.

31. Manuel Marcúe Padiñas et al., "La crisis de la educación en México. La ocupación del Instituto Politécnico Nacional," *Problemas de Latinoamérica* 3, no. 13 (November 20, 1956); and Rodríguez Álvarez et al., IPN: 50 años, 114. On the close relationship between the state and CONCAMIN during the 1940s, see Stephen Niblo, *Mexico in the 1940s: Modernity Politics and Corruption* (Wilmington, DE: Scholarly Resources, 1999), 225, 297.

32. On the militancy of politécnicos and younger students from the secondary schools in 1968 see Igor de León, *La noche de Santo Tomás* (Mexico City: Ediciones de Cultura Popular, 1988); Jaime García Reyes, Fernando Hernández Zárate, and David Vega, "Las batallas en el Politécnico," in *Pensar el 68*, ed. Gilberto Guevara Niebla and Raúl Álvarez Garín, 81–90 (Mexico City: Ediciones Cal y Arena, 2008); Raúl Jardón, *1968: El fuego de la esperanza* (Mexico City: Siglo XXI, 1998); Ariel Rodríguez Kuri, "Los primeros días: Una explicación de los orígenes inmediatos del movimiento estudiantil de 1968," *Historia Mexicana* 53, no. 1 (July–September 2003): 179–228.

33. *New York Times*, April 18, 1956; *Excélsior*, April 12, 1956; *El Popular*, April 11, 1956; Department of State documents, Washington, D.C.: Mexico–Internal Affairs, 1955–59, (hereafter DSDW, M-IA), Desp. 1348, June 8, 1956.

34. Students also demanded more financial resources. See Rodríguez Álvarez et al., IPN: 50 años, 146.

35. "Mexico," *Hispanic American Review* 9, no. 4 (1956): 163.

36. DSDW, M-IA, Desp. 1191, April 20, 1956.

37. AGN/DFS-63-3-1956/L-2/H-253–255; DSDW, M-IA, Desp. 1191, April 20, 1956; *La Voz de México*, April 20, 1956.

38. Author's interview with Jorge Oceguera, February 5, 2005, Mexico City.

39. Author's interview with Jesús Flores Palafox, January 26, 2005, Mexico City.

40. "¡No Ceder, Poli! La Agresión a los Internos, Primer Paso del Programa del Gobierno Contra el Instituto Politécnico," *Fuerza de la ESIME* no. 3 (October 1956), in Fondo Reservado de la UNAM—Impresos Sueltos, Movimientos Socio-Políticos (hereafter FR-U-IS, MS-P), vol. 26.

41. Author's interview with Jesús Flores Palafox, January 26, 2005, Mexico City.

42. "¡No Ceder!"; and "Testimonio: El Poli Habla," in IPN: 50 años, 150.

43. Rodríguez Alvarez et al., IPN: 50 años, 150, 144.

44. Ramón Ramírez, *El Movimiento estudiantil mexicano*, vols. I and II (Mexico City: Era, 1969); Sergio Zermeño, *Mexico City: Una democracia utópica* (Mexico City: Siglo XXI,

1978); César Gilabert, *El hábito de la utopía: Análisis del imaginario sociopolítico en el movimiento estudiantil de México: 1968* (Mexico City: Porrúa, 1993).

45. *La Chispa*, n.d., AGN/DFS-63-3-1956/L-3/H-32.

46. Author's interview with Oscar González, Mexico City, January 7, 2005. On the labor strikes of 1958, see Antonio Alonso, *El movimiento ferrocarrilero en México, 1958–1959: De la conciliación a la lucha de clases* (Mexico City: Era, 1972); Barry Carr, *La izquierda mexicana a través del siglo XX* (Mexico City: Era, 1996).

47. Author's interview with Nicandro Mendoza, May 14, 2005, Mexico City. On the use of these tactics in 1968, see Zermeño, *Mexico City*.

48. Author's interview with Oscar González, Mexico City, January 7, 2005. See also "Ahí va el golpe . . . !," in Marcúe Padiñas, "La crisis," 53.

49. *Siempre!*, June 27, 1956; Rodríguez Kuri, "Los primeros días."

50. Gómez Nashiki, "El Movimiento y la Violencia Institucional."

51. On the distribution of propaganda as a key element of porrismo, see Pensado, *Rebel Mexico*.

52. See, for example, *Excélsior*, April 21, 1956, and DSDW, M-IA, Desp. 1248, May 11, 1956.

53. *El Tiempo*, October 1, 1956, 4.

54. *Excélsior*, April 20, 1956; *Siempre!*, May 23, 1956.

55. *Excélsior*, April 21, 1956; *El Universal*, June 4, 1956.

56. *El Tiempo*, October 1, 1956.

57. See, for example, *La Nación*, June 18, 1956.

58. DSDW, M-IA, Desp. 28, June 10, 1956; *La Nación*, June 18, 1956; *El Universal*, June 20, 1956; Raúl Jardón, *El espionaje contra el movimiento estudiantil: Los documentos de la Dirección Federal de Seguridad y las agencias de "inteligencia" estadounidenses en 1968* (Mexico City: Itaca, 2003); Ariel Rodríguez Kuri, "El lado oscuro de la luna: El momento conservador en 1968," in *Conservadurismo y derechas en la historia de México*, ed. Erika Pani, 512–59 (Mexico City: FCE, 2009).

59. *Excélsior*, May 17, 21, and 29, and June 6, 1956.

60. *El Popular*, June 21, 1956.

61. *Excélsior*, June 21, 1956.

62. DSDW, M-IA, Desp. 116, September 3, 1956; *Washington Post*, September 22, 1956.

63. *Excélsior*, August 25, 1956. On movements outside Mexico City, see Antonio Gómez Nashiki, "El movimiento y la violencia institucional"; and Donald Russell Morris, "Political Violence and Political Modernization in Mexico: 1952–1964" (PhD dissertation, University of Wisconsin, 1971).

64. Born into a successful entrepreneurial family (his brother was the owner of the Hotel Regis), Alejo Peralta began his industrial career at the age of eighteen when he founded a small mechanical shop, which he named Peralta Hermanos. Three years later he graduated from ESIME (the Superior School of Mechanical Engineering, associated with the IPN), expanded his shop, and renamed it IUSA. In 1945 he founded one of Mexico's largest electrical industries, Compañía Electrocerámica, S.A. Nine years later he became one of Mexico's most prosperous millionaires after investing in the baseball teams "Azteca" and "Tigres Capitalinos." See Luis Suárez, *Alejo Peralta, un patrón sin patrones* (Mexico City: Grijalbo, 1992).

65. *Excélsior*, August 25, 1956.

66. *Excélsior*, August 24, 1956.

67. Marcúe Padiñas, "La crisis," 43.

68. On "*porrismo*" or "student thuggery," see Pensado, *Rebel Mexico*; Carmen Guitán Berniser, "Las porras: Estudio de caso de un grupo de presión universitaria" (thesis, UNAM, 1975); Olga Durón, *Yo Porro (Retrato hablado)* (Mexico City: Editorial Posada, 1984); Larissa Lomnitz, "The Uses of Fear: Porro Gangs in Mexico," in *Peace and War. Cross-Cultural Perspectives*, ed. Mary LeCron Foster and Robert A. Rubinstein (New Brunswick, NJ: Transaction Books, 1986); Hugo Sánchez Gudiño, *Génesis, desarrollo, y consolidación de los grupos estudiantiles de choque en la UNAM, 1930–1990* (Mexico City: UNAM, 2006).

69. *Excélsior*, August 13 and 27, 1956.

70. *Excélsior*, August 27, 1956; Hidalgo, *Trazos y mitos*, 173–74.

71. *Excélsior*, August 22 and 25, 1956.

72. *Excélsior*, September 24, 1956. In comparison, Operation Condor, the much-lauded 1970s antidrugs program that confronted well-armed drug traffickers and covered much of mountainous northern Mexico, involved only twenty-three hundred troops. Richard Craig, "Operation Condor: Mexico's Antidrug Campaign Enters a New Era," *Journal of Interamerican Studies and World Affairs* 22, no. 3 (August 1980): 345–63.

73. AGN/DFS-63-3–56/L-6/H-216.

74. Assorted letters, editorial pages of *Excélsior* and *El Universal*.

75. *Excélsior*, September 24, 1956; *La Nación*, May 20 and June 10, 1956.

76. *Novedades*, September 25, 1956.

77. *Excélsior*, September 20, 1956.

78. DSDW, M-IA, Desp. 358, October 10, 1956.

79. *Excélsior*, September 26, 1956; *Tiempo*, October 1, 1956.

80. AGN/DFS-63-3–56/L-6/H-266; AGN/DFS-63-3–56/L-6/H-319; *Excélsior*, October 24, 1956; Karl M. Schmitt, *Communism in Mexico: A Study in Political Frustration* (Austin: University of Texas Press, 1965), 84–85.

81. Author's interview with David Vega, February 12, 2005, Mexico City.

82. Both Alfonso Corona del Rosal, governor of the Federal District (1966–70), and labor union leader Jesús Robles Martínez would later be implicated in the violent repression of students during the 1968 movement. Jardón, *1968*; Ramírez, *El movimiento estudiantil Mexicano*; and Sergio Aguayo Q., *1968: Los Archivos de la Violencia* (Mexico City: Grijalbo, 1998).

83. Durón, *Yo Porro*.

FINAL COMMENTS | *Jeffrey W. Rubin*

CONTEXTUALIZING THE REGIME

What 1938–1968 Tells Us about Mexico, Power, and Latin America's Twentieth Century

Contextualization: What Story Do These Chapters Tell?

In this concluding chapter, I suggest that the history of Mexico recounted in these chapters is the story of power in twentieth-century Latin America, an account of politics and economic development and the tensions and pageantry of citizenship from the depression of 1929 through the establishment of neoliberalism in the 1990s. The Mexican Revolution was the first and most dramatic event in what we might call "the people coming on the scene" in twentieth-century Latin America, and it set the stage for much that was to follow. It was an explosive arrival in terms of ordinary people coming to "count" in national public narratives and politics.

Since colonial times and throughout the nineteenth century, ordinary and often poor Latin Americans—peasants, small farmers, Indians, domestic servants, women, slaves, blacks, factory workers, unemployed youth, students, small artisans, and shopkeepers—were at times able to stir up trouble or make themselves heard, but they were not recognized as having a right to a political voice or economic well-being. The running of the nation and the enjoyment of its material benefits, from capital cities to the smallest town halls, were the province of elites.

In the decades following the Mexican Revolution, ordinary people in Latin America came on the scene in country after country, making claims to *ser gente*—to be fully human and count as citizens—and having those claims recognized. In general, these efforts were less violent—and the results in national policymaking less thoroughgoing—than in Mexico. But across the hemisphere grassroots pressures and prescient leaders brought to center stage the claims of those previously excluded. The efforts that began with the Mexican Revolution continued through other national projects, including Colombia's Revolución en Marcha, Getúlio Vargas's dictatorship and the subsequent first round of Brazilian democracy, and Peronism in Argentina.

As in Mexico, Latin American elites tended to oppose the popular claims put forward in the name of political inclusion and new economic bargains, and people mobilizing to secure rights and resources suffered political manipulation and violent repression. Indeed, the very leaders who promoted reform from the 1930s to the 1950s, such as Cárdenas, Vargas, and Perón, themselves undermined the progressive aspects of their policies by acting to control mobilization from the center, respond to business demands, and quash autonomous labor and peasant movements.

From the 1950s to the 1970s, when activists in Latin America made use of new democratic mechanisms to continue the struggle for socioeconomic reform—and again stirred up people in the process—military officers staged coups in country after country with the support of business elites, landowners, and parts of the middle class, as well as the U.S. government and the police forces it had trained. By 1976, when the Argentine military seized power and initiated its "dirty war" against a wide swathe of the country's civilians, all but a small handful of nations in Latin America were firmly in the grip of military rule. As is well known, the generals in Latin America presided over the closing down of legislatures, the torture and disappearance of activists, and the annihilation of Indian villages. Military governments annulled labor rights, instilled fear through near-random slaughter, welcomed foreign corporations, and emphasized women's domestic responsibilities as wives and mothers.

In the context of this twentieth-century history of repression, this book does more than account for why the Mexican Revolution turned conservative, or was rolled back, or gave way to the inequalities of capitalist industrial development and, much later, free trade and the North American Free Trade Agreement. It offers far more than a judgment of whether Mexico was authoritarian (soft or not so soft), if that means that the central government used great manipulation, coercion, and violence to oppose and undermine efforts to forge instances of autonomy, democracy, voice, or equality in sustainable form. Of course the Mexican government was authoritarian, as were most of the other governments mentioned above.

Rollback and repression in Mexico were documented by John Womack's 1986 examination of the economic continuities linking the Porfiriato to the postrevolutionary 1920s and 1930s and by Nora Hamilton's 1982 study of "the limits of state autonomy."[1] In Hamilton's analysis, by the end of the 1930s, actors in the private sector became willing and able to oppose even the partial efforts to foster a "humane capitalism" that might be said to have constituted Cardenismo. As Paul Gillingham and Benjamin Smith observe in the introduction to this volume, revisionists before and especially after 1968 saw through the mask of the state to one agonizing component after another of how repression operated in Mexico,[2] most dramatically in the violence given public face at Tlatelolco, but stretching in a long line both before and after in the countryside and the cities and bleeding into what the revisionists labeled corporatism—an ability to structure political organization as and even before it happened.[3]

The vast mobilizations and disruptions of the revolution, together with the international context of worldwide depression, the United States' New Deal, and Soviet five-year plans, made Cardenismo possible, as did Cárdenas's effective and negotiated cultural project. But I think we can say now that Cárdenas's vision of land reform and labor rights, however qualified and amenable to capitalism, was a doomed and even impossible dream, as were the range of less and more radical proposals that followed in the hemisphere in subsequent decades, as various components of "the people" ever more determinedly pressed for new politics; some politicians responded and, for their own reasons, even took the lead.

What the chapters in this book do, with keen new research and interpretive vision, is plunge us into the middle of how the give and take of the twentieth century worked on the ground, for, I would argue, the knot of Mexico in 1938–68 rehearses the history of much of the twentieth century in this hemisphere. Those pivotal decades in Mexico, along with the three that followed, show us how state political and military might, visions and practices of economic development, ongoing resistance and rethinking on the part of tenacious activists, the multivalent weight of the Cold War, and the cultural productions of artists, governments, and media empires all yielded and sustained capitalist economic growth, anti-communist nationalism, severely restricted citizenship, and the highest levels of inequality on the planet.

This book follows the work of the state-centered revisionists of the 1960s through the 1980s, who identified authoritarianism in Mexico and showed the Mexican regime to rule through co-optation and repression.[4] It follows as well the work of those who were subsequently influenced (as I was) by combinations of neo-Marxist political economy and poststructuralism (in differing combinations and to different conclusions) as we sought to bring a newly theorized "culture" into political analysis and—relatedly but distinctly—decenter the Mexican regime in a variety of ways.[5] All of this is up for grabs in the new scholarship put forward in this volume.

Why up for grabs? Because we are still struggling, and arguing, to figure out what it all adds up to: how power works, where it is located, why developmentalism and neoliberalism both so effectively suppressed political voices and deepened economic inequality, and whether and where forms of resistance and opposition achieved a modicum of success. Why, in a sense, the Mexican government could do what it did from 1938–68 and thereafter—down to the horrific violence at the nexus of state power and drug trafficking today—and the developmentalist and populist, military, neoliberal, and democratic governments of the rest of the hemisphere could seemingly do the same over the long haul.

As we wonder now what Brazil under the Partido dos Trabalhadores (PT), or a multiethnic Bolivia with Evo Morales as president, or Chávez's Bolivarian Revolution, or Peru as it acquires wealth from mineral extraction might achieve in the way of meaningful democratic voice and economic well-being for their citizens—and know as we ask that the chances for enduring progressive reform are slim, stuck as we seem to be in global neoliberalism and wars on terror—we confront just what historians confront when examining the ongoing inequality and political repression of postrevolutionary Mexico.

If we are no longer surprised *that* this happens, for scholarly and political reasons we avidly search out *how* this happens. Even if the big picture does not change, we seek to understand the world in which we live. We seek as well to identify fissures, possible pathways for significant change. We wonder if reform can endure, particularly in democratic contexts. And we simultaneously know that game-changing moments occur and don't know what might happen in and through them to set things on now unimaginable paths of better or worse.

What does this book contribute to answering these "how" and "why" questions? First, the authors underscore the centrality of violence to political rule between 1938 and 1968 in Mexico. Through extensive work in newly opened intelligence archives, these scholars show not only the extent to which the central government in Mexico regularly and repeatedly used violence to quash opposition but also how the Mexican government came to systematically plan and execute this violence.[6] This is indeed a contribution, not because scholars did not already know the broad outlines of repression, but because its scope and meticulousness are sobering and provide, on first reading, a counterweight to analyses that emphasize negotiation, subaltern agency, and cultural resistance. The force of repression, and the tenacity with which practices of repression were learned, points these authors back to a notion of power amassed and exercised at the center.

The second contribution of the chapters in this book is their delineation, also rooted in close archival analysis, of the density and diversity of experience regarding such key matters as control of the military (Rath), electoral competition (Gillingham), tax collection (Smith), student radicalism (Pensado and Padilla), cultural understandings of politics (Piccato), and church-state relations (Blancarte). All of these are shown to have escaped the control of the center for periods of time. Third, and building on this density of experience, the book's authors show the complexity of local and regional histories and the ways *campesino*, activist, *cacique*, electoral, and military experiences intertwined to produce new realities and changing configurations of power. Finally, and significant in the framing of the book, several of the contributors, such as Knight, Hernandez, Rath, McCormick, and Gillingham, set out a moment of "closing down," sometime between the late 1930s and early 1950s, when the center, with its repressive apparatus, triumphed over density and complexity—indeed, made use of them—to enable an "authoritarian system" to consolidate. In this final chapter, I question this conclusion and suggest an alternative approach.

Mexico

The accounts and analyses offered here reveal what transpired beneath the surface of apparent political order, behind the story the regime told about itself and manufactured, and in tandem with artistic and cultural processes and institutions in its "golden age."[7] In their introduction, Gillingham and Smith set out the diversity of what happened from the late 1930s to the mid-1960s and the forms of protest, mobilization, dissent, and alternative views that characterized those years. Drawing on themes common to the book's diverse chapters, Gillingham and Smith observe that "rural communities across Mexico protested vigorously and at times violently against stolen elections, against crooked politicians, tax collectors, alcohol inspectors or forestry wardens, and against enduring poverty." Urban protests were similarly vigorous and constant, including cross-class movements that shaped government initiatives through petitioning, extempore organization, and collective bargaining by riot. In both arenas, there was active if frequently indirect dissent in the public sphere, including "a muckraking oppositional press *en provincia*" and "modern-day troubadours [corrido sellers] equipped with thin sheets of popular songs, which were read out and sung in markets, cantinas, and town squares."

In chapter 8, Gladys McCormick, writing about sugar producers in Morelos, shows the process by which the Jaramillo family and fellow *campesinos* staked out changing relationships to workers, mill bosses, and the government in the course of the 1940s and 1950s, their position steadily weakening in the face of the government's refusal to tolerate a worker-peasant alliance. Wil Pansters demonstrates in chapter 5 the unevenness of even the forceful Santos *cacicazgo* in San Luis Potosí, its places of weakness and negotiation, and the opposition it engendered, while in chapter 3 Thomas Rath uses military archives to show how the regime "aimed to camouflage the PRIísta state and the military's continuing autonomy, corruption, and repression."

Each author makes these points with specific examples, such as the way peasant activists forged in 1947 a strategy markedly different from the 1942 peasant-worker strike led by Rubén Jaramillo, which brought on army intervention. In 1947 Jaramillo's older brother Antonio, along with Miguel Torres Ortiz, used new local organizations, action through legal channels, and a language of modernization and integral development (rather than social justice) to secure for the mill a new general manager who was more open to social welfare policies and more popularly supported forms of corruption. Pansters identifies the "pragmatic and goal-oriented negotiations" between Santos and dissident miners, railroad workers, and *ejidatarios*. Rath provides us with the professional biography of General Miguel Z. Martinez, well known within the military as a specialist in state violence who, "after playing a prominent role fighting cristeros . . . led gangs of street fighters against Almazanistas during the 1940 election in Mexico City; he intimidated opponents with cries of 'give yourselves up *hijos de la chingada*, here comes *huevos de oro!*'[8] He then led Mexico City's police force and numerous military zones until the 1960s, by which point he had acquired a host of landed properties through dubious procedures."

In the course of these analyses, McCormick shows, as do Pansters and Rath, that regional movements and patterns of behavior that formed in one period maintained lives of their own during interaction with national directives and unraveled and engendered challenges in part by their own regional logic. In his conclusion concerning church-state relations in chapter 2, Blancarte underscores the way arrangements forged in one decade become something quite different just two decades later. While during the 1940s church and state formed an alliance characterized by nationalism and anticommunism, by the mid-1960s the church, "despite professing complete support for the regime . . . for the first time adopted a more radical stance than the government in social policy, as demands for social justice and democratization bled into church pastorals and bishops' epistles."

These chapters suggest that we be careful what we look for—we might find it but in the process not notice what we are *not* looking for. As Blancarte shows, soon after an antisocialist alliance became the official story of church-state relations, a very different set of positions began to develop beneath the surface. We know from Chiapas that this did not occur only or even predominantly by way of changes in outside theologies but by way of the experiences of clergymen with their parishioners and regional social relations. McCormick states eloquently the need to look for nuance when she describes the way Rubén Jaramillo's brothers and other opposition leaders disappeared from the oral history of family members and compatriots (while Rubén himself did not): "Perhaps the most important reason why the peasant leaders of the 1947–1948 mobilization have been forgotten is because many went on to support La Engorda in the 1950s, thus losing the heroic sheen of their earlier actions. . . . In the dichotomous recollections of good versus bad, or revolutionary versus anti-revolutionary, little room remains for those who straddled both camps at different moments."

One key result of this book will be to create room to see "those who straddle both camps" and, further, to see a political regime uneven in its centralization and power, whose "provincial, local, and central monsters" battle it out over matters "as deep as class and as shallow as envy."[9] McCormick herself, however, is ambivalent about opening up this room, siding with the peasant who states straightforwardly that the "government sent soldiers, sent the army, to force peasants to allow their sugar cane to be cut without any chance of dialoguing." Despite—or because of—the nuanced story of changing grassroots alliances, repression, new strategies, corruption, and open revolt she uncovers, McCormick sees Morelos as a school for state authoritarianism: "The regime successfully shut down grassroots organizing in communities with a long track record of protecting their autonomy and encouraged these same communities to forget the historical memory of such a legacy." In McCormick's view, this was "how this political order was constructed": through a "learning process" by which the Mexican government developed its particularly effective form of authoritarian rule.

Wil Pansters uses an approach and sensitivity similar to that of McCormick to show the dynamism that underlies the rule of regional bosses as well as the ways successful forms of control came out of and engendered challenges, which in turn led to new relations of power. Gonzalo N. Santos understood the performative and narrative dimensions of politics, holding command of the cultural codes of Mexico City and San Luis Potosí. With that knowledge and with armed supporters, Santos ran the state for fifteen years by jockeying with landowners, miners, railroad workers, and ejidatarios, bringing pragmatism to bear on "negotiation with dissident groups and their incorporation in some form in local administration."

Santos built his cacicazgo from above through a clique of "intermediate" local bosses tied to particular localities, combining brokered electoral participation with a relatively spare use of violence. Santos's forms of rule eventually led to the formation of opposition groups both within and outside the PRI, including doctors who led forceful and enduring civic opposition movements in the capital and in the northeastern city of Matehuala. These groups opposed Santos in the 1958 elections, and during this period López Mateos intervened decisively against him, leading swiftly to Santos's downfall. Like McCormick, Pansters presents an account of politics in which submission outweighs autonomy. But he does not suggest, as McCormick does, that San Luis Potosí was a training ground for regime authoritarianism. Rather, he starts his story with the years of political uncertainty that followed the demise of the cacicazgo of Saturnino Cedillo and ends with the opposition coalition that ousted Santos. "In the second half of the 1950s," he concludes, "opposition against the Santos cacicazgo also arose to a great degree from below, which points to the enduring importance of local political arenas as sources of political change (and stability)."

Benjamin Smith (chapter 10) shows us "political change (and stability)" through contestation over taxes, another arena in which disjunctive and circuitous pathways of political practice were created and sustained. Smith shows us that the federal government "couldn't" collect taxes from rural ejidatarios and urban market women and in response chose at times to support and enable the protest struggles of these groups, which served to quiet tense situations, garner support, and provide the appearance of supporting popular groups. At the same time, federal and state officials fomented a system of bribes and kickbacks to fund public projects while also ceding authority over public projects to the Catholic church. The need for recourse to such alternatives does not suggest an all-controlling state, although it is—as numerous authors of this book show—a means by which the state learned "forms of rule and ruling."[10] This strength and learning brought with it weakness as well as power, producing a state that was centralized but poorly financed, one that could dialogue with the urban poor through concessions on tax collection, but only in a framework of corruption and inequality. When Echeverría sought unsuccessfully to reform this system and create a more secure fiscal base for the state, he ended up resorting to printing money to fund his social welfare efforts. In Smith's analysis, the Mexican state did not have the funds to be monolithic.

Military entrepreneurialism and moving key military personnel from job to job similarly created networks that both abetted and stymied federal actors across decades and into the present (Rath). Paul Gillingham shows us contested elections and a way to consider elections as significant contestations over power even when they were not fairly run. Pablo Piccato underscores the complexity of cultural production and popular sentiment by taking us into the police and crime pages—the second sections—of urban newspapers. There, in contrast to the official political reporting on the front pages, the corruption of politicians could be described and savored in salacious detail. For example, coverage of secretary Ema Martínez's murder of a senator publicized her claims about politicians "who used their positions to get rich and have sexual adventures with female subordinates." This crime page coverage of immorality at the higher echelons of the regime unfolded as López Mateos was repressing the railroad workers. In the second sections of newspapers, ideas were circulated that represented and created alternative popular understandings of the regime, shoring up but also potentially undermining state power in the process.

Tanalís Padilla shows us continuing alternative worldviews in rural normal schools and the affiliated Federación de Estudiantes Campesinos Socialistas de México. The student federation, formed in 1935, linked student and *campesino* grievances well into the 1960s, drawing renewed inspiration from the Cuban Revolution and functioning as a link between the *normales* and radical initiatives such as the UGOCM in the north and guerrilla movements in the south. In addition, schoolteachers formed independent union movements in the 1950s and 1970s and played a key role in the 2006 protests in Oaxaca. Ironically, Padilla finds, "the very schools the revolutionary government had once designed to create a loyal citizenry were now producing its most militant foes." Pensado analyzes student organizing at the IPN, which was repressed in 1956, only to reappear in another form, with great effect, a decade later.

None of these authors leave out the repression, which weaves through virtually every story in the book. The IPN strike Pensado chronicles was broken through harsh military and legal attacks, "a series of systematic acts of violence and provocation against the students," culminating in the occupation of the Instituto by "eighteen hundred soldiers, more than three hundred granaderos, more than a hundred officers from the Judicial Police, and an indeterminate number of agents from the Federal Security Directorate (DFS)." Padilla reports that following the repression of the student movement in 1968, the SEP shut down fourteen of the country's twenty-nine rural normal schools, turning them into agricultural training schools; in the fifteen schools that remained the first three years of study, during which students completed their secondary education, were eliminated.

In his work on the significance of violence and the military to PRIísmo, Rath finds that in the 1940s, "in the name of public order, the military violently raided ejidos and municipalities, broke strikes, and intimidated, detained, and fined protesters en masse." In the 1950s "its core role was the application of force, and sometimes terror," characterized by military interventions in strategic economic zones as well as attacks on Indian communities. In 1955 a rebellion of indigenous villagers in the region of La Trinitaria, Chiapas, was defeated with a "display of military terror, mass executions and beheadings [that] shocked even the intelligence agent sent to investigate," but which the army insisted was "standard (if secretive) practice." In his account of government takeover of industrial unions, Snodgrass observes that "military deployments subdued dissidence in old communist strongholds, from the railway shops of Monterrey to the Gulf Coast oil refineries."

On the electoral front, the government's "combination of promises of reform, primaries, presidential denunciations of *caciquismo*, and tightening central control" subverted a powerful, pragmatic enthusiasm for competitive elections. In San Luis Potosí, "when things became more complicated and disturbances and violence might be the outcome of enduring political stalemates, Santos would dispatch the chief of the state police with a contingent of armed men and appoint a member of the military to control the situation, as happened in Salinas throughout the 1940s." In Morelos, when four thousand workers and peasants struck at the Zacatepec sugar cooperative, "government officials sent in soldiers from the nearby headquarters of the twenty-fourth military zone to surround the sugar mill and, by the following morning, take over the refinery." In his study of mid-century pistoleros, Piccato finds that "the pistolero was the bodyguard and enforcer for a politician or a criminal, or both . . . they operated against opposition or independent union leaders, students or electoral rivals." "Today," Piccato observes, "as in 1948 or 1959, when senators Angulo and Altamirano were killed, politics could not be clearly separated from the criminal use of violence and there was a consensus in favor of bending of the rule of law to achieve swift justice."

Power

How do we theorize centralized power that uses ongoing, evolving, premeditated repressive policy[11] but coexists with multiple locations and kinds of power that change over time in accord with their own dynamics? How do we put together "the relentless and increasing pressure from Mexico City" (which this book documents in detail), "the war between the provincial, the local, and the central monsters," and tenacious and innovative forms of popular opposition?[12]

We know that over time we see fewer of the old forms of peasant and worker mobilization that characterized and grew out of the revolution and gained renewed room to maneuver under Cárdenas's rule. Indeed, the regime learned to deal with those in the course of the 1940s and 1950s, but that does not mean conflict stopped happening. Officials in Mexico City had, from their point of view, systematized ways of dealing with familiar forms of grassroots opposition. But the regime was much less effective in dealing with new kinds of challenges, from the regional (and often multiclass) movements for political and economic reform in the 1960s and the student rebellion of 1968, to the guerrilla, popular, and clandestine movements of the 1970s, to the intertwined urban civil society and rural indigenous organizing that precipitated startling changes in the 1980s and 1990s. Indeed, if the 1950s was a resting point, as several authors in this book suggest, nothing stayed in place for long.

The question is how to interpret this historical moment—the 1940s and 1950s—looking backward and forward simultaneously. Mexicanists have long converged on the idea of everything eventually folding in to form a system. In chapter 1 Alan Knight shows high-level political officials and bosses turning away from Cárdenas and falling into line behind a conservative program. Knight presents compelling reasons for this shift: generational change; routinization of bureaucratic procedures; the belief on the part of new and old political leaders that Cárdenas had turned too far Left; and popular sentiments of disenchantment. Knight places these changes in the context of economic downturn and the growing political presence of businesspeople within the PRM, and he dates "closure"—the "turning point" between the end of revolutionary social reform and the beginning of a conservative "national project"—to 1937–38.

Paul Gillingham places the end of meaningful electoral competition, even within the official party and at the municipal level, in 1952. Gillingham shows that, throughout the 1940s, the "partial, patchwork, and negotiated nature of provincial electoral control" provided concessions and negotiation to opposition candidates and their supporters in municipal elections, even as it precluded outright opposition victories. Protest after elections, what Gillingham deems to be "collective bargaining by riot," produced yet further shifts and accommodations: "Postelectoral resistance was a risky strategy but one with three realistic aims: an immediate veto of opponents' entry to government, seats on a compromise municipal council, and a greater sensitivity to future demands." In the face of ongoing competition, however, "the steamroller in Mexican politics" placed restrictions on both primaries and general elections, and by the end of 1949 President Alemán felt strong enough to ban primaries. As a result of this final move, "flawed but competitive elections" gave way by 1952 to "the spectacle of an election."

Rogelio Hernández Rodríguez (chapter 4) describes regional strongmen who contributed to Mexican political stability through the 1950s by handling the states' "complex local socioeconomic, cultural, and political differences." However, Hernández finds regional *caudillos* to have been effectively eliminated by the end of the López Mateos *sexenio*, when presidential tolerance for ceding power to potentially interventionist regional bosses wore out. Going further, Paxman and Snodgrass argue that film and television (for the former) and workers and *braceros* (for the latter) were fully controlled by the regime through almost the entire period from 1938 to 1968, albeit with some negotiating space for media moguls and a relatively good economic deal for workers within government-controlled unions.

If many chapters of this book suggest arcs of contestation that resulted in centralized control achieved by a discernible date, others underscore the centrality of multiple shifting arrangements of politics and social life that provide different groups in Mexican society with forms of (limited) room to maneuver throughout the period, however unequal and shot through with power this room to maneuver may have been. We find this in Smith's descriptions of those who resisted urban taxes and the state's decisions to raise money by other means, Pansters's Santos cacicazgo, McCormick's peasant leaders, Piccato's second sections, Pensado's students, Padilla's schools for teachers, and Blancarte's churchmen, all of whom carve out and maintain practices or spaces that are alternative enough to enable people to live and compromise somewhat differently or even nudge the path of history in unexpected directions.

I think "hegemonic process" is a more useful concept here than authoritarianism. In these chapters, when the word *hegemony* is used at all, it means complete control, politically or culturally. Instead, I would use it to describe the ongoing tension between power that is imposed and power that is negotiated, as well as the complex interplay between regions and center.[13] Hegemonic process also provides a useful way of conceptualizing interactions among the diverse factions that constitute the state. Following William Roseberry's discussion in *Everyday Forms of State Formation*, we might use hegemony not to characterize consent or stable control "but to understand struggle."[14] Like those who see centralized authoritarianism in Mexico, Roseberry sees domination, but he finds this domination to be actively contested, reinscribed, and changed through time: "The field of force is much more complex, as the laws, dictates, programs, and procedures of the central state are applied in particular regions, each of which is characterized by distinct patterns of inequality and domination, which in turn are the uniquely configured social products of historical processes that include prior relations and tensions of center and locality."[15]

In Roseberry's view, hegemonic process is not uniquely cultural; it involves economy, politics, and military force as well. Hegemony characterizes a *shifting* system in which various forces of power and inequality reproduce themselves over time, performing considerable "work" to do so, and they are themselves changed in the process. In the words of Raymond Williams, hegemony "has to be seen as more than the simple transmission of an (un)changing) dominance." Rather, "it has continually to be renewed, recreated, defended, and modified. It is also continually resisted, limited, altered, challenged by pressures not at all its own."[16]

When characterizing and evaluating the changes that constitute enduring hegemony, it is important to problematize how the knowledge people gain from the second section of the newspaper—where the corrupt and repressive character of the regime can be revealed in discussions about crime—affects the decisions they make in living their everyday lives. This can be difficult to specify by any model and involves close readings of culture and politics in particular locations. People's dual knowledge of the official story and the stories behind the scenes leads sometimes to selling out for cash, sometimes to pleasure in the consumption of shoes or movies, and sometimes to launching an anti-tax campaign in the market or rallying in the zócalo in support of the Zapatistas. Mary Louise Pratt suggests that theory resists homogeneity "and multiplies its terms and categories only if someone with access to the process insists on the need to do so."[17] Through their access to new intelligence archives, this book's authors enable us to see, hold, and analyze the variety of on-the-ground experiences out of which domination was constructed, resisting homogeneity and multiplying our terms as we do so. It is similarly difficult to specify, but important to know, which intelligence information enabled which faction of the national political elite to win out in a particular time period or region and how each partial victory shifted regional and national politics in particular directions. Faced with the multiplicity that is the strength and insight of this book, I think "hegemonic process"—better than "authoritarianism"—gets to the nuances out of which history is made.

If I question the use of the term *authoritarian*—for being a model drawn from political science, being reductionist, setting up a reified "popular" and "state," and most of all suggesting that the arc of contestation that began with the revolution concluded by one date or another in an authoritarian "system"—there is something more appealing about the term *dictablanda*. "Dictablanda" evokes a wink, knowledge not only or simply of the *mano dura*, the repression, what's happening to the railroad workers or to the peasants supplying sugar mills in Morelos. Dictablanda also acknowledges the pleasure people take in "golden age" consumption, in their daily personal and collective cultural and family lives, and in new technologies, possibilities, and events.[18] Not just that Mexicans are being bought off, but that two things are happening at once: pleasure and optimism on the one hand, distrust and foreboding on the other. Dictablanda is aware and proud of the economic growth that is happening over the decades described in this book, the benefits to urban workers, the system of bargaining that maintains wages, even the notion of the PRI and the ideas that the PRI is the party that came out of the revolution and that the rough and tumble that is Mexican politics happens in part within and through the PRI.[19]

Dictablanda also encompasses the fear and desperation bred of decades of corruption and a Mexican "crisis" that has continued unabated from the 1980s to the present.[20] The expression *dictablanda* is humorous, albeit darkly, in its construction and meaning. It knows that there are some things that happen and other things that don't happen, and that Mexicans make these part of who they are and what they do in creative and different ways. This is what Pablo Piccato is getting at when he talks about the second section, what cultural historians try to discern in their deconstructions of Mexican elite and popular cultural production, and what scholars of Mexican politics and popular movements uncover when they leave the halls of power and go to the *barrios* or the provinces. In a more somber way, the depths and ironies of Mexican experience were reflected back to the nation in Subcomandante Marcos's famous communiqués, from "who shall ask forgiveness and who shall grant it?" to his increasingly long and quixotic missives about suffering and struggle in the southeast.[21]

I think that *authoritarianism* subsumes all that, and even the translation "soft authoritarianism" and the more descriptive "competitive authoritarianism" do the same. Soft authoritarianism and competitive authoritarianism know that hard authoritarianism is worse and democracy is better. Dictablanda, in contrast, knows that what existed yesterday and exists today might be bad, but what comes next might well be worse (as we have seen in today's violence that occurs beyond imagined limits). In its uncertainty about the future, dictablanda perhaps captures much better something about the twentieth century in Latin America.

Latin America in the Twentieth Century

Is Mexico a unique steamroller for repression and the manufacture of domination and cynicism? The startling opening of the 1990s, which saw the Zapatista rebellion and the establishment of the Instituto Federal Electoral and electoral democracy, brought this formulation into question because these openings had clear origins in the preceding decades. Indeed, the Zapatista rebellion could be traced in part to Samuel Ruiz's transformation from conservative to organizer as he made the rounds of PRI-controlled Mayan villages in the 1960s, and the clandestine leftists who left the cities after Tlatelolco to make the revolution in the countryside. Furthermore, the drug trafficking violence of the present and the state's complicity in it, while they point to state corruption and institutional reach common to state-centered analyses, indicate as well that the ways in which the power that was constructed between 1938 and 1968 has followed circuitous and unexpected pathways long out of central government control.[22]

In his analysis of the Mexican economy in the early decades of the twentieth century, John Womack Jr. argues that the "main historical meaning" of the Mexican Revolution is "capitalist tenacity in the economy and bourgeois reform of the state."[23] While this controversial statement downplays other significant historical meanings (not least Womack's own attributions of meaning to the Zapatista struggle in 1970), his observation dovetails with this volume's emphasis on the closing down of the revolution through a process of repression carried out from the center. At the same time, Womack opens up his stark conclusion by linking it to a political process within an economic context: "What really happened was a struggle for power, in which different revolutionary factions contended not only against the old regime and foreign concerns, but also, often more so, against each other . . . the victorious factions managed to dominate peasant movements and labor unions for the promotion of selected 'American' and native businesses."[24]

Here I believe Womack provides a path we can follow to link Mexico between 1938 and 1968 to twentieth-century Latin America more broadly, where overall a changing set of "victorious factions" pretty effectively "dominated[d] peasant movements and labor unions"—and other forms of grassroots and/or democratic resistance, alternatives, and rebellions—and promoted "selected 'American' and native businesses," including the business of the Cold War. This occurred as twentieth-century Latin American nations faced the task of conceptualizing and implementing "development" and adapting to and managing urbanization, with "the people coming on the scene" in new and increasingly creative and insistent ways. Mexico is perhaps the limiting case of what looks like a system but is in fact more diffuse, vectored, and multilayered, with three (or more) sorts of monsters fighting it out on a varied terrain.

At the same time, Mexico shows clearly the many ways in which power in twentieth-century Latin America was wielded against any sort of popularly driven, democratically controlled project that benefited the poor and marginalized, any project permitting local alternatives and autonomy or state-led moves toward "socialism" and even "social democracy" as it is broadly understood. If there is something particularly, repetitively repressive and corrosive about the legacy of PRI rule—rather than something particularly visible and theorized about that legacy—we might see it as a stand-in for the paths from 1910 to the military governments of the 1960s to 1980s and for the violence so deeply embedded in Latin America's democracies today.[25]

The lessons of mid-twentieth-century Mexico so incisively analyzed in this book include the routinized, skillful, and studied practice of "limited" repression; the use of brutal repression as a backup; effective means of disguising and denying the ongoing use of violence; a vast repertoire—much but not all of it illegal—for outmaneuvering leftist oppositions (together with the tenacity and innovation of grassroots resistance and mobilization); ongoing and determined support for private sector growth; little willingness or ability to stand up to private sector threats and discontent or to international economic forces and institutions; cultural projects that shore up nationalism while minimizing democratic content; and, importantly, diverse regional political formations that provide flexible, not fully controllable underpinnings for the perpetuation of inequality.

These phenomena do not seem uniquely Mexican. Nor do they characterize a "system" in any clear fashion. Indeed, we might wonder why Mexico presses scholars to want to see a system in the first place. We also wonder, with so much at stake, about whether the now lengthening arc of the transitions to democracy of the 1980s will produce something more than domination of ordinary people and the promotion of business. There is much to hope for and much to fear as we look from Mexico to Central America, from Venezuela to Brazil, from Bolivia to Chile. Will the tried and true mechanisms of repression and antidemocratic regional politics give way to alternatives of autonomy and democratic citizenship? For the most part, we will follow events to find the answer. At the same time, we are best poised to do so if we discern the modalities of repression, the regional pathways of politics and power through time, the interactions between center and region, the second sections of cultural production, and the depth of particular forms of political and economic experience delineated with such scholarly tenacity and imagination in this book.

Notes

1. John Womack Jr., "The Mexican Revolution, 1910–1920," in *Mexico Since Independence*, ed. Leslie Bethell, 125–200 (Cambridge: Cambridge University Press, 1991); Nora Hamilton, *The Limits of State Autonomy: Post-revolutionary Mexico* (Princeton, NJ: Princeton University Press, 1982).

2. Philip Abrams, "Notes on the Difficulty of Studying the State," *Journal of Historical Sociology* 1, no. 1 (1988 [1977]): 58–89; Jeffrey W. Rubin, "The State as Subject," *Political Power and Social Theory* 17 (2002): 107–31.

3. José Luis Reyna and Richard S. Weinert, eds., *Authoritarianism in Mexico* (Philadelphia: Institute for the Study of Human Issues, 1977).

4. Pablo González Casanova, *Democracy in Mexico*, trans. Danielle Salti (Oxford: Oxford University Press, 1970 [1965]); Judith Adler Hellman, *Mexico in Crisis* (New York: Holmes and Meier, 1983).

5. Gilbert M. Joseph and Daniel Nugent, eds., *Everyday Forms of State Formation: Revolution and the Negotiation of Rule in Modern Mexico* (Durham, NC: Duke University Press, 1994); Jeffrey W. Rubin, *Decentering the Regime: Ethnicity, Radicalism, and Democracy in Juchitán, Mexico* (Durham, NC: Duke University Press, 1997); Hispanic American Historical Review, *Mexico's New Cultural History: ¿Una Lucha Libre?* (Durham, NC: Duke University Press, 1999).

6. This is demonstrated with stunning force in Gabriela Soto Laveaga's study of the doctors' strike in Mexico City in 1964–65. Soto Laveaga shows that the repressive tactics eventually used to suppress the strike were outlined in explicit detail by govern-

ment officials within a short time of the strike's initiation. Gabriela Soto Laveaga, "The Emperor Has a New Lab Coat: Doctors' Strikes, Repression and the Mexican State, 1964–65" (unpublished manuscript, 2009).

7. Gilbert M. Joseph, Anne Rubenstein, and Eric Zolov, eds., *Fragments of a Golden Age: The Politics of Culture in Mexico Since 1940* (Durham, NC: Duke University Press, 2001); Mary Kay Vaughan and Stephen E. Lewis, eds., *The Eagle and the Virgin: Nation and Cultural Revolution in Mexico, 1920–1940* (Durham, NC: Duke University Press, 2006).

8. Gonzalo N. Santos, *Memorias* (Mexico City: Grijalbo, 1984), 714.

9. Womack, "The Mexican Revolution," 128; personal communication, John Womack, 2010.

10. Philip Corrigan, "State Formation," in Joseph and Nugent, *Everyday Forms of State Formation*, xvii–xix.

11. On the premeditation and relentlessness of rule from the center, see Aaron W. Navarro, *Political Intelligence and the Creation of Modern Mexico, 1938–1954* (University Park: Pennsylvania State University Press, 2010).

12. I thank John Womack for several ideas to which I refer in this conclusion: the dual formulation of "relentless pressure" and "three monsters"; the recognition that the lessening of old forms of mobilization does not signify the absence of conflict; and the notion that we should be careful what we look for (2010).

13. Joseph and Nugent, *Everyday Forms of State Formation*; see also Gillingham on "force and consent" in Gramsci's understanding of hegemony (preface in this volume).

14. William Roseberry, "Hegemony and the Language of Contention," in Joseph and Nugent, *Everyday Forms of State Formation*, 360–61.

15. Roseberry, "Hegemony and the Language of Contention," 365.

16. Raymond Williams, *Marxism and Literature* (Oxford: Oxford University Press, 1977), 112.

17. Mary Louise Pratt, "Where to? What Next?," in *Cultures of Politics/Politics of Cultures: Revisioning Latin American Social Movements*, ed. S. E. Alvarez, E. Dagnino, and A. Escobar (Boulder, CO: Westview Press, 1998).

18. Mary Kay Vaughan, "Transnational Processes and the Rise and Fall of the Mexican Cultural State: Notes from the Past," in Joseph, Rubenstein, and Zolov, *Fragments of a Golden Age*, 471–87.

19. Rubin, *Decentering the Regime*, chapter 4.

20. Laura Roush, "The Language of 'Crisis' and the Uses of Indefinition in Mexico City" (PhD dissertation, The New School, 2009).

21. Subcomandante Marcos, *Shadows of Tender Fury* (New York: Monthly Review Press, 1995).

22. Howard Campbell, *Drug War Zone: Frontline Dispatches from the Streets of El Paso and Juárez* (Austin: University of Texas Press, 2009).

23. Womack, "The Mexican Revolution," 129.

24. Womack, "The Mexican Revolution," 128.

25. Enrique Desmond Arias and Daniel M. Goldstein, *Violent Democracies in Latin America* (Durham, NC: Duke University Press, 2010).

SELECT BIBLIOGRAPHY

Aboites Aguilar, Luis. *Excepciones y privelegios: Modernización tributaria y centralización en México, 1922–1972*. Mexico City: El Colegio de México, 2003.
Abrams, Philip. "Notes on the Difficulty of Studying the State." *Journal of Historical Sociology* 1, no. 1 (1988 [1977]): 58–89.
Ackroyd, William S. "Military Professionalism, Education, and Political Behavior in Mexico." *Armed Forces and Society* 18, no. 1 (1991): 81–96.
Adler Lomnitz, Larissa. *Networks and Marginality: Life in a Mexican Shanty Town*. New York: Academic Press, 1977.
Aguayo Alvarez, José Luis. *Salaices Escuela Normal Rural: Formadora de maestros*. Chihuahua: Ediciones del Azar, 2002.
Aguayo Alvarez, José Luis, ed. *Un paseo por los recuerdos*. Chihuahua: La Asociación Civil de Exalumnos de Salaices, 2007.
Aguayo Quezada, Sergio. *1968: Los Archivos de la Violencia*. Mexico City: Grijalbo, 1998.
Aguayo Quezada, Sergio. *La Charola: Una historia de servicios de inteligencia en México*. Mexico City: Grijalbo, 2001.
Aguilar Camín, Hector, and Lorenzo Meyer. *In the Shadow of the Mexican Revolution: Contemporary Mexican History, 1910–1989*. Translated by Luis Fierro. Austin: University of Texas Press, 1993.
Aguilar Camín, Hector. *La Frontera Nomada, Sonora y la Revolución Mexicana*. Mexico City: Siglo XXI, 1977.
Aguirre Beltrán, Gonzalo, and Ricardo Pozas. "Instituciones indígenas en el siglo XX." In *Métodos y resultados de la política indigenista en México*. Edited by Alfonso Caso, Gonzalo Aguirre Beltrán, and Ricardo Pozas Arciniega. Mexico City: Instituto Nacional Indigenista, 1954.
Aguirre Beltrán, Gonzalo. *El pensar y el quehacer antropológico en México*. Puebla: Benemérita Universidad Autónoma de Puebla, 1994.
Aguirre Beltrán, Gonzalo. *El proceso de aculturación y el cambio sociocultural en México.* Mexico City: Universidad Iberoamericana, [1958] 1970.
Aguirre Beltrán, Gonzalo. *Formas de gobierno indígena*. Mexico City: UNAM, 1953.

Aguirre Beltrán, Gonzalo. *La población negra de México*. Mexico City: Fondo de Cultura Económica, [1946] 1972.
Aguirre Beltrán, Gonzalo. *Problemas de la población indígena en la cuenca del Tepalcatepec*. Mexico City: Instituto Nacional Indigenista, 1952.
Agustín, José. *Tragicomedia mexicana 1: La vida en México de 1940 a 1970*. Mexico City: Planeta, 1998.
Alcaraz, Agustín García. *Tinujei: Los Triquis de Copala*. Mexico City: Centro de Investigaciones y Estudios Superiores en Antropología Social, 1997.
Alder Hellman, Judith. *Mexico in Crisis*. New York: Holmes and Meier, 1983.
Alegre, Robert. "Las Rieleras: Gender, Politics, and Power in the Mexican Railway Movement, 1958–1959." *Journal of Women's History* 23, no. 2 (2011): 162–86.
Alisky, Marvin. "CONASUPO: A Mexican Agency Which Makes Low Income Workers Feel Their Government Cares." *Inter-American Economic Affairs* 27, no. 3 (winter 1973): 47–59.
Allen, Craig. *Eisenhower and the Mass Media*. Chapel Hill: University of North Carolina Press, 1993.
Almond, Gabriel A., and Sidney Verba. *The Civic Culture: Political Attitudes and Democracy in Five Nations*. Newbury Park, CA: Sage Publications, 1989.
Alonso, Ana. "The Politics of Space, Time and Substance: State Formation, Nationalism, and Ethnicity." *Annual Review of Anthropology* 23 (1994): 379–405.
Alonso, Antonio. *El movimiento ferrocarrilero en México, 1958–1959*. Mexico City: Era, 1972.
Alonso, Jorge. *El rito electoral en Jalisco, 1940–1992*. Guadalajara: Centro de Investigaciones y Estudios Superiores en Antropología Social, El Colegio de Jalisco, 1993.
Althusser, Louis. *Lenin and Philosophy and Other Essays*. New York: Monthly Review Press, 1972.
Alvarado, Arturo. *El portesgilismo en Tamaulipas: Estudio de la constitución de la autoridad pública en México posrevolucionario*. Mexico City: El Colegio de México, 1992.
Alvear Acevedo, Carlos. "La Iglesia de México en el período 1900–1962." In *Historia general de la Iglesia en América Latina, V. México*, 313–41. Mexico City: Paulinas, 1984.
Amador, María Luisa, and Jorge Ayala Blanco. *Cartelera cinematográfica, 1940–1949*. Mexico City: UNAM, 1982.
Amador, María Luisa, and Jorge Ayala Blanco. *Cartelera cinematográfica, 1950–1959*. Mexico City: UNAM, 1985.
Anderson, Martin Edwin. "Civil-Military Relations and Internal Security in Mexico: The Undone Reform." In *The Challenge of Institutional Reform in Mexico*, edited by Riordan Roett, 155–82. Boulder, CO: Lynne Rienner, 1995.
Anguiano Equihua, Roberto. *Las Finanzas del Sector Público en México*. Mexico City: UNAM, 1968.
Ankerson, Dudley. *Agrarian Warlord: Saturnino Cedillo and the Mexican Revolution in San Luis Potosí*. DeKalb: Northern Illinois University Press, 1984.
Ankerson, Dudley. *El caudillo agrarista: Saturnino Cedillo y la revolución Mexicana en San Luis Potosí*. Mexico City: INHERM, [1984] 1994.
Ankerson, Dudley. "Saturnino Cedillo, a Traditional Caudillo in San Luis Potosí, 1890–1938." In *Caudillo and Peasant in the Mexican Revolution*, edited by David A. Brading, 140–68. Cambridge: Cambridge University Press, 1980.

Aquino Casas, Arnulfo, and Jorge Perezvega. *Imágenes y símbolos del 68: Fotografía y gráfica del movimiento estudiantil*. Mexico City: UNAM, 2004.

Ard, Michael J. *An Eternal Struggle: How the National Action Party Transformed Mexican Politics*. Westport, CT: Praeger, 2003.

Arias, Enrique Desmond, and Daniel M. Goldstein, eds. *Violent Democracies in Latin America*. Durham, NC: Duke University Press, 2010.

Aronowitz, Stanley, and Peter Bratsis, eds. *Paradigm Lost: State Theory Reconsidered*. Minneapolis: University of Minnesota Press, 2002.

Ashby, Joe C. *Organized Labor and the Mexican Revolution under Lázaro Cárdenas*. Chapel Hill: University of North Carolina Press, 1963.

Aspe Armella, María Luisa. *La formación social y política de los católicos mexicanos: La Acción Católica y la Unión Nacional de Estudiantes Católicos, 1929–1958*. Mexico City: Universidad Iberoamericana, 2008.

Aviña, Alexander. *Specters of Revolution: Peasant Guerrillas in the Cold War Mexican Countryside*. Oxford: Oxford University Press, forthcoming.

Azuela, Mariano. *Nueva burguesía*. Mexico City: Fondo de Cultura Económica, 1985.

Babb, Sarah. *Managing Mexico: Economists from Nationalism to Neoliberalism*. Princeton, NJ: Princeton University Press, 2001.

Báez-Jorge, Félix. *¿Líderes indios o intermediarios indigenistas?* Mexico City: Escuela Nacional de Antropología e Historia, 1984.

Bailey, David C. "Revisionism and the Recent Historiography of the Mexican Revolution." *Hispanic American Historical Review* 58, no. 1 (February 1978): 68, 70–71.

Bantjes, Adrian A. *As if Jesus Walked on Earth: Cardenismo, Sonora, and the Mexican Revolution*. Wilmington, DE: Scholarly Resources, 1998.

Barkin, David, and Timothy King. *Regional Economic Development: The River Basin Approach in Mexico*. Cambridge: Cambridge Latin American Studies, 1970.

Barnouw, Erik. *Tube of Plenty: The Evolution of American Television*. New York: Oxford University Press, 1977.

Bartolomé, Miguel A., and Alicia M. Barabas. *La presa Cerro del Oro y el Ingeniero Gran Dios: Relocalización y etnocidio chinanteco*. Mexico City: Instituto Nacional Indigenista, 1990.

Barton Bray, David, Leticia Merino Pérez, and Deborah Barry, eds. *The Community Forests of Mexico: Managing for Sustainable Landscapes*. Austin: University of Texas Press, 2005.

Bartra, Armando. *Guerrero bronco: Campesinos, ciudadanos y guerrilleros en la Costa Grande*. Mexico City: Ediciones Era, 2000.

Bartra, Armando. *Los herederos de Zapata: Movimientos campesinos posrevolucionarios en México, 1920–1980*. Mexico City: Ediciones Era, 1985.

Bartra, Armando, Juan M. Aurrecoeche, Gisela Espinosa, and Lorena Paz Paredes, eds. *De haciendas, cañeros, y paraestatales: Cien años de historia de la agroindustria cañero-azucarera en México, 1880–1980*. Mexico City: Escuela Nacional de Estudios Profesionales Acatlán, Universidad Nacional Autónoma de México, 1993.

Bartra, Roger. *Caciquismo y poder político en el México rural*. Mexico City: Siglo XXI, 1975.

Bartra, Roger. *Anatomía del mexicano*. Mexico City: Random House Mondadori, 2005.

Basauri, Carlos. *La población indígena de México*. 3 vols. Mexico City: Departamento de Asuntos Indígenas, 1940.

Basurto, Jorge. *Del avilacamachismo al Alemánismo (1940–1952)*. Mexico City: Siglo XXI, 1984.

Basurto, Jorge. "The Late Populism of Luis Echeverría." In *Latin American Populism in Comparative Perspective*, edited by Michael L. Conniff, 93–111. Albuquerque: University of New Mexico Press, 1982.

Bassols Batalla, Angel. *El noreste de Mexico: Un estudio geografico-económico*. Mexico City: UNAM, 1972.

Bauman, Zygmunt. *Culture as Praxis*. London: Sage Publications, 1999.

Beals, Ralph L. "Anthropology in Contemporary Mexico." In *Contemporary Mexico: Papers of IV International Congress of Mexican History*, edited by James W. Wilkie, Michael C. Meyer, and Edna Monzón de Wilkie, 753–68. Berkeley: University of California Press for the UCLA Latin American Center/El Colegio de México, 1976.

Beardsell, Peter. *A Theatre for Cannibals: Rodolfo Usigli and the Mexican Stage*. Rutherford, NJ: Associated University Presses, 1992.

Beer, Caroline C. *Electoral Competition and Institutional Change in Mexico*. Notre Dame, IN: University of Notre Dame Press, 2003.

Beezley, William H., Cheryl English Martin, and William E. French, eds. *Rituals of Rule, Rituals of Resistance: Public Celebrations and Popular Culture in Mexico*. Wilmington, DE: Scholarly Resources, 1994.

Bellingeri, Marco. *Del agrarismo armado a la guerra de los pobres, 1940–1974*. Mexico City: Ediciones Casa Juan Pablos, 2003.

Bellinghausen, Hermann, ed. *Pensar el 68*. Mexico City: Cal y Arena, 2008.

Beltrán, Enrique. *La batalla forestal: Lo hecho, lo no hecho, lo por hacer*. Mexico City: Editorial Cultura, 1964.

Benjamin, Thomas, and Mark Wasserman, eds. *Provinces of the Revolution: Essays on Regional Mexican History, 1910–1929*. Albuquerque: University of New Mexico Press, 1990.

Benjamin, Thomas. *A Rich Land, a Poor People: Politics and Society in Modern Chiapas*. Albuquerque: University of New Mexico Press, 1989.

Benjamin, Thomas. *La Revolución: Mexico's Great Revolution as Memory, Myth and History*. Austin: University of Texas Press, 2000.

Bergquist, Charles. *Labor in Latin America: Comparative Essays on Chile, Argentina, Venezuela, and Colombia*. Palo Alto, CA: Stanford University Press, 1986.

Bernal, Rafael. *El complot mongol*. Mexico: Joaquín Mortiz, 1969.

Bethell, Leslie, and Ian Roxborough. "Latin America between the Second World War and the Cold War: Some Reflections on the 1945–1948 Conjuncture." *Journal of Latin American Studies* 20, no. 1 (1988): 167–89.

Blacker, O'Neill. "Cold War in the Countryside: Conflict in Guerrero, Mexico." *The Americas* 66, no. 2 (2009): 181–210.

Blair, Calvin P. "Nacional Financiera, Entrepreneurship in a Mixed Economy." In *Public Policy and Private Enterprise in Mexico*, edited by Raymond Vernon, 192–240. Cambridge, MA: Harvard University Press, 1964.

Blancarte, Roberto. *Historia de la Iglesia católica en México*. Mexico City: Fondo de Cultura Económica-El Colegio Mexiquense, 1992.

Blanco Moheno, Roberto. *Memorias de un reportero*. Zacatecas: Litográfia Zacatecana, 1966.

Boege, Eckart. *Los mazatecos ante la nación: Contradicciones de la identidad étnica en el México actual*. Mexico City: Siglo Veintiuno Editores, 1988.

Bonnell, Victoria E., and Lynn Hunt, eds. *Beyond the Cultural Turn: New Directions in the Study of Society and Culture*. Berkeley: University of California Press, 1999.

Booth, John A., and Mitchell A. Seligson. "The Political Culture of Authoritarianism in Mexico: A Reexamination." *Latin American Research Review* 9, no. 1 (1984): 106–24.

Bortz, Jeffrey L., and Marcos Aguila. "Earning a Living: A History of Real Wage Studies in Twentieth-Century Mexico." *Latin American Research Review* 41, no. 2 (2006): 112–38.

Bortz, Jeffrey L. *Industrial Wages in Mexico City, 1939–1975*. New York: Garland Publishers, 1987.

Bortz, Jeffrey L. "Wages and Economic Crisis in Mexico." In *The Mexican Left, the Popular Movements, and the Politics of Austerity*, edited by Barry Carr and Ricardo Anzaldúa Montoya, 41–46. San Diego: Center for U.S.–Mexican Studies, 1986.

Boyer, Christopher R. "Revolución y paternalismo ecológico: Miguel Ángel de Quevedo y la política forestal, 1926–1940." *Historia Mexicana* 57, no. 1 (2007): 91–138.

Boyer, Christopher R., and Emily Wakild. "Social Landscaping in the Forests of Mexico: An Environmental Interpretation of Cardenismo, 1934–1940." *Hispanic American Historical Review* 92, no. 1 (February 2012): 73–106.

Brachet-Marquez, Viviane. *The Dynamics of Domination: State, Class, and Social Reform in Mexico, 1910–1990*. Pittsburgh: University of Pittsburgh Press, 1994.

Braham, Persephone. *Crimes against the State, Crimes against Persons: Detective Fiction in Cuba and Mexico*. Minneapolis: University of Minnesota Press, 2004.

Brandenburg, Frank. *The Making of Modern Mexico*. Hoboken, NJ: Prentice-Hall, 1964.

Braun, Herbert. "Protest of Engagement: Dignity, False Love, and Self-Love in Mexico during 1968." *Comparative Studies in Sociology and History* 39, no. 3 (1997): 511–49.

Brautigam, Deborah A., Odd-Helge Fjeldstad, and Mick Moore, eds. *Taxation and State-Building in Developing Countries, Capacity and Consent*. Cambridge: Cambridge University Press, 2008.

Brockington, Dan. *Fortress Conservation: The Preservation of the Mkomazi Game Reserve*. Bloomington: University of Indiana Press, 2002.

Brooks, Tim. "A Short History of Network Television." In *The Complete Dictionary to Prime Time Network and Cable TV Shows 1946–Present*, 6th ed., edited by Tim Brooks and Earle Marsh, x–xxi. New York: Ballantine, 1995.

Brown, Jonathan C., and Alan Knight, eds. *The Mexican Petroleum Industry in the Twentieth Century*. Austin: University of Texas Press, 1992.

Buffington, Robert, and Pablo Piccato, eds. *Mexican Crime Stories: Case Studies, Causes Célèbres, and Other True-to-Life Adventures in the Social Construction of Deviance*. Albuquerque: University of New Mexico Press, 2009.

Caballero, José Antonio. "Amparos y Abogángsters: La justicia en México entre 1940 y 1968." In *Del nacionalismo al neoliberalismo, 1940–1994*, edited by Elisa Servín. Mexico City: Fondo de Cultura Económica, 2010.

Calderón Mólgora, Marco Antonio. *Historias, procesos políticos y cardenismos: Cherán y la Sierra Purépecha*. Zamora: El Colegio de Michoacán, 2004.

Calva Téllez, José Luis. *Economía política de la explotación forestal en México: Bibliografía comentada, 1930–1984*. Mexico City: Universidad Autónoma Chapingo/Universidad Nacional Autónoma de México, 1989.

Camp, Roderic Ai. *Biografías de políticos mexicanos, 1935–1985*. Mexico City: Fondo de Cultura Económica, 1992.

Camp, Roderic Ai. *Generals in the Palacio: The Military in Modern Mexico*. Oxford: Oxford University Press, 1992.

Camp, Roderic Ai. *Mexican Political Biographies, 1935–1993*, 3rd ed. Austin: University of Texas Press, 1995.

Camp, Roderic Ai. *Mexico's Mandarins: Crafting a Power Elite for the Twentieth Century*. Berkeley: University of California Press, 2002.

Camp, Roderic Ai. *Politics in Mexico*. Oxford: Oxford University Press, 1993.

Camp, Roderic Ai. "Women and Political Leadership in Mexico: A Comparative Study of Female and Male Political Elites." *Journal of Politics* 41, no. 2 (May 1979): xxvii, 468.

Campa, Valentín. *Mi testimonio: Memorias de un comunista mexicano*. Mexico City: Cultura Popular, 1978.

Campbell, Howard. *Drug War Zone: Frontline Dispatches from the Streets of El Paso and Juárez*. Austin: University of Texas Press, 2009.

Campbell, Howard. *Zapotec Renaissance: Ethnic Politics and Cultural Revivalism in Southern Mexico*. Albuquerque: University of New Mexico Press, 1994.

Campbell, Hugh C. *La derecha radical en México, 1929–1949*. Mexico City: SepSetentas, 1976.

Cancian, Frank. *The Decline of Community in Zinacantán: Economy, Public Life, and Social Stratification, 1960–1987*. Palo Alto, CA: Stanford University Press, 1992.

Cano, Gabriela. "Ciudadanía y sufragio femenino: el discurso igualitario de Lázaro Cárdenas." In *Miradas feministas sobre las mexicanas del siglo xx*, edited by Marta Lamas, 151–90. Mexico City: Fondo de Cultura Económica, 2007.

Cano, Gabriela. *Se llamaba Elena Arizmendi*. Mexico City: Tusquets Editores, 2010.

Cárdenas, Enrique, Jose Antonio Ocampo, and Rosemary Thorpe, eds. *Industrialización y estado en al America Latina, la leyenda negra de la Posguerra*. Mexico City: El Trimestre Económico, 2003.

Cárdenas, Enrique. *La hacienda pública y la política económica, 1929–1958*. Mexico City: Fondo de Cultura Económica/El Colegio de México, 1994.

Cárdenas, Lázaro. *Apuntes*. Mexico City: UNAM, 1986.

Carmagnani, Marcello. "El liberalismo, los impuestos internos y el estado federal mexicano, 1857–1911." *Historia Mexicana* 38, no. 3 (1989): 471–96.

Carr, Barry. *La izquierda mexicana a través del siglo xx*. Mexico City: Era, 1996.

Carr, Barry. *Marxism and Communism in Twentieth-Century Mexico*. Lincoln: University of Nebraska Press, 1992.

Carr, Barry. "The Many Meanings of 1968: The Student-Popular Movement Thirty Years After." http://www.latrobe.edu.au/history/news/digital/carr1.htm.1.

Cassigoli, Rossana. *Liderazgo sindical y cultura minera en México: Napoleón Gómez Sada*. Mexico City: Porrua, 2004.

Castañeda Jiménez, Héctor C. *Marcelino García Barragán: Una vida al servicio de México.* Guadalajara: UNED, 1987.

Castellano, Laura. *México Armado, 1943–1981.* Mexico City: Ediciones Era, 2007.

Castillo Gómez, Antonio. "Cultura escrita y sociedad." *Cultura Escrita & Sociedad* 1 (2005): 10–13.

Caulfield, Norman. "Mexican State Development Policy and Labor Internationalism, 1945–1958." *International Review of Social History* 42, no. 1 (1997): 45–66.

Ceceña, José Luis. *México en la orbita imperial.* Mexico City: Ediciones El Caballito, 1970.

Cedillo Vasquez, Luciano. *De Juan Soldado a Juan Rielero.* Mexico City: Publicaciones Mexicanas, 1963.

Centeno, Miguel Angel, and Fernando López-Alves, eds. *The Other Mirror: Grand Theory through the Lens of Latin America.* Princeton, NJ: Princeton University Press, 2000.

Centeno, Miguel Angel. *Blood and Debt: War and the Nation-State in Latin America.* University Park: Pennsylvania State University Press, 2002.

Chassen-López, Francie. "A Patron of Progress: Juana Catarina Romero, the Nineteenth-Century Cacica of Tehuantepec." *Hispanic American Historical Review* 88, no. 3 (2008): 393–426.

Chaturvedi, Vinayak, ed. *Mapping Subaltern Studies and the Postcolonial.* London: Verso, 2000.

Cisneros S., Armando. *La ciudad que construimos: Registro de la expansión de la ciudad de México, 1920–1976.* Mexico City: UNAM, 1992.

Civera Cerecedo, Alicia. *La escuela como opción de vida: La formación de maestros normalistas rurales en México, 1921–1945.* Toluca: El Colegio Mexiquense, A.C., 2008.

Cline, Howard F. *Mexico: Revolution to Evolution, 1940–1960.* New York: Oxford University Press, 1962.

Close, Glen S. *Contemporary Hispanic Crime Fiction: A Transatlantic Discourse on Urban Violence.* New York: Palgrave Macmillan, 2008.

Cockcroft, James D. "Mexico." In *Latin America: The Struggle with Dependency and Beyond*, edited by Ronald H. Chilcote and Joel C. Edelstein, 222–304. New York: John Wiley and Sons, 1974.

Cohen, Jeffrey H. "Transnational Migration in Rural Oaxaca, Mexico: Dependency, Development, and the Household." *American Anthropologist* 103, no. 4 (December 2001): 954–67.

Contreras, Ariel José. *México 1940: Industrialización y crisis política: Estado y sociedad civil en las elecciones presidenciales.* Mexico City: Siglo XXI, 1977.

Córdova, Arnaldo. *La ideología de la Revolución Mexicana: La formación del nuevo régimen.* Mexico City: Era, 1973.

Cornelius, Wayne. *Politics and the Migrant Poor in Mexico City.* Palo Alto, CA: Stanford University Press, 1975.

Corrales, Javier. "The Gatekeeper State: Limited Economic Reforms and Regime Survival in Cuba, 1989–2002." *Latin American Research Review* 39, no. 2 (2004): 35–65.

Corro, Salvador, and José Reveles *La Quina: El lado oscuro del poder.* Mexico City: Planeta, 1989.

Cosío Villegas, Daniel. *Ensayos y notas.* 2 vols. Mexico City: Editorial Hermes, 1966.

Cosío Villegas, Daniel. *La Constitución de 1857 y sus críticos.* Mexico City: Editorial Hermes, 1957.

Cosío Villegas, Daniel. *La Crisis de México*. Mexico City: Clio, [1947] 1997.
Cosío Villegas, Daniel. *La sucesión presidencial*. Mexico City: Joaquín Mortiz, 1975.
Craig, Ann L. *The First Agraristas*. Berkeley: University of California Press, 1983.
Craig, Richard. "Operation Condor: Mexico's Antidrug Campaign Enters a New Era." *Journal of Interamerican Studies and World Affairs* 22, no. 3 (August 1980): 345–63.
Crehan, Kate. *Gramsci, Culture and Anthropology*. Berkeley: University of California Press, 2002.
Crespo, Horacio, and Enrique Villanueva. *Estadísticas históricas del azúcar en México*. Mexico City: Azúcar S.A., 1988.
Crespo, Horacio, ed. *Historia del azúcar en México*. 2 vols. Mexico City: Editorial del Fondo de Cultura Económica, 1988.
Cross, John C. *Informal Politics, Street Vendors and the State in Mexico City*. Palo Alto, CA: Stanford University Press, 1988.
Crumrine, N. Ross. *The Mayo Indians of Sonora*. Tucson: University of Arizona Press, 1977.
Cummings O'Hara, Julia. "Transforming the Sierra Tarahumara: Indians, Missionaries and the State in Chihuahua, Mexico, 1890–1960." PhD dissertation, University of Indiana, 2004.
Dahl, Robert. *On Democracy*. New Haven, CT: Yale University Press, 2000.
Dahl, Robert. *Polyarchy: Participation and Opposition*. New Haven, CT: Yale University Press, 1971.
Dávila Peralta, Nicolás. *Las Santas Batallas: El Anticomunismo en Puebla*. Puebla: Gobierno del estado de Puebla, 1978.
Davis, Diane. "Policing and Mexican Regime Change: From Post-authoritarianism to Populism to Neo-liberalism." Working Paper No. 2. London: Crisis States Research Center, Development Studies Institute, London School of Economics, 2007.
Davis, Diane. "The Political and Economic Origins of Violence and Insecurity in Contemporary Latin America: Past Trajectories and Future Prospects." In *Violent Democracies in Latin America*, edited by Desmond Arias and Daniel Goldstein, 35–62. Durham, NC: Duke University Press, 2010.
Davis, Diane. *Urban Leviathan: Mexico City in the Twentieth Century*. Philadelphia: Temple University Press, 1994.
Dawson, Alexander Scott. *Indian and Nation in Revolutionary Mexico*. Tucson: University of Arizona Press, 2004.
De Grammont, Hubert C. "La Unión General de Obreros y Campesinos." In *Historia de la Cuestión Agraria Mexicana: Política estatal y conflictos agrarios 1950–1970*, vol. 8, 222–60. Mexico City: Siglo Veintiuno Editores, 1989.
de la Cerda, José E. *Contra el Cacicazgo Santista nació la Alianza Cívica Potosina*. San Luis Potosí: n.p., 1958.
de la Fuente, Julio. "Cambios raciales y culturales en un grupo indígena." *Acta Anthropológica* 3 (1948): 48–67.
de la Fuente, Julio. *Monopolio de aguardiente y alcoholismo en los Altos de Chiapas*. Mexico City: Comisión Nacional para el Desarrollo de los Pueblos Indígenas, 2009.
de la Fuente, Julio. *Yalálag: Una villa zapoteca serrana*. Mexico City: Museo Nacional de Antropología, 1949.

de la Garza, Enrique, Tomás Ejea León, and Luis Fernando Macias. *El otro movimiento estudiantil*. Mexico City: Extemporáneos, 1986.

de la Peña, Guillermo, and Renée de la Torre. "Microhistoria de un barrio tapatio: Santa Teresita (1930–1980)." In *Vivir en Guadalajara, La ciudad y sus funciones*, edited by Carmen Castañeda, 119–38. Guadalajara: Ayuntamiento de Guadalajara, 1992.

de la Peña, Guillermo. "Civil Society and Popular Resistance: Mexico at the End of the Twentieth Century." In *Cycles of Conflict, Centuries of Change: Crisis, Reform, and Revolution in Mexico*, edited by Elisa Servín, Leticia Reina, and John Tutino, 305–45. Durham, NC: Duke University Press, 2007.

de la Peña, Guillermo. "Corrupción e informalidad." In *Vicios públicos, virtudes privadas: La corrupción en México*, edited by Claudio Lomnitz-Adler, 113–28. Mexico City: CIESAS, 2000.

de la Peña, Guillermo. *A Legacy of Promises: Agriculture, Politics, and Ritual in the Morelos Highlands of Mexico*. Manchester, UK: Manchester University Press, 1982.

de la Peña, Guillermo. "Poder local, poder regional: Perspectivas socio-antropológicas." In *Poder local, poder regional*, edited by Jorge Padua and Alain Vanneph, 27–56. Mexico City: El Colegio de México/Centre d'Etudes Mexicaines et Centramericaines, 1986.

de la Peña, Guillermo. "Populism, Regional Power, and Political Mediation: Southern Jalisco, 1900–1980." In *Mexico's Regions: Comparative History and Development*, edited by Eric Van Young, 191–223. San Diego: Center for U.S.–Mexican Studies, UCSD, 1992.

de la Peña, Guillermo. "Social and Cultural Policies Towards Indigenous Peoples: Perspectives from Latin America." *Annual Review of Anthropology* 34 (2005): 717–39.

de la Peña, Moises. *Guerrero Económico*. Chilpancingo: Gobierno del Estado de Guerrero, 1949.

de la Peña, Sergio, and Marcel Morales Ibarra. *El agrarismo y la industrialización de México, 1940–1950: Historia de la cuestión agraria mexicana*, vol. 6. Mexico City: Siglo Veintiuno Editores, 1989.

de la Vega, Eduardo. "Origins, Development and Crisis of the Sound Cinema." In *Mexican Cinema*, edited by Paulo A. Paranaguá, 79–93. London: British Film Institute, 1995.

de León, Igor. *La noche de Santo Tomás*. Mexico City: Ediciones de Cultura Popular, 1988.

de Quevedo, Miguel Angel. *Algunas consideraciones sobre nuestro problema agrario*. Mexico City: Imprenta Victoria, 1916.

de Quevedo, Miguel Angel. "El problema de la deforestación en México: Solución práctica del mismo." *México Forestal* 2, no. 7–8 (1924): 64–69.

de Vries, Pieter. "The Performance and Imagination of the Cacique: Some Ethnographic Reflections from Western Mexico." In *Caciquismo in Twentieth-Century Mexico*, edited by Alan Knight and Wil Pansters, 327–46. London: Institute for the Study of the Americas, 2005.

Deere, Carmen Diana, and Magdalena León, eds. *Género, propiedad y empoderamiento: Tierra, estado y mercado en América Latina*. Mexico City: UNAM, PUEG, FLACSO, 2002.

Deininger, Klaus, and Lyn Squire. "A New Data Set Measuring Income Inequality." *World Bank Economic Review* 10 (1996): 565–91.

Del Castillo Troncoso, Alberto. "El movimiento estudiantil de 1968 narrado en imágenes." *Sociológica* 23, no. 68 (September–December 2008): 63–114.

Demmers, Jolle. *Friends and Bitter Enemies: Politics and Neoliberal Reform in Yucatán, Mexico.* Thela Latin America series, vol. 14. Utrecht, The Netherlands: Thela, 1998.

Diamond, Larry. "Elections without Democracy: Thinking about Hybrid Regimes." *Journal of Democracy* 13, no. 2 (April 2002): 21–25.

Dion, Michelle. *Workers and Welfare: Comparative Institutional Change in Twentieth-Century Mexico.* Pittsburgh: University of Pittsburgh Press, 2010.

D'Olmo, Leo. *El Otro: Aventuras de Chucho Cárdenas, El Gran Reportero-Detective Mexicano. Serie Escrita Especialmente Para "La Prensa."* Mexico City: La Prensa, 1947.

Dormady, Jason H. *Primitive Revolution: Restorationist Religion and the Idea of the Mexican Revolution, 1940–1968.* Albuquerque: University of New Mexico Press, 2011.

Doyle, Kate. "After the Revolution: Lázaro Cárdenas and the Movimiento de Liberación Nacional," National Security Archive Electronic Briefing Book no. 124. http://www2.gwu.edu/~nsarchiv/NSAEBB/NSAEBB124/.

Durón, Olga. *Yo Porro (Retrato hablado).* Mexico City: Editorial Posada, 1984.

Eckstein Raber, Salomón. *El ejido colectivo en México.* Mexico City: Fondo de Cultura Económica, 1966.

Eisenstadt, Todd A. *Courting Democracy in Mexico: Party Strategies and Electoral Institutions.* Cambridge: Cambridge University Press, 2004.

Elízaga, Raquel Sosa. *Los códigos ocultos del Cardenismo,* part 3. Mexico City: UNAM, 1996.

Elizondo, Juan Manuel. *De historia y política.* Monterrey: UANL, 2000.

Espinosa, Gisela D. "La reforma agraria y el nuevo modelo agroindustrial, 1935–1947." In *De haciendas, cañeros y paraestatales: Cien años de historia de la agroindustria cañero-azucarera en México, 1880–1980,* edited by Armando Bartra, 125–58. Mexico City: de mentaje UNAM, 1993.

Estrada Urroz, Rosalina. *Del telar a la cadena de mentaje: La condición obrera en Puebla, 1940–1976.* Puebla: Benemérita Universidad Autónoma de Puebla, 1997.

Falcón, Romana. *La semilla en el surco: Adalberto Tejeda y el radicalismo en Veracruz (1883–1960).* Mexico City: Gobierno del Estado de Veracruz, 1986.

Falcón, Romana. *Revolución y caciquismo: San Luis Potosí, 1910–1938.* Mexico City: El Colegio de México, 1984.

Fallaw, Ben. *Cárdenas Compromised: The Failure of Reform in Postrevolutionary Yucatan.* Durham, NC: Duke University Press, 2001.

Fallaw Ben. *Religion and State Formation in Postrevolutionary Mexico.* Durham, NC: Duke University Press, 2013.

Fallaw, Ben, and Terry Rugeley, eds. *Forced Marches: Soldiers and Military Caciques in Modern Mexico.* Tucson: University of Arizona Press, 2012.

Fein, Seth. "Hollywood and United States–Mexican Relations in the Golden Age of Mexican Cinema." PhD dissertation, University of Texas, Austin, 1996.

Fernández Aceves, María Teresa. "Engendering Caciquismo. Guadalupe Martínez and Heliodoro Hernández Loza and the Politics of Organized Labor in Jalisco."

In *Caudillo and Cacique in Twentieth-Century Mexico*, edited by Alan Knight and Wil Pansters, 201–24. London: Institute for Latin American Studies, 2005.

Fernández Aceves, María Teresa. "Voto femenino." In *Enciclopedia de Época: Política*, edited by Jorge Alonso. Guadalajara: Universidad de Guadalajara, in press.

Fernández Christlieb, Fatima. *Los medios de difusión masiva en México*. Mexico City: Juan Pablo, 1996.

Fernández, Claudia, and Andrew Paxman. *El Tigre: Emilio Azcárraga y su imperio Televisa*. Mexico City: Grijalbo-Mondadori, 2001.

Figueroa, Alejandro. *Por la tierra y por los santos*. Mexico City: Consejo Nacional para la Cultura y las Artes, 1994.

Fleischer, David, and Robert Wesson. *Brazil in Transition*. London: Praeger, 1983.

Flores García, Alejandro. *Cinecompendio 1971–1972*. Mexico City: A Posta, 1972.

Fowler-Salamini, Heather. *Agrarian Radicalism in Veracruz, 1920–1938*. Lincoln: University of Nebraska Press, 1978.

Fowler-Salamini, Heather. "Caciquismo, sindicalismo y género en la agroindustria cafetalera de Córdoba, Veracruz, 1925–1945." In *Integrados y marginados en el México posrevolucionario: Los juegos del poder local y sus nexos con la política nacional*, edited by Nicolás Cárdenas García and Enrique Guerra Manzo, 205–45. Mexico City: UNAM-Xochimilco, Miguel Ángel de Porrúa, 2009.

Fowler-Salamini, Heather, and Mary Kay Vaughan, eds. *Women of the Mexican Countryside: Creating Spaces, Shaping Transitions*. Tucson: University of Arizona Press, 1994.

Friedrich, Paul. "A Mexican Cacicazgo." *Ethnology* 4, no. 2 (April 1965): 190–209.

Friedrich, Paul. *The Princes of Naranja: An Essay on Anthropological Method*. Austin: University of Texas Press, 1986.

Fuentes, Carlos. *La región más transparente del aire*. Mexico City: Fondo de Cultura Económica, [1958] 1996.

Gamio, Manuel. *Forjando patria. Pro-nacionalismo*. Mexico City: Porrúa, 1916.

Gamio, Manuel. *La población del Valle de Teotihuacan*. 3 vols. Mexico City: Talleres Gráficos de la Nación, 1922.

García Riera, Emilio. *Breve historia del cine mexicano*. Zapopan, Jalisco: Mapa, 1998.

García Riera, Emilio. *Historia documental del cine mexicano*. 2nd ed. Guadalajara: University de Guadalajara, 1992.

Garrido, Luis Javier. *El partido de la revolución institucionalizada: La formación del nuevo Estado en México (1928–1945)*. 2nd ed. Mexico City: Siglo XXI, 1991.

Gauss, Susan M. *Made in Mexico: Regions, Nation, and the State in the Rise of Mexican Industrialism, 1920s–1940s*. University Park: Pennsylvania State University Press, 2010.

Gaxiola, Fernando Arce. "El caciquismo obrero: Joaquín Hernández Galicia en Ciudad Madero." In *Partido Revolucionario Institucional, 1946–2000: Ascenso y caída del partido hegemónico*, edited by Víctor Manuel Muñoz Patraca. Mexico City: Siglo XXI, 2006.

George, Alexander L., and Andrew Bennett. *Case Studies and Theory Development in the Social Sciences*. Cambridge, MA: MIT Press, 2004.

Gerth, Hans Heinrich, and Charles Wright Mills. *From Max Weber: Essays in Sociology*. New York: Oxford University Press, 1958.

Gilabert, César. *El hábito de la utopía: Análisis del imaginario sociopolítico en el movimiento estudiantil de México: 1968.* Mexico City: Porrúa, 1993.

Gill, Mario, ed. *La huelga de Nueva Rosita.* Mexico City: MAPRI, 1959.

Gillingham, Paul. "Ambiguous Missionaries: Rural Teachers and State Facades in Guerrero, 1930–1950." *Mexican Studies/Estudios Mexicanos* 22, no. 2 (summer 2006): 331–60.

Gillingham, Paul. *Cuauhtémoc's Bones: Forging National Identity in Mexico.* Albuquerque: University of New Mexico Press, 2011.

Gillingham, Paul. "Force and Consent in Mexican Provincial Politics: Guerrero and Veracruz, 1945–1953." PhD dissertation, Oxford University, 2005.

Gillingham, Paul. "Maximino's Bulls: Popular Protest after the Mexican Revolution, 1940–1952." *Past & Present* 206 (February 2010): 145–81.

Gillingham, Paul. "Mexican Elections, 1910–1994: Voters, Violence, and Veto Power." In *The Oxford Handbook of Mexican Politics*, edited by Roderic Ai Camp, 53–76. Oxford: Oxford University Press, 2011.

Gillingham, Paul. "Military Caciquismo in the Priísta State: General Mange's Command in Veracruz, 1937–1959." In *Forced Marches: Soldiers and Military Caciques in Modern Mexico*, edited by Ben Fallaw and Terry Rugeley, 210–37. Tucson: University of Arizona Press, 2012.

Gillingham, Paul. "Who Killed Crispín Aguilar? Violence and Order in the Postrevolutionary Countryside," in *Violence, Coercion and State-Making in Twentieth-Century Mexico: The Other Half of the Centaur*, edited by Wil Pansters, 91–111. Palo Alto, CA: Stanford University Press, 2012.

Gleizer Salzman, Daniela. *México frente a la inmigración de refugiados judíos, 1934–1940.* Mexico City: CONACULTA-INAH, 2000.

Gojman de Backal, Alicia. *Camisas, escudos y desfiles militares: Los dorados y el antisemitismo en México (1934–1940).* Mexico City: Fondo de Cultura Económica, 2000.

Gómez Nashiki, Antonio. "El movimiento estudiantil mexicano: Notas históricas de las organizaciones políticas, 1910–1971." *Revista Mexicana de Investigación Educativa* 8, no. 17 (2003): 187–220.

Gómez Nashiki, Antonio. "El Movimiento y la Violencia Institucional: La Universidad Michoacana de San Nicolás de Hidalgo, 1956–1966." *Revista de Investigaciones Educativa* 12, no. 35 (October–December 2007): 1179–208.

Gómez, Pablo. *1968: La historia también está hecha de derrotas.* Mexico City: Porrúa, 2008.

González, Luis. *Los días del Presidente Cárdenas.* Mexico City: Colegio de México, 1981.

González, Luis. *San José de Gracia: Mexican Village in Transition.* Austin: University of Texas Press, 1974.

González Bustamante, Celeste. "1968 Olympic Dreams and Tlatelolco Nightmares: Imagining and Imaging Modernity on Television." *Mexican Studies/Estudios Mexicanos* 26, no. 1 (winter 2010): 1–30.

González Casanova, Pablo. *Democracy in Mexico*, translated by Danielle Salti. London: Oxford University Press, [1965] 1970.

González Casanova, Pablo. *Internal Colonialism and National Development.* St. Louis: Social Science Institute, 1965.

González Casanova, Pablo. *La democracia en México.* Mexico City: Ediciones Era, 1975.

González Casanova, Pablo, ed. *Las elecciones en México: Evolución y perspectiva*. Mexico City: Fondo de Cultura Económica, 2004.

González Compeán, Miguel, and Leonardo Lomelí, eds. *El partido de la revolución. Institución y conflicto (1928–1999)*. Mexico City: Fondo de Cultura Económica, 2000.

González de Bustamante, Celestine. "*Tele-Visiones* (Tele-Visions): The Making of Mexican TV News, 1950–1970." PhD dissertation, Univeristy of Arizona, 2006.

González Navarro, Moisés. *Población y sociedad en México (1900–1970)*. 2 vols. Mexico City: UNAM, 1974.

González y González, Luis. *Pueblo en vilo*. Mexico City: SEP, 1984.

Gotkowitz, Laura. *A Revolution for Our Rights: Indigenous Struggles for Land and Justice in Bolivia, 1880–1952*. Durham, NC: Duke University Press, 2007.

Gradante, William. "'El Hijo del Pueblo': José Alfredo Jiménez and the Mexican *Canción Ranchera*." *Latin American Music Review* 3, no. 1 (1982): 36–59.

Gramsci, Antonio. *Selections from the Prison Notebooks*. London: Lawrence and Wishart, 1996.

Grandin, Greg. *The Blood of Guatemala: A History of Race and Nation in Guatemala*. Durham, NC: Duke University Press, 2000.

Grandin, Greg. *The Last Colonial Massacre: Latin America in the Cold War*. Chicago: University of Chicago Press, 2004.

Greenberg, James. *Blood Ties: Life and Violence in Rural Mexico*. Tucson: University of Arizona Press, 1989.

Greene, Graham. *The Lawless Roads*. London: Heinemann, 1939.

Grindle, Merilee S., and Pilar Domingo, eds. *Proclaiming Revolution: Bolivia in Comparative Perspective*. Cambridge, MA: Harvard University Press, 2003.

Guardino, Peter. *Peasants, Politics, and the Formation of Mexico's National State: Guerrero, 1800–1857*. Palo Alto, CA: Stanford University Press, 1996.

Guardino, Peter. *The Time of Liberty: Popular Political Culture in Oaxaca, 1750–1850*. Durham, NC: Duke University Press, 2005.

Guback, Thomas. *The International Film Industry: Western Europe and America since 1945*. Bloomington: University of Indiana Press, 1969.

Guerra, François-Xavier. *Modernidad e independencias: Ensayos sobre las revoluciones hispánicas*. Madrid: Editorial MAPFRE, 2000.

Guevara Niebla, Gilberto, and Raúl Álvarez Garín, eds. *Pensar el 68*. Mexico City: Cal y Arena, 2008.

Guevara Niebla, Gilberto. *La libertad nunca se olvida: Memoria del 68*. Mexico City: Cal y Arena, 2004.

Gutiérrez, Hermenegildo. *La reconstrucción de México: El problema de la ganadería*. Mexico City: Editorial Polis, 1943.

Haber, Stephen, Armando Razo, and Noel Maurer, eds. *The Politics of Property Rights: Political Instability, Credible Commitments and Economic Growth in Mexico, 1876–1929*. Cambridge: Cambridge University Press, 2003.

Haber, Stephen, ed. *How Latin America Fell Behind: Essays on the Economic Histories of Brazil and Mexico, 1800–1914*. Palo Alto, CA: Stanford University Press, 1997.

Habermas, Jürgen. *The Structural Transformation of the Public Sphere: An Inquiry into a Category of Bourgeois Society*. Cambridge, MA: MIT Press, 1991.

Hamilton, Nora. *The Limits of State Autonomy: Post-revolutionary Mexico*. Princeton, NJ: Princeton University Press, 1982.

Hanson, Roger D. *The Politics of Mexican Development*. Baltimore: Johns Hopkins University Press, 1971.

Hay, Colin, Michael Lister, and David Marsh, eds. *The State: Theories and Issues*. London: Palgrave, 2006.

Hayes, Joy. *Radio Nation: Communication, Popular Culture, and Nationalism in Mexico, 1920–1950*. Tucson: University of Arizona Press, 2000.

Hellman, Judith Adler. *Mexico in Crisis*. New York: Holmes and Meier, 1983.

Helú, Antonio. *La obligación de asesinar*. Mexico City: CNCA, 1991.

Hernández, Alicia. *La mecánica cardenista: Historia de la Revolución Mexicana, no. 16*. Mexico City: El Colegio de México, 1979.

Hernández Chávez, Alicia. *Mexico: A Brief History*. Berkeley: University of California Press, 2006.

Hernández Lomelí, Francisco. "Obstáculos para el establecimiento de la televisión comercial en México (1950–1955)." *Comunicación y Sociedad* 28 (September–December 1996): 147–71.

Hernández Rodríguez, Rogelio. *Amistades, compromisos y lealtades: Líderes y grupos en el Estado de México*. Mexico City: El Colegio de México, 1998.

Hernández Rodríguez, Rogelio. *El centro dividido: La nueva autonomía de los gobernadores*. Mexico City: El Colegio de México, 2008.

Hernández Rodríguez, Rogelio. *La formación del político mexicano: El case de Carlos A. Madrazo*. Mexico City: El Colegio de México, 1991.

Herrera Calderón, Fernando, and Adela Cedillo, eds. *Challenging Authoritarianism in Mexico: Revolutionary Struggles and the Dirty War, 1964–1982*. London: Routledge, 2011.

Herzfeld, Michael. *Cultural Intimacy: Social Poetics in the Nation-state*. London: Routledge, 2005.

Herzog, Jesús Silva. *El agrarismo mexicano y la reforma agrarian*. Mexico City: Fondo de Cultura Económica, 1985.

Hewitt de Alcantara, Cynthia. *La modernización de la agricultura Mexicana*. Mexico City: Siglo XXI, 1978.

Hinojosa Ortiz, Manuel. *Los bosques de México: Relato de un dispilfarro y una injusticia*. Mexico City: Instituto Mexicano de Investigaciones Económicas, 1958.

Hobsbawm, E. J. "Revolution." In *Revolution in History*, edited by Roy Porter and Mikulás Teich, 5–46. Cambridge: Cambridge University Press, 1986.

Hodges, Donald C., and Ross Gandy. *Mexico under Siege: Popular Resistance to Presidential Despotism*. London: Zed Books, 2002.

Hofstadter, Dan. *Mexico, 1946–1973*. New York: Facts on File, 1974.

Horcasitas de Pozas, Isabel, and Ricardo Pozas. "Del monolingüismo en lengua indígena al bilingüismo en lengua indígena y nacional." In *Pensamiento antropológico e indigenista de Julio de la Fuente*, edited by Aguirre Beltrán, Gonzalo Pozas Arciniega, Ricardo Báez-Jorge et al., 145–95. Mexico City: Instituto Nacional Indigenista, 1980.

Huntington, Samuel P. *Political Order in Changing Societies*. New Haven, CT: Yale University Press, 1968.

Hurtado, Javier. *Familias, política y parentesco: Jalisco, 1919–1991*. Mexico City: Fondo de Cultura Económica, 1993.

Iturriaga de la Fuente, José. *La revolución hacendaria: La hacienda pública con el presidente Calles*. Mexico City: SEP, 1976.

Izquierdo, Rafael. *Política hacendaria del desarrollo establizador, 1958–1970*. Mexico City: Colegio de México, 1995.

Jacobs, Ian. *Ranchero Revolt: The Mexican Revolution in Guerrero*. Austin: University of Texas Press, 1982.

Jaramillo, Rubén. *Rubén Jaramillo: Autobiografía y Asesinato*. Mexico City: Editorial Nuestro Tiempo, 1967.

Jardón, Raúl. *1968: El fuego de la esperanza*. Mexico City: Siglo XXI, 1998.

Jardón, Raúl. *El espionaje contra el movimiento estudiantil: Los documentos de la Dirección Federal de Seguridad y las agencias de "inteligencia" estadounidenses en 1968*. Mexico City: Itaca, 2003.

Jessop, Bob. *State Theory: Putting the Capitalist State in Its Place*. Cambridge: Polity 1990.

Jiménez, Armando. *Picardía Mexicana*. Mexico City: Libro Mex, 1960.

Joseph, Gilbert M., ed. *Reclaiming the Political in Latin American History: Essays from the North*. Durham, NC: Duke University Press, 2001.

Joseph, Gilbert M. "What We Now Know and Should Know: Bringing Latin America More Meaningfully into Cold War Studies." In *In from the Cold: Latin America's New Encounter with the Cold War*, edited by Gilbert M. Joseph and Daniela Spenser, 3–46. Durham, NC: Duke University Press, 2008.

Joseph, Gilbert M., Anne Rubinstein, and Eric Zolov, eds. *Fragments of a Golden Age: The Politics of Culture in Mexico Since 1940*. Durham, NC: Duke University Press, 2001.

Joseph, Gilbert M., Catherine C. LeGrand, and Ricardo D. Salvatore, eds. *Close Encounters of Empire: Writing the Cultural History of U.S.–Latin American Relations*. Durham, NC: Duke University Press, 1998.

Joseph, Gilbert M., and Daniel Nugent, eds. *Everyday Forms of State Formation: Revolution and the Negotiation of Rule in Modern Mexico*. Durham, NC: Duke University Press, 1994.

Joseph, Gilbert M., and Daniela Spenser, eds. *In from the Cold: Latin America's New Encounter with the Cold War*. Durham, NC: Duke University Press, 2008.

Joyce, Patrick. "What Is the Social in Social History?" *Past and Present* 206, no. 1 (2010): 213–48.

Kaldor, Nicholas. *Reports on Taxation II*. New York: Holmes and Meirer, 1980.

Kapelusz-Poppi, Ana María. "Physician Activists and the Development of Rural Health Postrevolutionary Mexico." *Radical History Review* 80 (spring 2001): 35–50.

Kaplan, Temma. "Female Consciousness and Collective Action: The Case of Barcelona, 1910–1918." *Signs* 7, no. 3 (1982): 545–66.

Kaufman Purcell, Susan. "Business-Government Relations in Mexico: The Case of the Sugar Industry." *Comparative Politics* 13, no. 2 (January 1981): 211–33.

Keller, Renata. "A Foreign Policy for Domestic Consumption: Mexico's Lukewarm Defense of Castro, 1959–1969." *Latin American Research Review* 47, no. 2 (2012): 100–119.

King, John. *Magical Reels*. London: Verso, 2000.

Klooster, Dan. "Campesinos and Mexican Forest Policy during the Twentieth Century." *Latin American Research Review* 38, no. 2 (2003): 94–126.

Klubbock, Thomas. *Contested Communities: Class, Gender, and Politics in Chile's El Teniente Copper Mine, 1904–1951.* Durham, NC: Duke University Press, 1998.

Knight, Alan. "Cárdenas and Echeverría: Two 'Populist' Presidents Compared." In *Populism in Twentieth Century Mexico: The Presidencies of Lázaro Cárdenas and Luis Echeverría,* edited by María L. O. Muñoz and Amelia M. Kiddle, 15–37. Tucson: University of Arizona Press, 2010.

Knight, Alan. "Cardenismo: Juggernaut or Jalopy?" *Journal of Latin American Studies* 26, no. 1 (February 1994): 73–107.

Knight, Alan. "México y Estados Unidos, 1938–40: Rumor y realidad." *Secuencia* 34 (January–April 1996): 129–54.

Knight, Alan. *The Mexican Revolution.* 2 vols. Lincoln: University of Nebraska Press, 1990.

Knight, Alan. "The Weight of the State in Modern Mexico." In *Studies in the Formation of the Nation-State in Latin America,* edited by James Dunkerley, 212–53. London: Institute for Latin American Studies, 2002.

Knight, Alan, and Wil Panster, eds. *Caciquismo in Twentieth-Century Mexico.* London: Institute for Latin American Studies, 2006.

Krauze, Enrique. *La presidencia imperial: Ascenso y caída del sistema político mexicano (1940–1996).* Mexico City: Fabula, 1997.

Krauze, Enrique. *Mexico: Biography of Power.* New York: Harper Perennial, 1998.

Krauze, Enrique. *Por una democracia sin adjetivos.* Mexico City: Joaquín Mortiz, 1986.

Lawson, Chappell H. *Building the Fourth Estate: Democratization and the Rise of a Free Press in Mexico.* Berkeley: University of California Press, 2002.

Le Roy Ladurie, Emmanuel. *Carnival: A People's Uprising at Romans.* New York: George Braziller, 1979.

Leñero, Vicente. *Asesinato: El doble crimen de los Flores Muñoz.* Mexico City: Plaza y Valdés, 1997.

Lerdo de Tejada, Sebastián C., and Antonio Godina. *El lobbying en México.* Mexico City: Miguel Ángel de Porrúa, 2004.

Lerner, Jesse. *The Shock of Modernity: Crime Photography in Mexico City.* Mexico City: Turner, 2007.

Lerner, Victoria. *La educación socialista.* Mexico City: El Colegio de México, 1979.

Lettieri, Michael. "Wheels of Government: The Alianza de Camioneros and the Political Culture of PRI Rule, 1929–1981." PhD dissertation, University of California, San Diego, 2013.

Levitsky, Steven, and Lucan A. Way. *Competitive Authoritarianism: Hybrid Regimes after the Cold War.* Cambridge: Cambridge University Press, 2010.

Levy, Daniel C., and Kathleen Bruhn. *Mexico: The Struggle for Democratic Development.* 2nd ed. Berkeley: University of California Press, 2006.

Lewis, Oscar. *The Children of Sánchez: Autobiography of a Mexican Family.* New York: Random House, 1961.

Lewis, Stephen E. *The Ambivalent Revolution: Forging State and Nation in Chiapas, 1910–1945.* Albuquerque: University of New Mexico Press, 2005.

Lewis, Stephen E. "The National Indigenist Institute and the Negotiation of Applied

Anthropology in Highland Chiapas, Mexico, 1951–1955." *Ethnohistory* 55, no. 4 (2008): 609–32.

Lieuwen, Edwin. *Mexican Militarism: The Political Rise and Fall of the Revolutionary Army.* Albuquerque: University of New Mexico Press, 1968.

Linz, Juan J. *Totalitarian and Authoritarian Regimes.* Boulder, CO: Lynne Rienner, 2000.

Loaeza, Soledad. *Clases Medias y Política en México, La Querella Escolar, 1959–1963.* Mexico City: Colegio de México, 1985.

Loaeza, Soledad. *El Partido de Acción Nacional: La larga marcha, 1939–1994.* Mexico City: Fondo de Cultura Económica, 2000.

Lomnitz-Adler, Claudio. *Exits from the Labyrinth: Culture and Ideology in the Mexican National Space.* Berkeley: University of California Press, 1992.

Lomnitz, Larissa. "The Uses of Fear: Porro Gangs in Mexico." In *Peace and War: Cross-Cultural Perspectives*, edited by Mary LeCron Foster and Robert A. Rubinstein, 15–24. New Brunswick, NJ: Transaction Books, 1986.

López Portillo, José. *Mis tiempos.* Mexico City: Fernández Editores, 1988.

Lorey, David E. *The University System and Economic Development in Mexico since 1929.* Palo Alto, CA: Stanford University Press, 1993.

Los maestros y la cultura nacional, 1920–1952, vols. 1–5. Mexico City: Museo Nacional de Culturas Populares/Dirección General de Culturas Populares, 1987.

Loyo, Engracia, ed. *Casa del pueblo y el maestro rural mexicano.* Mexico City: SEP, 1985.

Loyola Díaz, Rafael. *El ocaso del radicalismo revolucionario.* Mexico City: UNAM, 1991.

Loyola Díaz, Rafael, ed. *Entre la guerra y la estabilidad política: El México de los 40.* Mexico City: Consejo Nacional para la Cultura y las Artes, 1990.

Loyola Díaz, Rafael. "Manuel Avila Camacho: El preámbulo del constructivismo revolucionario." In *Presidentes mexicanos (1911–2000).* 2 vols. Edited by Will Fowler, 209–26. Mexico City: INEHRM, 2004.

Loyola Rocha, Jaime. "La visión integral de la sociedad nacional, 1920–1934." In *La antropología en México: Panorama histórico. 2. Los hechos y los dichos.* Edited by Carlos García Mora and Esteban Krotz. Mexico City: Instituto Nacional de Antropología e Historia, 1987.

Lozoya, Jorge Alberto. *El Ejército Mexicano.* Mexico City: Colegio de Mexico, 1965.

Luna, Ana Luisa. *La Crónica Policíaca en México: Nota Roja 40s.* Mexico City: Diana, 1993.

Mabry, Donald J. "Changing Models of Mexican Politics: A Review Essay." *The New Scholar* 5, no. 1 (1976): 31–37.

Mabry, Donald J. *Mexico's Acción Nacional: A Catholic Alternative to Revolution.* Syracuse, NY: Syracuse University Press, 1973.

Mabry, Donald J. *The Mexican University and the State: Student Conflict, 1917–1971.* College Station: Texas A&M University Press, 1982.

Magaloni, Beatriz. *Voting for Autocracy: Hegemonic Party Survival and Its Demise in Mexico.* Cambridge: Cambridge University Press, 2006.

Makarenko, Anton. *Poema pedagógico.* Mexico City: Ediciones de Cultura Popular, 1975.

Mallon, Florencia. *Peasant and Nation: The Making of Postcolonial Mexico and Peru.* Berkeley: University of California Press, 1995.

Mallon, Florencia. "The Promise and Dilemma of Subaltern Studies: Perspectives from Latin American History." *The American Historical Review* 99, no. 5 (December 1994): 1491–515.

Mares, David. "The National Security State." In *A Companion to Latin American History*, edited by Thomas Holloway, 386–405. Oxford: Blackwell, 2011.

Marichal, Carlos, and Steven Topik. "The State and Economic Growth in Latin America: Brazil and Mexico, Nineteenth and Early Twentieth Centuries." In *Nation, State and the Economy in History*. Edited by Alicia Teichova and Herbert Matis, 349–72. Cambridge: Cambridge University Press, 2009.

Martínez Assad, Carlos R. *El henriquismo, una piedra en el camino*. Mexico City: Martin Casillas, 1982.

Martínez Assad, Carlos R., ed. *Estadistas, caciques y caudillos*. Mexico City: UNAM, 1988.

Martínez Assad, Carlos R. *Los sentimientos de la región: Del viejo centralismo a la nueva pluralidad*. Mexico City: INEHRM, 2001.

Martínez, María Antonia. *El despegue constructivo de la Revolución: Sociedad y política en el alemanismo*. Mexico City: Miguel Angel Porrua Editorial, 2004.

Martínez de la Vega, Pepe. *Aventuras del detective Péter Pérez*. Mexico City: Plaza y Valdez, 1987.

Martínez della Rocca, Salvador, ed. *Voces y ecos del 68*. Mexico City: Porrúa, 2009.

Marwick, Arthur. *The Sixties: Cultural Revolution in Britain, France, Italy, and the United States, c. 1958–c. 1974*. Oxford: Oxford University Press, 1998.

McDonald, Terence J. "Introduction." In *The Historic Turn in the Human Sciences*, edited by Terence J. McDonald, 1–17. Ann Arbor: University of Michigan Press, 1996.

McGillivray, Gillian. *Blazing Cane: Sugar Communities, Class, and State Formation in Cuba, 1868–1959*. Durham, NC: Duke University Press, 2009.

Meade, Everard Kidder. "Anatomies of Justice and Chaos: Capital Punishment and the Public in Mexico, 1917–1945." PhD dissertation, University of Chicago, 2005.

Medina, Luis. *Del cardenismo al avilacamachismo: Historia de la Revolución Mexicana, no. 18*. Mexico City: El Colegio de México, 1978.

Medina, Luis. *Historia de la Revolución Mexicana, periodo 1940–1952. Vol. 20, Civilismo y modernización del autoritarismo*. Mexico City: Colegio de México, 1979.

Mejía Barquera, Fernando. *La industria de la radio y la televisión y la política del estado mexicano (1920–1960)*. Mexico City: Fundación Manuel Buendía, 1989.

Mendieta y Nuñez, Lucio. "La clase media en México." *Revista Mexicana de Sociología* 17, no. 2/3 (May–December 1955): 517–31.

Mendoza Ávila, Eusebio. *La educación tecnológica en México*. Mexico City: IPN, 1980.

Meyer, Jean. *El Sinarquismo: Un fascismo mexicano? 1937–47*. Mexico City: Joaquín Mortiz, 1979.

Meyer, Jean. *La Cristiada*. 3 vols. Mexico City: Siglo XXI Editores, 1977.

Michaels, Albert L. "The Crisis of Cardenismo." *Journal of Latin American Studies* 2, no. 1 (1970): 51–79.

Middlebrook, Kevin. *The Paradox of Revolution: Labor, the State, and Authoritarianism in Mexico*. Baltimore: Johns Hopkins University Press, 1995.

Migdal, Joel S. *Strong Societies and Weak States: State-Society Relations and State Capabilities in the Third World*. Princeton, NJ: Princeton University Press, 1988.

Miller, Michael Nelson. *Red, White, and Green: The Maturing of Mexicanidad, 1940–1946*. El Paso: Texas Western Press, 1998.

Molina, Alicia, ed. *José Vasconcelos: Textos sobre educación*. Mexico City: SEP, 1981.
Moncada, Carlos. *Del México violento: Periodistas asesinados*. Mexico City: Edomex, 1991.
Monsiváis, Carlos. *Días de Guardar*. Mexico City: Ediciones Era, 1970.
Monsiváis, Carlos. *El 68: La tradición de la resistencia*. Mexico City: Ediciones Era, 2008.
Monsiváis, Carlos. *Los mil y un velorios: Crónica de la nota roja*. Mexico City: Consejo Nacional para la Cultura y las Artes/Alianza Editorial, 1994.
Monsiváis, Carlos. "Vino todo el pueblo y no cupo en la pantalla." In *A través del espejo: El cine mexicano y su público*, edited by Carlos Monsiváis and Carlos Bonfil, 49–98. Mexico City: El Milagro, 1994.
Mora, Carl. *Mexican Cinema: Reflections of a Society, 1896–1980*. Berkeley: University of California Press, 1982.
Moreno-Brid, Juan Carlos, and Jaime Ros. *Development and Growth in the Mexican Economy: A Historical Perspective*. Oxford: Oxford University Press, 2009.
Moreno Flores, José. *Ametrallando! Periodismo humorístico, político, social*. Puebla: El Liberal Poblano, 1966.
Mottier, Nicole. "What Agricultural Credit and Debt Can Tell Us About the State in Mid-Century Mexico." Paper presented at the 126th Annual Meeting of the American Historical Association, January 5–8, 2012, Chicago.
Mraz, John. *Looking for Mexico: Modern Visual Culture and National Identity*. Durham, NC: Duke University Press, 2009.
Mraz, John. "Made on Rails in Mexico." *Jump Cut: A Review of Contemporary Media* 39 (June 1994): 113–21.
Nahmad, Salomón. *Fuentes etnológicas para el estudio de los pueblos ayuuk (mixe) del Estado de Oaxaca*. Mexico City: CIESAS, 1987.
Navarrete, Ifigenia. "La distribución del ingreso en México, tendencias y perspectivas." In *El perfil de México en 1980: La economía y la población*, 15–71. Mexico City: Siglo XXI, 1971.
Navarro, Aaron W. *Political Intelligence and the Creation of Modern Mexico, 1938–1954*. University Park: Pennsylvania State University Press, 2010.
Negrete, Martaelena. *Relaciones entre la iglesia y el estado en México, 1930–1940*. Mexico City: Colegio de México, 1988.
Newcomer, Daniel. *Reconciling Modernity: Urban State Formation in 1940s Leon, Mexico*. Lincoln: University of Nebraska Press, 2004.
Niblo, Stephen R. *Mexico in the 1940s: Modernity, Politics, and Corruption*. Wilmington, DE: Scholarly Resources, 2000.
Niblo, Stephen R. *War, Diplomacy, and Development: The United States and Mexico, 1938–1954*. Wilmington, DE: Scholarly Resources, 1995.
Nicholson, Irene. *The X in Mexico: Growth with Tradition*. New York: Doubleday, 1966.
Noble, Andrea. *Mexican National Cinema*. London: Routledge, 2005.
Novelo, Victoria. "De huelgas, movilizaciones y otras acciones de los mineros del carbón de Coahuila." *Revista Mexicana de Sociología* 42, no. 4 (1980): 1355–77.
Nugent, David. "Conclusion: Reflections on State Theory Through the Lens of the Mexican Military." In *Forced Marches: Soldiers and Military Caciques in Modern Mexico*,

edited by Ben Fallaw and Terry Rugeley, 238–68. Tucson: University of Arizona Press, 2012.

Nugent, David, ed. *Locating Capitalism in Time and Space: Global Restructuring, Politics, and Identity*. Palo Alto, CA: Stanford University Press, 2002.

Nutini, Hugo G., and Barry Isaac. *Social Stratification in Central Mexico, 1500–2000*. Austin: University of Texas Press, 2010.

Nye, Joseph S., Jr. *Soft Power: The Means to Success in World Politics*. New York: PublicAffairs, 2004.

Ochoa, Enrique C. *Feeding Mexico: The Political Uses of Food Since 1910*. Wilmington, DE: Scholarly Resources, 2000.

Ochoa, Enrique C. "Lic. Moisés T. de la Peña: The Economist on Horseback." In *The Human Tradition in Mexico*, edited by Jeffrey Pilcher, 165–80. Wilmington, DE: Scholarly Resources, 2003.

O'Donnell, Guillermo A. *Modernization and Bureaucratic-Authoritarianism: Studies in South American Politics*. Berkeley: University of California Press, 1979.

O'Donnell, Guillermo A., and Philippe C. Schmitter. *Transitions from Authoritarian Rule: Tentative Conclusions about Uncertain Democracies*. Baltimore: Johns Hopkins University Press, 1986.

Oikión, Verónica. *Michoacán en la vía de la unidad nacional, 1940–1944*. Mexico City: INEHRM, 1995.

Oikión Solano, Verónica, and Marta Eugenia García Ugarte, eds. *Movimientos armados en México, siglo XX*. 3 vols. Zamora: Colegio de Michoacán, 2008.

Olague, Jesús Flores, ed. *Historia mínima de Zacatecas: La fragua de una leyenda*. Mexico City: Noriega Editores, 2002.

Olcott, Jocelyn. *Revolutionary Women in Postrevolutionary Mexico*. Durham, NC: Duke University Press, 2005.

Olcott, Jocelyn, Mary Kay Vaughan, and Gabriela Cano. *Sex in Revolution: Gender, Politics, and Power in Modern Mexico*. Durham, NC: Duke University Press, 2006.

Olivera Sedano, Alicia, Rina Ortiz Peralta, Elisa Servín, and Tania Hernández Vicencio, eds. *Los matices de la rebeldía: Las oposiciones políticas y sociales*. Mexico City: INAH, 2010.

Padilla, Tanalis. *Rural Resistance in the Land of Zapata: The Jaramillista Movement and the Myth of the Pax Priísta, 1940–1962*. Durham, NC: Duke University Press, 2009.

Padilla Rangel, Yolanda. *Despues de la tempestad: La reorganización católica en Aguascalientes, 1929–1950*. Zamora: Colegio de Michoacán, 2001.

Pani, Alberto J. *La política hacendaria y la Revolución*. Mexico City: Cultura, 1926.

Pansters, Wil G. "Citizens with Dignity: Opposition and Government in San Luis Potosí, 1938–1993," in *Dismantling the Mexican State?*, edited by Rob Aitken, Nikki Craske, Gareth A. Jones, and David E. Standsfield, 248–54. Basingstoke, UK: Macmillan, 1996.

Pansters, Wil G. *Politics and Power in Puebla: The Political History of a Mexican State, 1937–1987*. Amsterdam: CEDLA Edita, 1990.

Pansters, Wil G. *Política y poder en Puebla: Formación y ocaso del cacicazgo avilamachista, 1937–1987*. Mexico City: Fondo de Cultura Económica, 1998.

Pansters, Wil G., ed. *Violence, Coercion and State-Making in Twentieth-Century Mexico: The Other Half of the Centaur*. Palo Alto, CA: Stanford University Press, 2012.

Partridge, William L., Antoinette Brown, and Jeffrey Nugent. "The Papaloapan Dam and Resettlement Project: Human Ecology and Health Impacts." In *Involuntary Migration and Resettlement: The Problems and Responses of Dislocated Peoples*, edited by Art Hansen and Anthony Oliver-Smith, 245–63. Boulder, CO: Westview Press, 1982.

Paxman, Andrew. "William Jenkins, Business Elites, and the Evolution of the Mexican State: 1910–1960." PhD dissertation, University of Texas, Austin, 2008.

Pellicer de Brody, Olga. *México y la revolución cubana*. Mexico City: Colegio de México, 1972.

Pellicer de Brody, Olga, and José Luis Reyna. *Historia de la Revolución Mexicana, 1952–1960: El afianzamiento de la estabilidad política*. Mexico City: El Colegio de México, 1978.

Pensado, Jaime. "Between Cultured Young Men and Mischievous Children: Youth, Transgression, and Protest in Late Nineteenth-Century Mexico." *Journal of the History of Childhood and Youth* 4, no. 1 (2011): 26–57.

Pensado, Jaime. "The (forgotten) Sixties in Mexico." *The Sixties: A Journal of History, Politics and Culture* 1, no. 1 (June 2008): 83–90.

Pensado, Jaime. *Rebel Mexico: Student Unrest and Authoritarian Political Culture During the Long Sixties*. Palo Alto, CA: Stanford University Press, 2013.

Pérez Islas, José A., and Maritza Urteage Castro-Pozo, eds. *Historias de los Jóvenes en México: Su presencia en el siglo XX*. Mexico City: Instituto Mexicano do la Juventud Archivo General de la Nación, 2004.

Pérez Montfort, Ricardo. "El discurso moral en los noticieros fílmicos de 1940 a 1960." In *Los archivos de la memoria*, edited by Alicia Olivera de Bonfil, 147–63. Mexico City: INAH, 1999.

Perló Cohen, Manuel. "Política y vivienda en México 1910–1952." *Revista Mexicana de Sociología* 41, no. 3 (July–September 1979): 769–835.

Piccato, Pablo. "Altibajos de la esfera pública en México, de la dictadura republicana a la democracia corporativa: La era de la prensa." In *Independencia y Revolución: Pasado, presente y futuro*, edited by Gustavo Leyva, Brian Connaughton, Rodrigo Díaz et al., 240–91. Mexico City: Fondo de Cultura Económica-Universidad Autónoma Metropolitana, 2010.

Pilcher, Jeffrey M. *Cantinflas and the Chaos of Mexican Modernity*. Wilmington, DE: Scholarly Resources, 2001.

Plancarte, Francisco M. *El problema indígena tarahumara*. Mexico City: Instituto Nacional Indigenista, 1954.

Portes Gil, Emilio. *Autobiografía de la Revolución Mexicana*. Mexico City: Instituto Mexicano de Cultura, 1964.

Portilla, Jorge. *Fenomología del relajo y otros ensayos*. Mexico City: Fundo de Cultura Ecónomica, 1984.

Pozas Horcasitas, Ricardo. *La democracia en blanco: El movimiento médico en México, 1964–1965*. Mexico City: Siglo XIX, 1993.

Pozas Horcasitas, Ricardo. "La democracia fallida: La batalla de Carlos A. Madrazo por cambiar el PRI." *Revista Mexicana de Sociología* 70, no. 1 (2008): 47–85.

Pratt, Mary Louise. *Imperial Eyes: Travel Writing and Transculturation*. London: Routledge, 1992.

Preston, Julia, and Samuel Dillon. *Opening Mexico: The Making of a Democracy.* New York: Farrar, Straus and Giroux, 2004.
Prewett, Virginia. *Reportage on Mexico.* New York: E. P. Dutton, 1941.
Quezada, Abel. *El mejor de los mundos imposibles.* Mexico City: CNCA, 1999.
Quijano, Manuel. "La medicina en México de 1940–2000." *Revista de la Facultad de Medicina de la UNAM* 46, no. 6 (2003): 215–16.
Quiles Ponce, Enrique. *Henríquez y Cárdenas, ¡Presentes! Hechos y realidades en la campaña henriquista.* Mexico City: Costa-Amic Editores, 1980.
Quintana, Alejandro. *Maximino Ávila Camacho and the One-Party State: The Taming of Caudillismo and Caciquismo in Post-Revolutionary Mexico.* Lanham, MD: Lexington Books, 2010.
Ramírez, Gabriel. *Miguel Contreras Torres, 1899–1981.* Guadalajara: Universidad de Guadalajara, 1994.
Ramírez, Ramón. *El Movimiento estudiantil mexicano,* Vols. I–II. Mexico City: Era, 1969.
Ramírez Berg, Charles. *Cinema of Solitude: A Critical Study of Mexican Film, 1967–1983.* Austin: University of Texas Press, 1992.
Rangel Hernández, Lucio. *La Universidad de Michoacana y el movimiento estudiantil, 1966–1989.* Morelia: IIH, 2009.
Rath, Thomas. *Myths of Demilitarization in Postrevolutionary Mexico, 1920–1960.* Chapel Hill: University of North Carolina Press, 2013.
Rath, Thomas. "'Que el cielo un soldado en cada hijo te dio': Conscription, Recalcitrance and Resistance in Mexico in the 1940s." *Journal of Latin American Studies* 37, no. 3 (August 2005): 507–31.
Ravelo Lecuona, Renato. *Los jaramillistas: La gesta de Rubén Jaramillo narrada por sus compañeros.* Cuernavaca, Morelos: Editorial la rana del sur, [1978] 2007.
Reyes Heroles, José Jesús. *Mis tiempos.* Mexico City: Fernández Editores, 1988.
Reygadas, Luis. *Proceso de trabajo y acción obrera. Historia sindical de los mineros de Nueva Rosita (1929–1979).* Mexico City: Instituto Nacional de Antropología e Historia, 1988.
Reyna José Luis, and Richard S. Weinert, eds. *Authoritarianism in Mexico.* Philadelphia: Institute for the Study of Human Issues, 1977.
Reynolds, Clark. *The Mexican Economy: Twentieth-Century Structure and Growth.* New Haven, CT: Yale University Press, 1970.
Ribeiro, Darcy. *Fronteras indígenas de la civilización.* Mexico City: Siglo Veintiuno Editores, 1971.
Riding, Alan. *Distant Neighbors: A Portrait of the Mexicans.* New York: Vintage, 1984.
Ríos Molina, Andrés. *Memorias de un loco anormal: El caso de Goyo Cárdenas.* Mexico City: Editorial Debate, 2010.
Rivas, René O. *La izquierda estudiantil en la UNAM: Organizaciones, movilizaciones y liderazgos (1958–1972).* Mexico City: UNAM, 2007.
Rodríguez, Victoria E. *Women's Participation in Mexican Political Life.* Boulder, CO: Westview, 1998.
Rodríguez Kuri, Ariel. "Adolfo López Mateos y la gran política nacional." In *Adolfo López Mateos: La vida dedicada a la política.* Mexico City: Gobierno del Estado de México, 2010.
Rodríguez Kuri, Ariel. "El lado oscuro de la luna: El momento conservador en 1968."

In *Conservadurismo y derechas en la historia de México*, edited by Erika Pani, 512–59. Mexico City: Fondo de Cultura Económica, 2009.

Rodríguez Kuri, Ariel. "Los años maravillosos: Adolfo Ruiz Cortines." In *Gobernantes mexicanos: 1911–2000*, edited by Will Fowler, vol. 2, 263–86. Mexico City: Fondo de Cultura Económica, 2008.

Rodríguez Kuri, Ariel. "Los primeros días: Una explicación de los orígenes inmediatos del movimiento estudiantil de 1968." *Historia Mexicana* 53, no. 1 (July–September 2003): 179–228.

Rodríguez Kuri, Ariel. "Secretos de la idiosincracia: Urbanización y cambio cultural en Mexico, 1950–1970." In *Ciudades mexicans del sigl XX, Siete estudios historicos*, edited by Carlos Lira Vásquez and Ariel Rodríguez Kuri, 19–56. Mexico City: Colegio de México, 2009.

Rodríguez Ledesma, Xavier. *El pensamiento político de Octavio Paz: Las trampas de la ideología*. Mexico City: Plaza y Valdés, 1996.

Rodríguez Munguía, Jacinto. *La otra guerra secreta: Los archivos prohibidos de la prensa y el poder*. Mexico City: Random House Mondadori, 2007.

Rodríguez Prats, Juan José. *El poder presidencial: Adolfo Ruiz Cortines*. Mexico City: Porrúa, 1992.

Román Román, Salvador. *Revuelta Cívica en Guerrero 1957–1960*. Mexico City: INERHM, 2003.

Ronfeldt, David. *Atencingo: Politics of Agrarian Struggle in a Mexican Ejido*. Palo Alto, CA: Stanford University Press, 1973.

Ronfeldt, David, ed. *The Modern Mexican Military: A Reassessment*. San Diego: Center for US–Mexican Relations, 1984.

Roseberry, William. *Anthropologies and Histories: Essays in Culture, History, and Political Economy*. New Brunswick, NJ: Rutgers University Press, 1991.

Ross, Stanley, ed. *Ha muerto la Revolución Mexicana?* 2 vols. Mexico City: SepSetentas, 1972.

Ross, Stanley, ed. *Is the Mexican Revolution Dead?* New York; Knopf, 1966.

Rozental, Sandra. "Mobilizing the Monolith: Patrimonio, Collectivity and Social Memory in Contemporary Mexico." PhD dissertation, University of Columbia, forthcoming.

Rubenstein, Anne. *Bad Language, Naked Ladies, and Other Threats to the Nation: A Political History of Comic Books in Mexico*. Durham, NC: Duke University Press, 1998.

Rubenstein, Anne. "Mass Media and Popular Culture in the Postrevolutionary Era." In *The Oxford History of Mexico*, edited by William H. Beezley and Michael C. Meyer, 598–634. New York: Oxford University Press, 2010.

Rubin, Jeffrey W. "Decentering the Regime: Cultural and Regional Politics in Mexico." *Latin American Research Review* 31, no. 3 (1996): 85–126.

Rubin, Jeffrey W. *Decentering the Regime: Ethnicity, Radicalism, and Democracy in Juchitán, Mexico*. Durham, NC: Duke University Press, 1997.

Rubin, Jeffrey W. "Popular Mobilization and the Myth of State Corporatism." In *Popular Movements and Political Change in Mexico*, edited by Joe Foweraker and Ann L. Craig, 247–67. Boulder, CO: Lynne Rienner, 1990.

Rubin, Jeffrey W. "The State as Subject." *Political Power and Social Theory* 17 (2002): 107–31.

Ruiz, Ramón Eduardo. *Mexico: Why a Few Are Rich and the People Poor*. Berkeley: University of California Press, 2010.

Sáenz, Moisés. *México íntegro*. Lima, Peru: Imprenta Torres Aguirre, 1939.

Salvia Spratte, Agustín. *Los laberintos de Loreto y Peña Pobre*. Mexico City: Ediciones el Caballito, 1989.

Sánchez Gudiño, Hugo. *Génesis, desarrollo, y consolidación de los grupos estudiantiles de choque en la UNAM, 1930–1990*. Mexico City: UNAM, 2006.

Sánchez Gutiérrez, Arturo. "La política en el México rural de los años cincuenta." In *The Evolution of the Mexican Political System*, edited by Jaime E. Rodriguez, 215–44. Berkeley: University of California Press, 1993.

Sánchez Hidalgo, Joaquín B. *Trazos y mitos de una utopía: La Institución Politécnica*. Mexico City: SAIPN, 2000.

Sánchez Susarrey, Jaime. "Mecanismos de negociación y concertación política." In *Historia política, 1940–1975: Jalisco desde la revolución*, edited by Jaime Sánchez Susarrey and Ignacio Medina Núñez. Guadalajara: Gobierno del Estado de Jalisco, 1987.

Sanders, Nichole Marie. *Gender and Welfare in Mexico: The Consolidation of a Postrevolutionary State*. University Park: Pennsylvania State University Press, 2011.

Sanderson, Steven E. *Agrarian Populism and the Mexican State: The Struggle for Land in Sonora*. Berkeley: University of California Press, 1981.

Sandos, James, and Harry Cross. *Across the Border: Rural Development in Mexico and Recent Migration to the United States*. Berkeley, CA: Institute of Governmental Studies, 1981.

Santiago, Myrna I. *The Ecology of Oil: Environment, Labor, and the Mexican Revolution, 1910–1938*. New York: Cambridge University Press, 2006.

Santos, Gonzalo N. *Memorias*. Mexico City: Grijalbo, 1986.

Santos Cenobio, Rafael. *El movimiento estudiantil en la UAS (1966–1972)*. Culiacán: Universidad Autónomia de Sinaloa, 2005.

Santoyo, Antonio. *La Mano Negra: Poder regional y estado en México (Veracruz, 1928–1943)*. Mexico City: Consejo Naciónal para la Cultura y Artes, 1995.

Saragoza, Alex M. "Behind the Scenes: Media Ownership, Politics, and Popular Culture in Mexico (1930–1958)." In *Los intelectuales y el poder en México: Memorias de la VI Conferencia de Historiadores Mexicanos y Estadounidenses*, edited by Roderic Ai Camp, 749–63. Mexico City: Colegio de México, 1991.

Saragoza, Alex M. *The Monterrey Elite and the Mexican State*. Austin: University of Texas Press, 1988.

Saragoza, Alex M. "Television." In *Encyclopedia of Mexico: History, Society, and Culture*, 2 vols., edited by Michael S. Werner, 2: 488–93. Chicago: Fitzroy Dearborn, 1997.

Sariego, Juan Luis. *El indigenismo en la Tarahumara*. Mexico City: Instituto Nacional Indigenista, 2002.

Sariego, Juan Luis. *Enclaves y minerales en el Norte de México: Historia social de los mineros de Cananea y Nueva Rosita, 1900–1970*. Mexico City: CIESAS, 1988.

Schatz, Edward. "Transnational Image Making and Soft Authoritarian Kazakhstan." *Slavic Review* 67, no. 1 (spring 2008): 50–62.

Schedler, Andreas, ed. *Electoral Authoritarianism: The Dynamics of Unfree Competition*. Boulder, CO: Lynne Rienner, 2006.

Schell, Patience. *Church and State Education in Revolutionary Mexico City*. Tucson: University of Arizona Press, 2003.

Scherer García, Julio, and Carlos Monsiváis. *Tiempo de saber: Prensa y poder en México*. Mexico City: Aguilar, 2003.

Schlefer, Jonathan. *Palace Politics: How the Ruling Party Brought Crisis to Mexico*. Austin: University of Texas Press, 2008.

Schmitt, Karl M. *Communism in Mexico: A Study in Political Frustration*. Austin: University of Texas Press, 1965.

Schryer, Frans J. *Ethnicity and Class Conflict in Rural Mexico*. Princeton, NJ: Princeton University Press, 1980.

Schryer, Frans J. *The Rancheros of Pisaflores: The History of a Peasant Bourgeoisie in Twentieth-Century Mexico*. Toronto: University of Toronto Press, 1980.

Schuler, Friedrich E. *Mexico Between Hitler and Roosevelt: Mexican Foreign Relations in the Age of Lázaro Cárdenas, 1934–1940*. Albuquerque: University of New Mexico Press, 1998.

Scott, James C. *Domination and the Arts of Resistance: Hidden Transcripts*. New Haven, CT: Yale University Press, 1990.

Scott, James C. *Weapons of the Weak: Everyday Forms of Peasant Resistance*. New Haven, CT: Yale University Press, 1985.

Segovia, Rafael. *La politización del niño mexicano*. Mexico City: Colegio de México, 1975.

Semo, Enrique, ed. *México, un pueblo en la historia*. Vol. 5, *Nueva Burgesia, 1938–1957*. Mexico City: Editorial La Patria, 1989.

Serrano, Monica. "The Armed Branch of the State: Civil-Military Relations in Mexico." *Journal of Latin American Studies* 27 (1996): 423–48.

Serrano Alvarez, Pablo. *La batalla del espíritu: El movimiento sinarquista en El Bajío, 1932–1951*. 2 vols. Mexico City: Consejo Nacional para la Cultura y las Artes, 1992.

Servín, Elisa. *La oposición política, Herramientas para la historia*. Mexico City: Fondo de Cultura Económica, 2006.

Servín, Elisa. "Reclaiming Revolution in the Light of the Mexican Miracle: Celestino Gasca and the Federacionistas Leales Insurrection of 1961." *The Americas* 66, no. 4 (2010): 527–57.

Servín, Elisa. *Ruptura y oposición: El movimiento henriquista, 1945–1954*. Mexico City: Cal y Arena, 2001.

Sewell, William B. *Logics of History: Social Theory and Social Transformation*. Chicago: University of Chicago Press, 2005.

Sherman, John W. *The Mexican Right: The End of Revolutionary Reform, 1929–1940*. Westport, CT: Praeger, 1997.

Siegel, Barry. *Inflación y desarrollo: Las experiencias de México*. Mexico City: Centro de Estudios Monetarios Latinoamericanos, 1960.

Silva Herzog, Jesús. *Un ensayo sobre la revolución Mexicana*. Mexico City: Cuadernos Americanos, 1946.

Simon, Joel. *Endangered Mexico: An Environment on the Edge*. San Francisco: Sierra Club Books, 1997.

Simonian, Lane. *Defending the Land of the Jaguar: A History of Conservation in Mexico*. Austin: University of Texas Press, 1995.

Singer, Morris. *Growth, Equality and the Mexican Experience*. Austin: University of Texas Press, 1970.

Smith, Benjamin T. "Inventing Tradition at Gunpoint: Culture, Caciquismo and State

Formation in the Región Mixe, Oaxaca (1930–1959)." *Bulletin of Latin American Research* 27, no. 2 (April 2008): 215–34.

Smith, Benjamin T. *Pistoleros and Popular Movements: The Politics of State Formation in Postrevolutionary Oaxaca.* Lincoln: University of Nebraska Press, 2009.

Smith, Benjamin T. *The Roots of Conservatism in Mexico: Catholicism, Society, and Politics in the Mixteca Baja 1750–1962.* Albuquerque: University of New Mexico Press, 2012.

Smith, Peter H. *Labyrinths of Power: Political Recruitment in Twentieth-Century Mexico.* Princeton, NJ: Princeton University Press, 1979.

Snodgrass, Michael. *Deference and Defiance in Monterrey: Workers, Paternalism and Revolution in Mexico, 1890–1950.* Cambridge: Cambridge University Press, 2003.

Snodgrass, Michael. "'New Rules for the Unions': Mexico's Steel Workers Confront Privatization and the Neoliberal Challenge." *Labor: Working-Class History of the Americas* 4 (fall 2007): 81–103.

Snodgrass, Michael. "Patronage and Progress: The Bracero Program from the Perspective of Mexico." In *Workers Across the Americas: The Transnational Turn in Labor History.* Edited by Leon Fink, 245–66. New York: Oxford University Press, 2011.

Solis, Leopoldo. *Economic Policy Reform in Mexico: A Case Study for Developing Countries.* New York: Pergamon Press, 1981.

Sorensen, Diana. *A Turbulent Decade Remembered: Scenes from the Latin American Sixties.* Palo Alto, CA: Stanford University Press, 2007.

Soto Correa, José Carmen. *El rifle sanitario, la fiebre aftosa y la rebelión campesina.* Mexico City: Instituto Politécnico Nacional, 2009.

Soto Laveaga, Gabriela. *Jungle Laboratories: Mexican Peasants, National Projects, and the Making of the Pill.* Durham, NC: Duke University Press, 2010.

Spenser, Daniela, ed. *Espejos de la Guerra fría: México, América Central y el Caribe.* Mexico City: CIESAS, 2004.

Stavans, Ilan. *Antihéroes: México y su novela policial.* Mexico City: Joaquín Mortiz, 1993.

Stepan, Alfred. *The Military in Politics: Changing Patterns in Brazil.* Princeton, NJ: Princeton University Press, 1974.

Stepan, Alfred. *Rethinking Military Politics.* Princeton, NJ: Princeton University Press, 1988.

Stevens, Evelyn P. *Protest and Response in Mexico.* Cambridge, MA: MIT Press, 1974.

Stevens, Evelyn P. "Protest Movement in an Authoritarian Regime: The Mexican Case." *Comparative Politics* 7, no. 3 (1975): 361–82.

Suárez, Luis. *Alejo Peralta, un patrón sin patrones.* Mexico City: Grijalbo, 1992.

Suárez, Luis, ed. *Lucio Cabañas, el guerrillero sin esperanza.* Mexico City: Roca, 1976.

Szekely, Miguel. "Pobreza y desigualdad en México entre 1950 y 2004." *El Trimestre Económico* 72, no. 4 (October–December 2005): 913–31.

Tannenbaum, Barbara A. *The Politics of Penury: Debts and Taxes in Mexico, 1821–1856.* Albuquerque: University of New Mexico Press, 1986.

Taussig, Michael. *Mimesis and Alterity: A Particular History of the Senses.* London: Routledge, 1993.

Thirlwall, Anthony P. *Nicholas Kaldor.* New York: New York University Press, 1987.

Tibón, Gutierre. *Pinotepa Nacional, mixtecos, negros y triquis.* Mexico City: n.p., 1961.

Tocqueville, Alexis de. *Democracy in America.* 2 vols. Translated by Henry Reeves. Cambridge: Sever and Francis, 1863.

Torres, Blanca. *Hacia la utopía industrial*. Mexico City: Colegio de México, 1984.

Torres, Blanca. "México en la Segundal Guerra Mundial." In *Historia de la Revolución Mexicana*, vol. 19. Mexico City: El Colegio de México, 1979.

Townsend, William. *Lázaro Cárdenas, demócrata mexicano*. Mexico City: Biografías Gandesa, 1959.

Trejo Delarbre, Raúl, ed. *Televisa, el quinto poder*. Mexico City: Claves Latinoamericanas, 1985.

Trinkunas, Harold. *Crafting Civilian Control of the Military in Venezuela*. Chapel Hill: University of North Carolina Press, 2005.

Tsebelis, George. "Decision Making in Political Systems: Veto Players in Presidentialism, Parliamentarism, Multicameralism and Mutipartyism." *British Journal of Political Science* 25 (July 1995): 289–325.

Tuñón Pablos, Enriqueta. *¡Por fin . . . ya podemos elegir y ser electas!* Mexico City: CONACULTA, INAH, Plaza y Valdes Editores, 2002.

Tutino, John. *Making a New World: Founding Capitalism in the Bajío and Spanish North America*. Durham, NC: Duke University Press, 2011.

Usigli, Rodolfo. *El gesticulador (pieza para demágogos en tres actos)*. Mexico City: Editores Mexicanos Unidos, 1985.

Valdés, Luz María. *Los indíos en los censos de población*. Mexico City: UNAM, 1995.

Valle, Eduardo. *El año de la rebelión por la democracia: Con una cierta mirada*. Mexico City: Oceano, 2008.

Vanderwood, Paul J. *Juan Soldado: Rapist, Murderer, Martyr, Saint*. Durham, NC: Duke University Press, 2004.

Vargas Llosa, Mario. "La dictadura perfecta," in *Desafios a la libertad*. Madrid: El Pais, 1994.

Vaughan, Mary Kay. "Cultural Approaches to Peasant Politics in the Mexican Revolution." *Hispanic American Historical Review* 79, no. 2 (1999): 269–308.

Vaughan, Mary Kay. *Cultural Politics in Revolution: Teachers, Peasants, and Schools in Mexico, 1930–1940*. Tucson: University of Arizona Press, 1997.

Vaughan, Mary Kay. "Modernizing Patriarchy: State Policies, Rural Households, and Women in Mexico, 1930–1940." In *Hidden Histories of Gender and State in Latin America*, edited by Maxine Molyneux and Elizabeth Dore, 194–215. Durham, NC: Duke University Press, 2000.

Vaughan, Mary Kay, and Stephen E. Lewis, eds. *The Eagle and the Virgin: Nation and Cultural Revolution in Mexico, 1920–1940*. Durham, NC: Duke University Press, 2006.

Vázquez Mantecón, Alvaro, and Sergio Raúl Arroyo. *Memorial del 68*. Mexico City: UNAM, Dirección General de Publicaciones y Fomento Editorial, 2007.

Veledíaz, Juan. *El general sin memoria*. Mexico City: Debate, 2010.

Vélez-Ibañez, Carlos. *Rituals of Marginality: Politics, Process, and Culture Change in Urban Central Mexico, 1969–1974*. Berkeley: University of California Press, 1983.

Ventura Patiño, María del Carmen. *Disputas por el gobierno local en Tarecuato, Michoacán, 1942–1999*. Zamora: Colegio de Michoacán, 2003.

Vera Estañol, Jorge. *La revolución Mexicana: Origenes y resultados*. Mexico City: Porrúa, 1957.

Villa Rojas, Alfonso. *Los mazatecos y el problema indígena de la cuenca del Papaloapan*. Mexico City: Instituto Nacional Indigenista, 1955.

Viotti da Costa, Emilia. "New Publics, New Politics, New Histories: From Economic Reductionism to Cultural Reductionism—in Search of Dialectics." In *Reclaiming the Political in Latin American History: Essays from the North*, edited by Gilbert M. Joseph, 17–31. Durham, NC: Duke University Press, 2001.

Vogel, Harold. *Entertainment Industry Economics*. New York: Cambridge University Press, 2007.

Wahl, Ana-Maria. "Economic Development and Social Security in Mexico, 1945–1985." *International Journal of Comparative Sociology* 35, no. 1/2 (1994): 59–81.

Wakild, Emily. *An Unexpected Environment: National Park Creation, Resource Custodianship, and the Mexican Revolution*. Tucson: University of Arizona Press, 2011.

Warman, Arturo. *De eso que llaman antropología mexicana*. Mexico City: Editorial Nuestro Tiempo, 1970.

Warman, Arturo. *Y venimos a contradecir: Los campesinos de Morelos y el estado nacional*. 2nd ed. Mexico City: Casa Chata, 1978.

Wasserman, Mark. *Persistent Oligarchs: Elites and Politics in Chihuahua, Mexico 1910–1940*. Durham, NC: Duke University Press, 1993.

Weinberg, Bill. "Mexico: Lacandón Selva Conflict Grows." NACLA *Report on the Americas* 36, no. 6 (2003): 26–47.

Whetton, Nathan L. *Rural Mexico*. Chicago: University of Chicago Press, 1948.

White, Christopher M. *Creating a Third World: Mexico, Cuba, and the United States during the Castro Era*. Albuquerque: University of New Mexico Press, 2007.

Whiting, Van R. *The Political Economy of Foreign Investment in Mexico*. Baltimore: Johns Hopkins University Press, 1992.

Whitney, Robert. "The Architect of the Cuban State: Fulgencio Batista and Populism in Cuba, 1937–1940." *Journal of Latin American Studies* 32, no. 2 (May 2000): 435–59.

Wiarda, Howard, ed. *Authoritarianism and Corporatism in Latin America—Revisited*. Gainesville: University Press of Florida, 2004.

Wilkie, James W., and Edna Monzón de Wilkie. *México visto en el siglo xx*. Mexico City: Instituto Mexicano de Investigaciones Económicas, 1969.

Wilkie, James W. *The Mexican Revolution: Federal Expenditure and Social Change since 1910*. Berkeley: University of California Press, 1970.

Wolf, Eric. "Aspects of Group Relations in a Complex Society: Mexico." *American Anthropologist* 58, no. 5 (October 1956): 1065–78.

Womack, John, Jr. "The Mexican Revolution, 1910–1920." In *Mexico Since Independence*, edited by Leslie Bethell, 125–200. Cambridge: Cambridge University Press, 1991.

Womack, John, Jr. *Zapata and the Mexican Revolution*. New York, Knopf, 1968.

Wood, Andrew Grant. *Revolution in the Street: Women, Workers, and Urban Protest in Veracruz, 1870–1927*. Wilmington, DE: Scholarly Resources, 2001.

Yates, Paul. *El desarollo regional de México*. Mexico City: Banco de México, 1962.

Zaremberg, Gisela. *Mujeres, votos y asistencia social en el México priísta y la Argentina peronista*. Mexico City: FLACSO-México, 2009.

Zepeda Lecuona, Guillermo. *Crimen sin castigo: Procuración de justicia penal y ministerio público en México*. Mexico City: Fondo de Cultura Económica-Cidac, 2004.

Zermeño, Sergio. *Mexico City: Una democracia utópica*. Mexico City: Siglo XXI, 1978.

Zieger, Robert. *The CIO, 1935–1955*. Chapel Hill: University of North Carolina Press, 1995.

Zolov, Eric. "¡Cuba sí, Yanquis no! The Sacking of the Instituto Cultural México-Norteamericano in Morelia, Michoacán, 1961." In *In from the Cold: Latin America's New Encounter with the Cold War*, edited by Gilbert M. Joseph and Daniela Spenser, 214–52. Durham, NC: Duke University Press, 2008.

Zolov, Eric. *Refried Elvis: The Rise of the Mexican Counterculture*. Berkeley: University of California Press, 1999.

CONTRIBUTORS

Roberto Blancarte is Professor at the Centro de Estudios Sociológicos of the Colegio de México and author of Historia de la Iglesia Católica en México.

Christopher R. Boyer is Associate Professor of History and Latin American and Latino Studies at the University of Illinois at Chicago, and author of Becoming Campesinos: Politics, Identity, and Agrarian Struggle in Postrevolutionary Michocán, 1920–1935.

Guillermo de la Peña is Professor of Social Anthropology at the Centro de Investigaciones y Estudios Superiores en Antropología Social—Occidente and author of A Legacy of Promises: Agriculture, Politics and Ritual in the Morelos Highlands of Mexico.

María Teresa Fernández Aceves is Professor of History at the Centro de Investigaciones y Estudios Superiores en Antropología Social—Occidente and author of Mujeres en el cambio social en el siglo XX mexicano.

Paul Gillingham is Lecturer in Latin American History at the University of Pennsylvania, and author of Cuauhtémoc's Bones: Forging National Identity in Modern Mexico.

Rogelio Hernández Rodríguez is Professor of Political Science at the Centro de Estudios Internacionales at the Colegio de México and author of El centro dividido: La nueva autonomía de los gobernadores.

Alan Knight is Professor of the History of Latin America at the University of Oxford and author of The Mexican Revolution (2 vols).

Gladys McCormick is Assistant Professor of History at Syracuse University and author of "The Political Economy of Desire in Rural Mexico: Authoritarianism and Revolutionary Change, 1935–1965."

Tanalís Padilla is Associate Professor of History at Dartmouth College and author of Rural Resistance in the Land of Zapata: The Jaramillista Movement and the Myth of the Pax Priísta, 1940–1962 (Duke University Press).

Wil G. Pansters is Professor of Latin American Studies at the University of Groningen, and Associate Professor of Anthropology at Utrecht University. He is the editor of *Violence, Coercion and State-Making in Twentieth-Century Mexico: The Other Half of the Centaur*.

Andrew Paxman is Assistant Professor of Latin American History at Millsaps College, and coauthor of *El Tigre: Emilio Azcárraga y su imperio Televisa*.

Pablo Piccato is Professor of Latin American History at Columbia University and author of *City of Suspects: Crime in Mexico City, 1900–1931* (Duke University Press).

Jaime M. Pensado is Carl E. Koch Assistant Professor of Latin American History at the University of Notre Dame and author of *Rebel Mexico: Student Unrest and Authoritarian Political Culture During the Long Sixties*.

Thomas Rath is Lecturer in Latin American History at University College London, and author of *Myths of Demilitarization in Postrevolutionary Mexico, 1920–1960*.

Jeffrey W. Rubin is Associate Professor of History at Boston University and author of *Decentering the Regime: Ethnicity, Radicalism, and Democracy in Juchitán, Mexico* (Duke University Press).

Benjamin T. Smith is Associate Professor of Latin American History at the University of Warwick and author of *Pistoleros and Popular Movements: The Politics of State Formation in Postrevolutionary Oaxaca*.

Michael Snodgrass is Associate Professor of Latin American History at Indiana University-Purdue University and author of *Deference and Defiance in Monterrey: Workers, Paternalism, and Revolution in Mexico, 1890–1950*.

INDEX

Aboites Aguilar, Luis, 257, 258
Abrams, Philip, 5, 6
Acapulco, 17, 99, 171, 268
Acatlipa, Morelos, 205
Acción Católica Mexicana (ACM), 15, 24, 59, 74, 76, 80, 250, 269
acculturation, 282, 284–86, 288, 292, 293
advocates, 237–39, 242–44
Africa, 2, 3, 219
agrarian reform (*reparto agrario*), 7, 12, 120, 224, 226, 236, 237, 240, 241, 242, 252, 255; and cardenismo, 49, 50, 53, 56–58, 64, 92; church opposition to, 72; and forestry, 217–18, 222, 226; rollback of, 12, 227, 250, 381; and women, 245–46
agraristas, xi, 57, 131, 136, 157, 158, 160, 239, 259
Aguascalientes, 17, 235, tax protests in, 264–67
Aguilar, Cándido, 161, 166
Aguilar, Francisco, 91
Aguirre Beltrán, Gonzalo, 283–90, 293
Aguirre, José Angel, 345
Aguirre, Vicente, 119
Ahualulco de Mercado (Jalisco), 245
Ajuchitlán (Guerrero), 157, 158
Alcabala, 262–64, 267, 268
alcohol, 186, 219, 305; politics of, 12, 153, 263, 287, 344, 383; tax evasion and, 257, 258–59
Aldrett, Pablo, 134, 138–43
Alemán Valdés, Miguel; and presidency, 14, 17, 23, 49, 112, 114, 119, 132, 151, 152, 154, 161, 243, 250, 283, 329, 333, 334, 335; and humor, 18, 19, 20; and the church, 77, 78;

and army, 92, 94, 95, 96, 98, 102; and anticommunism, 162; and unions, 177, 179, 205; and forestry management, 218, 219, 221, 225, 228; and taxation, 257, 258; and *indigenismo*, 284; and the media, 300, 304, 308–11; and teachers, 389
Alemanismo, 305. *See also* Miguel Alemán
Alianza Cívica Potosina, 140
Allá en el Rancho Grande, 302
Almazán, Juan Andreu, 49, 51, 52, 334; and the 1940 elections, 54, 56, 58–60, 65, 67, 69, 91, 92, 97, 112; links with Emilio Azcárraga, 14, 113, 305, 307
Altamirano, Rafael, 324, 325, 336, 388
Althusser, Louis, xii
Alvarez Garín, Raúl, 351
Alvarez, Manuel, 126–28, 132, 134, 136, 139
Amanecer, 325
Amaro, Joaquín, 49, 56, 59, 96, 102
American Smelting and Refining Company (ASARCO), 139, 176, 182
Amparo, 331, 334, 335
Ampudia del Valle, Rodrigo, 204, 206–9
Angangueo (Michoacán), 229
Angulo, Mauro, 330–36, 388
anticlericalism, 7, 15, 49, 50, 59, 72, 74, 363
Apaxtla (Guerrero), 157
Apizaco (Tlaxcala), 17, 333, 334
Appalachia, 175
Argentina, 179, 380; and bureaucratic authoritarianism, 21; labor history of, 181; military expenditure in, 95, 98; taxation and social spending in, 259, 260

Arias, Manuel, 345–48, 352
Armenta Barradas, Armando, 329, 334
Armenta, Marciano, 330, 334, 335
Armenta, Teodoro, 334
army. *See* military
Ataturk, Kemal, 61
Atencingo (Puebla), 196, 203, 211
Atl, Dr., 56
attorney general, 26, 134, 137, 140, 335
Auscultación, 155, 156, 158
Austria, Honorato, 119
authoritarianism, ix, x, xii–xiii, 2, 4, 7, 10, 11, 20–27, 55, 59, 135, 149, 151, 152, 154, 166, 181, 197, 198, 209, 211, 212, 237, 248, 256, 261, 280, 342, 356, 361–63, 366, 368, 372, 380, 381, 383, 385, 386, 390–93; bureaucratic, xii, 21; competitive, xii–xiii, xv, 22, 24, 25, 27, 149, 166, 171, 392; critique of, 390–91; electoral, 22, 27; soft, xiii, 27, 166, 392
Autlán (Jalisco), 247, 248
Avila Bretón, Rafael, 333, 334
Avila Camacho, Manuel: and presidency, 48–52, 58, 60, 62, 133, 161; and church, 73, 74, 75, 76; and army, 89–93, 96, 99, 102; and Puebla, 110–19; and peasants, 200–202; and forestry management, 218, 219, 225; and taxation, 257, 258; and *indigenismo*, 282; and the media, 301–6, 314; and teachers, 343
Avila Camacho, Maximino, 52, 53, 110, 111, 117, 304, 305
Avila Camacho, Rafael, 99, 111
Ayotzinapa (Guerrero), 351, 355
Azcárraga Milmo, Emilio, 313
Azcárraga Vidaurreta, Emilio, 14; emergence of television monopoly, 307–11; punished for support of Almazán, 305; and radio monopoly, 303–5; support for PRI from Televisa, 313–14
Azcárraga, Gastón, 303
Azuela, Mariano, 4

Bachelor, Steven, 7
Baja California, 26, 114, 161
Bajío, 2, 60, 61
Balas de plata, 321
Banco de México, 6, 110, 259
Banco Nacional Cinematográfico (BNC), 306, 309
Bank of Ejidal Credit, 58, 63

Barthes, Roland, 19
Bartlett Bautista, Manuel, 267
Bausauri, Carlos, 281
Bautista, Gonzalo, 118
Baz, Gustavo, 242, 243
Beals, Ralph, 268
Beltrán, Agapito, 139, 140
Beltrán, Enrique, 223, 231
Bernal, Rafael, 329
Blancarte, Roberto, 9, 11, 16, 383, 384, 390
Blanco Moheno, Roberto, 19
Boas, Franz, 284
Bolaño, Roberto, 321, 322
Bolivia, 48–49; contemporary politics of, 382, 394; revolution in, 55; taxation in, 260
Bonfil Batalla, Guillermo, 293
Booth, John A., 164
Boyer, Christopher, 8, 14, 35
braceros, 177, 179, 389; permits as rewards, 9, 14, 178; *corrido del bracero*, 17; as seasonal migrants from Jalisco, 188–91; remitting money for hospital construction, 242–43
Brand Sánchez, Humberto, 265
Brandenburg, Frank 3, 4, 155
Bravo Izquierdo, Donato, 93, 96
Brazil, 63; and bureaucratic authoritarianism, 21; contemporary politics of, 380, 382, 394; income inequality, 2–3; *indigenismo* in, 293; labor history, 179; military, 95, 98; structural hypocrisy in, 97; sugar production in, 198; and taxation and social spending, 259–61; television, 305
Buñuel, Luis, 309

Cabañas, Lucio, 24, 55, 350, 351, 353, 356
cacica, 16, 237–39
cacicazgo, 15, 383, 385, 386, 390; avilacamachista, 61, 97, 117–18; Cedillo, 129–31; García Barragán, 247, 249; and *pistolerismo*, 328, 331; Rojo Gómez, 118–20; Santos, 128–31, 135–42; in theory, 237–39; union, 13
cacique, 11, 16, 25, 52, 98, 100, 108, 109, 111, 114, 118, 119, 120, 121, 122, 127, 135, 136, 138–43, 150, 157, 159, 236–39, 247, 248, 250, 251, 267–70, 281, 285, 289, 322, 323, 334, 336, 341, 383
caciquismo, x, 142, 162; and historiography, 5, 7, 27, 121, 128–31, 238, 251, 329, 336–37, 388; military, 92–98; at state level, 108–25

430 INDEX

California, 190
Calles, Plutarco Elías, 51, 52, 53, 54, 56; and anticlericalism, 74; and cardenista reform, 49, 57, 63, 74, 85; and lumber industry, 343; and regional strongmen, 110–12, 117, 118, 127, 224
Camacho Barreto, Jesús, 248
Cámara, Fernando, 283
Camp, Roderic, 53
Campa, Valentín, 183
Campbell, Hugh, 58
Campeche, 114, 312
campesina, 246
campesino, 17, 102, 223, 225, 231, 301, 343, 344, 350, 351, 354, 355, 383
Campos, Tomás, 143
Cananea (Sonora), 14, 177, 184, 185, 186, 188
Cananea Cattle Company, 13
Cano, Gabriela, 244
Cantinflas, 4, 7, 20, 301
Caravan of Hunger, 176, 180
Cárdenas, Chucho, 331
Cárdenas, Francisco "Goyo," 323, 325, 326
Cárdenas del Río, Lázaro: and presidency, 1, 2, 48–54, 56, 58–63, 117, 118, 131, 132, 175, 177, 239, 241, 343, 355, 356, 380, 381, 388, 389; and army, 90–94, 96; and caciques, 108, 110, 111, 114, 139; and church, 71–75, 85; and Ciudad Madera, 13; and collectives, 198; and democracy, 165; and forestry management, 218–20, 222, 224, 225, 227, 228, 232; and *indigenismo*, 281, 282, 289, 291; and the media, 302, 305; and the Movimiento de Liberación Nacional (MLN), 24; nostalgia for, 20, 201–4; and students, 361, 363, 364, 370; and unions, 178, 179, 184
cardenismo, 47, 50, 52, 63, 91, 177, 211, 232, 302, 381. *See also* Lázaro Cárdenas
Cardoso de Oliveira, Roberto, 293
Carillo, Nabor, 361
Carillo, Raymundo, 266
Carr, Barry, 23
Carranza, Venustiano, 47, 239
Carrasco, Jesús, 180
Carrera Peña, Severino, 200, 204, 207
Carrillo Puerto, Elvia, 250
cartoons, 4, 7, 14, 19, 101, 155, 247, 301, 309
Casas Alemán, Fernando, 114
Casimiro, Francisco, 345

Caso, Alfonso, 284
Castrejón, Adrian, 102
Castro, Fidel, 23, 81, 351, 353
Castro, Pedro J., 335, 336
Catholic church, 11, 221, 384, 386; church/state relations, 9, 15, 49–50, 70–87; and the radical Right, 59–60; and social Catholicism, 82–84, 238, 269–70; and women, 250
Catorce (San Luis Potosí), 130, 139, 140
Ceballos, Alfonso G., 239
Cedillo, Saturnino, 49, 54, 56, 59–62, 108, 110, 111, 129–31, 134, 136, 139, 386
Cedral (San Luis Potosí), 130, 140, 141, 143
censorship, 17, 19, 101, 102, 303, 313, 325
Centeno, Miguel Angel, 25
Centro Coordinador Indigenista (CCI), 284, 286, 287, 291, 293
Chamula (Chiapas), 291
Charcas (San Luis Potosí), 130, 135, 136, 139
Charrismo, 13, 178–92, 341, 366, 371, 372
Chávez, Carlos, 307
Chávez, Hugo, 382
Chiapas, 91, 102, 158, 160, 268, 287, 288, 291, 324; anthropology in, 283–87; cardenismo in, 53, 57, 67; *Centro Coordinador Indigenista* in San Cristóbal, 284; counterinsurgency in, 12, 35, 99, 102, 387; electoral massacre in Tapachula, 157, 161; ñeo-Zapatismo, 55, 384
Chihuahua, 61, 97, 208; concentration of militia units, 91, 99; elections in, 161, 165, 166; forestry, 217, 219, 221, 228, 230, 231, 234, 235; guerrillas, 13, 16, 351–52; land reform, 13; taxation in, 258, 268, 273; *Centro Coordinador Indigenista*, 284; normalistas, 345, 347, 350, 351, 352
Chile, 3, 21, 95, 175, 181, 260, 394
Chilpancingo, 26, 268
China, 2, 55, 82
Christlieb Ibarrola, Adolfo, 24
Churubusco film studio, 312
Cienfuegos, Jesús, 258–59
cinema, 3, 4, 7, 18, 153, 154, 258, 299–315
citizenship, 77, 285–86, 292, 326, 379, 381, 394
Ciudad del Maíz (San Luis Potosí), 128
Ciudad Hidalgo (Michoacan), 24
Ciudad Juárez (Chihuahua), 166
Ciudad Madera (Chihuahua), 13, 351, 352, 353

Ciudad Nezahualcóyotl (Estado de México), 15, 18
Ciudad Valles (San Luis Potosí), 132
Clasa Filmes Mundiales, 17, 302
class consciousness, 57, 97, 286, 348, 355
Coahuayutla (Guerrero), 157
Coahuila, 175, 179, 181, 191, 192, 210, 259, 267
Coatepec (Veracruz), 154
Cocula (Guerrero), 157
Cold War, xii, 22–24, 175, 181, 361, 365, 368, 381, 393
Colima, 13, 235, 265
Collier, John D., 282
Colombia, 3, 56, 259, 260, 380
Colonia Roma, 324
Colosio, Luis Donaldo, 165
Columbia Teacher's College, 365
Columbia University, 223
Comisariado de Bienes Comunales, 289
Comisariado Ejidal, 137, 206, 289
communism, 1, 23, 24, 41, 55, 68, 150, 160, 325, 381, 384; and Alemán, 163; and cardenismo, 51, 52, 56, 57, 63, 64, 67, 91, 282, 303; and the church, 70–86; and students, 361, 368, 371; and teachers, 245, 348, 354; and unions, 175, 176, 177, 179, 180, 181, 388. *See also* Partido Comunista de México
community-based conservation, 218, 232, 233
Compañía Mexicana de Luz y Fuerza Motríz, 269
Compañía Nacional de Subsistencias Populares (CONASUPO), 182
Comunidad Revolucionaria Institucional, 291
Confederación de Cámaras Industriales (CONCAMIN), 364, 375
Confederación de Trabajadores de América Latina (CTAL), 23, 53
Confederación de Trabajadores de México (CTM), 49, 52, 53, 56, 59–61, 77, 92, 94, 138, 178, 199, 200, 225, 264
Confederación General de Trabajadores (CGT), 205-7
Confederación Nacional Campesina (CNC), 24, 199, 202, 203, 205, 206, 241, 245, 246, 247, 248, 249, 266
Confederación Nacional de Organizaciones Populares (CNOP), 15, 249
Confederación Patronal de la República Mexicana (COPARMEX), 60

Confederación Regional Obrera Mexicana (CROM), 53
congress, 16, 157; national, 76, 110, 117, 127, 133, 150, 151, 158, 161, 162, 163, 164, 186, 225, 227, 237, 244, 246, 247, 248, 306, 307, 323; state, 110, 117, 131, 132, 134, 158, 189, 236, 262, 264
Consejo Episcopal Latinoamericano (CELAM), 81
Consejo Supremo Tarahumara, 288, 289, 291
constitution (1917), 48, 51, 70, 71, 73, 75, 77, 79, 80, 82, 122, 222, 224, 250, 258, 269, 281, 289, 291, 355, 356, 364
Contreras, Manuel, 95
cooperatives: forest, 217; school, 269; sugar, 196–210, 388; union, 186, 188
co-option, 13, 15, 20, 157, 183, 186, 197, 198, 245, 256, 268, 381; difficulties financing same, 13–14, 256, 261; of rural populations, 202–8, 211–12, 267
Coordinadora Nacional de Trabajadores de la Educación (CNTE), 342
Coracero, Silvestre, 240
Coral Martínez, Blas, 94
Córdoba (Veracruz), 16, 157
Córdova, Arnaldo, 120
Corona del Rosal, Alfonso, 119, 120, 372
Coronil, Fernando, xii
Corrido, 17, 18, 25, 153, 184, 383
Corrigan, Philip, 5
corruption, 12, 14, 59, 100, 166, 310, 391–92; in the army, 90, 97–98, and state agents, 67, 197, 204–5, 207, 209, 210, 220, 226–27, 228, 229, 231, 256, 261, 267, 290–91, 324, 384–86; and justice, 325, 326; and labor, 56, 180, 184, 185, 191; and local politics, 143, 152, 285, satirized, 18–19; substitute for tax revenues, 268, 270; in universities, 362, 365–66, 371, 372
Cosío Vidaurri, Guillermo, 249
Cosío Villegas, Daniel, 4, 48, 150
Coss, Francisco, 56
Costa Chica (Oaxaca), 263
Costa Rica, 95, 98, 260, 261
Cristeros, 24, 59, 61, 70, 71, 79, 91, 93, 189, 239, 384. *See also* Cristiada
Cristiada, 49, 60, 211, 239, 240
crony capitalism, 217–35, 300
Cruz, Ezequiel "Scarface," 18
Cuaxocota (Puebla), 12,

Cuba, 23, 24, 81, 82, 86, 198, 305, 308, 342, 350–53, 356, 387
Cuban Revolution, 81–82, 86, 342; and Mexican guerrillas, 23–24, 351–53, 387; and students, 82; and teachers, 342, 350–57, 387
Cuetzala del Progreso (Guerrero), 158
Cuevas, Belén, 353
Culiacán (Sinaloa), 154, 165, 321
cultural missions, 280, 282, 343

D'Olmo, Leo, 331
Dahl, Robert, 48, 156, 166; and cost of repression, 26; and cost of toleration, 22, 156
dams, 99, 236, 249, 262, 287–88
De la Fuente, Julio, 283, 284, 287, 290
De la Madrid, Miguel, 120
De la Peña, Guillermo, 9
De la Peña, Moisés, 262, 263
De la Vega, Eduardo, 308
De Quevedo, Miguel Ángel, 221, 222, 224, 227
defensa rural, 90, 91, 97, 99. *See also* militia
Del Río, Dolores, 301
democracy, ix, xi, xii, 4, 11, 15, 22, 48, 62, 149, 152, 153, 161, 162, 163, 165, 176, 177, 181, 187, 188, 191, 266, 285, 346, 362, 372, 380, 392–94
Department of Agriculture, 206, 224, 227, 231
Department of Defense, 55, 90, 93, 95, 96
Department of Education, 2, 241, 280, 341–44, 348, 354, 369
Department of Health and Welfare, 16
Departamento Autónoma de Asuntos Indígenas (DAAI), 281, 282, 283, 289
Department of Press and Publicity (DAPP), 302
Department of Public Works, 6, 230
Department of the Economy, 201, 206
Department of the Interior, 8, 55, 74, 119, 132, 138, 150, 152, 155–57, 160, 162–64, 361
development, xi, 7, 10, 11, 14, 97, 109, 120, 139, 211, 258, 379–86, 393–94; and braceros, 188; church criticism of, 78–79, 82–84, 85, 86; and clientelism, 202–8; and forestry, 218–19, 231–32; and indigenismo, 280–90; and industry, 175, 177–84, 196, 199; and local elections, 155; and rural education, 342–44
Díaz, Juan, 248

Díaz, Pascual, 71
Díaz de León, Jesús, 180
Díaz Muñoz, Vidal, 166
Díaz Ordaz, Gustavo: and presidency, 118; and humor, 18, 19; and media, 313; and students, 362, 372; and teachers, 343, 355
Díaz Soto y Gama, Antonio, 56, 128
dictablanda, ix, xii–xiii, xv, 10, 11, 20, 27, 102, 121, 149, 167, 267, 270, 301, 342, 391–92
dictatorship, ix, x, xii, 1, 4, 27, 72, 156, 160, 206, 285, 380
Dominican Republic, 260
Doña Bárbara, 301
Dorantes, Ana María, 323
drugs, 14. *See also* narcotics
Durango, 53, 91, 94, 219, 228

Echeverría, Luis, 324; in the presidency, 118, 291; as populist, 55; and tax reform, 270, 386
Ecuador, 260
education, 1, 5, 16, 61, 91, 109, 188, 223, 236, 241, 305, 331, 360–72; Catholic, 85; Catholic opposition to, 15, 71, 73, 74–75, 76–77; and indigenismo, 280, 282, 283, 286, 293; and media programming, 312; and political dissidence, 16, 82; socialist, 2, 49, 58, 342–43, 364; and elimination of, 343, 348, 364; spending on, 259; teacher training colleges, 341–57; and women, 240, 246; and workers, 181, 182, 186; and the U.S., 181, 365
ejidatario, 12, 58, 90, 135–38, 140, 141, 203, 206, 207, 210, 217, 222, 226, 228, 242, 248, 258, 262, 263, 384, 385, 386
ejido, 13, 14, 25, 56, 57, 59, 63, 72, 101, 136, 137, 153, 176, 188, 198, 199, 205, 206, 209, 217, 220, 222, 223, 226, 227, 243, 248, 262, 263, 289, 342, 387
El Chapulín, 17, 268
El complot mongol, 329
El Diario de México, 19
El Diario de Xalapa, 17, 165
El Informador, 17, 246–48
El Momento, 329
El Mundo, 17
El Salvador, 260
El Sol del Centro, 17
El Universal, 101, 102, 227, 309, 324, 325, 354, 360, 367

elections, xii–xiii, 2, 8, 9, 11, 12, 13, 16, 20, 21, 22, 24, 25, 27, 60, 80, 82, 97, 100, 116–18, 126–72, 286, 290, 291, 383–86, 388, 389; and the army, 25–26, 91–93; and collective bargaining by riot, 13, 158, 160–61; local, 24, 116, 126–48, 158–72, 289–90, 291; and the Partido Acción Nacional (PAN), 24, 80, 158–61, 163, 164, 247; presidential, 11, 56, 58, 59, 66–67, 91, 96, 100, 112–16, 118, 265, 305, 313; primaries, 11, 129, 131, 133–37, 142, 149, 150–54, 157, 162–67, 388, 389; rigging and representation, 25, 100, 151–62, 181; union, 180, 181, 183, 184–88, 371; unseen, 149–51; and women, 15, 16, 80, 164–65, 246–51, 266
Emiliano Zapata Sugar Production Cooperative of Peasants and Workers, 198
England, 2
Ensayo de un crimen, 331
Escuela Nacional de Antropología e Historia (ENAH), 283
Everyday Forms of State Formation, 390
Excélsior, 102, 165, 262, 329, 335, 360, 361, 367

Fabela, Isidro, 54
Fabila, Alfonso, 281, 290
Faenas, 268
Fagen, Richard R., 164
Federación de Estudiantes Campesinos Socialistas de México (FECSM), 349, 350, 352, 354, 356, 387
Federación Popular del Pueblo Mexicano (FPPM), 163
Federal District, 16, 90, 91, 96, 124, 231, 326, 332, 333, 334, 335, 370. See also Mexico City
Federal Electoral Commission, 162, 392
Federal Radio and TV Law, 312, 313
Federal Security Directorate (DFS), 41, 96, 324, 370, 387
Fein, Seth, 303
Félix, María, 301, 314
Fernández Aceves, María Teresa, 16
Fernández Christlieb, Fátima, 313
Fernández, Emilio "El Indio," 309
Finland, 62
Flores Monroy, Rosario, 239
Flores Muñoz, Gilberto, 110, 113–16, 131, 133, 137
Flores, Gloria, 335
Flores, Higinio, 137

Ford Motor Company, 184
Forest Industry Management Units (UIEFS), 218, 225
forest service, 218–32
Formas de Gobierno Indígena, 285, 286
Forzán, Elías, 154
fortress conservation, 219–20, 225, 231, 232
Fowler-Salamini, Heather, 16, 238
Fox, Vicente, 18
France, 2, 54, 314
Franco, Francisco, 21, 59, 60, 62
Frente Nacional de Estudiantes Técnicos (FNET), 361, 363, 366, 368, 370, 371, 372
Frente Unico Pro Derechos de la Mujer, 244
Fuentes, Carlos, 4, 155, 209

Galeana, Morelos, 212
Galindo, Hermilia, 250
Gamio, Manuel, 279, 280, 281, 283, 284, 285, 293
Gamíz, Arturo, 350, 351, 352, 356
Garate, Raúl, 97
Garcés, Mauricio, 314
García Barragán, Marcelino, 239, 241, 247
García Moreno, Antonio, 175, 176, 180
García Tadeo, Tomás, 248
García Tellez, Ignacio, 52
García Valseca, Antonio, 221
García Zamora, José, 138
García, Basilio, 137
García, Filiberto, 329
García, Jesús, 81
García, León, 131, 132, 133
Garduño, Eduardo, 309
Garibi Rivera, José, 72
Garizurieta, Cézar, 19
Garrido Canabal, Tomás, 49, 108, 110, 111
Garza Zamora, Tiburcio, 97, 98
Gasca, Celestino, 12, 24, 94
Gavaldón, Roberto, 309
Gaxiola, Francisco, 201
General Directorate of Political and Social Investigations (IPS), 6, 7, 8, 155. See also spies
General Motors, 184
gender, 6; and caciquismo, 238–39; inequality, 244; and traditional roles, 241, 244, 246, 248; transgression, 351
Germany, 21, 23, 63, 76
Giner Durán, Práxedes, 352

Gómez Morín, Manuel, 161
Gómez Sada, Napoleón, 184, 186–88, 191, 192
Gómez, Alma, 353
Gómez, Herminia, 347
Gómez, Marte R., 49, 114
Gómez, Pablo, 351, 356
González Camarena, Guillermo, 307
González Casanova, Pablo, 114, 150, 258, 268
González Luna, Efraín, 160, 247
González Navarro, Moisés, 4
González Soto, Armando, 166
Gordillo, Elba Esther, 122
Gramsci, Antonio, x, xiv, 166, 395
Granaderos, 362, 365, 367, 370, 387
Grandin, Greg, 24
Greene, Graham, 62
Grupo Atlacomulco, 6, 54
Guadalajara, 17, 58, 73, 93, 188, 189, 190, 240, 241, 245, 248, 269, 270
Guanajuato, 185, 266, 355; and Cárdenas, 53; high concentration militia, 91; electoral massacre, 157, 161; town hall occupations, 158; sinarquismo, 160, 161
Guasave (Sinaloa), 157
Guatemala, 24, 259, 260, 261, 324
Guerrero, 16, 53, 334; and state weakness in, 25, 93, 99, 263; and rebellions, 53, 99, 158, 351; taxation in, 262, 263, 265, 268; and elections, 150, 152–65; and forestry, 219, 227, 232
Guevara, Che, 23, 24, 353, 354
Guichard, Eduardo, 329
Guiteras-Holmes, Calixta, 283
Gutiérrez, Hermenegildo, 136, 137

Haiti, 98
Hamilton, Nora, 5, 380
Handbook of Middle American Indians, 283
Hank González, Carlos, 19, 125
Hansen, Roger, 260, 261, 363
hegemony, x–xxii, 6, 27, 54, 250, 256, 279, 390–91
Helú, Antonio, 331
Henríquez Guzmán, Miguel: presidential campaign of 1952, 26, 56, 92, 94, 95, 113, 114, 124, 248, 287, 313; corruption, 92; party abolished, 163
Henriquismo, 6, 12, 96, 115, 129
Hermosillo (Sonora), 160
Hernández Corso, Rodolfo, 365, 366, 368

Hernández Rodríguez, Rogelio, 150, 383, 389
Hidalgo, 96, 224; strongmen in, 110, 111, 112, 114, 116–20
Hobsbawm, Eric, 13, 47
Hollywood, 300, 306–9, 314
Honduras, 2, 260
hospitals, 16, 25, 199, 237, 247, 249, 250, 251, 267, 269, 288; campaign to construct one in San Martín Hidalgo, 242–44; church-funded, 269–70
Huachinango (Puebla), 269
Huajuapan (Oaxaca), 24
Huasteca, 114, 119, 126, 127, 128, 130, 142, 143
Huerta, Victoriano, 48
humor, 3, 7, 17–20, 93, 98, 126, 261, 391, 392
hybrid regimes, ix, x, xii, 9

Ibargüengoitia, Jorge, 19
Iguala (Guerrero), 158, 165, 264, 265, 266
Import Substitution Industrialization (ISI), 11, 12, 179, 292, 310
India, 3, 166
indigenismo, 9, 25, 279–93
Instituto del Fondo Nacional de la Vivienda para los Trabajadores (INFONAVIT), 186
Instituto Mexicano de Seguro Social, 179, 182, 183, 186
Instituto Nacional de Antropología e Historia (INAH), 283
Instituto Nacional Indigenista (INI), 284–93
Instituto Politécnico Nacional (IPN), 281, 360–73, 387
intelligence, x, 7, 9, 96, 98, 102, 105, 349; problems and possibilities as source, 8, 95, 382, 391, 395
Ireta, Félix, 97, 98
Isthmus of Tehuantepec, 290
Italy, 314
Izquierdo Ebrard, Arturo, 335
Izquierdo Ebrard, Hugo, 335

Jalisco, 8, 16, 37, 57, 113, 124, 178, 192, 224, 235, 301, 302; and bracero program, 188–91, 195; concentration of militia in, 91; and counterinsurgency, 99; development in, 236–37, 241–46; and elections, 158, 186, 245, 246–49; military policing in, 100, 113
Jamay (Jalisco), 100
Japan, 3, 166

Jaramillo, Antonio, 196, 197, 204–11
Jaramillo, Porfirio, 196, 197
Jaramillo, Reyes, 196
Jaramillo, Rubén, 101, 196–210, 356, 383–85; as bureaucrat, 202, 211; *corrido de*, 17; and elections, 162; ideology of, 24, 55, 198; and rebellion, 196, 202; and strikes, 200–202; murder of, 101, 196, 356; women as soldiers for, 15
Jenkins, William, 11, 61, 303–7, 309, 310, 312, 316
Jessop, Bob, 6
Jiménez Delgado, Ramón, 133, 134
Jiménez, José Alfredo, 305
Jocotepec, Jalisco, 239, 249
John XXIII, 82
Jojutla, Morelos, 212
Jokes. *See* humor
Joseph, Gilbert, 5
Juárez, Benito, 150, 239
Juchitán (Oaxaca), 160

Kaldor, Nicholas, 255, 259, 260, 261
Kansas City, México y Oriente railroad, 230
Kaplan, Temma, 244
Kefauver, Estes, 311
Kelly, Isabel, 283
Kenya African National Union (KANU), 156
Kirchhoff, Paul, 283
Knight, Alan, 6, 11, 21, 237, 260, 302, 383, 389
Korea, 24
Krauze, Enrique, xv, 48
Kuomintang, 156

La ley de hérodes (Herod's Law), 155
La Trinitaria massacre, 12, 102, 387
Lagos de Moreno (Jalisco), 57
Laguna, 347; agrarian reform in, 57, 198; land invasions in, 13
Lara, Agustín, 301, 302
Law on Federal Executive Powers in Economic Matters, 13
Law of Social Dissolution, 183, 361, 362, 369, 371
League of Nations, 61
Leal Cienfuegos, Patricia, 266
Leduc, Renato, 19
Legorreta, Luis, 303
León (Guanajuato): electoral massacre in, 100, 129, 157, 161; tax protest in, 264–67

León, Congressman Aurelio, killing of, 333–35
Leviathan, 4, 55, 120–21
Lewis, Oscar, 255
Ley fuga (extrajudicial execution), 25, 26, 101, 102, 321, 332–37, 387
Leyva Mancilla, Baltazar, 227
Limantour, José Yves, 150
Limón, Gilberto, 93
Linz, Juan, 20, 27
literacy, 11, 182, 246, 288, 355
living standards, 2, 363, 391; and Import Substitution Industrialization, 11–12; of indigenous populations, 281–82, 286, 288; and media consumption, 304, 314–15, 320; of peasantry, 12, 21, 242, 345; and taxation, 259; of unionized workers, 13, 182–83, 186, 189; of women, 16, 246
Loera, Julián, 137
logging bans (*vedas*) 217–32
Loma Bonita (Oaxaca), 152
Lombardo Toledano, Vicente, 52, 59; and indigenismo, 282; role in 1940 presidential election, 56, 65; sympathy for USSR, 62; and student movements, 366, 371; and union leadership, 52–53, 57, 58
Lomnitz, Claudio, xiv, 128, 148
López, Jacinto, 13
López Mateos, President Adolfo, 13, 115, 124, 223, 250, 324; and communism, 81–82, 325; and clampdown on regional strongmen, 114, 118, 128, 248, 385, 389; and fiscal centralization, 257; and media policy, 311–14, 387; and student politics, 371
López Portillo, Guillermo, 101
López Portillo, President José, 48, 120, 125; and bank nationalization, 61
Loret de Mola, Senator Carlos, 165
Lorey, David E., 364
Los Mochis, 13, 58
Lugo Guerrero, José, 119
Lugo Verduzco, Adolfo, 120

Macías Valenzuela, Pablo, 94
Madero, Francisco, 54, 177
Madrazo, Carlos, 20, 165
Maestros rurales. *See* teachers
Magaña, Gildardo, 56, 66
Malaysia, xiii

Malinowski, Bronislaw, 283
Manchuria, 61
Mange, Alejandro, 95–96; and military caciquismo, 94
Mano negra, 53, 259
Mao, 55
Marcos, Subcomandante, 16, 392
market traders, politics of, 15, 16, 17, 255, 261, 264, 266, 268, 367, 383, 386, 391
Márquez, Enrique, 142
Martínez, Archbishop Luis María, 73
Martínez, Ema, 324–26, 337
Martínez, José María "Chema," 189
Martínez, Miguel Z., 93, 96, 384; and military repression, 93
Martínez de la Vega, Francisco, 136, 139
Martínez de la Vega, José, 331
Mascarúa, Alfonso, 330
Matamoros (Tamaulipas), 162, 264–65
Marx, Karl, 72
Marxism, 5, 24, 27, 59, 72, 77, 82, 179, 283, 381
Matehuala (San Luis Potosí), 130, 132, 134, 139–40
Mayo, 2, 13, 67
Mayoral Heredia, Manuel, 267, 269
Maximato, 71
McCormick, Gladys, 9, 14, 194, 383–86, 390
Medina, Genoveva, 16
Mendoza, Genaro, 135–36
Mendoza, Nicandro, 361, 369
Mérida, 160
"Mexican miracle," 11, 191, 363; inequality inside, 12, 179–80, 218; unpaid rural labor in, 269
Mexico City, 10, 11, 14, 18, 19, 25, 90, 91, 96, 98, 99, 119, 120, 126, 128, 132, 133, 135, 138, 141, 157, 186, 187, 202, 227, 238, 242, 255; anti-Semitism in, 67; cinemas in, 304, 310; elections in, 17, 100–101, 154, 164; homicide in, 323–26, 329, 334, 335; police in, 93, 331–32; protest caravans/delegations to, 176–77, 184, 197, 203, 207, 210, 225; student politics in, 26, 351, 360–77
Miahuatlán (Oaxaca), 269
Michel, Concha, 245
Michoacán, 14, 25, 66, 74, 91, 100, 101, 161, 291; as cardenista stronghold, 96, 114; forestry in, 219, 221, 228–29, 232; indigenista projects in, 281–82, 284, 286; military corruption in, 97–98; and normal schools, 343, 356; student movement, 367
Middlebrook, Kevin, 13
Migdal, Joel, 24
military, 9, 11, 21, 22, 24–26, 89–107, 380; and censorship, 97–98; counterinsurgency, 12–13, 94, 99, 103, 210, 287; crisis of 1948, 95–96; and elections, 26, 132, 136, 154, 158, 161, 166; and regional development schemes, 241, 268–69; officers in local government, 101, 131–33, 142–43, 160; in national politics, 11, 60, 62, 92–98, 113–14; official image of, 90–92; obligatory military service, 54, 98; occupation of the Instituto Politécnico Nacional, 370–71; policing/repression, 98–102, 227, 334–35; revolts, 56, 89, 96; as strike breakers, 176, 180, 182, 201, 369; structure of, 90–91, 98–99
militia (*defensas rurales*), 90–91, 93, 97, 99–100
Miller, Michael Nelson, 301
Mixteca, 159, 284, 290
Moctezuma, Fernando, 134
Moctezuma (San Luis Potosí), 130, 137, 142, 143
modernization of patriarchy, 236, 241, 250
Monclova (Coahuila), 160
Mongolia People's Revolutionary Party, 1
monopolies: commercial, 11, 17, 229, 263, 286–87, 300–301, 303–6, 309–11, 317; 1934 Monopolies Law, 303, 311
Monsiváis, Carlos, 19, 35, 308, 374
Monsiváis, Olivo, 137, 142
Monterrey, 2, 14, 50, 60, 130, 175, 177, 178, 180; business elites, 2, 50, 60; and mining/steel unions, 184–88, 191–92, 306, 388
Montes de Oca, Timoteo, 206
Morelos, 57, 194, 353; *agrarismo* in, 15, 57, 99; army actions in, 101; building peasant support in, 196–215; elections in, 162; *jaramillismo* in, 15, 17, 24, 55, 101, 196–215, 353, 356, 383–85
Moreira, Francisco, 137
Morelia Congress of 1963, 362
Moreno Valle, Rafael, 118
Morones, Luis, 53
Morones Prieto, Ignacio, 115–16, 124
Movimiento de Liberación Nacional (MLN), 24
Movimiento Nacional Revolucionario (MNR), Bolivia, 48, 55

Movimiento Revolucionario del Magisterio (MRM), 341–42
Mújica, Francisco, 49, 52, 302
municipio libre, 152, 286
Museo del Ejército, 92
Mussolini, Benito, 61
Mustieles, Agustín, 101–2

Nacional Financiera (NAFINSA), 17, 110
nationalism, xi, 5–6, 20, 25, 381, 384, 394; and cardenismo, 49–50, 54; and the church, 73–78; deployed against students, 367–68; economic, 184, 218, 220–23, 365; and education, 342–44; and indigenismo, 279–98; and media policy, 299–303, 305–8, 315
Naranja (Michoacán), 252
narcotics, 14, 320–22, 328, 336–37, 377, 382, 392
National Commission for the Development of Indigenous Peoples, 291–92
National Institute for Indigenous Languages, 292
National School of Anthropology and History (ENAH), 283, 293
Nava, Dr. Salvador, 140, 160
Nava Castillo, Antonio, 118
Navarrete, Ifigenia M., 260
Nayarit, 121; Flores Muñoz cacicazgo, 110–11, 114–16, 124; land invasions, 13, 197, 210
Nazi Germany, 21, 63, 76, 161
negotiation, x–xi, 5–6, 13–15, 261, 382–85, 389–90; and elections, 128–29, 141–44, 156–61, 163–64; and collective contracts, workers' benefits, 185–89; and peasant politics, 197–202; and taxation, 258, 264–67; and indigenous political authorities, 289; and media policy, 302, 315
Negrete, Jorge, 301, 314, 315
neoliberalism, 192, 279, 379, 382
newspapers, 17, 19, 149, 162, 221, 246–47, 264, 304, 324, 386–87, 391; controlled, closed down, 19, 97–98, 101, 325–26; crime in, second section and tabloids, 321–40, 386–87, 392, 394; and political dissent, 17, 19, 246–47, 268, 323, 366; and propaganda, 101, 302, 354, 360–61, 367–70; *Amanecer* (Querétaro), 325; *Don Paco, Don Roque* (both Apizaco), 17, 333; *El Chapulín* (Oaxaca), 17,

268; *El Diario de México*, 19, *El Diario de Xalapa*, 17; *El Informador de Guadalajara*, 17, 246–47, 248; *El Momento* (Oaxaca), 329; *El Mundo* (Tampico), 17; *El Nacional*, 17, 73; *El Sol del Centro* (Aguascalientes), 17; *La Trinchera de Culiacán*, 165; *El Universal*, 360; *Excélsior*, 102, 165, 262, 329, 335, 360–61, 367; *La Prensa*, 102, 222, 325–26, 331, 333, 335; *La Verdad de Acapulco*, 17; *Novedades*, 102, 205, 360, 370; *Presente*, 19; *Tiempo*, 360, 367, 368
newsreel, 17, 68, 299, 302, 304; CLASA Films Mundiales SA's *Noticiario*, 17, 302
Nieto, Juan, 205
Nochebuena, Juvencio, 119, 125
North American Free Trade Agreement (NAFTA), 380
Normales rurales (rural teacher training colleges), 23, 341–59, 364, 372, 387
Novo, Salvador: 1948 report on public vs. private media ownership, 307–8
Nueva Rosita (Coahuila), 175–78, 186
Nuevo León, 97, 99, 100, 115, 175, 257
Nugent, David, xiii, 283
Nugent, Daniel, 5

O'Farrill, Rómulo, 307–8; covert partnership with Alemán, 308; merger with Azcárraga, 310–11
Oaxaca, 12, 18, 25, 91, 97; anthropology in, 283, 284; army repression in, 99, 101, 102, 161, 171; church social programs, 269–70; elections in, 150, 152, 159, 160; federal spending in, 257, 261; forced labor in, 268–69, forestry in, 219, 232; social movements in, 15–16, 18, 26, 264, 266–68, 342, 387; satirical press in, 17, 329; taxation in, 261, 263–65
Obregón, President Alvaro, 47, 112; and agrarian reform, 49; moratoria on logging, 224; sense of humor, 18
oil industry, 178, 271; nationalization of, 49, 58, 60, 62, 63, 73, 74, 177, 365
oilworkers, 181; charrismo and, 185, 186; living standards of, 182, 187; militancy of, 175, 179, 180; repression of, 25, 201, 356, 388
Ojeda, Nabor, 166, 266
Olachea, Agustín, 93, 123–24
Olcott, Jocelyn, 165
Ometepec (Guerrero), 25, 263

Orientación, 154, 165, 206
Orizaba (Veracruz), 157, 264–65
Ortiz, Eulogio, 132
Ortiz Mena, Antonio, 255
Orwell, George, 27
Ortega, Edmundo, 266
Othón de Mendizábal, Miguel, 281–82
Ossorio, León, 67
Otatitlán (Veracruz), 162

Pabello Acosta, Rubén, 149
Pacelli, Cardinal Eugenio, 74, 75
Pachuca, 96, 118–20, 125
Padgett, Vincent, 135, 140, 142
Padilla, Ezequiel, 314
Padilla, Tanalís, 16, 41, 198, 364, 375, 383, 387, 390
Palillo, Jesús Martínez, 4, 19, 20
Pan-American Highway, 284
Pani, Alberto J., 62, 303
Pansters, Wil, xiv, 9, 111, 117, 144, 160, 169, 170, 251, 265, 273, 383–85, 386, 390
Papaloapan Basin, 284, 287; dam and resettlement of Mazatecs, 287–88
paper industry, 218–20, 224–25; state control of newsprint supply via PIPSA, 17
Parra, Manuel, 2, 53, 259, 338
Parral (Chihuahua), 350
Partido Acción Nacional (PAN), 7, 24, 61, 68, 134, 146, 160–64, 246–47, 269, 370; and electoral reform, 161, 164; successes in municipal politics, 159, 160–61; and tax protests, 265–66; and women, 16, 54, 80, 165
Partido Agrario Obrero Morelense (PAOM), 162, 290
Partido Auténtico de la Revolución Mexicana (PARM), 97
Partido Católico Nacional (PCN), 70
Partido Comunista Mexicano (PCM), 62, 282; and church, 77; and feminism, 15; Thirteenth Congress in brothel, 23; repression of, 325; schism in, 23; taken off ballot, 163; and weakness of, 23
Partido Nacional Revolucionario (PNR), 59; and army, 110, 112; radio propaganda, 314; weakness in regions, 150
Partido Nacional de Salvación Pública, 67
Partido de la Revolución Mexicana (PRM), 51, 60, 63, 74, 75, 131, 137; colonized by business right, 61; colonized by caciques, 141; consolidation at federal level, 158; dissolved, 161; failure and reliance on caudillos in 1940, 59, 112–13, 150; rise of popular sector and centrism, 54, 55; in San Luis Potosí, 131–34
Partido Obrero-Campesino Mexicano (POCM), 23
Partido Político Félix U. Gómez, 136
Partido Popular (PP), 158, 162, 164–65
Partido Revolucionario Chihuahuense, 150
Partido Revolucionario de Unificación Nacional (PRUN), 51
Partido Revolucionario Institucional (PRI), 1, 10, 20; and business, 61; and Cárdenas, 54; and the Cold War, 24; compared to other authoritarian parties, xii–xiii, 21–22, 27, 55–56, 156; decline, fall, and resurrection thereof, 27, 122, 166–67, 291–92; and elections, 11, 16–17, 22, 128–29, 135–44, 149–67, 246–51; in graffiti, 18; image of invincibility thereof, 4, 25; and indigenous populations, 279–80, 283–84, 289–91; and labor, 177–80, 186–88; and Leviathan, 55, 66, 121; and media policy/press control, 17, 79, 101, 299–300, 305, 313–14, 323, 356; and the military, 92–98; and nationalism, 50, 78, 299–300; and peasants, 196–97, 210–12; and regional strongmen, 113–16, 126–28; and teachers, 341–42, 354–57; and women, 16, 164–65, 244–48, 250–51
Partido Socialista de las Izquierdas, 150
Partido Socialista Fronterizo, 112
Paso del Macho (Veracruz), 165
Pátzcuaro (Michoacán), 282; First Inter-American Indigenista Congress, 282, 284, 293
pax priísta, 1, 177, 183, 301, 315
Paxman, Andrew, 9, 10, 14, 17, 35, 40, 68, 272, 389
Paz, Octavio, xv
Pensado, Jaime, 9, 11, 36, 42, 359, 383, 387, 390
Peralta, Alejo, 368–71
Pérez Gallardo, Reynaldo, 131–32, 139, 142, 143, 145
Pérez Treviño, Manuel, 56
perfect dictatorship, xii, xv, 1, 27
Peronism, 181, 380
Perote (Veracruz), 156; and illegal logging, 225–27

INDEX 439

Peru, 259, 260, 382
Pétain, Marshal, 62
Petróleos Mexicanos (PEMEX), 58, 135, 185, 258
Pineda Flores, Carlos, 247
Pinedismo, 53
Pinochet, Agustín, 21
pistoleros (gunmen), 12, 25, 94, 97, 99, 100, 134, 143, 154, 157, 158, 202, 321–40; *cuerudos* (often ex-army paramilitaries), 102; culture, 361, 369, 388
Pius XI, 71, 72
police, 8, 12, 14, 21, 102, 132, 321, 361, 380, 384, 386, 387, 388; army officers in command of, 93, 98; and corruption, 227, 268, 270, 331; roles in elections, 101, 132, 138, 141, 142–43, 153, 154, 155, 163; low public opinion of, 100, 322, 330–31, 336; Mexico City Police Department Secret Service, 323, 331, 332, 370; multiple agencies, 333; and "Operation P" (occupation of university), 370; and political killings, 202, 328; police news (*nota roja*), 321–40; policewomen, 323; riot police (*granaderos*), 362, 365, 367, 370, 387; and tax protests, 267; and torture, 331–32, 334; and unions, 182, 210. *See also* Federal Security Directorate (Dirección Federal de Seguridad, DFS), General Directorate of Political and Social Investigations (Dirección General de Investigaciones Políticas y Sociales, IPS)
Plan de las Hayas (Veracruz), 330
Plancarte, Francisco, 289
Politécnico (Instituto Politécnico Nacional, IPN), 281–82, 360–77, 387
polyarchy, 27, 166
Porfiriato, 47, 50, 149, 150, 164, 206, 221–22, 238, 256, 262, 263, 285, 303, 355, 380
Portes Gil, President Emilio, 52, 53, 112, 114
Pozas, Ricardo, 283, 284, 286–87
Prado, Eugenio, 208–10
Pratt, Mary Louise, 280, 391
presidentialism, 4–5, 122
priests, 18, 63, 70–88, 176, 238, 269
primary elections, 11, 129, 131, 133–37, 142, 149, 150–54, 157, 162–67, 388, 389
Puebla, 75, 96, 99, 101, 121, 160, 178, 179, 198, 235, 258, 307, 310, 334; avilacamachista cacicazgo in, 61, 97, 99, 110–11, 114, 116–18, 144, 304; army policing popular in, 100; army repression in, 12, 35; forced labor in, 269; peasant organization in, 196; student movements in, 14, 82, 118
public sphere, xii, 16–17, 383; deliberately fragmented, x, xiii, 103; and murder, 321–37
Puente de Ixtla (Morelos), 212
Purépecha/Tarascans, 281–84, 286, 289, 291

Querétaro, 53, 235, 325, tax protests in, 264–65
Quevedo, Rodrigo, 93, 96
Quevedo, Miguel Ángel de, 221–22, 224, 227
Quezada, Abel, 4, 19, 42, 155
Quintana, Valentín, 330
Quintana Roo, 114, 232
Quintero, Colonel Eugenio, 133, 138, 160
Quiroga (Michoacán), 228
Quiróz Cuarón, Alfonso, 330

radio, 301–15; Azcárraga's network, Radio Programas de México, 304–5; *la hora nacional*, 305; O'Farrill's XEX, 308; party radio, XE-PNR, 302; Radio Habana Libre, 23, 353–54; increasing set ownership, 301, 305, 313
railroads, 224, 229, 230
railworkers, 131, 141, 175, 177, 180, 189, 201, 311, 391; and nationalization, 58, 63; 1959 strike, 11, 55, 81, 182–83; media coverage of, 313, 325, 356, 387; and San Luis Potosí politics, 140, 141, 384, 385; union, 178, 179, 180, 181, 191, 266
Ramírez, José Santos, 140–41
Ramírez, Margarito, 114
Ramírez, Rafael, 343, 348
Ramos, Genaro, 269
Ramos Santos, Matías, 101, 370
Rath, Thomas, 12, 35, 36, 170, 382, 383, 384, 386, 387
Redfield, Robert, 282, 283
real wages, 2, 13, 21, 182, 259, 318, 363
relajo, 18, 20
remittances, 179, 193
repression, 11–13, 25–26, 41, 63, 380, 382–84, 387–88, 392–94; army's role in, 98–103; of dissident election campaigns, 141, 154, 158–61, 166; of indigenous rebels, 287; media coverage of, 313, 356; of peasants,

440 INDEX

196–97, 201–2, 204, 208, 227, 232; of railroad workers, 81, 182–83, 311, 313, 325, 387, 391; of satire, 18–19; of students, 360–77; of rural teachers, 354–56
resistance ix–xii, 2, 5, 14–15, 390, 393; and taxation, 262–70; indigenous, 290–95; postelectoral, 157–58; of students, 364–67; of teachers, 342–43, 356–57
resource regulation, 13–14, 27, 218
revisionists, 4, 66, 120–21, 144, 261, 381
Revolution, Mexican, 1–2, 26, 43, 109–10, 120, 199, 224, 239, 256–57, 379–81; and the church, 70–75; constitution of 1917, 48–50, 70, 355–56; discourse/myth of, xi, 6, 10, 13, 17, 25, 26, 55–56, 103, 152, 156, 161, 165, 177, 183, 185, 197, 204, 207, 341, 349, 353, 363, 366; and rural education, 342–44; end of, 47–69, 389–93; historiography, 4–6; and indigenismo, 279–82, 292; veterans of, 56–57, 90, 100, 136, 140, 204, 206; and women, 15, 54, 245
revolutionary family, 3, 59, 311
Reyes Heroles, Jesús, 125, 165
Reynolds, Clark W., 264
Reynosa, military caciquismo in, 97–98
Reynoso, Leobardo, 110, 111, 114, 115, 116, 118, 262
Río Balsas irrigation scheme, 24
riots, 14, 131; collective bargaining by, 13, 15, 27, 158, 160–61, 267, 383, 389; riot police (*granaderos*) 362, 365, 367, 369–70, 387
Ríos Thivol, Colonel Manuel, 21, 40
Ríos Zertuche, Antonio, 96,
Rius, 19
Rivas Guillén, 131–33
roads, 7, 21, 92, 99, 199, 218, 229, 241, 262, 268, 270, 288; unpaid labor to build, 268–69
Robles Martínez, Jesús, 341, 372, 377
Rocha, Antonio, 134, 137
Rodríguez, President Abelardo, 14, 52, 93, 114, 310, 318
Rodríguez, Luis, indigenous cacique of Región Mixe, 269
Rodríguez, Luis I., secretary to Cárdenas, 145, 370
Rodríguez, Mónico, 200, 203
Rodríguez Kuri, Ariel, 7
Rodríguez Silva, Santiago, 332
Rojo Gómez, Jorge, 110–14, 118–20

Romania, jokes in, 20
Rome, 59, 60, 83
Roosevelt, Franklin Delano, 58, 62, 303
Roosevelt, Theodore, 162
Roque (Guanajuato), 355
Roseberry, William, 390
Rubin, Jeffrey, xii, 122
Rueda, Andrés, 206
Rueda, Quintín, 119
Ruiz, Samuel, 392
Ruiz Cortines, President Adolfo, 3, 81, 111, 161, 250; and the church, 79; and extrajudicial execution, 336; and forestry, 226; and graft allegations, 318; and media policy, 308–11; and regional strongmen, 113–15, 123–24; and satire, 3, 18; and students, 368, 370–71; and tax, 258; and women, 244
Rus, Jan, 291
Russia/Soviet Union, xiii, 1, 2, 21, 23, 48, 62, 63, 76, 77, 78, 171, 346

Sáenz, Moisés, 280–82, 284, 285, 293, 343, 348
Salaices (Chihuahua), 345, 350, 351, 354–56
Salas, Ismael, 134, 138, 139, 142, 143
Saldívar Martínez, Luis, 329–30
Salinas (San Luis Potosí), 130, 138–39, 143, 160
Salinas Leal, Bonifacio, 94, 96, 97
Saltillo, Coahuila, 130, 265
San Andrés Tuxtla (Veracruz), 155, 226
San Cristobal (Guerrero), 99
San Cristóbal de las Casas (Chiapas), *Centro Coordinador Indigenista*, 284, 287
San Jerónimo (Guerrero), 160
San José de Gracia (Michoacán), 54, 63, 101
San Luis de la Paz (Guanajuato), 160
San Luis Potosí, 8, 94, 383, 385, 386, 388; caciquismo in, 9, 110, 114, 115, 121, 160; and Cedillo revolt, 56–57; local politics in, 126–48, 157, 158; taxation in, 132, 262; social movements in, 14, 264–65
San Marcos (Zacatecas), 347, 350
San Martín Hidalgo (Jalisco), 237, 239–42, 245, 247, 248; campaign for hospital, 242–44
Santa Anna, 150
Sánchez, Manuel, 255
Sánchez Cano, Edmundo, 267

Sánchez Celis, Leopoldo, 165
Sánchez Taboada, Rodolfo, 114
Sánchez Vite, Manuel, 119–20
Sansores Pérez, Carlos, 114
Santo Domingo (San Luis Potosí), 130, 136–37, 147
Santos, Gonzalo N., 9, 110–16, 155, 250, 383, 385–86, 388, 390; and humor, 18, 19; and local elections, 126–48, 160; and pistoleros, 100, 329; and presidential succession, 115–16, 118, 124
Santos Valdés, Jesús, 352
Saucedo, Francisco, 143
Saucillo (Chihuahua), 347, 350–51, 353–55
Sayer, Derek, 5, 31
Schmitter, Philip, xii
Scott, James, 3
Secretariado Social Mexicano (SSM), 74, 79
Segovia, Rafael, 16
Seligson, Mitchell A., 164
senate, 80, 178, 186, 267, 333; "informal senate," 151; and regional checks and balances, 123
Serdán, Pablo and Davíd, 203
Serdán, Félix, 210
Serviço Nacional de Informaçoes, 21
sesentaocheros (leading figures in 1968 student movement), 362
Sewell, William, 10
Sierra Leone, 3
Silva Herzog, Jesús, 4
Sinaloa, 13, 198, 321; dam construction in, 288; forestry in, 228, 235; political violence in, 94, 157; social movements in, 171, 197, 210
sinarquismo, 2, 7, 59–61, 146, 160, 162–63, 189, inside the PRI, 160, 290
Sindicato de Trabajadores de Sales, 138
Smith, Peter, 150
Snodgrass, Michael, 8, 13, 14, 36, 40, 42, 202, 388, 389
social benefits, 13–14, 96, 182–88, 189, 191–92, 209
social landscaping, 218–20, 232
social movements, 7, 11–15, 55, 109, 379–94; and Catholics, 59–60, 70, 83–86; and indigenous communities, 287, 290–94; and media coverage, 313; and miners, 175–78; and peasant communities, 141, 198–208, 227–28; and students, 118,

360–77; and taxation, 255–75; and teachers, 350–51, 356–57
soft power, xv, 20, 27
Solaña, Caterino, 266
soldiers. *See* military
Solórzano, Antonio, 201, 213
Sonora, 53, 67, 91, 187, 190, 262, 281; Abelardo Rodríguez as state's boss, 93; and forestry, 228, 235; land invasions in, 13, 197, 210; and primary elections, 185; student movements in, 14
Soto Correa, José Carmen, 101
Soto Laveaga, Gabriela, 7, 394
Spain, 21, 60, 63, 183
Spanish Civil War, 62, 68
spies, 3, 7, 8, 12, 21, 155
squatters (*paracaidístas*), 10, 14, 15, 351, 353
Stalin, 56, 68
state prosecutor (*ministerio público*), 333
statistics, 2, 7–8, 229, 230, 269, 326, 327, 363
steel industry, 175, 178, 191, 219; production increases, 184
steel workers, 175, 176, 179, 182, 183, 185, 191, 192
strikes, 20, 25, 49, 60, 175, 179, 181–85, 356; army role in breaking, 25, 101, 176, 180, 182, 201, 207; doctors (1964–65), 394–95; portrayal in the media, 313, 360–61, 367–68; Nueva Rosita miners, 175–77; railroad workers (1959), 182–83; students (1956), 360–77; tax strikes, 262–68; Zacatepec sugar refinery, 200–201, 207
students, 11, 14, 26, 82, 86, 103, 118, 183, 283, 291, 293, 313, 329, 333, 379, 387, 388, 390; movement of 1968, 313, 351, 354, 361–62, 365, 366, 372, 374, 375, 377, 387; normalistas, 342–59, Politécnico strike of 1956, 360–77; porros, 360–61, 369, 371–72; protest tactics, 366–67
sugar industry, 130, 198–99, 303
sugar workers, 13, 25, 58, 177, 178, 183, 185, 186, 194, 304, 383, 385, 388, 391; and bracero program, 188–91; and peasant politics, 196–215
Summer Institute of Linguists, 282
Supreme Court, 6, 52, 307, 309, 319

Tabasco, 61, 110, 267, 288
Tacámbaro (Michoacán), 343
Taft-Hartley Act, 181

Taibo, Paco Ignacio II, 184
Taiwan, 3, 156
Tajín Totonac, 283
Tamaulipas, 72, 99, 112, 114, 162, 171, 194, 198; military caciquismo in, 97–98
Tamazunchale (San Luis Potosí), 134
Tamiahua (Veracruz), 269
Tanzania, xiii, 3
Tapachula (Chiapas), 67, 157, 265
Tapia, José María, 93
Tarahumara, 2, 25, 281, 284–86, 288–91, 345
Taussig, Michael, x
Tax, Sol, 283
taxation, 12, 14, 15, 17, 39, 179, 186, 221, 255–75, 383, 386, 390, 391; "black fiscal economy," 21, 261–70; fiscal centralization, 109, 113, 256–58; evasion of, 21, 25, 258–59, 261, 304; on media, 304, 306; protest movements, 121, 132, 136, 262–66, 306; regressive, 259–60
Taxco (Guerrero), 154, 156, 165, 166, 268
teachers, xi, 2, 57, 73, 92, 239, 241, 245, 246, 247, 248, 283, 341–59, 371, 390; and agrarismo, 342–43; anticlericalism, 71, 73, 76; as caciques, 291, 341; and elections, 153, 155, 157, 160; and guerrillas, 16, 350–57; and independent unions, 341–42, 387; and indigenismo, 280, 289, 291; training colleges (*normales*), 240, 243, 341–59, 365; violence against, 60
Tecolotlán (Jalisco), 247
Tehuacán (Puebla), 268
Tehuixtla (Morelos), 212
Tejeda, Adalberto, 108
telegraph, 102, 268, 356
television, 14, 17, 186, 299–320; Alemán family covert stake in, 308, 318; Alemán's 1950 informe on TV, 305; National Microwave Network, 313; telenovelas, 313, 315; TeleSistema Mexicano (TSM), 17, 310–11, 313–14; Televisa, 17, 313
Tepalcatépec Commission, 284, 288
tequio (communal/forced labor), 268, 290
Tequixtepec (Oaxaca), 268
Tezoatlán (Oaxaca), 18
theater, 4, 18–19, 164, 241, 268, 301, 345; movie theaters, 302–7, 309–12, 319
Tierra Colorado (Guerrero), 268
Tixtla (Guerrero), 157

timber industry, 8, 12, 14, 130, 217–35, 273, 293, 350, 383
Tlaquiltenango (Morelos), 205
Tlatelolco massacre, 4, 26, 313, 355, 356, 381, 392
Tlaxcala, 93, 158; federal beer tax in, 257–58; pistoleros kill Senator Angulo, 329–36
Tocqueville, Alexis de, xv, 55
Torreón (Coahuila), 178, 306
Torres Ortiz, Mateo, 205–9
torture, 101, 331–32, 334, 380
Treasury (Secretaría de Hacienda), 6, 242, 257, 263
Trejo, Captain Trujillo, 102
Treviño, Jacinto B., 114
Triquis, 2, 12, 101
Trotsky, 55, 61
True Whig Party of Liberia, 1
Tsebelis, George, x, 169
Tseltal, 286
Tuohy, William S., 164
Turkey, 3
Tuxtla Gutiérrez, 102
Tzotzil, 286, 291

Ugarte, Senator Gerzayn, 334
Unión Campesina Obrera Morelense, 207–8
Unión General de Obreros y Campesinos de México (UGOCM), 12, 13, 290, 351, 353, 356, 387
Universidad Nacional Autónoma de México (UNAM), 283, 361, 362, 368; UNAM students as middle class, 364
Unión Nacional Sinarquista. See sinarquismo
United States, 22, 52, 54, 90, 94, 162, 181, 183, 184, 219, 255, 302, 303, 307, 381; and braceros, 177, 179, 188–91, 243; and Cárdenas, 62, 69, 93; and the church, 76, 77, 82; and the Cold War, 22–24, 41, 78, 181–82, 353, 365, 380; and dependency theory, 40; and the film industry, 303–7, 317, 319; and indigenous peoples, 280, 282–83, 285, 293, 343; and television, 300, 307, 311, 314
unwritten rules/*reglas no escritas*, 21, 103, 198
Urbina, Erasto, 57
Uruapan (Michoacán), 227–28
Uruchurtu, Ernesto, 15, 124
Urzúa Flores, Guadalupe, 16, 236–54; and lupistas, 248–49
Usigli, Rodolfo, 4, 19, 161, 331

Valdés, Juan Matías, 152
Vallejo, Demetrio, 183
Vanegas (San Luis Potosí), 130, 140, 141
Vargas, Getulio, 380
Vargas Llosa, Mario, xv
Vasconcelos, José, 62, 280, 344
Vatican II, 82–86
Vázquez, Genaro, 24, 158
Vaughan, Mary Kay, xiii, 6
Vejar Vázquez, Octavio, 92
Velasco, Augusto, 360
Velasco de Alemán, Beatriz, 243
Velázquez, Elpidio, 94
Velázquez, Fidel, 53, 180
Velázquez, Padre Pedro, 79, 80–81
Vélez-Ibañez, Carlos, 15, 18
Venado (San Luis Potosí), 130
Vera Estañol, Jorge, 4
Veracruz, 16, 35, 53, 91, 194, 198, 219, 259, 302, 310; anthropology in, 283; elections in, 150–53, 156–57, 159–60, 161, 163–64; forestry in, 219, 224, 225–27, 228; military caciquismo in, 94, 100, 269; pistoleros in, 329, 330, 334–36, 338
veto players, x, 159
Vietnam, 24
Villa, Pancho, 54, 183, 302, 355
Villa Cardel (Veracruz), 160
Villa de Guadalupe (San Luis Potosí), 130
Villa de la Paz (San Luis Potosí), 130, 139
Villa de Ramos (San Luis Potosí), 130
Villa Rojas, Alfonso, 283, 287–88
Villahermosa (Tabasco), 264–65
Villegas, Otilio, 119
Villistas, 91, 100

water, 14, 130, 137, 176; political control of, 137, 176; provision of drinking, 15, 187, 236, 247, 270, 352
weapons of the weak, 3, 18, 27
Weber, Max, x, 5–6, 25, 322, 336

Wilkie, James, 259
Williams, Raymond, 390
Wolf, Eric, 9, 297
Womack, John, Jr., 380, 392–93, 395
women, 15–16, 100, 101, 309, 321, 379, 380, 386; as caciques/cacicas, 16, 237–39; and the church, 80, 250; and development programs, 242–46; and female consciousness, 244–46, 250; and murder/sexual violence, 12, 100, 240, 321, 323–25, 327, 332, 334; as normalistas, 343, 351, 353; in politics, 54, 57, 80, 155, 164–65, 236–54; and social movements, 18, 256, 264–66
World War II, 15, 48, 62, 77, 90, 102, 218, 219, 220, 230, 306, 363

Xalapa, 14, 17, 163, 164, 165, 259, 336

Yaquis, 13, 281, 290
Yocupicio, Román, 53
Yucatán, 53, 57, 113, 283; land reform in, 57, 198

Zabludovsky, Jacobo (TV presenter, media consultant to presidency), 313
Zacatecas, 95, 130, 262, 347; caciquismo in, 110, 114, 116, 118, 121; riots in, 161
Zacatepec (Morelos), 9, 25, 196–215, 388
Zamora, Gregorio, 140
Zapata, Emiliano, 54, 196, 198, 199, 202, 206, 210, 355, 366
Zapata, Nicolás, 210
Zapatistas, 55, 56, 100, 183, 204, 206, 207, 232, 391, 392, 393
Zapotecs, 2, 290
Zavala, Manolo, 190
Zimapán (Hidalgo), 119
Zinacantán (Chiapas,) 160
Zirándaro (Michoacán), 25
Zolov, Eric, 353
Zumacarregui, Dr., 140